EUtROPEs
The Paradox of European Empire

Edited by:

John W. Boyer
Berthold Molden

I0889639

Cahiers Parisiens
Parisian Notebooks
Volume 7
Paris, France • Chicago, Illinois
2014

Copyright © 2014 by the University of Chicago

All rights reserved. Published in 2014
Produced by the Office of the Dean of the College

Printed in the United States of America

ISBN 978-2952596268

This volume contains papers presented at a capstone conference held December 5-7, 2013, at the University of Chicago Center in Paris. The authors are 20 scholars from Europe who, over a five-year period (2008-2013), each spent six months in residence at the University of Chicago teaching and conducting research.

With special thanks to the Christian A. Johnson Endeavor Foundation and the Andrew W. Mellon Foundation for their support of these scholars and this volume.

TABLE OF CONTENTS

INTRODUCTION

THE PRESENT COLLECTION OF ESSAYS OWES ITS TITLE TO A CONFERENCE held December 5-7, 2013, at the University of Chicago Paris Center with the sponsorship of the Andrew W. Mellon and Christian A. Johnson Endeavor Foundations. Bringing together historians, linguists, cultural scientists, musicologists and scholars of philosophy, urban studies and film studies, the conference explored the meanings that "Europe" has held for different actors at different times. With the symbolic dissection of Europe as their common project, the participants deliberately chose an open-ended term—"EUtROPEs"—to capture the conceptual agenda of the conference, a neologism that indicates several meanings and therefore calls for some preliminary explanation. To begin, a range of historical references comes to mind, such as the figures of late antiquity who bore the name. One was the 4th-century Roman historian Eutropius, who held the office of *magister memoriae* and was best known for his portraits of the heroes of the decadent Empire. His name literally meant "he who turns to have a better view." Another was the Syrian wife of emperor Maximian, Eutropia, who could reasonably symbolize the (postcolonial) entanglements of Europe and the Eastern Mediterranean.

EUtROPEs may also call to mind a Utopia, an ideal, peaceful society that far surpasses the imagination even of Thomas More. This is Europe as the realization of a Kantian ideal, the Hegelian world spirit that is "coming into itself," albeit not on a fictive island, but on the continent long seen as the "center of modern civilization." It is not uncommon to hear Europe described today as a global power that has overcome its dark past of exploitation and genocide crystallized in Colonialism and the Holocaust, which has mastered its missionary hubris to become the symbol of a bright, global future. But is this accurate? After all, the term EUtROPE may also signify the translocation of Europe to the tropical zones of the globe, and not only in the predictable sense of Claude Lévi-Strauss' *tristes tropiques* or Joseph Conrad's deeply Catholic and Eurocentric Congolese apocalypse. Here EUtROPE may also indicate the inversion of Europe's position in the economic and political global system, from the center to the periphery, wherein European concepts, phantasies and desires themselves become exoticized. Such a "tropification" of Europe clearly builds upon the diagnosis of Dipesh Chakrabarty, the keynote speaker of the conference, of a "provincializing" of Europe. In fact, to paraphrase a thesis of Chakrabarty's, EUtROPEs may even transcend the anthropocentric realms of history, politics and culture to connote an ecosystemic phenomenon—"eutrophication"—defined by the oversupply of nutrition.

While the contributors to this volume acknowledge these diverse associations, they intend to highlight the narrower literary and semiotic term "trope," meaning a common, figurative theme or device whose use is unreflective and imaginative. As such, they understand EUtROPEs primarily as codes that endow Europe with meaning. The significance of any one of these codes depends upon the speaker, the audience and the political goals that motivate the discourse. The imaginings of Europe thus deployed may even be mutually exclusive given the varied social and cultural locations of speakers, who may or may not have considered themselves a part of Europe (regardless of whether they resided within its physical boundaries), and may have been perceived differently by others. Still, they allow that additional perspectives could prove illuminating, particularly if one expands the field of vision within the broader Paris-St. Petersburg-Vienna triangle in which the contributors reside. One could entwine Roland Barthes' work on semiotics with Ludwig Wittgenstein's writings on the relations between language and reality, or utilize Mikhail Bakhtin's model of heteroglossia so often used in cultural history and memory studies. One could further apply Michel Foucault's concepts of power and counter-memory, or Walter Benjamin's theory about the translatability of meaning and his famous historical metaphor of the Angel of History. The exploration of EUtROPEs could well accommodate Tzvetan Todorov's writings about the alterity of the colonial, non-European world and its consequences for the construction of a European identity. In fact, many of these approaches figure into the essays in this book, which expresses a polyphonic and richly layered analysis of the "discourse of Europe" in its own right.

Over the course of the conference, the discussions of the meaning of Europe evolved in two directions that now enrich the contributions to this volume. The first revolved around the question of legacy. What have been the consequences of the many ideas of Europe proposed and deployed over time? In the second, participants explored what has and continues to constitute Europe. That is, if Europe is a discourse and idea that invokes a non-local, regional, and transnational entity, what has been the binding, shared content of that discourse? Both discussions tried to bridge the past, present, and future of Europe in its economic, political, social, and cultural dimensions. Throughout this vivid debate, in which Dipesh Chakrabarty and other faculty from the University of Chicago served as active interlocutors, several broad reconsiderations emerged, which pointed towards new framings for inquiries into Europe as a historical idea and a set of constitutive practices.

What binds Europe?

In the following essays, phenomena ranging from political institution building, religious practices, movements of people and ideas and popular culture to memories all express elements of a shared past and present, through which it is possible to read—or question—something called "Europe." On these terms, the individual essays discuss Christianity; the Enlightenment; linguistic structures; music and cinema; imperial, authoritarian, and nationalist political pasts; and common struggles with the politics of memory. From these themes, the volume demonstrates ways in which Europe has been both consciously constructed through alliances and political or religious discourses, as well as tacitly forged, either through the dissemination of similar categories of thought and aesthetic orientations or through the construction of historical parallels. Thus, the essays collectively bring together a picture of Europe as both a conscious goal and a byproduct of autonomous, but still interconnected historical developments.

Next to this discussion of the practices that have constituted Europe runs a related theme about the physical and symbolic space of Europe. If Europe is an idea forged by common institutions, histories, and heritages, which nonetheless unfold in diverse patterns and temporalities, then the geographical space of Europe seems fated to constantly shift as well. These shifts do not always come "from below." While certain imagined spaces, such as Central Europe, have long proved resilient and compelling for reasons of shared culture, they have also been marginalized by Cold War politics that divide the world into East and West (Hanáková). The shifting geographical boundaries of "Europe," "East," and "West" are of particular interest to the contributors in light of Saidian and post-colonial theoretical influences, which highlight the processes of discursive and practical exclusion, as well as in light of the pressing politics of EU expansion, which, still echoing the Cold War, trigger their own discussions of inclusion and exclusion. Several of the essays express concern that the politics of difference at work in the European community still reflect "the symbolic geography of modernity and development," which has been critically scrutinized in other contexts (Bodnar).

In general, the contributors' work articulates a fair amount of skepticism with regard to the politics of deliberate community making. Here, the urgent politics of the European Union serve as a significant interlocutor for the essays. Taken together, they argue that the project for a European Union privileges an economistic perspective of integration and to rest on a political and economic vision of Europe as a space with no room for the socialist or communist past experienced by so many Europeans (Molden). At other places, the essays explore the institutional structure of the EU and its interest in fiscal order, which seems increasingly to come into tension with the particular interests of the nations (Ghervas). Beneath the EU's claims to inclusiveness and democracy, is there is a "hidden structure" that excludes certain memories and viewpoints from representation? Is the project of political-economic unity creating unnecessary division in the name of a coherent European culture? Is the EU homogenizing European culture or triggering reactionary reassertions of regional distinctiveness? If the project of Europe is worth pursuing, what are its costs?

Building on discussions at the conference, several essays provide a historical framework within which to consider the EU project. For some, that project seems to draw from earlier imaginaries of a united Christian and imperial Europe, but without having solved the historical tensions between the idea of a European family and the centrifugal forces of national particularity. If Europe could not function as a Christian-imperial family in the past, can it today be a political-economic family? What place is there for Christianity in this process? Does a shared Christian history facilitate secular integration? Or, amidst the active configuration of transnational financial and political institutions, does Christianity, as a fount of cultural forms, tacitly offer an alternative path to European unity, as in the form of pilgrimage songs that create a transnational space? (Kokorz) Finally, where does this leave other voices of European culture, such as European Jewry and Islam, with their histories as victims of expulsion and extermination?

Yet the contributions also show how a shared past presses toward disintegration rather than integration. While the goal of a united Christian Europe foundered on the shoals of national particularity and self-determination that pointed toward new forms of state and society, the past may now pose serious challenges to European peace and unity. If one cannot discount the notion that democracy requires critical historical consciousness, the contributors give due attention to mounting evidence that the present politics of memory in Europe endangers the very existence and possibility for such consciousness. The essays on Austria (Dreidemy) and Hungary (Bartha) demonstrate powerful ways in which the process of coming to terms with the past can prohibit critical engagement with that past.

The weight of the past figures prominently in this volume, suggesting the importance of memory and the politics of memory as a resource that both binds Europe and provides the material for self-reflexively conceiving Europe. The essays on commemoration demonstrate how remembrance can turn the past into an unstable ground upon which to construct the present. This past may some day disappear as its marks on the physical world subside to a new growth of trees, weeds, and wildflowers—both metaphorically and literally speaking (Sendyka). At other moments, the process of remembering shifts the ground of memory from the event itself to the commemorative process, causing subtle shifts in the psyche of the body politic (Łysak). And while commemoration studies have long stressed that the politics of commemoration is deeply influenced by *whose* memory it is commemorating, these contributions put forward a different consideration: that *what* is remembered is no less problematic and political. In sum, they suggest that how Europe understands its present and envisions its future will continue to be tied up in reconfigurations of its violent past. The idea of Europe as a peaceful, inclusive project will continue to face the mirror image of its destructive exclusions.

In light of the persistence of memory as a political issue, the contributors also explore how Europe will bear the weight of its own memory. What does it mean to move about a place such as Berlin, whose sidewalks are peppered with brass plaques testifying to victims of the Holocaust? What are the effects of constantly engaging in the politics of memory while one is building the present? How has the genre of "disastrous" memory been experienced in previous periods, and what can we learn from the comparison with the present? (Lavocat) The past, as Charkrabarty suggested in his final comments on the conference, is not always a route to democracy. He raised two considerations that have influenced the present volume. First, history writing is a process of interrogation: as a form of testimony, one needs to interrogate memory as rigorously as one would archival documents. Second, such interrogation will not necessarily always lead to liberation: "The poor also invent tradition when it suits them," he noted. In these instances, critical historical consciousness would go against the interests of the oppressed. The relationship between history and democracy remains a question, he proposed, rather than a technically dogmatic proposition. This intervention points to a broader reconsideration that should be integrated into future research: is Europe, so caught up in remembering, commemorating, and debating its past, neglecting other potential paths to a democratic future?

In looking to future research, a second broad reconsideration emerges. What will be the future idea of Europe? Is Europe a synthetic project or is it a unity in which difference is possible? Building from an awareness of

Europe's historical relationship to the "other," the contributions approach the question of self and other in dialectical terms: is Europe a project of synthesis in which the self and the other become one? Or is it possible to conceive of difference within the synthesis? The latter possibility, Chakrabarty suggested, would require us to rethink questions of self, place and identity in terms such as heteroglossia and de-identification. This would mean thinking about Europe as one might think through a symphony by Mahler: a polyphony of different voices and styles providing a "heterogeneity that mirrors the social diversity from which it originates" (Celestini), possibly in terms of a "historico-political polyphony" (Molden). This polyphonic approach may also be connected fruitfully to phenomenological analyses, which could use a "slow, universal history of human beings" and their common, evolved capacities as starting points for a hermeneutical understanding of human experience.

What is Europe's legacy?

The second major theme of the contributions is the question of Europe's legacy. This question, visible in the preoccupation of both the public and the academy with how to rethink Europe for the future of politics, cannot be considered apart from the question of historical Europe. In the contributions, discussions of the practices, ideologies and histories binding and dividing Europe point to many possible legacies. Some of these, like the nation-state and democratic governance, are explicitly political, even though the nation-state, with extraordinary integrative power, has provided negative lessons for how to democratically "deal with" multiethnic and multicultural societies—lessons that call for models like that of "cultural autonomy" (Shcherbak). Others are material, namely modern urban (De Frantz) and secularly sacred (Sendyka) spaces. Additionally, there are Europe's many cultural products—symphonies (Celestini), plays (Ospovat), films (Bagrov), and the underlying languages themselves (Nykiel)—each of which substantiates the past and carries it into the future. But the examination of legacy also takes place across a more abstract geographical and conceptual plane.

Readers will find consensus in this book that Europe was first and foremost an idea that has contributed in no small way to the fundamental structures of global modernity. In this creative capacity, Europe has appeared as model of social relations and offered a perspective on the relationship between humans and the natural world. As the Enlightenment produced universal claims about humans, nature, and social order, Europeans used them to make sense of a heterogeneous world of practices and beliefs. The emergence of critical schools of thought in modernity reflected changes in the forms and genres of cultural expression and analysis, which both embodied and perceived social reality in ways that transcended the formalism of earlier epochs

(Rejniak-Majewska). In one case, the projection of politics into the arts created new visions of pan-European Absolutism (Ospovat). This process entailed a range of colonial and critical engagements, the legacies of which are still evident. Understanding the nature of this encounter remains a historical project of significant scope and urgency (Spector), while the legacy of the encounter reappears in continuing engagements on unequal political or fiscal footing between Europe and "non-Europe" (Cohen). As Chakrabarty argued, it is this epistemological and ideological heritage, more than geopolitical centrality, that has proved the most resilient legacy of Europe.

The contributors' approach to this legacy contains a tension that forcefully captures the volume's line of inquiry. On one hand, the authors reconstruct the ways in which Europe has produced global categories of self-understanding. Universal categories of philosophy, religion, and science, generated by the Enlightenment, became, through translations in a variety of contexts, integrated with local particularities. The legacies of these projects and the shadows of doubt surrounding them, Chakrabarty suggests, include not only imbalances and inequalities, but also terms of judgment (such as equality before the law, reason and science) that forecast new historical possibilities, greater equality and self-determination. On the other hand, following Chakrabarty and departing from those earlier scholarly engagements that end with Europe's complex legacy, the authors have attempted to press beyond "Europe" as a unit of analysis. Given the needs of the present day, which require thinking on an ecological and planetary scale, perhaps it is too anthropocentric to continue thinking exclusively in terms of Europe—or Asia or India, for that matter.

Europe has been the site of many fruitful world-historical utopias in the past. Let us hope that European scholars, policy makers, and enlightened citizens have the creative capacity to fashion new understandings of the future of their civilization in the decades to come.

We would remiss in concluding this introduction without expressing our profound gratitude to the two foundations that joined forces to sponsor these 20 scholars over the course of five years. With the generous support of the Christian A. Johnson Endeavor and Andrew W. Mellon Foundations, each year's scholars came together in Paris for an orientation to the teaching and research climate at the University of Chicago, and then joined our community in Hyde Park for two quarters. We also wish to thank the faculty who helped to build the program, most of whom then came to Paris for the final conference to continue their mentorship and collegial commentary about research and teaching: Leora Auslander, Robert Bird, Philip Bohlman, Robert Morrissey, Bozena Shallcross, and Tara Zahra. Finally, we wish to thank Martha Merritt and Dan Bertsche for their extraordinary efforts in the preparation of the conference and this volume.

CIVILIZATION AND CORRUPTION: EUROPE IN THE PHILOSOPHICAL HISTORY OF THE FRENCH ENLIGHTENMENT

Céline Spector*

Abstract

Over some thirty years, much research in the field of postcolonial studies has debunked the very idea of a history of Europe as a civilization. With civilization and colonization as two sides of the same coin, it has seemed only right and proper to demystify the concept of which the West claimed paternity. Europe has been called upon to "provincialize" itself, in Dipesh Chakrabarty's provocative formulation. In tune with a more general critique of the Enlightenment, in which the advance of Reason always threatens to become the reign of domination, this postcolonial critique has had a certain raison d'être, insofar as it was necessary to flatten the shaky edifice of a universalism that was nothing other than Eurocentric. But the assaults of "subaltern studies" have also had the effect of denying the reality that Europe was conceived as a civilization at the very time when the critique of its colonization process was beginning to take shape.

In this paper, I will offer a defence of the Enlightenment's anti-colonialism. Some will consider provocative the underlying thesis that eighteenth-century Europe century did not necessarily commit a "theft of history" by taking away the

* Céline Spector is a Professor in the Department of Philosophy at the Bordeaux Montaigne University.

dignity of historical agents from colonized peoples or those left on the margins of 'civilized' spaces. But the truth is that several great philosophers of the French, Scottish, and Dutch Enlightenment paved the way for a new theory of world history capable of accommodating other civilizations as well as that of Europe. Although Europe was credited with a particular destiny, it was also thought of as the site of an ever threatening barbarism and the source of possible crimes against humanity (the first being those which followed the encounter with the Indians of the New World).

To assay the "postcolonial studies critique" is not to throw out its contribution, but to mitigate what today appears to be its one-sided emphasis. After looking at a number of fashionable conceptions of Europe as a "civilization" (what J. G. A. Pocock calls the "Enlightened narrative"), I shall focus on an author of central importance for the further elaboration of the history of Europe (especially in the Scottish Enlightenment); namely, Montesquieu. On questions such as the "Chinese model," the civilization of Russia, or the genocide of New World "savages," Montesquieu was more often than not the springboard for an analysis centered on Europe, whether as model or anti-model. Montesquieu offered the very first reflections on modern Europe as a "civilization," or rather a differentiated civil society, marked by political and religious pluralism (monarchies and republics, Catholic and Protestant nations). This Europe was an economic entity based on the "spirit of commerce," but also a civil society united by its customs and operating as a veritable engine of history in the modern age; a society that, since the discovery of America, had defined itself as different from its others, the continents that it colonized or subjugated.

"END OF A MYTH?"[1] IN 1975 RAYMOND ARON'S DISILLUSION WITH THE process of European construction was already a sign. Today the hope of a federal Europe seems well and truly dead. The post-war golden age that presided over the rebirth of the European project—between the Soviet empire and the American imperial republic—was short-lived. So here we are now, nearly forty years later, at a point where the disenchantment is growing ever deeper.

Yet Europe does not have to be viewed with such forlorn eyes. A single market, more or less regulated, is not necessarily all that remains if the goal of a federation falls by the wayside. We can return to a different history that is also ours, to the idea of Europe as it existed before the simplistic opposition of federation and market took hold. After the moment of birth (the Renaissance[2]) and the moment of hiatus (the Reformation), the eighteenth century, and particularly its second half, forged rich and promising theories of Europe.

---

[1] R. Aron, "Fin d'un mythe?" in *L'Europe des crises* (Brussels: Bruylant, 1976), 123.

[2] J. Hale, *The Civilization of Europe in the Renaissance* (London: Harper Collins, 1993).

During the Enlightenment, Europe was first conceived as a federation in a line of descent from projects for perpetual peace. It was also envisaged as a kind of civil society, uniting peoples or societies beyond the divisions created by the rise of rival nation-states. Europe embodied both the reality of the world market (associated with colonial expansion and imperial rivalries) and the utopia of an association of states delegating part of their sovereignty to guarantee peaceful coexistence. At a deeper level, however, Europe was theorized for the first time as a "civilization."[3]

Over some thirty years, much research in the field of postcolonial studies has debunked the very idea of Europe as a civilization. With civilization and colonization as two sides of the same coin, it has seemed only right and proper to demystify the concept of which the West claimed paternity. Europe has been called upon to "provincialize" itself, in Dipesh Chakrabarty's provocative formulation.[4] Even Braudel's project of a "grammar" of civilizations suddenly appeared scandalous, since it seemed to freeze moving entities and to open the door to the peddlers of a "clash of civilizations."[5] In tune with a more general critique of the Enlightenment, in which the advance of Reason always threatens to become the reign of domination, this postcolonial critique had a certain *raison d'être,* insofar as it was necessary to flatten the shaky edifice of a universalism understood as Eurocentrism. But the assaults of "subaltern studies" also had the effect of denying the reality that Europe was conceived as a civilization at the very time when the critique of its colonization process was beginning to take shape.

In this paper, I will offer a defense of the Enlightenment's anti-colonialism. Some will consider provocative the underlying thesis that Europe did not necessarily commit a "theft of history"[6] in the eighteenth century by taking away the dignity of historical agents from colonized peoples or those left on the margins of "civilized" spaces. But the truth is that several great philosophers of the French, Scottish, and Dutch Enlightenment paved the way for a new theory of world history capable of accommodating other civilizations as well as that of Europe. Although Europe was credited with a particular destiny, it was also thought of as the site of an ever-threatening barbarism and the source

---

[3] The first use of this term in the modern sense dates from 1756, but for the sake of convenience we shall employ it here for a slightly earlier period (the first half of the century).

[4] D. Chakrabarty, *Provincializing Europe: Postcolonial Thought and Historical Difference* (Princeton: Princeton University Press, 2000). See also Edward Said's pioneering *Orientalism: Western Conceptions of the Orient* (London: Routledge & Kegan Paul, 1978).

[5] Originally a manual for final year school students, this was first published in 1963. For an English translation, see F. Braudel, *The History of Civilizations* (London: Penguin, 1995).

[6] J. Goody, *The Theft of History* (Cambridge: Cambridge University Press, 2006).

of possible crimes against humanity (the first being those which followed the encounter with the Indians of the New World).

To assay the "postcolonial studies critique" is not to throw out its contribution, but to mitigate what today appears to be its one-sided emphasis. After looking at a number of fashionable conceptions of Europe as a "civilization" (what J. G. A. Pocock calls the "Enlightened narrative"),[7] I shall focus on an author of central importance for the further elaboration of the history of Europe (especially in the Scottish Enlightenment); namely, Montesquieu.[8] The starting point here will be *The Spirit of the Laws* (1748)—a work that served as a matrix for reflections on Europe (whether to eulogize or criticize it) by eighteenth-century philosophers. From Voltaire to Herder, taking in Diderot, Raynal, and Robertson, the major contributors to the philosophical history of Europe before the French Revolution were all readers of *The Spirit of the Laws*: they attempted either to build upon it or to find an answer to it. On questions such as the "Chinese model," the civilization of Russia, or the genocide of New World "savages," Montesquieu was more often than not the springboard for an analysis centered on Europe, whether as model or anti-model. Montesquieu offered the very first reflections on modern Europe as a "civilization," or rather, a differentiated *civil society* marked by political and religious pluralism (monarchies and republics, Catholic and Protestant nations). This Europe was an economic entity based on the "spirit of commerce," but also a civil society which, since the discovery of America, had defined itself as different from its others, the continents that it colonized or subjugated.

---

[7] See J. G. A. Pocock, "Some Europes in Their History," in *The Idea of Europe: From Antiquity to the European Union*, ed. A. Pagden (Cambridge: Cambridge University Press, 2002), 55–71; *Barbarism and Religion* (Cambridge: Cambridge University Press, 1999), 2:278–88; K. O'Brien, *Narratives of Enlightenment: Cosmopolitan History from Voltaire to Gibbon* (Cambridge: Cambridge University Press, 1997); S. Sebastani, *I limiti del progresso. Razza Europe genere nell'Illuminismo scozzese* (Bologna: Il Mulino, 2008), 229–54; A. Lilti, "'Et la civilisation deviendra générale': L'Europe de Volney ou l'orientalisme à l'épreuve de la Révolution," *La Révolution française* [Online], Dire et faire l'Europe à la fin du XVIIIe siècle, online since 10 June 2011, http://lrf.revues.org/290.

[8] See C. Spector, "Science des mœurs et théorie de la civilisation: de *L'Esprit des lois* de Montesquieu à l'école historique écossaise," in *Les Equivoques de la civilisation*, ed. B. Binoche (Seyssel: Champ Vallon, 2005), 136–60. On William Robertson and his introduction to the *History of the Reign of Charles the Fifth*, 1769 (4 vols.), see S. Sebastiani, "*L'Esprit des lois* nel discorso storico dell'Illuminismo scozzese," in *Montesquieu e i suoi interpreti*, ed. D. Felice (Pisa: ETS, 2005), 211–45; " L'Amérique des Lumières et la hiérarchie des races. Disputes sur l'écriture de l'histoire dans l'*Encyclopaedia Britannica* (1768–1788)," *Annales HSS* 2 (April–June 2012): 327–61; C. Spector, "Penser l'Europe au XVIIIe siècle: le miroir américain dans l'œuvre de William Robertson," *La Révolution française*, Dire et faire l'Europe à la fin du XVIIIe siècle, 14 June 2011, http:/lrf.revues.org/index259.html.

A brief word here about method. This study is not a work of social or cultural history. It does not seek to trace a new awareness of Europe among cultured elites or, more randomly, among the peoples of the continent—a task that a number of other authors have attempted with a greater or lesser degree of success.[9] My aim will not be to uncover in history the matrix of European identity, in the sense in which certain historians have defined Europe as a continent of the mind with a single vocation blending together Greek humanism, Roman legalism, and Christian universalism; nor to deconstruct that mind once again, on the pretext that, although Europe invented liberty, humanism, progress, and tolerance, it also invented servitude and barbarism.[10] Rather, I intend to analyze how the idea of Europe became an object of historical and philosophical knowledge, within the framework of a philosophical history that was not yet a true philosophy of history.[11]

I. EUROPE AS A CIVILIZATION?

Modernity: Europe and Its Others

Since the event known as "the discovery of America," the narrative of European history has started from the figures of otherness with which Europe has found itself confronted: the savage otherness of the Americas, after Columbus and subsequent voyages of discovery; Oriental otherness of the great Persian and

---

[9] See D. Hay, *Europe, The Emergence of an Idea* (Edinburgh: Edinburgh University Press, 1957); J.-B. Duroselle, *L'Idée d'Europe dans l'histoire* (Paris: Denoël, 1965); L. Febvre, *L'Europe. Genèse d'une civilisation, Cours professé au Collège de France en 1944–1945* (Paris: Perrin, 1999); B. Voyenne, *Histoire de l'idée européenne* (Paris: Payot, 1964); R. Barlett, *The Making of Europe: Conquest, Colonization and Cultural Change, 950–1350* (London: Penguin, 1994); *L'Europe à la recherche de son identité*, ed. C. Villain-Gandossi (Lille: Éditions du CTHS, 2002); D. Heater, *The Idea of European Unity* (New York: St. Martin's Press, 1992); F. Draus, *Critique historique de l'idée européenne* (Paris: Guibert, 2009); J.-F. Schaub, *L'Europe a-t-elle une histoire?* (Paris: Albin Michel, 2008); F. Chabod, *Storia dell'idea d"Europa* (Bari: Laterza, 1971). And, more specifically on the eighteenth century: J. Meyer, *L'Europe des Lumières* (Le Coteau: Horvath, 1989); P.-Y. Beaurepaire, *Le Mythe de l'Europe française au XVIIIe siècle. Diplomatie, culture et sociabilités au temps des Lumières* (Paris: Autrement, 2007); G. Py, *L'Idée d'Europe au siècle des Lumières* (Paris: Vuibert, 2004).

[10] See *Facing Each Other: The World's Perception of Europe and Europe's Perception of the World*, ed. A. Pagden (ldershot, UK: Ashgate, 2000); A. Pagden, "Deconstructing Europe," *History of European Ideas*, 18/3 (1994), 329–46; A. Pagden, "Vous autres Européens—or Inventing Europe," *Acta Philosophica* 14/2 (1993): 141–58.

[11] See M. Verga, "European Civilization and the "Emulation of the Nations": Histories of Europe from the Enlightenment to Guizot," *History of European Ideas* 34 (2008), 353–60; *Storie d'Europa. Secoli XVIII–XXI* (Rome: Carocci, 2004).

Ottoman empires, which gave rise to the static fiction of "Oriental despotism" and the erotic fantasy of the harem; Asiatic (especially Chinese) otherness of a great civilization which, before Europe, successfully mastered the arts, including the art of government; and Russian otherness, which prompts questioning about civilization as *process* and *project*, as reality and *task* or *ideal*, since the whole point is to know how Russia can be "civilized" by importing European sciences, arts, and politics. For a long time too—and this tendency has grown continually stronger—historiography has emphasized that the question "how did Europe become European?" is inseparable from how Europe could be so barbaric (philosophers have never stopped reflecting on its *original sin*, the massacre of the Amerindians).

Thus, the idea of Europe proceeds from a reflection on the specificity of its history: How is it that Europe could be free and prosperous, in contrast to the decline of the Ottoman Empire and the regimes of servitude that it embodied? How could Europe overtake China, having previously been inferior to its civilization? And how could Russia become European by civilizing itself through the import of foreign customs? These threads come together in a philosophical question: what are the causes (economic, cultural, and political) of the rise of European civilization since the fall of the Roman Empire and the preceding collapse of Greco-Roman civilization?

In short, the advent of the European idea in the eighteenth century was linked to two guiding threads: the projects of perpetual peace that underlay European unification (the path to federation later embodied in the League of Nations); and the theories of a civilizing process, sometimes accompanied with colonization projects or "plans."[12] The former track, pointing toward cosmopolitan institutions, reached its highpoint in Saint-Pierre or Kant, and its principal critique in Rousseau or Hegel.[13] The latter theories met their

---

12 See, among recent works: E. Easley, *The War over Perpetual Peace: An Exploration into the History of a Foundational International Relations Text* (New York: Palgrave Macmillan, 2004); B. Arcidiacono, *Cinq types de paix, Une histoire des plans de pacification perpétuelle (XVIIe–XXe siècles)* (Paris: Presses Universitaires de France, 2011); J.-P. Bois, *La paix. Histoire politique et militaire* (Paris: Perrin, 2012).

13 See C. Spector, "Le *Projet de paix perpétuelle*: de Saint-Pierre à Rousseau," in Rousseau, *Principes du droit de la guerre. Ecrits sur le Projet de Paix Perpétuelle de l'abbé de Saint-Pierre*, ed. B. Bachofen and C. Spector (Paris: Vrin, 2008), 229–94; "Who is the Author of the *Abstract of Monsieur l'Abbé de Saint-Pierre's* Plan for Perpetual Peace? From Saint-Pierre to Rousseau," *History of European Ideas* 39/3 (2013): 371–393; F. Markovits, "L'Europe en question: Castel de Saint-Pierre et Mably," in "Le Grand Danger", ed. J.-P. Faye, *Passages d'encres*, n° 42, June 2011. For a contemporary reprise, see U. Beck and E. Grande, *Cosmopolitan Europe* (Cambridge: Polity, 2007).

fiercest opponents in such eighteenth-century figures as Anquetil Duperron, who heaped scorn on Montesquieu, and in the late twentieth-century current of post-colonial studies. One side offered a critique of the idealism or utopianism that still hangs over European federalism; the other, a critique of the imperialism and ethnocentrism of the Enlightenment. Scylla and Charybdis, perhaps.

The second track, however—the affirmation and critique of civilization—remains the less well known. Among the first great theorists of the European "spirit," Europe is not associated with a system of institutions but is rather seen as the privileged site of the modern civilizing process. The analysis most commonly focuses on the causes of its ever-vaunted "exceptionalism." Critical minds today may denounce the dead end into which that kind of thinking led. But the Enlightenment was less naïve than people often claim, and it would be wrong to project onto it the schema that first appeared in the nineteenth century with the great philosophers of history. At least one cannot credit the major eighteenth-century philosophers (Montesquieu, Rousseau, Diderot, Voltaire, Robertson, Herder ...) with the illusion shared by numerous defenders of the "Christian roots" of the European Union. Among the *philosophes*, modern European history is often used as a kind of war machine against Christianity and the blind alleys of missionary evangelism. Although the *philosophes* sometimes allied Islam with Oriental despotism, they also reflected on the causes and consequences of the Reformation, without prejudging the Christian unity of Europe. Above all, reflection on the "modernity" of Europe went together with a secularization of providential world history so that "civilization" enshrined a new teleology of emancipation.

European History as a History of Emancipation?

The emergence in the eighteenth century of histories of *Europe* (rather than of individual countries, as Pufendorf still proposed), together with philosophies of history (Voltaire) or historical *tableaux* (Robertson), was a key moment in the construction of Europe as a theoretical object. With his *Essay on the Manners of Nations*, Voltaire launched a radical critique of Eurocentric providential history in the style of Bossuet. Europe was no longer the natural (or divine) subject of universal history but one civilization among others, following China and India in the work's order of exposition.[14] The history of Europeanization after the fall of the Roman Empire is here not only one of emancipation (the victory of reason over prejudices, enlightenment over fanaticism and superstition,

[14] See Voltaire, *Essai sur les mœurs,* ed. B. Bruno et al. (Oxford: Voltaire Foundation, 2009–2012 et seq.).

civilization over barbarism, gentleness over cruelty, the sciences and arts over ignorance, and liberty over the serfdom and servitude associated the feudal system). The invention of the "history of Europe" also testifies to its wrong-doing (the Crusades, the Inquisition, the extermination of the Amerindians, the enslavement of Africans) and to its steps backward (the wars of religion). Above all, it places a question mark over the dominant Eurocentrism, either by invoking older models of civilization (China, Ancient India[15]) or by reversing the roles à la Montaigne so that "civilized" man appears more barbaric than those he calls "savages," or by rehabilitating age-old enemies (the Ottoman Empire), or by cutting the ground from under perennial customs (so that hereditary nobility becomes an absurd practice of which nine-tenths of the planet rightly has no knowledge).

In this light, the laborious advances of reason in Europe do not make it the cradle of civilization, or even its main area of expansion: Voltaire's reflections on the fate of civilizations after colonial expansion betray a profoundly ambivalent attitude to Europe's hold over the rest of the world. Defined by a backlash from the great discoveries, but also by its splits and schisms, Europe has its strength in economic development but also in its philosophical capacity for self-criticism. In his contribution to the *History of the Two Indies*, Diderot would convert the denunciation of injustice into a call for emancipation—although one could suspect that his rejection of forcible colonization ends only in an appeal for "soft colonization," using the economy of desire and cross-breeding to obtain the consent of colonized subjects to their domination.[16]

Europe as Civil Society

Before this radical exposure of the imperialist attitude of the great European powers, Rousseau had formulated a powerful critique (quite unrelated to the issue of colonization[17]) of Europe as a market-oriented civil society. His argument is developed in the "Extrait du Projet de paix perpétuelle de M. l'abbé

[15] On William Robertson's *Historical Disquisition*, see G. Carnhall, "Robertson and Contemporary Images of India," in *Robertson and the Expansion of Empire,* ed. S. J. Brown (Cambridge: Cambridge University Press, 1997), 210–30.

[16] Diderot, *Histoire des deux Indes,* in *Œuvres,* III (Paris: Robert Laffont, 1995), 689–97 (cf. Diderot, "Extracts from the *Histoire des Indes*," in *Political Writings*, ed. J. H. Mason and R. Wokler [Cambridge: Cambridge University Press, 1992], 165–214); see S. Muthu, *Enlightenment against Empire* (Princeton: Princeton University Press, 2003), chap. 3; S. M. Agnani, "'Doux commerce, douce colonisation': Diderot and the Two Indies of the French Enlightenment," in *The Anthropology of the Enlightenment,* ed. L. Wolff (Stanford: Stanford University Press, 2007), 65–84; S. M. Agnani, *Hating Empire Properly: The Two Indies and the Limits of Enlightenment Anticolonialism* (New York: Fordham University Press, 2013).

[17] This surprising silence is polemically underlined in C. W. Mill, *The Racial Contract* (New York: Cornell University Press, 1999).

de Saint-Pierre," published in 1761.[18] Trying to improve Saint-Pierre's political thought, Rousseau actually invents an argument that in his view does more justice to the thesis of the *Projet de paix perpétuelle* (before refuting it in his own *Jugement* on the Project).[19] Here Europe acquires a new dimension: history, Rousseau argues, has created a space where different peoples, whether they like it or not, are caught up in a common destiny.[20] The European powers form "a sort of system among themselves which unites them by one single religion, the same international law, morals, literature, commerce, and a sort of equilibrium that is the necessary effect of all this."[21] Rousseau mentions a "society among the nations of Europe" and tries to explain its birth. Rome—which, following its conquests, awarded citizenship to all its subjects and imposed the rule of a single law—was initially responsible for the "political and civil union" that "formed among all the members of a single empire."[22] After the empire of politics and law came the empire of religion: "A third bond, stronger than the preceding ones, was that of Religion, and one cannot deny that it is above all to Christianity that Europe still owes today the sort of society that has endured among its members."[23]

According to Rousseau, then, European society emerges through its social bonds: here one finds historical continuity, despite the decay of political forms. Priesthood and empire shaped the link among peoples that previously had no real community of rights or interests. Even the decay of the Roman Empire did not abolish that community of peoples. The European cultural space owes its unity not to the drawing of geographical frontiers but to the appearance of a "real society" endowed with common mores and, to some degree, even common laws:

"All these causes joined together form out of Europe, not merely an ideal collection of Peoples who have nothing in common but a name like Asia or Africa, but a real society which has its morals, its Religion, its customs and even its laws, which none of the Peoples who compose it can set aside without soon causing disturbances.[24]"

---

[18] Rousseau, "*Abstract of Monsieur l'Abbé de Saint-Pierre's* Plan for Perpetual Peace," in *Collected Writings of Rousseau* [CWR], vol. 11, trans. C. Kelly (Hanover, NH: University Press of New England, 1995), 27–48.

[19] Rousseau, *The Confessions*, in CWR, vol. 5, book 9, 354–56. On Saint-Pierre, see C. Spector, "L'Europe de l'abbé de Saint-Pierre," in *Les Projets de l'abbé Castel de Saint-Pierre (1658–1743)*, ed. C. Dornier and C. Poulin (Caen: PUC, 2011), 39–49.

[20] See B. Bernardi, "Rousseau et l'Europe: sur l'idée de société civile européenne," and C. Spector, "Le *Projet de paix perpétuelle*: de Saint-Pierre à Rousseau," in *Principes du droit de la guerre, Écrits sur le Projet de Paix Perpétuelle de l'abbé de Saint-Pierre*, ed. B. Bachofen and C. Spector (Paris: Vrin, 2008), 295–330 and 229–294.

[21] Rousseau, *Abstract*, 29.

[22] Ibid., 30.

[23] Ibid.

[24] Ibid., 31.

Rousseau thus speaks of Europe as a "real society" or "real community," before considering it as a political entity (a federation of sovereign states agreeing on a social contract). He dwells on its singularity: Europe is more fertile, more populous, better "joined up in its parts" than the rest of the world; it is streaked with rivers that make communication easier. Rousseau even mentions the situation of its inhabitants, their restlessness and propensity to travel, their urge to communicate all the time since the invention of printing, and their inclination for trade as a way of satisfying their numerous desires. This *Europe of commerce*, in the broad sense that the term had in those days—material and cultural commerce as the vehicle of communication among people—is by no means the Europe that corresponds to Rousseau's wishes. But it is certainly the one he describes here, in the service of Saint-Pierre's thought. For since this Europe of commerce is unable to regulate itself, since it is shot through with conflicting ambitions that cannot be stabilized, it seems necessary to create a federation endowed with a common interest (peace)—although it is not feasible in a monarchical Europe, where power rivalries cannot be called off. While regarding Saint-Pierre's projected federation as virtually impossible to achieve, Rousseau therefore invents a new theoretical object: Europe as *civil society*, not just a political society.

Nevertheless, Rousseau uncovers this cultural unity of Europe only by displaying its many-sided corruption: the perverse effects of the sciences and arts on liberty and virtue, the reign of self-interest that makes all Europeans "bourgeois." Since the Renaissance, the Europe of the arts and sciences, of commerce, luxury, and finance, has also been the Europe of inequality and servitude. Montaigne's presentiment finds confirmation here. Europe is homogenous insofar as the structure of its social relations is the same. It forms the worst breeding ground for the urges of distinction and domination. Europe has one and the same "spirit" insofar as commerce, the primacy of self-interest, and the emergence of political economy have abolished local and national idiosyncrasies, producing a bland uniformity at the level of Europe: "[now] there are only Europeans. All have the same tastes, the same passions, the same morals."[25]

II. MONTESQUIEU: *DOUX COMMERCE* AND CIVILIZATION

But a less bleak reading of European history is still possible. A couple of years before Rousseau, Montesquieu considered the commercial spirit as the true engine of history, prosperity, peace, and political liberty. In *The Spirit of the Laws*, Europe features as a subject of history, warding off a certain

---

25 Rousseau, *Considerations on the Government of Poland*, in CWR, 11: 174–75.

type of empire, which would transform it from the soil of liberty and "gentle commerce" (*doux commerce*)[26] into a place of servitude. According to Montesquieu, the move from conquest to commerce is the only option for Europe.[27]

Europe and Asia: Western Liberty Facing Oriental Despotism?

In *The Spirit of the Laws*, Europe is conceived primarily as a *plural* geographical entity. Sketching the wide expanse of a continent (its Eastern frontiers include Moscow and part of Turkey[28]), Montesquieu highlights the climatic, geographical, and topographical characteristics that predispose it towards moderation: the temperate zone in which it is located follows an imperceptible gradation, which explains the difficulty of conquering a neighboring people with a similar degree of courage (according to climate-based theories[29]). The division of Europe into Mediterranean and Northern countries does not alter the substance of the matter. What counts is the *differential* within a particular area. This is the explanation of the "strength of Europe" and its liberty:

> In Asia the strong and weak nations face each other; the brave and active warrior peoples are immediately adjacent to effeminate, lazy and timid peoples; therefore, one must be the conquered and the other the conqueror. In Europe, on the other hand, strong nations face the strong; those that are adjacent have almost the same amount of courage. This is the major reason for the weakness of Asia and the strength of Europe, for the liberty of Europe and the servitude of Asia: a cause that I think has never before been observed. This is why liberty never increases in Asia, whereas in Europe it increases or decreases according to the circumstances.[30]

---

[26] See A. O. Hirschman, *The Passions and the Interests* (Princeton: Princeton University Press, 1977).

[27] See A. Pagden, *Lords of all the World* (New Haven: Yale University Press, 1995), 115–23; *Peoples and Empires* (New York: The Modern Library, 2001), chap. 7.

[28] See Montesquieu, *The Spirit of the Laws,* ed. A. M. Cohler et al. (Cambridge: Cambridge University Press, 1989), henceforth SL, cited by volume, chapter and/or page numbers. See also *Persian Letters*, trans. C. J. Betts (London: Penguin, 1973), henceforth PL.

[29] We cannot enter here into the assumptions behind such theories. See D. de Casabianca, *Montesquieu. De l'étude des sciences à l'esprit des lois* (Paris: Champion, 2008); C. Spector, *Montesquieu. Liberté, droit et histoire* (Paris: Michalon, 2010).

[30] SL, 17: 3.

Such a characterization of Oriental "weakness," structurally opposed to European "strength," seems to reinforce the idea of a set of knowledge and powers underpinning the European claim to hegemony. Not only is Europe endowed "by nature" with an aptitude for liberty that others lack, but Asia exhibits characteristics (effeminacy, laziness, timidity) that seem to cry out for its potential civilizers, or possible conquerors, to assert energetic mastery over it. The contrast is truly striking: "In Asia there reigns a spirit of servitude that has never left it, and in all the histories of this country it is not possible to find a single trait marking a free soul; one will never see there anything but the heroism of servitude."[31]

Topological factors operate in the same way: because of the vast plains that facilitate its conquest, "in Asia one has always seen great empires; in Europe they were never able to continue to exist."[32] According to Montesquieu, "natural divisions" [high mountains and wide rivers, not vast plains] delineate a territory that is fragmented and resistant to empire. Unlike the Oriental world, Europe is therefore governed by "a genius for liberty, which makes it very difficult to subjugate each part and to put it under a foreign force other than by laws and by what is useful to its commerce."[33] Here arises the theme of European dynamism versus "Oriental inertia." Not only do physical causes incline Orientals to idleness, voluptuousness, cowardice, and *ipso facto* servitude, but moral causes (religion, economics, politics) most often accentuate those effects: such is the case especially in India, where the dominant religion supposedly reinforces the passivity bound up with climate.[34] China, though despotic, is an exception in this regard.[35]

The difficulty, however, is to assess the naturalization of the three forms of servitude (political, civil, and domestic) in the vast torrid plains of Asia. Are non-European peoples dominated by nature, with no politics or history? Should one follow the great Orientalist Anquetil-Duperron, who systematically criticized the conception of Oriental despotism in *The Spirit of the Laws*, and conclude that "on some points perhaps Europeans need to take a

---

[31] SL, 17: 6. See F. Chabod, *Storia dell'idea d'Europa* (Rome: Laterza, 2007), 87f.; P. Rolland, "Montesquieu et l'Europe," in *L'Europe entre deux tempéraments politiques: idéal d'unité et particularismes régionaux. Etudes d'Histoire des Idées Politiques* (Aix-en-Provence: Presses Universitaires d'Aix-Marseille, 1994), 41–60; S. M. Mason, "Montesquieu's Vision of Europe and its European Context," *SVEC* 341 (Oxford: Voltaire Foundation, 1996), 61–87.

[32] SL, 17: 6; cf. *Réflexions sur la monarchie universelle* (henceforth RMU), § VIII.

[33] Ibid.

[34] SL, 14: 5.

[35] SL, 8: 21; 19: 16–19. See J. Pereira, *Montesquieu et la Chine* (Paris: L'Harmattan, 2008).

lesson from Orientals"?[36] No doubt the "facts" mentioned by Montesquieu (following Chardin, Tavernier, or Ricaut) are sometimes questionable. No doubt the theory of despotism is knowingly a caricature. Yet one should avoid a simplistic reading: unlike many nineteenth-century theorists of progress, Montesquieu does not express the notion of Europe's intangible superiority. In the *Persian Letters*, as in *The Spirit of the Laws*, the portrait of Oriental despotism emerges from a complex process in which travel accounts combine with criticisms of absolute monarchy. Montesquieu's harem, for example, with its system of favors, has echoes of Versailles—so much did Louis XIV pay heed to "Oriental politics."[37]

The truth of despotism is not that of a reflection: far from being confined to the Orient, Persia, Turkey, China, or Japan, it represents the threat weighing on all forms of government, republican or monarchical. A moderate predisposition may come up against conquest and political hyper-centralization, two dimensions of power abuse. For Montesquieu, the genius of European liberty remains precarious: "Most European peoples are still governed by mores. But if, by a long abuse of power or by a great conquest, despotism becomes established at a certain time, neither mores nor climate would hold firm, and in this fine part of the world, human nature would suffer, at least for a while, the insults heaped upon it in the other three."[38] Political liberty may increase or decrease according to circumstances. And the state of war among great European powers acts against liberty and prosperity, so much so that Montesquieu cites Turkey as an example because of its greater frugality. On account of the balance of powers—a continental equilibrium involving the excessive arming of nations—Europe escapes empire only at an exorbitant cost: "We are poor with the wealth of the whole universe."[39] In no way does Europe have a perennial solution at its disposal: "Oriental despotism" provides it only with the mirror of its possible destiny.

---

[36] Anquetil Duperron, *Législation orientale* (Amsterdam: Marc-Michel Rey, 1778), 7. See S. Stuurman, "Cosmopolitan Egalitarianism in the Enlightenment. Anquetil Duperron on India and America," *Journal of the History of Ideas* 68/2 (April 2007): 255–278.

[37] PL, 37. On the *Persian Letters*, see A. Grosrichard, *Structure du sérail. La fiction du despotisme asiatique dans l'Occident classique* (Paris: Seuil, 1979); C. Spector, *Montesquieu, Les* Lettres persanes. *De l'anthropologie à la politique* (Paris: P.U.F., 1997); D. J. Schaub, *Erotic Liberalism: Women and Revolution in Montesquieu's* Persian Letters (London: Rowman & Littlefield Publishers, 1995).

[38] SL, 8: 8. See P. Rétat, "La représentation du monde dans *L'Esprit des lois*. La place de l'Europe," in *L'Europe de Montesquieu, Cahiers Montesquieu,* ed. A. Postigliola and M. G. Bottaro Palumbo (Oxford: Voltaire Foundation, 1995), 7–16 (and the whole of the volume).

[39] SL, 13: 17; cf. RMU, § 24.

Christianity and Barbarism

One still needs to examine the birth of Europe and its "spirit," which has nothing to do with any inherent essence. The main aspect is Christianity: "Separated from the rest of the world by religion, by vast seas, and by deserts," Europe is opposed to the Muslim world, which, a footnote points out, surrounds it almost everywhere.[40] The gentleness (*douceur*) of Christian religion is expressed in its contribution to political rights and international law: "The Christian religion is remote from pure despotism; the gentleness so recommended in the gospel stands opposed to the despotic fury with which a prince would mete out his own justice and exercise his cruelties."[41] The eulogy extends to its social and political usefulness: since Christianity does not encourage separation (of men and women, prince and subjects), it supposedly excludes the spirit of despotism. Is the justification for its civilizing project contained here *in nuce*? "In spite of the size of the Ethiopian empire and the vice of its climate, the Christian religion has kept despotism from being established there and has carried the mores and laws of Europe to the middle of Africa."[42] The homage is even more applicable with regard to international law, or *jus publicum europeanum*. This is how Montesquieu explains the existence of a kind of unity of modern Europe beyond its wars and conflicts:

> This right of nations, among ourselves, has the result that victory leaves to the vanquished these great things: life, liberty, laws, goods, and always religion, when one does not blind oneself. *One can say that the peoples of Europe today are no more disunited than were the peoples and the armies, or the armies themselves, in the Roman Empire when it became despotic and military*; on the one hand, the armies waged war with one another, and, on the other, they were allowed to take the spoils of the towns and to divide or confiscate the lands.[43]

However, the praise of the European spirit—as opposed to the ferociously destructive spirit of Oriental despots—has more than one side to it. On the one hand, the state of war that undermines Europe is attenuated by

---

[40] SL, 23: 25.
[41] SL, 24: 3.
[42] Ibid.
[43] Ibid., emphases added. Cf. SL, 10: 3.

the existence of international law, which supposedly protects nations from the mad ambitions of princes. On the other hand, Montesquieu sees between European moderation and the genius of Christianity only a link of expediency, which owes nothing to the *truth* of the religion of the Gospels.[44] Furthermore, this contribution is by no means unequivocal: the utility of Catholicism for imperialist ends is demonstrated by the conquest, enslavement, or actual extermination of the Amerindians. In France, it was the pretext of evangelization that led Louis XIII to ship slaves into his colonies so that they could be converted.[45] As to the Spanish, they invoke the mission assigned to them by Pope Alexander VI to reenact the role of the *Imperium Romanum*, seeking to export Christianity to a climate that cannot receive it.[46] One of the greatest crimes in history (the enslavement and genocide of the Amerindians) was committed in the name of religion. The so-called civilized nations, as Montaigne saw, are the real barbarians.[47]

From Spirit of Conquest to Spirit of Commerce

But Montesquieu also outlines Europe's political future. Whereas the *Considerations on the Causes of the Greatness of the Romans and Their Decline* shows that the enlargement of empire can only result in its decline, the *Reflections on Universal Monarchy* provides a demonstration of this for the benefit of modern politics: no constant hegemony like that of the Romans is possible any longer in Europe.[48] In *The Spirit of the Laws*, universal monarchy is considered senseless: "nothing would have been more deadly for Europe" than the success of Louis XIV's project.[49] Facing the twin risk of invasion from without and insurrection from within, every earthly empire is doomed to dissolution or despotism.[50]

---

[44] SL, 24: 4.

[45] SL, 15: 4. In the *Persian Letters*, Montesquieu is even more severe (PL, 75).

[46] SL, 29: 24.

[47] See the "very humble remonstrance" to the Inquisitors: "We must warn you of one thing; it is that, if someone in the future ever dares to say that the peoples of Europe had a police in the century in which we live, you will be cited to prove that they were barbarians, and the idea one will have about you will be such that it will stigmatize your century and bring hatred on all your contemporaries." (SL, 25: 13).

[48] In the end, the text of the *Reflections* was never published (Montesquieu having destroyed the copies of it out of prudence), but many individual passages were incorporated into *The Spirit of the Laws*. On the *Considerations*, see the introduction and notes by C. Larrère in *Oeuvres Complètes*, vol. 2 (Oxford: Voltaire Foundation, 2000).

[49] SL, 9: 7.

[50] RMU, 10, 349; *Mes Pensées* (MP), 1829; SL, 8: 17 and 9: 6.

Yet the rejection of empire does not entail any yearning for a federal Europe based on a permanent Congress of States. Montesquieu has no faith in Saint-Pierre's or Leibniz's conception of a European republic.[51] *The Spirit of the Laws* outlines another option for Europe: the path of commerce rather than war. The passage from the spirit of conquest to the spirit of commerce induces profound changes, since commercial powers cannot gain lasting hegemony.[52] Whereas war separates peoples, commerce is supposed to unite them. The reciprocal satisfaction of needs is the source of the interdependence of societies. Europe is now conceived as a civil society: "A prince thinks he will become greater through the ruining of a nearby state. On the contrary! Things in Europe are such that all countries depend on one another. France needs the opulence of Poland and Muscovy, as Guyenne needs Brittany, and Brittany, Anjou. Europe is a country made up of a number of provinces."[53]

The Spirit of the Laws therefore contributes to the idea of Europe as an *economic* subject of history.[54] Now at the center of trade with the world, "Europe has reached such a high degree of power that nothing in history is comparable to it."[55] But new questions arise: Has Europe been diverted from the dream of imperial unity only to constitute new forms of empire outside its own territory? Does the emancipatory project of modernity serve as the vehicle of a negative dialectic bearing forms of domination more insidious than those it claims to abolish? Commerce, wedded as it is to sociability, may help to reduce violence on the soil of Europe. But does it not lead to the export of imperial violence elsewhere and to a new kind of colonization?

Sea Empire and Land Empire

Book XXI of *The Spirit of the Laws* sets out a history of Europe in its relations with the rest of the world. In tracing the paths whereby Europe developed the premises of a world history, Montesquieu aims to refute those who claim Rome as a model for modern nations. In the name of a drive to civilize and convert others, Spain and Portugal were even more cruel and "barbaric" than

---

[51] Letter to the Baron of Stain, 17 October 1729. On Montesquieu's relation to Saint-Pierre, see C. Spector, "Montesquieu, critique du *Projet de Paix Perpétuelle*?" in *Montesquieu et l'Europe,* ed. J. Mondot et al. (Bordeaux: Académie Montesquieu, 2006), 139–75.

[52] RMU, 2, 342–43. Cf. *Considérations sur les causes de la grandeur des Romains*, 4: 114. See C. Larrère, "Montesquieu on Economics and Commerce," in *Montesquieu's Science of Politics,* ed. D. Carrithers et al. (New York: Rowman & Littlefield, 2001), 335–74.

[53] MP, 318; cf. RMU, 18. The texts supporting this thesis are cited in C. Spector, *Montesquieu et l'émergence de l'économie politique* (Paris: Honoré Champion, 2006), chap. 4.

[54] On this transition, see M. Foucault, *Security, Territory, Population: Lectures at the Collège de France 1977–1978* (Basingstoke, UK: Palgrave Macmillan, 2007), Lecture of 22 March 1978, 285–310.

[55] SL, 21: 21.

Rome: not only did they fail in their project of domination, but they fueled destructive rivalries within European nations through the logic of land-grabbing that followed the discovery of the New World.[56] Montesquieu contrasts several forms of empire: while colonial expansion is destructive when based on an outdated identification of wealth with gold and silver, as in Mexico or Peru, it contributes to prosperity when it is based on the exchange of wealth rooted in agriculture, manufacturing, and commerce—foreign trade bringing internal trade in its wake.

Yet like the scorpion in the fable, Europe could not give up empire. In *The Spirit of the Laws*, modernity was associated with the invention of a new, more refined figure of colonization: the colonies of settlement favored by the Spanish and Portuguese gave way to the trading posts or commercial colonies established by the maritime powers (Holland, England). Europe was now associated with the system of colonial exclusion. Montesquieu describes this system as a "fundamental law" of Europe, stipulating economic advantages that the mother country enjoys in return for military and civil advantages offered to the colonies:

> Thus, in Europe it remains a fundamental law that any commerce with a foreign colony is regarded as a pure monopoly enforceable by the laws of the country; and one must not judge this by the laws and examples of ancient peoples, which are hardly applicable. It is acknowledged that the commerce established between mother countries does not include permission to trade in the colonies, where it continues to be prohibited to them. *The disadvantage to the colonies, which lose the liberty of commerce, is visibly compensated by the protection of the mother country, which defends them by her arms or maintains them by her laws.* What follows from this is a third law of Europe, that, when foreign commerce is prohibited with the colony, one can navigate its seas only when this is established by treaties.[57]

Now, this argument of colonial protection by weapons and laws seems dubious. Obviously, these colonies did not benefit from reciprocal trade, nor did they really consent to "the laws of Europe" imposed upon them. Commercial exchanges in favor of Europe made it the dominant economic player since Columbus's voyages of discovery,[58] so much so that Montesquieu

---

[56] Ibid.

[57] SL, 21: 21, emphases added.

[58] 'Father du Halde says that the internal commerce of China is greater than that of all Europe. This might be, if our external commerce did not increase our internal commerce. Europe carries

makes the colonial powers (Holland, England, France) true "tyrants" of Europe and the world.[59] Of course, as commerce blossoms in places of liberty, every situation is in theory reversible. But the historical rootedness of the "genius of servitude" and the "spirit of liberty" makes it difficult to argue that the globalization of trade so beneficial to Europe could work to the advantage of another continent instead (America aside).[60] Although the universality of commerce is certainly a de-centering force—it does not establish any privileged position around which the rest of the world must forever circle[61]—the privilege granted here to Europe is quite patent.

Montesquieu's attitude to the slave trade shares in this ambivalence. Although Montesquieu offers one of the earliest philosophical condemnations of slavery, complete with flashes of irony ("The peoples of Europe, having exterminated those of America, had to make slaves of those of Africa in order to use them to clear so much land"[62]), he also speaks of the "necessity" of servile labor to maintain the triangular commerce:

> The consequence of the discovery of America was to link Asia and Africa to Europe. America furnished Europe with the material for its commerce in that vast part of Asia called the East Indies. Silver, that metal so useful to commerce as a sign, was also the basis for the greatest commerce of the universe as a commodity. Finally, voyages to Africa became necessary; they furnished men to work the mines and lands of America.[63]

The contradiction is in the thing itself. While denouncing the abuses of slavery in all its forms (domestic, civil, and political), Montesquieu reveals Europe's new imperial tendencies, to the detriment of the rest of the world. Yet he never argues from the superiority of European customs to justify the general imposition of a model of civilization: such imperialism is potentially

---

on the commerce and navigation of the other three parts of the world, just as France, England and Holland carry on nearly all the navigation and commerce of Europe.' (SL, 21: 21).

[59] MP, 568.

[60] Africa suffers from the same spirit of servitude as Asia, but America, "destroyed and newly repopulated by the nations of Europe and Africa, can scarcely demonstrate its own genius today." (SL, 17: 6–7).

[61] See C. Larrère, *Actualité de Montesquieu* (Paris: Presses de la Fondation nationale des Sciences politiques, 1999), 125–26.

[62] SL, 15: 5. See C. Spector, ""Il est impossible que nous supposions que ces gens-là soient des hommes": la théorie de l'esclavage au livre XV de *L'Esprit des lois*," *Lumières* 3 (2004): 15–51; J. Ehrard, *Lumières et esclavage* (Brussels: André Versaille, 2008).

[63] SL, 21: 21.

tyrannical, as in the case of Peter the Great, who sought to foist European sciences, arts, and mores on Russia.[64] In his short *Encyclopédie* article, "Europe," the Chevalier de Jaucourt would develop much more vigorously the "grand narrative" of European superiority linked to its civilizing process, while compiling several passages from *The Spirit of the Laws*.

CONCLUSION

The Enlightenment philosophers were not naïve young innocents. They became trapped in their contradictions as they tried to leave behind a violent system of colonization and subjugation and aimed at one of peaceful reciprocal trade between Europe and the rest of the world. But one should not too hastily fault their attempt to analyze the "spirit" of modern Europe or to account for its gradual civilizing process. In the work of Montesquieu, Rousseau, Voltaire, Robertson, Diderot-Raynal, or Herder,[65] Europe is thought of in an ambiguous manner. On the one hand, it is the territory where the great monarchical (and sometimes despotic) powers compete with one another to grab the largest share of the world cake, using raw materials, native peoples, and slaves for their purposes. On the other hand, facing the immobility of the "savage" nations or "Oriental despotism," Europe is the main locus of a civilizing process that is also a process of emancipation. After the Roman Empire, the barbarian invasions, and the feudal system, modern commercial Europe is the soil of political and civil liberty, the birthplace of commerce, luxury, taste, sociability, sciences, and arts.

After Edward Said, it is thus tempting to denounce the roots of a suspect "Orientalism" that projected the West's desire for hegemony onto the Orient and to deplore the construction of a mythical Asia and America destined to showcase Europe's superiority. The question arises all the more because several Enlightenment philosophers (above all, Montesquieu, Robertson, and Raynal) praised the invention, in modern Europe, of a new form of commercial colonization. It is but one step from that to inculpating those who were sometimes also behind the "four-stages" theory, which detected the advent of "civilized" societies out of nomad societies. Truly, the Enlightenment philosophers did invent a grand narrative of civilization in which Europe was the core area.

---

[64] SL, 19: 14.

[65] On Diderot and Raynal, see K. Ohji, "Civilisation et naissance de l'histoire mondiale dans l'*Histoire des deux Indes* de Raynal," *Revue de synthèse* 129/1 (2008): 57–83. See also *Penser l'Europe au XVIIIe siècle. Commerce, Civilisation, Empire,* ed. A. Lilti and C. Spector, Oxford: Oxford University Studies in the Enlightenment, 2014.

Yet we should not jump to the conclusion that the Enlightenment philosophers were committed to a "theft" of other people's history. Just as "civilization" became the keyword of a certain philosophy of history only around the turn of the nineteenth century (reaching its climax in Guizot[66]), it may be that the changeover from sharply anti-imperial philosophers such as Diderot, Smith, Bentham, Burke, and Constant to philosophers of liberty, such as Condorcet or John Stuart Mill, who defended colonization in the name of civilization,[67] took place at the beginning of the nineteenth century. "Orientalism," then, was not intrinsic to the conception of Europe as "civilization."

BIBLIOGRAPHY

Agnani, S. M. "'Doux commerce, douce colonisation': Diderot and the Two Indies of the French Enlightenment." In *The Anthropology of the Enlightenment,* ed. L. Wolff, 65–84. Stanford: Stanford University Press, 2007.

———. *Hating Empire Properly: The Two Indies and the Limits of Enlightenment Anticolonialism*. New York: Fordham University Press, 2013.

Anquetil Duperron, A. H. *Législation orientale*. Amsterdam: Marc-Michel Rey, 1778.

Arcidiacono, B. *Cinq types de paix, Une histoire des plans de pacification perpétuelle (XVIIe–XXe siècles)*. Paris: Presses Universitaires de France, 2011.

Aron, R. "Fin d'un mythe?" In *L'Europe des crises*. Brussels: Bruylant, 1976.

Barlett, R. *The Making of Europe: Conquest, Colonization and Cultural Change, 950–1350*. London: Penguin, 1994.

Beaurepaire, P.- Y. *Le Mythe de l'Europe française au XVIIIe siècle. Diplomatie, culture et sociabilités au temps des Lumières*. Paris: Autrement, 2007.

Beck, U., and E. Grande. *Cosmopolitan Europe*. Cambridge: Polity, 2007.

Bernardi, B. "Rousseau et l'Europe: sur l'idée de société civile européenne." In *Principes du droit de la guerre, Écrits sur le Projet de Paix Perpétuelle de l'abbé de Saint-Pierre*, ed. B. Bachofen and C. Spector, 295–330. Paris: Vrin, 2008.

Bois, J.-P. *La paix. Histoire politique et militaire*. Paris: Perrin, 2012.

[66] F. Guizot, *The History of Civilization in Europe* [1830] (London: Penguin, 1997). See the introduction by P. Rosanvallon to the modern French edition: *Histoire de la civilisation en Europe* (Paris: Hachette, 1985).

[67] See Condorcet, *Sketch for a Historical Picture of the Progress of the Human Mind*, London: Weidenfeld and Nicholson, 1955. On the turning point in liberalism, see J. Pitts, *A Turn to Empire: The Rise of Imperial Liberalism in Britain and France* (Princeton: Princeton University Press, 2005); S. Muthu, *Enlightenment against Empire* (Princeton: Princeton University Press, 2003).

Braudel, F. *The History of Civilizations*. London: Penguin, 1995.

Carnhall, G. "Robertson and Contemporary Images of India." In *Robertson and the Expansion of Empire,* ed. S. J. Brown, 210–30. Cambridge: Cambridge University Press, 1997.

Casabianca, D. de. *Montesquieu. De l'étude des sciences à l'esprit des lois*. Paris: Champion, 2008.

Chabod, F. *Storia dell'idea d'Europa*. Bari: Laterza, 1971; Rome: Laterza, 2007.

Chakrabarty, D. *Provincializing Europe: Postcolonial Thought and Historical Difference*. Princeton: Princeton University Press, 2000.

Condorcet, N. de. *Sketch for a Historical Picture of the Progress of the Human Mind*, London: Weidenfeld and Nicholson, 1955.

Diderot, D. "Extracts from the *Histoire des Indes.*" In *Political Writings*, ed. J. H. Mason and R. Wokler, 165–214. Cambridge: Cambridge University Press, 1992.

Draus, F. *Critique historique de l'idée européenne*. Paris: Guibert, 2009.

Duroselle, J.-B. *L'Idée d'Europe dans l'histoire*. Paris: Denoël, 1965.

Easley, E. *The War over Perpetual Peace: An Exploration into the History of a Foundational International Relations Text*. New York: Palgrave Macmillan, 2004.

Ehrard, J. *Lumières et esclavage.* Brussels: André Versaille, 2008.

Febvre, L. *L'Europe. Genèse d'une civilisation, Cours professé au Collège de France en 1944–1945*. Paris: Perrin, 1999.

Foucault, M. *Security, Territory, Population: Lectures at the Collège de France 1977–1978*. Basingstoke, UK: Palgrave Macmillan, 2007.

Goody, J. *The Theft of History*. Cambridge: Cambridge University Press, 2006.

Grosrichard, A. *Structure du sérail. La fiction du despotisme asiatique dans l'Occident classique*. Paris: Seuil, 1979.

Guizot, F. *The History of Civilization in Europe* [1830]. London: Penguin, 1997.

Hale, J. *The Civilization of Europe in the Renaissance*. London: Harper Collins, 1993.

Hay, D. *Europe, The Emergence of an Idea*. Edinburgh: Edinburgh University Press, 1957.

Heater, D. *The Idea of European Unity.* New York: St. Martin's Press, 1992.

Hirschman, A. O. *The Passions and the Interests*. Princeton: Princeton University Press, 1977.

Larrère, C. *Actualité de Montesquieu*. Paris: Presses de la Fondation nationale des Sciences politiques, 1999.

———. "Montesquieu on Economics and Commerce." In *Montesquieu's Science of Politics,* ed. D. Carrithers et al., 335–74. New York: Rowman & Littlefield, 2001.

Lilti, A. "'Et la civilisation deviendra générale': L'Europe de Volney ou l'orientalisme à l'épreuve de la Révolution." *La Révolution française* [Online], Dire et faire l'Europe à la fin du XVIIIe siècle. 10 June 2011. http://lrf.revues.org/290.

Markovits, F. "L'Europe en question: Castel de Saint-Pierre et Mably." In "Le Grand Danger," ed. J.-P. Faye, *Passages d'encres* 42 (June 2011).

Mason, S. M. "Montesquieu's Vision of Europe and its European Context." *SVEC* 341. Oxford: Voltaire Foundation, 1996.

Meyer, J. *L'Europe des Lumières*. Le Coteau: Horvath, 1989.

Mill, C. W. *The Racial Contract*. New York: Cornell University Press, 1999.

Montesquieu. *Persian Letters*. Translated by C. J. Betts. London: Penguin, 1973.

———. *The Spirit of the Laws*. Edited by. A. M. Cohler et al. Cambridge: Cambridge University Press, 1989.

Muthu, S. *Enlightenment against Empire*. Princeton: Princeton University Press, 2003.

O'Brien, K. *Narratives of Enlightenment: Cosmopolitan History from Voltaire to Gibbon*. Cambridge: Cambridge University Press, 1997.

Ohji, K. "Civilisation et naissance de l'histoire mondiale dans l'*Histoire des deux Indes* de Raynal." *Revue de synthèse* 129/1 (2008): 57–83.

Pagden, A. "Deconstructing Europe." *History of European Ideas* 18/3 (1994): 329–46.

———. *Lords of all the World*. New Haven and London: Yale University Press, 1995.

———. *Peoples and Empires*. New York: The Modern Library, 2001.

Pagden, A., ed., *Facing Each Other: The World's Perception of Europe and Europe's Perception of the World*. ldershot, UK: Ashgate, 2000.

Pereira, J. *Montesquieu et la Chine*. Paris: L'Harmattan, 2008.

Pitts, J. *A. Turn to Empire: The Rise of Imperial Liberalism in Britain and France*. Princeton: Princeton University Press, 2005.

Pocock, J. G. A. *Barbarism and Religion*. Cambridge: Cambridge University Press, 1999.

———. "Some Europes in Their History." In *The Idea of Europe: From Antiquity to the European Union*, ed. A. Pagden, 55–71. Cambridge: Cambridge University Press, 2002.

Py, G. *L'Idée d'Europe au siècle des Lumières*. Paris: Vuibert, 2004.

Rétat, P. "La représentation du monde dans *L'Esprit des lois*. La place de l'Europe." In *L'Europe de Montesquieu, Cahiers Montesquieu*, ed. A. Postigliola and M. G. Bottaro Palumbo, 7–16. Oxford: Voltaire Foundation, 1995.

Robertson, W. Introduction to *The History of the Reign of Charles the Fifth*, 1769 (4 vols.).

Rolland, P. "Montesquieu et l'Europe." In *L'Europe entre deux tempéraments politiques: idéal d'unité et particularismes régionaux. Etudes d'Histoire des Idées Politiques,* 41–60. Aix-en-Provence: Presses Universitaires d'Aix-Marseille, 1994.

Rosanvallon, P. Introduction to *Histoire de la civilisation en Europe*, by F. Guizot. Paris: Hachette, 1985.

Rousseau, J.-J. *Abstract of Monsieur l'Abbé de Saint-Pierre's* Plan for Perpetual Peace. In *Collected Writings of Rousseau.* Translated by C. Kelly. Hanover, NH: University Press of New England, 1995), 11: 27–48.

———. *The Confessions.* In *Collected Writings of Rousseau.* Translated by C. Kelly. Hanover, NH: University Press of New England, 1995), 5 (9): 354–56.

Said, E. *Orientalism: Western Conceptions of the Orient.* London: Routledge & Kegan Paul, 1978.

Schaub, D. J. *Erotic Liberalism: Women and Revolution in Montesquieu's* Persian Letters. London: Rowman & Littlefield, 1995.

Schaub, J.-F. *L'Europe a-t-elle une histoir.,* Paris: Albin Michel, 2008.

Sebastiani, S. *I limiti del progresso. Razza Europe genere nell"Illuminismo scozzese*. Bologna: Il Mulino, 2008, 229-54.

———. "*L'Esprit des lois* nel discorso storico dell'Illuminismo scozzese." In *Montesquieu e i suoi interpreti*, ed. D. Felice, 211–45. Pisa: ETS, 2005.

———. "L'Amérique des Lumières et la hiérarchie des races. Disputes sur l'écriture de l'histoire dans l'*Encyclopaedia Britannica* (1768–1788)." *Annales HSS* 2 (April–June 2012): 327–61.

Spector C., *Montesquieu, Les* Lettres persanes. *De l'anthropologie à la politique.* Paris: Presses Universitaires de France, 1997.

———. "Il est impossible que nous supposions que ces gens-là soient des hommes": la théorie de l'esclavage au livre XV de *L'Esprit des lois.*" *Lumières* 3 (2004): 15–51.

——— "Science des mœurs et théorie de la civilisation: de *L'Esprit des lois* de Montesquieu à l'école historique écossaise." In *Les Equivoques de la civilisation*, ed. B. Binoche, 136–60. Seyssel: Champ Vallon, 2005.

———. "Montesquieu, critique du *Projet de Paix Perpétuelle*?" In *Montesquieu et l'Europe,* ed. J. Mondot et al., 139–75. Bordeaux: Académie Montesquieu, 2006.

———. *Montesquieu et l'émergence de l'économie politique.* Paris: Honoré Champion, 2006.

———. "Le *Projet de paix perpétuelle*: de Saint-Pierre à Rousseau." In *Principes du droit de la guerre, Écrits sur le Projet de Paix Perpétuelle de l'abbé de Saint-Pierre*, ed. B. Bachofen and C. Spector, 229–94. Paris: Vrin, 2008.

———. *Montesquieu. Liberté, droit et histoire*. Paris: Michalon, 2010.

———. "L'Europe de l'abbé de Saint-Pierre." In *Les Projets de l''abbé Castel de Saint-Pierre (1658–1743),* ed. C. Dornier and C. Poulin, 39–49. Caen: PUC, 2011.

———. "Penser l'Europe au XVIIIe siècle: le miroir américain dans l'œuvre de William Robertson." *La Révolution française*, Dire et faire l'Europe à la fin du XVIIIe siècle. 14 June 2011. http:/lrf.revues.org/index259.html.

———. "Who is the Author of the *Abstract of Monsieur l'Abbé de Saint-Pierre's* Plan for Perpetual Peace? From Saint-Pierre to Rousseau." *History of European Ideas* 39/3 (2013): 371–393.

Stuurman, S. "Cosmopolitan Egalitarianism in the Enlightenment: Anquetil Duperron on India and America." *Journal of the History of Ideas* 68/2 (April 2007): 255–278.

Verga, M. *Storie d'Europa. Secoli XVIII–XXI.* Rome: Carocci, 2004.

———. "European Civilization and the 'Emulation of the Nations': Histories of Europe from the Enlightenment to Guizot." *History of European Ideas* 34 (2008): 353–60.

Villain-Gandossi, C., ed. *L'Europe à la recherche de son identité*. Lille: Éditions du CTHS, 2002.

Voltaire. *Essai sur les mœurs*. Edited by B. Bruno et al. Oxford: Voltaire Foundation, 2009–2012.

Voyenne, B. *Histoire de l'idée européenne*. Paris: Payot, 1964.

"GREATER BRITAIN" INTO "GREATER RUSSIA": A CASE OF IMAGINING EMPIRE AND NATION IN THE EARLY TWENTIETH CENTURY RUSSIAN EMPIRE

Alexander Semyonov*

Abstract

This chapter revises the historiographic assumption that Russian intellectuals and politicians turned to Europe in search of models and authoritative strategies of nation-building. Exploring the case of the translation into Russian of John Robert Seeley's The Expansion of England *and its adaptation to Russian politics by Petr Struve, the author argues that Russian ideologues and politicians recognized the imperial character of European ideologies and politics and sought in Europe models and blueprints for a modernizing empire. The chapter traces the intellectual and political evolution of Petr Struve from Marxism to right wing liberalism and argues that Struve was attracted to Seeley by his desire to modernize the language of political conversation about empire and nationalism at a moment of crisis in the dynastic imperial regime in Russia. Struve also found in Seeley a novel vision of imperialization of sovereignty and a combination of empire and nationalism in the politics of the composite state. The translation of "Greater Britain" into "Greater Russia" was far from perfect, as is the case with any political or intellectual transfer, yet the explored*

* Alexander M. Semyonov is Dean and Professor in the Department of History at the National Research University-Higher School of Economics in St. Petersburg.

episode does call into question the purported hegemony of nationalism in the history of the twentieth century and provides ground to contend that equally widespread and influential at the time were imaginaries of transformative and modernizing empires.

Historians no longer take for granted the association of certain cultural-political characteristics with physical geography. Scholars from Edward Said through Larry Wolff have demonstrated that the process of consolidating one's own sense of Europe was dependent on the construction of the significant Other in the form of the Orient or Eastern (Oriental) Europe. A coherent and homogenous notion of Europe is easier to mold from the self-proclaimed periphery. Perhaps the first and most enduring discourse of a single Europe was formulated by the Slavophiles in Russia in the first half of the nineteenth century. Slavophiles, or "Nativists" as they called themselves, spoke of Europe as the epistemological power that oppressed Russia and made it into a colony.[1]

The construction of a homogenous Europe in the discourse of Slavophiles was simultaneous with the quest for organicist foundations for Russia's emancipation: the "Russian people." The integrity of Russia and the Russian people in this discourse of romanticism was paralleled in the discursive construction of the integrity of Europe: "Some can say that Western European life cannot be subsumed in the concepts and forms of Latinism; Western Europe did discover a new spiritual way in Protestantism. But I answer that Protestantism is the same Latinism, only in its dialectical rejection."[2] As is argued in a recent article by historians of the Russian Empire, the Slavophiles were the first postcolonial or subaltern intellectuals whose case demonstrates an intimate link between the discourse of subalternity and nationalism.[3]

This invention of a national tradition at the foundation of the Russian state overshadowed the composite and multinational and supranational character of the Russian Empire. The powerful discourse of romantic nationalism and its subsequent spread into representations of the Russian monarchy and the politics of the Russian imperial government[4] muted the languages of imperial diversity and made the Russian Empire in turn a different type of subaltern, unable to

[1] Ilya Gerasimov, Marina Mogilner, and Sergey Glebov, "The Post-Imperial Meets Post-Colonial: Russian Historical Experience and the Post-Colonial Moment," *Ab Imperio* 2 (2013): 97–135.

[2] Yuri Samarin, "Sovremennyi ob'em pol'kogo voprosa," by Boris Nolde, *Yuri Samarin i ego vremia* (Moscow: Algoritm, 2003), 435.

[3] Gerasimov, Mogilner, and Glebov, "The Post-Imperial Meets Post-Colonial," 101.

[4] Richard Wortman powerfully demonstrated how nationalism was incorporated by the Russian monarchy into its scenarios of power as a way to adapt the dynastic rule to the challenges of modern society and politics, see Richard Wortman, *Scenarios of Power: Myth and Ceremony in Russian Monarchy*, 2 vols. (Princeton: Princeton University Press, 1995, 2000). Anatoly

articulate itself in the authoritative languages of politics and science until the second half of the nineteenth century.[5] The dynastic logic of the supranational empire persisted in a sedimented form in its central institution, the Russian monarchy, but its presence could not help but reveal the acute tensions between the hegemonic post-romantic nationalizing discourse of the Russian people and Russian national state on the one hand, and the praxis of empire on the other.

At the height of World War I nationalist mobilization, Nicholas II, being the most populist-nationalist and anti-Semitic tsar of the Romanov dynasty,[6] still dutifully complied with the historical tradition of the Russian monarchy, which cast him as the emperor rather than the Russian Orthodox Tsar. In November 1914, Nicholas II made a tour of the empire, paying a visit to the western front, southern cities, and the Caucasus. During his stay in Tiflis, Nicholas II met a delegation of the Georgian nobility; attended a prayer service in the Orthodox Cathedral; toured the "temple of glory" of the Caucasian, Russo-Turkish, and Russo-Persian wars; visited with the Armenian Catholikos during a service in the Van Cathedral and again in a separate meeting; watched prayer services and talked with the mufti in Shiite and Sunni mosques; received delegations from various nationalities, confessions, and religious sects of the region; asked the Armenians and Muslims, but not the Georgians, to "spread his good word" to all of their brethren; and graciously received an ancient Bible from the Syrians and Torah from the Jews.[7]

Yet, this full-of-political-sense, symbolic praxis of the dynastic ruler made no sense to ideologues and politicians of the empire, regardless of whether they were conservative or liberal. For the leader of the liberal opposition, Paul Miliukov, the ritualized performances and monologues of Nicholas II's reign were pitiful replicas of the bygone Byzantine Empire.[8] For conservative

---

Remnev demonstrates how the logic of the nationalizing regime went hand in hand with the technocratic dispositions of the imperial government, how it caused rethinking of the policy of colonization, and how in practice the discourse on Russian nationhood clashed with the lack of Russian ethnicity or bounded cultural coherence in the social reality of the Russian Empire, see Antoly Remnev and Natalia Suvorova, "'Russkoe delo' na aziatskikh okrainakh: 'Russkost'' pod ugrozoi ili somnitel'nye 'kul'turtreggery'," *Ab Imperio* 2 (2008): 157–222.

[5] For a fully developed argument of this transformation, please see Ilya Gerasimov, Sergey Glebov, Jan Kusber, Marina Mogilner, and Alexander Semyonov, "New Imperial History and the Challenges of Empire," in *Empire Speaks Out: Languages of Rationalization and Self-Description in the Russian Empire*, edited by Ilya Gerasimov, Jan Kusber, and Alexander Semyonov (Leiden: Brill, 2009), 3–32.

[6] On the transformation of politics of the Russian monarchy in the reign of Nicholas II, see Wortman, chap. 7 in *Scenarios of Power,* vol. 2, and Sergey Podbolotov, "Tsar and narod: Populistskii natsionalizm imperatora Nikolaia II," *Ab Imperio* 3 (2003): 199–223.

[7] *Letopis' voiny 1914 g*, 16 (1914): 251–255, and 17 (1914): 272–274.

[8] [P.N. Miliukov], "Derzhavnyi maskarad," *Osvobozhdenie* 19 (1903): 321.

technocrat Vladimir Gurko, the ceremonial performances of the Russian emperor betrayed the inferior culture of an Oriental empire.[9]

Public intellectuals, ideologues, and politicians of the Russian Empire in the second half of the nineteenth and early twentieth century sought to find new authoritative discourses for the composite and diverse space of the Russian Empire. A part of them was acutely aware that Europe was not homogenous in its historical experience, that European history could not be boxed in national containers, and that the constitutive part of Europe as a role model was its non-European imperial and colonial experience. In their search for new authoritative languages of empire, this group of Russian intellectuals and politicians was part of the global discussion of the dilemmas of empire.[10] I will elucidate their search by investigating the translation into the Russian political imagination of John Robert Seeley's ideological vision of "Greater Britain."

From the Other Shore: A Redescription of the British Empire in the 19th Century

During the 1879–80 academic year, the Regius Professor of Modern History of Cambridge University, Sir John Robert Seeley gave a lecture course on the Holy Roman Empire. It traced the evolution of a premodern polity and its impact on the contemporary world of nation-states, including the many paradoxes that Seeley, according to the testimony of his students, loved to stress and explore.[11] The lecture on the eighteenth century explored the ambiguous relations between nation-state and empire. During the 1881–82 academic year, Seeley developed the lecture on the eighteenth century into a new two-part course.[12] Scholarship and politics went hand in hand, so that course was attended by applicants seeking entry to British colonial service. Seeley's friends

---

[9] V. I. Gurko, *Cherty i siluety proshlogo* (Moscow: NLO, 2000), 551–552.

[10] The history of entanglement of the imperial imagination in the Russian Empire and its alternative versions (the discourse of imperial diversity, discourse of modern colonialism, discourse of the nationalizing empire) is just starting to being written, see Vladimir Bobrovnikov, "Russkii Kavkaz i frantsuzskii Alzhir: Sluchainoe skhodstvo ili obmen opytom kolonial'nogo stroitel'stva [Russian Caucasus and French Algeria: Accidental Commonality or Exchange of Experience in Colonial Government]," Martin Aust, Ricarda Vulpius, and Aleksei Miller, eds., *Imperium inter pares: Rol' transferov v istorii Rossiiskoi Imperii, 1700–1917* (Moscow: NLO, 2010), 182-209; and Marina Mogilner, *Homo imperii: A History of Physical Anthropology in Russia* (Lincoln: University of Nebraska Press, 2013).

[11] J. R. Tanner, "John Robert Seeley," *The English Historical Review* 10, no. 39 (July 1895): 507–514.

[12] One lecture from this course was published as John Robert Seeley, "The Expansion of England in the Eighteenth Century," *Macmillans Magazine* 46 (1882): 456–65.

persuaded him to publish this course of lectures as a book, and after many hesitations he agreed. In 1883, *The Expansion of England* was published. It went through seventeen editions up until 1901 and went out of print only in 1956.[13] Before *The Expansion of England,* Seeley was known as an expert on the history of Christianity, the history of European international relations, the author of a biography of Freiherr vom Stein, and an advocate of the rigorous German understanding of history as a science.[14] After the publication of his lectures, Seeley's name became irrevocably associated with the political program of imperialism and the political project of "Greater Britain."[15]

Seeley's vision of "Greater Britain" coalesced with one of the phases of intensive growth of the British Empire, and its ideological reconfiguration. It is important to take note that this period witnessed the growing connection between imperialist imaginations and the policies of different European states. Historians of imperial Germany have recently reminded us that the formation of the German Reich was accompanied by the entry of this new German power into the worldwide competition for colonial division of the world.[16] The elites of the new German state were conscious of the presence and experience of European colonial empires, particularly that of the British

---

[13] John Robert Seeley, *The Expansion of England: Two Courses of Lectures* (London, 1883); extracts from this edition were also published as: Idem, *Our Colonial Expansion* (London, 1887, rev. eds. 1900 and 1910); and Idem, *The Expansion of England*, edited by John Gross (Chicago: University of Chicago Press, 1971), xxvii.

[14] Adolf Rein, *Sir Lohn Robert Seeley: Eine Studie über den Historiker* (Langensalza, 1912); John Robert Seeley, *Life and Times of Stein, or Germany and Prussia in the Napoleonic Age*, 3 vols. (Cambridge: Cambridge University Press, 1878).

[15] Duncan Bell, *The Idea of Greater Britain: Empire and the Future World Order, 1860–1900* (Princeton: Princeton University Press, 2007); Deborah Wormell, *Sir John Seeley and the Uses of History* (Cambridge: Cambridge University Press, 1980). The actual idiom came from Sir Charles Dilkes' travelogue, surveying the "white colonies": C. W. Dilke, *Greater Britain: A Record of Travel in the English-Speaking Countries during 1866 and 1867*, 3 vols. (London, 1868). This provenance of the linguistic formula in the early-modern legal and political order rather than in racial or ethnic mapping is pointed out by David Armitage, *The Ideological Origins of the British Empire: Ideas in Context* (Cambridge: Cambridge University Press, 2000). On the unintended and paradoxical impact of Seeley that led to the separation of British imperial history from English history, see Peter Burroughs, "John Robert Seeley and British Imperial History," *Journal of Imperial and Commonwealth History* 1 (1972): 191–211; J. G. Greenlee, "A 'Succession of Seeleys': The 'Old School' Re-examined," *Journal of Imperial and Commonwealth History* 4 (1976): 266–82; David Fieldhouse, "Can Humpty-Dumpty Be Put Together Again? Reflections on Imperial History in the 1980s," *Journal of Imperial and Commonwealth History* 12 (1984); and Linda Colley, "What is Imperial History Now?," in *What is History Now?*, edited by David Cannadine (Basingstoke, G.B.: Palgrave MacMillan 2002), 132–147.

[16] George Steinmetz, *The Devils Handwriting: Precoloniality and the German Colonial State In Qingdao, Samoa, And Southwest Africa* (Chicago: University of Chicago Press, 2007), 148, 150.

Empire, which was often seen as the model empire. The entry of the new German state into the imperialist competition for colonial possessions prompted the intensification of rivalry and the growing interrelatedness of ideological justifications of imperialist policies.[17]

It is possible to see a link between Seeley's ideological intervention into the shaping of British identity on the one hand and the more assertive politics and optimistic vision of British imperialism at the end of the nineteenth century, on the other.[18] One of the underlying messages of Seeley's treatise was the call to transgress the isolationist and archipelagic understanding of the English past and to open up the British public mind to the presence of empire in the present. Consequently, Seeley attacked the view of English history that would be later called the "Whig interpretation of history." His criticism of the Whig interpretation of history pointed out the relationship between history that is focused on the progress of democracy, and the archipelagic view of history, which truncated the imperial dimension of English history and polity. Seeley's famous phrase about acquiring empire "in a fit of absence of mind" should be seen in the context of the development of post-romantic European historiographies, which produced the effect of nationalizing complex imperial pasts and led to the loss of cognizance of the imperial dimension of European nation-states.

To be sure, opening the British public mind to the presence of empire involved the construction of an interpretative framework for the manifold connections that existed between the metropole and its diverse periphery. It also involved a redefinition of the concept of empire. As such, it was both a scholarly and a political move, notwithstanding Seeley's presentation of his research as positivist and following the rigorous standards of German *Wissenschaft*. The political message of Seeley's treatise was encapsulated in the reframing of the space and diversity of the empire. Instead of juxtaposing the metropole and periphery, he juxtaposed India, "where the English nation . . . is just a drop in the ocean of Asiatic people" to the white settler colonies.[19] According to Seeley, the latter were bound together by race, culture, and political ties and therefore could be viewed as one "nation." Seeley further noted that with respect to the colonial empire of white settler colonies, "our empire is not an Empire at all in the ordinary sense of the word. It does not consist

---

[17] Ibid.

[18] Andrew S. Thompson, "The Language of Imperialism and the Meanings of Empire: Imperial Discourse in British Politics, 1895–1914," *Journal of British Studies* 36, no. 2 (1997): 147–177; idem, *The Empire Strikes Back?: The Impact of Imperialism on Britain From the Mid-Nineteenth Century* (New York: Pearson Longman/Routledge, 2005).

[19] Seeley, *The Expansion of England*, 56.

of congeries of nations held together by force, but in the main of one nation, as much as it is were no Empire but an ordinary state."[20]

The conceptual reframing of the diverse space of the British Empire did not end by bracketing India as an exception.[21] In his treatise, Seeley also elaborated the point of shared and composite space of the white settler colonies. He acknowledged the fact that some of these white settler colonies were not populated by the uniform English nation. Yet pressing his juxtapositional grid of India-versus-the-rest, Seeley insisted that these white settler colonies did not inherit a complex web of sovereignties, as was the case with the Indian subcontinent, and that they did not encounter substantial cultural resistance to the superior "civilization." Invoking the historical analogy of Pax Romana, Seeley shifted the argument from the Englishness of white settler colonies to their shared "European civilization."[22] This argument made the Dutch settlers in South Africa and Francophone population in Canada seem to fall within the single imagined community.

Furthermore, Seeley employed relativistic arguments of two kinds in order to emphasize the shared and composite space of Greater Britain. First of all, he relativized the imagined uniformity of the island-based metropole: "If in these islands we feel ourselves for all purposes one nation, though in Wales, in Scotland and in Ireland there is Celtic blood and Celtic languages utterly unintelligible to us are still spoken, so in the Empire a good many French and Dutch and a good many Caffres and Maories may be admitted without marring the ethnological unity of the whole." He further reminded the British public that the formation of the archipelagic metropolitan polity and identity was dialectically connected to outward colonial expansion, that Scotland was a separate kingdom, and in Ireland the English were just a colony among the "alien" population.[23] In other words, the formation of the supposedly exclusive and clearly demarcated national core of the British Empire was synchronous to and interrelated with the formation of the British Empire, and Seeley labored to restore this interrelatedness for the benefit of the project of "Greater Britain."

Second, Seeley noted the cultural difference between the white settler colonies and the islands but countered this argument with an observation that in the near future the English culture in the metropole would be transformed under the impact of democratization and entry of the lower classes into public

---

[20] Ibid., 62.

[21] See also Nicholas Dirks, *Scandal of Empire: India and the Creation of Imperial Britain* (Cambridge: Belknap Press, 2006), 317, 342.

[22] Seeley, *The Expansion of England*, 250–256.

[23] Ibid., 18.

politics. These relativistic arguments undermined the rigid boundary between the metropole and white settler colonies and presented the British *imperium* (in contradistinction to British India as *dominium*) as a single continuum of differentiated spaces and cultures. The most suitable political form for the British *imperium,* or Greater Britain, according to Seeley, was a federation or federative union.[24]

Finally, the most interesting feature of Seeley's treatise for the purpose of the present analysis is the explicit comparative framework in which the present state and preferred future shape of the British Empire were discussed. As has been noted, Seeley had a keen interest in the history of composite European polities, particularly the Holy Roman Empire. He was of the opinion that the historical destiny of large composite political formations was far from being spent. In one of his articles prior to the publication of the *Expansion of England,* he argued in favor of the Unites States of Europe, an ambitious project involving a federative political union of European states for the purpose of preventing European wars.

As the basis for his argument, Seeley pointed to the existence of composite states in Europe, such as the Habsburg Empire.[25] In the *Expansion of England,* he differentiated the historical experience of the British Empire from that of the Habsburg Empire, which in his mind was "a mere mechanical forced union of alien nationalities."[26] He likened his project of Greater Britain with the experience of the United States of America and Russia: "As soon as the distance is abolished by science, as soon as it proved by the examples of the United States and Russia that political union over vast areas has begun to be possible, so soon Greater Britain starts up, not only a reality, but a robust reality."[27]

Furthermore, Seeley underscored the point that those comparative cases of large political unions were not just abstract models for emulation but that competitors could encroach upon the space of the British Empire.[28] He was also convinced that inaction would result in the growing movement for independence in white settler colonies, and this would threaten the position of Great Britain as a member of the club of European great powers, especially in view of the rise of the German Empire.[29]

---

24 Ibid., 178.
25 J. R. Seeley, "United States of Europe," *Macmillan Magazine* 23 (1870–1871): 436–448.
26 Seeley, *The Expansion of England*, 56–57.
27 Ibid., 86–87.
28 Ibid., 24–25, 130–132, 302–304.
29 Ibid., 24–25.

Intellectual Travels

In 1903, the publishing house of O. N. Popova released a new book. It was a Russian translation of *The Expansion of England*.[30] The publication of this translation was made possible, among other ways, by the decision of the Tambov governor in 1896 to refuse the appointment of Vladimir Aleksandrovich Gerd as the local agronomist.[31] Vladimir Gerd, by that time a graduate of both the St. Petersburg Imperial University and Agricultural Institute in New Alexandria, was the son of Aleksandr Yakovlevich Gerd, the famous popularizer of natural sciences and new pedagogical methods, and the grandson of James Arthur Heard, who resettled in the Russian Empire in 1819 and brought in his luggage Joseph Lancaster's schooling system. Left without income by the decision of the governor, Vladimir Gerd started to earn his keep by making translations from English into Russian. One of the commissioned translations was *The Expansion of England*.

His family tradition provided the background for Vladimir Gerd's interest in public education and "enlightenment" and endowed him with a mastery of English, a rarity among Russian intellectuals at the close of the nineteenth century. Student contacts at the university ushered him into the network of left-wing circles embracing Marxism and evolving into a Social-Democratic intellectual and political movement. This network included, inter alia, Petr Struve, who in 1897 assumed the post of the editor of *Novoe Slovo*, a periodical that was transferred from the Populist to the Social-Democratic camp by the deal between Posse and Semyonov, on the one hand, and the publisher Olga Nikolaevna Popova, on the other.[32]

Struve was drawn into the work of editing the book series on natural sciences, philosophy, psychology, sociology, and history produced by the Popova publishing house. Seeley's treatise was published in that series, in accordance with Struve's vision of how to use this book series. Struve envisaged the series as a modernizing instrument with respect to the general intellectual debate and the language of modern politics that was emerging in late imperial Russia. Gerd produced a high quality translation that creatively tackled the conceptual discrepancies between Russian and English. Seeley's concept of "Greater Britain" was not lost in translation but noted and explained to the Russian reader.[33]

---

[30] John Robert Seeley, *Rasshirenie Anglii* (St. Petersburg: O.N. Popova Publishing House, 1903).
[31] L. N. Nikonov, B. E. Raikov, "V. A. Gerd," in *Ekskursionnoe delo* (Moscow-Leningrad, 1928), 5–16.
[32] Richard Pipes, chaps. 7 and 8 in *Struve, Liberal on the Left, 1870–1905* (Cambridge, MA: Harvard University Press, 1970).
[33] Seeley, *Rasshirenie Anglii*, 7–8.

Seeley's trace in Struve's intellectual and political biography did not lapse after 1903. During the period of the 1905–1907 revolution, Struve returned to Seeley in the context of thinking about the diagnosis and consequences of the revolutionary upheaval. Struve's political position after the revolutionary experience was expressed in a series of articles in *Russkaia Mysl'* (Russian Thought) and, most famously, in the *Vekhi* (Landmarks) collection. One of the articles in *Russkaia Mysl'* was entitled "Greater Russia: Reflections on the Problem of Russian Power."[34]

Struve's writings after 1907 caused turmoil in Russian progressive public opinion and engendered a series of political debates pertaining to the most fundamental issues of Russian politics after the revolution. With reference to the aforementioned article on "Greater Russia," Struve was accused by progressive political commentators of abandoning the liberal political platform and walking into the camp of right wing politics and "official Russia."[35] To substantiate this claim, Struve's critic pointed to the fact of Struve's borrowing the concept of "*Velikaia Rossiia*" from a speech by Petr Stolypin in the imperial parliament (State Duma) on improvement of the socio-economic life of peasants and the right of property, in which the head of the government eloquently opposed the path of radicalism and proclaimed the goal of his policy to be "*Velikaia Rossiia*."

In response to this criticism, Struve pointed to the fact that he did not need Stolypin's dictum to express his political ideas. Stolypin's phrase was only "words," while Struve was interested in "ideas" or programmatic political thinking. Struve further stated that the expression was used in "the special political sense" and was "the Russian way of putting the slogan, which was used by a Cambridge university professor, John Robert Seeley, to articulate and propagate British imperialism."[36] Struve stressed that his critics were not able to substantially discuss the ideas of "Greater Russia" because of their mistaking the words of a Cambridge professor for the words of "official Russia."

In 1916, Struve again stressed the conceptual rather than rhetorical impact of *The Expansion of England*, while giving a public talk at Cambridge University:

> Looking back on the intellectual history of the Cambridge University and of its members, we should not find it difficult

---

[34] P. B. Struve, "Velikaia Rossiia: iz razmyshlenii o probleme russkogo mogushchestva," *Russkaia Mysl'* 1 (1908): 143–157. The key concept could be backtranslated from Russian as both "Great Russia" and "Greater Russia."

[35] A. V. Peshekhonov, "Na ocherednye temy: novyi pokhod protiv intelligentsii," *Russkoe Bogatstvo* 4 (1909): 100–125.

[36] P. B. Struve, "Na ocherednye temy," *Russkaia Mysl'* 1 (1909), 194.

> to demonstrate how greatly even distant Russia is obliged to the work of your Cambridge men. But, personally, I feel just now especially urged to recall and to honor with you one name, the name of John Robert Seeley, that great teacher of historical insight and thought. And this led me a good many years ago to have his *Expansion of England* published in Russia, and every year I recommend my students at the beginning of their course to read this masterpiece, which makes it possible for every thinking man to enter into the spirit of English history, and to realize the political genius of the English people.[37]

Thus, the British intellectual connection—to be sure one among many in the mindset of this versatile thinker—followed Struve's political engagement with problems of nationalism, empire, and imperialism, which were constituent of early twentieth century dilemmas of the Russian Empire.

Empire and Nationalism: The Story of Petr Struve's "Greater Russia"

Petr Struve was an unusual figure among the ranks of the Russian intelligentsia. This intellectual and scholar made a debut at the end of the nineteenth century as an Orthodox Marxist. Together with other late nineteenth century Marxist political economists, Struve dealt a blow to widespread populist economic and sociological views, proving the case for the development of capitalism and irreversible social change in the Russian Empire. Scholarship and politics went hand in hand, and Struve also penned the manifesto of the Russian Social Democratic Labor Party. He then resurfaced on the Russian political scene as a liberal and advocate of the idealistic conception of political freedom. Together with other idealists, Struve came up with a critique of positivism and populism suggesting that the belief in ironclad laws of socio-economic development prevents the development of a moral personality and defense of political freedom. Struve became editor of the liberal opposition mouthpiece "*Osvobozhdenie*" (Liberation) and therefore held one of the most influential positions in the Constitutional-Democratic party, the preeminent liberal party of post–1905 politics.

After the end of the first Russian Revolution, Struve became known for his critique of the revolutionary utopianism of the Russian intelligentsia, including Orthodox Marxism and Social Democratic politics. This critique

---

[37] P. B. Struve, "Past and Present of Russian Economics," in *Russian Realities and Problems,* edited by J. D. Duff (Cambridge: Cambridge University Press, 1917), 47–48.

was also aimed at reorienting Russian liberalism from its radical politics of confrontation with the state to the politics of cooperating with the state for the purpose of assuring post–1907 constitutionalism, bourgeois democracy, and economic modernization of the country. In these years he stood for pronounced Russian nationalism. Struve's Russian nationalism led him to a political confrontation with Ukrainian nationalism. Polemical interventions by Struve in these years initiated widespread public debates and caused re-alignment of political affinities in the broad progressive political milieu. In 1917, Struve opposed the Bolsheviks and joined the anti-Bolshevik movement during the Civil War. In the emigration years, Struve continued his economic studies, participated in émigré politics, and moved politically to the monarchist camp and defense of the Orthodox religion as the mystical foundation of Russia.

In short, Struve dramatically and sometimes radically changed his political views, and these changes reflected the dynamic pace and complexities of Russian politics at the beginning of the twentieth century. Struve himself believed that abstract philosophical and political ideas recur in history. What makes them political phenomena (and interesting to study), Struve contended, is their social functioning in historically specific realities.[38] The best biography of Struve, written by Richard Pipes, claims that Struve had always been a Russian nationalist. Pipes ahistorically located the origins of Struve's nationalism in the tradition of Russian Slavophile and conservative thought.[39] A careful study of Struve's intellectual and political evolution prior to his announcement of the program of "Greater Russia" suggests a different and much more complicated genealogy of Struve's nationalism.

In his Marxist analysis of the development of capitalism in Russia, Struve found that the development of market-oriented production was determined by the peculiarity of Russian economic geography. Whereas agricultural production flourished in the South, the Northern regions developed a specialization in handicraft industries. The structural economic relations between the North and South led to the emergence of a system of exchange of craft products from the North for the agricultural produce from the South. This axis of necessary economic relations between the North and South provided the "organic" foundation for the later emergence of a capitalist system of

---

[38] [P. B. Struve], "Is istorii obshchestvennykh idei i otnoshenii v Germanii v XIX v.," *Novoe Slovo* 8 (1897): 161–164; idem, "Is istorii obshchestvennykh idei i otnoshenii v Germanii v XIX v.," *Nauchnoe Obozrenie* 4 (1898): 784–795.

[39] Richard Pipes, "Introduction," in *Struve, Liberal on the Left, 1870–1905* (Cambridge, MA: Harvard University Press, 1970).

production. More importantly, this structural peculiarity of Russian geography provided the foundation for the emergence of the national economy.

Struve understood the notion of national economy in terms of Friedrich List; i.e., an economy that encompasses a division into agricultural and industrial sectors and thus relies on a sufficient internal market.[40] In 1894 Struve did not relate his economic analysis of the Russian "organic" capitalist system to the problem of cultural diversity in the Russian Empire or to the question of political reorganization of the empire. In particular, he did not pay attention to the problematic designation of the "Russian South" as a culturally homogenous region. His main preoccupation was to refute the dominant perspective of populist economists who refused to accept the fact and the value of capitalist development for Russia. Yet this map of the "organic" capitalist system would neatly correspond to the territorial map of "Greater Russia."

Struve's European academic sojourns, which were a must in Russian professional academic training before World War I, brought him to the Habsburg Empire. There he discovered a socio-cultural dimension for capitalist development. He observed that capitalist development had caused a disruption in the balance of nationalities in the Habsburg Empire.[41] In particular, this research led Struve to conclude that the cultural-linguistic-territorial map could significantly change during the transition from a traditional peasant economy to the economy of capitalist exchange and production. The position of elite, high culture was not guaranteed during this transition. Later, during his years of parliamentary politics, Struve repeatedly drew attention to the inadequacy of defining modern politics on the basis of the ethnographic classification of the Russian Empire's population and to the transformative potential of modern state politics, which could be applied to the reshaping of socio-cultural identities. The combined output of capitalism and modern politics produced a "nation in the making," as he once put it.

The foundation of Struve's nationalism was not derived from the veneration of the pre-modern organic community and culture promoted by Slavophiles. Rather, his understanding of the disruptive impact of capitalist development and the "creative" function of modern politics led him to embrace a strikingly constructivist and modernist approach to nationalism and nation-formation. In his confrontation with Ukrainian nationalism, Struve

---

[40] P. B. Struve, *Kriticheskie zametki k vorposu ob ekonomicheskom razvitii Rossii* (St. Petersburg, 1894), 240; idem, "Osnovnye momenty v razvitii krepostnogo khoziastva v Rossii v XIX veke," *Mir Bozhii* 11 (November 1899), 275.

[41] P. B. Struve, "Avstriiskoe krest'ianstvo i ego bytopisateli," *Vestnik Evropy* 6 (June 1893): 569–585; idem, "Nemtsy v Avstrii i krest'ianstvo," *Vestnik Evropy* 2 (February 1894): 796–828.

did not dispute the possibility of forming a modern Ukrainian nation with a literary language and exclusive identity. This was, for him, one of the potential scenarios for development. Commenting on efforts by the Ukrainian national movement to promote a distinct Ukrainian language and claim political representation of the Ukrainian nation in electoral politics, Struve contended that

> the sharpening of Ukrainian particularism is primarily the intelligentsia's goal and its invention. The masses of the population have not yet invested in this struggle. Everything depends on the involvement of the masses in this struggle. The degree of their involvement will determine the very possibility of such a struggle and its magnitude. [. . .] As far as I can see, what is happening among the Ukrainian people's masses is the chaotic process of transformation of the Little Russian way of life and language under the impact of new urban and industrial culture, universal military conscription, schooling in the Russian language, Russian book printing, and Russian newspapers. The spread of Russian book printing and newspapers is limited, but it still supersedes the spread of book printing and newspapers in the Ukrainian language. [. . .] I proceed from the assumption that there exists a common Russian culture and its instrument—the common Russian language. The role of the common Russian language [in relation] to local dialects and other Russian [East Slavic] languages is similar to the one played by Hochdeutsch toward other German dialects. I do not see how one can refute this thesis, though I understand that one can channel all efforts toward the goal of attainment of a different status and different role for the Ukrainian language.[42]

In other words, Struve did not refute the Ukrainian nation-building project on the basis of its artificiality. The modern Russian nation was as artificial as the Ukrainian one in the sense that it had not been a primordial social reality. Its formation, or the nationalization of the masses (*narodnye massy*), depended on the work of social mechanisms and political choices. This constructivist insight made Struve realize that his polemics against Ukrainian nationalism were themselves a factor in determining the outcome of the competition between

---

[42] P. B. Struve, "Obshcherusskaia kul'tura i ukrainskii partikuliarizm, otvet ukraintsu," *Russkaia Mysl'* 1 (1912): 65–86, 70–71, 76–77. The polemics were started by Struve's reply to Vladimir Zhabotinsky and continued with a reply to Bogdan Kistiakovsky: P. Struve, "Chto zhe takoe Rossiia," *Russkaia Mysl'* 1, no. 1 (1911): 175–178.

Russian and Ukrainian nation-building projects. This contributed to the aggressive tone of Struve's polemics against Ukrainian nationalism, which evolved during World War I into accusations of cultural and political separatism.[43]

Struve's polemics with Ukrainian nationalism are often treated by historians in isolation from his overall political views of this period.[44] Seen in the framework of competition between modern Ukrainian and Russian nationalisms, Struve appears to be an ideologue for nationalization of the Russian Empire. However, Struve's entry route into this polemics was through his political and intellectual engagement with the dilemmas of modernizing the empire, and not through a preoccupation with Russian nationalism alone.

In the wake of the radical parliamentary experiment of the first two Dumas, to the second of which he was elected as a deputy, Struve grew disillusioned with what he called "intelligentsia politics." It was "irresponsible," by which he meant that it repudiated the value of the state's interventionist function in modern social and economic life, it disregarded questions of "racial and national" diversity in the empire, and it obscured the vital importance of *Weltpolitik* and international relations in the epoch of intense competition among empires. In addition to offering a vehement critique of intelligentsia politics, he came up with an alternative program of politics for the future.

Struve called this program of alternative politics "Greater Russia," in an explicit reference to Seeley's project of "Greater Britain." Struve's representation of the connection between his and Seeley's imaginative politics wields a symbolic clout. It suggested the proximity of the Russian Empire to the archetypical empire of modern times, sort of a membership in the club of the powerful and advanced. But there was a substantive reason for Struve to use Seeley's reformist vision of the British Empire as a blueprint for rethinking the questions of sovereignty, power, and diversity in the Russian Empire after the 1905 revolution. Struve found in Seeley's text a way to estrange the

---

43 P. B. Struve, "Velikaia Rossiia i Sviataia Rus'," *Russkaia Mysl'* 12 (1914): 176– 180. See also N.A. Gredeskul, "Lozhnaia ideia: K voprosu o kul'turnom separatizme," *Natsional'nye problemy* 2 (1915 [1914]): 2– 5; F. F. Kokoshkin, "Liberalizm i nationalism," *Russkie Vedomosti*, November 9, 1914; P. Miliukov, "Ukrainskii vopros i P. B. Struve," *Rech'*, November 9, 1914; S. Petliura, "Otritsatel'nye cherty polemiki po ukrainskomu voprosu," *Ukrainskaia zhizn'*, 11–12 (1914): 13; B. Kistiakovskii, "Chto takoe natsionalizm: dva osnovnykh tipa natsionalizma," *Natsional'nye problemy* 1 (1915).

44 Olga Andriewsky, "Medved' iz Berlogi: Vladimir Jabotinsky and the Ukrainian Question, 1904–1914," *Harvard Ukrainian Studies* 14, no.3–4 (December 1990): 249–268; idem, "The Russian-Ukrainian Discourse and the Failure of the 'Little Russian Solution,' 1782–1917," *Culture, Nation, and Identity: The Ukrainian-Russian Encounter, 1600–1945*, edited by Andreas Kappeler et al. (Edmonton: Canadian Institute of Ukrainian Studies Press, 2005), 182–214.

reality of empire in Russia and de-center the conventional political lexicon of discourse about the dilemmas of empire.

The first Russian revolution transformed the field of politics. Particularly, it revealed the irreducibility of the problem of empire to the question of transformation of the autocracy into a bourgeois democracy. The common belief among Russian progressive forces was that the introduction of a constitution and democracy ought to solve all the tensions and conflicts in the culturally, confessionally, and ethnically heterogeneous space of empire. It turned out that, quite to the contrary, the crisis of the dynastic order opened up new, and exacerbated old, conflicts in the space of empire.

The logic of democracy turned out to be impervious to the problem of the constitutive boundaries of the political community that sought to be represented and self-ruled. Offering equal individual rights and integration, the ideal of democracy bracketed off the possibility that society could consists of groups rather than individuals and that some of these groups could be interested in retention of their distinctiveness rather than in integration.[45] Finally, it did not account for the existence of the autonomous logic of the sovereign state, which defined the boundaries of sovereignty in relation to other sovereign states, rather than through the process of "internal" self-determination.[46]

In the program of "Greater Britain," Struve found a critique of the "Whig interpretation of history" that was congenial to his own critique of the progressive intelligentsia's democratic mindset. He also found in Seeley a vision of a complex strategy for reshaping the relationship between sovereignty, power, and diversity in the context of empire. Struve's "Greater Russia" differed from Seeley's "Greater Britain" in Struve's modernist and constructivist understanding of the processes of nation-building, but it followed the major premises of Seeley's vision of politics for the modernizing empire. Like Seeley, Struve identified the primary point of departure as the competition among empires for restructuring the world order, which occurred in the phase of high imperialism. He keenly observed the rise of competition between the British Empire and the *Kaiserreich*, the changing balance of power in Central Europe as a result of the defeat of the Habsburg Empire against the *Kaiserreich*, the outreach of the *Kaiserreich* to the Middle East, and the effects of the defeat of the Russian Empire in the Russo-Japanese war. This competition among empires

[45] On the conflict between democratic and particularistic logic in the imperial space of public politics, see Alexander Semyonov, "The Real and Live Ethnographic Map of Russia: The Russian Empire in the Mirror of the State Duma," in *Empire Speaks Out: Languages of Rationalization and Self-Description in the Russian Empire,* edited by Ilya Gerasimov, Jan Kusber, and Alexander Semyonov (Leiden: Brill, 2009), 191–228.

[46] P. B. Struve, "Predislovie," in Woodrow Wilson, *Printsipy demokratii* (Berlin, 1924), v– xiv.

defined the "external" logic of sovereignty: "The supreme law for the life of the state is that each healthy and strong . . . state desires to be a great power."[47]

According to Struve, the Russian Empire could not extricate itself from imperial entanglements in the western borderlands, southeastern Europe, the Middle East, and the Far East. Struve saw the primary locus of Russian imperial entanglements in the western and southern regions of the European part of the empire, which involved the Polish and Jewish questions and was linked to the strategic positioning of "Greater Russia" in the basin of the Black Sea. An escape from these entanglements meant that other great powers would step in to fill the vacuum. Also, as a modernist-nationalist, Struve (unlike romantic nationalists) was keenly aware of the fact that there was no natural, territorial, national unit to which the escape from empire could proceed.

At the same time, the "external" logic of sovereignty was inseparable from its "internal" logic. According to Struve, the modern empire could not function without a national core and dynamic economic development.[48] Both elements of the modern empire required liberalization and democratization of the political regime. But the logic of democracy with its antinomies, according to Struve, could not define the boundaries of the political community that ought to be the subject and the agency of liberalization and democratization.

To resolve this complex problem of modernizing the empire, Struve, following Seeley's vision, proposed a combination of two forms of sovereignty to serve as the foundation of "Greater Russia." For Poland and other imperial peripheries, Struve envisioned the development of a partial or divided sovereignty. A regime of political autonomy should be combined with overlordship and the abandonment of attempts to russify Poland:

> The Kingdom of Poland's belonging to Russia is exclusively a question of power. [. . .] Prussia seeks . . . to germanize Poznan; the idea of russifying Poland, following the example of the attempts by Germans to germanize their Polish lands, is an absolutely unattainable utopia. The de-nationalization of Russian Poland could not be achieved by the Russian people or the Russian state. There cannot be any cultural or national competition between the Russians and the Poles on the territory of the

---

47 P. B. Struve, "Velikaia Rossiia: iz razmyshlenii o probleme russkogo mogushchestva," *Russkaia Mysl'* 1 (1908), cited in P. B. Struve, *Patriotica: Politika, kul'tura, religia, sotsializm* (Moscow, 1997), 51.

48 P. B. Struve, "Ekonomicheskaia problema 'Velikoi Rossii': Zametki ekonomista o voine i narodnom khoziastve," in *Velikaia Rossiia: Sbronik Statei po voennym i obshchestvennym voprosam*, part 2, edited by V.P. Riabushinksii (Moscow, 1910), 143–154.

> Kingdom of Poland: the Russian element on this territory is represented only by the army and civil service.[49]

The situations in Poland and other peripheries helped to define the boundaries of the potential national core of the new Russian Empire. The imagined map of the national core was supposed to include all population groups seeking integration into Russian high culture and the territories of the Russian "organic" capitalist system, which were mapped by Struve in his earlier economic analysis of Russian capitalism. An inclusive, national sovereignty was imagined by Struve as an important condition for rapid economic development and national integration of the empire's core. This applied to the legal, political, and cultural integration of both the peasant ("Little Russian" and "Great Russian") masses and whatever distinct national groups had been so marked by the defunct regime of autocracy: "The kernel of the solution of the Jewish question is the abolition of the Pale of Settlement. From the viewpoint of Russian power, the Jewish question is not so essential as is usually regarded in . . . conservative circles . . . In fact, despite all the anti-Semitic shrieks, the Jews, out of all the "*inorodtsy*" of Russia, can be most easily enlisted into the service of Russian statehood and assimilated to Russian culture."[50]

Thus, in Struve's project of "Greater Russia," one finds a significant departure from the traditional political pathways of autocracy and imperial rule. Fearing his strategy would be wrongly associated with autocracy, Struve populated his publications with neologisms and even used Latin in the middle of his Russian-language publications, calling the Russian imperial situation "imperium" to emphasize the novelty of his political designs and the fact that he was not talking about autocracy.[51] His conceptualization of empire was located in the context of the 1905 crisis of the Russian dynastic empire, as well as in the context of modern politics, the growing relevance of sociological and

---

[49] Struve, *Patriotica: Politika, kul'tura, religia, sotsializm*, 57–58. Compare Struve's description of the presence of the Russian cultural potential in Poland with Seeley's description of the British presence in India, "where the English nation . . . is just a drop in the ocean of Asiatic people." (Seeley, *The Expansion of England*, 56.)

[50] Struve, *Patriotica. Politika, kul'tura, religia, sotsializm*, 56.

[51] Struve, "Ekonomicheskaia problema 'Velikoi Rossii': Zametki ekonomista o voine i narodnom khoziastve," 154. The term "estrangement" was coined in 1917 by Viktor Shklovsky, a founding father of the Russian Formalist tradition of literary criticism, to describe the process of enhancing the perception of an object's deeper meaning by alienating it and making the object look strange, unfamiliar, or unpredictable (Viktor Shklovsky, "Iskusstvo kak priem," in *Sborniki po teorii poeticheskogo iazyka*, vol. 2 (Petrograd, 1917): 3–14; English translation: Viktor Shklovskij, "Art as Technique," in *Literary Theory: An Anthology*, edited by Julie Rivkin and Michael Ryan (Malden, MA: Blackwell Publishing, 1998), 15–21.

economic analysis, and the emerging hegemony of Russian and non-Russian nationalism. Even though Struve was a modern Russian nationalist, his nationalism was not discrete from concerns about the empire. As I have tried to show, Struve's nationalism was part of a larger, complex strategy, in which imperialization of sovereignty helped to limit the politics of nationalism, and the politics of nationalism helped to resolve the antinomies of democracy and sustain the politics of imperialism. Rather than facing each other as antagonists, empire and nationalism were imagined and propagated by Struve as compatible and mutually reinforcing political strategies for post–1905 politics.

Meeting with representatives of the German High Command in Kiev in 1918, Pavel Miliukov, a rival of Struve for influence in Russian liberal politics, used the concept of "Greater Russia" to undergird the demarcation of a new political map of the region. The context for the discussion was the collapse of the Russian Empire and advance of the German army.[52] Speaking of Poland, Miliukov reiterated his commitment to the declaration of the Provisional Government on the creation of an independent Polish state, but observed that the declaration did not specify the territorial boundaries of the future Polish state. In his view, the future Polish state should not include Lithuania and the Ukraine, which were "subject to return to Greater Russia."

Thus, even in the face of the creation of independent states and the triumph of the model of the nation-state, Russian politicians continued to embrace the imperialist vision of territory and sovereignty. It is telling that Miliukov did not use other political imageries of the time, such as the "one and indivisible Russia" or "Rus'."[53] This suggests both the intransigence of imperialism in Russian political discourse and the lack of appeal in Russian politics of the time of a more integral and Jacobite vision of sovereignty and ethnicity, such as the one that underpinned the politics of the Young Turks in the wartime Ottoman Empire.

Imports or Mirrors of Imperial Imagination?

The practitioners of transnational and comparative imperial history rightly note that the focus on the historical development of a particular empire or a particular type of empire often obscures the influences and intensive learning of empires from each other.[54] Although one can find cases of learning and

---

52 P. N. Miliukov, *Dnevnik* (Moscow: ROSSPEN, 2005), 36.

53 Struve himself adopted the more exclusive language of religiously and ethnically bounded community of *Rus'* at the start of World War I, P. B. Struve, "Velikaia Rossiia i Sviataia Rus'," *Russkaia Mysl'* 12 (1914): 176–180.

54 Ann Stoler, "Considerations on Imperial Comparisons," in *Empire Speaks Out*, 33–55.

the instrumental importation of political models of imperialism in Russian history, I stress in the present story the process of reading and constructing political meaning in a situation of acute political need to create distance from the conventional vocabulary, conceptions, and spatial imagery of empire. The story of translation is usually a story of misunderstanding. Seeley misjudged the national pillars of the imperial expansion and integrity of the Russian Empire in Central Asia. Similarly, Struve overlooked the importance of legal and political culture in Seeley's definition of the prospective national cohesion of "Greater Britain."

Yet the story of attempts to translate and adopt other empires' political visions is very telling for the situation of imperial crisis and imperial renewal on the receiving end of the translation. The attempt to approximate "Greater Britain" with "Greater Russia" helps correct the conventional view of continuity of the dynastic and territorial empire in Russian history and the futility in comparing colonial and maritime empires with continental ones. Struve's assumption that the work of an "English genius" could be of use in rethinking Russian imperial politics does suggest the feeling held by politicians and intellectuals of a rupture and the opening of new ways in Russian politics. Contrary to the simple teleology from empire to nation, the project of "Greater Russia" highlights the persistence of imperial discourses and dispositions. The fact that the particular project failed should not divert historians' attention from the general context of the persistent imperialist political imagination, of which "Greater Russia" was a part. The project of the Soviet ethno-territorial federation was closer to that context of political imagination than to the ideal of the nation-state. After all, no one expects to find in the mirror the exact reflection of the role model.

BIBLIOGRAPHY

Andriewsky, Olga. "Medved' iz Berlogi: Vladimir Jabotinsky and the Ukrainian Question, 1904–1914." *Harvard Ukrainian Studies* 14, nos. 3–4 (1990): 249–268.

———. "The Russian–Ukrainian Discourse and the Failure of the 'Little Russian Solution,' 1782–1917." In *Culture, Nation, and Identity: The Ukrainian–Russian Encounter, 1600–1945*, edited by Andreas Kappeler et al., 182–214. Edmonton: Canadian Institute of Ukrainian Studies Press, 2005.

Armitage, David. *The Ideological Origins of the British Empire: Ideas in Context.* Cambridge: Cambridge University Press, 2000.

Bell, Duncan. *The Idea of Greater Britain: Empire and the Future World Order 1860–1900.* Princeton: Princeton University Press, 2007.

Bobrovnikov, Vladimir. "Russkii Kavkaz i frantsuzskii Alzhir: Sluchainoe skhodstvo ili obmen opytom kolonial'nogo stroitel'stva [Russian Caucasus and French Algeria: Accidental Commonality or Exchange of Experience in Colonial Government]." In *Imperium inter pares: Rol' transferov v istorii Rossiiskoi Imperii, 1700–1917* [Imperium inter pares: The Role of Transfers in the History of the Russian Empire, 1700–1917], edited by Martin Aust, Ricarda Vulpius, and Aleksei Miller, 182–209. Moscow: NLO, 2010.

Burroughs, Peter. "John Robert Seeley and British Imperial History." *Journal of Imperial and Commonwealth History* 1 (1972): 191–211.

Colley, Linda. 2002. "What is Imperial History Now?" In *What is History Now?,* edited by David Cannadine, 132–147. Basingstoke, G.B.: Palgrave MacMillan.

Dilke, C. W. *Greater Britain: A Record of Travel in the English-Speaking Countries during 1866 and 1867.* 3 vols. London, 1868.

Dirks, Nicholas. *Scandal of Empire: India and the Creation of Imperial Britain.* Cambridge: Belknap Press, 2006.

Dubenskiy, D. N. *Letopis' voiny 1914 g.* [The Chronicle of the War, 1914.]16: 251–255; 17: 272–274. n.p., 1914.

Fieldhouse, David. "Can Humpty-Dumpty Be Put Together Again? Reflections on Imperial History in the 1980s." *Journal of Imperial and Commonwealth History* 12 (1984): 9–23.

Gerasimov, Ilya, Sergey Glebov, and Marina Mogilner. "The Post-Imperial Meets Post-Colonial: Russian Historical Experience and the Post-Colonial Moment." *Ab Imperio* 2 (2013): 97–135.

Gerasimov, Ilya, Jan Kusber, Marina Mogilner, and Alexander Semyonov. "New Imperial History and the Challenges of Empire." In *Empire Speaks Out: Languages of Rationalization and Self-Description in the Russian Empire*, edited by Ilya Gerasimov, Jan Kusber, and Alexander Semyonov. Leiden: Brill, 2009.

Gredeskul, N. A. "Lozhnaia ideia: K voprosu o kul'turnom separatizme. [A False Idea: On the Question of Cultural Separatism]" *Natsional'nye problemy* 2 (1915 [1914]): 2– 5.

Greenlee, J. G. "A 'Succession of Seeleys': The 'Old School' Re-examined." *Journal of Imperial and Commonwealth History* 4 (1976): 266–282.

Gurko, V. I. *Cherty i siluety proshlogo* [Features and Figures of the Past]. Moscow: NLO, 2000.

Kistiakovskii, B. "Chto takoe natsionalizm: dva osnovnykh tipa natsionalizma. [What is Nationalism: Two Basic Types of Nationalism]" *Natsional'nye problemy* 1 (1915): 3–5.

Kokoshkin, F. F. 1914. "Liberalizm i nationalism [Liberalism and Nationalism]." *Russkie Vedomosti* 9 (November 1914): 2.

Miliukov, P. N. "Derzhavnyi maskarad [Royal masquerade]." *Osvobozhdenie* 19 (1903).

———. "Ukrainskii vopros i P. B. Struve [The Ukrainian Question and P. B. Struve]," *Rech'* 9 (November 1914): 3.

Mogilner, Marina. *Homo imperii: A History of Physical Anthropology in Russia.* Lincoln: University of Nebraska Press, 2013.

Nikonov, L. N. and B. E. Raikov. "V. A. Gerd." In *Ekskursionnoe delo*, 5–16. Moscow–Leningrad, 1928.

Peshekhonov, A. V. "Na ocherednye temy: novyi pokhod protiv intelligentsii [On Current Debates: A New Charge Against Intelligentsia]." *Russkoe Bogatstvo* 4 (1909): 100–125.

Petliura, S. "Otritsatel'nye cherty polemiki po ukrainskomu voprosu [Negative Features of the Debate on the Ukrainian Question]." *Ukrainskaia zhizn'*, 11–12 (1914): 12–16.

Pipes, Richard. *Struve, Liberal on the Left, 1870–1905.* Cambridge, MA: Harvard University Press, 1970.

Podbolotov, Sergey. "Tsar and narod: Populistskii natsionalizm imperatora Nikolaia II [Tsar and the People: Populist Nationalism of the Emperor Nicholas II]." *Ab Imperio* 3 (2003): 199–223.

Rein, Adolf. *Sir Lohn Robert Seeley: Eine Studie über den Historiker.* Langensalza, 1912.

Remnev, Antoly, and Natalia Suvorova. "'Russkoe delo' na aziatskikh okrainakh: 'Russkost'' pod ugrozoi ili somnitel'nye 'kul'turtreggery' [The Russian Cause in the Asian Peripheries: Russianness under Threat or Doubtful Kulturtraeger]." *Ab Imperio* 2 (2008): 157–222.

Samarin, Yuri. "Sovremennnyi ob'em pol'kogo voprosa [The Current Scope of the Polish Question]." In *Yuri Samarin i ego vremia*, by Boris Nolde. Moscow, 2003.

Seeley, John Robert. *The Expansion of England*, edited by John Gross, xxvii. Chicago: University of Chicago Press, 1971.

———. "The Expansion of England in the Eighteenth Century." *Macmillans Magazine* 46 (1882): 456–465.

———. *The Expansion of England: Two Courses of Lecture.* London, 1883.

———. *Life and Times of Stein, or Germany and Prussia in the Napoleonic Age.* 3 vols. Cambridge: Cambridge University Press, 1878.

———. *Our Colonial Expansion.* London, 1887.

———. *Rasshirenie Anglii.* St. Petersburg: O.N. Popova Publishing House, 1903.

———. "United States of Europe." *Macmillan Magazine* 23 (1870–1871): 436–448.

Semyonov, Alexander. "The Real and Live Ethnographic Map of Russia: The Russian Empire in the Mirror of the State Duma." In *Empire Speaks Out: Languages of Rationalization and Self-Description in the Russian Empire*, edited by Ilya Gerasimov, Jan Kusber, and Alexander Semyonov, 191–228. Leiden: Brill, 2009.

Shklovsky, Viktor. 1917. "Iskusstvo kak priem [Art as Technique]." In *Sborniki po teorii poeticheskogo iazyka*, 2: 3–14. Petrograd, 1917.

———. "Art as Technique." In *Literary Theory: An Anthology*, edited by Julie Rivkin and Michael Ryan, 15–21. Malden, MA: Blackwell Publishing, 1998.

Steinmetz, George. *The Devils Handwriting: Precoloniality and the German Colonial State In Qingdao, Samoa, And Southwest Africa*. Chicago: University of Chicago Press, 2007.

Stoler, Ann. "Considerations on Imperial Comparisons." In *Empire Speaks Out: Languages of Rationalization and Self-Description in the Russian Empire*, edited by Ilya Gerasimov, Jan Kusber, and Alexander Semyonov, 33–55. Leiden: Brill, 2009.

Struve, P. B. "Avstriiskoe krest'ianstvo i ego bytopisateli [Austrian Peasantry and Its Literary Accounts]." *Vestnik Evropy* 6 (1893): 569–585.

———. "Chto zhe takoe Rossiia [What Is Russia?]." *Russkaia Mysl'* 1, no. 1 (1911): 175–178.

———. "Ekonomicheskaia problema 'Velikoi Rossii': Zametki ekonomista o voine i narodnom khoziastve [The Economic Problem of 'Greater Russia': Notes of an Economist on War and Economy]." In *Velikaia Rossiia: Sbronik Statei po voennym i obshchestvennym voprosam*, edited by V. P. Riabushinksii, part 2, pages 143–154. Moscow, 1910.

———. "Is istorii obshchestvennykh idei i otnoshenii v Germanii v XIX v. [From the History of Social Ideas and Relations in Germany in the 19th Century]." *Novoe Slovo* 8 (1897): 161–164.

———. "Is istorii obshchestvennykh idei i otnoshenii v Germanii v XIX v. [From the History of Social Ideas and Relations in Germany in the 19th Century]." *Nauchnoe Obozrenie* 4 (1898): 784–795.

———. *Kriticheskie zametki k vorposu ob ekonomicheskom razvitii Rossii* [Critical Notes on the Question of Economic Development of Russia]. St. Petersburg, 1894.

———. "Na ocherednye temy." *Russkaia Mysl'* 1 (1909): 194–198.

———. "Nemtsy v Avstrii i krest'ianstvo [Germans in Austria and the Peasantry]." *Vestnik Evropy* 2: 796–828.

———. "Obshcherusskaia kul'tura i ukrainskii partikuliarizm, otvet ukraintsu [All-Russian Culture and Ukrainian Particularism, A Response to a Ukrainian]." *Russkaia Mysl'* 1 (1912): 65–86.

———. Osnovnye momenty v razvitii krepostnogo khoziastva v Rossii v XIX veke [Basic Features in the Development of the Serf Economy in 19th Century Russia]." *Mir Bozhii* 8, no. 10 (1899): 180–194; 8, no. 11 (1899): 271–289; 8, no. 12 (1899): 254–283.

———. "Past and Present of Russian Economics." In *Russian Realities and Problems*, edited by J. D. Duff, 47–48. Cambridge: Cambridge University Press, 1917.

———. "Predislovie [Foreword]." In *Printsipy demokratii*, edited by Woodrow Wilson, 5–14. Berlin, 1924.

———. "Velikaia Rossiia: iz razmyshlenii o probleme russkogo mogushchestva [Greater Russia: Reflections on the Problem of Russian Power]." *Russkaia Mysl'* 1 (1908): 143–157.

———. "Velikaia Rossiia i Sviataia Rus' [Greater Russia and the Holy Rus']."*Russkaia Mysl'* 12 (1914): 176– 180.

Tanner, J. R. "John Robert Seeley." *The English Historical Review* 10, no. 39 (July 1895): 507–514.

Thompson, Andrew S. *The Empire Strikes Back?: The Impact of Imperialism on Britain From the Mid-Nineteenth Century*. New York: Routledge, 2005.

———. "The Language of Imperialism and the Meanings of Empire: Imperial Discourse in British Politics, 1895–1914." *Journal of British Studies* 36, no. 2 (1997): 147–177.

———. *Patriotica: Politika, kul'tura, religia, sotsializm* [Patriotica: Politics, Culture, Religion, Socialism]. Moscow, 1997.

Wormell, Deborah. *Sir John Seeley and the Uses of History*. Cambridge: Cambridge University Press, 1980.

Wortman, Richard. *Scenarios of Power: Myth and Ceremony in Russian Monarchy*. 2 vols. Princeton: Princeton University Press, 1995, 2000.

ANTIDOTES TO EMPIRE: FROM THE CONGRESS SYSTEM TO THE EUROPEAN UNION*

Stella Ghervas**

Abstract

Is the European Union a "non-imperial empire"? This is what the President of the European Commission, José Manuel Barroso, once stated in 2011. This oxymoron is doubly paradoxical because the term empire has long had a negative connotation for both supporters and opponents of European integration. It is therefore appropriate to return to historic precedents for the argument against a continental empire in Europe, and to examine past alternatives. This paper will look at the experiment of the Congress System *(1815–1825) born out of the Congress of Vienna, when diplomatic delegations from all over Europe congregated after the cataclysm of the Napoleonic Wars. In particular, the treaty of the Holy Alliance, a collective covenant for peace, was signed in September 1815 by three great powers (Russia, Austria, and Prussia) that had in common their aversion to the empire of Napoleon. Yet the imperial element could not be removed from the picture, since Russia and Austria*

* Earlier versions of this article were presented at the Visiting Scholars Seminar "New Research on Europe" at Harvard University's Center for European Studies, and the interdisciplinary Conference "EUtROPEs. The Paradox of European Empire," organized by the University of Chicago in Paris. I wish to thank Laurent Franceschetti, Dustin Simpson, David Armitage, Dipesh Chakrabarty, William Graham, Mark Jarrett, and Robert Morrissey for having kindly reviewed and commented on this paper, as well as Alain d'Iribarne and Jean-Jacques Rey, who read previous versions. It was completed with the generous support of the Fondation pour Genève and the Fondation des archives de la famille Pictet.

** Stella Ghervas is a Visiting Scholar at Harvard University's Center for European Studies.

were themselves empires. Hence the discourse of the Holy Alliance inevitably led to fatal contradictions. Out of the paradoxes of that case study, we will highlight the fact that the European Union is less liable to become an empire than a directorate of great powers, with its attendant risks.

How far, or how close, is the European Union to becoming a pan-European empire? It is worth noting that this analogy is increasingly proposed for the EU.[1] Its vogue is likely due to the rapid expansion of the Union to the east over the last decade and its resulting size, which now spans a large part of the continent.[2] A wide range of personalities have made this comparison, in what seems a rather chaotic trend: the former Soviet dissident Vladimir Bukovsky characterized the EU as the "old Soviet system presented in Western guise";[3] Jeremy Rifkin claims that the Holy Roman Empire "from the eighth (sic) to the early nineteenth centuries is the only faint historical parallel";[4] even the president of the European Commission, José Manuel Barroso, calls it a "non-imperial empire"[5]—in a seemingly Orwellian doublethink. Jan Zielonka makes a much more detailed case, by proposing a paradigm for the EU as a benign form of "neo-Medieval empire."[6]

---

[1] Ole Waever, "Imperial Metaphors: Emerging European Analogies to Pre-Nation-State Imperial Systems," in *Geopolitics in Post-Wall Europe: Security, Territory and Identity*, ed. Ola Tunander, Pavel Baev, and Victoria Ingrid Einagel (London: Sage Publications; Oslo: International Peace Research Institute, 1997), 59–93; Madalina V. Antonescu, *Uniunea Europeana, Imperiile antice si Imperiile medievale. Studiu comparativ.* [The EU, Ancient, and Medieval Empires: A Comparative Study] (Bucharest: Cartea Universitara, 2008); Christopher S. Browning, "Westphalian, Imperial, Neomedieval: The Geopolitics of Europe and the Role of the North," in *Remaking Europe in the Margins: Northern Europe after the Enlargements*, ed. Christopher S. Browning (Aldershot, UK: Ashgate, 2005), 85–101.

[2] Paul-Augustin Deproost, "*Hic non finit Roma*. Les paradoxes de la frontière romaine, un modèle pour l'Europe?" in *Imaginaires européens. Les frontiers pour ouvrir l'Europe*, ed. Paul-Augustin Deproost and Bernard Coulie (Paris: L'Harmattan, 2004), 29–50; James Anderson, "Singular Europe: An Empire Once Again?" in *Geopolitics of European Union Enlargement: The Fortress Empire*, ed. Warwick Armstrong and James Anderson (London: Routledge, 2007), 9–29.

[3] Vladimir Bukovsky, "The European Union: The New Soviet Union?" http://www.youtube.com/watch?v=js40QG3UEE8.

[4] Jeremy Rifkin, *The European Dream: How Europe's Vision of the Future is Quietly Eclipsing the American Dream* (Cambridge: Polity, 2004), 198.

[5] José Manuel Barroso (President of the European Commission): "Sometimes I like to compare the European Union, as a creation, to the organization of empires. Empires! Because we have [the] dimension of empires," Video press conference EUX.TV, 2007, http://www.youtube.com/watch?v=c2Ralocq9uE.

[6] Jan Zielonka, *Europe as Empire: The Nature of the Enlarged European Union* (New York: Oxford University Press, 2006), 164–91.

More generally, the resurgence of academic interest in empires as political entities is in our *Zeitgeist*. After the collapse of the Soviet Union and the accession of the United States of America to the status of hyper-power (especially in light of its change of policy in 2001), it was predictable that the case of empires would be reopened; it also became a "hot ticket," whose merits are sometimes exaggerated.[7]

But beyond the events of the last two decades, this renewed interest is yet another avatar of a time-honored intellectual debate in Europe, between Empire and the Westphalian states—or more accurately, between the traditional hierarchical (top-down) conception of political order on the continent, and other models proposed as alternatives. The question had already been framed at the time of the Enlightenment. Authors such as Abbé de Saint-Pierre, Rousseau, and Kant, with their plans of perpetual peace, attempted to theorize some form of multilateral order in Europe, as a middle ground between the two radically opposed views of the time: on the one hand, a *continental empire* ("universal monarchy") that would abruptly impose a "hegemonic peace" upon all states, which could amount to servitude; on the other, the European *balance of power*, an organized anarchy liable to degenerate into regular, furious, and often petty wars between states.[8] In the early twentieth century, the concept of "balkanization" was introduced to describe extreme cases of the latter phenomenon.[9] These paradigms led, of course, to very distinct concepts of peace for the continent,[10] as well as of center-periphery relations. In a way, the scholars who espouse the imperial thesis are attempting to reset the intellectual pendulum back to the top-down order.

There is, however, another darker aspect to empires. In a previous article, I argued that this subject has considerable relevance, *beyond* the boundaries of academic institutions: the image of empire plays a crucial and measurable

---

[7] See Alexander J. Motyl, "Is Everything Empire? Is Empire Everything?" *Comparative Politics* 38, no. 2 (2006): 229–49; David Armitage, "Introduction," in *Theories of Empire, 1450–1800*, ed. David Armitage (Aldershot, UK: Ashgate, 1998), xv–xxxiii.

[8] Stella Ghervas, "La paix par le droit, ciment de la civilisation en Europe? La perspective du Siècle des Lumières," in *Penser l'Europe au XVIIIe siècle: Commerce, Civilisation, Empire*, ed. Antoine Lilti and Céline Spector (Oxford: Voltaire Foundation, 2014), 47–70.

[9] Maria N. Todorova, *Imagining the Balkans* (New York: Oxford University Press, 1997), 33–34.

[10] On these different types of peace (hegemonic, peace of balance, federal, confederal, and directorial), see Bruno Arcidiacono, *Cinq types de paix. Une histoire des plans de pacification perpétuelle (XVIIe–XXe siècles)* (Paris: PUF, 2011); Stella Ghervas, "Peace perpetually reconsidered," *Books & Ideas*, November 12, 2012, http://www.booksandideas.net/Peace-perpetually-reconsidered.html.

role in the political and public attitudes of Europeans toward Brussels.[11] It frames mental geographies and influences center-periphery perceptions. But in that context, its connotation is definitely negative, because it awakens the memories of two continental empires of the twentieth century—the Third Reich and the Soviet Union—particularly their totalitarian approach to society, ruthless military occupations, and harsh treatment of civilians. Those were traumatic experiences that, as Hannah Arendt wrote, led to the realization that progress and doom were two sides of the same coin.[12] Not all evolutions are for the best.

That observation is very apt for the debate at hand: *empire*, considered by some as a possibly desirable model for Europe, awakens at the same time a "historical specter" that not only feeds Eurosceptic attitudes, but is also a concern that shapes the policies of the EU itself. Going farther back, to the early eighteenth century, we find that there existed already a common agreement in the Law of Nations that no single power should ever extend a *universal monarchy* (hence, a continental empire) over Europe. Preventing such a thing from occurring was precisely the purpose of the *balance of power*, the principle of multilateral equilibrium included in the Treaty of Utrecht in 1713.[13] In short, *does the return of "empire" (as a paradigm describing the EU) amount to a self-denial of the European project, or worse, self-defeat?*

To help us answer this question, it might be fruitful to return to historical precedents of the argument for or against a pan-European empire, and to the alternatives proposed at the time. This paper traces the arguments of a group of statesmen of the Congress System (1815–25), who had in common their aversion to the empire of Napoleon and the intention to establish a collective covenant of peace among sovereign states. The tale would be interesting all by itself. Yet the paradoxes of that experiment, translated into modern terms, should raise some doubts about whether the EU truly qualifies as an "empire," suggesting that its challenges might lie instead in a different direction: the risk of becoming an oligarchy of "great powers" that would no longer satisfy the aspirations of European citizens.

---

[11] Stella Ghervas, "From Empires to the Anti-Empire: National Imaginaries toward Political Europe," *Journal of Contemporary European Studies*, 2015.

[12] Hannah Arendt, "Preface," in *The Origins of Totalitarianism* (San Diego: Harcourt, 1973), vii.

[13] See Michael Sheehan, *The Balance of Power: History and Theory* (New York: Routledge, 1996), 97–120; Paul Schroeder, *The Transformation of European Politics, 1763–1848* (Oxford: Oxford University Press, 1994), 3–52; Stella Ghervas, "Balance of Power vs. Perpetual Peace: Paradigms of European Order from Utrecht to Vienna, 1713–1815 ," in *The Art of Peacemaking: Lessons learned from Peace Treaties*, ed. A. H. A. Soons (Leiden: Martinus Nijhoff Publishers/Brill, 2015).

FROM THE HOLY ALLIANCE TO THE CONGRESS SYSTEM

From 1802 to 1815, the title to preeminence in Europe was unexpectedly stolen by the vast territorial formation created by the French Emperor Napoleon, an empire *par excellence*.[14] According to a first interpretation, it was a "reconstruction" of the European order, issuing a beneficial *Pax Napoleonica* modeled after the *Pax Romana*.[15] Accordingly, the rhetoric and ideals of the vast Napoleonic Empire, particularly the glory and hopes for political/social/economic progress that it conveys up to our times, have been carefully studied.[16] In a second and opposite interpretation, especially outside of France, it was a near-apocalyptic period that upset and nearly destroyed the European political order based on the balance of power. After the defeat of Napoleon's Empire, the Allied Powers manifested a clear and unambiguous intention to rebuild a new continental system based on the *status quo*, where no power would ever again be allowed to achieve predominance over all others.

Such was in particular the viewpoint of the authors of the pact of the Holy Alliance, signed in Paris by three of the Allied Powers (Russia, Austria, and Prussia) on September 26, 1815,[17] then ratified by the majority of the states on the continent. That treaty presents us with three major difficulties, which obscured its real significance for a long time. In the first place—and in contrast to the Final Act of the Congress of Vienna (June 9, 1815) and the military alliances of the great powers signed at the time (all rather conventional documents)—the Holy Alliance stands out as a singularity: a manifesto, a broad declaration of intents not followed by immediate effects. Secondly, its form was imbued with an intriguing Christian rhetoric, an unlucky fact that has prompted several historians to dismiss it as gibberish. Third, a polarized interpretation, especially in France, has long held that the "Holy Alliance"

---

[14] The interest in the Napoleonic Empire shows no signs of abating. Among the abundant literature in recent years we can mention: Michael Broers, *Europe under Napoleon, 1799–1815* (New York: Edward Arnold, 1996); Annie Jourdan, *L'Empire de Napoléon* (Paris: Flammarion, 2000); Gunther Rothenberg, *Die Napoleonischen Kriege* (Berlin: Brandenburger Verlagshaus, 2000); Charles Esdaile, *Napoleon's Wars: An International History, 1803–1815* (London: Penguin, 2007); Thierry Lentz, *Nouvelle Histoire de l'Empire* (Paris: Fayard, 2002–2004); Jean Tulard, *Napoléon, chef de guerre* (Paris: Tallandier, 2012).

[15] See e.g., *L'Empire napoléonien: Une expérience européenne?*, ed. François Antoine, Jean-Pierre Jessenne, Anne Jourdan, and Hervé Leuwers (Paris: Armand Colin, 2014).

[16] Among recent contributions, see e.g., Robert Morrissey, *Napoléon et l'héritage de la gloire* (Paris: PUF, 2010).

[17] "Traité de la sainte Alliance entre les Empereurs de Russie et d'Autriche et le Roi de Prusse, signé à Paris le 14/26 septembre 1815," in *Le Congrès de Vienne et les traités de 1815*, ed. Comte d'Angeberg (Léonard Chodzko) (Paris: Amyot, 1863–1864), vol. 4 (1864), 1547–49.

(a term improperly applied to the broad policies of the great powers after the fall of Napoleon, and even to the Concert of Europe up to the 1850s)[18] had only been an intellectual, social, and political regression.[19] By contrast, a few twentieth-century Swiss historians provided a more careful analysis of the pact; in that, they were undoubtedly stimulated by the presence of the League of Nations in their homeland.[20]

Closer to us, a more balanced reinterpretation of the post-Napoleonic period is underway, thanks to a renewal of historiography carried out, in good part, by Anglo-American scholars.[21] This is parallel to the aforementioned revival of interest in the concept of "empire" (including the Napoleonic one) in history.[22] From these advances, we can engage in study of this manifesto from a fresh perspective. We then discover a long-matured thought process, with layers as various as the plans for perpetual peace of

---

[18] For the sake of clarity, we will use the term "Holy Alliance" here to refer to the treaty itself, and *not* to the new European order that was established in this period. We will rather use terms such as "Congress System," "Concert of Europe," or "Post-Napoleonic period," as applicable.

[19] French historians have traditionally framed the nineteenth century in an elementary dialectics between two opposed blocs: Holy Alliance/Restoration/Reaction/Conservatism on one side, and Enlightenment/French Revolution/"the Peoples' Spring"/progress on the other. The questioning of these interpretations is making headway: see Emmanuel de Waresquiel, *L'histoire à rebrousse-poil: les élites, la Restauration, la Révolution* (Paris: Fayard, 2005), 2–53; Sylvie Aprile, *La révolution inachevée, 1815–1870* (Paris: Berlin, 2010), 531–47. It would be fruitful to explore the historical process by which these associations of ideas came to be formed first in elites, then in national imaginaries.

[20] Werner Näf, *Zur Geschichte der Heiligen Allianz* (Bern: Paul Haupt, 1928); Hans W. Schmalz, *Versuche einer gesamteuropäischen Organisation 1815–1820* (Aarau: Sauerländer, 1940); Maurice Bourquin, *Histoire de la Sainte-Alliance* (Geneva: Georg, 1954). Also published in Switzerland was the work by Belgian historian Jacques-Henri Pirenne, *La Sainte-Alliance. Organisation européenne de la paix internationale,* 2 vols. (Neuchâtel: Ed. de la Baconnière, 1946–1949). See also, more recently, Stella Ghervas, *Réinventer la tradition: Alexandre Stourdza et l'Europe de la Sainte-Alliance* (Paris: Honoré Champion, 2008).

[21] Notably: Adam Zamoyski, *Rites of Peace: The fall of Napoleon and the Congress of Vienna* (New York: Harper Collins, 2007); *Napoleon's Legacy: Problems of Government in Restoration Europe,* ed. David Laven and Lucy Riall (Oxford: Berg, 2000); Paul Schroeder, *The Transformation of European Politics, 1763–1848* (Oxford: Oxford University Press, 1994); Alan Sked, *Metternich and Austria: An Evaluation* (Houndsmill, UK: Palgrave Macmillian, 2008); Mark Jarrett, *The Congress of Vienna and Its Legacy: War and Great Power Diplomacy After Napoleon* (London: I.B. Tauris, 2013).

[22] See e.g., the recent work of Frederick Cooper and Jane Burbank, *Empires in World History: Power and the Politics of Difference* (Princeton: Princeton University Press, 2010). The authors pose two essential questions with reference to the Napoleonic Empire: "Did his empire represent a new, post-revolutionary notion of empire politics, less aristocratic and hierarchical, more centralized and bureaucratic? How French was the French empire under Napoleon?" (229).

the Enlightenment, Christian tradition (including its Orthodox and Protestant branches), and early nineteenth century mysticism. More importantly, it expressed a political ecumenism that broke away from the traditional paradigm of the duality of Roman Emperor/Papacy in Europe, effectively destroying it. Finally, this treaty explicitly endorsed a condemnation of wars of aggression in Europe, thus heralding a profound change in the political mentalities of the Continent—a concept that would come to be known as *pacifism*. In summary, the Holy Alliance initially staked out a middle ground between the reactionary tendencies that demanded a return to the *Ancien Régime*, and the radical movements toward popular and national representation.

RUSSIA AT THE DOWNFALL OF NAPOLEON'S EMPIRE

In what circumstances did the Holy Alliance come into being? It is necessary here to recount briefly some events related to the final years of the Napoleonic Wars. The dismal debacle of the Russian Campaign of 1812 (which remained impressed in the minds of the Russians as the *Great Patriotic War*) led to a dramatic reversal of military fortunes: after the French army crossed the Berezina in the last days of November 1812, the Russian army led a furious counter-offensive across Eastern Europe that brought it to Berlin on March 4, 1813, after covering 1,000 kilometers in only three months.[23] It was in the wake of that sensational advance that Prussia, and later Austria, regained their freedom and joined the Anglo-Russian coalition, in what German historiography has come to call the *wars of liberation* (*Befreiungskriege*).[24] For the first time ever, four great powers of Europe were in a position to field their forces simultaneously against France, in what became the climax—and the turning point—of the Napoleonic Wars: the gigantic battle of Leipzig (also known as the Battle of the Nations). On October 16, 1813, over half a million soldiers on both sides clashed, with a third injured or killed, possibly the largest and bloodiest battle in recorded history until

[23] Adam Zamoyski, *Moscow 1812: Napoleon's Fatal March* (New York: Harper Collins, 2004), 520–43; Dominic Lieven, *Russia against Napoleon: The Battle for Europe, 1807 to 1814* (London: Penguin Books, 2009), 285–328.

[24] See Ferdi Akaltin, *Die Befreiungskriege im Geschichtsbild der Deutschen im 19. Jahrhundert* (Frankfurt: Verlag Neue Wissenschaft, 1997); Volker Sellin, *Die geraubte Revolution. Der Sturz Napoleons und die Restauration in Europa* (Gottingen: Vandenhoeck und Ruprecht Verlag, 2001), 11–39; David A. Bell, *The First Total War: Napoleon's Europe and the Birth of Warfare as We Know It* (Boston: Houghton Mifflin Company, 2007), 294–301; Alan Sked, *Radetzky: Imperial Victor and Military Genius* (London: I.B. Tauris, 2011).

World War I.[25] After four days, the *Grande Armée* was defeated. Having lost control of Europe, Napoleon started retreating to France.

On March 31, 1814, the first allied unit that had the honor of entering Paris along the Champs-Elysées was the Cossack cavalry in full uniform.[26] This symbolic fact, very revealing of the relations among the Allies, powerfully struck the imaginations of contemporaries; despite this, it has remained largely ignored by Western (especially French) historiography, but also by Russian historians. In September of the same year there began in Vienna the famous Congress, the task of which was to reorganize the map of Europe following the political and territorial upheavals caused by the Napoleonic Wars. Quite logically, the Russian delegation was the focus of attention. After the Hundred Days and the final abdication of Napoleon (June 1815), it was again the Russian army that was assigned the task of occupying the Paris region.[27] All in all, while the Austrian, Prussian, and British armies had been the hammer of the coalition that finally broke the French army, the Russian army had played all along the role of the anvil.

Against this background, it is easier to understand how the Russian Empire of Tsar Alexander I (1777–1825) established itself for a decade as a European superpower *avant la lettre*, at the forefront of the reconstruction of the political order. The tendency to forget the prominent military and political role of Russia in those days is all the more paradoxical because the Russian army had never pushed so far west, and would never again return.

THE HOLY ALLIANCE: THE LETTER AND THE SPIRIT OF THE TREATY

It was in the late summer of 1815, after the final defeat of the French empire, that Tsar Alexander I proposed the pact of the Holy Alliance to the emperor of Austria, Francis I, and the Prussian king, Frederick William III. It was

---

[25] Gunther E. Rothenberg, *The Art of Warfare in the Age of Napoleon* (Bloomington: Indiana University Press, 1978), 81; David A. Bell, *The First Total War*, 251. See also Gerd Fesser, *1813. Die Völkerschlacht bei Leipzig* (Jena/Quedlinburg: Verlag Bussert & Stadeler, 2013); Digby Smith, *1813—Leipzig: Napoleon and the Battle of the Nations* (London: Greenhill Books, 2001), 55–74.

[26] Dominic Lieven, *Russia against Napoleon,* 494–520; Emmanuel de Waresquiel and Benoit Yvert, *Histoire de la Restauration, 1814–1830: Naissance de la France moderne* (Paris: Perrin, 1996), 31–33; Michael V. Leggiere, *The Fall of Napoleon. Volume I: The Allied Invasion of France, 1813–1814* (Cambridge: Cambridge University Press, 2007), 48–62; Adam Zamoyski, *Moscow 1812*, 546–50.

[27] See Jacques Hantraye, *Les Cosaques aux Champs-Elysées: les occupations étrangères en France après la chute de Napoléon* (Paris: Belin, 2005), 217–31; Vasily K. Nadler, *Imperator Aleksandr I i ideja Svjaschennogo Sojuza* [Emperor Alexander I and the Idea of the Holy Alliance], 5 vols. (Riga: N. Kimmel, 1886–1892), vol. 5, 1–114;

unprecedented that this document, signed in Paris on September 26, 1815, would be ratified by most states of Europe, great and small, with two notable exceptions: the Holy See and Britain (for opposite reasons that we will briefly explain).

As already mentioned, it is essential that we clearly distinguish the Holy Alliance from the multiplicity of treaties signed during the same year, notably the *Final Act of the Congress of Vienna* of June 9, 1815, which formally redefined and guaranteed the borders of European States and provided for practical matters related to the new order, such as navigation on the Danube. We should also not confuse it with the *two* treaties signed on November 20, 1815; namely, the *Treaty of Paris* (again a post-war territorial settlement, reinstating the Bourbon monarchy), and the military *Quadruple Alliance* of Prussia, Austria, Russia, and Britain, which guaranteed the application of the peace settlements of the "Vienna Order" (later extended to France in 1818).

The Holy Alliance is of another kind altogether. This surprising and rather short document (written in French, the diplomatic language of the time) consists of a preamble and three articles. While referring to the "Most Holy and Indivisible Trinity" and to "Divine Providence," the preamble commands that the sovereigns follow "the Holy Religion of our Savior" and accept the "necessity of submitting the reciprocal relations of the Powers, upon [its] sublime truths." The first article declares that the three monarchs are "united by the bonds of a true and indissoluble fraternity" and are "fellow countrymen" called to protect "Religion, Peace, and Justice." The second article requires that sovereigns and their subjects do each other "reciprocal service," that they manifest "mutual affection" with "the most tender solicitude," and that they consider themselves members of the "One family" of Austria, Prussia, and Russia, and more broadly, of "the Christian world" united to the end of "enjoying Peace." The third article invites all states that wish so to join in this treaty, to contribute to "the happiness of nations, too long agitated."[28]

A reader used to the conventions of modern language may no doubt find this lumbering prose rather obscure. It may become clearer if we consider that it relocates the metaphor of a Christian family piously united (as in *fraternity, affection, solicitude, service*) squarely into the political sphere, alongside more explicit terms like *compatriots, fellow countrymen, nations,* and *subjects.*

---

[28] "Traité de la sainte Alliance," in *Comte d'Angeberg*, t. 4, 1547–49. See Andrei Zorin, *Kormia dvuglavogo orla: Literatura i gosudarstvennaia ideologiia v Rossii v poslednei treti XVIII–pervoi treti XIX veka* [Feeding the Two-headed Eagle: Literature and State Ideology in Russia from the last third of the eighteenth century to the first third of the nineteenth century] (Moscow: Novoe literaturnoe obozrenie, 2001), 297–335.

The incomprehension of posterity began, however, very soon thereafter: much was written and said on the subject, as early as the second decade of the nineteenth century. Of particular interest is the associated legend, according to which the pact was the invention of a female mystic, Barbara Juliane von Krüdener, who supposedly suggested it to the Tsar.[29] The facts on the origins of the Holy Alliance are both more prosaic and more fascinating: the author was Alexander I himself. He wrote the preliminary notes in pencil and then gave them to his Head of Chancery, Count John Capodistrias, so that he could render them in a diplomatic language. In his turn, Capodistrias passed the document to a brilliant and cultivated secretary named Alexandre Stourdza. Stourdza later provided a detailed explanation of the text of the treaty in an unpublished piece called "Considérations sur l'acte d'alliance fraternelle et chrétienne du 14/26 septembre 1815," held by the Pushkin House in St. Petersburg.[30]

Without delving too deeply into hermeneutic analysis that might take us away from our purpose, suffice it to say that the pact of the Holy Alliance encloses an essential concept (in modern terminology) of *a peaceful alliance of hereditary kings and their states, extendable to all Christian states.* In his "Considérations," Stourdza sought to demonstrate that the pact was grounded on a solid theoretical and ideological base, in order to overcome the suspicions of those who opposed the pact and to refute their objections. In his theoretical construction, Napoleon was the heir of French Revolution, and his fall the end of an epoch of social and political disorder. Referring to the recent victory of the Allies following the Hundred Days, Stourdza wrote, "The *principle of subversion* against all religious and social institutions has just been slain a second time."[31] This European unrest found its origin, according to him, in the Seven Years' War (1765) and included the American Revolution, the French Revolution, and the succeeding Napoleonic epoch. Hence the sole solution was to restore a *principle of order* in public life, and therefore to "proclaim [...] the sole conservative principles, which had been too long relegated to the subordinate sphere of domestic life."[32] There lies the explanation for the intentional but otherwise incomprehensible intrusion of Christian principles into the political sphere. In fact the Tsar had already expressed that very idea nine months earlier, on December 31, 1814, in a diplomatic note that he had

---

[29] See Vasily K. Nadler, *Imperator Aleksandr I i ideja Svjaschennogo Sojuza,* vol. 5, 251–356.

[30] I discovered that document in 1993 at the Department of Manuscripts of the Pushkin House (also known as the Institute of Russian Literature) in St. Petersburg (hereafter RO IRLI). See Stella Ghervas, *Réinventer la tradition,* 186–91.

[31] Alexandre Stourdza, "Considérations sur l'acte d'alliance fraternelle et chrétienne du 14/26 septembre 1815," RO IRLI, 288/1, no. 21, f. 1 (emphasis added).

[32] Ibid., f. 2.

sent to the plenipotentiaries of the three great powers (and lest there remain any doubt, it was long before he had even met Baroness Krüdener).[33] More generally, the feeling from many contemporaries that they had just escaped a near-apocalyptic experience largely explains the wave of mysticism that washed over Europe in those years.

Stourdza's testimony thus confirms that the Holy Alliance did pursue a conservative, religious, and counter-revolutionary agenda. For all that, it would be a mistake to call it a reactionary or ultra-royalist manifesto. Between these two extremes, there existed not only a vast spectrum of ideas, but also profound divergences. We should sooner speak of a middle ground, a "defensive modernization," which sparked a storm of criticism from both sides.[34]

The Legacy of the Enlightenment: State Reform and the Ideal of Perpetual Peace

One way of illustrating how the treaty was controversial in the eyes of contemporaries is to recount how the text was reformulated during its drafting. The Austrian emperor, after consulting the original version of the treaty, passed it along to his minister Klemens Wenzel von Metternich, a man of rather conservative dispositions. Metternich modified the sentence "the subjects of the three contracting parties will remain united by a true fraternity" into "the *three monarchs* will remain united."[35] Similarly the initial version stated that the three Powers were three *provinces* of a sole nation—a notion that the Austrian minister amended by presenting them as three *branches* of the same

[33] "Pénétrés...des principes immuables de la religion chrétienne commune à tous, c'est sur cette base unique de l'ordre politique comme de l'ordre social que les souverains, fraternisant entre eux, épureront leurs maximes d'Etat et garantiront les rapports entre les peuples que la Providence leur a confiés". ["Convinced…of the immutable principles of the Christian religion shared by all, it is on this single basis of both political and social order that the Sovereigns, acting as brothers toward each other, will purify their State maxims and guarantee the relationships between the peoples that Providence entrusted to them." (translation mine)] A copy of that note ("Diplomatic note of Tsar Alexander I to the plenipotentiaries of Austria, Great Britain, and Prussia") is kept in the archives of St. Petersburg: [Alexandre Stourdza], "Venskij Kongress" [The Congress of Vienna], RO IRLI, 288/2, no. 6, ff. 35–41. See Maurice Bourquin, *Histoire de la Sainte-Alliance*, 134; Stella Ghervas, *Réinventer la tradition*, 72–73; Mark Jarrett, *The Congress of Vienna*, 173.

[34] Stella Ghervas, *Réinventer la tradition*, 430–31.

[35] "Les *sujets des trois parties contractantes* demeureront unis par les liens d'une fraternité véritable" into "les *trois monarques* demeureront unis…" See Francis Ley, *Alexandre Ier et sa Sainte-Alliance* (Paris: Fischbacher, 1975), 149–53 (emphasis added). On this subject, see also: Werner Näf, *Zur Geschichte der Heiligen Allianz*, 34–37; H. G. Schenk, *Aftermath of Napoleonic Wars—An Experiment* (Oxford: Oxford University Press, 1947), 31–43.

family. Metternich, having obviously grasped that there was an attempt to pass political reformism under the guise of religious rhetoric (both of which he disliked), had therefore been quick to temper the enthusiasm of the Tsar. His was also the paternalist idea that the monarchs were "benevolent fathers." However, the idea that Europe represented a "Christian nation" still made it into the final version of the text.

It is obvious from the original proposition that Alexander I had sought to found a European nation "essentially one" and living in peace, of which the various states would be *provinces*. We can easily guess the reason for Metternich's amendments: the original wording would have united the peoples of Europe in a position, so to speak, "over the heads of the sovereigns," while placing unprecedented constraints on the monarchs; the text would have smacked of a constitution.[36] The original version even provided that the military forces of the respective powers would have to be considered as forming a single army—130 years before the aborted project of the European Defense Community of the early 1950s! Even though Tsar Alexander I had initially envisaged a sort of *league of nations* united under the authority of the sovereigns, what eventually emerged was an *alliance of kings*.

From this point of view, the pact of the Holy Alliance stemmed from a line of thought of the Enlightenment. We should keep in mind that the monarchs and ministers[37] of the post-Napoleonic era considered themselves as heirs of that movement *as a matter of course*: after all, they were the direct descendants of the sovereigns Frederick II of Prussia, Catherine of Russia, and Joseph II of Austria, all of whom had surprised their epoch with their intellectual audacity and rivaled one another to host in their courts philosophers such as Voltaire, Rousseau, Diderot, and Kant, much to the chagrin of the conservative minds of their respective kingdoms. On the other hand, the three sovereign signatories of the Holy Alliance rejected the French Revolution with their utmost energy.

---

[36] See Olga V. Orlik, *Rossija v mezhdunarodnyh otnoshenijah, 1815–1829: Ot Venskogo kongressa do Adrianopolskogo mira* [Russia in International Relations, 1815–1829: From the Congress of Vienna to the Peace of Andrinople] (Moscow: Nauka, 1998), 16–24.

[37] As a representative example of that posterity of the "enlightened" rulers, the tsar Alexander I appointed the Duke of Richelieu (future president of the Council of Ministers of Louis XVIII) Governor of Novorossiya ("New Russia," an area including Odessa and Crimea) from 1803 to 1814. Richelieu was assigned in particular the mission of turning Odessa into an ideal port city, complete with all the urban and civic refinements. His memory is still honored today in that city. See Emmanuel de Waresquiel, *Le duc de Richelieu, 1766–1822* (Paris: Perrin, 1990), 136–73; Stella Ghervas, "Odessa et les confins de l'Europe: un éclairage historique," in *Lieux d'Europe. Mythes et limites*, ed. Stella Ghervas and François Rosset (Paris: Editions de la MSH, 2008), 107–24.

How can we explain the terms of this *painful divorce* of the kings from liberal ideals? If we draw a line between moderate and radical Enlightenment thinking, things become clearer.[38] The sovereigns had been receptive, indeed keenly so, to novel ideas, as long those ideas assisted them in their efforts to reform the institutions of the state, develop administrative structures, and modernize urban infrastructure and transportation. They were more than content if that could assist them in their efforts to curb the most conservative forces of their states, particularly the higher aristocracy and the Church, which they sought to subordinate to the authority of the state. There was, however, a line that could never be crossed: as soon as a thinker ventured to criticize the mores of a nation or its autocracy (notably in the case of Russia),[39] he could no longer expect to keep a sympathetic ear of the sovereigns or their inner circles. In their minds, there had never been any question of challenging the thrones themselves or stirring up the populace. The executions in 1793 of Louis XVI and Marie Antoinette—who was none other than the aunt of Francis I, emperor of Austria[40]—then the coronation of Napoleon I in 1804, were two unexpected and particularly dramatic developments in this tragedy.

As for Tsar Alexander, his grandmother, the emperor Catherine the Great, had wanted him to have a Western education steeped in the new ideas. To that end, she enlisted as her tutor Frédéric-César de La Harpe, a Swiss from the Canton of Vaud. As a young Archduke, Alexander had thus been committed to the liberal thought of Enlightenment thinkers. In the early years of his reign, he sympathized with Polish progressives. Unsurprisingly, we find the Polish patriot Prince Adam Jerzy Czartoryski at the head of his diplomatic service from 1804 to 1806. Alexander similarly upheld the constitution of the Grand Duchy of Finland in 1809.[41] He also appointed as chief of his government Mikhail Speransky (1809–1812), considered as one of the

---

[38] Jonathan Israel explains how the Enlightenment saw an opposition between a radical movement (rationalist and committed to the reform of political institutions) and a moderate movement (also open to the use of sensitivity and tradition, and politically loyal to constitutional monarchy): see Jonathan Israel, *A Revolution of the Mind: Radical Enlightenment and the Intellectual Origins of Modern Democracy* (Princeton: Princeton University Press, 2010).

[39] On the ambiguous attitude of Catherine II about her famous "Nakaz," see Stella Ghervas, "La réception de *L'Esprit des lois* en Russie: histoire de quelques ambiguïtés," in *Le Temps de Montesquieu*, ed. Michel Porret and Catherine Volpilhac-Auger (Geneva: Droz, 2002), 391–404.

[40] At the time Marie Antoinette was executed, he had just risen to the position of Archduke of Austria and Emperor of the Holy Roman Empire, under the name of Francis II.

[41] See Päiviö Tommila, *La Finlande dans la politique europééene en 1809–1815* (Helsinki: Finnish Historical Society, 1962).

founders of Russian liberalism.[42] Later, at the time of the Congress of Vienna, we find a Greek patriot, John Capodistrias, at the head of his diplomatic corps (a function that he shared, however, with a more conservative Baltic-German, Karl Nesselrode).[43] On the other hand, Alexander did not wish to upset, or could not risk upsetting, the delicate balance on which the imperial regime of Russia rested; in that, he did not differ from Catherine the Great. After all, Russia was a country where riots and conspiracies were commonplace.[44] Being nonetheless an admirer of the British system, the Tsar declared himself in favor of the establishment of a constitutional monarchy in France in 1814,[45] and in the following year he granted a liberal constitution to the Kingdom of Poland under his authority.[46]

Another idea that had been developing in the mind of Tsar Alexander was *perpetual peace*, a plan promoted by Charles-Irénée Castel de Saint-Pierre just after the treaty of Utrecht of 1713 and later re-elaborated by Rousseau and then Kant. Its chief goal was to replace the system of the balance of power, which had so far defined the relations between states in Europe, with a more pacific and stable legal order under a federation.[47] That idea had remained a matter of lighthearted conjecture in the eighteenth century, but later events in Europe had given credit to it, and for good reason: had the supposedly "regulating" device of the balance of power not miserably broken down in the face of the Revolution and Napoleon's Empire? In fact, and as early as September 1804, the Tsar had issued "Secret Instructions" (finalized by Adam Czartoryski) to his minister Nikolai Novossiltsev that required him to forge an alliance with Britain, and beyond, a European "federation" that would be founded on the law of nations. These

---

[42] See Marc Raeff, *Michael Speransky: Statesman of Imperial Russia, 1772–1839* (The Hague: Nijhoff, 1957).

[43] Capodistrias, a figurehead for philhellenism, later openly supported the revolt of the Greeks against the Ottoman Empire; he was elected president of Greece in 1827. Czartoryski associated with the Polish insurrection of 1830 against Russia.

[44] Alexander came into power in 1801, following the assassination of his father Paul I; his own death on December 1, 1825, coincided with the Decembrist revolt, which the new Tsar Nicholas I brutally suppressed. See Nicolai K. Schilder, *Imperator Aleksandr I: ego žizn' i carstvovanie* [The Emperor Alexander I: his life and his reign], 4 vols. (St. Petersburg: 1897–1898).

[45] Emmanuel de Waresquiel and Benoît Yvert, *Histoire de la Restauration*, 20–23, 42–48.

[46] Alexandre Arkhaguelski, *Alexandre Ier: le feu follet* (Paris: Fayard, 2000), 253–58; Marie-Pierre Rey, *Alexandre Ier* (Paris: Flammarion, 2009), 405–408; W. H. Zawadzki, *A Man of Honour: Adam Czartoryski as a Statersman of Russia and Poland, 1795–1831* (Oxford: Oxford University Press, 1993), 278–79.

[47] Stella Ghervas, "La paix par le droit, ciment de la civilisation en Europe?".

instructions referred explicitly to Saint-Pierre, even if they distanced themselves from his ideas.[48] As could be expected, the English cabinet declined to accept the proposal as it stood; the treaty eventually signed was a more conventional military alliance.

In the spring of 1815, uniting the European powers was no longer a dream out of the blue, but a pressing concern: Napoleon had unexpectedly returned to power. Just before leaving Vienna, Alexander I commissioned a "Projet d'instruction générale pour les missions de Sa Majesté Impériale,"[49] dated the 13/25 of May, aimed at tightening his links with his brothers in arms. In this memoir, his immediate concerns curiously merge with his grand designs of old. We find in particular a reference to the "grand European family," anxiety that he might have to face a new alliance directed against him, yet also a conviction imbued with mysticism, that he was "visibly protected by a superior force."[50] The step toward the Holy Alliance was all the more momentous because, under the influence of the Tsar, the three victorious powers of continental Europe were themselves about to take it.

Romantic Mysticism: From Philosophical Speculation to Political Weapon

On the other hand, how are we to account for the striking religious tone in the text of the Holy Alliance, even the ostentatious religiosity? In the first place, it was part of a *Zeitgeist* directly connected to the menace of doom that Napoleon's Empire had cast over the European continent. In Russia particularly, the French invasion of 1812 had created a wave of devotion around the Tsar, in which religious fervor visibly played a part. In Germany, a mystical movement also emerged in the years 1810–20. Among its chief representatives, two are particularly relevant: the Protestant thinker Jung-Stilling and the Catholic

---

[48] The text of the *Instructions secrètes* is reproduced in *Vnešnjaja Politika Rossii XIX i načala XX–go veka* [*The Foreign Policy of Russia in the nineteenth and early twentieth centuries*] (Moscow: Politizdat, 1961), Series I, t. II: 138–51. A few years later, Roxandra Sturdza, the sister of Alexander, would write in her memoirs that the Holy Alliance was "the realization of the grandiose concept of Henri IV and Charles Irénée Castel, the Abbé de Saint-Pierre" (Roxandre Edling-Stourdza, *Mémoires de la comtesse Edling, née Stourdza*, Moscow: Imprimerie du St-Synode, 1888, 242). See Constantin de Grunwald, *Trois siècles de diplomatie russe* (Paris: Calmann-Lévy, 1945), 146–59; Andrei Zorin, *Kormia dvuglavogo orla,* 305–15; Marie-Pierre Rey, *Alexandre Ier*, 131–70.

[49] "Project of General Instruction for the Missions of his Imperial Majesty."

[50] Nikolai K. Schilder, *Imperator Aleksandr I*, t. 3, 542–47; Stella Ghervas, *Réinventer la tradition*, 264–65.

philosopher Baader,[51] who were both personal acquaintances of the Tsar. That *mysticism* of romantic inspiration was a philosophical movement pursuing transcendence beyond perceptible reality, or where sentiment and intuition replaced rational knowledge of divinity. Essentially a personal endeavor, mysticism inevitably led to questioning the dogmas of the established Churches to a greater or lesser extent, and—worse still—to a rapprochement of the mystics across the boundaries of the faiths.[52] Religious convergence in pursuit of a higher truth was thus a recurrent theme, which elicited dire warnings from the major Christian Churches, alarmed to see their followers turning away from the traditionally established beliefs.

Much may be explained by the fact that Alexander I was residing in southern Germany (in Baden) as well as in Austria for a few months between 1814 and 1815. It was on that occasion that he met Jung-Stilling and Baader, as well as the baroness Krüdener. The baroness,[53] who had had a stormy youth and then converted to pietism in 1804 (becoming a prophetess of sorts in the process), was convinced that the Tsar had been conferred a messianic duty to liberate Europe from Napoleon, whom she considered an incarnation of the devil—a view that no doubt flattered the Tsar and comforted him in his aims. Historical testimonies—notably that of Stourdza—indicate, however, that the baroness played no political role, something for which she likely would not have been qualified anyway. In any case, she cannot be credited for having invented the design of a European alliance, since (as mentioned above) Alexander I had already been entertaining this notion for a decade. What is more, the sovereign quickly forgot his "muse," who went on to die in disgrace in the Crimea.

While the sincerity of the religious faith of Alexander I is not generally in question,[54] a caution is in order: there was also shrewd political calculation in the wording of the Holy Alliance. The concept of a "Christian nation" in Europe, an ecumenism embracing the Catholic, Protestant, and Orthodox faiths was, in fact, an insidious attack aimed at the Holy See. Somewhat

---

[51] An essay by Franz von Baader that did influence the Tsar is *Über das durch die französische Revolution herbeigeführte Bedürfnis einer neuen und innigern Verbindung der Religion mit Politik* [*On the necessity created by the French Revolution for a new and closer relation of religion and politics*] (Nuremberg: Friedrich Campe, 1815).

[52] Stella Ghervas, *Réinventer la tradition*, 233–96.

[53] On this historical character, see Francis Ley, *Madame de Krüdener, 1764–1824: Romantisme et Sainte-Alliance* (Paris: Honoré Champion, 1994).

[54] The Tsar ordered the Holy Alliance to be posted in St. Petersburg on Christmas day, and starting in March 1816 it was to be read in all churches of his Empire. See Werner Näf, *Zur Geschichte der Heiligen Allianz*, 34–37; Robert de Traz, *De l'Alliance des rois à la Ligue des peuples: Sainte-Alliance et SDN* (Paris: Grasset, 1936), 68.

surprisingly, it has not been noted that the Pope of Rome, a major political actor of European history for centuries, was now being banned from the continental chess game of the Congress of Vienna and would never recover his former status.

In fact, the statement in the treaty of the Holy Alliance that "the three sovereigns make up a single nation with the same Christian faith" amounted to a notice of liquidation of the thousand-year-old political system of Western Europe, which had been founded (at least ideologically) on the alliance between the Catholic Pope and the Holy Roman Emperor. By putting Catholicism, Protestantism, and Orthodoxy on equal footing, thus making the political organization of Christian Europe "non-confessional," the sovereigns of the three powers were plainly declaring that the Pope's claim to supremacy in Europe was null and void. From that angle, it takes the aspect of a backstage revolution. Napoleon had already damaged the prestige of the Sovereign Pontiff with his own sacrilegious coronation in 1804. Two years later, the abolition of the Holy Roman Empire[55] had sealed the bankruptcy of the temporal side of the fellowship between the Pope and the Holy Roman Emperor. In 1815, it was the turn of the spiritual side to be liquidated. As a result, the political role of the Sovereign Pontiff was reduced to that of a sovereign of an Italian state. This ideological backlash profoundly upset Pope Pius VII; therein lies the reason why the Holy See refused to sign the pact of the Holy Alliance.[56]

Why had the sovereigns of the great powers engaged in such a radically *anti-clerical* maneuver that deliberately ousted the Pope from European politics? Tsar Alexander I was an autocrat of the Eastern Christian rite who had just come to extend his influence over Western Europe. The caesaropapist organization of society, inherited from the Byzantine Empire and which inspired imperial Russia, considered the head of state (Caesar) as the representative of Christ on earth; the role of the Church was to organize the community of believers *within* the borders of the state. It appeared thus inconceivable that a foreign patriarch could ever be politically placed above others, a fact that would have put him beyond the authority of the ruler. From Alexander's point of view, a Patriarch of Rome who not only considered himself independent of the sovereigns, but historically claimed to be their suzerain, was a contestant on the European political scene that had to be remorselessly shoved out of the way.

---

[55] Caused by the abdication of the Emperor Francis II of Habsburg on August 6, 1806.

[56] Sophie Olszamowska-Skowronska, *La correspondance des papes et des empereurs de Russie (1814–1878)* (Rome: Pontificia Universita Gregoriana, 1970), 14–15 (Miscellanea Historiae Pontificiae, XXIX).

That rather unfriendly attitude toward the Catholic Church was shared, but for entirely different reasons, by the Protestant king of Prussia (a hereditary enemy of Roman supremacy) and the sovereign of Austria—the same who had liquidated the Holy Roman Empire and crowned himself emperor of Austria under the name of Francis I. The latter was also the nephew of the archduke Joseph II (1741–90), who had applied a policy known as *Josephism*, aimed precisely at subordinating the Church to the State and at restraining pontifical power. Hence, beyond the mysticism of the epoch, would it be appropriate to speak of a strand of *mystification* in the Holy Alliance, especially when considering the amendments from a character as down-to-earth as Metternich?[57] In any case, there was a shared interest on the part of the three Powers to put the final nail in the coffin of Papal political authority.

In firm opposition to the Holy Alliance, there arose, naturally enough, representatives of Roman Catholic thought, such as the Jesuits, as well as Louis de Bonald and Joseph de Maistre. In defiance of all odds, they kept advocating an alliance of sovereigns under the auspices of the Pope, as well as a return to the prerogatives of the aristocratic class.[58] It is those views that most impressed minds in France, especially the alliance of the Bourbon monarchy and the Church of Rome, despite the fact that both were now only secondary pieces on a rather complicated European chessboard. In addition, Maistre knew the Tsar well, since he had spent several years in Saint Petersburg;[59] if he mistrusted him, it was not for failing to know him. Maistre wrote about the Holy Alliance, even before its publication: "Let us note that the spirit behind it is not Catholic, nor Greek or Protestant; it is a peculiar spirit that I have been studying for thirty years, but to describe it here would be too long; it is enough to say that it is as good for the separated Churches as it is bad for Catholics. It is expected to melt and combine all metals; after which, the statue will be cast away."[60] Maistre was exposing what he had rightly perceived as a

---

[57] See Alan J. Reinerman, *Austria and the Papacy in the Age of Metternich,* Vol. I: *Between Conflict and Cooperation, 1809–1830* (Washington: Catholic University Press, 1979), 7–19.

[58] A witness to the clash between Catholic and Orthodox visions of the social and political role of the Church, was the polemic pamphlet, *Considérations sur la doctrine et l'esprit de l'Eglise orthodoxe* (Stuttgart: J. G. Cotta, 1816), written by Alexander Stourdza, to which Joseph de Maistre angrily responded with his famous *Du Pape* (see Stella Ghervas, *Réinventer la tradition*, 313–34). As a sidenote, it is Stourdza's book that introduced the term *orthodoxe* in French to refer to the Eastern Christian rite, and from there into all Western languages.

[59] He had been the ambassador of the king of Piedmont-Sardinia from 1803 to 1817.

[60] Letter from Joseph de Maistre to Count Vallaise, dated October 1815, in Joseph de Maistre, *Œuvres complètes* (Geneva: Slatkine Reprints, 1979), vol. 13: 163–64 (translation mine); see also Robert Triomphe, *Joseph de Maistre. Étude sur la vie et sur la doctrine d'un matérialiste mystique* (Geneva: Droz, 1968), 309–10.

cunning maneuver: by adopting the Christian religion as the guiding principle, but diluting it at the same time into a vague whole, the three sovereigns had meant to undermine the Pope's sphere of influence. By a process that our age would call "embrace, extend, and extinguish," they had deliberately opened the door to a European political sphere that would henceforth be free of ecclesiastical influence (though not of religion).

Finally, the wording "Christian family" offered yet another advantage in the geopolitical context of the time: it covered all states of Europe, but left out the Ottoman Empire, a Muslim state. Russia, which had concluded a war with Turkey only three years before,[61] had been entertaining definite ambitions over it since the epoch of Peter the Great. Thus the Holy Alliance potentially gave the Russian Empire a free hand on the rather complex Eastern Question—in other words, the competition among the great powers to partition the territory of the declining Ottoman Empire.[62]

THE IDYLL'S END

The "black legend" surrounding the Holy Alliance often leads us to forget that this treaty was generally well received in Europe and that *public opinion* (an emerging phenomenon at this time, even if limited to elites) made Tsar Alexander I into a kind of hero for European and even American pacifists.[63] His popularity also extended to France—a country that objectively owed him some gratitude, since he had decisively stepped in to prevent its being carved into pieces by the occupying powers.[64]

The treaty of the Holy Alliance accompanied the birth of the *Congress System*, which led the great powers to convene regularly in European cities, such as Vienna, Aix-la-Chapelle, or Verona, in order to discuss matters related

---

61 Eighth Russo-Turkish War (1806–1812), concluded by the Treaty of Bucharest.

62 On the ensuing debates around the Greek insurrection, see Stella Ghervas, "Le philhellénisme d'inspiration conservatrice en Europe et en Russie," in *Peuples, Etats et nations dans le Sud-Est de l'Europe* (Bucharest: Ed. Anima, 2004), 98–110; Stella Ghervas, "Philhellénisme et ambitions russes dans le contexte de la question d'Orient," in *Φιλελληνισμός. Το ενδιαφέρον για την Ελλάδα και τους Έλληνες από την Επανάσταση ως σήμερα* [Philhellenism: Sympathy for Greece and the Greeks, from the Revolution to Our Days], ed. Anna Mandilara, Georgios Nikolaou, Lambros Filitouris and Nikolais Anastassopoulos (Athens: Herodote, 2014), 739–66.

63 W. P. Cresson, *The Holy Alliance: The European Background of the Monroe Doctrine* (New York: Oxford University Press, 1922), 83–94; Jacques-Henri Pirenne, "Les tentatives russes en vue d'obtenir l'adhésion des Etats-Unis à la Sainte-Alliance d'après quelques documents connus, 1816–1820," *Revue belge de philologie et d'histoire* no. 34, fasc. 2 (1956): 433–41.

64 Stella Ghervas, *Réinventer la tradition*, 73–74.

to peacekeeping in Europe.[65] It is paradoxically in this context of frequent meetings that the idyll was cut short in just a few years. In 1819, under the influence of Metternich, Austria and Prussia issued the Carlsbad Decrees, which constrained freedom of the press, as well as that of the German universities, thus generating a wave of popular unrest.[66] That same year, the Tsar suspended the parliament of Poland and abolished freedom of the press there. At the congresses of Troppau (1820) and Laibach (1821), again under the influence of Metternich, the Great Powers agreed that they should exercise a right of intervention if the domestic situation of a given state threatened the peace of its neighbors. All this was happening in a period when public opinion in Europe aspired to greater liberty and to political representation, leading to the first national aspirations to self-rule. Violent revolts spread throughout Europe in the 1820s, particularly in Germany, in northern Italy occupied by Austria, in Spain, Poland, and even some territories of the Ottoman Empire (Serbia, Greece, and the Danubian Principalities). The armies of Austria, Prussia, Russia, and eventually France assisted each other in campaigns of brutal repression. Tsar Alexander I, who felt bitterly what he saw as the failure of his liberal policies, finally surrendered to the views of Metternich. Thus was the transition from moderate reformism to reaction completed.

In reality, the failure was less ideological than practical: the vision of the Tsar had encountered obstacles that it could not predict, much less overcome. These can be summarized in five paradoxes:

1. *The treaty of the Holy Alliance was at odds with the main political movements of the time.* By invoking God and universal Christianity as the core principle of legitimacy and the "glue" holding the European states together, it was clearly flying in the face of that strain of Enlightenment thinking (notably that of Kant) that advocated a strictly secular approach to politics, founded on a social pact among citizens and—at a higher level—among nations. According to liberal opinion, therefore, the Holy Alliance came to be perceived as a symbol of obscurantism. It is all the more ironic that this treaty did not find favor with the Catholic Church either, for the precise reason that it permanently excluded it from European politics. Rejected by liberals for being too conservative, detested by the Catholic ultra-royalists for being too progressive, the Holy Alliance was satisfactory to no one.

---

[65] On the "Congress System," see Mark Jarrett, *The Congress of Vienna*, 158–205.

[66] Stella Ghervas, *Réinventer la tradition*, 204–17.

2. *The idea of the "Christian family" was no sufficient counterweight for national aspirations.* The most pressing issue of the time was the popular demand for representation; yet the Holy Alliance, by invoking the divine legitimacy of monarchs, closed the door to any debate. Because of this "design flaw," the treaty was ideologically inadequate to counteract the development of centrifugal movements of national affirmation. After 1848, the idea of a "European family" contained in the Holy Alliance had to give way to the rising nation-states. It would not be until 1919 that the world would see the reemergence of a League of Nations, to which Alexander I had confusedly aspired. But this time it would be firmly grounded on the self-determination of the various peoples.
3. *In the field of foreign policy of the great powers, the dream of a fraternity of states also had to yield to the traditional policies of the balance of power.* Briefly united in order to liquidate the legacy of Napoleon, the European states quickly reverted to their natural inclinations, each leading a separate political life according to its own strategic and commercial interests. As early as 1821 and the Greek War of Independence against the Ottoman Empire, the powers of France, Austria, Britain, and Russia all found themselves increasingly in competition on the Eastern Question. The situation degenerated to such a point that three decades later, all the powers of Europe found themselves allied against Russia, which now posed a military threat to Constantinople; this led in 1853 to the Crimean War and the capture of Sevastopol (1855).
4. *The friendly ties among the European powers rested in large part on Russia, and more accurately on the shoulders of a rather unusual ruler with vast, if not always consistent, ambitions: Tsar Alexander I.* Not the least of the contradictions that he presented was that he had received an enlightened education in a rigidly traditional Orthodox environment. Furthermore, Russia almost stood as "another world" from Europe: it was autocratic, authoritarian, and socially backward, having not even yet come to abolishing serfdom (not to mention the considerable number of Russian soldiers of the Napoleonic Wars who were detained for life as virtual serfs in "military colonies").[67] At the end of Alexander's reign, and even more so after his death in 1825, Russia became a champion of the Reaction, in the face of a European continent that was increasingly

[67] See generally, Janet Hartley, *Russia, 1762–1825: Military Power, the State and the People* (Westport, CT: Praeger, 2008), 190–208; Michael Jennings, *Arakcheev: Grand Vizier of the Russian Empire, 1769–1834* (New York: Dial Press, 1969), 141–47, 183–98.

aspiring to liberalism. The new Tsar, Nicholas I, was quick to liquidate the progressive movements in Russia and abroad, earning himself the moniker, "the Policeman of Europe." The defeat in the Crimean War eventually put an end to the only truly pan-European intermezzo that Russia has ever known, thus relegating it to the eastern periphery of the continent.

5. *The final, and perhaps most profound, paradox of the Holy Alliance is that despite the fact that it strongly condemned the Napoleonic Empire, Russia and Austria were themselves continental empires with all the trappings of such political entities*; Prussia for its part was ruling over Eastern provinces that were little more than colonies. Fortunately (and quite realistically), none of the three entertained the dangerous ambition to rule *all* of Europe, as Napoleon had once done. But even though a *directorate of great powers* sounded better than a universal monarchy, a legitimate question remains: did it truly make a difference for the secondary powers excluded from regular negotiations or the nations that aspired to self-rule? Was this shared hegemony significantly better than one man's hegemony? Therein lies a fundamental contradiction in the terms of the Holy Alliance.

Could that help explain the critiques that were leveled at the Holy Alliance in the nineteenth century? Viscount Castlereagh, the English Foreign Minister (1812–22), offered a *bon mot* that made it into history when he said that the Holy Alliance was a "piece of sublime mysticism and nonsense."[68] No doubt he feigned not to discern that this European project was not only pursuing a long matured political purpose, it was also steeped in the ideals of the Enlightenment. While Castlereagh recommended that the Prince Regent sign the treaty after all, as a means to both satisfy and restrain the Tsar, such a unification of the European political order was clearly unwelcome to the English government: the doctrine of the balance of power required a modicum of *disunity* among the European states to function properly. Only the military Quadruple Alliance was in order, as a means to restore and consolidate the political balance against a possible reoccurrence of the French menace. Aside from that, active interference in the political affairs of the continent was simply not in the cards. This may clarify why the British cabinet felt that the Prince Regent of England could not sign the treaty.[69]

---

[68] Sir Charles Kingsley Webster, *The Foreign Policy of Lord Castlereagh, 1812–1815: Britain and the Reconstruction of Europe* (London: G. Bell and Sons, 1931), 481–83.

[69] Mark Jarrett, *The Congress of Vienna*, 176–80.

As for the public image, it is at the time of the Congress of Verona (1822) and the French intervention in Spain that the idea emerged in the public opinion of that later country that the Holy Alliance was only a coalition of "northern powers" seeking absolute monarchy and opposing any and all manifestations of liberalism. Elsewhere on the continent,[70] the name evoked the notion of a coalition of empires hostile to popular representation and to national claims, and prompt to intervene to suppress popular insurrections. It was again to be used in a negative sense in France after 1830, during the government of the July Monarchy, when the country found itself in opposition to the rest of the continent.[71] But it is only after the revolutions of 1848 that the "black legend" firmly took root. In France, new characters who revived the ideals of the French Revolution came to the fore. For them, the term "Holy Alliance," used derogatorily, lumped together a return to the *Ancien Régime*, anti-liberal spirit, and military repression. This explains why many sources from that period reflect such a dark image of the treaty.

While the eventual failure of the treaty is unquestionable, quite a few historians displayed a lack of objectivity in perpetuating a biased interpretation of its initial intentions.[72] At least in the mind of the Tsar, the Holy Alliance had been born progressive and moderate, as a legacy of the enlightened monarchies; most importantly, it sought peace as a response to the despotism and militarism of Napoleon. If it was fundamentally opposed to the French Revolution, it was not because it was rejecting the ideas of the Enlightenment (of which it was also a legitimate heir); it was because it sought to protect the foundations of monarchical regimes.

It remains, nevertheless, that the sovereigns were taken off guard by the magnitude and rapid growth of the liberal movements in Europe, and that they indeed fell back after a few years to a policy of censorship and reduction of liberties, followed by military suppression. It is thus necessary to draw a

---

[70] Attacks on the Holy Alliance began in the British press even earlier than the Congress of Verona: the *Morning Chronicle*, a paper associated with the Whigs, condemned the "Holy Alliance" as tyrannical in early 1821. See e.g., Mark Jarrett, *The Congress of Vienna*, 278–79.

[71] See, for example, Edgard Quinet, *La France de la Sainte-Alliance en Portugal* (Paris: Joubert, 1847). Talleyrand wrote to Louis-Philippe: "Ce serait voir d'une manière trop sombre ce qui vient de se passer que de l'attribuer à un retour vers la Sainte-Alliance [...], cette ligue formée contre la liberté des peuples" ["It would be seeing the latest events in too somber a manner to attribute them to a return to the Holy Alliance, that league formed against the liberty of the people." (translation mine)], in *Mémoires du prince de Talleyrand*, ed. Albert de Broglie (Paris: Calmann-Lévy, 1891), vol. 4: 369. See also *La Sainte-Alliance*, ed. Guillaume de Bertier de Sauvigny (Paris: Armand Colin, 1972), 322–23.

[72] Emile Bourgeois and Antonin Debidour, among others: see Guillaume de Bertier de Sauvigny, *La Sainte-Alliance*, 345–72.

clear line between the initial motives of the treaty of the Holy Alliance (as proposed by Alexander I), the general Congress System, and the political drift that eventually led to the Reaction. The initially benevolent ideology of the Holy Alliance failed to establish a durable peace within the borders of the states themselves because it neglected to take into account key aspirations of the people it embraced: On one hand, the principle of divine legitimacy ignored the demands for political representation from emerging social classes, particularly in France, Prussia, Spain, Portugal, Naples, and Sardinia. On the other hand, the principle of *status quo ante* of the political borders also denied the claims to recognition of a number of groups ignored by the Vienna settlement, notably the Poles, Norwegians, Belgians, Saxons, and Genoese (not to mention the Greeks in the Ottoman Empire). In the first case, this led to revolutions of the oppressed against the ruling class; in the second, to general insurrections against the foreign occupant, often led by the local aristocracy itself. All that was left to it was to *keep the peace*, with the force of arms. In that simple statement lies the essence of the Reaction.

All in all, the text of the Holy Alliance has gone down in history as a palimpsest, which leaves us with the task of separating its various layers of meaning. Beyond its mysticism, its Christian ecumenism was a double-edged sword: it was directed both against the political supremacy of the Papacy and against the Ottoman Empire. From the viewpoint of a historian, however, it contains a key feature that makes it truly innovative: almost all states of the continent endorsed a project for a peaceful political order in Europe, one that would no longer be based on the balance of powers or the military might of an emperor of exceptional stature (like Charles V or Napoleon), but rather on active and pacific cooperation—what came to be called the "Concert of Europe."[73]

THE LASTING LEGACY OF THE CONGRESS SYSTEM

One can thus perceive that the modern history of Europe has seen recurrent impulses to establish a durable system of peace in Europe—as a workable to alternative to *pax hegemonica*—after each major continental conflict. In

[73] According to Jacques-Alain de Sédouy, the term "Concert of Europe" did not appear until around 1830, and Metternich was the first to use it: Jacques-Alain de Sédouy, *Le concert européen: Aux origines de l'Europe, 1814–1914* (Paris: Fayard, 2009), 11. But reality preceded the appearance of the word, with the Congress of Vienna, the treaty of the Holy Alliance and the later Congresses. See also Carsten Holbraad, *The Concert of Europe: A Study in German and British International Theory, 1815–1914* (London: Longman, 1970); René Albrecht-Carrié, *The Concert of Europe* (New York: Walker, 1968); Matthias Schulz, *Normen und Praxis: Das Europäische Konzert der Grossmächte als Sicherheitstrat, 1815–1860* (Munich: Oldenbourg, 2009).

1713, after the War of Spanish Succession (when the France of Louis XIV had threatened to acquire the vast colonial empire of Spain),[74] the solution adopted had been the balance of power. That same year, Saint-Pierre had come forward with his *Plan for Perpetual Peace*, in which he sought to replace war with arbitration as an instrument of dispute resolution.

After the balance of power had been upset in the Napoleonic era, and all of Europe had nearly escaped domination by the French Empire—at the cost of considerable destruction and loss of life—it certainly makes sense that the great powers would briefly try to replace their self-reliant and egotistical policies with a concerted peacemaking effort. One aim was to close the door on a possible return of universal monarchy; a second was to maintain that hard-won peace. That policy was all the more rational on the part of Alexander I, in that he had carefully considered it during the years of the war, in spite of any feelings of resentment. This time, the system would be *directorial*; i.e., dominated by a select club of great powers actively engaging in mutual cooperation with each other, even on military matters.[75] It is the same principle of territorial integrity and ban on war that would later be explicated and generalized in 1919 in the Covenant of the League of Nations.[76] But in the latter case, the principle of self-determination of the people would seek to outlaw *regional* empires in Europe.

Both epochs were, however, profoundly different, each conceiving its own solutions from the *horizon of experience*[77] available to it. Nor are these various attempts direct descendants of each other; they are rather examples of

---

[74] See *La pérdida de Europa. La Guerra de Sucesión por la Monarquía de España*, ed. Antonio Álvarez-Ossorio, Bernardo J. García, and Virginia León (Madrid: Fundacion Carlos de Amberes, 2007); Lucien Bély, *L'art de la paix en Europe: Naissance de la diplomatie moderne, XVIe–XVIIIe siècle* (Paris: PUF, 2007).

[75] See Bruno Arcidiacono, *Cinq types de paix. Une histoire des plans de pacification perpétuelle (XVIIe–XXe siècles)* (Paris: PUF, 2011), 168–78; Paul W. Schroeder, "Did the Vienna System Rest on a Balance of Power?" in Paul Schroeder, *Systems, Stability, and Statecraft: Essays on the International History of Modern Europe* (New York: Palgrave Macmillan, 2004), 37–57; Stella Ghervas, "Peace Perpetually Reconsidered," *Books & Ideas*, November 12, 2012, http://www.booksandideas.net/Peace-perpetually-reconsidered.html.

[76] For a recent work, see Mark Mazower, *Governing the World: The History of an Idea* (New York: The Penguin Press, 2012).

[77] Jürgen Habermas elaborates on the approach by horizon of experience, in "Kants Idee des Ewigen Friedens: aus dem historischen Abstand von 200 Jahren," *Kritische Justiz* 28, no. 3 (1995): 293–319; for the English translation, see: "Kant's Idea of Perpetual Peace: With the Benefit of 200 Years Hindsight," in *Perpetual Peace: Essays on Kant's Cosmopolitanism*, ed. James Bohman and Matthias Lutz-Bachmann (Cambridge, MA: MIT Press, 1997), 113–54. For an application to the period of the Congress System, see Mark Jarrett, *The Congress of Vienna*, 353–79.

convergent evolution.[78] The Holy Alliance necessarily took the form of a mere letter of intent. It was nevertheless a complete break with the European order of both the *Ancien Régime* and the Empire of Napoleon, since it elevated pacific multilateralism to the rank of a written principle. Admittedly, the principle of a "veritable and indissoluble brotherhood" within a "common nation" was rather convoluted. All the same, it outlawed any state that would aspire to conquer another in Europe. It can therefore be considered a decisive step forward in the foundation of international relations as we know them today.

Yet, the paradigm of empire (and thus the *pax hegemonica*) still had great prospects in Europe: not only did the Austrian and Russian empires survive and even prosper for decades, but Germany as well was united in 1871 under a German, national *Reich*. After World War I, Europe had a brief respite when the empire of the tsars succumbed to the October Revolution, and Wilson's principle of self-determination in the Treaty of Versailles led to the downfall of the Austrian, Russian, and Ottoman Empires. Nonetheless, the Soviet Union was born within a few years and the Third German Reich was proclaimed in 1933, an entity with Pan-German ambitions at first, which would soon become continental. It would take a Second World War to crush the latter, leaving the continent a field of ruins. It is barely more than two decades ago, in 1991, that the Soviet Empire collapsed under its own weight.

From these attempts at a multilateral European order in modern history—and in particular from the experiment of the Congress System—we can infer that the idea of pan-continental empire (at least in the sense it had in the nineteenth and twentieth centuries) has been profoundly antipathetic to the political ethos of Europe. The Congress System and the League of Nations might seem today no more than pious resolutions, in view of the two World Wars, the Cold War, and our current period of power readjustment.[79] Yet, the moral and legal condemnation of arbitrary recourse to war remains today a prerequisite to any effort at pacification.

Today, the European integration process started in the 1950s is taking the place of an interrupted line of continental empires, in a geographical area that has never known anything of that size other than an empire. Hence, a last question remains: could political leadership in Europe ever be distinguished from uncivil bullying by a hegemon, or the exclusive rule by a club of great powers? In 1946, Winston Churchill proposed a "sovereign remedy" to the

---

[78] For a comparison between the two epochs, see Robert de Traz, *De l'Alliance des rois à la Ligue des peuples.*

[79] See James Sheehan, *Where Have All the Soldiers Gone: The Transformation of Modern Europe* (Boston: Houghton Mifflin, 2008), 161–62, 172–227.

plight of wars and destructions, that would be "to re-create the European Family, or as much of it as we can, and to provide it with a structure under which it can dwell in peace, in safety and in freedom."[80] Those words eerily echo those of the Holy Alliance. Later, the preamble of the Treaty of the European Union recalled "the historic importance of the ending of the division of the European continent and the need to create firm bases for the construction of the future Europe." By this, they asserted their commitment to end wars between nation-states. But as if to repel the specter of a pan-European empire, the signatories confirmed immediately thereafter "their attachment to the principles of liberty, democracy, and respect for human rights and fundamental freedoms and of the rule of law."[81]

It is observable that the European Union has sought so far to find a politically acceptable middle path between the balance of powers and the authoritarian rule of an empire, with a view to maintaining peace and economic prosperity. Hence it is not very likely that the EU is to become an empire *stricto sensu* in the near future. But whether or nor it will truly succeed in its original intent of equal representation of interests remains open to debate, especially now that "concentric circles" are being formed for the handling of European affairs in response to the economic crisis. In particular, the Eurozone is a precedent of a "Union within the Union," directed by an informal "Eurogroup" that smacks of a conference of Great Powers.[82] Accordingly, the movements of *indignados* in Greece, Spain, and Portugal, as well as the Europolls, suggest that the feelings of popular representation ("demos legitimacy") are faltering in some countries: this is the so-called "democratic deficit."

Though they certainly do not have the revolutionary character of the revolts of the 1820s, the recent popular movements raise a similar question: could the EU ever become a directorial system ruled by a select club of powers, thereby repeating—again out of the best intentions—the same ruinous error committed by the Congress System of Vienna? Might the key to political peace, both *among* the European states and *within* their borders, lie in taking popular aspirations into account?

---

[80] Winston Churchill, "Speech at Zurich" (September 19, 1946), in *Blood, Toil, Tears and Sweat: The Speeches of Winston Churchill*, ed. David Cannadine (Boston: Houghton Mifflin Company, 1989), 309–14.

[81] "Consolidated version of the Treaty on European Union" (Lisbon Treaty, 2007), Preamble.

[82] Roger Liddle, Olaf Cramme, and Renaud Thillaye, "Where Next for Eurozone Governance? The Quest for Reconciling Economic Logic and Political Dilemmas," *Policy Network Paper* (July 2012): 1–20.

BIBLIOGRAPHY

Akaltin, Ferdi. *Die Befreiungskriege im Geschichtsbild der Deutschen im 19. Jahrhundert*. Frankfurt: Verlag Neue Wissenschaft, 1997.

Albrecht-Carrié, René. *The Concert of Europe*. New York: Walker, 1968.

Álvarez-Ossorio, Antonio, Bernardo J. García, and Virginia León, ed. *La pérdida de Europa: La Guerra de Sucesión por la Monarquía de España*. Madrid: Fundacion Carlos de Amberes, 2007.

Anderson, James. "Singular Europe: An Empire Once Again?" In *Geopolitics of European Union Enlargement: The Fortress Empire*, ed. Warwick Armstrong and James Anderson, 9–29. London: Routledge, 2007.

Antoine, François, Jean-Pierre Jessenne, Anne Jourdan, and Hervé Leuwers. *L'Empire napoléonien: Une expérience européenne?* Paris: Armand Colin, 2014.

Antonescu, Mădălina V. *Uniunea Europeană, Imperiile antice şi Imperiile medievale: Studiu comparativ* [The EU, Ancient, and Medieval Empires: A Comparative Study]. Bucharest: Cartea Universitară, 2008.

Aprile, Sylvie. *La révolution inachevée, 1815–1870*. Paris: Berlin, 2010.

Arcidiacono, Bruno. *Cinq types de paix: Une histoire des plans de pacification perpétuelle (XVIIe–XXe siècles)*. Paris: PUF, 2011.

Arkhaguelski, Alexandre. *Alexandre Ier: le feu follet*. Paris: Fayard, 2000.

Arendt, Hannah. *The Origins of Totalitarianism*. San Diego: Harcourt, 1973.

Armitage, David. "Introduction." In *Theories of Empire, 1450–1800*, ed. David Armitage, xv–xxxiii. Aldershot, UK: Ashgate, 1998.

Baader, Franz von. *Ueber das durch die französische Revolution herbeigeführte Bedürfnis einer neuen und innigern Verbindung der Religion mit Politik*. Nuremberg: Friedrich Campe, 1815.

Barroso, José Manuel. "European Union is 'Empire,'" 2007. Accessed July 3, 2014. http://www.youtube.com/watch?v=c2Ralocq9uE.

Bell, David A. *The First Total War: Napoleon's Europe and the Birth of Warfare as We Know It*. Boston: Houghton Mifflin Company, 2007.

Bély, Lucien. *L'art de la paix en Europe: Naissance de la diplomatie moderne, XVIe–XVIIIe siècle*. Paris: PUF, 2007.

Bertier de Sauvigny, Guillaume de, ed. *La Sainte-Alliance*. Paris: Armand Colin, 1972.

Bukovsky, Vladimir. "The European Union: The New Soviet Union?" Accessed July 3, 2014. http://www.youtube.com/watch?v=js40QG3UEE8.

Bourquin, Maurice. *Histoire de la Sainte-Alliance*. Geneva: Georg, 1954.

Broers, Michael. *Europe under Napoleon, 1799–1815*. New York: Edward Arnold, 1996.

Browning, Christopher S. "Westphalian, Imperial, Neomedieval: The Geopolitics of Europe and the Role of the North." In *Remaking Europe in the Margins: Northern Europe after the Enlargements*, ed. Christopher S. Browning, 85–101. Aldershot, UK: Ashgate, 2005.

Churchill, Winston. "Speech at Zurich. September 19, 1946. In *Blood, Toil, Tears and Sweat: The Speeches of Winston Churchill*, ed. David Cannadine, 309–14. Boston: Houghton Mifflin Company, 1989.

Consolidated Version of the Treaty on European Union (Preamble). Lisbon Treaty, 2007.

Cooper, Frederick, and Jane Burbank. *Empires in World History: Power and the Politics of Difference*. Princeton: Princeton University Press, 2010.

Cresson, W. P. *The Holy Alliance: The European Background of the Monroe Doctrine*. New York: Oxford University Press, 1922.

Deproost, Paul-Augustin. "*Hic non finit Roma*: Les paradoxes de la frontière romaine, un modèle pour l'Europe?" In *Imaginaires européens: Les frontiers pour ouvrir l'Europe*, ed. Paul-Augustin Deproost and Bernard Coulie, 29–50. Paris: L'Harmattan, 2004.

Edling-Stourdza, Roxandre. *Mémoires de la comtesse Edling, née Stourdza*. Moscow: Imprimerie du St-Synode, 1888.

Esdaile, Charles. *Napoleon's Wars: An International History, 1803–1815*. London: Penguin, 2007.

Fesser, Gerd. *1813. Die Völkerschlacht bei Leipzig*. Jena/Quedlinburg: Verlag Bussert & Stadeler, 2013.

Ghervas, Stella. "Balance of Power vs. Perpetual Peace: Paradigms of European Order from Utrecht to Vienna, 1713–1815." In *The Art of Peacemaking*, ed. A. H. A. Soons. Leiden: Martinus Nijhoff Publishers/Brill, 2014.

———. "From Empires to the Anti-Empire: National Imaginaries toward Political Europe." *Journal of Contemporary European Studies*, 2015.

———. "Odessa et les confins de l'Europe: un éclairage historique." In *Lieux d'Europe: Mythes et limites*, ed. Stella Ghervas and François Rosset, 107–24. Paris: Editions de la MSH, 2008.

_____. "La paix par le droit, ciment de la civilisation en Europe? La perspective du Siècle des Lumières." In *Penser l'Europe au XVIIIe siècle: Commerce, Civilisation, Empire*, ed. Antoine Lilti and Céline Spector, 47–70. Oxford: Voltaire Foundation, 2014.

———. "Peace Perpetually Reconsidered." *Books & Ideas*. November 12, 2012. http://www.booksandideas.net/Peace-perpetually-reconsidered.html.

_____. "Le philhellénisme d'inspiration conservatrice en Europe et en Russie." In *Peuples, Etats et nations dans le Sud-Est de l'Europe,* 98–110. Bucharest: Ed. Anima, 2004.

———. "Philhellénisme et ambitions russes dans le contexte de la question d'Orient." In *Φιλελληνισμός: Το ενδιαφέρον για την Ελλάδα και τους Έλληνες από την Επανάσταση ως σήμερα* [Philhellenism: Sympathy for Greece and the Greeks, from the Revolution to Our Days], ed. Anna Mandilara, Georgios Nikolaou, Lambros Filitouris, and Nikolais Anastassopoulos, 739–66. Athens: Herodote, 2014.

———. "La réception de *L'Esprit des lois* en Russie: histoire de quelques ambiguïtés." In *Le Temps de Montesquieu*, ed. Michel Porret and Catherine Volpilhac-Auger, 391–404. Geneva: Droz, 2002.

_____. *Réinventer la tradition: Alexandre Stourdza et l'Europe de la Sainte-Alliance*. Paris: Honoré Champion, 2008.

Grunwald, Constantin de. *Trois siècles de diplomatie russe*. Paris: Calmann-Lévy, 1945.

Habermas, Jürgen. "Kants Idee des Ewigen Friedens: aus dem historischen Abstand von 200 Jahren." *Kritische Justiz* 28, no. 3 (1995): 293–319.

_____. "Kant's Idea of Perpetual Peace: With the Benefit of 200 Years Hindsight." In *Perpetual Peace: Essays on Kant's Cosmopolitanism*, ed. James Bohman and Matthias Lutz-Bachmann, 113–54. Cambridge, MA: MIT Press, 1997.

Hantraye, Jacques. *Les Cosaques aux Champs-Elysées: les occupations étrangères en France après la chute de Napoléon*. Paris: Belin, 2005.

Hartley, Janet. *Russia, 1762–1825: Military Power, the State and the People*. Westport, CT: Praeger, 2008.

Holbraad, Carsten. *The Concert of Europe: A Study in German and British International Theory, 1815–1914*. London: Longman, 1970.

Alexander I, Tsar: Instructions secrètes; In Vnešnjaja Politika Rossii XIX i načala XX–go veka [*The Foreign Policy of Russia in the Nineteenth and Early Twentieth Centuries*], vol. 2. Moscow: Politizdat, 1961.

Israel, Jonathan. *A Revolution of the Mind: Radical Enlightenment and the Intellectual Origins of Modern Democracy*. Princeton: Princeton University Press, 2010.

Jarrett, Mark. *The Congress of Vienna and Its Legacy: War and Great Power Diplomacy After Napoleon*. London: I. B. Tauris, 2013.

Jennings, Michael. *Arakcheev: Grand Vizier of the Russian Empire, 1769–1834*. New York: Dial Press, 1969.

Jourdan, Annie. *L'Empire de Napoléon*. Paris: Flammarion, 2000.

Laven, David, and Lucy Riall. *Napoleon's Legacy: Problems of Government in Restoration Europe*. Oxford: Berg, 2000.

Leggiere, Michael V. *The Fall of Napoleon*, vol. 1, *The Allied Invasion of France, 1813–1814*. Cambridge: Cambridge University Press, 2007.

Lentz, Thierry. *Nouvelle Histoire de l'Empire*. Paris: Fayard, 2002–2004.

Ley, Francis. *Alexandre Ier et sa Sainte-Alliance.* Paris: Fischbacher, 1975.

_____. *Madame de Krüdener, 1764–1824: Romantisme et Sainte-Alliance.* Paris: Honoré Champion, 1994.

Liddle, Roger, Olaf Cramme, and Renaud Thillaye. "Where Next for Eurozone Governance? The Quest for Reconciling Economic Logic and Political Dilemmas." *Policy Network Paper* (July 2012): 1–20.

Lieven, Dominic. *Russia against Napoleon: The Battle for Europe, 1807 to 1814.* London: Penguin Books, 2009.

Maistre, Joseph de. *Du Pape*. Lyons: Rusand, 1819.

_____. *Joseph de Maistre to Count Vallaise, October 1815*. Letter. In Joseph de Maistre, *Œuvres completes*, vol. 13. Geneva: Slatkine Reprints, 1979.

Mazower, Mark. *Governing the World: The History of an Idea*. New York: Penguin Press, 2012.

Morrissey, Robert. *Napoléon et l'héritage de la gloire*. Paris: PUF, 2010.

Motyl, Alexander J. "Is Everything Empire? Is Empire Everything?" *Comparative Politics* 38, no. 2 (2006): 229–49.

Näf, Werner. *Zur Geschichte der Heiligen Allianz.* Bern: Paul Haupt, 1928.

Nadler, Vasily K. *Imperator Aleksandr I i ideja Svjaschennogo Sojuza* [Emperor Alexander I and the Idea of the Holy Alliance], 5 vols. Riga: N. Kimmel, 1886–1892.

Olszamowska-Skowronska, Sophie. *La correspondance des papes et des empereurs de Russie (1814–1878).* Rome: Pontificia Universita Gregoriana, 1970.

Orlik, Olga V. *Rossija v mezhdunarodnyh otnoshenijah, 1815–1829: Ot Venskogo kongressa do Adrianopolskogo mira* [Russia in International Relations, 1815–1829: From the Congress of Vienna to the Peace of Andrinople]. Moscow: Nauka, 1998.

Pirenne, Jacques-Henri. *La Sainte-Alliance. Organisation européenne de la paix internationale,* 2 vols. Neuchâtel: Ed. de la Baconnière, 1946–1949.

_____. "Les tentatives russes en vue d'obtenir l'adhésion des Etats-Unis à la Sainte-Alliance d'après quelques documents connus, 1816–1820." *Revue belge de philologie et d'histoire* 34, fasc. 2 (1956): 433–41.

Quinet, Edgard. *La France de la Sainte-Alliance en Portugal.* Paris: Joubert, 1847.

Raeff, Marc. *Michael Speransky: Statesman of Imperial Russia, 1772–1839.* The Hague: Nijhoff, 1957.

Reinerman, Alan J. *Austria and the Papacy in the Age of Metternich*, vol. 1, *Between Conflict and Cooperation, 1809–1830.* Washington: Catholic University Press, 1979.

Rey, Marie-Pierre. *Alexandre Ier*. Paris: Flammarion, 2009.

Rifkin, Jeremy. *The European Dream: How Europe's Vision of the Future is Quietly Eclipsing the American Dream*. Cambridge: Polity, 2004.

Rothenberg, Gunther E. *The Art of Warfare in the Age of Napoleon*. Bloomington: Indiana University Press, 1978.

———. *Die Napoleonischen Kriege*. Berlin: Brandenburger Verlagshaus, 2000.

Schenk, H. G. *Aftermath of Napoleonic Wars—An Experiment.* Oxford: Oxford University Press, 1947.

Schilder, Nicolai K. *Imperator Aleksandr I: ego žizn' i carstvovanie* [The Emperor Alexander I: His Life and His Reign], 4 vols. St. Petersburg: 1897–1898.

Schmalz, Hans W. *Versuche einer gesamteuropäischen Organisation 1815–1820.* Aarau: Sauerländer, 1940.

Schroeder, Paul W. "Did the Vienna System Rest on a Balance of Power?" In Paul Schroeder, *Systems, Stability, and Statecraft: Essays on the International History of Modern Europe*, 37–57. New York: Palgrave Macmillan, 2004.

———. *The Transformation of European Politics, 1763–1848*. Oxford: Oxford University Press, 1994.

Schulz, Matthias. *Normen und Praxis: Das Europäische Konzert der Grossmächte als Sicherheitstrat, 1815–1860*. Munich: Oldenbourg, 2009.

Sédouy, Jacques-Alain de. *Le concert européen: Aux origines de l'Europe, 1814–1914*. Paris: Fayard, 2009.

Sellin, Volker. *Die geraubte Revolution: Der Sturz Napoleons und die Restauration in Europa*. Gottingen: Vandenhoeck und Ruprecht Verlag, 2001.

Sheehan, Michael. *The Balance of Power: History and Theory*. New York: Routledge, 1996.

Sked, Alan. *Metternich and Austria: An Evaluation*. Houndsmill, UK: Palgrave Macmillian, 2008.

———. *Radetzky: Imperial Victor and Military Genius*. London: I. B. Tauris, 2011.

Smith, Digby. *1813—Leipzig: Napoleon and the Battle of the Nations*. London: Greenhill Books, 2001.

Stourdza, Alexandre. "Considérations sur l'acte d'alliance fraternelle et chrétienne du 14/26 septembre 1815." RO IRLI, 288/1, no. 21.

_____. *Considérations sur la doctrine et l'esprit de l'Eglise orthodoxe*. Stuttgart: J. G. Cotta, 1816.

Talleyrand, Charles Maurice de. *Mémoires du prince de Talleyrand*, ed. Albert de Broglie, vol. 4. Paris: Calmann-Lévy, 1891.

Todorova, Maria N. *Imagining the Balkans*. New York: Oxford University Press, 1997.

Tommila, Päiviö. *La Finlande dans la politique européeene en 1809–1815*. Helsinki: Finnish Historical Society, 1962.

Traz, Robert de. *De l'Alliance des rois à la Ligue des peuples: Sainte-Alliance et SDN*. Paris: Grasset, 1936.

Triomphe, Robert. *Joseph de Maistre: Étude sur la vie et sur la doctrine d'un matérialiste mystique*. Geneva: Droz, 1968.

Tulard, Jean. *Napoléon, chef de guerre*. Paris: Tallandier, 2012.

Waever, Ole. "Imperial Metaphors: Emerging European Analogies to Pre-Nation-State Imperial Systems." In *Geopolitics in Post-Wall Europe: Security, Territory and Identity*, ed. Ola Tunander, Pavel Baev, and Victoria Ingrid Einagel, 59–93. London: Sage Publications; Oslo: International Peace Research Institute, 1997.

Waresquiel, Emmanuel de. *Le duc de Richelieu, 1766–1822*. Paris: Perrin, 1990.

———. *L'histoire à rebrousse-poil: les élites, la Restauration, la Révolution*. Paris: Fayard, 2005.

Waresquiel, Emmanuel de, and Benoit Yvert. *Histoire de la Restauration, 1814–1830: Naissance de la France moderne*. Paris: Perrin, 1996.

Webster, Sir Charles Kingsley. *The Foreign Policy of Lord Castlereagh, 1812–1815: Britain and the Reconstruction of Europe*. London: G. Bell and Sons, 1931.

Zamoyski, Adam. *Moscow 1812: Napoleon's Fatal March*. New York: Harper Collins, 2004.

———. *Rites of Peace: The Fall of Napoleon and the Congress of Vienna*. New York: Harper Collins, 2007.

Zawadzki, W. H. *A Man of Honour: Adam Czartoryski as a Statesman of Russia and Poland, 1795–1831*. Oxford: Oxford University Press, 1993.

Zielonka, Jan. *Europe as Empire: The Nature of the Enlarged European Union*. New York: Oxford University Press, 2006.

Zorin, Andrei. *Kormia dvuglavogo orla: Literatura i gosudarstvennaia ideologiia v Rossii v poslednei treti XVIII–pervoi treti XIX veka* [Feeding the Two-headed Eagle: Literature and State Ideology in Russia from the Last Third of the Eighteenth Century to the First Third of the Nineteenth Century]. Moscow: Novoe literaturnoe obozrenie, 2001.

L'EUROPE N'EXISTE PAS? ABOUT THE CONSTRUCTION OF A EUROPEAN MUSICAL SPACE

Gregor Kokorz

Abstract

This essay explores cultural and, more specifically, musical constructions of identity and space, analyzing the dynamics in which art functions as a medium for identity construction and, more precisely, how art is utilized for the construction of "Europaness." What makes Europe? Who makes Europe? What kind of Europe, and when and where is Europe constructed? Adopting the notion of space as culturally constructed, the essay investigates how music contributes to the construction of Europe as a cultural space, not by defining or analyzing a given musical space, but by focusing on processes of transformation in the conception of space and by exploring the role of music in such processes. The present investigation is conducted by means of two case studies, each focusing on one popular song that bears aspects of national and transnational construction of space and identity. The first study focuses on the history and significance of the Ave Maria of Lourdes, *a nineteenth-century French pilgrim song related to the famous Marian sanctuary. The second study analyzes* La Montanara, *an Italian mountain song from the 1920s, and its national and transnational reception.*

"*Musik baut Europa*"—Music builds Europe. In 2012 one could read this sentence written in big letters on the trams running through the city of Karlsruhe. It advertised the 21st edition of the *European Cultural Days*, a festival taking place every other year since 1983 and contributing to

Karlsruhe's identity as a city in the center of Europe, situated at the river Rhine only a few kilometers from the French–German border. Referring to the words of the former president of the European Commission, Jacques Delors, "one cannot fall in love with Europe's internal market," Michael Heck, Karlsruhe's former councilor for cultural affairs and the main initiator of the festival, described the motivation for taking this initiative as follows: "In our days we are stating the question: what constitutes the bond that unites Europe spiritually? Does this kind of bond exist, and if so, do we have consciousness about its existence? And how can we foster the further development of such a bond?"[1]

Looking at today's European map and listening to the European soundscape one can easily identify a large number of other music-related initiatives with similar intentions, which cover a wide range of different musical genres. The *Eurosonic Festival* has taken place since 1996 in the Dutch town of Groningen and every year brings together up to 300 pop bands from all over Europe.[2] The *European Border Breakers Award (EBBA)* is a prize launched by the European Commission to stimulate the cross-border circulation of new popular music, awarded every year on the occasion of the Groningen festival to ten European bands for their first international music album.[3] The *Klangkondensat Europe* is an experimental music project based on dozens of sound fragments of the European soundscape condensed into a one-hour radio transmission, thus literally composing the European soundscape.[4] Let's not forget, moreover, the *European Youth Orchestra,* founded already in 1978, and its more renowned spin-off, the *Chamber Orchestra of Europe*, existing since 1981, both co-financed by the European Commission.[5] European politicians have not only given financial support to musical initiatives, such as those mentioned above, but they have also created Europe's own musical symbol: since 1971, when the Parliamentary Assembly of the Council of Europe

---

[1] "Wir stellen in der heutigen Zeit die Frage, was ist das Band, das Europa als geistiges Band verbindet? Gibt es dieses Band überhaupt und wenn es dieses Band gibt, ist es uns bewusst? Wie kann es weiter entwickelt werden?" Interview with Michael Heck, KA-News.de, April 12, 2004, accessed June 5, 2013, http://www.ka-news.de/nachrichten/karlsruhe/Karlsruhe-Heck-Sprache-ist-ein-Kulturgut;art86,19948.

[2] Accessed June 5, 2013, http://festival.eurosonic-noorderslag.nl/en/about-us/about/history/.

[3] Accessed June 5, 2013, http://ec.europa.eu/culture/our-programmes-and-actions/prizes/european-border-breakers-awards_en.htm.

[4] Accessed June 5, 2013, http://alien.mur.at/vaportrails/index.html?page=projekt&lang=en.

[5] See Erna Metdepennighen, "Musikförderung der europäischen Gemeinschaft," in *Musik und Kulturbetrieb: Handbuch der Musik im 20. Jahrhundert*, vol. 10, edited by Sabine Arndt (Laaber: Laaber Verlag, 2006), 333–335, and *Music and the European Union: European Union Youth Orchestra, European Border Breakers Award, European Union Baroque Orchestra* (General Books LLC, 2010).

decided on a musical anthem, the European Union has been represented not only by yellow stars on blue ground, but also by Beethoven's *Ode to Joy*.[6]

All of this shows a rich and manifold kaleidoscope of European music, which also represents a plurality of ways in which music is connected to political and cultural processes, referring to some kind of "Europeannes" through simple involvement and instrumentalization, or as a reaction. Such plurality mirrors the ongoing intentional processes of transnational identity construction in the building and financing of music institutions, organizations, and networks; in the raising of transnational awareness; by the granting of specific awards; and by the creation and utilization of music as a symbolic representation in the form of an anthem. In this sense, a title such as "*Musik baut Europa*" stands indeed for a process of identity transformation directed towards the future. It also seems to be informed—or at least paralleled—by a critical understanding of space, as it has been shaped by the ongoing debate and problematization of the category itself of space in cultural studies.[7] Europe is not addressed as something given, but as an entity under construction, and at the same time music is addressed as an essential agent for the construction of such European space.

Homogenization versus Diversity

The effects of the increased transnationalization of music were the subject of a recent volume on *Postnational Musical Identities*.[7] With a specific focus on the Americas, the authors Corona and Madrid have given support to the idea that processes of transnationalization and new transnational identity constructions generate a new epistemology for music. That is, in a globalized world, both music repertoires and mechanisms of music distribution and consumption undermine the formerly discursive homogenization of the nation-state. In particular, urban areas metamorphose into post-national lands, which, with their visible and audible heterogeneity, undermine the importance of national and territorialized cultures.

However, recent European developments show evidence that such processes of transnational identity construction do not necessarily have to follow a new and different epistemology compared to that of former national identity constructions. The decision to have a European anthem and the adoption of

---

[6] Resolution 492/1971; for further details refer to Albrecht Riethmüller, "Die Hymne der Europäischen Union," in *Europäische Erinnerungsorte*, vol. 2, edited by P. den Boer, H. Duchhardt, G. Kreis, and W. Schmale (Munich: Oldenbourg Verlag, 2012), 89–96.

[7] Ignacio Corona and Alejandro L. Madrid, eds., *Postnational Musical Identities: Cultural Production, Distribution, and Consumption in a Globalized Scenario* (Lanham, MD: Lexington Books, 2008).

Beethoven's *Ode to Joy* for such a purpose indeed show parallels and even direct references to nineteenth-century processes of nation-building. Other aspects, such as the role of orchestras, can be analyzed under such premises as well.[8] Even though European cultural politics frequently stresses the role of culture for Europe's diversity,[9] in the afore mentioned examples the institutions and modes of representation aim mainly at homogenization, in the sense of representing unifying audible symbols as a common locus for European identification.[10] This view receives further confirmation from widespread ideas on the oneness of European culture, such as that mentioned by the Italian author, theater playwright, and Nobel prize winner Dario Fo, who is prominently quoted in the European document on the importance of culture for the European Union: "Even before Europe was united at the economic level or was conceived at the level of economic interests and trade, it was culture that united all the countries of Europe. The arts, literature, music are the connecting link of Europe."[11]

Past versus Future

Differently than in "*Musik baut Europa,*" in Dario Fo's vision, European culture is not to be built in the future, but is something already existing as a cultural heritage that Europeans have in common. As much as European identity

---

[8] With regard to the Berlin and Viennese philharmonic orchestras, such role for political and national discourses has been recently analyzed by Fritz Trümpi, *Politisierte Orchester: Die Wiener Philharmoniker und das Berliner Philharmonische Orchester im Nationalsozialismus* (Vienna, Köln, Weimar: Böhlau Verlag, 2011).

[9] Most prominently in Article 167 (formerly 151) of the European Treaty: "The Community shall take cultural aspects into account in its action under other provisions of this Treaty, in particular in order to respect and to promote the diversity of its cultures." *Official Journal of the European Union*, October 26, 2012, C326/123, http://eurlex.europa.eu/LexUriServ/LexUriServ.do?uri=OJ:C:2012:326:0047:0200:EN:PDF, accessed June 25, 2013.

[10] This is certainly true for the initiative of the European Anthem and institutions such as the European orchestras. Even though the latter recruit their members from different European countries and thus internally create a diverse multitude, as a whole and in their mode of representation, e.g., as European ambassadors, they function as a unity. The Border Braker Award aims at an increasing transnationalization, with a strong emphasis on facilitating access to different national markets, and could thus be interpreted in the sense of emphasizing the post-national situation described by Corona and Madrid. For a critical discussion of the use of culture in general in the context of European political discourses, see: Heidemarie Uhl, "Zwischen Pathosformal und Baustelle: Kultur und europäische Identität," in *Kulturerbe als soziokulturelle Praxis,* edited by Moritz Csáky and Monika Sommer (Innsbruck: Studienverlag, 2005), 129–146.

[11] Accessed 25 June 2013, http://eur-lex.europa.eu/LexUriServ/LexUriServ.do?uri=COM:2007:0242:FIN:EN:PDF. This concept also finds frequent parallels in the academic literature.

construction can refer to an ongoing process directed toward the creation of a transnational future yet to be built, it can also relate to the past: "The heritage of the remembered past and the communal visions of the future are without any doubt the two most important sources from which a collective identity can be created."[12] Indeed, many academic studies on European identity frame the issue as a historical or history-related problem, referring to places of memory (*lieux de mémoire*) and discussing the relevancy of history for European self-understanding.[13] The debate on different *lieux de mémoire*, initiated by Pierre Nora[14] with regard to the French nation and adopted by similar projects for other national and transnational[15] contexts, has now reached the European level. In some of these cases, music has been considered as a relevant aspect of identity construction.[16] In the project *Europäische Erinnerungsorte*,[17]

---

[12] "Das Erbe der erinnerten Vergangenheit und gemeinsame Zukunftsvisionen sind sicherlich die zwei wichtigsten Quellen, aus denen kollektive Identitäten schöpfen können." Kornelia Konzal, "Europäische Erinnerungsorte—Bericht von einer Baustelle," in *Europäische Geschichtskultur—Europäische Geschichtspolitik: Vom Erfinden, Entdecken, Erarbeiten der Bedeutung von Erinnerung und Geschichte für das Verständnis und Selbstverständnis Europas,* edited by Christoph Kühberger and Clemens Sedmak (Innsbruck: Studien Verlag, 2009), 9–18.

[13] E.g., Kühberger and Sedmak, *Europäische Geschichtskultur—Europäische Geschichtspolitik.*

[14] Pierre Nora, ed., *Les lieux de mémoire*, 3 vols. (Paris: Gallimard, 1984–1992).

[15] E.g., *Steinbruch—Deutsche Erinnerungsorte: Annäherungen an eine deutsche Gedächtnisgeschichte*, ed. by Constanze Cacenac-Lecomte et al. (Frankfurt a. M., Vienna, Bern: Lang, 2000); Etienne François and Hagen Schulze, eds., *Deutsche Erinnerungsorte*, 3 vols. (Munich: Beck, 2001); Emil Brix, Ernst Bruckmüller, and Hannes Stekl, eds., *Memoria Austriae*, 3 vols. (Vienna, Munich, Oldenburg: Verlag für Geschichte und Politik, 2004–2005); *Lieux de mémoire au Luxembourg: Usages du passé et construction nationle,* edited by Sonja Kmec et al. (Luxembourgh: Saint Paul, 2007); Mario Isnenghi, ed., *I luoghi della memoria: Simboli e miti dell' Italia unita* (Roma, Bari: Gius. Laterza & Figli, 1996), Jacques Le Rider, Moritz Csáky, and Monika Sommer, eds., *Transnationale Gedächtnisorte in Zentraleuropa* (Innsbruck: Studien-Verlag, 2002).

[16] In the case of Austria, these musical *lieux de mémoire* are not limited to single composers, in this case to Mozart, but refer to music in general as the construction of Austria as a music nation. See Cornelia Szabo-Knotik, "Mythos Musik in Österreich: die Zweite Republik," in *Memoria Austriae*, vol.1, edited by Emil Brix, Ernst Bruckmüller, and Hannes Stekl (Vienna, Munich, Oldenburg: Verlag für Geschichte und Politik, 2004), 243–270; Gernot Gruber "Wolfgang Amadeus Mozart," in *Memoria* Broca *Austriae*, vol.1, edited by Emil Brix, Ernst Bruckmüller, and Hannes Stekl (Vienna: Verlag für Geschichte und Politik, 2005), 304–335, 48–78. For Italy, the Italian opera has been recognized as a *lieux de mémoire*, see Giovanni Morelli "L' opera," in *I luoghi della memoria: Simboli e miti dell' Italia unita*, edited by Mario Isnenghi (Roma, Bari: Gius. Laterza & Figli, 1996), 89–160.

[17] Boer et al., *Europäische Erinnerungsorte* 2; see also *Jahrbuch für Europäische Geschichte* 2002, which contains the proceedings of an international conference that was the initial starting point for the project on the *Europäische Erinnerungsorte*; Kirstin Buchinger, Claire Gantet, and Jakob Vogel, eds., *Europäische Erinnerungsräume* (Frankfurt a. M.: Campus Verlag 2009); Kühberger and Sedmak, *Europäische Geschichtskultur—Europäische Geschichtspolitik.*

Verdi's Aida and Beethoven's 9th Symphony as well as the chanson,[18] have thereby received the honor of being recognized as European musical *lieux de mémoire*.

Methodological Problems

A closer look at the above examples reveals, however, a series of problems and a certain fatigue in defining them as European musical *lieux de mémoire*. The proposed choices differ remarkably in their methodological focus, as well as in the general conception of what "Europeannes" is or how it comes to be constituted. One can find "Europeannes" in a single opus of a great composer, in structural and thematic parallels that constitute a musical genre, in the composer's explicit intention of creating a memorial space, and in the history of interpretation, such as the use of Beethoven's 9th Symphony as the source of the European anthem. Even though the authors of the project *Europäische Erinnerungsorte* admit a certain randomness in the selection of their examples, one still has to wonder about the underpinning consensus of such examples, as all three belong to the musical sphere of the bourgeoisie, whereas popular musical genres have been left aside.

Projects such as the above have provoked several critiques and a certain degree of skepticism. The heterogeneity and lack of a communal European history, the inadequacy of a well-developed theoretical frame, and the risk that the desire for a locus of European identification reflects political self-fulfillment have been maintained as arguments against the relevance of reflections on communal symbolic places as a constitutive basis for Europe.[19]

Identity and Space

My own interest in this topic has developed from working on the relation of music and space, and more specifically, how music contributes to the

---

[18] Markus Engelhardt, "Verdis Aida," in *Europäische Erinnerungsorte*, edited by Pim den Boer, Heinz Duchhardt, Georg Kreis and Wolfgang Schmale (Munich: Oldenbourg Verlag, 2012), 2: 247–254; Konrad Küster, "Beethovens Neunte Sinfonie," in *Europäische Erinnerungsorte* 2: 239–246; Ursula Mathis-Moser, "Das Chanson," in *Europäische Erinnerungsorte* 2: 255–262.

[19] See, for example, Etienne François, "Europäische lieux de mémoire," in *Transnationale Geschichte*, edited by Gunilla Budde, Sebastian Conrad, and Oliver Janz (Göttingen: Vandenhoeck & Ruprecht, 2006), 290–303; Kornelia Konzal, "Europäische Erinnerungsorte—Bericht von einer Baustelle," in *Europäische Geschichtskultur—Europäische Geschichtspolitik*, edited by Christoph Kühberger and Clemens Sedmak (Innsbruck: Studien Verlag 2009), 54–64.

construction of space and how, at the same time, the analysis of music can yield information about the construction of space.[20] Questions of space and identity are not necessarily connected to each other, and indeed most recent academic research on both topics, whether in music or other fields, has been developed without any cross-reference.[21] Yet questions of identity relate to questions of space, and they can develop a strong spatial dimension when collective identity constructions, such as national or transnational European ones, are negotiated.

Still, the imaginative processes of the creation of a communal identity can refer to different aspects. They may be based on communal values or a common history, and thus are not necessarily based on geographical and spatial aspects. The spatial component does, however, become a core issue for identity construction wherever space is not self evident, but is the subject of multiple and conflicting attributions that result in diverse spatial imaginations and in conflicting territorializations, such as is the case with the multiethnic situation of nineteenth-century Central Europe. Furthermore, recent changes in the theoretical conception of space, which is no longer conceived as a given and fixed category, have provided research on identity and space with a common theoretical basis, that of constructiveness. These changes also engender the possibility for a musicology based on cultural studies to engage a reflection upon the category of space.

Space matters, but if space is a subject of construction and imagination, and thus is *per se* unstable and subject to change, the aim cannot be that of defining a given national or supranational space. Obstacles to such an undertaking with regard to Europe have been formulated by Wolfgang Schmale in the volume *Europäische Erinnerungsorte*. Using the figure of the mythos—with reference to Europe, the Phoenician king's daughter seduced by Zeus as the mythical eponym of the continent—he comes to the following conclusion:

---

[20] My recent research on this topic has therefore focused on the Central European region, in particular on nineteenth-century Trieste and the role of music in this multiethnic region in a situation of increasing nationalisms, see Gregor Kokorz, "Triest 1848—Musik im Spannungsfeld nationaler Diskurse," in *Die Revolution 1848/49 und die Musik,* edited by Barbara Boisits (Vienna: Böhlau, 2014), 157–176.

[21] See, for example, Andrew Leyshorn, David Matless, and George Revill, "Introduction: Music, Space, and the Production of Place," in *The Place of Music*, edited by Andrew Leyshorn, David Matless, and George Revill (New York: Guilford Press, 1998), 1–30. Reverberations—such as Durkheim's idea of the social construction of space—from Maurice Halbwach's conception of a cultural memory reveal, however, a different prospective on the relation between space and identity, see Markus Schroer, *Räume, Orte, Grenzen: Auf dem Weg zu einer Soziologie des Raums* (Frankfurt a. M.: Suhrkamp, 2006), 59f.

> Myths have the property of the ambiguous and the ambiguity, their origins are obscure, they elude definition, they are changeable, adaptable. All this seems to apply to Europe as soon as one tries to fix it in a definition, an image, a historical account, the concept of European identity and European culture. It is always possible to deconstruct such an account as a myth. The myth of Europe encompasses the indefinable, those aspects of Europe, which cannot be grasped.[22]

Rather than trying to grasp the ungraspable and attempt to define a European musical space, it seems more important to focus on the dynamics; that is, on processes that contribute to the construction and transformation of space, as well as on how music is involved and may contribute to such a construction. For this purpose, I will analyze two music examples, and I will investigate their potential spatial aspects. I will first focus on the history and significance of a nineteenth-century French pilgrim song related to the sanctuary of Lourdes. My second example will follow, on its way across the Alps, an Italian mountain song from the 1920s. What happens to musical analysis, how does the focus change, and what answers can we receive when we bring music and space into conversation? These two case studies will investigate such spatial aspects, and the comparison of national and transnational significations will provide us with some answers on the European space and music's contribution to its dynamics.

Lourdes—The National and Transnational Dimensions of a Pilgrim Song

Last summer, looking out of my Roman window, within view of the magnificent pine trees of Villa Borghese, I was listening to the soundscape pouring from the city into my window. Besides the sound of the screeching trams, and the disco music intermingling with Beethoven's symphonies performed in the

[22] "Mythen besitzen die Eigenschaft des Vieldeutigen und der Vieldeutigkeit, ihre Ursprünge sind dunkel, Definitionen entziehen sie sich; sie sind wandelbar, anpassbar. Alles das scheint auf Europa zuzutreffen, sobald es auf irgendeine Weise festgehalten werden soll – in einer Definition, in einem Bild, in einer historischen Darstellung, im Begriff der europäischen Identität, der europäischen Kultur. Immer ist es möglich, das Gesagte oder Dargestellte zu dekonstruieren, als Mythos zu entlarven. 'Mythos Europa' umgreift das Nichtdefinierbare, das nicht Festhaltbare an Europa." Wolfgang Schmale, "Der Mythos Europa," in *Europäische Erinnerungsorte*, edited by Pim den Boer, Heinz Duchhardt, Georg Kreis, and Wolfgang Schmale (Munich: Oldenbourg Verlag, 2012), 1:16.

nearby Villa Giulia *all'aperto* on Saturday evenings, there was another sound regularly scratching my ear. It was series of bell sounds coming from a church tower every day at noon, which not only announced *mezzogiorno*—the noon hour—but also transported other information while the bell sounds connected in my mind to the well-known melody of the refrain of the pilgrims' song to the Lady of Lourdes. The double message of those bell sounds—signaling the noon hour and forming the notes of a song of pilgrimage—holds an interesting answer to the question of the importance of memory for the understanding of music. In this particular case, the main significance of this event becomes accessible only through memory. It is a musical event that points beyond its immediate musical presence. Even though it receives some significance as the traditional announcement of the noon hour through the specific time of day when the bell tolls, its main significance occurs only through an act of remembrance of the song's lines.

One can suppose that the intention for introducing this pilgrims' song as a signal for the noon hour was not the creation of a transnational European soundscape, but rather was religiously motivated, signifying Christianity and more particularly the veneration of the Virgin Mary as it is celebrated in Lourdes, a sanctuary dedicated to her in Southern France close to the Spanish border. Still, the usage of this melody creates a strong spatial dimension, as it not only connects to Christian content, but also links the song to a specific geographical place, thus spanning an acoustic bridge between Rome and Lourdes, between Italy and France. There has been a vital practice of pilgrimages to Lourdes from the second half of the nineteenth century till today, which have spurred the erection of several copies of the sanctuary (the grotto with the sculpture of the Madonna) and the tuning of bells according to the melody of the pilgrims' song, motivated by the initial line of the song itself, "*Es schallet der Glocken geheiligter Mund*."[23] For such reasons, the above-described acoustic bridge takes place in different

[23] "Toll the bells a holy sound." Today the text exists in slightly different versions, the above-quoted one refers to the oldest German version, which can be found in Arthur Schott, *Die Wunder von Lourdes* (Stuttgart: Verlag der Süddt. Verlagsbuchhandlung, 1887), 328–331; however, it does not correspond to the original French version, which refers to the biblical text of the apparition of the angel and not to the sound of the bells: "*L 'heure était venue, Ou l'airain sacré, De sa voix connue, Annonçait l'Ave*"; see Gaignet, *Cantique-Récit de L'apparition de N.D. de Lourdes* (Rodez: H. de Broca, 1875), 3. For the melody's socio-cultural background and origin, refer to Fritz Abel, "Aquelas Montanhas, Tradition et vitalite d'une chanson populaire occitance," in *Romana Cantat. Lieder in alten und neuen Chorsätzen mit sprachlichen, literarischen und musikwissenschaftlichen Interpretationen*, edited by Francisco J. Oroz Arizcuren (Tübingen: Gunter Narr Verlag, 1980), 2: 363–386.

places[24] and creates a sonic network all over Europe, a kind of a transnational sound space that can be described as Christian and European.

This transnational dimension is first constituted in Lourdes itself. The sanctuary attracts about six million pilgrims and tourists every year from different countries. The majority come from France, Italy, and Spain, followed by the Netherlands, Great Britain, Ireland, Belgium, and Germany, as well as an increasing number of Eastern European pilgrims since the 1990s.[25] Whereas many of the pilgrims' activities at the sanctuary take place on an individual or group level (such as taking water from the sacred fountain, walking inside the grotto of the apparition, or the celebration of Masses), the central religious event, the Marian procession, which takes place every evening, reunites all different pilgrims' groups into one single religious action and at the same time creates a transnational, multilingual, and multinational space. Truly, it creates unity in plurality. It is thereby the musical action, the song *Ave, Ave, Ave Maria,* which is continuously repeated during this rosary procession, which lasts one to two hours, that bridges the national and language differences and unites the participants.

The singing of the song holds relevant memorial and performative components with distinct significations, which are both constitutive of the song in its formative function. The strophic song, written by Abbé Gaignet in 1873 for Lourdes and used ever since, relates in 60 strophes, each of 4 verses followed by the refrain "*Ave, Ave, Ave Maria,*" some central aspects of the narrative of the shrine: the apparition of the Virgin Mary to Bernadette Soubirous, the finding of the fountain, the messages of the Virgin, and the first pilgrimages to Lourdes.[26] While this commemoration constitutes the Christian content and identity, the performative action of communal singing not only creates a religious but also a strong transnational space by bridging national gaps. The organization of the pilgrimages shows various national aspects, partly demanded by different language needs. It includes the visibility of national presences. For example, the provenance of the different pilgrim groups is signaled by national colors on the sanctuary's calendar, and groups identify

---

[24] Refer, e.g., to Heidi Christ, "'Das staunende Volk, es kniet betend umher …' Recherchen zum 'Großen Lourdes-Lied' " *Forschungsstelle für Fränkische Volksmusik*, accessed 27 June 2013, http://www.volksmusik-forschung.de/index.php?id=142.

[25] France (30%), Italy (30%), Spain (10%), Great Britain (5%), Ireland (5%), Germany (5%), Belgium (5%); source: Marie Caujolle, *Lourdes* (Vic-en-Bigorre Cedex: MSM, 2009), 51.

[26] Gaignet, *Cantique-Récit de L'apparition de N.D. de Lourdes* (Rodez: H. de Broca, 1875); for further information on the origin of the song, refer to Henry Branthomme "Un evenement qui bousule et entraine (1858–1901)" in *Histoire de Lourdes,* edited by Stephane Baumont (Toulouse, 1993), 149–246.

themselves by carrying national symbols, such as little flags, during the procession. The space, marked by national connotations expressing difference, receives unity and homogenization through the performative activities, which become stronger through the singing, literally unifying all pilgrims into one single voice.

Lourdes' Origin as a National Sanctuary

This transnational dimension is anything but self-evident, as Lourdes, like many other sanctuaries, such as Medjugorje in Bosnia, Monte Grisa in Trieste, Mariazell in Austria, and the Lithuanian Hill of the Crosses near Siauliai, just to mention a few, has served not only religious but also political and in particular national functions.[27] The early success of Lourdes was partly based on the alliance with modernity—the early access to the railway system (1866) and the vast media presence, in particular through Henri Lasserre's pious history of the sanctuary, *Notre-Dame de Lourdes* (1869)—but to a good amount also by its political function as a national sanctuary, when after the Franco-Prussian war Lourdes became the destination of a series of national pilgrimages of penance and was central to the attempts to restore the Bourbon monarchy.[28]

Such nationalist origins become evident also in Lourdes' main pilgrims' song, the *Ave, Ave, Ave Maria*. The narrative of the song, whose structure follows the rosary, leaves behind in the last ten stanzas the story of Bernadette and the apparition and elevates an appeal to the French nation, thus transforming the private history of Bernadette into a public, national suffering:

Pieux Sanctuaire,
Tu les vis présents
De la France entière
Les nobles enfants

[27] This nexus between religion and nationalism has become a well researched topic; for further general information, refer, for example, to: Anthony W. Marx, *Faith in Nation* (Oxford: Oxford University Press, 2003); for the political instrumentalization of the Madonna, see Anna Bravo, "La madonna pellegrina," in *I luoghi della memoria: Simboli e miti dell' Italia unita,* edited by Mario Isnenghi (Rome: Gius, Laterza & Figli, 1996), 587–598; Mart Bax, *Medjugorje: Religion, Politics, and Violence in Rural Bosnia* (Amsterdam: VU Uitg, 1995), Christian Stadelmann, "Mariazell," in *Memoria Austriae II: Bauten, Orte, Regionen,* edited by Emil Brix, Ernst Bruckmüller, and Hannes Stekl (Vienna: Verlag für Geschichte und Politik, 2005), 304–335.

[28] Ruth Harris, *Lourdes: Body and Spirit in the Secular Age* (London: Penguin Press, 1999); Andreas J. Kotulla, *Nach Lourdes! Der französische Marienwallfahrtsort und die Katholiken im Deutschen Kaiserreich* (Munich: Martin Meidenbauer, 2006); *Le Jubilé du Pèlerinage national a Lourdes 1873–1897* (Paris: Maison de la Bonne Presse, 1897); Em. Bougaud, *La Sainte Vierge & La France: Discours prononcé au pèlerinage national de cléry* (Orléans: Blanchard, 1874).

This national intention becomes even more evident in eight other additional strophes entitled *Ave Maria des Vendéens,* which are dedicated to the use of the pilgrims on their arrival. The title itself frames the song in a French national context, referring to the rural region of the Vendée, which had become the center of royalist and Catholic resistance during the French Revolution, and for the royalist movement after 1873 a new center for the reawakening of the French nation. The 4th strophe makes this evident through a direct appeal to the entire French nation: "*La France l'écoute.*" Opening with "*La France,*" a position that in the preceding strophes was held by "*L' enfant,*" referring to the frightened girl Bernadette, the strophe makes most explicit the metaphoric comparison between the suffering French nation and the pain of Bernadette. Like many sick pilgrims, the nation can expect miraculous healing from its own suffering ("*Se lève soudain,*" 4th strophe) if it follows the call of the sanctuary ("*Venez ici!,*" 5th strophe), and Lourdes can become the new Vendée ("*C'est notre Vendée,*" 5th strophe); that is, a locus of the resurrection of the French nation.

1. Sur cette colline
Marie apparut:
Au front qu'elle incline
Rendons le salut: Ave…

2. A l'enfant timide
Priant au vallon,
Au Gave rapide
Elle a dit son nom. Ave…

3. L'enfant le répète
Comme un doux écho;
La Gave lui prête
La voix de son flot. Ave…

4. La France l'écoute
Se lève soudain,
Et se met en route,
Chantant ce refrain: Ave …

5. La voix maternelle
Dit: Venez ici!
Le people fidèle
Répond: Me voici! Ave…

6. Un souffle de grâce
Pousse vers ce lieu;
Ce souffle qui passe
Est celui de Dieu. Ave …

7. C'est notre Vendée
Qui vient à son tour
A l'Immaculée
Dire son amour. Ave…

8. Reçois la prière
de tes Pèlerins;
Montre-toi leur Mère,
De tous fais des saints. Ave…[29]

[29] All quotations are from J. Gaignet, *Cantique-Récit de L'apparition de N.D. de Lourdes* (Rodez: H. de Broca, 1875), 12.

All this marks Lourdes in the first place as a national *lieux de mémoire*, but history also shows a significant transformation of the place towards a transnational space,[30] which according to the motto "unity in plurality" can be interpreted as a European space, not through memory but through the communal performative activity of singing.

La Montanara—Alpine Border Crossings?

In 1973, when I was four year old, the German pop singer Heino[31] had one of his greatest successes. *La Montanara (Das Lied von den Bergen)* dominated the German hit parade for 24 weeks, reaching third place.[32] The song was still popular about six or seven years later when I spent my summer holidays at a farm in the Styrian alps, and I got to know it through *Ö-Regional*, the regional Austrian radio station, which was the favorite and most likely the only radio program available to Steffi, the farmer's wife, who was listening while doing her housework. Listening to the lines of the song and looking out onto the alpine landscape that surrounded me, the song seemed so correctly placed, describing so well my own experience.

It was many years later that I found out that Heino had not written the song, nor it was related to a German or Austrian alpine context,[33] which seemed so very much to have inspired the song. At this time Bach had conquered the

---

[30] The formation of Lourdes as an international pilgrimage site starts as early as in the 1870s and develops parallel to the formation of Lourdes as a national *lieux de mémoire*. This demonstrates ambivalence and a multitude of possible semantic attributions and constructions. Already the nineteenth-century discourse contributes to the construction of Lourdes as an international and humankind–reuniting place: "*Beim Anblick der Weltwallfahrt nach Lourdes ist klar und einleuchtend wahrzunehmen, dass dieselbe in geschichtlicher Hinsicht eine völkervereinigende Bedeutung hat. Schon der nächste Hinblick lehrt es, wenn wir so die Pilger von allen Nationen zur gemeinsamen Mutter hinziehen sehen und bemerken, wie sie brüderlich als Christen und Menschen ohne Unterschied und Zwiespalt, zu ihren Füßen sich vereinigen.*" Arthur Schott, *Die Wunder von Lourdes* (Stuttgart: Verlag der Süddt. Verlagsbuchhandlung, 1887), 379.

[31] Heino, German pop singer, born as Heinz Georg Krammer on December 13, 1938; see Heino, *Und sie lieben mich doch: Die Autobiografie* (Munich: Ed. Ferenczy bei Bruckmann, 1995).

[32] Taking the German hit parade as reference, only one other song outperformed this result. The year before, in 1972, *Blau blüht der Enzian*—another alpine theme—reached second place and stayed in the charts for 28 weeks.

[33] This association of a German and Austrian cultural context is also evoked by the other titles with which *La Montanra* was released. On the B-side of the single there was *Der Schneewalzer*, and on the LP album *La Montanara* was published together with songs such as *Das Kufsteinlied*, or *Am Brunnen vor dem Tore*, and *Das Wandern ist des Müllers Lust*. See the artist's homepage, accessed June 4, 2013, http://www.heino.de/diskografie.html.

position of my personal musical hero, and I was on my way to becoming a musicologist. In the Piedmont Alps, at the *Pian della Mussa (Balme),* close to the Italian-French border at the very end of a romantic alpine valley, a shining silver plaque caught my attention. It read:

LA MONTANARA
1927 –1987
di Toni Ortelli

QUESTI MONTI ISPIRINO NEL TUO ANIMO
SENTIMENTI DI PACE E D'AMORE

CHE "LA MONTANARA" ESPRIME
NEL CANTO CHE QUI NACQUE

"*La Montanara*/1927–1987/by Toni Ortelli/May these mountains inspire in your heart those feelings of peace and love which *La Montanara* expresses, the song that was created in this place." (See insert, figure 1.)

In reality, the song, which was so deeply engrained into my childhood's musical memory, had been written in 1927 for the choir *Coro della SAT,*[34] and its remarkable popularity and diffusion is closely related to, and dependent on, such choir's history. Both the melody and the lyrics were by Toni Ortelli, remembered on the plate. Responsible for its harmonization and choir adaptation was Luigi Pigarelli (1875–1964), the president of the concert society in Trento and an early supporter of the choir, who wrote many of its four-part settings.[35] The choir's popularity started soon after its foundation in the late 1920s and early 1930s, first winning the prestigious prize of the *Guido d' Arezzo* choir competition, which was followed, in 1933, by an early recording for Columbia records and, in 1935, by the printed edition of the choir's core repertoire, *Canti della Montagna: dal repertorio del Coro della SOSAT*. This strong media presence added remarkably to the choir's reputation and

[34] SAT = Società degli Alpini Tridentini, the choir of the Society of the Tridentin Alpinists. The first concert was on May 25, 1926. This and all the following information on the song and the choir, *Coro della SAT,* are based on Piero De Martini, *Il Conservatorio delle Alpi. Il Coro della SAT: storia, documenti, testimonianze* (Milan: Bruno Mondadori, 2009).

[35] The biographical background of musicians such as Pigarelli reveals an even more complex situation, which, however, cannot further be explored in the realm of this paper. Pigarelli was born as a citizen of the Habsburg Monarchy, studied law in Graz, and was introduced to the repertoire of popular music through a research project of the Austrian academy of science, for which he collected the Trientin repertoire of popular songs in the 1910s.

popularity, and also to the diffusion of its repertoire, of which Toni Ortelli's *La Montanara* had become a central part. (See insert, figure 2.[36])

Through such historical circumstances, however, the song also became deeply embedded in Italians' national and fascist context. Evidence for this comes from the choir's early repertoire, which drew on Italian First World War soldiers' songs, *Canti di Soldati,*[37] and the use of the popular choir for fascist propaganda.[38] How much in the course of the years *La Montanara* has come to be identified with a specific representation of Italian national identity is best shown by the fact that, in 1959, the Italian poet Salvatore Quasimodo received the Nobel Price for Literature from the hands of the Swedish king to the sound of Toni Ortelli's popular melody. The song indeed received such popularity that its author began to be called "*Goffredo Mameli delle Alpi,*"[39] thus making a direct reference to the creator of the song *Fratelli d'Italia*.[40]

A Heterogeneous Lieu de Mémoire Musicale

The plaque commemorating the creation of the melody transforms the *Pian della Mussa* into a musical *lieu de mémoire*. But what significance does it give to the place? What kind of *lieu de mémoire* is thereby created? Obviously the melody evokes different memories, and what is remembered has nothing to do with my childhood memories. One can suppose that the initiators of this *lieu de mémoire musicale* had in mind supporting the reawakening tourism of an alpine village by remembering the glorious times, when in the 1920s Balme became the center of the rising winter sports and Toni

---

[36] The frontispiece of this edition (showing three Alpinists, a section of the Italian Army, with their characteristic caps) and dedicating the edition to the reconstruction of the Alpine Shelter Cesare Battisti, a citizen of Trento and deputy to the *Reichsrat* in Vienna, executed by the Habsburg authorities in 1916 for his Italian national activities, can be read in an Italian national context.

[37] *Canti di Soldati, raccolti da Piero Jahier armonizzati da Vittorio Gui* (1919).

[38] E.g., a concert given in Rijeka in March 1938 and a performance on the occasion of Hitler's visit to Rome in 1938. The information is based on the newspaper article: "Sosat contro Sat. La Guerra dei cori trentini," *Trentino Corriere Alpi*, December 17, 2009. These aspects would need further investigation, which in the realm of this paper cannot be provided. Publications dedicated to the choir's history focus on nostalgic and artistic aspects but do not further investigate these political issues of the choir's activities.

[39] Elisabetta Zanellato, "L'inno delle Montagne: La Montanara," *Barmes News* 32 (2009), 13.

[40] For the importance and implications of Goffredo Mameli's Fratelli d' Italia, refer to *Fratelli d' Italia: Goffredo Mameli e Genova nel 1847,* edited by Emilio Costa, Giulio Fiaschini, and Leo Morabito (Genova: Istituto Mazziniano, 1998).

Ortelli and his song may have been part of this context. Granting him honorary citizenship on the occasion of the 60th birthday of the song gave importance and publicity to the place itself.[41] However, because of its history and its use, the melody bears other memories that make of this *lieu de mémoire* a national place of remembrance. This reading is reinforced by the geographical position of the memorial plate, only a few kilometers from the French border, with other monuments of military and national significance in sighting distance, such as the monument for the fallen *Bersaglieri* (an elite corps of the Italian army) in remembrance of their fight for the founding of the Italian state:

SUBIRONO IL MARTIRIO
CADDERO I FIGLI PREDILETTI

NEL CENTENARIO
DELL' UNITÀ D'ITALIA
I BERSAGLIERI
DELLA SEZIONE MEDAGLIA D' ORO
GUGLIELMO SCOGNAMIGLIO
DI CIRIÈ E VALLI DI LANZO
NON DIMENTICANDO
OFFRONO A LORO
IL SIMBOLO DELL' AMORE E DELLA PACE

30 LUGLIO 1961 ZAFFIRI

They suffered martyrdom/fell the elected sons/On the occasion of the 100th year/of the Italian unification/the Bersaglieri/of the gold medal section/ "Guglielmo Scognamiglio"/of Ciriè and Lanzo valleys/never forgetting/offer to them/the symbol of love and peace. (See insert, figure 3.)

"*Il simbolo dell'amore e della pace*"—The symbol of love and peace. This is not only the formula for the remembrance of the unification of the Italian state, but the identical wording is used again for commemorating the creation of *La Montanara* some thirty years later, in 1987: "*Sentimenti di pace e d' amore che la Montanara esprime*"—May these mountains inspire in your heart those feelings of peace and love which *La Montanara* expresses. All of this turns the remembrance of the melody into an Italian national musical landmark.

---

[41] Elisabetta Zanellato, "L'inno delle Montagne: La Montanara," *Barmes News* 32 (2009), 12–13.

Conclusions

Music creates space. It gives significance to a place and thus forms and transforms its meaning. Music can develop this signifying spatial power in different ways. In the case of *Pian della Mussa,* it is the remembrance of the creation of a song that signifies this alpine valley and transforms it not so much into a creative spot which by the force of its unique genius loci has inspired the popular melody, neither into a place of remembrance for a great musician, but into a national *lieu de mémoire*. Such a place receives its significance not through specific musical elements, which is why the approach of musical analysis is not able by itself to reveal these strata of meanings, but through the diverse contextualization of the song and its remembrances. These sociocultural frames are essential for the construction of meaning and, for this very reason, memory is of central importance for the signifying process and the creation of space. The Lourdes pilgrimage song offers, instead, a different dynamic for the production of space. Here space is created through performative practice, the repeated singing in the place that connects the song to the place itself, and makes of music an essential part of it. The song is thereby embedded within a series of other elements and performative actions, which taken together constitute the place as the religious space of the miraculous apparition of the Virgin of Lourdes.

In both cases, however, in the Lourdes song as well as in *La Montanara,* the musical structure is also involved and contributes to the spatial construction. This happens in the first instance at the textual level, where in the frame of the composition space is described and developed: the history of the apparition at the grotto of Marsabielle that the Lourdes song narrates and thus remembers, and the alpine landscape, populated by mountain peaks, waterfalls, and trees, without any specific geographical reference, which for this very reason can become the subject of an alpine border crossing and can be perceived as part of a German as well as Italian national alpine sphere.

But the musical structure also, the melodic line, adds to the construction of space, most evidently in the case of the Lourdes song played by the bells in Rome. Without being in Lourdes and without any explicit textual reference, the melodic line works as an evocation of place and identity, as an act of remembrance similar to a Wagnerian "*Erinnerungsmotiv,*" that connects the present musical event to the one heard in the past. Recognition and reconnection are essential moments and make the Roman bell sounds become a part of the spatial construction, as they signify and transform the sound of the noon hour into a remembrance, and thus into a part of Lourdian piety and Lourdian space.

As much as remembrance reveals itself to be an essential part of spatial production, processes of oblivion and acts of de-signification become equally relevant for the musical production of space. Both the examples developed a strong and even dominant national significance, but at the same time, they also trespassed the boundaries of national framing and developed transnational importance. In my personal remembrance, neither the Lourdes song nor *La Montanara* has national significations, even though the musicological analysis reveals precisely the importance of such significations. What at first shows the interpretative plurality and ambivalence of a diverse contextualization and different memories, brings back the question of a European musical space, particularly in the relation and oscillation between national and transnational interpretative frames.

The transnational seems thereby to be at the same time a prerequisite and a consequence of processes of de-semantization and the oblivion of national interpretations and memories. As transnational significations develop alternatives to the existing national ones, they also contribute to the destabilization of such national interpretations and framings. The transnationalization of a (previously) dominant national content has to be supported, however, by a weakening of a national interpretation. The Lourdes song never would have been able to develop its role as a communal pilgrims' song had its perception been that of a French national utterance. At the same time the use of this song by foreign—that is, not French—pilgrims, has hindered an exclusively national framing of the biographical and religious content of the song. The ambivalence of the text, which offers the possibility of multiple and different interpretations, has supported from the beginning different significations. The transnational that we observe in this case is not its primary intention, but rather a consequence of the widespread religious practice of Catholic pilgrimages.

Transnational presence can thus develop different qualities. The transnational dissemination of the Lourdes song generated by international pilgrimages tends towards the development of a communal religious interpretation and thus towards a communal space. *La Montanara's* transnational presence, instead, does not develop a communal (European) interpretation on the ground of a shared alpine experience, as evoked in the lyrics, but hints to a transformative process of cultural transfer, which results in diverse contextualizations that share the melodic line but differ in their significations.

Communal space, however, needs shared interpretation. Music can contribute to the construction of such a communal space, but because of its specifics and in particular its semantic openness, it can also allude to the existence of a community. It follows further that trans-nationalization, as a key concept of present European development, needs similar semantic grounding. This can be found in the remembrance and (re)construction of a communal past, as well as in the building of a communal European future.

BIBLIOGRAPHY

Abel, Fritz. "Aquelas Montanhas, Tradition et vitalite d'une chanson populaire occitance." In *Romana Cantat. Lieder in alten und neuen Chorsätzen mit sprachlichen, literarischen und musikwissenschaftlichen Interpretationen*, vol. 2, edited by Francisco J. Oroz Arizcuren, 363–386. Tübingen: Gunter Narr Verlag, 1980.

Bax, Mart. *Medjugorje: Religion, Politics, and Violence in Rural Bosnia*. Amsterdam: VU Uitg, 1995.

Boer, Pim den, and Heinz Duchhardt, Georg Kreis, Wolfgang Schmale. *Europäische Erinnerungsorte*, vol. 2. Munich: Oldenbourg Verlag, 2012.

Bougaud, Emile. *La Sainte Vierge & La France: Discours prononcé au pèlerinage national de cléry.* Orléans: Blanchard, 1874.

Branthomme, Henry. "Un evenement qui bousule et entraine (1858–1901)." In *Histoire de Lourdes,* edited by Stephane Baumont, 149–246. Toulouse, 1993.

Bravo, Anna. "La madonna pellegrina." In *I luoghi della memoria: Simboli e miti dell' Italia unita,* edited by Mario Isnenghi, 587–598. Rome: Gius, Laterza & Figli, 1996.

Brix, Emil, Ernst Bruckmüller, and Hannes Stekl, eds. *Memoria Austriae*, 3 vols. Vienna: Verlag für Geschichte und Politik, 2004–2005.

Buchinger, Kirstin, Claire Gantet, and Jakob Vogel, eds. *Europäische Erinnerungsräume*. Frankfurt a. M.: Campus Verlag 2009.

Cacenac-Lecomte, Constanze et al., eds. *Steinbruch—Deutsche Erinnerungsorte: Annäherungen an eine deutsche Gedächtnisgeschichte*. Frankfurt a. M.: Lang, 2000.

Canti di Soldati, raccolti da Piero Jahier armonizzati da Vittorio Gui (1919).

Caujolle, Marie. *Lourdes*. Vic-en-Bigorre Cedex: MSM, 2009.

Christ, Heidi. "'Das staunende Volk, es kniet betend umher . . .' Recherchen zum 'Großen Lourdes-Lied.'" Forschungsstelle für Fränkische Volksmusik. Accessed 27 June 2013. http://www.volksmusik-forschung.de/index.php?id=142.

Commission of the European Communities. *Communication from the Commission to the European Parliament, the Council, the European Economic and Social Committee and the Committee of the Regions on a European Agenda for Culture in a Globalizing World*, COM 242. Brussels: Commission of the European Communities, 2007.

Costa, Emilio, Giulio Fiaschini, and Leo Morabito, eds., *Fratelli d' Italia: Goffredo Mameli e Genova nel 1847*. Genova: Istituto Mazziniano, 1998.

Heino [Heinz Georg Krammer]. *Und sie lieben mich doch: Die Autobiografie*. Munich: Ed. Ferenczy bei Bruckmann, 1995.

Corona, Ignacio, and Alejandro L. Madrid, eds., *Postnational Musical Identities: Cultural Production, Distribution, and Consumption in a Globalized Scenario*. Lanham, MD: Lexington Books, 2008.

Engelhardt, Markus. "Verdis Aida." In *Europäische Erinnerungsorte*, vol.2, edited by Pim den Boer, Heinz Duchhardt, Georg Kreis, and Wolfgang Schmale, 247–254. Munich: Oldenbourg Verlag, 2012.

François, Etienne. "Europäische lieux de mémoire" In *Transnationale Geschichte,* edited by Gunilla Budde, Sebastian Conrad, and Oliver Janz, 290–303. Göttingen: Vadenhoeck & Ruprecht, 2006.

François, Etienne, and Hagen Schulze, eds. *Deutsche Erinnerungsorte*, 3 vols. Munich: Beck, 2001.

Gaignet. *Cantique-Récit de L'apparition de N.D. de Lourdes*. Rodez: H. de Broca, 1875.

Gruber, Gernot. "Wolfgang Amadeus Mozart." In *Memoria Austriae I: Menschen, Mythen, Zeiten,* edited by Emil Brix, Ernst Bruckmüller, and Hannes Stekl, 304–335. Vienna: Verlag für Geschichte und Politik, 2005.

Harris, Ruth. *Lourdes: Body and Spirit in the Secular Age*. London: Penguin Press, 1999.

Heck, Michael. "Sprache ist ein Kulturgut." Interview in *KA-News.de*, April 12, 2004. Accessed 27 June 2013. http://www.ka-news.de/nachrichten/karlsruhe/Karlsruhe-Heck-Sprache-ist-ein-Kulturgut;art86,19948.

Isnenghi, Mario, ed., *I luoghi della memoria: Simboli e miti dell' Italia unita*. Rome: Gius, Laterza & Figli, 1996.

Le Jubilé du Pèlerinage national a Lourdes 1873–1897. Paris: Maison de la Bonne Presse, 1897.

Martini, Piero De. *Il Conservatorio delle Alpi. Il Coro della SAT: storia, documenti, testimonianze*. Milan: Bruno Mondadori, 2009.

Kmec, Sonja et al., eds., *Lieux de mémoire au Luxembourg: Usages du passé et construction national*. Luxembourgh: Saint Paul, 2007.

Kokorz, Gregor. "Triest 1848—Musik im Spannungsfeld nationaler Diskurse." In *Die Revolution 1848/49 und die Musik,* edited by Barbara Boisits, 157–176. Vienna: Böhlau, 2014.

Konzal, Kornelia. "Europäische Erinnerungsorte—Bericht von einer Baustelle." In *Europäische Geschichtskultur—Europäische Geschichtspolitik: Vom Erfinden, Entdecken, Erarbeiten der Bedeutung von Erinnerung und Geschichte für das Verständnis und Selbstverständnis Europas,* edited by Christoph Kühberger and Clemens Sedmak, 9–18, 54–64. Innsbruck: Studien Verlag, 2009.

Kotulla, Andreas J. *Nach Lourdes! Der französische Marienwallfahrtsort und die Katholiken im Deutschen Kaiserreich*. Munich: Martin Meidenbauer, 2006.

Kühberger, Christoph, and Clemens Sedmak, eds., *Europäische Geschichtskultur—Europäische Geschichtspolitik: Vom Erfinden, Entdecken, Erarbeiten der Bedeutung von Erinnerung und Geschichte für das Verständnis und Selbstverständnis Europas.* Innsbruck: Studien Verlag, 2009.

Küster, Konrad. "Beethovens Neunte Sinfonie." In *Europäische Erinnerungsorte,* vol. 2, edited by Pim den Boer, Heinz Duchhardt, Georg Kreis, and Wolfgang Schmale, 239–246. Munich: Oldenbourg Verlag, 2012.

Le Rider, Jacques, Moritz Csáky, and Monika Sommer, eds., *Transnationale Gedächtnisorte in Zentraleuropa.* Innsbruck: Studien-Verlag, 2002.

Leyshorn, Andrew, David Matless, and George Revill. "Introduction: Music, Space, and the Production of Place." In *The Place of Music,* edited by Andrew Leyshorn, David Matless, and George Revill, 1–30. New York: Guilford Press 1998.

Marx, Anthony W. *Faith in Nation.* Oxford: Oxford University Press, 2003.

Mathis-Moser, Ursula. "Das Chanson." In *Europäische Erinnerungsorte,* vol. 2, edited by Pim den Boer, Heinz Duchhardt, Georg Kreis, and Wolfgang Schmale, 255–262. Munich: Oldenbourg Verlag, 2012.

Metdepennighen, Erna. "Musikförderung der europäischen Gemeinschaft." In *Musik und Kulturbetrieb: Handbuch der Musik im 20. Jahrhundert,* vol. 10, edited by Sabine Arndt, 333–335. Laaber: Laaber Verlag, 2006.

Morelli, Giovanni. "L' opera." In *I luoghi della memoria: Simboli e miti dell' Italia unita,* edited by Mario Isnenghi, 89–160. Rome: Gius, Laterza & Figli, 1996.

Music and the European Union: European Union Youth Orchestra, European Border Breakers Award, European Union Baroque Orchestra. General Books LLC, 2010.

Nora, Pierre, ed. *Les lieux de mémoire,* 3 vols. Paris: Gallimard, 1984–1992.

Riethmüller, Albrecht. "Die Hymne der Europäischen Union." In *Europäische Erinnerungsorte,* vol. 2, edited by Pim den Boer, Heinz Duchhardt, Georg Kreis, and Wolfgang Schmale, 89–96. Munich: Oldenbourg Verlag, 2012.

Schmale, Wolfgang. "Der Mythos Europa." In *Europäische Erinnerungsorte,* vol. 1, edited by Pim den Boer, Heinz Duchhardt, Georg Kreis, and Wolfgang Schmale, 15–20. Munich: Oldenbourg Verlag, 2012.

Schott, Arthur. *Die Wunder von Lourdes.* Stuttgart: Verlag der Süddt. Verlagsbuchhandlung, 1887.

Schroer, Markus. *Räume, Orte, Grenzen: Auf dem Weg zu einer Soziologie des Raums.* Frankfurt a. Main: Suhrkamp, 2006.

"Sosat contro Sat. La Guerra dei cori trentini." *Trentino Corriere Alpi.* December 17, 2009.

Stadelmann, Christian. "Mariazell." In *Memoria Austriae II: Bauten, Orte, Regionen,* edited by Emil Brix, Ernst Bruckmüller, and Hannes Stekl, 304–335. Vienna: Verlag für Geschichte und Politik, 2005.

Szabo-Knotik, Cornelia. "Mythos Musik in Österreich: die Zweite Republik." In *Memoria Austriae I,* edited by Emil Brix, Ernst Bruckmüller, and Hannes Stekl, 243–270. Vienna: Verlag für Geschichte und Politik, 2004.

Trümpi, Fritz. *Politisierte Orchester: Die Wiener Philharmoniker und das Berliner Philharmonische Orchester im Nationalsozialismus.* Vienna: Böhlau Verlag, 2011.

Uhl, Heidemarie. "Zwischen Pathosformal und Baustelle: Kultur und europäische Identität." In *Kulturerbe als soziokulturelle Praxis,* edited by Moritz Csáky and Monika Sommer, 129–146. Innsbruck: Studienverlag, 2005.

Zanellato, Elisabetta. "L'inno delle Montagne: La Montanara." *Barmes News* 32 (2009): 12–13.

MNEMONIC HEGEMONY? THE POWER RELATIONS OF CONTEMPORARY EUROPEAN MEMORY

Berthold Molden

Abstract

In his inauguration speech as President of the European Parliament in February 2007, Hans-Gert Pöttering suggested, "the founding of a 'House of European History.' It should [be] a place where our memory of European history and the work of European unification is jointly cultivated." This historico-political intervention by the highest European officials indicates a new stage in the creation of a transnational framework for the interpretation of the past. Debates on official representations of European history, however, have raised doubts concerning this transnationality: Is the European politics of history dedicated to the "dialogical memory" (Aleida Assmann) between nation-states? Is the historico-political tendency that Ute Frevert has called the Europeanization of Germany's twentieth century, really the "nightmare" of a Germanization of European memory (Jan-Werner Müller)? Will the museum's storyline blot out existing conflict in order to promote desired unity? And most importantly, will the twentieth century memories of most Europeans, which according to recent research defy European master narratives, be sacrificed to the salvific history of EU integration? Critically assessing some of the recent German and European contributions on European memory, this paper interprets these tensions between grand narratives and communicative memories as relations of power within a theoretical concept of mnemonic hegemony.

'East' and 'West' are notions that contain real history, whereas 'Europe' is an empty sound. [. . .] Everything we imply by the term European Culture came into existence between the Vistula and the Adriatic and the Guadalquivir and, even if we were to agree that Greece, the Greece of Pericles, lay in Europe, the Greece of today certainly does not.

Oswald Spengler[1]

Introduction

The pessimistically conservative philosopher-historian Oswald Spengler hid this strong verdict in the first footnote of his magnum opus, *The Decline of the West*, the first volume of which was published towards the end of World War I in Vienna, capital of an empire in decay. Had his remark been made a century later, at a time when the quite different empire of "Europe" faces a distinct crisis of identity and cohesion, it would still reflect much of the controversy currently surrounding the notion of European history and memory: Is a Greek state shattered by economic crisis and torn apart by ideological schisms still considered part of a European community that claims to have overcome ideological confrontations, let alone Fascism and Communism, as political forces to be reckoned with? Or, put in more general terms: What defines Europe? Who is part of it? Are East and West in fact the most "real" fault lines between inner-European communities of shared experience and thus identity? Which are Europe's most important historical ingredients worthy of remembrance? Who defines this canon of history? And what are the conceptual, epistemic, and ideological categories guiding this definition?

When the founding moment of post-World War II European integration came around for the fiftieth time, the president of the European Parliament, Hans-Gert Pöttering—together with another German Christian democrat, the European Council president, Angela Merkel; and the president of the European Commission, Manuel Barroso, formerly a man of the Left—signed a solemn declaration about Europe's past, present, and future. At the beginning of this text, known as the "Berlin Declaration," it says: "Thanks to the yearning for freedom of the peoples of Central and Eastern Europe, the unnatural division of Europe is now consigned to the past. European unification shows that we have learnt the painful *lessons of a history* marked by bloody conflict." And its finale proclaims: "With European unification, a *dream of earlier generations* has become a reality. Our history reminds us that we must protect this for the good of future generations."[2] As so often happens, history is invoked

[1] O. Spengler, *The Decline of the West. Volume I: Form and Actuality* (New York: Knopf, 1926, 1950), 16.

[2] Declaration on the occasion of the 50th anniversary of the Treaty of Rome, March 25, 2007.

as a teacher, and the speaker claims to have learned an important lesson. Also, as in many teleological discourses on historical development, the current political project is portrayed as the true fulfillment of the hopes and dreams of earlier generations, incorporating—especially in the case of Europe—a highly heterogeneous ancestry in its entirety.

Yet Mr. Pöttering's ambitions concerning representations of European history have not been limited to anniversary discourses. In his inauguration speech as President of the European Parliament, he declared:

> I would like to suggest a locus for history and for the future, where the concept of the European idea can continue to grow. I would like to suggest the founding of a "House of European History." It should not be a dry, boring museum, but a place where our memory of European history and the work of European unification is jointly cultivated, and which at the same time is available as a locus for the European identity to go on being shaped by present and future citizens of the European Union.[3]

This historico-political intervention by the highest European officials indicated a new stage in a process that had more or less started with the Declaration on European Identity in 1973:[4] the creation of a transnational framework for the interpretation of the past. Only after, although not necessarily because of, the 1973 declaration did European history and memory once again become preferred topics of academic, intellectual, and political

---

[3] H.-G. Pöttering, *Inaugural Address*, February 13, 2007, accessed August 3, 2013, http://www.europarl.europa.eu/sides/getDoc.do?pubRef=-//EP//TEXT+CRE+20070213+ITEM-003+-DOC+XML+V0//EN. A written draft of this speech pointed out Mr. Pöttering's involuntarily constructivist—and in fact egocentric—self-perception more explicitly: "I should like to create a locus for history and for the future." Cf. Committee of Experts for the House of European History, *Conceptual Basis for a House of European History* (Brussels 2008), 5, accessed August 3, 2013, http://www.europarl.europa.eu/meetdocs/2004_2009/documents/dv/745/745721/745721_en.pdf.

[4] Historians Małgorzata Pakier and Bo Stråth compare the identity politics of the European Union since 1973 to the efforts of symbolic integration to be observed in nation-building processes in the nineteenth century (and call upon historians not to write legitimizing narratives as their predecessors had). This analogy transforms the different European value and/or memory cultures and nation-states (France, England, Germany, Poland, or Italy) into competing parties about the definition of Europeanness in the constitutional controversy of 2004. It is seen as representative for a whole number of seemingly irreconcilable differences among the representations of European history. Cf. *A European Memory? Contested Histories and Politics of Remembrance*, Studies in Contemporary European History, vol. 6, edited by B. Stråth and M. Pakier (New York: Berghahn, 2012), 1–3.

debate. Although the "return of memory" in the 1980s came about within the framework of methodical nationalism, the transnationalization of this phenomenon followed suit.

In fact, as is often noted, Pierre Nora's recovery of the Halbwachsian concept of collective memory is more than methodological nationalism, it is normative nationalism. Nora created a canon of mnemonic reference points that was intended to strengthen French identity, not unlike museums and the unification of language had served the creation of the French nation in the first place. Just as Nora's model of "realms of memory" has been applied to other European and non-European nation-states, it is now being tried out on Europe. The project is no less normative and constructivist, which accounts for the fact that even those historians who promote these identity markers admit that they are embarking on a "quest for European realms of memory," as well as for European memory in general.[5] Others have Europeanized Aleida Assmann's term "spaces of memory," and they too are still charting uncertain territory.[6]

The emergence of a "European memory," irrespective of its concrete form, is generally agreed upon as desirable by most academics and politicians. With the successful integration of Europe as its goal, European memory studies tend to come up with categories that are both political and analytical. Their normativity and often-open political involvement (advocating a mediating and reconciliatory approach) becomes evident when we look at a statement made by Bernd Faulenbach. This historian's name is associated with the famous compromise in post-unification German politics of history, the so-called Faulenbach formula, to neither relativize Nazi crimes nor trivialize Stalinist crimes in a careful calibration of totalitarianism theory.[7] In 2004 he answered affirmatively to the rhetorical question of whether creating a European memory culture was a mission.[8] This is but one of many exemplifications

---

[5] E. François, "Auf der Suche nach den europäischen Erinnerungsorten," in *Europas Gedächtnis. Das neue Europa auf der Suche zwischen nationalen Erinnerungen und gemeinsamer Identität*, edited by H. König et al. (Bielefeld: 2008), transcript, 85–104; E. François, "Auf der Suche nach dem europäischen Gedächtnis," in *Europa und die Europäer. Quellen und Essays zur modernen europäischen Geschichte*, edited by R. Hohls et al. (Stuttgart: Steiner Verlag, 2005), 250–255.

[6] K. Buchinger et al., eds., *Europäische Erinnerungsräume* (Frankfurt am Main: Campus, 2009).

[7] *Schlussbericht der Enquette-Kommission "Überwindung der Folgen der SED-Diktatur im Prozess der deutschen Einheit,"* 240, June 10, 1998, accessed August 13, 2013, http://dip21.bundestag.de/dip21/btd/13/110/1311000.pdf.

[8] B. Faulenbach, "Konkurrenz der Vergangenheiten? Die Aufarbeitung des SED-Systems im Kontext der Debatte über die jüngere deutsche Geschichte," in *1945 bis 2000. Ansichten zur deutschen Geschichte*, edited by A. Stephan (Opladen: Leske & Budrich, 2002, 17–32; and "Eine europäische Erinnerungskultur als Aufgabe? Zum Verhältnis gemeinsamer und trennender Erinnerungen," *Storia della Storiografia* 46 (2004), 205–219.

of the commonly shared hope of most scholars to see some form of European memory culture emerge. Just as the post-1945 integration process was a peace project putting an end to centuries of wars between European powers, the construction of a European memory is intended to pacify the wars of attrition among the continent's national memory cultures.

Hence what is characteristic of most of these endeavors is the casualness with which not only politicians but also academics admit and embrace the normative nature of their work. One might have thought that the legitimizing role that historians held during the formative phase of European nation-states had changed significantly towards a more critical function in society. Against this backdrop, a seemingly frivolous observation has been made: that for many of the prestigious historians and cultural scientists involved, "searching for *lieux the mémoire* can be fun," as this search is seen as "an instrument to construct [. . .] national identities."[9] The very fact that the often-advocated "European identity" and "European memory" evidently do not exist yet[10] seems to provide even stronger incentive for their architects to continue on their path.

Memory in a Post-Ideological Europe?

The formation of any dominant canon of historical narratives omits some social experiences while putting others at the center, thus producing "historical truth." Such a process can be recognized in all sorts of less assertive narratives, as well as in formerly important leitmotifs that have been "vanquished" and therefore disposed of with particular vehemence. Unless the overcome ideology and its concept of history are instrumentalized as an absolutely evil Other of the victorious model of development (such as everything connected with National Socialism[11]), its manifestations are mostly being stored in the more remote, rarely frequented repositories of latent memory.[12] One case in point: the concepts of history and future created in formerly Communist Eastern Europe, including ideas of European integration that for decades had

---

[9] E. Pfister and K. Prager, "How We Learned to Stop Worrying and Utilize European *Lieux de Mémoire* as an Historical Instrument," in *Der Donauraum. Zeitschrift des Institutes für den Donauraum und Mitteleuropa* 51/1 (2011), 21-33, here: 22 and 24.

[10] Cf. the respective Eurobarometer-surveys on questions of identity in Europe: http://ec.europa.eu/public_opinion/archives/eb/eb64/eb64_en.htm (July 3, 2009), and http://ec.europa.eu/public_opinion/archives/eb/eb60/eb60_en.htm (July 3, 2009).

[11] E. Traverso, *Gebrauchsanweisungen für die Vergangenheit: Geschichte, Erinnerung, Politik* (Münster: UNRAST 2007), 71–77.

[12] The use of storage-related metaphors calls for an emphasis on the important distinction between individual and collective memory, which will be discussed in more detail later. Paul

co-determined the political *imaginaire* of millions of Europeans and naturally did not evaporate overnight with the disappearance of the Iron Curtain. As the question of power in the creation of a collective is central, the equalization of Socialist ideas with Communism and eventually with totalitarianism—and thus the delegitimization of Socialism—is a hegemonic practice in Europe and in the West in general.

When analyzing a set of power relations, one must first ask how the stigmatization of Communism and Socialism in European history is a hegemonic practice that seeks to ever more firmly establish the unquestionable primacy of liberalism as the only non-contingent path in a teleological philosophy of history. The implication, if not the outright assertion, of a post-ideological age is part of a larger narrative of victory of the West after 1989 that casually does away with Socialism as a political ideology. Hence demanding, in the words of historian Gregor Thum, a "pan-European perspective"[13] does not mean a homogenizing discourse determined by a dominant ideology, but an open vision capable of showing those forces active in the past, even if they do not have a leading function in the present. Similar issues have been raised concerning the politics of European memory.[14]

The cultural critic Boris Buden writes of the "infantilization" of Eastern Europeans, who are deprived of the political maturity proven throughout the 1989 process, as well as the validity of their historical experience in general. They become mere apprentices on the path to democracy.[15] Buden asks: "In whose interest does this happen? Who incapacitates the actors of historical

---

Ricœur pointed out that from a phenomenological perspective we can only speak of individual memory and that collective memory is but an operative term; cf. P. Ricœur, *Das Rätsel der Vergangenheit. Erinnern–Vergessen–Verzeihen* (Göttingen: Wallstein, 2000), 79. In this sense, we should accept the notion of memory as a repository of latent residues of the past only on a collective, but not on an individual level. Individual memory would be erroneously described with the metaphor of a repository where all experiences would be stored and readily available; for a community, however, partial group memories or certain bodies of sources may function as such "repositories" from where certain contents can find their way into a historical canon.

13 G. Thum, "'Europa' im Ostblock. Weiße Flecken in der Geschichte der europäischen Integration," in *Zeithistorische Forschungen* 1/3 (2004), 379–395.

14 K. Schlögl, "Europa neu vermessen: Die Rückkehr des Ostens in den europäischen Horizont," in *Europas Gedächtnis. Das neue Europa auf der Suche zwischen nationalen Erinnerungen und gemeinsamer Identität*, edited by H. König et al. (Bielefeld: transcript, 2008), 147–168; B. Gremek, "Ost und West: Geteilte europäische Erinnerung," in *Europas Gedächtnis. Das neue Europa auf der Suche zwischen nationalen Erinnerungen und gemeinsamer Identität*, edited by H. König et al. (Bielefeld: transcript, 2008), 133–146.

15 B. Buden, *Zone des Übergangs. Vom Ende des Postkommunismus* (Frankfurt a. Main: Suhrkamp, 2009), 36–38.

change, who deprives them of their status as subjects?"[16] These questions about the power relations in the representation of contemporary European history are so important precisely because of the strategies of essentialization and dehistoricization that can be observed. If we transpose Buden's thoughts into the context of European museums, we arrive at the issue of curatorial agency, the conditions of production in museums and other institutions, public or private, as well as independent artistic practice. Which history is being told in the exhibitions of public museums? Whose experiences and/or interpretations enter into these sites of representation? Who conceives of the storylines, to whom are they directed, and which historical meaning should they be endowed with? Which historico-political relations of power are expressed in curatorial decisions?

The infantilization and incapacitation of the revolutionary subjects of 1989 aim at the classifiability of the history of Communism within a teleological world history—by sidelining it to a historical holding track, an error, an episode rather than a period in history. In the classic mode of developmentalism, this means, "Back to the start!" for all those millions who have lived in a different social system for seven or four decades, who had known different experiences of socialization. Their entire experience is often delegitimized as something to be overcome in order to be absorbed by the already (albeit not completely or perfectly) realized ideal form of human society exemplified by the democracies of Western Europe. This practice revives the Enlightenment's normative-linear concept of history, the utopic dimension of which is pragmaticized through irony, to paraphrase Boris Buden. What Buden calls ironic is the "critical distance" of Western decision-making elites rooted in their leading protagonists' recognition of existing inherent problems of market-oriented liberal democracy—and the induced delusion of greatness to embody the ideal society.[17] While some have prematurely invoked the coming of the End of History, others rightly lament the End of Utopia,[18] with the claim of the former presupposing the acceptance of the latter and essentializing the presently dominant political and social zeitgeist as non-ideological and natural.

To depict the history of Marxism (both the idea and its political application) as an historical error reveals the victors' will to power that aspires to deprive, at least in the sense of its lasting disempowerment, the overcome

---

[16] B. Buden, *Zone des Übergangs*, 43.

[17] B. Buden, *Zone des Übergangs*, 17–33.

[18] The obvious references to these two discourses on the (not-so neo-)liberal side and among the (not-so New-)Left are F. Fukuyama, *The End of History and the Last Man* (New York: The Free Press, 1992); and R. Jacoby, *The End of Utopia: Politics and Culture in an Age of Apathy* (New York: Basic Books, 1999).

Socialism of its most dangerous potency: the critical analysis of asymmetric distribution of wealth and power and the possible courses for action and social alternatives derived from it. The option to consider other social orders different from the presently dominant one, and not to rule out radical changes, distinguishes contingent and open concepts of history and society from deterministic ones (and thus, to a certain degree, from Marxism itself as post-Marxist criticism would suggest). The historical victor—the "West"—which strives to disempower the potential of the outgunned ideology proves how desperately it is fighting to maintain its hegemony. This is all the more true in a global (and, for that matter, European) constellation in which the democratic market's promises of salvation do not seem to be self-evident or infallible anymore. Post-1989 Europe—that is, the very "European Family" whose enlargeable "house" the misdirected Eastern kinship has been invited to join[19]—has equipped itself with a master narrative in the form of a salvific history: the narration of the European peace project, of irresistible economic growth, of a victory over Communism allegedly achieved through historical consistency rather than by military strength. This narrative is characterized by the high degree of inevitability innate to many neo-Hegelian diagnostics of an end of history.

This post-1989 narrative has its roots in the Cold War. Led by France, Western Europe after World War II defined itself—since the Schuman Declaration in May 1950 at the latest—as the continent of peace[20] and freedom, in the sense of pluralistic democracy[21] (with the exceptions of Spain, Portugal, and Greece) and of anti-Communism. The term "free world" (although originally coined in reference to the anti-Hitler alliance) was, in the Truman terminology, soon to describe every country on Earth except those of the Socialist bloc, thus including non-democratic countries; e.g., in the Middle East and in Latin America. Conflating Fascism and Communism, it constituted a

---

[19] F. Stern, "The Common House of Europe," in *The New York Review of Books* 36/19, December 7, 1989.

[20] "The contribution which an organized and living Europe can bring to civilisation is indispensable to the maintenance of peaceful relations." Cf. K. Rothschild, "Peace and Security via Interdependence and Cooperation in Europe," in *Österreichische Zeitschrift für Außenpolitik* 19/1 (1979), 14–25; D. Krüger, *Sicherheit durch Integration? Die wirtschaftliche und politische Integration Westeuropas 1947 bis 1957* (Munich: Oldenbourg Wissenschaftsverlag, 2003).

[21] In Art. 1 of the 1973 Document on European Identity, the nine EC states declared: "Sharing as they do the same attitudes to life, based on a determination to build a society which measures up to the needs of the individual, they are determined to defend the principles of representative democracy, of the rule of law, of social justice—which is the ultimate goal of economic progress—and of respect for human rights." It is interesting that the document refers to the signing parties as the "Nine European States"—implicitly binding Europeanness to this "core Europe."

"bridge by which the USA could pass from the anti-Fascism of the wartime coalition to the anti-totalitarianism of the Cold War era,"[22] a strategy to which Western European countries eagerly subscribed. The sphere of influence of Stalin's Soviet Union thereby became the factual Non-Europe—even though Western European media and public opinion usually distinguished between the regimes and the peoples governed by them. Defining market capitalism as the "European social system" practically excluded Communist regimes from this Europe. Furthermore, the "otherness" of Eastern European Communist societies was additionally crystallized by Orientalizing these countries[23]—an externalization strategy well practiced since the Enlightenment.[24] The Austrian historian Andrea Komlosy thus wrote: "The East of Europe does in large parts not belong to this Europe [Western Europe as a center of global economy]."[25]

Such a perception does not make it too surprising that the political and academic literature after 1989 frequently features the ideas of the "Europeanization" of Eastern Europe[26] and of its "Return to Europe."[27] Eastern European history is being interpreted as a "Soviet 'non-European' past" in

[22] D. Geppert, "'Proclaim Liberty Throughout all the Land': Berlin and the Symbolism of the Cold War," in *The Postwar Challenge: Cultural, Social, and Political Change in Western Europe, 1945–1958* (Studies of the German Historical Institute, London), edited by D. Geppert (Oxford: Oxford University Press, 2003), 339–363, here: 348.

[23] P. Chilton, *Security Metaphors: Cold War Discourse from Containment to Common House* (New York: Peter Lang, 1996).

[24] L. Wolff, *Inventing Eastern Europe: The Map of Civilization on the Mind of the Enlightenment* (Stanford: Stanford University Press, 1994); M. Todorova, *Imagining the Balkans* (Oxford: Oxford University Press, 1997); V. Goldsworthy, *Inventing Ruritania: The Imperialism of the Imagination* (New Haven: Yale University Press, 1998).

[25] A. Komlosy, "Der Marshall-Plan und der Eiserne Vorhang in Österreich," in *80 Dollar. 50 Jahre ERP-Fonds und Marshall-Plan in Österreich 1948–1998*, edited by G. Bischof and D. Stiefel (Vienna: Überreuter, 1999), 261–297, here: 266.

[26] From a broad range of publications, cf. e.g., J. Olsen, "The Many Faces of Europeanization," *Journal of Common Market Studies* 40/5 (2002), 921–952; *The Politics of Europeanization*, edited by K. Featherstone and C. Radaelli (Oxford: Oxford University Press, 2003); J. DeBardeleben, "Introduction," in *Soft or Hard Borders? Managing the Divide in an Enlarged Europe*, edited by J. DeBardeleben (Aldershot: Ashgate, 2005), 1–22.

[27] J. Batt, *The New Slovakia: National Identity, Political Integration and the Return to Europe* (London: Royal Institute of International Affairs, 1996); *Polens Rückkehr nach Europa. Geistige Überwindung des Kommunismus*, edited by P. Eisenmann and B. Rill (Regensburg: Friedrich Pustet, 1993); G. Santangelo, *The Baltic States Return to Europe: The Baltic Re-integration Problem between the Nordic and the EU Option* (=Jean Monet Working Paper No. 11, September 1997), University of Catania 1997, accessed September 9, 2013, http://www.fscpo.unict.it/EuroMed/jmwp11.htm; A. M. Smith, *The Return to Europe: The Reintegration of Eastern Europe into the European Economy* (Basingstoke: Palgrave Macmillan, 2000); H.-J. Wagener, *Rückkehr nach Europa* (Frankfurt a.d.O.: Frankfurter Institut für Transformationsstudien, 1999).

which, as Joan DeBardeleben remarked, it was not the idea of Marxism as such which was banned from the perspective of post-war peace and liberty values, but its authoritarian and totalitarian implementation.[28] However, given the dramatic changes not only of political structures but also of the economic mechanisms of the social distribution of wealth in the ex-communist EU-debutants, this assessment has to be questioned. Despite its historical origin, the allegedly failed Socialist utopia of justice did not rank among the conversion criteria of the transformation period. The Copenhagen Criteria did not allude to social questions.[29] But six years later the Amsterdam Treaty made the problem of social marginalization a topic of European integration. In connection with the crisis of the EU constitution, the "social question" seems to reestablish itself in the catalog of European values and to soften the neoliberal paradigm of the 1990s from a bottom-up perspective. The swift mutability of elements of European identity indicates that much attention has to be given to the diachronic development lines of our object of research.

After 1989 the East-West borderline of inclusion and exclusion experienced an interesting transformation. This had to do with the fact that after the end of the Cold War the "self-conception" of the European integration process ran into a crisis of definition. Initially the EU's reaction to the challenges of enlargement seemed more pragmatic than visionary. The Schengen-Agreement had created the possibility of free citizen movement between the signatory states, whose number grew rapidly. With the initiation of accession negotiations with former COMECON countries and the states succeeding former Yugoslavia, the EU's external border was projected farther to the east, while the Schengen border was first drawn along the former Iron Curtain, and remained there ever after the first wave of accession in 2004. With this, a thrice-tiered Europe was established: Schengen, EU, and non-EU. Concerning the further liquidation of the EU's inner borders and the localization of its external frontiers, two issues are of high relevance.

First, as Malcolm Anderson wrote, "The intention of the Schengen system was to [provide anxious public opinion with] 'compensation' for the

---

[28] J. DeBardeleben, "Introduction," 4.

[29] "Membership requires that the candidate country has achieved stability of institutions guaranteeing democracy, the rule of law, human rights and respect for and protection of minorities, the existence of a functioning market economy as well as the capacity to cope with competitive pressure and market forces within the Union. Membership presupposes the candidate's ability to take on the obligations of membership including adherence to the aims of political, economic and monetary union." Cf. European Council in Copenhagen, *Conclusions of the Presidency (21–22 June 1993)*, SN 180/93 (Brussels: Council of the European Communities, 1993), 10–15.

security 'deficit' allegedly caused by the abolition of border controls through a series of new cooperative security measures."[30] The stricter controls at the external borders of the supranational European block had to calm Western European citizens who were unsettled by the drastic changes brought about by economic globalization and liberalization and by European integration. Second, the governing of external border control by a supranational[31] agreement meant that the EU for the first time assumed territorial competences. In connection with the EU occupying the term "Europe," this implied a highly explosive consequence for political imagery: "Europeans who are not citizens of EU member states are no longer simply excluded from a set of nation-states: they are excluded from a unit which goes by the name of 'Europe.'" "Schengenized," according to Timothy Snyder, means "excluded from Europe."[32]

This political history of bordering the identity of a victorious anti-Communist European peace project created a corresponding historical practice of disempowerment, a decisive dimension of which is the reduction of Socialist history to its repressive elements; that is, equalizing Communism with Stalinism or with Mao's Cultural Revolution. And yet, by no means do I want to imply that all "Western" interpretations of European history remain at the level of extreme simplification. On the contrary, the liberal doctrine of pluralism has also produced a demand for historico-political polyphony. Historiography and museums can be understood as condensed fields of observation for discursive processes of construction that ultimately can also be found in the political rhetoric of accession speeches or public retrospections on the occasion of official anniversaries, among others. It is this very commitment to polyphony that we can recognize in the debates surrounding the House of European History, for example, but these debates also clearly indicate how this diversity in the representation of historical experience is meant to serve a specific political universalism.

Another example would be the emphasis on totalitarianism theory–a theory often leading to the relative equalization of National Socialism and Communism–implicit in the memory politics of the European Commission, such as the international traveling exhibition "Totalitarianism in Europe," curated under the auspices of the Commission's Platform of European Memory and

---

[30] M. Anderson, "The Transformation of Border Controls: A European Precedent?," in *The Wall around the West: State Borders and Immigration Controls in North America and Europe*, edited by P. Andreas and T. Snyder (Lanham, MD: Rowman & Littlefield, 2000), 15–29, here: 21.

[31] And binding for all accession candidates, as opposed to "old" EU members like Great Britain.

[32] Both quotes: T. Snyder, "Conclusion: The Wall around the West," in *The Wall around the West*, 219–227, here: 223.

Conscience. The same international network of memorial institutions and museums recently protested against the appointment of a Communist as director of the Institute for the Study of Totalitarian Regimes in Prague, while it has not formulated any similar criticism against the controversial Institute of National Remembrance in Poland.[33]

Public representations of this interpretation of history produce a particularly strong claim to validity in museums and historical exhibitions. In almost all public museums in post-communist countries, the permanent exhibits on history were created in the spirit of "transitionology."[34] Hence their storylines often follow the characteristics of anti-communist triumphalism described before: delegitimization, relativization of potential social advantages of Socialism (education, position of women on the labor market, distributional justice), and criminalization. Museologists and historians have analyzed these features of post-communist depictions of Communism, but rarely criticized them. Again, the normative assumption of the need for a new European master narrative seems to blot out analytical reservations. Rather, case studies commonly referred to as standard works tend to affirm these story lines.[35] At best, critique is formulated in view of particularly extreme representations of revisionism or instrumentalization of history.

As far as the official or socially hegemonic politics of history are concerned, the history of Stalinist repression and Communist regimes is prominently represented in many parts of Eastern Europe as one of the enormous experiences of evil, often placed side by side with the Nazi-occupation and the Holocaust. Commonly cited examples include the House of Terror in Budapest and the Museum of the Occupation of Latvia: the first shows the pitfalls of displaying historical violence in a blatant and sensational manner, while the second ascribes to the crimes of National Socialism a lesser horror than to Stalinism; and both—although the Hungarian case in a more extreme way—construct powerful stories of collective victimhood and national suffering. Leading Western narratives tend to contribute to a homogenizing interpretation of this past as one of suffering and despair, although generally opposing any analogies with the Holocaust. The discussion about the Ukrainian term "Holodomor" indicates the strong Western European reservations

---

[33] Platform for European Memory and Conscience, *Letter to the Institute for the Study of Totalitarian Regimes*, August 15, 2013, accessed October 6, 2013, http://www.memoryandconscience.eu/wp-content/uploads/2013/08/Letter-to-USTR-Council-15.8.2013.pdf.

[34] S. Cohen, *Failed Crusade: America and the Tragedy of Post-Communist Russia* (New York: Norton, 2001), 23–31.

[35] *Der Kommunismus im Museum. Formen der Auseinandersetzung in Deutschland und Mitteleuropa*, edited by V. Knigge and U. Mählert (Cologne: Böhlau, 2005).

against concepts of genocidal history that seem to resonate with comparisons or relativizations of the crimes against European Jewry.

Although these remarks might indicate a homogeneous discourse among decisive political and intellectual elites in Eastern and Western Europe, such an always-partial consensus ends beyond the realm of anti-Communism and falls apart when it comes to the interpretation of the Second World War and the Holocaust. Issues of co-responsibility and victimhood have triggered fervid controversies, but have also raised questions about the role of Eastern European agency in the events of 1989. Again, the House of European History and the German influence on its original curatorial concept provide a perfect example.

When the Committee of Experts commissioned by the European Parliament presented its "Conceptual Basis for the House of European History" in October 2008, critical voices followed suit. On December 3, 2008, several Polish members of the European Parliament, under the leadership of the parliament's vice chairman Adam Bielan, sent a letter to President Pöttering naming twenty-two of the "most serious omissions and misinterpretations of the said document." These reservations solicited further emphasis on Catholicism as a foundation of Europe, the Polish role in the defeat of the Ottoman troops in Vienna 1683, stronger emphasis on "Bolshevik atrocities," the recalibration of the impact of Polish troops in the Second World War, and the call to omit the deportation of Germans from Eastern Europe "if mass Nazi and Soviet deportations of other nations, both during and after World War Two, are not mentioned." And in point two, the undersigned called for "a special attention to the historical sensitivity of smaller nations of Europe."[36]

Much of this criticism was directed against the dominant role of Germany in the composition of the European historical narrative, and regardless of the domestic Polish hegemony expressed in this letter—after all, Polish historian Włodzimierz Borodziej[37] was part of the Committee of Experts and therefore co-author of the criticized concept—in the context of international debates about European memory, Polish protagonists pretended to defend

---

[36] A. Bielan et al., *Letter to Hans-Gert Pöttering*, Brussels, December 4, 2008. This criticism has since been taken up and supported by anti-European parties. Nigel Farage, member of the European Parliament for the UK Independence Party, declared that "the rewriting of history has some dangerous precedents"; cf. B. Waterfield, "Anger at Plans for Official European History," in *The Telegraph*, January 2, 2009, accessed September 22, 2013, http://www.telegraph.co.uk/news/worldnews/europe/4077245/Anger-at-plans-for-official-European-history.html.

[37] Borodziej himself had been the object of an anti-Communist witch-hunt accusing him and his family of collaboration with the Communist secret service.

the marginalized, subaltern voices in Europe against the hegemonic conductors in Berlin and Paris, as Maria Mälksoo notes:

> "Polish and Baltic political elites' endeavor to wrench the 'European mnemonical map' apart in order to become more congruent with the different historical experiences within the enlarged EU, as well as to gain EU support for influencing Russia to acknowledge its responsibility for the crimes of the communist regimes in Eastern Europe and the Soviet occupation in the Baltic states, demonstrate the curious trademark of their politics of becoming European: a combination of simultaneously seeking recognition from and exercising resistance to the hegemonic 'core European' narrative of what 'Europe' is all about."[38]

From this perspective, the mnemonic hegemon is indeed identifiable as the dominant Western powers within the European Union, with the insurrection against it arising from the East. Eastern struggle for change in an allegedly emerging "European memory culture" concerns itself with the breaking of this hegemony in order to transform Eastern European societies into real partners and actors in this culture, instead of, once again, into subaltern satellites. It is interesting to note that, in the author's opinion, the national politics of history in Poland and the Baltic states do in fact represent the experience of their peoples. The individual mass memory in Eastern Europe is neither voiceless nor passive but has found an anti-hegemonic avant-garde in its governments.

This confrontation is not limited to the issue of World War II. While the interpretative predominance about historical responsibilities in World War II and the Holocaust may be the most highly valued currency in Europe's historico-political debates, the question of agency in the events of 1989 is even more significant in terms of the current political processes. The history of anti-regime protests in the German Democratic Republic and their alleged causal function for the implosion of Soviet power in Eastern Europe is a case in point. In a recent book on the representation of Europe in museums and exhibitions, the authors emphasize how this focus intends to put Germany, once again, at the center of events in Europe, thus ignoring the much more polycentric and complex developments that led to the demise of the Iron Curtain. Polish historians rightly stress the important contribution of

---

[38] M. Mälksoo, "The Memory Politics of Becoming European: The East European Subalterns and the Collective Memory of Europe," in *European Journal of International Relations* 15/4 (2009), 653–680, here: 655.

Solidarnosć to this process, and similar trends of reevaluation come from Hungary and especially the Soviet Union itself.[39]

One question of German dominion over European narratives has been uttered by several analysts and could be synthesized into a bipolar equation: How does the historico-political tendency that Ute Frevert has called the "Europeanization of Germany's twentieth century"[40] relate to the "nightmare" of a Germanization of European memory?[41] As the above-mentioned Polish example shows, the "German Industrial Norm" for coming to terms with the past (Timothy Garton Ash)—now extended to the production design of European memory—does not meet with unanimous joy. Some have tried to explain German interpretative power over these issues not only through its experience with Holocaust remembrance, but also with the fact that German *lieux de mémoire* (as Central European) are more transnational than, for example, those of France.[42]

Nevertheless, Jan-Werner Müller's thoughts transcend the Germanization trope and tackle an issue that seems much more relevant and interesting for politico-historical analysis: a class-sensitive gaze at the question of whose experience is being incorporated into cultural memory and whose is not. Although Müller does not explicitly write of class, he does indeed differentiate between collective or national memory, on the one hand, and individual mass memory, on the other.[43] And while he himself confesses to be mostly interested in "collective memories and public claims about these memories—not private, unarticulated or even involuntary memories"[44]—unlike many of his colleagues he at least acknowledges that historical experience does indeed define the quality of memory.[45] The following pages are dedicated to this neglected issue.

---

[39] W. Kaiser et al., *Europa ausstellen. Das Museum als Praxisfeld der Europäisierung* (Cologne: Böhlau, 2012), 146.

[40] U. Frevert, "Europeanizing Germany's Twentieth Century," in *History & Memory* 17 (Spring/Summer 2005), 87–116.

[41] J.-W. Müller, "On 'European Memory': Some Conceptual and Normative Remarks," in *A European Memory?*, edited by M. Pakier and B. Stråth, 25–37.

[42] E. Pfister and K. Prager, "How We Learned to Stop Worrying," 25–28.

[43] J.-W. Müller, "On 'European Memory,'" 29.

[44] J.-W. Müller, "On 'European Memory,'" 29.

[45] A decade before the previously cited essay, Jan-Werner Müller dedicated the better part of a collective volume to this juxtaposition: J.-W. Müller, "Introduction," in *Memory and Power in Post-War Europe*, edited by J.-W. Müller (Cambridge: Cambridge University Press, 2002), 1–35. In this book, Timothy Snyder's article seems to have had the most impact on the distinction of these two forms of memory: T. Snyder, "Memory of Sovereignty and Sovereignty over Memory: Poland, Lithuania, and Ukraine, 1939–1999," in J.-W. Müller, *Memory and Power in Post-War Europe*, 39–58.

Historical Experience and the Material Dimension of Memory

In the controversies about European memory, Aleida Assmann formulated a mediating response: dialogical memory, defined as the "politics of memory between two or more states that are connected with each other through a common history of violence, recognize their own part in the traumatized history of the other and empathically include the suffering of the other in their own memory."[46] While this model does explain the historico-political dynamics between nation-states, it remains at the level of active politics of history and excludes their interaction with those communicative memories that are not politically articulate. Aleida and Jan Assmann have been aware of the importance of the contingent crossings between communicative and cultural memory since the beginning of their work on the topic. Regarding Holocaust remembrance, Aleida Assmann points out that "the eyewitnesses' memory of their experiences, if it is not to be lost to posterity, must be translated into the cultural memory of future generations."[47]

This categorical imperative for the memory of the Holocaust and of other histories of genocide and repression basically applies to all representations of the past. Jan Assmann calls this process "formation:" "The objectivation or crystallization of communicated meaning and collectively shared knowledge is a prerequisite of its transmission in the culturally institutionalized heritage of a society."[48] And elsewhere he asserted, "what is at stake is the transformation of communicative [. . .] memory into cultural [. . .] memory."[49] There is no doubt that the dynamics of mnemonic selection in the canonization of the past have been recognized and addressed by both scholars as "creating tension and transition between the various poles."[50]

---

[46] A. Assmann, *Auf dem Weg zu einer europäischen Gedächtniskultur: Lecture on the occasion of receiving the Paul Watzlawick Price*, 18, March 30, 2009, accessed August 2, 2013, http://www.watzlawickehrenring.at/loadfile.php?f=5808.

[47] A. Assmann, *Erinnerungsräume. Formen und Wandlungen des kulturellen Gedächtnisses* (Munich: Beck, 1999), 15. English translation quoted from: D. Levy and N. Sznaider, *The Holocaust and Memory in a Global Age* (Philadelphia: Temple University Press, 2006), 34.

[48] J. Assmann, "Memory and Cultural Identity," in *Cultural History/Cultural Studies = New German Critique* 65 (Spring/Summer 1995), 125–133, here: 130. The German original was published in 1988.

[49] J. Assmann, "Die Katastrophe des Vergessens. Das Deuteronomium als Paradigma kultureller Mnemotechnik," in *Mnemosyne. Formen und Funktionen der kulturellen Erinnerung*, edited by A. Assmann and D. Harth (Frankfurt: Suhrkamp, 1991), 337–355, here: 343. English translation quoted from: D. Levy and N. Sznaider, *The Holocaust*, 33.

[50] J. Assmann, "Communicative and Cultural Memory," 113.

Nevertheless it is noteworthy that in Jan Assmann's famous model, the aspect of transmission is still associated with a "floating gap." This notion, although meant to describe a group's or society's vanishing memory of a certain period of the middle-term past (as opposed to its rich memory of the immediate and long-gone pasts), also seems to indicate a sort of cultural black box moving through time, in which experience is subject to veiled processes of transformation that escape our analysis. The concept of mnemonic hegemony can be used to unfold this box into a field of agency and emphasize its political nature.

I am certainly not the first to suggest this, and many groundbreaking historical thinkers and philosophers have ventured into this difficult terrain. But so far we have been lacking an operational memory theory that simultaneously highlights discursive agency in specific political contexts (interests), the public adscription of narrative credibility, and access to media and spheres of social knowledge production and signification; that tackles not only the competitive relations between hegemonic and proactively counter-hegemonic agencies often described as memory wars, but also the coexisting communities of passive remembrance; that describes the interactions between these fields; and that thus allows for a more embracing analysis of the dialectics between memory and politics.

I encountered several contradictions and limitations of current historico-political concepts in my research both in Central America and in Europe. One seemingly evident observation did not cease to fascinate me: What is transformed or incorporated into the great narrations that explain history to later generations is much less the experience of the majorities (social and everyday history) than military antagonisms and diplomatic crisis events. So, while cultural memory enjoys a certain (albeit never unchallengeable) stability, communicative memory on the other hand, although passively powerful at the time, faces the challenge of a form of social selection in which it rarely participates actively. Historical experiences and their immediate representations produce frames of communicative memory that may be specific to a small town, but may also span over a whole continent. In neither case, however, is the survival of such a historical perception guaranteed or even likely. If it is not picked up by a modern Homer—and could (or should) anthropologists, sociologists, or oral historians assume this role?—the power of the narration ends with the lifespan of its carriers.

It is such a process that I observed between 2005 and 2010, when I designed and directed a project on different representations of European post-1945 history: the "many memories of the Cold War" in Austria, the Czech Republic, Germany, Hungary, Italy, Poland, Romania, Slovakia, and Slovenia, as well as, on a preparatory level at the time, in Bulgaria and Turkey.[51] We conducted hundreds of oral history interviews and collected contemporary media sources and archival documents in order to analyze everyday history and the construction of memory in different public spheres and social realities east and west of the former Iron Curtain. One, although by no means the only, particularly significant feature of the extremely widespread strands of social memory was that the patterns contradicted some of the eminent narratives on the history of the Cold War and its aftermath.

To begin with, the very term "Cold War" was not a very widespread designation among our interviewees in the West and completely absent from the *imaginaire* of formerly Communist societies. Nor did the period's prevalent representations—in history books, TV documentaries, etc.—as a period of constant crises and/or the struggle of democratic versus repressive regimes structure the signifying narratives that we identified in our interviews. Instead, these narrations were endowed with meaning mostly by accounts of stability, continuity, and options to accommodate oneself in a given situation. Ideological binaries were less important for collective distinction and othering than the ethno-national conflicts dating back at least to the nineteenth century.

Evidently, personal experience had a bigger structuring impact than big politics; thus, the grand communication events of the Cold War (the Berlin Crises of 1948 and 1961, the Budapest uprising of 1956, the Prague Spring in 1968, for example) were hardly mentioned, and the turning point of 1989 itself received surprisingly little attention in our interviews.[52] While some of these findings, such as the importance of personal experience in life stories, may not be surprising, the far-ranging difference (albeit not necessarily dissent) from the dominant historical accounts of this period demands attention—and all the more so as other research endeavors have produced similar results, even if the researchers have not always emphasized these contradictions in their conclusions,[53] while others have done so:

> In a similar way [as it may contribute to the relativization of quantitative sociological findings] ethnographic research can

[51] Cf. http://www.bertholdmolden.net/index.php?/projekte/ (accessed September 24, 2013); for later developments cf. http://ehp.lbg.ac.at/node/375 (accessed September 24, 2013).

[52] B. Molden, "The Cold War in the European Memory Matrix," in *Clashes in European Memory: The Case of Communist Repression and the Holocaust*, edited by M. Blaive et al. (Piscataway, NJ: Transaction, 2011), 212–227.

[53] Cf., e.g., *Living (with) Borders: Identity Discourses on East-West Borders in Europe*, edited by U. Meinhof (Aldershot: Ashgate, 2002); *Post-Communist Nostalgia*, edited by M. Todorova and Z. Gille (New York: Berghahn, 2010); Pakier and Stråth, *A European Memory?*; *Remembering Communism: Genres of Representation*, edited by M. Todorova (New York: Social Science Research Council, 2010).

> question some *topoi* in the borderland discourse of political elites or hint at their collision with the everyday experiences of those who live in these borderlands.[54]

Indeed, several contradictions become visible if we juxtapose empirical studies in social and cultural history with the official politics of history of the European Union and its member states. The combination of some factors mentioned in the second section of this essay—the all-embracing criminalization of Communism and the disempowerment of the subjects formerly living under its rule—implies the collective and involuntary victimization of all these subjects (except those actively collaborating with the repressive system). However, contrary to this tendency, research on this subject has for some time found that this victimization is at odds with many individual and group memories of state Socialism.[55] A recent study of historical memory among Slovenian textile workers illustrates that the history of state Socialism in Yugoslavia (as well as elsewhere in East and Southeastern Europe) is highly complex and cannot be reduced to simple formulas:

> Socialism as remembered by workers is not a story of the former political system. Memories of everyday socialist life have obviously been depoliticized [. . .]. Most people miss the 'good, old days,' but that does not mean that they identify with the politics of the former Socialist Federal Republic of Yugoslavia. [. . .] This type of social memory is inspired not by abstract national interests but rather because people feel that their values have been undermined and they seek justice.[56]

Similar assessments can be found in other articles in two recent volumes edited by Maria Todorova, assessments that also rebut the common simplification of positive memories of Socialism as "Eastalgia" among "modernization losers."[57] But this knowledge not withstanding, some of the most influential

---

[54] P. Lozoviuk, "Einleitung," in *Grenzgebiet als Forschungsfeld. Aspekte der ethnografischen und kulturhistorischen Erforschung des Grenzlandes*, edited by P. Lozoviuk, Schriften zur sächsischen Geschichte und Volkskunde 29 (Leipzig: Leipziger Universitätsverlag, 2009), 7–14, here: 12.

[55] Long before the above-cited more recent studies, a groundbreaking work in this regard was: L. Niethammer et al., *Die volkseigene Erfahrung. Eine Archäologie des Lebens in der Industrieprovinz der DDR. 30 biographische Eröffnungen* (Berlin: Rohwolt, 1991).

[56] N. Vodopivec, "Past for the Present: The Social Memory of Textile Workers in Slovenia," in Todorova, *Remembering Communism*, 213–234, here: 228–229.

[57] Todorova, *Remembering Communism*; and Todorova and Gille, *Post-Communist Nostalgia*.

public intellectuals in Western Europe subscribe to such a simplifying narrative, as illustrated by the following quote of Claus Leggewie catering to the needs of EU identity construction:

> For Eastern Europe this perspective is tinged by misery and envy, since the success and happiness of the West were qualified by the failures and unhappiness on the other side of the Iron Curtain during the Cold War. We can hardly claim that the opening toward the East since 2004 has already healed this gap. But neither should we hesitate to build a museum of Europe that broaches the issue of this success story.[58]

Critical analysts have shown that such outright mnemonic-historical corroborations of a political agenda through "success stories" penned or curated by professional academic authorities serve hegemonic purposes and intend to "draw a line under agonistic struggles and conflicting interpretations."[59] Instead of subscribing to the grandiose top-down project of creating a European memory, I suggest we try to widen our gaze and include bottom-up dynamics, even if it turns out to be methodologically challenging.

Conclusion

So, what to expect from the House of European History and similar central representations of European history? First, there is the question of their penetrating power. Kaiser, Krankenhagen, and Poehls take a somewhat ambivalent position on the capability of grand international museum projects to build binding identity-markers of European integration. On the one hand, they claim that "only grand new museum projects like the Musée [del Europe] and the HEH can develop new master narratives like those of integration as the third phase of European unity and culmination point of European history,"[60] while on the other they assure us that "grand projects like the HEH only have a limited potential reach anyway."[61]

---

[58] C. Leggewie, "The Seven Circles of Pan-European Memory," in *Social Research* 75/1 (Spring 2008), 217–234, here: 231.

[59] R. Wodak and J. Richardson, "On the Politics of Memory (or not)," in *Critical Discourse Studies* 6/4 (November 2009), 231–235, here: 231.

[60] Kaiser et al., *Europa ausstellen*, 151.

[61] Kaiser et al., *Europa ausstellen*, 24.

This two-sided analysis reveals a conundrum of the many institutions involved in inventing a supranational tradition, or to put it less pointedly, institutions that cater to the growing demand for a sense-making explanatory narrative of the process of cohesion among formerly very antagonistic actors in the arena of European politics. This exhibitionary construction process[62] is not just a top-down affair coordinated by EU politicians; it rather takes place on several overlapping and mutually entwined fields of cultural politics and includes local, national, and regional museums and temporary exhibitions.

The most pressing question, however, appears to be about whose demands really are met by the dominant narratives of EUro-history. Analytic overviews certainly suggest that cultural Europeanization and the creation of a transnational cohesive narrative of European history are tasks set by European decision-making elites, both on economic-political and cultural levels and including national elites who may well oscillate between anti-European sentiments and pro-integration stances depending on their tactical position in their national arenas. Anti-European populism in the form of externalizing responsibility for issues of economic or cultural insecurity may answer to the growing anxiety in European populations regarding the increasing awareness of crisis in Europe.

On the other hand, national political elites (center conservative and center-left parties equally so, while the radicalized political class of Greece currently seems to break out of that hegemonic assumption and consider other paths) seem convinced that there is no reasonable economic alternative to European integration. It is therefore not surprising that one of the most attentive observers of European history, Tony Judt, had a rather skeptical perception of a "European memory" early in the process of its construction: "From Spain to Lithuania the transition from past to present is being recalibrated in the name of a 'European' idea which is itself a historical and illusory product, with different meanings in different places."[63]

When analyzing European history politics in hegemonic terms, the question will arise whether or not the European Union, the Commission, the Parliament, or the Council embody a "mnemonic hegemon." Obviously, a simple yes would not do justice to the complexity of relations of mnemo-hegemonic forces in Europe, nor would a simple no. In 2000, the historian Bo Stråth argued that the construction of the multiple discourses (rather than a

---

[62] In the broader sense of Tony Bennett's "exhibitionary complex"; cf. T. Bennett, "The Exhibitionary Complex," in *New Formations* 4 (1988), 73–102.

[63] T. Judt, "The Past is Another Country: Myth and Memory in Postwar Europe," in *Daedalus* 121/4 (1992), 83–118, here 112.

clearly describable region, people, or political system) that constitute Europe "cannot be understood simply in terms of hegemony or something that can easily be defined. The concept of hegemony is just as burdened by ideology, by an invisible hierarchy of values, as the system it pretends to demystify. Who defines the poles of the hegemony? Constructed Europe is contradictory and ambiguous."[64]

Although I agree with Bo Stråth's interpretation of "Europe" as a polyphonic discourse, I think that his assessment underrates the importance of the material level of hegemony and, as it were, of historical discourse. In historico-political hegemony theory, this material structure would imply both the power structures in a given society, including their relations to specific historical narrations, and the experience of living in a specific context at a specific time. While the former mainly determine the politics of history and relations between their actors, the latter is specifically important for the constitution of communicative memory outside the realm of the active politics of history. Hence, when analyzing European history politics in hegemonic terms, the question arises whether or not the European Union, the Commission, the Parliament, or the Council embody a "mnemonic hegemon." To answer it—and at the same time Stråth's question concerning the poles of hegemony—one has to look at their inter-relations to the European states, economic elites, and cultural power centers of knowledge-production. And eventually, to the often passive spheres of communicative memory.

---

[64] B. Stråth, "Introduction: Europe as a Discourse," in *Europe and the Other and Europe as the Other*, edited by B. Stråth (Brussels: Peter Lang, 2000), 13–44, here: 39. Ten years after the aforementioned quote, Stråth, together with Małgorzata Pakier, wrote in a less disallowing manner about hegemony: "Collective memories are not unequivocal but rather a product of social forces. Emerging in social contention and debate, such constructs reflect power relationships, which might take on more or less hegemonic proportions with a corresponding impact on recollections. However, even when the collective memory seems hegemonic, it remains a discourse without essence." (M. Pakier and B. Stråth, "Introduction: A European Memory?," in *A European Memory?*, edited by M. Pakier and B. Stråth: 1–20, here: 7. Despite their conception of memory in terms of power relations, and their using rather than dismissing the concept of hegemony, the authors employ the term still very much in the way of Stråth's constructivist argument a decade earlier. When he and Pakier assert a hegemonic/counter-hegemonic quality to the constructed and contentious nature of social remembrance, they think of it as "usually politically instrumentalized." This hint to political instrumentalization emphasizes an obvious point but, in my opinion, misses a more important one: rather than being "nothing but a discourse about past events and how to order and interpret them" (M. Pakier and B. Stråth, "Introduction," 7) the concept of hegemonic relations is strongly associated with the material conditions that coin the configurations of social forces in any particular historical period. And they do affect the relations of power.

BIBLIOGRAPHY

Anderson, Malcolm. "The Transformation of Border Controls: A European Precedent?" In *The Wall around the West: State Borders and Immigration Controls in North America and Europe*, edited by Peter Andreas and Timothy Snyder, 15–29. Lanham, MD: Rowman & Littlefield, 2000.

Assmann, Aleida. *Auf dem Weg zu einer europäischen Gedächtniskultur: Lecture on the Occasion of Receiving the Paul Watzlawick Prize*, 18, March 30, 2009, accessed August 2, 2013, http://www.watzlawickehrenring.at/loadfile.php?f=5808.

———. *Erinnerungsräume: Formen und Wandlungen des kulturellen Gedächtnisses*. Munich: Beck, 1999.

Assmann, Jan. "Die Katastrophe des Vergessens: Das Deuteronomium als Paradigma kultureller Mnemotechnik." In *Mnemosyne. Formen und Funktionen der kulturellen Erinnerung*, edited by Aleida Assmann and Dietrich Harth. Frankfurt: Suhrkamp, 1991.

———. "Memory and Cultural Identity." *Cultural History/Cultural Studies = New German Critique* 65 (Spring/Summer 1995): 125–133.

Batt, Judy. *The New Slovakia: National Identity, Political Integration and the Return to Europe*. London: Royal Institute of International Affairs, 1996.

Bennett, Tony. "The Exhibitionary Complex." *New Formations* 4 (1988): 73–102.

Buchinger, Kirstin, Claire Cantet, and Jakob Vogel, eds. *Europäische Erinnerungsräume*. Frankfurt am Main: Campus, 2009.

Buden, Boris. *Zone des Übergangs: Vom Ende des Postkommunismus*. Frankfurt am Main: Suhrkamp, 2009.

Chilton, Paul A. *Security Metaphors: Cold War Discourse from Containment to Common House*. New York: Peter Lang, 1996.

Cohen, Stephen F. *Failed Crusade: America and the Tragedy of Post-Communist Russia*. New York: Norton, 2001.

DeBardeleben, Joan. "Introduction." In *Soft or Hard Borders? Managing the Divide in an Enlarged Europe*, edited by Joan DeBardeleben, 1–22. Aldershot, GB: Ashgate, 2005.

Eisenmann, Peter, and Bernd Rill. *Polens Rückkehr nach Europa: Geistige Überwindung des Kommunismus*. Regensburg: Friedrich Pustet, 1993.

Faulenbach, Bernd. "Eine europäische Erinnerungskultur als Aufgabe? Zum Verhältnis gemeinsamer und trennender Erinnerungen." *Storia della Storiografia* 46 (2004): 205–219.

———. "Konkurrenz der Vergangenheiten? Die Aufarbeitung des SED-Systems im Kontext der Debatte über die jüngere deutsche Geschichte." In *1945 bis 2000: Ansichten zur deutschen Geschichte*, edited by Annegret Stephan, 17–32. Opladen, Germany: Leske & Budrich, 2002.

Featherstone, Kevin, and Claudio Radaelli, eds. *The Politics of Europeanization*. Oxford: Oxford University Press, 2003.

François, Etienne. "Auf der Suche nach den europäischen Erinnerungsorten." In *Europas Gedächtnis: Das neue Europa auf der Suche zwischen nationalen Erinnerungen und gemeinsamer Identität*, edited by Helmut König, Julia Schmidt, and Manfred Sicking, 85–104. Bielefeld: 2008. Transcript.

———. "Auf der Suche nach dem europäischen Gedächtnis." In *Europa und die Europäer: Quellen und Essays zur modernen europäischen Geschichte*, edited by Rüdiger Hohls, Iris Schröder, and Hannes Siegrist, 250–255. Stuttgart: Steiner Verlag, 2005.

Frevert, Ute. "Europeanizing Germany's Twentieth Century." *History & Memory* 17 (Spring/Summer 2005): 87–116.

Fukuyama, Francis. *The End of History and the Last Man*. New York: The Free Press, 1992.

Geppert, Dominik. "'Proclaim Liberty Throughout all the Land': Berlin and the Symbolism of the Cold War." In *The Postwar Challenge: Cultural, Social, and Political Change in Western Europe, 1945–1958*, edited by Dominik Geppert, 339–363. Studies of the German Historical Institute, London. Oxford: Oxford University Press, 2003.

Goldsworthy, Vesna. *Inventing Ruritania: The Imperialism of the Imagination*. New Haven: Yale University Press, 1998.

Graw, I. "'Das hat vielleicht mit dem Alter zu tun': Ein Interview mit Pierre Bourdieu." *Texte zur Kunst* 30/8 (1998): 77-86.

Gremek, Bronisław. "Ost und West: Geteilte europäische Erinnerung." In *Europas Gedächtnis. Das neue Europa auf der Suche zwischen nationalen Erinnerungen und gemeinsamer Identität*, edited by Helmut König, Julia Schmidt, and Manfred Sicking, 133–146. Bielefeld: 2008. Transcript.

Jacoby, Russell. *The End of Utopia: Politics and Culture in an Age of Apathy*. New York: Basic Books, 1999.

Judt, Tony. "The Past is Another Country: Myth and Memory in Postwar Europe." *Daedalus* 121/4 (1992): 83–118.

Kaiser Wolfram, Stephan Krankenhagen, and Kerstin Poehls. *Europa ausstellen: Das Museum als Praxisfeld der Europäisierung*. Cologne: Böhlau, 2012.

Knigge, Volkhard, and Ulrich Mählert, eds. *Der Kommunismus im Museum: Formen der Auseinandersetzung in Deutschland und Mitteleuropa*. Cologne: Böhlau, 2005.

Komlosy, Andrea. "Der Marshall-Plan und der Eiserne Vorhang in Österreich." In *80 Dollar: 50 Jahre ERP-Fonds und Marshall-Plan in Österreich 1948–1998*, edited by Günter Bischof and Dieter Stiefel, 261–297. Vienna: Überreuter, 1999.

Krüger, Dieter. *Sicherheit durch Integration? Die wirtschaftliche und politische Integration Westeuropas 1947 bis 1957*. Munich: Oldenbourg Wissenschaftsverlag, 2003.

Leggewie, Claus. "The Seven Circles of Pan-European Memory." *Social Research* 75/1 (Spring 2008): 217–234.

Levy, Daniel, and Nathan Sznaider. *The Holocaust and Memory in a Global Age*. Philadelphia: Temple University Press, 2006.

Lozoviuk, Petr. "Einleitung." In *Grenzgebiet als Forschungsfeld: Aspekte der ethnografischen und kulturhistorischen Erforschung des Grenzlandes*, edited by Petr Lozoviuk, 7-14. Schriften zur sächsischen Geschichte und Volkskunde 29. Leipzig: Leipziger Universitätsverlag, 2009.

Mälksoo, Maria. "The Memory Politics of Becoming European: The East European Subalterns and the Collective Memory of Europe." *European Journal of International Relations* 15/4 (2009): 653–680.

Meinhof, Ulrike, ed. *Living (with) Borders: Identity Discourses on East-West Borders in Europe*. Aldershot, GB: Ashgate, 2002.

Molden, Berthold "The Cold War in the European Memory Matrix." In *Clashes in European Memory: The Case of Communist Repression and the Holocaust*, edited by Muriel Blaive, Christian Gerbel, and Thomas Lindenberger, 212–227. Piscataway, NJ: Transaction, 2011.

Müller, Jan-Werner, ed. *Memory and Power in Post-War Europe*. Cambridge: Cambridge University Press, 2002.

———. "On 'European Memory': Some Conceptual and Normative Remarks." In *A European Memory? Contested Histories and Politics of Remembrance*, edited by Bo Stråth and Małgorzata Pakier, 25–37. Studies in Contemporary European History, vol. 6. New York: Berghahn, 2012.

Niethammer, Lutz, Alexander von Plato, and Dorothee Wierling. *Die volkseigene Erfahrung: Eine Archäologie des Lebens in der Industrieprovinz der DDR; 30 biographische Eröffnungen*. Berlin: Rohwolt, 1991.

Olsen, Johan P. "The Many Faces of Europeanization." *Journal of Common Market Studies* 40/5 (2002): 921–952.

Pfister, Eugen, and Katharina Prager. "How We Learned to Stop Worrying and Utilize European *Lieux de Mémoire* as an Historical Instrument." *Der Donauraum: Zeitschrift des Institutes für den Donauraum und Mitteleuropa* 51/1 (2011): 21-33.

Ricœur, Paul. *Das Rätsel der Vergangenheit. Erinnern–Vergessen–Verzeihen*. Göttingen: Wallstein, 2000.

Rothschild, Kurt. "Peace and Security via Interdependence and Cooperation in Europe." *Österreichische Zeitschrift für Außenpolitik* 19/1 (1979): 14–25.

Santangelo, Grazia D. *The Baltic States Return to Europe: The Baltic Re-integration Problem between the Nordic and the EU Option* (=Jean Monet

Working Paper No. 11, September 1997), University of Catania 1997. Accessed September 9, 2013. http://www.fscpo.unict.it/EuroMed/jmwp11.htm.

Schlögl, Karl. "Europa neu vermessen: Die Rückkehr des Ostens in den europäischen Horizont." In *Europas Gedächtnis: Das neue Europa auf der Suche zwischen nationalen Erinnerungen und gemeinsamer Identität*, edited by Helmut König, Julia Schmidt, and Manfred Sicking, 147–168. Bielefeld: 2008. Transcript.

Smith, Alan. *The Return to Europe: The Reintegration of Eastern Europe into the European Economy*. Basingstoke, GB: Palgrave Macmillan, 2000.

Snyder, Timothy. "Conclusion: The Wall around the West." In *The Wall around the West: State Borders and Immigration Controls in North America and Europe*, edited by Peter Andreas and Timothy Snyder, 219–227. Lanham, MD: Rowman & Littlefield, 2000.

———. "Memory of Sovereignty and Sovereignty over Memory: Poland, Lithuania, and Ukraine, 1939–1999." In *Memory and Power in Post-War Europe*, edited by Jan-Werner Müller, 39–58. Cambridge: Cambridge University Press, 2002.

Spengler, Otto. *The Decline of the West. Volume I: Form and Actuality*. New York: Knopf, 1950.

Stern, Fritz. "The Common House of Europe." *The New York Review of Books* 36/19, December 7, 1989.

Stråth, Bo. "Introduction: Europe as a Discourse." In *Europe and the Other and Europe as the Other*, edited by Bo Stråth, 13–44. Brussels: Peter Lang, 2000.

Stråth, Bo, and Małgorzata Pakier, eds. *A European Memory? Contested Histories and Politics of Remembrance*. Studies in Contemporary European History, vol. 6. New York: Berghahn, 2012.

Thum, Gregor. "'Europa' im Ostblock: Weiße Flecken in der Geschichte der europäischen Integration." *Zeithistorische Forschungen* 1/3 (2004): 379–395.

Todorova, Maria. *Imagining the Balkans*. Oxford: Oxford University Press, 1997.

Todorova, Maria, and Zsuzsa Gille, eds. *Post-Communist Nostalgia*. New York: Berghahn, 2010.

Traverso, Enzo *Le passé, modes d'emploi. Histoire, mémoire, politique*. Paris: La fabrique, Paris 2005.

Vodopivec, Nina. "Past for the Present: The Social Memory of Textile Workers in Slovenia." In *Remembering Communism: Genres of Representation*, edited by Maria Todorova, 213–234. New York: Social Science Research Council, 2010.

Wagener, Hans-Jürgen. *Rückkehr nach Europa*. Frankfurt a.d.O.: Frankfurter Institut für Transformationsstudien, 1999.

Waterfield, Bruno. "Anger at Plans for Official European History." *The Telegraph*, January 2, 2009.

Wodak, Ruth, and John Richardson, "On the Politics of Memory (or not)." *Critical Discourse Studies* 6/4 (November 2009): 231–235.

Wolff, Larry. *Inventing Eastern Europe: The Map of Civilization on the Mind of the Enlightenment*. Stanford: Stanford University Press, 1994.

MEMORY OF NATURAL DISASTERS: CONSTRUCTION AND REPRESENTATIONS OF EUROPE

Françoise Lavocat*

Abstract

We propose to analyze in this article some aspects of the discursive and aesthetic handling of natural disasters between the seventeenth and nineteenth centuries by making two hypotheses: the first is that construction of the recollection of disasters, in the form that they take from the seventeenth century onwards, is eminently political; the second is that this political dimension exists, notably, in connection with European conflicts (seventeenth century), with the way in which formative Europe defined its borders (eighteenth century), and, as disasters were transformed (the disappearance of the plague in Europe and the appearance of technological disasters), with the representation of Europe in relation to the rest of the world (nineteenth century). While the commemoration of past disasters becomes an issue in the context of the revolutions and restorations of the nineteenth century, putting ancient and contemporary disasters into historical perspective (as done by Chavannes de la Giraudière between 1855 and 1911) serves as an educational, religious, and political project aimed at young people.

We shall endeavor first of all to show some of the political issues found in the representation of the plague in the seventeenth century, by way of two contemporary literary examples of the Milan plague (1630), as well as the transformation of the

* Françoise Lavocat is a Professor in the Department of Comparative Literature at Université Paris 3-Sorbonne nouvelle.

plague columns in the context of the war between the Austrian monarchy and Turkey at the end of the seventeenth and beginning of the eighteenth centuries. Next, we will show how the plague, when it disappeared from Europe, was thought of as an inferior state of civilization; it then serves to accentuate the definition of a modern, Christian, non-Jewish Europe, separated from Turkey and the East by measures that are as effective as they are symbolic (the "cordon sanitaire," or quarantine line). Finally, the last part is devoted to an editorial phenomenon of the second half of the nineteenth century, Catastrophes célèbres *by Hippolyte de Chavannes de la Giraudière, showing how he summarizes, through the disasters, a certain vision of Europe and the world, just before its destruction through a disaster which eclipses all the others, the First World War.*

The seventeenth century is the period in which the relationship with natural disasters was radically transformed. People told stories about them, they painted them, and they immortalized them in monuments, with far more depth, detail, and splendor than in previous centuries.

There was nothing natural or simple about it. Louis XIV banned the press from mentioning the earthquakes in France during his reign for fear that they would be interpreted as bad omens and understood as metaphors for the country's situation.[1] Furthermore, if the monarchs did not want their descendants to keep a record of what had destroyed their reign, did the survivors not yearn above all to forget their hardships? Every narrator of disaster is said to be split between the duty to convey the report and the shared desire to bury the traumatic memory. Besides, what is there to tell? Each epidemic, each earthquake, is much like the next. What are people commemorating exactly when they erect a monument to the plague?

It is some aspects of the discursive and aesthetic handling of natural disasters between the seventeenth and nineteenth centuries (with some continuations to the current day) that we propose to analyze in this article by making two hypotheses: the first is that construction of the recollection of disasters in the form that they take from the seventeenth century onwards is eminently political; the second is that this political dimension is, notably, connected to European conflicts (seventeenth century); the way in which Europe, in formation, defined its borders (eighteenth century); and, as disasters were transformed (the disappearance of the plague in Europe and the appearance of technological disasters), the representation of Europe in relation to the rest of the world (nineteenth century). While the commemoration of past disasters becomes an

---

[1] Grégory Quenet, *Les Tremblements de terre aux XVIIe et XVIIIe siècles: La naissance d'un risque* (Seyssel: Champ Vallon, 2005).

issue in the context of the revolutions and restorations of the nineteenth century, putting ancient and contemporary disasters into historical perspective (as done by Chavannes de la Giraudière between 1855 and 1912) serves as an educational, religious, and political project aimed at young people.

We shall endeavor first of all to show some of the political issues embedded in the representation of the plague in the seventeenth century, by way of two examples: the story of the Milan plague of 1630 (by Giuseppe Ripamonti), and the transformation of the plague columns in the context of the war between the Austrian monarchy and Turkey at the end of the seventeenth and beginning of the eighteenth centuries. Next, we will show how the plague, when it disappeared from Europe, was thought of as an inferior state of civilization; it then serves to accentuate the definition of a modern, Christian, non-Jewish Europe, separated from Turkey and the East by measures that are as effective as they are symbolic (the "cordon sanitaire," or quarantine line). Finally, the last part is devoted to an editorial phenomenon of the second half of the nineteenth century, *Les Catastrophes célèbres* by Hippolyte de Chavannes de la Giraudière, showing how he summarizes, through the disasters, a certain vision of Europe and the world, just before its destruction through a disaster which eclipses all the others, the First World War.

The Invention of the Commemoration of the Plague in the 17th Century

It was when the plague epidemics in Europe became less frequent (starting in the sixteenth century)[2] that their inscription into the collective memory was implemented. This does not mean that before the seventeenth century there were no descriptions of the plague (one only need think of the prologue to *The Decameron*), no plague columns,[3] no pictorial representations according to a votive iconography, which is furthermore no longer spontaneously identified as linked to the plague.[4] But in all discursive and artistic genres, the

---

[2] They were all resurgences of the plague from 1348–1350.

[3] These appeared in the fourteenth century. The oldest one that we know of was built in 1381 in Klosterneuburg in what is now Lower Austria. See Marie Andree-Eysn, *Volkskundliches aus dem Bayerisch-Österreichischen Alpengebiet* (Braunschweig: Friedrich Vieweg und Sohn, 1910; reprint: Hildesheim: G. Olms, 1978), 26.

[4] This is perhaps the case for Raphael's Madonna of Foligno, surrounded by clouds which look very much like those on the Viennese plague column; see Elisabeth Schröter, "Raffael's Madonna di Foligno: Ein Pestbild?" *Zeitschrift für Kunstgeschichte* 50 (1987): 47–87, cited by Christine M. Boeckl, "Vienna's Pestsäule: The Analysis of a Seicento Plague Monument," *Wiener Jahrbuch für Kunstgeschichte* 49 (1996): 41–55. On the iconography of the plague in general, see Christine M. Boeckl, *Images of Plague and Pestilence: Iconography and Iconology* (Kirksville, MO: Truman State University Press, 2000).

seventeenth century and the following century[5] mark an important turning point in the representation of disasters, either through previously unseen or even experimental forms,[6] or through the radical transformation of existing generic traditions.

Here we will settle for giving two examples, one historical and literary, the other architectural,[7] which attest to the convergence between formal innovation and complication of the meaning of the disaster associated with the desire to pass the memory down to posterity. However, in both cases, the construction of this memory requires the overstretching, or perhaps the diversion, of the memory of the epidemic in favor of a political aim.

De peste Mediolani quae fuit anno 1630 by Giuseppe Ripamonti was published in 1641 by a historian who had served Cardinal Federico Borromeo until the latter's death (1631) and then the local authorities of Milan, who tasked him with writing the history of the city.[8] The work was drawn from the city's annals, as its title indicates,[9] extracted from this general history of Milan (in 23 books) and published separately—which highlights the interest aroused by the subject ten years after the epidemic.

The originality of this account of the plague lies first in the fact that it is indeed a historical work, coupled with a personal testimony.[10] In fact, the presentation of the event immediately highlights and develops at length the historical causes of the plague, going back to the wars between Charles V and Francis I, prior to the wars for the succession of the Duchy of Mantua in which the duchy of Milan was engulfed under Spanish domination: the governor of

---

[5] A number of works have recently been focused on the 18th century, to the detriment of the previous century. See, for example, Anne-Marie Mercier-Faivre and Chantal Thomas, eds., *L'invention de la catastrophe au XVIIIe siècle: Du châtiment divin au désastre naturel* (Geneva: Droz, 2008).

[6] This is the case for Benedetto Cinquanta's theatrical piece in Milan in 1632 (*La peste del MDCXXX Traggedia novamente composta dal padre Fra Benedetto Cinquanta*). On this exceptional text, we are taking the liberty of referring to our article "Donner forme au Chaos: Le théâtre de la peste de Benedetto Cinquanta" in *Pestes, incendies, naufrages: Ecritures du désastre au XVIIe siècle,* edited by Françoise Lavocat (Turnhout, Belgium: Brepols, 2011), 451–588.

[7] We are aware that reading a book and looking at a monument are unalike sensory experiences; this difference is probably relevant in the cognitive construction of collective memory. However, we do not develop this aspect in this article.

[8] *Chronistae Urbis mediolani historiae patriae* (1641–1643), in 23 books, translated in 1856: *Alcuni brani delle Storie patrie di Giuseppe Ripamonti, per la prima volta tradotti dall'originale latino per C. T. Dandolo* (Milan: Antonio Arzione, E. C., 1856).

[9] *De Peste quae fuit anno 1630 libri V, desumpti ex annalibus urbis, quos 60 decurionum auctoritate scribebat* (Milan: Malatestas, 1641).

[10] This is perhaps misleading because Ripamonti's presence during the epidemic has been contested.

Milan, the marquis of Spinola[11] was fully involved in the Siege of Casale.[12] This is the reason why taxes were raised, to support the imperial armies who were crossing over and ravaging the Milanese people, first bringing famine and then the plague. Opulent Milan was therefore ruined and contaminated by the troops of its masters, who were absent during the disaster (Spinola, and then his successors, were at the Siege of Casale). This was followed by serious mass anti-Spanish riots and demonstrations by the people,[13] which worried the local authorities, all the more because they did not stop demanding financial aid from Philip IV, in vain, to deal with the situation.[14]

Thus, one of the two essential issues of the plague in Milan in 1630, from a historical and political perspective, is the stability of the city, or even its upkeep under the aegis of Spain (the revolt of Naples was not far away[15]), the other being the controversy concerning the plague sowers (*untori*).[16] On this subject, Ripamonti prudently expresses a skeptical opinion:[17] tormented by the Inquisition in his youth,[18] he knows that his words are under surveillance. The insistence on human rather than divine causality is also noteworthy.

---

[11] He had previously been illustrated in his military victories in Flanders.

[12] He died during this siege in 1631. He was replaced, as both the head of Milan and in the siege, by Diego Felipez de Guzman.

[13] Spinola's predecessor, Fernandez de Córdoba, left Milan under a hail of stones (August 22, 1629).

[14] Ripamonti emphasizes that these subsidies were systematically refused by the Spanish monarch, whose finances had been drained.

[15] The Naples insurrection took place under Masaniello's leadership in 1647–1648.

[16] On these points, see William G. Naphy, *Plagues, Poisons and Potions: Plague Spreading Conspiracies in the Western Alps, c. 1530–1640* (Manchester: Manchester University Press, 2002), 185 ff., and Yves-Marie Bercé, "les semeurs de peste," in *La vie, la mort, la foi, le temps, mélanges offerts à Pierre Chaunu,* edited by J. P. Bardet and M. Foisil (Paris: PUF, 1993), 85–94.

[17] I am taking the liberty of referring to two of my own articles, "Raconter la catastrophe," in Lavocat, *Pestes, incendies, naufrages*, 31–151; "Narratives of Catastrophe in the Early Modern Period: Awareness of Historicity and Emergence of Interpretative Viewpoints," *Poetics Today* 33, no. 3 (2013): 254–299.

[18] Ordained as a priest in 1606 (at the age of 33), doctor of the Biblioteca Ambrosiana, he was arrested in 1618, at the instigation of his protector, Cardinal Federico Borromeo. He was accused of mocking, under the cover of fiction, his companions and superiors, of having irreverently evoked Saint Augustine and Saint Charles Borromeo, Federico's cousin; he was suspected of materialism, atheism, and even witchcraft. In 1622, he was sentenced to five years in prison, which was transformed into a summons for definitive residence in the Archbishop's palace in Milan; that is to say, subjected to the strict surveillance of Federico Borromeo, until his death in 1631. See the biography written by Francesco Cusani, published with his translation of Ripamonti's history of the Milan plague: *La peste di Milano del 1630, V libri cavati dagli annali della citta*, translated by F. Cusani [1841] (Milan: Muggiani, 1945).

It is these circumstances that would constitute the memory of the Milan plague, which required several actors and a chronological process of three centuries.

First it was drawn up by the various authorities of Milan. The Milan Senate, as all Italian children have known since Manzoni,[19] had a column that was said to be "infamous," erected on the site[20] of the razed house of the barber Giacomo Moro, the main defendant in the plague sowers' trial, combined with a plaque recalling the crime and its punishment. The senate is furthermore the silent partner in Ripamonti's history of Milan. During the plague, the bishop of Milan, Federico Borromeo, decreed the introduction of votive festivals;[21] on June 11, 1630, he also organized the procession of the body of Saint Charles Borromeo, his uncle (died in 1583, canonized in 1610), in the plague-stricken streets of Milan. Finally, the King of Spain offered Milan a precious coffin made of rock crystal to hold the saint's remains, which were transferred to it with great pomp in 1638.

This repeated exhibition of the body of Saint Charles has high symbolic and political importance. On one hand, the 1577–1578 plague, during which Charles Borromeo distinguished himself with his devotion and his abnegation, had been established as a model, particularly by Ripamonti. The idealized account of the management of the previous plague enables the historian to point the finger at the insufficiencies of the actors in the plague of 1630, insubordinate people and inadequate public powers. The benefit for Federico Borromeo being placed in the prestigious shadow of his uncle is clear.[22] As for Spain, it ostensibly places this hero of the Counter Reformation under its aegis, and Philip IV, through the mouth of the governor of Milan, Diego Felipez de Guzman, attributes the responsibility for the victories of the imperial armies to the Saint of the Plague.[23]

---

[19] He wrote *La Storia della colonna infame* as an appendix to *I Promessi sposi* (1830).

[20] Near the current Porta Ticinese.

[21] July 2, the festival of visiting the Virgin for liberation from the plague. (This would take place until 1868.)

[22] The reduction, for posterity, of Charles Borromeo to the icon of "saint of the plague" was for himself a godsend. The rigorous application of the Tridentine principles by Borromeo had been so contested that he was subjected to an assassination attempt by four members of a religious order that he was bullying (the "Umiliati"). Charles Borromeo also vigorously persecuted witches, Protestants, and Jews. He methodically destroyed the agreement between Christians and Jews in Cremona, until the latter were expelled; see Giovanni B. Magnoli, ed., *Gli ebrei a Cremona, Storia di una comunità fra Medioevo e Rinascimento* (Florence: Giuntina, 2002), 76 ff.

[23] "The support of San Carlo, who with a single favor brought victory to my armies, who without his help would not have been able to advance and leave the necessary defence of the State to attack the enemy territory"; *De peste*, 348 (author's translation).

This diversion seems to have been very effective, if we believe Ripamonti, who, on the occasion of this festival, describes the people of Milan as reconciled with their Spanish monarch.[24] He shares the ecstatic contemplation of a literally dazzling work of art with the crowd. A recent photograph of the precious coffin in rock crystal leaves one to think that it was effectively shining with a thousand fires. (See insert, figure 4.)

The recognition for the donors combined with the religious fervor for the relics credited with miraculous virtues made the rebellious people return to their duty. However, the description of this festival, included in Ripamonti's treatise on the plague, comes to an end on a dysphoric note: in the disorder of the devoted crowd and in the middle of the shouts of those possessed, bloody fights rise up; the German soldiers guarding the barriers beat some citizens to death. In the outer wall of the church, a quarrel about precedence occurs between the orders of magistrates of the city. Ripamonti did not conclude his treatise with the show of jubilation in unity and rediscovered obedience, but rather with the image of internal conflict, the chaos of the *plèbe*, and the violence of foreign domination.

What happened next is too well known for us to linger on it. The liberal Italians in the eighteenth century (Pietro Verri)[25] and the nineteenth century (Alessandro Manzoni), due to the plague of Milan of 1630, or rather due to these circumstances (the trial of the *untori* and foreign occupation), proposed arguments in favor of the abolition of torture, and Italian unity against the domination of the Habsburgs. This is really what ensured the entry of Manzoni's novel and the Milanese plague of 1630 into the patriotic repertoire and the Italian school canon, even more easily since Manzoni's novel had nothing anti-clerical in it: his tale of the plague expressed an anti-Spanish point of view, but one very favorable to Borromeo and the order of the Capuchins. In the wake of Manzoni's writing, historic interest and curiosity for the events of 1630 were developed: the historian and translator Francesco Cusani, who was

---

[24] "The citizens and the foreigners could be heard in one voice, praising King Philip for such a magnificent gift, wishing him a long life and a prosperous empire, for the Austrian dynasty and the Spanish name. Even the women were shouting, 'Long live the foreign kings and Long live our princes'"; *De peste*, 348.

[25] *Osservazioni sulla tortura e singolarmente sugli effetti che produsse all'occasione delle unzioni malefiche alle quali si attribuì la pestilenza che devastò Milano l'anno 1630*: in this important text (1777), Verri leaves the example of an analysis of the plague sowers' trial in Milan to pronounce an indictment against torture. Count Pietro Verri (1728–1797), despite having undertaken numerous responsibilities within the Austrian administration under Maria Theresa, favorably welcomed the French Revolution and the Napoleonic troops. He took part in the foundation of the Cisalpine Republic.

also in agreement with liberal and anti-Austrian ideas, translated Ripamonti's *De Peste* into Italian, in 1841. *La Storia della colonna infame* by Manzoni was published in 1840. In France, in 1843, *Le Magasin pittoresque*[26] published "The History of the Infamous Column"[27] in three issues, accompanied by an engraving of it (see insert, figure 5).

This view is, in all probability, imaginary, since the column had been removed one century earlier in 1777, by the wind or an unknown hand, according to the anonymous French author of the article in *Le Magasin Pittoresque,*[28] or at the instigation of Pietro Verri himself, according to Francesco Cusani, which would obviously make its disappearance more significant. The French article, which goes back to and resumes passages by Verri and Manzoni (all borrowed from Ripamonti), ends with a glowing report on the conquests of modernity in terms of penal justice and the hope expressed for additional progress: after the abolition of torture, the abolition of the scaffold must follow.

Even if this "infamous column" is not unique in Italy,[29] the one in Milan is the only one to be associated with the plague to the point where it has become the symbol of it and has eclipsed the epidemic itself. This column, through an inversion of its original significance,[30] is mobilized by the historic imagination of the nineteenth century like a picturesque curiosity, from a time far from iniquity and barbarism, from the standpoint of the Enlightenment, where the progress of modern civilization in terms of human rights are not in any doubt. However, the original so-called "infamous" column was itself paradoxical, insofar as the plague columns that were erected by the hundreds in the seventeenth and eighteenth centuries signified praise and actions of grace. Is this initial inversion of the signs, which made this column stand out and enabled it to play this role, in the collective memory?

---

[26] Magazine founded by Edouard Charton and which was published in installments between 1833 and 1938 in Paris.

[27] In the table of contents, these articles are referenced in the section "biographies and anecdotes," and can be found on pages 209–211, 279–280 and 326–327. *Le Magasin Pittoresque* can be consulted online on Gallica (Bibliothèque nationale de France, NUMP–360).

[28] *Le magasin pittoresque*, 1843, 326.

[29] In Bari there is a column, flanked by a lion, to which those condemned with light sentences are connected. It dates from middle of the sixteenth century.

[30] This inversion was really created by Manzoni. Formerly, the column instead testified to the existence of the crime and the guilt of the propagators of the plague sowers. These lines by Jean-Pierre Papon are testimony to this: "the fact that I am reporting was legally recorded; the guilty ones were taken and punished; the house where they made their strokes of death were razed to the ground, and on the first day of August 1630, on that site, a column was erected with an inscription, which, keeping the memory of this horrible infamy, is devoted to the loathing of those who committed it, for all time," Jean-Pierre Papon, *De la peste, ou époques mémorables de ce fléau et les moyens de s'en preserver* (Paris: Lavillette et Compagnie, 1800), 162–163.

In truth, there is another plague epidemic that resulted in a column: that of Vienna in 1679. The column was created between 1680 and 1692 following the wishes of Leopold I, Archduke of Austria. He is represented on his knees in the median part of the column, addressing his prayers to the Trinity, which dominates the entire edifice, while on the level below, an allegory of faith pushes the plague into Hell. (See insert, figure 6.)

Until the nineteenth century, the very impressive column dominated all the surrounding urban landscape, as demonstrated by a drawing allegedly by Johann August Corvinus.[31] (See insert, figure 7.)

This plague column is certainly not the first. Since the fourteenth century, stone crosses have frequently been erected during times of plague, in particular in France, in the Rhine, Bavaria, Westphalia, the Alps, and Austria.[32] Most often they served to signal the site of cemeteries dug during times of plague (the authors of writings on the plague also give themselves the duty of mentioning these places, destined for rapid invisibility, especially in cities[33]), or even to mark the borders of the plague-stricken areas.[34] They commemorate the deaths[35] (human, but also sometimes animal, in the case of epizootics), sometimes remembering an extraordinary event in relation to the epidemic.[36]

Moreover, the columns with statues on top representing the Holy Trinity or the Virgin Mary multiplied, in the same area, during the Counter-Reformation, with no systematic link to the plague: they are a common symbol of the fight against the Turks.

However, the *Pestsäule* of Vienna is exceptional for many reasons, not only through its dimensions and its decorative wealth, but also through its polysemy. Without carrying out a detailed analysis[37] or going back to the story of its long development,[38] we would like to emphasize the remarkable

[31] Johann August Corvinus, "Die Pestsäule in Wien," drawing based on an etching by Salomon Kleiner, Vienna, 1724.

[32] Marie Andree-Eysn, 1910, 1978, 26.

[33] This is the case for Ripamonti and Defoe.

[34] There is an inscription, "Sterb bis daher 1626 Pestsein," on a stone cross on the road between Adnet and Krispl in Salzburg state; see Andree-Eysn, 1910, 1978, 26.

[35] Found on a stone cross in Burgkirchen in Bavaria: "Zur frommen Erinnerung an die in der Pestzeit 1648–1649 hier begraben R.I.P."; see Andree-Eysn, 1910, 1978, 26.

[36] Rainer H. Schmeissner, *Steinkreuze in der Oberpfalz* (Regensburg: Studiodruck, 1977), 114–115; accessed August 20, 2013, at http://www.suehnekreuz.de/SKN/pestkreuze.html.

[37] See, in particular, Alexander Grünberg, *Pestsäulen in Österreich* (Vienna: Bergland Verlag, 1960); Christine M. Boeckl, "Vienna's Pestsäule": 41–55; Ingeborg Shemper-Sparholz, "Notice 211," in *Geschichte der bildenden Kunst in Österreich*, edited by Hellmut Lorenz (Munich: Prestel, 1999), vol. 4: 495.

[38] See Manfred Koller and Rainer Prandstetter, "Die Pest in Wien und Kaiser Leopold," *Restauratorenblätter* 6 (November 1982).

coincidence in the mutation of historical circumstances; namely, the affirmation of a political aim coinciding with the development of artistic innovation. There was a long way, indeed, between the final result and the initial project of the column, created in wood from a design by Joseph Frühwirth, and inaugurated in this primitive form in 1680, at a festival described by the famous preacher (attached to Leopold I's court in 1677) Abraham a Sancta Clara.[39] It is, then, only a traditional column dominated by the sculptural group of the Trinity. But its creation was halted because the city's finances were depleted and especially because of the Siege of Vienna by the Turks[40] in 1683.

After victory against the Turks and Austria's conquest of new territories in Bohemia and Hungary, the project was brought to completion with a completely different team,[41] which was linked to the court and knowledgeable about European innovations, particularly Italian and Venetian. Furthermore, it was no longer just about asking God to end the plague, already long gone (even if resurgences were still to come, in 1698 and especially in 1713), or even giving him thanks for having suspended his punishment, but about celebrating a victory and illustrating the glory of the house of Austria.[42] Also, as art historians have remarked, in the lower group sculpted by Paul Strudel (not yet completed in 1692, at the second inauguration of the monument), the plague personified in the emaciated face and pushed down into Hell by faith, or religion, greatly resembles heresy.[43] In a striking way, the body of evil slides into the void, outside of the scene, towards the spectator, at whose height the statue is found. (See insert, figure 8.)

Furthermore, the structure of the column dedicated to the Trinity is tripartite, both on the horizontal plane (Hell, Earth, Heaven) and the vertical

---

[39] He delivered a sermon, printed with an engraving representing the column and the decorations of the festival: *Oesterreichisches Deo Gratias, Das ist: Eine außführliche Beschreibung eines Hochfeyerlichen Danck-Fests, Welches Zu Ehren der Allerh. Dreyfaltigkeit wegen genädiger Abwendung der über uns verhängten schweren Straff der Pest in der Kaiserlichen Haupt- und Residentz-Statt Wienn den 17. Junii A. 1680 ... angestellet worden: Sambt einer kurtzen Predigt* (Vienna: Peter Paul Vivian, 1680).

[40] The same disastrous sequence happened in Vienna in the sixteenth century, with a plague epidemic (1521) and a siege on the city by the Turks (1529).

[41] Bernardt Fischer von Erlach, a young engraver, sculptor, and then imperial architect; Ludovico Octavio Burnacini, intendant of the imperial theaters; Paul Strudel, Italianized sculptor.

[42] On the collusion between religion and the exercise of power in the Habsburgs, see Anna Coreth, *Pietas Austriaca: Austrian Religious Practice in the Baroque Era* (1950), translated by William D. Bowman and Anna Maria Leitgeb (West Lafayette, IN: Perdue University Press, 2004).

[43] Gerolf Coudenhove: *Die Wiener Pestsäule. Versuch einer Deutung* (Vienna: Verlag Herold, 1958); Boeckl, 'Vienna's Pestsäule', 1996, 53.

plane (God, Christ, Holy Spirit). Each side of the triangular column is devoted to one of the Persons of the Trinity, to which several bas-reliefs correspond,[44] with inscriptions, the coats of arms of Austria and of conquered lands. Next to God, Austria. Next to Christ, Hungary. Next to the Holy Spirit, Bohemia. (See insert, figures 9-11.)

The interpretations of this erudite and complicated (in part due to the Jesuit Franciscus Menegatti) iconographic program differ: are the clouds that form the body of the column borrowed from Italian theatre décor,[45] or do they refer to the etiology of disease—people believed that disease was carried along by the wind? Probably both. It is both a monument commemorating (in a slightly conventional way)[46] the Viennese epidemic and a grandiose scenery, inspired by baroque theatre and demonstrating the legitimacy of monarchical power.

The column of Vienna in any case disrupts the iconography of the traditional *Pestsäule* in the Austrian monarchy (even if cases of very ornate columns also exist in Germany, for example). A very large number of towns, in particular within the monarchy, built monuments of this type between 1678 and 1775,[47] generally dedicated to the Trinity, without equaling the splendor of the one in the capital. Representations of the plague, through an allegory or a scene on a bas-relief, completely disappeared. On the other hand, several plague columns clearly symbolize the victory against the Turks, by the rather rare motif of the Virgin Mary standing on a crescent, or even, like in Klagenfurt (1689), of a cross mounted on a crescent, while the group of the Trinity appears at the next level down on the monument. The project of this column, designed in 1680, was also modified after 1683. (See insert, figure 12.)

This conversion of a death memorial into a monument dedicated to victory also matches the little story and the song that constitute the other constituent element of the memory of the plague of Vienna, as it has reached us today. Augustin, the bagpipe-player, having fallen asleep drunk, was buried in the grave of those who had died in the plague; awakening among the dead, he plays music until someone gets him out of the grave, safe and sound. It is a story of resurrection, told in a description of the plague of 1679 by Abraham

---

[44] Next to God is the plague and the creation of Eve; next to Christ, Easter and the Last Supper; and next to the Holy Spirit, Pentecost and the Flood.

[45] In accordance with Grünberg (*Petsäulen in Osterreich*, 1960, 12), among others.

[46] As C. M. Boeckl remarks, the bas-relief representing the plague of Vienna takes up, with no originality, the accepted motifs on this theme ('Vienna's Pestsaüle', 1996, 46).

[47] We are basing ourselves on the list of *Pestsäule* in Austria given by Grünberg (*Pestsäulen in Österreich,* 1960, 10–11).

a Sancta Clara,[48] who contributed in a decisive way to the construction of the memory of the Viennese epidemic.[49]

However, this little story does not belong to the plague of Vienna at all. It was told, almost identically, in 1576, in an account of the plague of Milan; it would be told again, in 1722, in the fictionalized history of the plague of London of 1665 by Daniel Defoe.[50] What is different, however, is the longevity of the anecdote and the popularity in Austria of this character, a sort of Papageno of the plague. It is once more an inversion, because under the pen of the colorful preacher (a Sancta Clara), the joyful Augustin was rather an image of the intemperance and the frivolity of the sinner. The lesson of the anecdote is naturally prone to many metamorphoses, which espouse the starts and jolts of the political and economic history of Europe: before the First World War, it gave its name to an operetta,[51] and later (1940) to a film played by a very popular Austrian actor, Paul Hörbiger:[52] (See insert, figure 13.)

Before the Second World War, "Der liebe Ausgutin" was also the name of a Jewish literary café[53]—which reopened its doors after the war with the name "Theater of Courage" ("Theater der Courage").[54] Currently, "Augustin" is a newspaper sold by homeless people and travelers.

The Austrian monarchy based the affirmation of its religious, judicial, and territorial unity on the symbolic plasticity of the plague. The *Pestsäule* represents the rejection of the enemy in all forms, in Hell and beyond the borders. The character of Augustin incarnates the persistence of the Austrian identity in and through its margins through the tribulations of history. These two memorial icons perhaps functioned in a complementary way.

---

[48] *Mercks Wienn, das ist: deß wütenden Todts Ein umständige Beschreibung, In der berühmten Haupt und Kays. Residentz Statt in Oesterreich, Im 1679. Jahr* (Vienna: Peter Paul Vivian, 1680).

[49] He also wrote a call to resistance against the Turks: *Auf, auf ihr Christen! Das ist Eine bewegliche Aufrischung. Der Christlichen Waffen wider den Türkischen Blut-Egel* (Vienna: Johannes Van Ghelen, 1683). His work had a significant reception, as far as Goethe, Schiller, Kierkegaard, and Heidegger mentioned it. See Franz Eybl, *Abraham a Sancta Clara: von Prediger zum Schriftsteller* (Tübingen: M. Niemayer, 1992); Jean Schillinger, *Abraham a Sancta Clara: pastorale et discours politique dans l'Autriche au XVIIe siècle* (Bern: Peter Lang, 1993).

[50] On this subject, see my article, "Raconter la catastrophe," 38.

[51] By Leo Fall; it was performed for the first time in Berlin on February 2–3, 1912. Augustin is a music teacher there, in love with a princess who ends up not being a princess.

[52] I thank Berthold Molden, who gave me this information.

[53] Founded in 1931 by Stella Kadmon and closed in 1938, it opened again with the artist's return from Palestine in 1948.

[54] An exhibition devoted to this character was held on the occasion of the tercentenary of the epidemic, in 1979. Many documents exhibited concern this cabaret. See Walter Obermeir, Gestaltung und Text: *Die Pest in Wien—300 Jahre lieber Augustin* (Vienna: Wechselausstellung der Wiener Stadt- und Landesbilbiothek, 1979).

We also note that to continue to make sense well after its historical existence, the plague must no longer be the plague, or no longer only the plague, an operation of shifting that the "infamous" counter-column of Milan carries out just as well as the founding column of the empire of Vienna.

Borders of Europe, Borders of the Plague

The territorial and judicial consolidation of the Habsburg Empire coincided with a collection of measures aiming to protect Austria and the monarchy's newly added territories by establishing a *cordon sanitaire* with the East. In 1713, the "pragmatic sanction" founded the unity of Austria, Hungary, and Bohemia[55] (which the *Pestsäule* assimilated to the indissoluble unity of the Trinity). In 1718, five years after the last outbreak of the plague in Austria (in 1713),[56] Banat, Slavonia, and a part of Bosnia were integrated into the Habsburg monarchy. In 1728, a barrier 1,900 km in length was created along the border between the monarchy and Turkey, from the arc of the Carpathian Mountains to the Adriatic Sea. The posts for checks, disinfection, and quarantine were staggered every 3,000 steps, or roughly every two kilometers. Between 5,000 and 11,000 people were examined daily, as well as goods and mail (in 1830, 30,000 letters per week to the only post in Semlin, today Zemun in the Republic of Serbia). Quarantine was twenty-one days for a man in good health and usually forty-two if there was a threat of plague. These measures employed large numbers of people and were very costly; at the start of the nineteenth century, they cost 80,000 florins a year. They slowed trade considerably and led to price increases. Joseph II relieved this a little in 1828, but the cordon was only dismantled in 1873 by Franz Joseph.[57]

The effectiveness of this measure is debatable. Certainly, no other plague afflicted Vienna again, in the eighteenth or nineteenth centuries. But plague centers sprang up in the eighteenth century in Transylvania, Slavonia, Croatia, Hungary, Galicia, and Dalmatia. According to H. Schmoltzer, the cordon sanitaire would have unduly prolonged the terror of the plague in Europe when it no longer threatened. (It was, however, threatened by

[55] Robert Walter et al., *Grundriss des österreichischen Bundesverfassungsrechts* (10th edition) (Vienna: Manz, 2007), 17 ff.

[56] This epidemic has stayed in the collective memory less so than the one in 1679. It did, however, lead to the building of a church dedicated to Saint Charles Borromeo (*Karlskirche*), who prolonged and developed the political programme of the *Pestsäule*.

[57] All this information was gained from Hilde Schmölzer, *Die Pest in Wien, "Deß wütenden Todts Ein umbständig Beschreibung…"* (Vienna: Österreichischer Bundesverlag, 1988).

cholera.) The plague cordon also focused the fear on Turkey. It was upon entering the strangely deserted Istanbul (like Moscow taken by the Napoleonic army?) that the Greek armies, in the science fiction novel by Mary Shelley, contracted the plague and transmitted it to the rest of the world, until the total extinction of humanity, with the exception of the narrator (*The Last Man*, 1823).[58]

However, even if fiction exploits the immemorial fear of the plague, this one at the beginning of the nineteenth century seems even more strange to Europe, while in the second half of the eighteenth century it ravaged Russia, Turkey,[59] Palestine, and North Africa,[60] some of which border Europe. Although objectively fragile, the European exception revealed, in the eyes of the abbot Jean-Pierre Papon,[61] for example, the superiority of its state of civilization. The plague, he remarks, has long been native to Europe. But this is no longer the case today; the plague reigns only "in Africa and in Asia"; the war in these regions, the intensification of trade with the Levant, and "the universal agitation in which we live"[62] expose Europe to the risk of contamination. The abbot also believes that the plague is unknown to primitive populations as it is to developed civilizations, which cultivate the arts and understand "the commodities of life":

> Formerly in France and Italy there was the same center of corruption which held the plague in Egypt and Ethiopia: the Enlightenment destroyed it. Why would they not penetrate these distant climates one day to carry out the same miracle there?
> *De la peste*, 1800, preface: 7 (author's translation)[63]

---

[58] In the novel, the plague also arrives in England by the intermediary of a contaminated boat that had set sail from America. In this work of fiction, the destruction of Europe comes from both the East and the New World.

[59] Daniel Panzac, *La peste dans l'empire ottoman, 1700–1850* (Leuven: Peeters, coll. Turcica, 1985).

[60] Lucette Valensi, "Calamités démographiques en Tunisie et en Méditerranée orientale aux XVIIIe et XIXe siècle," in *Annales: Économies, Sociétés, Civilisations* 24, 6 (1969), 1540–1561, accessed September 1, 2013, doi:10.3406/ahess.1969.42218, http://www.persee.fr/web/revues/home/prescript/article/ahess_0395-2649_1969_num_24_6_422187.

[61] Jean-Pierre Papon (1734–1803), from Nice, an orator, notably wrote the *Histoire de la Provence* (1777–1786), the *Histoire du Gouvernement français* (1788), and the *Histoire de la Révolution de France* (1815), as well as the *Relation de la peste de Marseille de 1720 et de celle de Montpellier de 1629* (1820). His perspective is historical and political. (He is a monarchist.)

[62] *De la peste, ou époques mémorables de ce fléau et les moyens de s'en préserver* (Paris: Lavillette et Compagnie, 1800) "préface," 1.

[63] "Il y avait autrefois en France et en Italie le même foyer de corruption qui entretient la peste en Egypte et en Éthiopie: les lumières l'ont détruit. Pourquoi ne pénètreraient-elles pas un jour dans ces climats éloignés pour y opérer le même miracle ?" *De la peste,* 1800, "préface," 7.

The expression of a lively faith in the Enlightenment is accompanied by a moralistic intention. The abbot, more enlightened than many authors of treatises on the plague of the following century, never suggests that the epidemic could be a divine punishment. In his opinion, it is solely due to the absence of hygiene and sanitary measures, insufficiently developed agriculture, and a bad government. But the contamination between an infected country and one that is not is always the consequence of an infringement and a mistake with regard to money and trade:

> Anyway, it must be admitted, the ease with which it [the Plague] slides amongst us is increasing on account of our becoming less delicate about methods for growing richer. Each trick that greed invents for introducing contraband goods, is for him an opportunity to overcome the barriers that separate him from Europe.
> *De la peste*, 1800, preface, 2 (author's translation).[64]

The abbot even goes so far as to claim that in the event of a plague epidemic, if the populations were not corrupted by the lure of profit, there would not even be ten people contaminated![65] Also, when he mentions the plague of Milan, he says it originated from "old clothes that people had stolen or bought from German soldiers."[66]

We find other examples in the nineteenth century of rewriting accounts of epidemics that took place in the seventeenth century, highlighting contamination due to fraud and trade. For Giovanni Casoni, an engineer and Venetian man of letters (1783–1857),[67] the history of the introduction of the plague to Venice in 1630 has clearly anti-Semitic accents:[68]

---

[64] "D'ailleurs, il faut l'avouer, la facilité qu'il a à se glisser parmi nous augmente en raison de ce que l'on devient moins délicat sur les moyens de s'enrichir. Chaque ruse que la cupidité invente pour introduire des marchandises de contrebande, est pour lui une occasion de franchir les barrières qui le séparent de l'Europe"; *De la peste*, 1800, "preface," 2.

[65] *De la peste*, 1800, 149.

[66] "hardes que les gens du peuple avoient volées ou achetées à des soldats allemands," *De la peste*, 1800, 149. It is true that Tadino had mentioned a certain Pietro Lovato, who allegedly transported clothes stolen from a German soldier (*Raguaglio dell'origine et giornali successi della gran Peste*, 1648, 50), but Papon generalizes (the guilty ones are "the people"), and assimilates trade and theft.

[67] Giovanni Casoni, engineer, architect, director of harbor installations in Venice and the writer of numerous historical works (*Dizionario Biografico degli Italiani* 21 (1978), accessed September 4, 2013, http://www.treccani.it/biografie/. According to the author of his funeral eulogy, he was an enthusiastic admirer of the grandeur that came from Venice, and he harbored anti-Austrian feelings. He gave his support to the revolution of 1848–1849; accessed September 4, 2013, www.istitutoveneto.it/.../D/.../BLOB%3AID%3D822.

[68] It must be remembered that the bull *Cum nimis absurdum* (1555) forbade Jews from any activity other than the trade of old rags, an impossible activity during times of plague, and in

> This old woman, who was a victim of the disease, revealed, almost by force and under the guise of a confession, that some Jews had given her some laundry to wash; before and after they gave it to her, they washed their hands with vinegar, which made some people suspect that this laundry, sold in a sordid way by the Israelites, allegedly arrived from Mantua, and others that it arrived on a clandestine path from the quarantined island of San Clemente (author's translation).[69]

The association of Jews and the plague is certainly not new: it has become—lately—inseparable from the memory of the Black Death of 1348.[70] The persecutions in the seventeenth century were, however, directed against other communities or against individuals (the French in Milan in 1577, Protestants in Lyon in 1629) because the Jews had been expelled before the epidemic (from Rome in 1569, from Milan and Lombardy in 1571 and 1597,[71] from Austria in 1669, etc.) or confined to ghettos.[72] However, Giovanni Casoni's account of the plague of 1630, two hundred years later, reveals, through the

fact always suspicious. Indeed, even if fleas had not yet been identified as a vector of the disease, the observation had long since been made that the fabric encouraged it.

[69] "questa vecchia che pure restò vittima de quella malattia, prima di morire, quasi in confessione e per forza, fece manifesto, che certi ebrei dieronle da lavar alcune biancherie, prima e dopo di consegnar le quali si erano lavate le mani con aceto; ciocché fece sospettar ad alcuni che quelle biancherie, negoziate sordidamente dagl' Israeliti, fossero pervenuto da Mantova, e ad altri che fossero capitate per via clandestina dalla contumaciale isola di S. Clemente"; *Peste di Venezia nel xdcxxx, Origine della erezione del Tempio a S. Maria della Salute* (Venice: G. Girardi, 1830), 11.

[70] See for example Johannes Nohl, *Der Schwarze Tod. Eine Chronik der Pest 1348 bis 1720. Unter Benutzung zeitgenössischer Quellen* (Kiepenheuer: Potsdam, 1924); Philip Ziegler, *The Black Death,* (London: Collins, 1969); Samuel K. Cohn Jr. "The Black Death and the Burning of Jews", *Past & Present* 196/1, 2007, 3-36.

[71] This does not mean that the Jews, who had supported France in the wars of succession of the Milanese, had not particularly suffered from the victory and the occupation of imperial armies. On this subject, see Francesca Cavarrochi, *La comunità ebraica di Mantova fra prima emancipazione e unità d'Itali* (Florence: Giuntina, 2002).

[72] In this case, it seems that the Jewish and Christian authorities had collaborated to face the plague, even if this did not always happen without tension. See in particular the account of the plague of Rome (1657) by Jacob Zahalon (*Ozar ha-Hayyim*, Venice: 1683), doctor of the ghetto of Rome; Harry Friedenwald, "Jacob Zahalon of Rome: Medieval Rabbi, Physician, Author and Moralist," *Bull. Med. Libr. Assoc.* (1918): 1-10; *The Jews and Medicine* (Baltimore: Johns Hopkins University Press, 1944); and the account by Abraham Ben Isaac Alluf Massarani of the plague and the taking of Mantua by the Imperials (*Ha–Galut ve-Ha-Pedut*, Venice, 1634). This account was translated into Italian in 1938. Large extracts of it can be found in Cavarrochi, *La comunità ebraica di Mantova,* 2002, 33–49.

choice and rewriting of its sources, the resurgence of the accusation against the Jews as the cause of the plague.

Conflicts Around the Memory of the Plague

In the nineteenth century the perpetuation of the memory of plague epidemics from the seventeenth century, and perhaps more broadly of disasters past, was very often[73] undertaken by the Catholic Church, which made sometimes this memory the source of political conflicts.

The Catholic Church's involvement is the direct consequence of the way in which the future memory of the event was programmed by the actors of the previous centuries. The construction of monuments dedicated to the plague in the seventeenth century or the beginning of the eighteenth century was in fact accompanied by vows. Throughout the epidemic, the prince, the bishop, and the local authorities promised God the building of a monument, to beg him to make the plague stop and to thank him for having done it. The completion time of this vow demanded this double aim, prospective and retrospective. The authors of the vow furthermore foresaw its durability, engaging the community and future generations. After the official inauguration of the monument,[74] column, or church, annual commemorative ceremonies took place. They had the function of renewing the vow, remembering the tribulations suffered by the town, celebrating the actions and the memory of those in power, and finally and in particular, commemorating the erection or inauguration of the monument itself. Add to this the homage paid to a religious character who distinguished himself particularly well during the plague: this is the case for Saint Charles Borromeo, who is the patron of plagues that he did not know of (Milan in 1630 and Vienna in 1713), and the bishop of Marseille, Belsunce (who inevitably qualified as the "new Borromeo").[75] These anniversaries, especially the centenaries, led to religious ceremonies, the republishing of ancient texts, and the production of rewritings.

It was exactly in this setting that Giovanni Casoni wrote in 1830, two hundred years after the plague of Venice. To his account is attached that of the novelist and man of letters Francesco Loredano (1607–1661), a contemporary

[73] This is not systematic. As we have seen, the memory of the plague of Milan is inseparable from Manzoni's work; however, this brings Federico Borromeo and the Capuchin order canonization through literature.

[74] There could be several, in the urgency of the disaster and once the monument was finished: this is the case for the *Pestsäule* of Vienna, in 1680 and in 1692.

[75] For example by Jean-Baptiste Sardou, in *La peste à Marseille Fête votive du sacré cœur et hommage rendus à Belsunce* (Marseille: Chauffard, 1879), 4.

of the event. The whole thing is presented as a gesture of devotion, aiming also to satisfy historical curiosity and local nationalism. In the case of Venice, these sentiments apparently still gather a consensus, since the festivals that commemorate the erection of the Church of Salute still take place.

The majority of festivals commemorating plagues, and monuments dedicated to the plague, however, did not survive to the nineteenth century.[76] The case of the plague of Marseille of 1720 and 1722 is particularly significant. In truth, from the start, conflict accompanied the figure and actions of the Bishop of Marseille, Monseigneur de Belsunce. Other than his presence at the sites of the epidemic occasionally being contested,[77] the organization of a procession,[78] at the peak of the epidemic, aroused strong opposition,[79] which was nothing that had not been seen before in these circumstances.[80] After a ceremony, on November 1, 1720, in which the bishop, reproducing the painful staging executed by Saint Charles Borromeo, appeared barefoot with a rope around his neck, walking towards an altar set up in open air, and asked the local authorities, in May 1722 (during the fresh outbreak of the epidemic), for the dedication of the town to the Sacred Heart of Jesus. The realization of this vow was met with tribulations. Interrupted during the French Revolution (but celebrated covertly), the votive ceremonies were reestablished in 1807. A statue of Belsunce was erected (in 1802), then moved. At the moment of the first centenary of the epidemic, in the middle of the Bourbon Restoration, the first stone of a church was laid, but the project did not continue.[81] The ceremonies were definitively abandoned in 1871, which motivated the writing of a large number of anti-Republican protest writings. This was generally the

---

[76] As we have previously seen (see note 19), the votive ceremonies that Federico Borromeo initiated stopped in 1868.

[77] This is also the case for Federico Borromeo, according to G. Ripamonti, 1640.

[78] According to J. Coste, however, Balsunce was allegedly opposed to the processions without managing to stop them; the processions were supposedly requested by the local authorities relaying the demands of the population, see *Représentations et comportements en temps d'épidémie dans la littérature imprimée de peste (1490–1725): Contribution à l'histoire culturelle de la peste en France à l'époque moderne* (Paris: Honoré Champion, 2007), 647. The presentation of events by Sardou in 1879 claims the contrary.

[79] "An assembly so numerous, so crammed in a likely time of crisis, must have seemed macabre to many people. Some of them even shouted that, with this inevitable calamity, without waiting for the event, they wrote to foreign countries that indiscreet and out of season devotion had given evil a new activity, and that everything was going to perish in Marseille"; *La peste à Marseille*, 1879, 5.

[80] *La relation historique de la peste de Marseille,* by the doctor Jean-Baptiste Bertrand, represents these conflicts (Cologne: Pierre Marteau, 1721), 20–25; see Coste (2002), 577.

[81] The town of Marseille, however, gave the name Belsunce to a neighborhood and a court.

political tone of French writing of the nineteenth century anyway, with regard to plagues of the past.[82]

The commemoration of the epidemics of the past, even today, is rarely independent from an ideological project, especially when they are restored after a period of interruption. We can cite the contemporary example of Český Krumlov in the Czech Republic, a small town in south Bohemia, which was once part of the Austrian monarchy and then the Austro-Hungarian Empire, in the region of the Sudetes. The year 2009, in fact, led to some important festivities (June 15–21), which started with the benediction by the bishop of a column of Mary (*Mariensäule*), erected in 1714–1716 in memory of the plague of 1680–1682, at the instigation of the Countess von Eggenberg, née Schwartzenberg, a princely family with numerous properties (including Český Krumlov) during the monarchy. According to the description of the festivals of 2009, the benediction of the plague column was followed by Mass and various festivities in costume (from the Middle Ages and the Renaissance), in addition to a prize being awarded to a scientific personality. Among the celebrations that year, a modern sculpture entitled "*Plastik Glockenturm für Europa*" by Petr Fidrich was inaugurated (the inclusion of the Czech Republic in Europe dates from 2004)[83]:

The communication department in the town emphasizes the fact that these festivals, with the name "Festival of the Rose with five petals" (*Fest auf der fünfblättrigen Rose*), "revive" the particularly brilliant festivals of 1909 organized by Prince Schwartzenberg. The history of these festivals, the origins of which are confused with those of the foundation of the town in 1309, closely follows that of the region. Suspended by the Communist regime, they were re-established in 1968, taking advantage of the Prague Spring. They again took place in 1969 and 1970, then were once more suspended until 1990—one year after the Velvet Revolution and the fall of the Communist regime. It was also in 2009 that the plague column was renovated and the fountain that was originally associated with it was rebuilt.

All of these demonstrations, on the event of the eighth centenary of the town, are heterogeneous. They illustrate the local pride, the nostalgia for

---

82 Viscount Victor d'Arlincourt, who wrote many theatrical pieces, published *La peste noire, ou Paris en 1334, drame en 5 actes et 7 tableaux* (Paris: Marchant, 1845). In *Les écorcheurs ou l'usurpation et la peste: Fragments historiques de 1418* (3rd ed., Paris: Renduel, 1833), he is not worried about making the plague an allegory of republican ideas. This work was translated into Italian (*Gli scorti ovvero l'usurpazione e la peste*, Milano, 1834).

83 Official website (English): http://www.ckrumlov.info/docs/en/atr280.xml. The development of the heritage of Český Krumlov is subsidized by Unesco.

the monarchy,[84] the past dissidence against the Communist regime, and the desire to fit into modernity (the homage to Europe and science), all at the same time. The opening of these festivities around the plague column gives everything a historical–religious tone, the exact impact of which is difficult to evaluate; but whatever this plague symbolizes, this festive and touristic undertaking seems to serve as a reconstitution of an era—before the First World War—that is over, a repair of the fractures of history, and a promotion of European integration.

If the disasters, in particular the plague, always signify something other than themselves from the moment that people devote monuments to them, the prolongation of their memory obligatorily makes them consistent with recent history. This is illustrated by a collection of disasters that saw great diffusion in the second half of the nineteenth century and up until the First World War.

Educational Disasters? *Les Catastrophes célèbres* by Hippolyte de Chavannes de la Giraudière

Between 1855 and 1912, the short work by Hippolyte de Chavannes de la Giraudière, entitled *Les Catastrophes célèbres,* had a new, larger edition published (in 1885) and twenty-two subsequent editions (the one in 1885 was already the eleventh).[85] The first edition was translated into German and was published in Vienna around 1860, anonymously. The French publications and republications went forth from the presses at Mame Publishing House in Tours, specialized in the publication of religious books and texts for young people. *Les Catastrophes célèbres* belongs to this niche: it belongs to the "Library of Christian schools" collection, and it publicized the endorsement of the Archbishop of Paris. The cover illustration on the Viennese publication emphasizes that the book was aimed at a young readership:[86] (See insert, figure 14.)

In the preface, which he later adds to his new edition, the French author does not much explain what could constitute the educational impact of his work: it is about satisfying "man's natural penchant to sympathies

---

[84] It is likely that the current descendant of the Schwarzenberg prince, Karel Schwarzenberg, a close collaborator of Václav Havel and involved in the dissidence during the Communist regime, Minister of Foreign Affairs in the Czech Republic from 2007 to 2009 and from 2010 to 2013, took part in the promotion of these festivals, largely inspired by his family history.

[85] In the development to follow, we are using the 1861 edition (available on Gallica) for the first edition, and the edition from 1891 for the second.

[86] We can also note that the children represented in this illustration are playing at war, which is not the subject of the book, except indirectly, as we will see.

with the misfortunes of others," and also his "curiosity." A collection of accounts of disasters involves distant lands and offers the opportunity for little lessons to be learned: "The firedamp explosion in the Jabin wells" enables some principles of chemistry to be shown (1892, 128), the fire at the theater in Nice, principles of architecture (1892, 153), the earthquakes, principles of physics, etc. This is also and perhaps in particular a history lesson, insofar as the author confirms, in his preface, that the details given by the witnesses of the disasters "explain little more than the era to which they belonged." (1892, 7). Indeed, in the second edition, the author systematically rendered a chronological order. Generally speaking, he discredits the old testimonies, feeling that they are often exaggerated (this is the case, among others, for the fire of Moscow in 1571, to which we will return)[87] and short of scientific understanding.[88] Ultimately, the distant countries and the long-past eras do not provide sufficiently detailed reports or reliable testimonies. They are only interesting due to the imagery of the irrational interpretations of the people.[89]

Also, the text primarily deals with disasters that occurred in Europe, according to this list made from the first edition onwards:

Total Europe	North America	Canada	Latin America (Peru)	Russia
14	1	1	1	2

In Europe, it is Italy and France that provide the most examples:

France	Germany	Mediterranean (from Genoa to Marseille)	Switzer-land	Italy	The Nether-lands	England	Portugal
4	1	1	1	4	1	1	1

[87] With regard to the number of inhabitants in the town of Pleurs, buried by a landslide in 1618, "an old traveler, Burdet, says three thousand. But he is exaggerating" (*Catastrophes*, 1861, 168). Author's translation.

[88] Concerning the earthquakes in Canada: "It seemed interesting to us to give this relationship here, written at a time when science had not yet appeared to explain these terrible phenomena, which overwhelmed the imaginations all the more greatly since their cause was more or less unknown, and that glimpsed through the magnifying glass of fear and ignorance, they often took on a strange, fantastical character" (*Catastrophes*, 1861, 157). Author's translation.

[89] Concerning the earthquakes in Peru: "Before being conquered by the Spanish, the Indian peoples in the villages that were most exposed to this terrible phenomenon imagined that the shaking of the ground came from the impact that the steps of their god made on the

The majority of them occurred recently, in the nineteenth century:

Series[90]	Antiquity	17th c	18th c	19th c
1169–1693				
1571–1812				
1170–1825				
1687–1787				
4	1	3	2	8

As far as the nature of the disasters is concerned, earthquakes and fires are best represented (even if the book did not particularly focus on natural disasters, as demonstrated by its title). The plague is notably absent; technological accidents, such as train derailments, make their appearance:

Eruptions, earthquakes	5 cities, 10 events	Pompeii, Lisbon, Sicily (4), Peru (3), Canada
Waterspout (tornado)	1	Monville
Landslides	2	Rossberg, Pleurs
Fires	4 towns	London, Moscow (2), Salins, Hamburg
Floods	2 cities, 12 events	Holland (11), Saint Petersburg
Train accidents	2	Versailles–Paris Norwalk
Shipwreck	1	Genoa–Rome
Collapsed bridge	1	Angers

The second edition strongly highlights these choices. The last two chapters from the first edition have disappeared ("Loss of the Hercules II liner in the Mediterranean on April 25, 1854" and "Norwalk Disaster, United States, May 4, 1854") and nine new chapters have been added, all of which happened between 1876 and 1881, which shows a realigning to recent, or even immediate history. Among them, one single non-European event is

ground when it descended from heaven and came to look over them. At the first tremor, men, women, and children would rush out of their huts shouting: 'We're here! We're here!'" (*Catastrophes*, 1861, 103–104).

90 Several chapters, in fact, associate a town or a region with a series of disasters of the same type (for example, the earthquakes in Sicily and the floods in the Netherlands), by giving a series of dates, which Chavannes de la Giraudière borrowed from the chronological lists of disastrous events or the collection of writings from different eras concerning one type of event or another (shipwrecks, plagues, fires, etc.). They were very frequent in the seventeenth century, just as they are today.

mentioned ("ch XIX: The cyclones in the Indian Oceans, 1789–1876"), five took place in France, three were accidents linked to new technologies or industry: "XXI: The Zenith balloon disaster"; "XXII: Firedamp explosion in the Jabin wells near Saint Etienne [...]," "XXXIII: Disaster of rue Bérangère" (an explosion); "XVII: Disaster of Charenton" (a train derailment). Two fires are dealt with, "Paris burnt by the Commune, 22–28 May 1871" and "The theater of Nice, on May 23, 1881."

The review establishes: modern and European disasters, which de Chavannes de la Giraudière prioritizes, are increasingly less natural. We can only make conjectures concerning the absence of the plague. Does it still belong to the register of the inexplicable—the discovery of the bacillus of the plague by Yersin took place in 1894—while the author is offering his young readers a rational and scientific reading of events, far from any kind of providentialism? Could it be that the plague would give this public too dreadful an image? The only diseases that the author briefly mentions are cholera and smallpox, following a flood in Calcutta (1892, 111). The plague is perhaps now considered an event which cannot happen in Europe, and which therefore loses much of its interest. While the European and modern disasters are frightening, they offer consoling aspects, especially when due to technology. On one hand, we can think that progress will make them disappear (thus, the dams in Holland are now quite effective for preventing flooding).[91] On the other hand, they are full of testimonials of courage, altruism, and selflessness. While the earthquakes in Peru led to pillaging and rebellion,[92] the inhabitants of Angers, in 1850, threw themselves into the water to save the soldiers who had fallen from a collapsed bridge (1861, 91), and the people in Monville, near Rouen, victims of a waterspout in 1845, were not worried about the loss of their belongings and were only concerned about human losses (1861, 144–146).

Contemporary catastrophes are in the end likely to be read politically when they themselves are not full of political events.

The chapter devoted to the fires of Moscow is evidence of a more pronounced orientation, from one edition to the next, towards the contemporary period. The first edition grouped two events in an inverted chronological order, that of 1802 with the arrival of the Napoleonic troops in Moscow, and

[91] "These disasters, nevertheless, have become increasingly rare, as experience has shown engineers the mistakes that their predecessors made, and as calculations in hydraulic science have gained more precision and reliability" (*Catastrophes*, 1861, 84). Author's translation.

[92] "as if it was not enough with all these disasters, thieves rushed up and pillaged from all sides, with no pity for the unfortunate souls who were shouting from under the ruins. Finally the Indians got out, and proudly said to themselves that they would not pay tribute any more" (*Catastrophes*, 1861, 111).

of 1571, with the siege of Moscow by the Tatars. In the second edition, the event from the sixteenth century has been removed. It was, however, a gripping and well-known narrative in previous centuries. The first occurrence of it can be found in *Les Histoires admirables et mémorables* by Simon Goulart (1608); it is mentioned in an account of the Great Fire of London in 1666.[93] But this interested Chavannes de la Giraudière little (he found it "exaggerated"), and he ended up removing it.[94]

The removal of the old text only highlights, in editions after 1881, the episode of the Napoleonic wars, told in the first person by an anonymous witness ("a historian"), who belongs to the French side and ostensibly sympathizes with it. This point of view, like that of the author expressed at the beginning of the chapter, emphasizes the glory of Napoleon and his army. However, even if the Russian arsonists are depicted as a drunken, demonic people, the destruction of Moscow under Rostopchin's orders is in the end presented as an "act of patriotism" not lacking in grandeur (1861, 64). In any case, the partial presentation of this episode of the Russian campaign was in tune with the new power: the first edition of *Les Catastrophes célèbres* was published in 1855 under the reign of Napoleon III. Perhaps it flattered him. The future Russian ally[95] was, however, spared.

Strangely, the German translation of *Les Catastrophes célèbres,* published in Vienna around 1860, brought this chapter to the front: the fire of Moscow opens the collection, which in the original French version had started with the destruction of Pompeii, while the chapter "Fires of Moscow" had only been fifth. The intention of the anonymous translator is undecipherable: this change is the only one he introduced in relation to the order of the chapters in the original French version, which otherwise he followed very faithfully. In the chapter devoted to "Fires of Moscow," de Chavannes de la Giraudière affirmed that the Russian government had spread the false rumor that the French were the arsonists. This manipulation, the author reckoned, was detrimental to the peace and harmony between the peoples.[96]

---

[93] On this subject, see my article, "Raconter la catastrophe," 2011, 38, and Pierre Kapitaniak, "La catastrophe au service de la couronne: l'incendie et *La Gazette* de Londres de 1666," in Lavocat, *Pestes, Incendies, Naufrages*, 381–455.

[94] De Chavannes de la Giraudière presents the adventure as if it had been experienced by Goulard himself, while Goulard says that it is an account by a Dutch trader.

[95] The alliance between France and Russia was signed in 1892.

[96] "It is one of these many means that politics implements to animate people against one another, and perpetuate international hatred, which often has no basis other than unjust prevention" (*Catastrophes,* 1861, 70). Author's translation.

Was the translator sensitive to this conciliatory or even pacifist declaration? Would he have wanted to make understood, in the country that was at the head of the anti-Napoleonic coalition, a point of view that was favorable to the former enemy? Or would he, on the contrary, have preferred to recall the disaster of the Russian campaign and the Napoleonic defeat? Indeed, Napoleon's armies' entry into Moscow was a Pyrrhic victory. Even if this is not what Chavannes de la Giraudière was highlighting, the translator perhaps ironically wanted to suggest it by changing the order of the chapters. We will never know, nor will we know if his gesture is in relation to the anonymity that he keeps; the turnaround in the alliance among the European powers in the nineteenth century makes an interpretation in this context risky.[97] This altered arrangement of the book is still significant, without our knowing why exactly, and the choice and the hierarchy of disasters clearly depends on the political interpretation that one makes of them. This explains the clear preference in the book for historical and modern disasters.

This feature is eminently the case for the fire of Paris extending from May 23–28, 1871. The Moscow fire was the only event handled in the book that was neither a natural nor a technological disaster. The fire of Paris by the Federates was, however, treated in a similar way, which probably strengthened the lesson that the author wanted his young readership to draw from this chapter, which concludes with these words: "God wants the lesson to be learnt, and for Paris never to have to submit to anything similar!" (1891, 122).

The thematic perspective of the fire emphasizes the extent of material losses and only alludes to the victims in a very selective way: only the "innocent who perished in the flames"[98] are briefly mentioned. The author transposes the comparative rhetoric common to collections of disasters (to have "the sad honor of occupying a few pages in this book," "intensity" and "extraordinary circumstances" are required[99]) to the depreciative outdoing of the insurgents—worse than Nero, Sardanapalus, the Vandals, Rostopchin . . .

Finally, under the guise of an eyewitness account that he inserts into almost every chapter, the narrator interlaces his own voice with the words of the "head of executive power" (1891, 115), a speech by Thiers (1891,

---

[97] At the moment when Chavannes de la Giraudière published his text, the Crimean War was in full swing, with France and Britain on one side, and Russia on the other (1854–1856). Austria remained neutral. Russia, however, had given active support to Austria during the crushing of the Hungarian Revolution in 1849.

[98] "How many children, women, and old people were asphyxiated, burnt alive, buried in the caves that they used as refuges!" (*Catastrophes*, 1891, 121).

[99] Concerning the earthquakes in Peru (*Catastrophes,* 1861, 104).

116–117), and an article from the official newspaper (1891, 119–121). The book thereby suggests a personal and collective point of view from the perspective of a coalition and does not conceal its partiality (the Versailles people are "our soldiers"). There is certainly no reason for Chavannes de la Giraudière to disguise it because his point of view is largely shared by his readers. The treatment of an event as a natural or technological disaster even reinforces the legitimacy of the bias: who could be favorable to an earthquake or the breaking of a train axle? By focusing on the ruins, rather than on the corpses (which would be especially those of the insurgents), he is able to present the Commune as a "revolt against civilization and humanity" (1891: 119), by explicitly skipping over its causes and its nature.[100]

The second edition of *Les Catastrophes célèbres* met undeniable success: the first edition had been republished ten times in thirty years, between 1855 and 1885; the second edition was republished ten times in the next twenty years, and a further three times before the First World War. The modernization of the corpus is perhaps not strange given this surprisingly long-lasting success; however, none of the disasters between 1870–1880 (except for the fire of Paris in the elimination of the Commune) has stayed in the collective memory. Disasters are, in fact, destined to be forgotten, unless a political and aesthetic handling of the event (such as the *Pestsäule* of Vienna excellently does) manages to perpetuate the memory, always through the means of a shift in meaning. The work by Chavannes de la Giraudière was not republished again after the First World War, which overshadowed landslides and train derailments of the nineteenth century. It is indeed possible that what made the volume such a success—its modernism—is what made it outdated. The few old disasters to survive being forgotten still had strong symbolic potential in the twentieth century, as shown by the Pompeii motif, which opens *Les Catastrophes célèbres* and the twentieth century, informing the beginnings of psychoanalysis[101] and cinema.[102]

---

[100] "We don't need to look here for the origins of the Commune, its organization, its reign, its main members [...] We simply need to concentrate on the conclusion of this sinister drama" (*Catastrophes*, 1891, 114).

[101] Wilhem Jensen, *Gradiva* (1903); Sigmund Freud, *Der Wahn und die Träume in Jensens "Gradiva,"* (1908).

[102] The first film entitled *The Last Days of Pompeii* dates from 1900 (English), the second from 1908 (Italian). Three different Italian films with this title were released in 1913. Subsequently, other films appeared in 1926, 1935, 1937, 1950, and 1959. Only the 1935 film is American. Pompeii at the cinema is a European affair; there were many films on this subject, especially before the First and Second World Wars, as if they were metaphorical foreshadowings.

Natural disasters do not just belong to the history of Europe—they made Europe.

First, some disasters certainly had a decisive impact on the movements of populations, the falls of empires, the swift development of new religions: it is only relatively recently (perhaps since global warming lets us foresee major disruptions) that we have highlighted the consequences of the plague of Justinian[103] on the disintegration of the Roman empire, the increase of barbaric invasions, and the expansion of Islam. People have also supposed that the Black Death of 1348 had favored the dawn of the Renaissance, through the redistribution of power and wealth brought about by the increase in mortality. On a smaller scale, the fire of London probably opened an era of modernity and prosperity for the capital, thanks to the rebuilding that it made necessary.[104] The divorce of the history of nature and that of man, which occurred in the seventeenth and eighteenth centuries,[105] validated in the twentieth century by the Annales School,[106] is now being reconsidered by historians.[107] From this perspective, we wanted to show that the fact that Europe had rid itself of the plague at the beginning of the nineteenth century, while its neighbors were continuing to be affected by it, consolidated the definition of its borders. The coincidence between the two last epidemics of Viennese plagues, the victory of the Habsburg monarchy over the Ottoman Empire, and the conquest of lands that would make up the Austro-Hungarian Empire, rather shows the overlapping of political history and the history of disasters. This interweaving involves artistic creations, whether the *Pestsäule* of Vienna, or, transforming the plague into a tool to denounce oppression, as in *I Promessi Sposi* by Manzoni.

Natural disasters are indeed also the facts of discourse, developed more or less depending on the era. For different reasons, which in part stem from

---

[103] William Rosen, *Justinian's Flea: Plague, Empire, and the Birth of Europe* (New York: Viking, 2007).

[104] Cynthia Wall, *The Literary and Cultural Spaces of Restoration London* (Cambridge: Cambridge University Press, 1998).

[105] On all these points, I take the liberty of referring to my foreword in *Pestes, Incendies, Naufrages*, 2011.

[106] Fernand Braudel, *La Méditerranée et le monde méditerranéen à l'époque de Philippe II* (Paris: A. Colin, 1949). Natural disasters belong, according to him, to the almost motionless time that defines the relationship of humanity with its environment.

[107] Serge Briffaud, "Vers une nouvelle histoire des catastrophes," *Sources, Travaux historiques* 33 (1993). Christian Desplat, "Pour une histoire des catastrophes naturelles," in *Les catastrophes naturelles dans l'Europe médiévale et moderne,* edited by Bartolome Bennassar (Toulouse: Presses Universitaires du Mirail, 1996), 115–163; Grégory Quenet, "La catastrophe, un objet historique," *Hypothèses,* Travaux de l'école doctorale d'histoire, Université de Paris I-Panthéon-Sorbonne (Paris: Publications de la Sorbonne, 2000).

the diffusion of the Counter-Reformation, the political and religious appropriation of natural disasters emerged in the seventeenth century, with a view to keeping the memory of them, and not without success. This memory, essentially managed by the church, was prolonged, not without conflict, until the twentieth century, if not, in certain cases, until today. The metaphorical potential of natural disasters, in particular the plague, in fact makes them likely to be of use for all sorts of shifts, or even manipulations—dealing with the Commune, as Chavannes de la Giraudière does, in the way of a natural disaster is certainly not neutral.

The study of the long duration of the metaphorical relationship between natural and non-natural disaster, the political implications of building memory (think of that of nine eleven…), the role that art plays in these memorial constructions, seems to us to be full of teachings in the current context, which is no longer European but globalized.

BIBLIOGRAPHY

A Sancta Clara, Abraham. *Auf, auf ihr Christen! Das ist Eine bewegliche Anfrischung der christlichen Waffen wider den Türkischen Blut-Egel.* Vienna: Johannes Van Ghelen, 1683.

———. *Oesterreichisches Deo Gratias, Das ist: Eine außführliche Beschreibung eines Hochfeyerlichen Danck-Fests, Welches Zu Ehren der Allerh. Dreyfaltigkeit wegen genädiger Abwendung der über uns verhängten schweren Straff der Pest in der Kaiserlichen Haupt- und Residentz-Statt Wienn den 17. Junii A. 1680 … angestellet worden: Sambt einer kurtzen Predigt.* Vienna: Peter Paul Vivian, 1680.

———. *Mercks Wienn, das ist: deß wütenden Todts Ein umständige Beschreibung, In der berühmten Haupt und Kays: Residentz Statt in Oesterreich, Im 1679. Jahr.* Vienna: Peter Paul Vivian, 1680.

Andree-Eysn, Marie. *Volkskundliches aus dem Bayerisch-Österreichischen Alpengebiet.* Braunschweig: Friedrich Vieweg und Sohn, 1910; reprint: Hildesheim: G. Olms, 1978.

Arlincourt, Victor d'. *Les écorcheurs ou l'usurpation et la peste. Fragments historiques de 1418.* 3rd ed. Paris: Renduel, 1833.

———. *La peste noire, ou Paris en 1334, drame en 5 actes et 7 tableaux.* Paris: Marchant, 1845.

Bercé, Yves-Marie. "Les semeurs de peste." In *La vie, la mort, la foi, le temps, mélanges offerts à Pierre Chaunu,* edited by J. P. Bardet and M. Foisil, 85–94. Paris: PUF, 1993.

Bertrand, Jean-Baptiste. *La relation historique de la peste de Marseille.* Cologne: Pierre Marteau, 1721.

Boeckl, Christine M. "Vienna Pestsaüle: The Analysis of a Seicento Plague Monument." *Wiener Jahrbuch für Kunstgeschichte* 49 (1996): 41–55.

———. *Images of Plague and Pestilence*: *Iconography and Iconology*. Kirksville, MO: Truman State University Press, 2000.

Casoni, Giovanni. *Peste di Venezia nel xdcxxx, Origine della erezione del Tempio a S. Maria della Salute*. Venice: G. Girardi, 1830.

Cavarrochi, Francesca. *La comunità ebraica di Mantova fra prima emancipazione e unità d'Itali*. Florence: Giuntina, 2002.

Charton, Edouard. *Le Magasin Pittoresque* (1843), online on Gallica Bibliothèque nationale de France, NUMP–360.

Chavannes de la Giraudière, Hippolyte de. *Les catastrophes célèbres*. Tours, Mame, 1855.

Cohn Jr., Samuel K. "The Black Death and the Burning of Jews." *Past & Present* 196, no. 1 (2007): 3–36.

Coreth, Anna. *Pietas Austriaca*: *Austrian Religious Practice in the Baroque Era* [1950]. Translated by William D. Bowman and Anna Maria Leitgeb. West Lafayette, IN: Perdue University Press, 2004.

Coste, Joel. *Représentations et comportements en temps d'épidémie dans la littérature imprimée de peste (1490–1725). Contribution à l'histoire culturelle de la peste en France à l'époque moderne*. Paris: Honoré Champion, 2007.

Coudenhove, Gerolf von, and Auer Paulus (Photos). *Die Wiener Pestsäule: Versuch einer Deutung*. Vienna: Herold, 1958.

Eybl, Franz. *Abraham a Sancta Clara: von Prediger zum Schriftsteller*. Tübingen: M. Niemayer, 1992.

Friedenwald, Harry. "Jacob Zahalon of Rome: Medieval Rabbi, Physician, Author and Moralist." *Bull. Med. Libr. Assoc*. 8, no. 1 (July 1918): 1–10

———. *The Jews and Medicine*. Baltimore: Johns Hopkins University Press, 1944.

Grünberg, Alexander. *Pestsäulen in Österreich*. Vienna: Bergland Verlag, 1960.

Koller, Manfred, and Rainer Prandstetter, eds. Die Wiener Pestsäule. Vienna: Österr. Sektion d. IIC, Internat. Inst. For Conservation of Historic and Artistic Works, 1982.

Lavocat, Françoise. "Donner forme au Chaos. Le théâtre de la peste de Benedetto Cinquant." In *Pestes, incendies, naufrages. Ecritures du désastre au XVIIe siècle,* edited by Françoise Lavocat, 2011, 451–588.

———. "Narratives of Catastrophe in the Early Modern Period: Awareness of Historicity and Emergence of Interpretative Viewpoints." *Poetics Today* 33, no. 3 (2013): 254–299.

———. "Raconter la catastrophe." In *Pestes, incendies, naufrages*, edited by Françoise Lavocat, 2011, 31–151.

Lavocat, Françoise, ed. *Pestes, incendies, naufrages: Ecritures du désastre au XVIIe siècle*. Turnhout, Belgium: Brepols, 2011.

Magnoli, Giovanni B., ed. *Gli ebrei a Cremona, Storia di una comunità fra Medioevo e Rinascimento*. Florence: Giuntina, 2002.

Mercier-Faivre, Anne-Marie, and Chantal Thomas, eds. *L'invention de la catastrophe au XVIIIe siècle. Du châtiment divin au désastre naturel*. Geneva: Droz, 2008.

Naphy, William G. *Plagues, Poisons and Potions: Plague Spreading Conspiracies in the Western Alps, c. 1530–1640*. Manchester: Manchester University Press, 2002.

Nohl, Johannes, *Der Schwarze Tod: Eine Chronik der Pest 1348 bis 1720. Unter Benutzung zeitgenössischer Quellen*. Potsdam: Kiepenheuer, 1924.

Obermeir, Walter. *Die Pest in Wien- 300 Jahre lieber Augustin*. Vienna: Wechselaussteilung der Wiener Stadt- und Landsbilbiothek, 1979.

Panzac, Daniel. *La peste dans l'empire ottoman, 1700–1850*. Leuven: Peeters, collection Turcica, 1985.

Papon, Jean-Pierre. *De la peste, ou époques mémorables de ce fléau et les moyens de s'en préserver*. Paris: Lavillette et Compagnie, 1800.

Quenet, Gregory. *Les Tremblements de terre aux XVIIe et XVIIIe siècles. La naissance d'un risque*. Seyssel: Champ Vallon, 2005.

Ripamonti, Giuseppe. *Chronistae Urbis mediolani historiae patriae* (1641–1643); *Alcuni brani delle Storie patrie di Giuseppe Ripamonti, per la prima volta tradotti dall'originale latino per C. T. Dandolo*. Milan: Antonio Arzione, E. C. 1856.

———. *De Peste quae fuit anno 1630 libri V, desumpti ex annalibus urbis, quos 60 decurionum auctoritate scribebat*. Milan: Malatestas, 1641. *La peste di Milano del 1630, V libri cavati dagli annali della citta*. Translated by F. Cusani [1841]. Milan: Muggiani, 1945.

Sardou, Jean-Baptiste. *La peste à Marseille Fête votive du sacré cœur et hommage rendus à Belsunce*. Marseille: Chauffard, 1879.

Schillinger, Jean. *Abraham a Sancta Clara: pastorale et discours politique dans l'Autriche au XVIIe siècle*. Bern: Peter Lang, 1993.

Schmeissner, Rainer H. *Steinkreuze in der Oberpfalz*. Regensburg: Studiodruck, 1977. Accessed August 20, 2013. http://www.suehnekreuz.de/SKN/pestkreuze.html.

Schmölzer, Hilde. *Die Pest in Wien, "Deß wütenden Todts Ein umbständig Beschreibung . . ."* Vienna: Österreichischer Bundesverlag, 1988.

Schröter, Elisabeth. "Raffael's Madonna di Foligno: Ein Pestbild?" *Zeitschrift für Kunstgeschichte* 50 (1987): 47–87.

Shemper-Sparholz, Ingeborg. "Notice 211." In *Geschichte der bildenden Kunst in Österreich*, vol. VI: Barock, edited by Hellmut Lorenz, Munich: Prestel, 1999.

Tadino, Alessandro. *Raguaglio dell'origine et giornali successi della gran Peste, contagiosa, Venefica, 1 Malefica seguita nella Città di Milano, & suo Ducato dall'Anno 1629 fino all Anno 1632*. Milan: Ghisolfi, 1648.

Valensi, Lucette. "Calamités démographiques en Tunisie et en Méditerranée orientale aux XVIIIe et XIXe siècle." *Annales. Économies, Sociétés, Civilisations*. 24, no. 6 (1969): 1540–1561. doi:10.3406/ahess.1969.42218. Accessed September 1, 2013. http://www.persee.fr/web/revues/home/prescript/article/ahess_0395-2649_1969_num_24_6_422187.

Verri, Pietro. *Osservazioni sulla tortura e singolarmente sugli effetti che produsse all'occasione delle unzioni malefiche alle quali si attribuì la pestilenza che devastò Milano l'anno 1630* (1804). Palermo: Sellerio, 2003.

Walter, Robert et al. *Grundriss des österreichischen Bundesverfassungsrechts*. 10th edition. Vienna: Manz, 2007.

Ziegler Philip. *The Black Death*. London: Collins, 1969.

ARTISTIC INTERVENTIONS: FROM COMMEMORATING POST-HOLOCAUST LOSSES TO CARVING A SPACE FOR JEWISH LIFE IN POLAND

Tomasz Łysak*

Abstract

Dominick LaCapra has brought into focus the relationship between the notions of trauma, absence, and loss, highlighting the need to differentiate these respective cultural phenomena. For the last two decades, Polish critical art has galvanized public opinion and shocked traditionally minded art critics. With time, artists have moved from waging a frontal attack on cultural taboos to a reassessment of the wartime past and its aftermath. Zbigniew Libera's Lego Concentration Camp *might serve as a proof of this transition. Recently, the focus has shifted again to the manifestations of Jewish presence in Poland, either in the past or in the future. As much as Mirosław Bałka's monumental* How It Is *(2009) represents absence, Yael Bartana's series of films,* Jewish Renaissance Movement in Poland: Mary Koszmary *("Nightmares"),* The Wall and Tower, *and* Assassination, *attempts to imaginatively reinstate Jewish life in Poland. Wojciech Wilczyk's photographic project,* There's No Such Thing as an Innocent Eye *(2008), cataloging the remaining synagogues and houses of prayer in Poland, traces the posthumous life of Jewish architecture not only in the wake of the Holocaust but also after four decades of Communism and twenty years of capitalist ingenuity. Łukasz Baksik's Matzevot*

* Tomasz Łysak is an Assistant Professor at the University of Warsaw.

for Everyday Use (2010) is another photographic project of interest. Last but not least, Rafał Betlejewski's I Miss You, Jew! *(2005–ongoing) proposes a reparative psychoanalysis of the body politic via a series of interventions in the public space.*

This paper is going to examine the aesthetic underpinnings of these representations of absence/loss and a recent shift of emphasis to political interventions in Polish Holocaust art. The aforementioned artworks expand the problematization proposed by LaCapra by engaging the audiences in the process of reinstating Jewish presence. The invitation extended to the Jews is possible in the realm of art, as it can play with the sociopolitical, triggering a reconsideration of the traumatic past.

Dominick LaCapra has brought into focus the relationship between the notions of trauma, absence, and loss, highlighting the need to differentiate these respective cultural phenomena.[1] In Holocaust art, modalities of absence and loss have been used to commemorate the victims, with the loss conspicuous across a broader spectrum of aesthetic strategies. For the last two decades, Polish critical art has galvanized public opinion and shocked traditionally minded art critics. With time, artists moved from waging a frontal attack on cultural taboos to a reassessment of the wartime past and its aftermath. Zbigniew Libera's *Lego Concentration Camp* (1996)[2] and Artur Zmijewski's *Berek* ("The Game of Tag, 1999")[3] might serve as proof of this transition.

Recently, the focus has shifted again to manifestations of Jewish presence in Poland, either in the past or in the future. As much as Mirosław Bałka's monumental *How It Is* (2009) represents absence, Yael Bartana's series of films, *Jewish Renaissance Movement in Poland*: *Mary Koszmary* ("Nightmares"), *The Wall and Tower*, and *Assassination*, attempts to imaginatively reinstate Jewish life in Poland. Wojciech Wilczyk's photographic project *There's No Such Thing as an Innocent Eye* (2008), cataloging the remaining synagogues and houses of prayer in Poland, traces the posthumous life of Jewish architecture not only in the wake of the Holocaust but also after four decades of Communism and twenty years of capitalist ingenuity. Łukasz Baksik's *Matzevot for Everyday Use* (2010) is another photographic

---

1 See Dominick LaCapra, "Trauma, Absence, Loss," in *Writing History, Writing Trauma* (Baltimore: Johns Hopkins University Press, 2001), 43–85.

2 The work was shown at the *Mirroring Evil: Nazi Imagery/Recent Art* exhibition at the Jewish Museum in New York in 2002.

3 Zmijewski had his naked actors play tag in a gas chamber at an undisclosed camp and in the cellar of a private house. Recently, the video was removed from an exhibition at Martin Gropius Bau in Berlin, see http://www.aica-int.org/spip.php?article1269.

project of interest.[4] Last but not least, Rafał Betlejewski's *I Miss You, Jew!* (2005–ongoing) proposes a reparative psychoanalysis of the body politic via a series of interventions in the public space.

This paper is going to examine the aesthetic underpinnings of these representations of absence/loss and a recent shift of emphasis to political interventions in Polish Holocaust art. It commences with a presentation of theoretical positions on the relationship between art and the Holocaust and the specific path taken by Polish artists in the postwar period. It then moves from Mirosław Bałka's aesthetics of absence to politically inclined interventions in public spaces, and ends with a comparison of the effectiveness of the different media and strategies adopted by the artists.

From the Aesthetics of Absence to the Politics of Presence

For two decades, theoretical considerations about post-Holocaust art have been dominated by the counter-art discourse propagated by James E. Young, building upon Adorno's aesthetics shunning the redemptive function of art.[5] Maeve Cooke argues for a more nuanced perspective on the intersection of the aesthetic and the ethical in late modern representations of the Holocaust.[6] For Adorno and Young, the anti-redemption qualities of art consist in art's avoiding closure; that is, offering an edifying experience to the audience and facilitating a degree of distance by means of aesthetic pleasure. Cooke warns against taking these claims at face value, pointing to the fluidity of the ethical in the perception of counter-art, which does very little to support ethical interpretations through its content.[7] Furthermore, she underscores the indispensability of the emotional in the process of perceiving art. In her reading, anti-representational art is a vital counterpart to more traditional types of art, the value of the former lying in its potential to unsettle ethical categories by engaging in a critical dialogue with them.[8]

There is a tendency to view Holocaust art as a separate artistic domain: "(. . .) critical scholarship suggests that art about the Holocaust has

---

[4] Łukasz Baksik, *Macewy codziennego uzytku/Matzevot for Everyday Use* (Wołowiec: Wydawnictwo Czarne, 2012).

[5] See James E. Young, *The Texture of Memory: Holocaust Memorials and Meaning* (New Haven: Yale University Press, 1993); *At Memory's Edge: After-Images of the Holocaust in Contemporary Art and Architecture* (New Haven: Yale University Press, 2000); and James. E. Young, ed., *The Art of Memory: Holocaust Memorials in History* (New York: Prestel, 1994).

[6] Maeve Cooke, "The Ethics of Post-Holocaust Art: Reflections on Redemption and Representation," *German Life and Letters* 59, no. 2 (2006): 266–279.

[7] Ibid., 276.

[8] Ibid., 279.

always been subject to its own set of norms which are basically politically and psychologically motivated."[9] These norms touch upon two aspects; namely, the impact on the audience and the visual conventions employed:

> Decidedly utilitarian, such art is prescriptive—in the sense that it is meant to heal—and pedagogical—in that it is intended to prevent future occurrences. In visual representation, what is typically considered permissible is either pure abstraction (in which the event is often indiscernible without a script) or direct, realistic representation where the event is immediately identifiable.[10]

Here Sarah Gendron draws a line between abstract art and realistic art: the former avoids the danger of misrepresentation but risks obliqueness in the absence of an accompanying explanation, the latter is "considered by many to be the more effective with regards to the aims of healing and prevention."[11] Recent realistic art has to face up to the problem of how to make use of the vast visual archives. This phenomenon has been examined by the critic Ernst van Alphen.[12] In his view, artists such as Christian Boltanski, Ydessa Hendeles, and Peter Forgacs work against the grain of archival tradition. The status of the archive in the works discussed in the present essay is far from uncomplicated as the artists produce their own archives, twisting the meaning of the already existing collections or complementing their omissions.

Has Polish art in the wake of the Holocaust provided a radically different response than Western artistic practices? Katarzyna Bojarska singles out two basic representational strategies:

> The tone which, as it seems, prevailed the longest in Holocaust art, was on one hand, serious meditation connected to lament and curbing visual expression, and, on the other hand, a scream associated with the injunction to witnessing.[13]

---

[9] Sarah Gendron, "It's the Real Thing: The Limits of Realism in Holocaust Visual Art," *Contemporary French and Francophone Studies* 13, no. 4 (2009): 415.

[10] Ibid., 415.

[11] Ibid., 416.

[12] Ernst van Alphen, "Visual Archives as Preposterous History," *Art History* 30, no. 3 (2007): 364–382.

[13] Katarzyna Bojarska, "Obecnosć Zagłady w twórczosci polskich artystów," ["The Holocaust in works by Polish artists,"], accessed May 25, 2013, http://www.culture.pl/baza-sztuki-pelna-tresc/-/eo_event_asset_publisher/eAN5/content/obecnosc-zaglady-w-tworczosci-polskich-artystow

In the immediate aftermath of the war, artists turned to their own experiences of imprisonment in the concentration camps, their miraculous salvation from death pits, or other traumatizing circumstances. Contesting a critical consensus in Poland about artists' failure in depicting the unspeakable horror, Bojarska tries to salvage two works: Władysław Strzeminski's *Moim przyjaciołom Zydom* ("To my Jewish Friends," 1945) and Oskar Hansen's project for the memorialization of Auschwitz–Birkenau (1957).[14] Strzeminski's collages continue interwar experiments with mixed media, combining: "the delicate lines of drawings with the shameless accuracy of photography, e.g. a pile of dead bodies." Hansen promoted the idea of "open form" by means of a symbolic erasure of Birkenau, slashing the ruins of the camp with an elevated tarmac road. Former prisoners rejected the negativity pivotal to the project, but its formal novelty was a forerunner to Western experiments with negative form, stemming from postmodernist practices in the 1970s. It is my hunch that Bałka follows Hansen's footsteps in the radical discarding of representation and entrusting the audience with the task of commemoration in *How It Is*. On the other hand, such art failed to secure public funding in Poland after the fall of Communism, with the exception of a new memorial at the site of the former Bełzec death camp (2004).

In a recent essay, Erica Lehrer and Magdalena Waligórska contribute to the present discussion by reading Bartana and Betlejewski as harbingers of a generational shift in representations of the Holocaust.[15] This consists in discarding ineffective institutional commemoration in favor of political interventions in performative art or using the Internet as an interactive platform. This new attitude is dubbed by the critics the "subjunctive politics of history": "Projects are expressly political, commemorating not for its own sake but for the purpose of social change. They refer to—and attempt to create new—memories of the past, address present-day social ills, and imagine different futures."[16] While Lehrer and Waligórska recognize the potential for "civic engagement or democratic agency," they perceive the danger of elitism and polarization of the audience.

Jacques Rancière's impact on the discussions of art and art practices in Poland requires a separate study.[17] Instead, I am going to concentrate on the

---

[14] Ibid.

[15] Erica Lehrer and Magdalena Waligórska, "Cur(at)ing History: New Genre Art Interventions and the Polish-Jewish Past," *East European Politics, Societies & Cultures* 27, no. 3 (2013): 510–544.

[16] Ibid., 512.

[17] Krytyka Polityczna, a left-wing publishing house and an important participant in public debate in Poland, has published translations of two books by the philosopher.

implications of his notion of the political located in the sphere of the sensible (subdivided into the visible and sayable), and the manner of policing discourse by rendering certain practices unfit for public discussion. Rancière's work is riddled with contradictions, as demonstrated by Gabriel Rockhill, but what interests me here is the theorization of the interplay between works of art and their political influence.

> Nevertheless, he continues to remind his reader that there is no fluid confluence between aesthetic dissensus and political dissensus. In one of his boldest claims, he asserts that the politicized art of those who purport to venture out into the real world or to provoke public mobilization is condemned either to disappear as art (by being indiscernible from politics) or to remain within the museum space, forever cut off from the real world.[18]

Rockhill builds on the above remarks in an attempt to conceptualize a popular misconception about political art; namely, the "talisman complex." "This complex is based on the naïve belief in the innate power of works of art to instigate social and political change."[19] It is my intention to shed light on the application of art for political ends (motivated by an ethical resistance to prevalent commemorative practices or lack thereof) in the context of post-Holocaust culture. What are the visual forms of the shift from the aesthetics of absence to the politics of presence? What is expected of the audience in both types of art when they take up the topic of the Holocaust? Finally, I wish to compare the effectiveness of these strategies in the public sphere.

AESTHETICS OF ABSENCE

Mirosław Bałka's *How It Is* can be seen as the epitome of anti-representational art, deliberately evading a concrete reference. A towering steel structure (10x13x30 meters), painted black, stood in the Turbine Hall at the Tate Modern in London inviting the audience to penetrate its darkness or, to be more accurate, to be penetrated by it. Elevated over the floor, it had an ascending ramp at its shorter end, leading into darkness inside, which thickened with each step. Thus, Bałka's giant container is an example of negative epiphany, in

---

[18] Gabriel Rockhill, "Rancière's Productive Contradictions: From the Politics of Aesthetics to the Social Politicity of Artistic Practice," *Symposium: Canadian Journal of Continental Philosophy* 15, no. 2 (2011): 37.

[19] Ibid., 39–40.

which entering darkness leads to being engulfed by it. While the sculptor declared Treblinka to be his source of inspiration,[20] it is by no means evident. To complicate matters even further, an exhibition catalog reproduces Bałka's list of references: "Plato's caves," "hell visions," "black holes," "Hades," "Babi Yar," "Leviathan (crossed out)," "my cellar entrance," "some Treblinka Stangl?[21] (crossed out)," "open graves," "whale," "Malevich's Black Square," etc.

Julian Heynen undermines the unqualified referentiality of this enumeration: "it is impossible to say what these words actually represent: concepts or images. Let's call them notions that can materialise in one form or another."[22] Paulo Herkenhoff warns against the pitfalls of blindly following the artist's hints, as: "Balka is simply offering a vast history of darkness, a layering of connections, concepts and facts, sources and references that are devoid of hierarchy and that propose conjunctions of personal and historical memory (. . .)."[23] Even though the critic places the container in the context of Bałka's other Holocaust works, the genocide of the Jews hardly takes center stage in his elaborate mapping of the history of darkness. If I were to ponder the possibility of a Holocaust reading of *How It Is*, I would point to the mobile gas chambers, which were retrofitted with lights inside the goods compartment in order to avoid panic. Furthermore, unlike Daniel Libeskind's *Holocaust Tower* at the Jewish Museum in Berlin, the black container lacks a door cutting off visitors from the outside, as the sculptor has no intention of playing with identification or suggesting a concrete reference. As with negative representations of the Holocaust, such as Peter Eisenman's *Memorial to the Murdered Jews of Europe* in Berlin (2005), the task of interpretation rests with the audience.

Earlier manifestations of Bałka's interest in Treblinka have alluded to little known aspects of the camp; e.g., a zoo set up by the commandant to display animals captured in the forest (*250x700x455, ø41x41/Zoo/T*, 2007). The title refers to the physical dimensions of the steel structure, its shape replicating the original building known from photographs.[24] The sculpture has

---

[20] http://www.theguardian.com/artanddesign/2009/sep/15/miroslaw-balka-interview-tate-modern.

[21] Bałka refers here to the camp commandant at Treblinka—Franz Stangl—interviewed by Gitta Sereny for her *Into that Darkness: from Mercy Killing to Mass Murder* (London: Deutsch, 1974).

[22] Julian Heynen, "That's How It Is," in *Miroslaw Balka: How It Is*, edited by Helen Sainsbury (London: Tate Publishing, 2009), 29.

[23] Paulo Herkenhoff, "The Illuminating Darkness of *How It Is*," in Helen Sainsbury, ed., *Miroslaw Balka*, 50.

[24] For the photographs, see: http://www.deathcamps.org/treblinka/zoo.html.

been scaled to reflect Bałka's body height with an arm stretched up. The choice of Treblinka is by no means accidental—the artist lives in Otwock, a prewar Jewish spa for respiratory diseases on the outskirts of Warsaw, whose Jewish inhabitants perished in this death camp. In addition to this, Bałka's interest in the genocidal past found expression in a video of deer grazing on grass poking through the snow at Birkenau (*Winterreise: Bambi 1* and *2* 2003), or a rectangular concrete tunnel, *AuschwitzWieliczka* (2009)—permanently exhibited in Kraków en route from Ghetto Heroes Square to Oskar Schindler's Enamel Factory—an accusation of commercialized tourism with its promise of "great entertainment."[25] The work is a reaction to commercial day trips taking in the former concentration camp and a famous salt mine in Wieliczka. Furthermore, he recorded numerous videos in Treblinka with a small handheld camcorder. Undeniably, the topic of the Holocaust has remained a vital source of inspiration, but this preoccupation is translated both into sculptures and videos. They offer a commentary on the aftereffects of the Holocaust on contemporary culture and forms of commemoration.

The artist and some critics have refuted the interpretation of *How It Is* as Holocaust art, deeming it an example of the facile superficial criticism characteristic of consumerist culture.[26] The sculptor prefers to perceive his art as a form of poetry without fixed meaning, open to a variety of interpretations.[27] Waldemar Pranckiewicz's comparative study of *How It Is* forgoes the genocidal undertones altogether, concentrating instead on the uses of darkness in art.[28] On the other hand, such a poetic work as *BlueGasEyes* (2004)

---

[25] "AUSCHWITZWIELICZKA—Nowa praca Mirosława Bałki" ["AuschwitzWieliczka—A New Work by Mirosław Bałka"], accessed August 20, 2013, http://www.culture.pl/kalendarz-pelna-tresc/-/eo_event_asset_publisher/L6vx/content/auschwitzwieliczka-nowa-praca-miroslawa-balki.

[26] In Jacek Tomczuk's "Uciec z szuflady na literę 'H'" (*Przekrój* 52 [2010], 53. ["Escape the H-marked drawer"]) Bałka complains that the Tate Modern advertized his container as the "gate to the Warsaw Ghetto" on their website. A similar warning against too facile an equation of his art with the Holocaust had been formulated earlier in connection with his video works ("Plakat Carla Andre i sól. O Mirosławie Bałce rozmawiają Andrzej Przywara i Rafał Jakubowicz część druga" ["Carl Andre's poster and salt: Andrzej Przywara and Rafał Jakubowicz talk about Mirosław Bałka], *Kresy—Kwartalnik Literacki* 1/2 (2010), 210–215.

[27] "Mój widz nie oczekuje sensacji. Wybitny polski rzezbiarz Mirosław Bałka przed wystawą w Tate Modern," ["My audience are not sensation seekers." Eminent Polish sculptor Mirosław Bałka before his Tate Modern exhibition], *Dziennik Polska Europa Swiat,* February 28–March 1, 2009, 13.

[28] Waldemar Pranckiewicz, "Materia ciemnosci" [The matter of darkness], *Oronsko* 2 (2010), 48–52. The critic compares Bałka's sculpture to works by Anish Kapoor, James Turrell, and a novel by Samuel Beckett, from which its title is borrowed.

has evoked chains of associations with the operation of the gas chambers.[29] A dual projection of a flickering blue flame on a gas cooker onto the salt covered floor is visually appealing but far from unambiguous. The fluidity of meaning and the elitist character of Bałka's art provoked a hostile reaction amongst Cracovians from Podgórze against *AuschwitzWieliczka,* leading to calls for it to be removed from its first location and more information to be provided about its meaning. Thus, the only presentation of Bałka's art in a public space in Poland, despite its artistic merits and intellectual depth, failed to communicate its message. There is no denying that the exhibition at the Tate Modern contributed to a belated wider recognition of Bałka's art in Poland, but its difficult, poetic character precludes any popular influence.

DOCUMENTING THE AFTERLIFE OF JEWISH PROPERTY

Wojciech Wilczyk's *There's No Such Thing as an Innocent Eye* (2009)[30] is a collection of photographs of former synagogues and houses of prayer in Poland. The buildings have been photographed from the front with a mid-format Hasselblad camera and in ambient light. Even though the inspiration for the artistic project came from a bona fide cataloging effort,[31] it is a far cry from the objectifying discourse of architectural catalogs. It seems fitting to use the word "inventory" instead. In Polish "*inwentarz*" has had multiple definitions broader than the English meaning: "an itemized list of current assets: as (1) a catalog of the property of an individual or estate (2): a list of goods on hand" (*Merriam Webster Dictionary*). *Słownik polszczyzny XVI wieku* ("Dictionary of Sixteenth Century Polish") defines an inventory as follows: "a list of things found in the bequest or the manor of the deceased (. . .) written by an heir or the supervisor of minors." Linde's dictionary from the early nineteenth century states: "Inventory, an official listing of things found in the bequest or the manor of the deceased or debtor." Finally, *Praktyczny słownik współczesnej polszczyzny* ("A Practical Dictionary of Contemporary Polish") writes about

---

[29] Edyta Gawron has compared it to the shape of fake showers in Auschwitz, the salt on which the images were projected to Zyklon B pellets, while the hissing sound accompanying the moving image was likened to killing by poisonous gas; see Monika Branicka and Edyta Gawron, "'B' jak Bałka, 'B' jak 'Beyond,' 'B' jak błąd, cyklon B i banalnosć zła," ["'B' for Bałka, 'B' for 'Beyond,' 'B' for blunder, Zyklon B, and the banality of evil"], accessed August 20 2013, http://www.obieg.pl/rozmowy/1429.

[30] Wojciech Wilczyk, *Niewinne oko nie istnieje/There's No Such Thing as an Innocent Eye* (Łódz: Atlas Sztuki, Korporacja Ha!Art, 2009).

[31] Jan Jagielski and Eleonora Bergman, *Zachowane synagogi i domy modlitwy w Polsce* [Remaining synagogues and houses of prayer in Poland] (Warsaw: ZIH, 1996).

inventory (in contradistinction to livestock) as "elements of farm property: devices, machines, tools, and buildings." In my view, this concept sheds light on the structure of the project, the photographer's responsibility as an heir, and by extension, the role of postwar Polish society as administrators of Judaica. Compiling such an inventory becomes an ethical undertaking for the photographer.

Therefore, Wilczyk's project is more than a mere list of objects, a photographic architectural catalog, delving into the ethical underpinnings of "the afterlife of buildings." I borrow this phrase from an architectural project, *Hotel Polonia: The Afterlife of Buildings* (2008).[32] Nicolas Grospierre and Kobas Laksa have created a visual illustration of the afterlife of signature buildings in Poland, including prestigious office spaces in Warsaw, Warsaw University Library, and the Lichen Sanctuary of Our Lady of Sorrows. Digitally manipulated photographs render the prospective functions of built environments after their initial purpose has run its course: the Roundabout One skyscraper turned into a funeral home/cemetery, the academic library transformed into a shopping center, and the sanctuary serving as an aqua park. The project won the Venice Biennale of Architecture in 2009, attracting much media attention in Poland. Wilczyk's endeavor has not been such a high profile success, but his exhibition has traveled to places such as Jerusalem and Paris. Wilczyk has documented the afterlife of Jewish buildings, which underwent transformation under Communism and recently were molded anew by capitalist ingenuity. Finally, searching for context, I could not omit Rafał Jakubowicz's *Pływalnia* ("Swimming pool," 1993)—an investigation into the Jewish character of a swimming pool converted by the Nazis from a synagogue in 1940 in Poznan.

It would be erroneous to treat *There's No Such Thing* as an impersonal cataloging effort: members of local communities hardly ignored the professional camera on a tripod and its operator. As some of the interactions had caught the photographer off guard, he started taking notes. In Burzenin a local "guardian of the synagogue" inquired as to whether the photography was commissioned by the Jewish council and had no objections once he had heard it wasn't. In Krasnystaw, things took a different turn as the photographer was threatened with physical violence and damage to his equipment by two drunken locals shouting from a neighboring lot. These threats made him retreat. Such interactions stem from the status of the photographed buildings: in spite of both a practical and symbolic takeover, local populations cannot get rid of a lingering fear that a day of reclamation might come. For this reason

---

[32] The project was curated by Jarosław Trybus and Grzegorz Piątek.

alone, photographing causes unease since any inventory of "leftover Jewish property"[33] fuels such fears.

I have chosen a single image to illustrate the fate of formerly Jewish buildings. Transformed into apartments and commercial space, the synagogue in Luban Sląski bears a large sign, "Skup złomu" ("Scrap metal recycling"), on the façade, a metaphorical commentary on the reuse of Jewish buildings after their original functions were terminated. Recycling synagogues and houses of prayer has been undertaken with different objectives in mind: commercial, cultural, residential, etc., with select buildings performing a variety of functions over time. On the other hand, scavenging for scrap metal has become synonymous with the shift from a socialist economy based on heavy industry to capitalism: entire plants fell prey to the ingenuity and industriousness of scavengers. Additionally, Wilczyk initially made his mark in the world of artistic photography by chronicling the decline of the industrial landscape of Silesia.[34]

The phrase "leftover Jewish property" highlights the historical presence of the original owners and their later disappearance, naturalizing the present-day proprietors. Who owns the "post-Jewish"? Poles do.[35] The domestication of this property, or rather acquisitive prescription, in good or bad faith, stirs fear when ghosts of former owners rear their heads. Therefore, photography reproaches; that is, it lays bare the domesticated reality, stripping it of safety. By dint of photography, objects slip out of the local population's control. Furthermore, photography is not disinterested, and the local community recognizes the act of picture taking as a sign of appropriation.

Łukasz Baksik's *Matzevot for Everyday Use*[36] can be seen as an extension of Wilczyk's idea of documenting the postwar fate of Jewish property. Baksik was struck by the widespread use of Jewish tombstones (*matzevot*) for all sorts of practical purposes, a process initiated by the Nazi occupants but continued by Polish neighbors and their descendants. Even though robbing graves is

---

33 "Leftover Jewish property" (*mienie pozydowskie*) is a neologism coined to refer to things left in Poland as a result of the war and the Holocaust. In a similar way, "leftover German property" refers to real estate taken away from Germans forced to leave after 1945. Jan Tomasz Gross speaks of "the so-called leftover Jewish property" in *Neighbors: The Destruction of the Jewish Community in Jedwabne, Poland* (Princeton: Princeton University Press, 2001), 109.

34 Andrzej Stasiuk, *Czarno-biały Śląsk*, with photographs by Wojciech Wilczyk [Silesia in black-and-white] (Kraków: Galeria Zderzak, 2004).

35 The history of the ownership of the photographed buildings can be complicated, as some buildings have been claimed by Jewish organizations and heirs in the last two decades. However, at times certain ones were sold back to Poles.

36 Łukasz Baksik, *Macewy codziennego uzytku/Matzevot for Everyday Use* (Wołowiec: Wydawnictwo Czarne, 2012).

an age-old phenomenon (including the desecration of Jewish cemeteries in modern times and the appropriation of tombstones for building purposes), the author is interested in the specific context of recycling matzevot for construction, surface reinforcement, street furniture, or grindstones during the war and in its aftermath. In an interview for *Gazeta Wyborcza,* he (with some reservations) identified his endeavor as a form of documentary photography.[37] *Matzevot* made its debut as an exhibition curated by Ewa Toniak at the Zamek Ujazdowski Contemporary Art Center in October–November 2010. The images fall short of a comprehensive catalog of the applications of the stones, only documenting objects with a conspicuous origin. Baksik searched for visible inscriptions, ideally in heavily used places such as school courtyards.

Bogdan Łopienski's famous photograph *Greetings from Piwniczna* (1974) attests to the practical invisibility of the matzevot in the postwar period: five teenage boys are having a picnic at a Jewish cemetery, sitting on a fallen tombstone. Two of them are shirtless, basking in the sunlight. On the rail tracks above, a steam locomotive occupies almost half of the frame with the driver looking out of the window, facing the camera.[38] The title might suggest that the image shows what the resort has to offer: great weather, a convenient railway connection, and "successful" integration of the traumatic past into the postwar life.

In the album a general view of the locale is printed on the even-numbered pages with a detail photograph reproduced opposite. The images have been rendered in black-and-white, with the general views in a tiny 5.5x8cm format. There is no uniform size for the detail photographs: a postcard format (10x15cm) with a few slightly larger images (13x19cm). In my view, the jump in size is a commentary on the perception of matzevot, which blend into the landscape to the point of disappearance. At times, this blending is so thorough that the photographer's intervention was indispensable in order to uncover the Hebrew inscriptions: in Zator the tombstones had been laid face down in a courtyard. In the innocuous establishing shot, the backs of several tombstones protrude from a lawn; then one has been flipped, exposing the inscriptions (as well as their imprint on the ground). In addition to being used for construction, tombstones have been transferred to Christian cemeteries, reinscribed with new names (for example, a black granite tombstone cut in half to embellish a family grave at an Evangelical necropolis in Gołkowice or a

---

[37] Ibid., 39.

[38] The photographer admits that he waited for about half an hour for the train to pass ("Zawód: fotoreporter. Rozmowa z Bogdanem Łopienskim" [Profession: photojournalist. A conversation with Bogdan Łopienski], accessed August 23, 2013, http://www.dwutygodnik.com/artykul/3233-zawod-fotoreporter.html.

Catholic tomb in Topczewo). The former used the blank reverse, whereas the latter appropriated the obverse with the name of the deceased and a plea for a "Hail Mary" in his memory engraved between Hebrew characters.

A separate section of the book is devoted to knife-sharpening sandstone grindstones. This time there is only one reproduction for each object accompanied by translations of the original inscriptions into Polish and English. Cutting stones to a cylindrical shape has rendered the inscriptions incomplete. Taken out of the workshops and sheds, grindstones have been placed on lawns or on cobblestones. A few discarded grindstones have ended up as debris (with their use a forgotten art); e.g., a grindstone in Milejczyce has shared the fate of a coal-fired stove covered in snow in a remote corner of a courtyard.

Baksik's ambitious aim—namely, returning the misused tombstones to cemeteries—does not seem feasible, but he nevertheless takes an ethical stance in relation to objects seen as spoils:

> A matzeva belongs in a cemetery. (. . .) What I want is to pose questions. To reflect on our society, history, and on ourselves. The answers interest me less, particularly black-and-white ones. When I began work on the project I was convinced that I knew all the answers and was capable of evaluating every situation unambiguously. The more photographs I took, the less sure I was of my opinions.[39]

JEWISH RENAISSANCE MOVEMENT IN POLAND

Yael Bartana's film triptych, *Mary Koszmary*, *Wall and Tower*, and *Assassination,* examines a political taboo in Poland and Israel; namely, the mass return of Jews to Poland. Bartana, an Israeli artist working in Europe, addresses the phantasmatic presence of Jewish ghosts in Poland in *Nightmares* (2007) via the genre of a communist propaganda film. A young left-wing activist, played by Sławomir Sierakowski,[40] admonishes Jews to return to Poland, acknowledging a widespread imaginary fear among Poles that such a return might lead to reclaiming lost property. A quilt—appropriated from Rivka, a Jewish girl murdered in the Holocaust—now insulates an old Polish woman from cold and is a material proof of these fears. Extending such an invitation is meant to have a reparatory function, as if 3,300,000 Jews killed in the Holocaust can supposedly change the present-day Polish population by

---

[39] Baksik, *Macewy* . . . , 40.

[40] A left-wing intellectual and a founder of Krytyka Polityczna.

virtue of turning Poles into Europeans cherishing the values of multiculturalism and openness to difference. *Nightmares* was recorded at the Decennial Stadium in Warsaw, a central arena for Communist celebrations in the past but also the site of Ryszard Siwiec's self-immolation on September 8, 1968.[41] Now replaced by the new National Stadium (2012), the Decennial had been a symbol of transition from a regulated economy to unbridled capitalism, hosting the largest open-air marketplace in Europe until its demolition. The counter-historical approach in the film is not meant to analyze the mistreatment of Jews under Communism, and it treats the stadium symbolically without taking its history seriously.

Wall and Tower (2009) refers to the colonization of Palestine in the interwar period, when encampments could be built under the cover of night without a building permit from the British authorities. The construction of a Zionist-type camp was staged at a historical site of Jewish martyrdom—between the Monument to the Ghetto Heroes and the then future Museum of the History of Polish Jews in Warsaw. The construction was a response to calls for a new Jewish "*aliyah*" to Poland, as opposed to the traditional "*aliyah*" to Israel. A visual style reminiscent of Communist newsreels showcases Zionist ideals of working for the future of the Jewish nation. What catches the eye is the physical attractiveness of the builders, the embodiment of the *sabra* ideal of strength and virility. Thus, phantasmatic Jewish returnees are to breathe new life into Poland. The movement would not be complete without its own coat of arms: a white-crowned eagle merged with the Star of David on a red background. A flag is offered to the Polish-Jewish pioneers by Sławomir Sierakowski and proudly flown from the camp's tower. Bartana criticizes current Israeli politics and the building of settlements in the occupied territories, but the wooden architecture of the encampment evokes associations with the makeshift architecture of death camps. The instruments of control: the barbed wire, the wall and tower, and the gate are reminders of the Holocaust.

The final installment of the triptych reenacted the 1922 right-wing assassination of the Polish president Gabriel Narutowicz[42] in a changed

---

[41] Ryszard Siwiec set himself on fire during a televised celebration of the central harvest festival in protest at the military intervention in Prague. The act was briefly recorded by cameras but excluded from broadcast and silenced by the authorities. It was only after the fall of Communism that Siwiec gained recognition, in the documentary film *Usłyszcie mój krzyk* ("Hear my cry," dir. Maciej J. Drygas, 1991) and recently in a memorial unveiled at the National Stadium.

[42] Gabriel Narutowicz was assassinated at the Zachęta Art Gallery on November 16, 1922, just five days after being elected President. The murder was triggered by an intense campaign of hatred and accusations of his siding with "freemasons and enemies of Poland."

political climate—the twenty-first century. In *Assassination* (2011), Sławomir Sierakowski's body is publicly displayed in the Congress Hall of the Palace of Culture in Warsaw, another historically significant site picked by Bartana.[43] A memorial service takes place in Piłsudski Square, with the platform for speakers occupying the place next to where John Paul II said mass in 1978 (with an ominous sermon about the need for change interpreted as a prophecy of the end of Communism). Speakers include the fallen leader's Israeli wife, Dana, reaching the heights of romantic rhetoric; Anda Rottenberg[44] highlighting the historical coexistence of different ethnic groups, only to be destroyed at the beginning of the twentieth century; and Alona Frankel—a child survivor from Kraków—who asserts the Polish citizenship she was forced to renounce before emigrating to Israel. Rivka's ghost joins the process of mourning, silently confronting the militant Zionism of an Israeli journalist. Offering commentary on the political situations in Poland and Israel, *Assassination* is a form of left-wing messianism touting the benefits of multiculturalism. It takes a stand against right-wing xenophobia and extends the invitation to non-Jewish victims of persecution. Therefore, the *Jewish Renaissance Movement in Poland* does not stop at a symbolical redressing of historical wrongs, but seeks solutions to contemporary problems.[45] Its reliance on socialist rhetoric can be read as a call to action, opposing the non-interventionist individualism of late capitalism, a fertile breeding ground for nationalistic hatred.

INCLUSION OF THE JEWS IN NATIONAL MEMORY

Rafał Betlejewski perceives his art as a long overdue psychoanalytic treatment of Poles meant to exorcize hostility. The grammatical form of the slogan "I miss you, Jew!"; namely, the first person singular, ought to facilitate fruitful relations with the lost object. (The artist is counting on an unenforced identification, which is out of the question when the first person plural is used).[46]

---

[43] It is the setting in which the Polish United Workers' Party was dissolved in 1990, after four decades of annual gatherings held there.

[44] Anda Rottenberg is an art critic and a former director of the Zachęta Art Gallery who lost her position in 2001 as a result of two scandals concerning critical art displayed there.

[45] The capstone event for the project—namely a congress for the JRMiP—took place in Berlin in May 2012, where the line between an actual social movement and an artistic provocation was constantly blurred to the point of diluting the initial purpose of the intervention. See Lehrer and Waligórska, "Cur(at)ing . . . " The Polish dimension was sidelined in favor of a discussion of internal Israeli conflicts and larger European considerations.

[46] This slogan might be read as a critical stance towards the propagandist uses of this grammatical form in Communist newspeak.

Let us scrutinize Betlejewski's ends. This call for analysis does not pass muster as any bona fide therapy, but verges upon Freudian "unfinished analysis." Negative reactions to murals with the slogan—typically, painting over or cleaning up the word "Jew"—might point to the loss, the lost object. Betlejewski tries to inculcate nostalgia, which is an acknowledgment of loss rather than a wish that its traces should disappear. There is an additional motto: "For Poles, 'loss' should be a synonym of the word 'Holocaust,'" legitimizing the present psychoanalytical interpretation.

Betlejewski's initiative started as an outreach project in which he gathered Polish inhabitants in various towns and cities with historically large Jewish populations around a chair covered with sheepskin and a kippah. Group photographs that were taken would subsequently have the "I miss you, Jew!" slogan digitally superimposed. The photo shoots were advertised in advance on the website www.tesknie.com, a media outlet for the project's photographic output. One of the locations for a photo shoot was Dworzec Gdanski in Warsaw (Gdansk Railway Station)—a point of departure for Polish Jews forced to leave the country without the right to return during an anti-Semitic campaign known as "March 1968." Time and again, Betlejewski underscores the personal dimension of his endeavor, claiming that this commemoration of murdered Polish Jews stems from his subject position as a Polish Catholic. Additionally, sympathetic imitators have produced their own versions of the empty chair photograph, at times complete with a personal story.

The formal simplicity conducive to imitation is also pivotal to another iteration of the project; namely, murals with the slogan painted in capital letters on walls in various Polish cities. The project targeted a number of symbolic locations, such as a garage that faces a memorial at 18 Miła Street, where Mordechai Anielewicz and other fighters involved in the Warsaw Ghetto Uprising died on May 8, 1943. Integrating Anielewicz into Polish history, Betlejewski envisions an inclusive conception of Polish patriotism acknowledging Jewish heroes. With this in mind, he placed a miniature Polish flag next to Israeli flags left at the monument by Jewish groups. Individuals and foundations across the country joined the effort, sending photographic documentation. Jews from all walks of life (including a Hassidic rabbi) participated as well, having their pictures taken in front of the murals, sitting for group portraits, or even lending a hand in painting slogans.

The reparative psychoanalytical character of *I Miss You, Jew!* found its climax in July 2010, when the artist reenacted a barn-burning, alluding to the immolation of Jews by their Polish neighbors in Jedwabne 69 years earlier. In preparation for the performance, a traditional wooden barn was purchased in Godaszewice, dismantled, and rebuilt in a field outside the village of Zawada, near Tomaszów Mazowiecki. The objective of the staging was kept secret from the inhabitants of the village. At the same time, an extensive "promotional" campaign was set in motion on the website and in the national media. As a result, the event was televised, with representatives of other media also in attendance.

Dressed in traditional peasant garb, Betlejewski staged a burning of Polish guilt: blank pieces of paper representing the sin of anti-Semitism fed the flames inside the wooden structure. A village administrator from Zawada, Krzysztof Ogórek, estimated that the event was watched by approximately 600 people. With the village in the eye of the storm of media attention, Ogórek spent four days researching the pogrom in Jedwabne on the Internet and came to understand the reenactment.[47] Despite harsh criticism from art critics and political commentators, Małgorzata Maciejewska supported it in a letter to *Gazeta Wyborcza*. She dispelled accusations of "producing kitsch," "appealing to drunkards," and "the destruction of a community of memory," etc., highlighting the therapeutic dimension of the reenactment. In her view, the barn-burning advocated coming to terms with the dark side of Polish-Jewish relations, raising the question of guilt and a national community that should not protect its core by pushing the burden of its crimes onto marginal groups of thugs.[48]

Betlejewski shuns the commercial value of art objects, relying instead on triggering social change. Public space is his chosen arena for correcting glaring omissions in Polish commemoration, with the artist playing on emotions, such as psychological mechanisms of identification, resistance, and transference. The grammatical first person used in the slogan calls for taking a stance towards the past, whereas the rejection of identification triggers resistance and transference in which hostile emotions towards Jews are shifted onto the artist (at times accused of spreading ethnic hatred; e.g., after being arrested by the police for painting a mural in Warsaw). The actual results of the artistic project are hard to gauge, but there is no denying that it polarized the public. Its function is to offer closure, a process of successful working through, freeing Poles from denial through staging a crisis or by confronting negative emotions. This denial obscures the loss of lives, Jewish culture, and the multi-ethnic character of the country. *I Miss You, Jew!* appeals to emotions (both positive and negative), placing less emphasis on a discussion of historical facts.

---

[47] Piotr Pacewicz, "Rozmowa z sołtysem Zawad, Krzysztofem Ogórkiem" ["Conversation with Zawada village administrator, Krzysztof Ogórek"], *Gazeta Wyborcza*, July 11, 2010, accessed September 4, 2013, http://wyborcza.pl/1,76842,8127187,Rozmowa_z_soltysem_Zawad__Krzysztofem_Ogorkiem.html.

[48] Małgorzata Maciejewska, "Nie nasza stodoła—list," ["Not our barn—a letter to the editor"], *Gazeta Wyborcza*, July 16, 2010, accessed September 4, 2013, http://wyborcza.pl/1,76842,8146511,Nie_nasza_stodola___list.html.

POLITICS OF LOSS AND REPARATION

The artworks selected for this presentation offer a political perspective on Holocaust commemoration. How does this political angle compare to earlier art that tackles witnessing and postmemory? Postmemory is understood here not only in the narrow context of art by descendants of Holocaust survivors,[49] but more widely as a response to decades of cultural commemoration, rather than to the event itself.

Wilczyk's reinterpretation of an architectural catalog sidesteps the aesthetics of postmemory. Neither the original catalog nor its artistic rendition belongs to the cultural repertoire of visual memory of the Holocaust. Baksik challenges accepted forms of cultural memory via recourse to the historical form and distribution of photographic images. Generic conventions of urban and rural landscapes and documentary photography have been employed to restore memory of the original use of objects. Such a strategy rings a bell, reminding us of Edgar Allan Poe's "The Purloined Letter,"[50] in which objects in plain view remain invisible until their incorporation into the visible. Thus, the photographers are like the detective Dupin, searching where nobody else has cared to look before. Baksik's photographic objects were found in backyards, cemeteries, workshops, flea markets, and city space, or as road reinforcement. Recently, the issue of the material remains of Jewish culture found cinematographic representation in Władysław Pasikowski's feature film *Pokłosie* (*Aftermath*, 2012). This controversial film narrates the rediscovery of a genocidal episode perpetrated by Polish neighbors on Jews during the war, sending shockwaves through a village at the turn of the twenty-first century. Fulfilling a deeply felt moral obligation, the main protagonist removes matzevot used to pave a road in order to erect them in a symbolic, more dignified resting place.

Yael Bartana employs postmemory but not the type connected to the Holocaust. Instead, the artist appropriates the visual codes of Communism (*Mary Koszmary*) and Zionism (*Wall and Tower*) and reenacts the interwar clash between utopian left-wing politics and homegrown forms of Fascism (*Assassination*). Betlejewski sees his project as a form of psychoanalytical work. The artist plays on the concept of resistance, which marks a therapeutic

---

[49] For a discussion of the multifarious meanings of postmemory see, Elke Heckner, "Whose Trauma Is It? Identification and Secondary Witnessing in the Age of Postmemory," in *Visualizing the Holocaust: Documents, Aesthetics, Memory*, edited by David Bathrick, Brad Prager, and Michael D. Richardson (Rochester, NY: Camden House, 2009), 62–85.

[50] Jacques Lacan's "Seminar on the Purloined Letter" tackled this famous short story, explaining the psychoanalytical mechanism of repression.

breakthrough; namely, fear associated with the discovery of the truth. Furthermore, he seeks to reclaim public space dominated by hostility from football hooligans employing anti-Semitic rhetoric. Interestingly, the crusade against anti-Semitism in the public space assumed an even more provocative form in Peter Fuss's billboard "Zydzi won z katolickiego kraju" ("Jews out of this Catholic country!," 2006), "outing" various figures in Polish political and public life as "Jews."[51]

A few of art's aims proposed by Rockhill are pertinent to the works discussed: "political pedagogy and perception management," "collective identity and counter-histories," and "critical intervention or complicity."[52] The first is realized in works pointing to obscured traces of prewar Jewish life (architecture or cemeteries); the second targets the ill-conceived view that Jewish history has no points of convergence with Polish identity and heritage; and finally, the majority of the works discussed herein have the potential for critical intervention. When their potential for closure is taken into consideration, only Bałka's installation rejects this notion. For Wilczyk and Baksik a degree of closure is connected to the ethical reckoning with visual traces of Jewish life and death: Bartana envisions a phantasmatic messianic redemption, while Betlejewski prescribes the psychoanalytical treatment of hostility/denial.

With the exception of Bałka, the political ends of these interventions consist in stimulating a public discussion by recourse to realistic representation. The reliance on the aesthetics of absence in *How It Is* requires a sophisticated rhetorical apparatus to unriddle its ambitious goals. Therefore, its poetics—the mainstay of aesthetic success—misses the mark as a stimulus for fruitful dialog. What are the mechanisms for the political effectiveness of other projects? Betlejewski has incorporated audience response into the structure of his performances, relying on popular participation and support. Wilczyk and Baksik have chosen to intervene in the sensible, meeting Rancière's definition of the political. Bartana relies on the visual style of propaganda to achieve a counter-historical reconciliation. Therefore, the replacement of the concept of absence with the notion of loss has facilitated a more productive relationship with the past. Last but not least, the late modern hegemony of

---

[51] The list was taken from the Internet—a hotbed of conspiracy theories about the alleged Jewish infiltration of Polish political, social, and cultural life. The location of the billboard—in front of a church in Koszalin—was the nail in the coffin for an exhibition of Fuss's works entitled "Jesus Christ, King of Poland." The prosecutor's office closed the gallery and had the billboard taken down. See Ala Kusiak-Brownstein and Izabela Kowalczyk, "Peter Fuss i antysemityzm obnazony" ["Peter Fuss and anti-Semitism laid bare"], accessed September 4, 2013, http://www.obieg.pl/artmix/1720.

[52] Rockhill, "Rancière's …," 50–52.

abstractionist responses to the Holocaust in Western art fails to describe the dynamics of commemoration in Poland.

BIBLIOGRAPHY

Alphen, van Ernst. "Visual Archives as Preposterous History." *Art History* 30, no. 3 (2007): 364–382.

"AUSCHWITZWIELICZKA—Nowa praca Mirosława Bałki." Accessed August 20, 2013. http://www.culture.pl/kalendarz-pelna-tresc/-/eo_event_asset_publisher/L6vx/content/auschwitzwieliczka-nowa-praca-miroslawa-balki.

Baksik, Łukasz. *Macewy codziennego uzytku/Matzevot for Everyday Use*. Wołowiec: Wydawnictwo Czarne, 2012.

Bojarska, Katarzyna. "Obecnosć Zagłady w twórczosci polskich artystów." Accessed May 25, 2013. http://www.culture.pl/baza-sztuki-pelna-tresc/-/eo_event_asset_publisher/eAN5/content/obecnosc-zaglady-w-tworczosci-polskich-artystow.

Branicka, Monika, and Edyta Gawron. "'B' jak Bałka, 'B' jak 'Beyond,' 'B' jak błąd, cyklon B i banalnosć zła." Accessed August 20, 2013. http://www.obieg.pl/rozmowy/1429.

Cooke, Maeve. "The Ethics of Post-Holocaust Art: Reflections on Redemption and Representation." *German Life and Letters* 59, no. 2 (2006): 266–279.

Gendron, Sarah. "It's the Real Thing: The Limits of Realism in Holocaust Visual Art." *Contemporary French and Francophone Studies* 13, no. 4 (2009): 415.

Gross, Jan Tomasz. *Neighbors: The Destruction of the Jewish Community in Jedwabne, Poland*. Princeton: Princeton University Press, 2001.

Heckner, Elke. "Whose Trauma Is It? Identification and Secondary Witnessing in the Age of Postmemory." In *Visualizing the Holocaust: Documents, Aesthetics, Memory*, edited by David Bathrick, Brad Prager, and Michael D. Richardson, 62–85. Rochester, NY: Camden House, 2009.

Herkenhoff, Paulo. "The Illuminating Darkness of *How It Is*." In *Miroslaw Balka: How It Is*, edited by Helen Sainsbury, 50–102. London: Tate Publishing, 2009.

Heynen, Julian. "That's How It Is." In *Miroslaw Balka: How It Is*, edited by Helen Sainsbury, 26–44. London: Tate Publishing, 2009.

Jagielski, Jan, and Eleonora Bergman. *Zachowane synagogi i domy modlitwy w Polsce*. Warsaw: ZIH, 1996.

Kusiak-Brownstein, Ala, and Izabela Kowalczyk. "Peter Fuss i antysemityzm obnazony." Accessed September 4, 2013. http://www.obieg.pl/artmix/1720.

LaCapra, Dominick. "Trauma, Absence, Loss." In *Writing History, Writing Trauma*, 43–85. Baltimore: Johns Hopkins University Press, 2001.

Lehrer, Erica, and Magdalena Waligórska. "Cur(at)ing History: New Genre Art Interventions and the Polish-Jewish Past." *East European Politics, Societies & Cultures* 27, no. 3 (2013): 510–544.

Maciejewska, Małgorzata. "Nie nasza stodoła—list." *Gazeta Wyborcza*, July 16, 2010. Accessed September 4, 2013. http://wyborcza.pl/1,76842,8146511,Nie_nasza_stodola___list.html.

"Mój widz nie oczekuje sensacji. Wybitny polski rzezbiarz Mirosław Bałka przed wystawą w Tate Modern." *Dziennik Polska Europa Swiat,* February 28–March 1, 2009, 13.

Pacewicz, Piotr. "Rozmowa z sołtysem Zawad, Krzysztofem Ogórkiem." *Gazeta Wyborcza*, July 11, 2010. Accessed September 4, 2013. http://wyborcza.pl/1,76842,8127187,Rozmowa_z_soltysem_Zawad__Krzysztofem_Ogorkiem.html.

Przywara, Andrzej, and Rafał Jakubowicz. "Plakat Carla Andre i sól. O Mirosławie Bałce rozmawiają Andrzej Przywara i Rafał Jakubowicz częśc druga." *Kresy—Kwartalnik Literacki* 1/2 (2010): 210–215.

Pranckiewicz, Waldemar. "Materia ciemnosci." *Oronsko* 2 (2010): 48–52.

Rockhill, Gabriel. "Rancière's Productive Contradictions: From the Politics of Aesthetics to the Social Politicity of Artistic Practice." *Symposium: Canadian Journal of Continental Philosophy* 15, no. 2 (2011): 37.

Sereny, Gitta. *Into that Darkness: From Mercy Killing to Mass Murder*. London: Deutsch, 1974.

Stasiuk, Andrzej. *Czarno-biały Sląsk*, with photographs by Wojciech Wilczyk. Kraków: Galeria Zderzak, 2004.

Tomczuk, Jacek. "Uciec z szuflady na literę 'H.'" *Przekrój* 52 (2010): 53.

Wilczyk, Wojciech. *Niewinne oko nie istnieje/There's No Such Thing as an Innocent Eye*. Łódz: Atlas Sztuki, Korporacja Ha!Art, 2009.

Young, James E. *At Memory's Edge: After-Images of the Holocaust in Contemporary Art and Architecture*. New Haven: Yale University Press, 2000.

———. *The Texture of Memory: Holocaust Memorials and Meaning*. New Haven: Yale University Press, 1993.

Young, James. E., ed. *The Art of Memory: Holocaust Memorials in History*. New York: Prestel, 1994.

"Zawód: fotoreporter. Rozmowa z Bogdanem Łopienskim." Accessed August 23, 2013. http://www.dwutygodnik.com/artykul/3233-zawod-fotoreporter.html.

Internet resources:

http://www.aica-int.org/spip.php?article1269.

http://www.theguardian.com/artanddesign/2009/sep/15/miroslaw-balka-interview-tate-modern.

http://www.deathcamps.org/treblinka/zoo.html.

PRISM: UNDERSTANDING NON-SITES OF MEMORY*

Roma Sendyka**
(Translated by Jennifer Croft)

Abstract

The article discerns a new object of memory studies; namely, a category of sites that fulfill the requirements to be memorialized but have not been so. An abundance of such locations is characteristic of Central and Eastern Europe. Thus, the sites in question are by no means exceptional: empty plots, abandoned buildings, lots overgrown with vegetation. Preliminary features that define such sites include the fact they have been the locations of various atrocities of the twentieth century (including the Shoah, the Roma and Sinti Holocaust, and other genocides, as well as other instances of mass violence like relocations and ethnic and totalitarian purges). A further characteristic these sites share is the presence of human remains (whether in the past or still today). The physical features of the sites are not strictly determinable or definitively discernible, as today they are often an organic–inorganic fusion of ruins, ashes, and flora. The victims that could have been remembered on the site are ethnically miscorrelated with the group presently living in direct proximity. The

* This paper is accompanied by eight diptychs, which can be found in the last 9 pages of the insert, prepared for the purposes of this publication by Jason Francisco, an artist, essayist, and photographer. Francisco's diptychs raise in visual language questions that the present article sets forward: the contemporary meaning of contested, forgotten memory sites, the usage of the sites, our presence within them, the habitable and the inhabitable, the ordinary and the inconceivable, the conflicts of past and present, life and death, the visible and the invisible.

** Roma Sendyka is an Assistant Professor in the Department of Polish Studies at the Jagiellonian University.

sites are not properly marked, nor are they attributed incorrectly. They are instead neglected, or hidden in other ways (often littered, overgrown, devastated). Lastly, the neglect of memorialization leads to revitalization, ethically problematic and often met with criticism.

Following a term employed in passing by Claude Lanzmann (1986), these sites will be named "non-sites of memory," in opposition to the seminal notion by Pierre Nora (1984). A term formulated by George Didi-Huberman—namely "lieux malgré tout" (1995)—will be used to counterbalance Lanzmann's overtly negative phrase.

After a preliminary endeavor to define such spaces, the article undertakes a search for a new, inclusive methodology that could be applied to the study of non-sites of memory. The article questions the usefulness of currently leading terms in memorialization discourse while also questioning the very possibility of conceiving of non-sites of memory with the use of traditional discreet categories and the textual paradigm of interpretation. It tests instead a series of terms from the natural sciences (hypostasis, detritus) and finally, inspired by the post-humanities, it borrows from geology the notion of "accretionary prism" as a conceptual model for its complexly vital object.

The idyllic river landscape that opens Claude Lanzmann's *Shoah* soon becomes scenes in which Szymon Srebrnik guides the filmmakers through the forest in order to finally stand before an empty clearing and say, "Es ist schwer zu erkennen, aber es war hier." (It is difficult to recognize, but it was here.)[1] "Here" is Chełmno/Kulmhof, one of the many sites of genocidal massacres perpetrated between Berlin and Moscow that now contain the remains of the victims.[2] Forest clearings, clumps of trees, grassy knolls—the residents of Central-Eastern Europe know these places, which on the surface are no different from their surroundings, though there does seem to be something disturbing in the air around them that sets them apart. My question is, what is it? Because it is not the driving force of symbols—of signs posted, or of tombstones—nor the language of ruins. Here nature covers over, transforms, and does not allow the visitor to view the past.

1 *Shoah*, Chapter 4, 00:07:05.

2 Following the reasoning of Timothy Snyder in *Bloodlands: Europe between Hitler and Stalin* (New York: Basic Books, 2010), I propose expanding the discussion of "non-sites of memory" to refer not only to Holocaust sites but also to the sites of other genocides or of other forms of mass violence, and to sites related to these events (including dilapidated areas of towns, abandoned houses, ruined cemeteries, etc.). A full inventory of these places would require further research.

Lanzmann provocatively calls his work a "topographical, geographical" film,[3] maintaining that it is not possible to really think the problem of the Holocaust without visiting its sites and combining knowledge of events with a spatial experience that is meant to be extended in a sort of reenactment, "hallucinations," attempts at imagining that "nothing has changed": "I was witness to the change," he says, "and yet, at the same time, I had to think that time had not actually completed its task."[4] This plane of dual temporality distorts space-time: quiet bends in the river, clearings, mounds become "disfigured sites [*les lieux défigurés*]" located simultaneously in the "here and now" as well as in the "there and then." Lanzmann defines such spaces as *les non-lieux de la mémoire* (non-sites of memory). Although the idea of "non-site"[5] (the image of the "voyage to nowhere," to "the unknown") crops up with some frequency in survivors' narratives,[6] the term, used in the title of a 1986 interview[7] is very clearly, according to Dominic LaCapra,[8] derived from Pierre

---

[3] Claude Lanzmann, "Le Lieu et la parole," in *Au sujet de Shoah: Le Film de Claude Lanzmann*, edited by Michel Deguy (Paris: Éditions Berlin, 1990), 294: "You have to learn and see. You have to see and learn. They're inseparable. If you go to Auschwitz but know nothing about the place or the history of the camp, you don't see anything, you don't understand anything. By the same token, if you do know but haven't been there, you don't understand anything, either. They have to go together. That's why the issue of places is such a fundamental one. I didn't make an idealistic film full of grandiose musings on metaphysics and theology about what happened to the Jews and why they were killed. It's a very grounded film, a film on topography, on geography."

[4] Lanzmann, "Le Lieu et la parole," 290: "I call these deformed places non-sites of memory. At the same time, it's essential that the traces endure. I have to give in to hallucinations and think that nothing has changed. I was witness to the change, and yet, at the same time, I had to think that time had not actually completed its task."

[5] Nora's term is translated into English as "sites of memory"; its reverse would thus be in English "non-sites of memory." The term "non-places," meanwhile, translates Marc Augé, as in his "non-lieux de la surmodernité." It is worth noting the etymology of the English words "site" and "place." "*Site* derives from the Latin *situs*, derived from the verb *sinere*, meaning 'to set aside, to leave be, to permit,' while *place* derives from the greek *plateîa*, meaning 'broad street' or 'open city space.' This is to say that a site, in the original conception of the English language, is a position designated in the action of leaving it or for the sake of being able to leave it, presumably so that it can be found again, which is to say encoding as part of its very designation the possibility of putting it out of mind, leaving it to inactivity, and perhaps to neglect. Place, on the other hand, presumes an experiencing subject there to constitute it as such—an experiencing subject seeing expansively into a location, which becomes a locus of attachment and activity. 'Place,' in other words, designates the fullness-in-experience of a 'site' when it is actually inhabited"; see: http://jasonfrancisco.net/to-go-to-lviv (Feb. 28, 2014).

[6] Cf. Anne Whitehead, *Trauma Fiction* (Edinburgh: Edinburgh University Press, 2004), 49.

[7] François Gantheret, "L'Entretien de Claude Lanzmann, Les non-lieux de mémoire," *Nouvelle Revue de Psychanalyse* 33 (1986), 293–305.

[8] "With implicit reference to a phrase of Pierre Nora, he also brings out how the sites that are so important in his film are 'non-lieux de la mémoire' in that they are traumatic sites that

Nora's conception of "sites of memory." Indeed, abandoned, unmarked sites of destruction do not serve either the local community or any other group as a memory anchor; there is no person whose "imagination would invest them with a symbolic aura,"[9] which essentially makes them the opposite of the places catalogued in *Les Lieux de mémoire* (1984–92)/*Realms of Memory* (1996–98).

I propose here to return to these special places "in spite of everything [*malgré tout*]"—"in spite of the fact that there is nothing, but nothing, left to see" there. It was Georges Didi-Huberman who, in his essay "*Lieux malgré tout*" from the collection *Phasmes* (1995),[10] proposed replacing Lanzmann's negative term "*non-lieu*" with "the site despite everything," which possesses a positive valence. He then proceeded to pose the question that, to me, successfully isolates the central problem of these sites; namely, "Why are these sites of slaughter *the* sites in spite of everything, the sites par excellence, the essential sites?"[11]

What makes these sites essential? Why and how do we conceive of them as sites *despite everything*, despite the fact that "there is nothing . . . left"? What exactly distinguishes them from the topographical fabric into which they have been sewn—because despite initially appearing to blend in with the surrounding landscape, there is in fact a distancing, an isolation here. Srebrnik was able to point out his execution site because it somehow stood out from the rest of the forest: someone had kept nature from completely absorbing this space. "Non-sites of memory" are not—I suggest—permanently forgotten, as Lanzmann alleged:[12] there does exist a performatively articulated memory around them, which would make them distant relatives of anti-monuments,[13] were it

---

challenge or undermine the work of memory." Dominic LaCapra, "Lanzmann's 'Shoah': 'Here There Is No Why,'" *Critical Inquiry* 2 (1997), 240; Lanzmann's term is now less clear due to the use of "non-lieu" in Marc Augé, *Non-Lieux, introduction à une antropologie de la supermodernité; Non-Places: An Introduction to Supermodernity*, trans. by John Howe, 2nd edition (London: Verso, 2009). (1992). A similar phrase also occurs in Georgio Agamben's *Remnants of Auschwitz: The Witness and the Archive*, trans. by Daniel Heller-Roazen (Zone Books: New York, 1999), 52: *non-place* is a site occupied by a *Muselmann*, with its extreme limit called "selection."

[9] Pierre Nora, "Between Memory and History: Les Lieux de Mémoire," *Representations* 26 (1989), 19.

[10] Georges Didi-Huberman, *Phasmes: essais sur l'apparition* (Paris: Minuit, 1995).

[11] Georges Didi-Huberman, "The Site, Despite Everything," trans. Stuart Liebman, in *Claude Lanzmann's Shoah: Key Essays*, edited by Stuart Liebmann (Oxford: Oxford University Press, 2007), 115.

[12] Ulrich Baer writes about places where "historical knowledge has burned out," see *Spectral Evidence: The Photography of Trauma* (Cambridge: MIT Press, 2002), 72.

[13] Cf. James E. Young, *Texture of Memory: Holocaust Monuments and Meanings* (New Haven, CT: Yale University Press, 1993).

not for the radically different origins of the actions performed upon and against them. These sites are actively present in the life of surrounding communities in such a way that they are bypassed, not named, not marked, not built up, unsown—as taboo places. The memory of them is not revealed at the level of material culture—markers are not placed there—but rather by way of negation, in turning away or turning a blind eye, and even through such radical gestures as littering and vandalizing: these acts appear to be related to ritual acts, magic, primal acts intended for cursed spaces, taboo places, which our culture has associated since Roman times (if not before) with death and catastrophe.[14]

The places I have in mind are numerous and diverse, and are the result of a variety of historical cataclysms, not only the Shoah. They are, in essence, burial places—mass graves or killing sites[15]—while also being sites of executions and of torture (like the terrains of former labor camps, concentration camps, and death camps) that have not been memorialized by being transformed into museums or monuments; and furthermore, places that remain connected to the events of genocide: demolished synagogues, vandalized cemeteries. These places may occur both in the city and in the countryside; they may be small, or even tiny, and they may also be extensive. They may stand out from the surrounding landscape in the sense that they are a kind of breach in its ordinary, familiar structure; they may not stand out at all, being mere clumps of grass or thickets. They share a certain affective aura that is difficult to rationalize—something in these spaces is perceptibly "off."

To develop a working definition of these places, I hazard an indication of the following qualities they have in common: they also cause in common a certain discomfort among the communities nearest them, for whom commemorating them is a greater threat for their collective identity than is neglecting to commemorate them, though this, too, puts them at risk of external critique. In other words, these places are not sites of memory in Pierre Nora's sense largely because the populations topographically ascribed to them do not need or even actively do not want to invest their memory in them. They want to forget these locales, to not-remember them. *Les lieux de la non-mémoire.* Or with the negative particle preceding the entire time, as Lanzmann has it: *Les non-lieux de la mémoire.*

---

[14] Cf. Eli Edward Burriss, *Taboo, Magic, Spirits: A Study of Primitive Elements in Roman Religion* (New York: Macmillan, 1931), 66–67. With regard to places, "taboo" referred not so much to prohibiting the disturbance of a site as it did to the behavior of individuals who found themselves on that site. Taboo places (e.g., places struck by lightning) were marked with (for example) stones that would prevent the passerby from accidentally wandering in.

[15] See Patrick Desbois, *The Holocaust by Bullets: A Priest's Journey to Uncover the Truth behind the Murder of 1.5 Million Jews* (New York: Palgrave Macmillan, 2009).

To address their "fundamental significance," I will give a concrete example: the site of the former German concentration camp at Krakow-Płaszów, which owes its fame to Thomas Keneally's book *Schindler's Ark* (1982) and to Steven Spielberg's film *Schindler's List* (1993).[16] It is estimated[17] that 25,000 prisoners passed through this camp, and that the remains of 8,000–10,000 predominantly Jewish victims are still located on these premises. After the war, the area continued to be undeveloped, with abundant vegetation taking its revenge for the period of the almost total destruction of the land during the life of the camp. A monument "in honor of the martyrs killed in Hitler's genocide from 1943–1945"[18] stands at the eastern edge of the site. As a result of rapid urbanization after 1989, the site of the camp, which people had previously perceived as being on the outskirts of the city, suddenly became a part of the very center of the city. Satellite photos on Google Maps show a gaping hole in the fabric of the city here, around the same size as the Old Town of Krakow so very beloved by tourists. These two splotches relate to one another like the twin blots of a Rorschach test, embodying the urban conscious and the urban unconscious, the visible and the invisible, the revealed and the concealed, the familiar and the uncanny.

Above

In his book *Spectral Evidence: The Photography of Trauma*, Ulrich Baer reads the image corresponding to the typical "non-site of memory" based on the site of the former Zwangsarbeitslager in Ohrdruf (part of Michael Levin's *War Story* [1995]), asserting that in fact "we are made to see an unfathomable void that will not be dispelled."[19] The idea of "picturing nothing" also facilitates the ekphrasis of the black-and-white photograph called "Sobibór" from the cycle *Deathly Still: Pictures of Former Concentration Camps* by Dirk Reinartz (1995).[20] Applying Baer's ideas to pictures that clearly do *not* display emptiness in any empirical sense seems to suggest that the

---

[16] The camp began as a work camp in late 1942 and was officially transformed into a concentration camp in January 1943. After expansions, it ultimately occupied 67 hectares. Its liquidation lasted from August 1944 until mid-January 1945.

[17] Cf. Ryszard Kotarba, *Niemiecki obóz w Płaszowie 1942–1945* (Warszawa - Kraków: Instytut Pamięci Narodowej, 2009), 161–175.

[18] Built in 1964 by architect Witold Cęckiewicz. In an interview I conducted with Cęckiewicz in October 2013, he told me that he did not recollect the source of funding or the originator of the memorialization.

[19] Ulrich Baer, *Spectral Evidence,* 75.

[20] New York: Scalo Publishers, 1995.

fundamental quality of "non-sites of memory" is their invisibility, their transparency, in the sense that they do not hold the gaze of the passerby. Difficult to recognize, they then surprise us with their lack of identifying markers; our awareness of these spaces' connections to instances of mass murder, meanwhile, heightens our sense of absence and abandonment—our sense of emptiness. A number of photographic projects dedicated to representing non-sites of memory would later opt for a similar poetics, including some of Alan Cohen's series *On European Ground* (2001), Susan Silas' *Helmbrechts Walk* (1993–2003), and even Wojciech Wilczyk's photographs from *There Is No Innocent Eye* (*Niewinne oko nie istnieje*; 2009), meticulously made devoid of any human presence.

Baer's interpretations are exemplars of a very typical practice in dealing with genocide sites. Their reception is generally formatted by a particular minimalist and monochromatic aesthetic consistent with the poetics of the artworks—like Levin's and like Reinhartz's. Lanzmann spoke similarly about the places he filmed in Poland in an interview for *Cahiers du Cinéma*: "there was nothing at all, sheer nothingness, and I had to make a film on the basis of this nothingness."[21] The expectations of the viewers inform the work to such an extent that it sometimes goes as far as to sacrifice authenticity—so vital to Holocaust history—to preserve its ascetic style.[22] Meanwhile, the stereotype of the monochrome is immediately undone, insofar as nature makes its way in the cognitive process from back- to foreground, where—compositionally—in the case of the representation of "non-sites of memory," it generally tends to be. The necessity of a reappraisal of over-exploited conventions of reception has been pointed out by Simon Shama, who writes that "we are accustomed to think of the Holocaust as having no landscape—or at best one emptied of features and color, shrouded in night and fog, blanketed by perpetual winter, collapsed into shades of dun and grey [. . .]. It is shocking, then, to realize that Treblinka, too, belongs to a brilliantly vivid countryside."[23] Putting the static poetics of reception to one side, we run into elements that are inconsistent with the Holocaust: colors, sunshine, and the vibrant filling in of the field of observation that is nature.

---

[21] Stuart Liebman, *Claude Lanzmann's* Shoah: *Key Essays* (Oxford: Oxford University Press, 2007), 39.

[22] One of the extras from *Schindler's List*, interviewed in the video project *Spielberg's List* (2003) by Omer Fast, mentions that Spielberg's set required the reconstruction of prisoners' barracks, with new boards being painted gray despite the fact that in 1943 they would have looked exactly like the ones freshly delivered in 1992: new and light-colored.

[23] Simon Schama, *Landscape and Memory* (New York: Vintage Books, 1996), 26.

Recent contributions of the newly non-anthropocentric humanities now equip us to better consider the properties of "non-sites of memory," beginning with the visible; that is, with the landscape: biotic and abiotic components of the local ecosystem. Nature, in the case of the spaces that interest me here, is the only immediate datum: if the site does still contain remnants of past tragedy, they are often hard to spot at first glance and may require some digging around in order to be discovered. Perceiving the intense, even lush layers of plant life demands the two steps just described: the deconstruction of the concept of "non-sites of memory" as places of voids, and the rejection of monochromatic poetics as the basic format of the imagination.

The question of whether biological material can provide insight into "non-sites of memory" leads in turn to more specific issues, such as the extent to which nature becomes representation, or even literally presentation in the sense of making the victims present. The two extremes in this debate are, on the one hand, the position that plant life is the worst enemy of remembering the victims, and on the other, the opposite: that nature is a faithful companion and suffering's most intimate witness. One of these stances is held by Armando, the Dutch painter and writer.

Born in 1929, Armando spent the years of World War II (and of his childhood) in Amersfoort, a township in which the Nazis placed a concentration camp. His experience of the silence and passivity that occurred alongside those atrocities has returned time and time again in his works. The landscape onto which the guilt of all of the "by-standers" has been projected has turned into a *schuldig Landschap* (guilty landscape). Armando's denouncement is a polyphonic soliloquy: "The edge of the forest, for example the trees towards the front, must have seen a thing or two. The trees in the back can hardly be blamed, they could never have seen anything. But the edge, the seam of the forest: that has seen it . . ."[24] Ernst van Alphen explains the position of the artist as follows: "The presence of the trees on that scene of violence, the continuity between the edge of the forest and the perpetrators of that violence, enables the trees to be blamed. The trees are witnesses, but they don't testify. Their refusal to testify, to serve as a trace of 'the war,' determines their guilt." The order of anthropomorphic nature is, then, radically distinguished from the order of the victims.

The reverse position is represented by Łukasz Surowiec, who presented a project entitled "Berlin–Birkenau" at the 2012 Berlin Biennale. A part of the work was the act of giving out birch seedlings from the site of the former Birkenau concentration camp. The artist explained his plan as follows: "I bring a live cemetery. The trees at Birkenau drink water from earth mixed with

---

[24] Ernst van Alphen, *Armando: Shaping Memory* (Rotterdam: NAi Publishers, 2000), 10–11.

ashes and breathe the same air that bore the smoke from the burnt bodies. Those trees contain something of those people."[25]

Surowiec's bioart project is one of the works that initiate and foment the idea that plants, in absorbing the mineral remains of human beings as they grow, become something more than simply the representation of the victims' suffering by becoming witnesses at the cellular level—their presence metonymically restores the existence of those now absent. Anthropomorphizing trees, either planted or spontaneously arising on Holocaust sites, results in a next step, that of taking the metaphor literally: "if we actually think about the organic contents of the trees, we realize that they all contain within themselves the remains of the victims," writes Jacek Małczyński in his piece tellingly titled "Trees: Living Monuments at the Museum and Place of Memory in Bełżec."[26] Trees are thus treated as transgenic objects—an extreme liberalization of a metaphor, since blending human with plant DNA is in fact an operation that must be carried out artificially in a lab.[27] It is an approach that renders habitat not as witness, but rather as a way of permitting the victims to endure.[28]

Below

Regardless of what position we take on what we find above ground, traces of the tragedy remain concealed below ground, and a full analysis of "non-sites of

---

[25] An interview conducted by Daniel Miller, accessed July 27, 2012, http://www.krytykapolityczna.pl/7BerlinBiennale/SurowiecBerlinBirkenau/menuid-427.html.

[26] Jacek Małczyński "Drzewa—Żywe pomniki w Muzeum-Miejscu Pamięci w Bełżcu," *Teksty Drugie* 1–2 (2009).

[27] Jacek Małczyński writes about a "laboratory" art project by Gregore Tremmel and Shiho Fukuhara entitled "Biopresence," accessed July 27, 2012, http://www.biopresence.com/description.html. There are also similar commercial projects; cf. Ian Sample, "Firm Plans Human DNA Tree Memorial," *The Guardian* (April 30, 2004), accessed 28 July 2012, http://www.theguardian.com/science/2004/apr/30/genetics.highereducation.

[28] Between these two limit points there are a number of intermediary interpretations also possible, of which I will mention only one here: Oskar Hansen's project of a "road memorial," in which the artist, along with a group of others, proposed cutting across the terrain of the camp at Birkenau with an asphalt road 65 meters across and conserving only those camp relics that could be found within the space of that road. The rest was to be consumed by nature. Jan Stanisław Wojciechowski cites an unpublished note written by Hansen: "The growing forest surrounding the 'Road' is a kind of 'watch' measuring the time that elapses since the tragic events of the camp, so it's an expression of the triumph of life over death . . . Then when you keep going you emerge from the "Road" into the open space of a field . . . You return to life, able to fully appreciate its value." Jan Stanisław Wojciechowski, "Oskara Hansena (i zespołu) projekt oświęcimskiego pomnika 'Drogi' w świetle jego teorii Formy Otwartej," in *Pamięć Shoah: Kulturowe reprezentacje i praktyki upamiętniania,* edited by T. Majewski and A. Zeidler-Janiszewska (Łódź: Wydawnictwo Officyna, 2011), 65.

memory" would have to consider the space traditionally occupied by archaeology and geology. The difficulty of this research is crucially heightened by the fact that according to Judaic law, land containing the remains of victims of the Holocaust cannot be touched, being cemetery land.[29] An analysis of what is hidden beneath the plant layer appears to aim primarily at the discovery of relics—proofs of the existence of places of torture and of bodies or human ashes. I would argue that the materiality of these objects is more complicated than this.

In 2006, the Municipality of Krakow announced an architectural competition to develop into a memory site the land of what was once the Płaszów camp. The team (Proxima) that won first place in the competition was asked to provide an inventory. The categories employed by the architects can enable us to imagine the "sub-plant" state of the "non-site of memory." Proxima presented the results of their research in ten charts: a geological map of the present state of the place; a map of Austrian remains from the First World War; a map reconstructing the borderlines of the pre-war Jewish cemeteries; a map of the concentration camp buildings from the Second World War; a map of extant camp relics; a map of postwar developments (roads, paths); and a map of recent technical installations (water pipes, electricity cables, etc., that now run through the camp's premises). The eighth map displays the ownership structure; the last-but-one pictures trees and shrubs; and the last map presents the proposed developments needed to complete the winning project.

These charts are a testament to how many discourses are at work within a single, topographically defined place: geographical, geodetic, geological, historical, administrative and legal, technical (systems); biological; religious (the cemeteries existing on this land prior to the war), artistic (the development planned), as well as memory discourse (existing monuments). We can imagine maps charting the walking paths and pausing places for local residents (the discourse of "free time"), mapping the places specified by camp inmates in their private narratives (the discourse of idiosyncratic memory), and mapping the "phantasmatic"—local residents have their own tales and legends about the land from after the war. The camp land is also impinged upon by aggressive advertising by a nearby shopping mall that closes off the view and that also

---

[29] Archeological investigations were conducted in preparation for the construction of the memorial site in Bełżec; cf. Małczyński, *Drzewa*, 211: "33 mass graves have been located. They take up a large part of the site. The minimally invasive method of drilling probes has been used." Sobibór was similarly investigated, see A. Kola, "Sprawozdanie z archeologicznych badań na terenie b. obozu Zagłady Żydów w Sobiborze," *Przeszłość i Pamięć* 3 (2000). Non-invasive Holocaust archaeology is a recent development; cf. Caroline Sturdy Colls, "Holocaust Archaeology: Archeoogical Approaches to Landscapes of Nazi Genocide and Persecution" *Journal of Conflict Archaeology* 7, no. 2 (2012).

makes it possible to add to the above list, economic discourse (the discourse of consumption and trade).

The way that the Proxima Group has physically rationalized the confusion of orders on camp land brings to mind the notion of a palimpsest as a basic cognitive model allowing the increasing complexity of the site under consideration to be reckoned with. The figure of the palimpsest is built upon an idea of sedimentation (the buildup of successive planes) and provides a consistent synchronic model[30] in which individual categories are easy to separate, group, and read. (This is how the Proxima study is organized.)

As much as the quality of simultaneity certainly describes the state of the discourses interwoven in the fabric of the camp terrain in Płaszów, the project does not attain functional data storage or readability. Let us note, however, the way in which Proxima presented their study: the first map becomes lighter when the second map is placed on top of it, etc. Let us imagine, meanwhile, all the maps placed upon one another without any shading allowances: the chaos of the symbols would make any recognition of the properties of the site impossible. The researcher confronted not with the model, but rather with the object, standing in the middle of the terrain in question, is confronted with a cacophony of unstructured data (data that is in fact encoded and that requires training in order to be decoded, which impedes the activity of understanding still further.) The layeredness of the palimpsest, then, is merely an a priori cognitive construction allowing for the pictorial representation of the elements of the "non-site of memory" and is most certainly *not* its ontological characteristic.

Therefore, it might be more effective to refer to a "technical" description of a palimpsest. Greco-Roman etymology unites the words *palin* ("again") and *psao* ("I scrape").[31] Some of the elements that make up the physical contours of the Płaszów grounds seem to support the "leveling" quality of the palimpsest: layers do not simply get added to one another, but are rather always erasing what came before, leaving only traces of the existence of the previous layer. As a new layer of soil and vegetation covered over and destroyed the remnants of the camp's buildings, so the construction of the camp itself razed the structures that had been built on that land in the era of the First World War, and so, too, the current construction of apartment buildings has erased all traces of the SS barracks.

---

[30] "The structural concept of the palimpsest is based on the text's ability to reveal explicitly its sources of precedent layers in order to make them totally visible and easily discernable," see Michał P. Markowski, "Wiping Out: The Palimpsest, the Subject, and the Art of Forgetting," edited by Bożena Shallcross and Ryszard Nycz (Frankfurt am Main: Peter Lang, 2011), 121.

[31] Cf. Justyna Beinek, "Inscribing, Engraving, Cutting: The Polish Romantic Album as Palimpsest," in *The Effect of Palimpsest: Culture, Literature, History,* edited by Bożena Shallcross and Ryszard Nycz (Frankfurt am Main: Peter Lang, 2011), 29.

But it strikes me that the figure of the palimpsest, whether the palimpsest that accentuates layeredness and lastingness or the palimpsest that refers more to the act of destruction, is unable to productively back up any analysis of the "non-site of memory," primarily because of one characteristic shared by both versions; namely, the basic concept of order, the succession of individual elements, the particular "syntactic logic" of both models based on the idea of sequence, on relationships of cause and effect, and on the assumption that the basic elements of the system are discrete, unconnected and discernable. Meanwhile the reality of physical objects on the grounds of the camps turns the idea of "layeredness" upside down—part of the installation is underground, part of it above; the ruins of the barracks are at once overgrown (as when vegetation covers extant structural elements of the camp) and also partly not (as when vegetation is nearby or underneath these elements); the human remains may be underneath but also above the earth's surface. In addition, some architectural projects (for example, the reinforcement of the Krakow fortress) functionally belong to several maps (several discourses): the trenches must simultaneously be included in the categories of ruins of the beginning of the twentieth century and mass graves from 1944. Furthermore, in treating layers as stable space, the metaphor of the palimpsest does not explain what happens *between* them:[32] it does not, then, serve the purpose of describing those "dynamic," "mixed," "diffuse" objects that are, without a doubt, the "living" grounds of "non-sites of memory."

Prism

The contested sites of genocide and atrocity—I repeat—cannot be explained with the use of concepts based on the logic of a sentence. The particular "mixed" character of "non-sites of memory" requires us to seek out metaphors from among terms suggesting disorder, and especially the type of disorder in which biological and non-biological elements are mixed, along with man-made items and natural elements, all of it in a state of constant agitation, of ongoing change. Elements disintegrate and are shuffled around, grow and die, are moved (e.g., by architects investigating the terrain, by visitors, by animals, by prisoners customarily sent in the spring to do light logging). Thus the metaphor I seek would need to include the idea of confusion and leftovers, of change and remaining, and perhaps the fullest reservoir of suitable ideas might be found in "rubbish theory."

---

[32] Ryszard Nycz, "The Palimpsest and the Spiderweb: Two Dimensions of the Textualisation of Experience" in Shallcross and Nycz, *The Effect of Palimpsest,* 23.

What unites the "non-site of memory" with the "garbage heap" is not only the metaphor of the "rubbish dump of history," which we could no doubt use for places like Płaszów, not only the habit of littering in deserted places, but their shared state of "potentiality" and "indeterminacy." If Jonathan Culler is correct that "as the transient moves towards rubbish, it can either be torn down to make way for something new (this is the transient view, the view from the system of transients) or else salvaged as durable: rebuilt, reconstructed."[33] The material contents of the "non-site of memory" possess a similar dual dynamic: the camp's remains, as well as human remains, undergo a process of decomposition, becoming soil for the plants, though they might also be preserved if the locale is selected for conservation and turned into a "lieu d'histoire." Yet it is difficult to ignore the fact that some elements of rubbish theory preclude its usage for "non-sites of memory." Firstly, it echoes the rhetoric of the perpetrators who originally sent "human garbage" off to these camps in the first place. Secondly, in order for it to be "rubbish," the locale must become useless and "inferior" within the system of exchange.[34] The most important components of "non-sites of memory," human remains, simply cannot be evaluated in terms of an economic system, nor can there be any idea of referring to them as "trivial."

Metaphors with their provenance in the language of the natural sciences may be more productive, including the (also Adornian) term "detritus," with its connotation of an unordered accumulation of many elements and the movement of their interaction, as well as the effect of their acting: departure, destruction, forgetting.[35] In biology, detritus is any form of non-living organic material, be it the bodies or components of dead organisms or the matter discarded by living organisms, such as feces.[36] Adorno utilized the term in a context convergent with the topic of this article insofar as it was connected with the operation of memory disturbed by the "detritus of things."[37] Detritus is synonymous in Adorno with the indiscriminate magma of stimuli brought to us by popular culture. Understood literally, "biologically," it carries connotations that are useful in thinking about the problematic of the "non-site of memory": the unordered accumulation of many elements, the movement of their interactions, as well as the effect of their activities: waste,

---

[33] Jonathan Culler, "Junk and Rubbish: A Semiotic Approach," *Diacritics* 15, no. 3 (Fall 1985), 9.

[34] Culler, 5.

[35] Zafar Reshi and Sumira Tyub, *Detritus and Decomposition in Ecosystems* (Delhi: New India Publisher, 2007), 1.

[36] Ibid.

[37] Tia DeNora, *After Adorno: Rethinking Music Sociology* (Cambridge: Cambridge University Press, 2003), 77.

ruin, homogenization. It emphasizes the influence on the surrounding community. (For biologists and ecologists, detritus has a major role in the proper functioning of the ecosystem.)

Detritus is thus the arena in which dead matter (the past) becomes transformed into fertile soil that is able to give rise to new life. In this sense, it serves to heal: in the case of "non-sites," what has been forgotten may *need* to have been forgotten in order for the surrounding areas to continue to live. The metaphor of detritus would thus describe the positive component of the decomposition of memory occurring at "non-sites of memory" and the restorative significance of this process for the communities residing around these "non-sites." On the other hand, the particularity of the "non-lieu de mémoire" is its conjunction of "detritus" with the opposite of this—not everything falls apart, and the very notion of visiting the places mentioned here is tied to the conviction that there is still evidence here incriminating the perpetrators—even if this evidence takes the form of a person capable of recalling the crime.

The material reality of "non-sites of memory" could also be described by means of an idea rejected by Giorgio Agamben in his *Remnants of Auschwitz.* "Hypostasis," in its original Greek meaning, "is a substratum, deposit, or sediment left behind as a kind of background or foundation by historical processes of subjectificaton and desubjectification."[38] I'm particularly interested here in this definition's mobilization of what I was pointing out in analyzing GP Proxima's charts: the multitude of discourses clashing on the post-camp terrain of Płaszów. The short-circuiting, the collision, or even the less violent compounding of the space's external qualities that produce its sedimentary, residual character as a "collection of traces" would direct our attention to geology, which has lately become a participant in historical discourses.[39] The term "anthropocene" has arisen to define a period in which human activity has become defining in the shaping of the earth, so that the "eternal humanist distinction between the history of humanity and natural history"[40] has collapsed before our very eyes. "Non-sites of memory" may, then, serve as spheres in which one can actually observe this intermingling of the traditional human and natural orders. In some of them, one can literally watch the functioning of "man as new geological force"—especially in Płaszów, built near a quarry and also working during the war as a place that intervened in the land's own structure. During the First World War, soldiers disrupted the limestone

---

[38] Giorgio Agamben, *Remnants of Auschwitz: The Witness and the Archive*, trans. Daniel Heller-Roazen (New York: Zone Books, 1999), 158.

[39] Cf. Dipesh Chakrabarty, "The Climate of History: Four Theses," *Critical Inquiry* 35 (2009): 197–222.

[40] Chakrabarty, 201.

present here by digging trenches; later, camp prisoners were forced to dig out cellars, break down rock, and remove the ensuing rubble. On these "non-sites of memory," natural history—the history of the rocks, trees, water—becomes an essential component of human history, making theoretically possible a discussion that would exceed the historical order.

Thus, the final metaphor I wish to propose here for the "non-site of memory" comes from the reservoir of geology. The term I have in mind is "prism." In Polish, "pryzma" is used to designate compost; that is, the place for organic garbage. In this term, therefore, both rubbish theory and detritus come into play. The term also holds the energy of hypostasis; i.e., the sediment necessary for development, growth, and change. Geology, meanwhile, defines prism, above all, as the "accretionary prism." This is an area of sedimentation produced by materials sloughed off by the force generated by friction between the largest tectonic plates, transferred and then left in the form of a wedge wherever it was that the tectonic movements ceased.

This definition of prism thus also incorporates a palimpsestic, continuous "scraping." Rock and organic material (e.g., from the bottom of the sea) are combined in no order and expelled from their original location as the result of overwhelming force, geological "violence." The prism is thus organic and non-organic, is "marred" and "illegible." It is produced by the activity of external forces, which can be compared to the activity of external discourses: history, politics, economy, memory. "The wedge," the physical presence of the object, does not allow itself to be dominated by these discourses, leaving the unsettling feeling that sweeps up the visitor, the feeling that there is still something there that threatens the organized order. The more common English meaning of the word prism,[41] i.e., an object that separates white light into a spectrum of colors, also generates a particular kind of metaphorical strength: "non-sites of memory" are locations deconstructing all homogenizing imaginaries purporting to understand them. They refract and complicate superficially monological discourse—both the discourse around itself and perhaps also the existing discourse on genocide sites in general.

A Question in Lieu of a Conclusion

That Lanzmann, in rejecting the notion of the "lieu de mémoire," added a negating particle to the first rather than to the second component of Nora's term ought to give us pause, for it could also be argued that in the locales he films, it is memory, not the site, that is deficient. Edward Relph was a

[41] Until recently, this meaning also existed in Polish.

precursor to Marc Augé and student of Martin Heidegger. His *Place and Placelessness* (1976) tied "placelessness" with a particular quality of topographical sites that strips the visitor of his or her sense of being an "existential participant" in a space of "givenness" for life. (I will bracket here for the moment the question of the modernity of the places described by Relph.) Baer, describing the effect of Levin's photograph, writes that it shows the "landscape without us."[42] "Non-sites of memory" are, then, not-for-life; they are always sentenced to death. The readily discernable other side of this phrasing is the critique of—even the indignation in the face of—the vacancy, the unmarkedness, the nondescriptness of these spaces. "Non-sites" ought instead to be cordoned off by some sort of "line" indicating their extent, allowing for the demarcation of the space of our symbolic engagement. Lanzmann's thinking clearly subscribes to this desire for demarcation: in an interview with François Gantheret for *La Nouvelle Revue de Psychanalyse*, in which he utilized the term "non-lieux de mémoire," he talked about arriving in Sobibór and meeting an old railway man. Lanzmann reconstructed the conversation as follows:

> "Please show me. Please show me where the camp started." "Okay," he said. "I'll show you." After taking a few steps he turned to me and said, "Okay, here there was a wood support, and then here was the next one." And I see myself crossing that line and saying, "Here I'm inside the concentration camp." I stepped back three meters. "And here I'm outside of the camp. On that side, you have death. On this side, life."[43]

It is hard for me to accept the dialectical nature of this "here you have death, there you have life." If you look at the actual "non-sites of memory" from the perspective of Eastern Europe, the limiting "line" that Lanzmann requires was never so obvious. The line was, for the Eastern European population, permeable (although the degree of its permeability was, of course, different for different groups of people), far more permeable than to the citizens of countries in the West, due to radical differences in the forms of Nazi occupation. In any case, those limits that were wooden structures did not defend against

---

[42] Ulrich Baer, 75.

[43] Cited (in a different translation reversing the order of the last two sentences of this passage) in Richard Brody, "Claude Lanzmann on 'Shoah,'" *The New Yorker* (December 10, 2010), http://www.newyorker.com/online/blogs/movies/2010/12/claude-lanzmann-on-shoah.html; cf. *Au sujet de Shoah: Le film de Claude Lanzmann* (Paris: Éditions Belin, 1990), 281–282; and Claude Lanzmann, *Patagonian Hare: A Memoir,* trans. Frank Wynne (New York: FSG, 2013).

death: at any moment, the whim of any of the perpetrators might cast anyone at all over onto the "side of death." That is why, given the location of my point of view between Moscow and Berlin, it seems to me that it is necessary in the face of "non-sites of memory"—which perhaps ought to be given another name—to ask a different set of questions. Access to them, as they are not yet fully articulable, would consist of deconstructing the third principle of the conceptualization of places of genocide: dialectical separation. Standing with a camera in the forests of Sobibór, at the clearing in Ohrdruf, in the landscape of Płaszów, we are there, we are at the non-site, we enter onto that terrain, consciously or unconsciously invading a place of death with life. The "non-site of memory" turns out to be the "landscape with us." In order to comprehend the "fundamental significance" of these sites, we need to try and understand how the forces of memory and forgetting together affect this space, how the vibrancy of these places coexists with their moribundity; hence, their "organic–nonorganic" character, inextricable.

Stepping out of the discursive frameworks set out above for a moment, I would like to ask a more basic question of those sites "of fundamental significance": where do we actually stand in relation to them? If not on the outside and not on the inside—then where? Are we excluded from them, or sucked into their untamed life after/in trauma? What are we to do, here in this part of Europe, as we enter onto "non-sites of memory," theoretically "unlivable," but in practice so shamelessly alive?

BIBLIOGRAPHY

Agamben, Georgio. *Remnants of Auschwitz: The Witness and the Archive.* Translated by Daniel Heller-Roazen. New York: Zone Books, 1999.

Augé, Marc. *Non-Lieux, introduction à une antropologie de la supermodernité.* Paris: Le Seuil, 1992.

———. *Non-Places: Introduction to an Anthropology of Supermodernity.* Translated by John Howe. Verso: New York, 1995.

Baer, Ulrich. *Spectral Evidence: The Photography of Trauma.* Cambridge: MIT Press, 2002.

Beinek, Justyna. "Inscribing, Engraving, Cutting: The Polish Romantic Album as Palimpsest." *The Effect of Palimpsest: Culture, Literature, History,* edited by Bożena Shallcross and Ryszard Nycz. Frankfurt am Main: Peter Lang, 2011.

Brody, Richard. "Claude Lanzmann on 'Shoah.'" *The New Yorker.* 10 December 2010.

Burriss, Eli Edward. *Taboo, Magic, Spirits: A Study of Primitive Elements in Roman Religion.* New York: Macmillan, 1931.

Chakrabarty, Dipesh. "The Climate of History: Four Theses." *Critical Inquiry* 35 (2009): 197–222.

Colls, Caroline Sturdy. "Holocaust Archaeology: Archeoogical Approaches to Landscapes of Nazi Genocide and Persecution." *Journal of Conflict Archaeology* 7, no. 2 (2012).

Culler, Jonathan. "Junk and Rubbish: A Semiotic Approach." *Diacritics* (Fall 1985).

DeNora, Tia. *After Adorno: Rethinking Music Sociology.* Cambridge: Cambridge University Press, 2003.

Desbois, Patrick. *The Holocaust by Bullets: A Priest's Journey to Uncover the Truth behind the Murder of 1.5 Million Jews.* New York: Palgrave Macmillan, 2009.

Didi-Huberman, Georges. *Phasmes : essais sur l'apparition,* Paris: Minuit, 1995.

———. "The Site, Despite Everything." Translated by Stuart Liebman. In *Claude Lanzmann's Shoah: Key Essays*, edited by Stuart Liebmann. Oxford: Oxford University Press, 2007.

Gantheret, François. "L'Entretien de Claude Lanzmann, Les non-lieux de mémoire." *Nouvelle Revue de Psychanalyse* 33 (1986).

Kotarba, Ryszard. *Niemiecki obóz w Płaszowie 1942-1945.* Warszawa–Kraków: Instytut Pamięci Narodowej, 2009.

LaCapra, Dominic. "Lanzmann's 'Shoah': 'Here There Is No Why.'" *Critical Inquiry* 2 (1997).

Lanzmann, Claude. "Le Lieu et la parole." *Au sujet de Shoah: Le Film de Claude Lanzmann*, edited by Michel Deguy. Paris: Éditions Berlin, 1990.

———. *Patagonian Hare: A Memoir.* Translated by Frank Wynne. New York: FSG, 2013.

Liebman, Stuart. *Claude Lanzmann's* Shoah: *Key Essays.* Oxford: Oxford University Press, 2007.

Małczyński, Jacek. "Drzewa—Żywe pomniki w Muzeum-Miejscu Pamięci w Bełżcu." *Teksty Drugie* 1–2 (2009).

Markowski, Michał P. "Wiping Out: The Palimpsest, the Subject, and the Art of Forgetting." *The Effect of Palimpsest: Culture, Literature, History*, edited by Bożena Shallcross and Ryszard Nycz. Frankfurt am Main: Peter Lang, 2011.

Norra, Pierre. "Between Memory and History: Les Lieux de Mémoire." *Representations* 26 (1989).

Nycz, Ryszard. "The Palimpsest and the Spiderweb: Two Dimensions of the Textualisation of Experience." *The Effect of Palimpsest: Culture, Literature, History*, edited by Bożena Shallcross and Ryszard Nycz. Frankfurt am Main: Peter Lang, 2011.

Pamięć Shoah. Kulturowe reprezentacje i praktyki upamiętniania, edited by T. Majewski and A. Zeidler-Janiszewska. Łódź: Wydawnictwo Officyna, 2011.

Reshi, Zafar, and Sumira Tyub. *Detritus and Decomposition in Ecosystems.* Delhi: New India Publisher, 2007.

Schama, Simon. *Landscape and Memory.* New York: Vintage Books, 1996.

Snyder, Timothy. *Bloodlands: Europe between Hitler and Stalin.* New York: Basic Books, 2010.

van Alphen, Ernst. *Armando: Shaping Memory*. Rotterdam: NAi Publishers, 2000.

Whitehead, Anne. *Trauma Fiction*, Edinburgh: Edinburgh University Press, 2004.

Young, James E. *Texture of Memory: Holocaust Monuments and Meanings*. New Haven: Yale University Press.

THE THEATER OF WAR AND PEACE: THE "MIRACLE OF THE HOUSE OF BRANDENBURG" AND THE POETICS OF EUROPEAN ABSOLUTISM*

Kirill Ospovat

Abstract

This paper addresses the cultural poetics of pan-European absolutist politics, as revealed during the Seven Years' War (1756–1763) and in its outcome, known as the "miracle of the house of Brandenburg." I argue that political self-fashioning of the war's two major actors, the Russian emperor Peter III and Frederick II of Prussia, and their reading of events were shaped by "scenarios of power" elaborated in tragedy and opera seria, *the two major theatrical genres of pan-European absolutist theater specifically suited to negotiate fundamental visions of sovereignty. For Frederick, himself a man of letters and a poet, tragedy provided a paradigm of royal charisma paradoxically affirmed by defeats threatening its very essence. Theatrical interest for a misfortunate hero, the fundamental aesthetic effect of tragedy, served as a model for patriotic mobilization around the figure of the defeated rather than the triumphant king. On the other hand, the instant restitution of all conquered Prussian territory by Peter III immediately after his ascension to the throne was conceived as a spectacular gesture inaugurating a scenario of clement rule, canonized in some of the central texts of the neoclassical dramatic canon, and extended*

* This paper was written with the support of the Early Modern European Drama and the Cultural Net, which is funded by the European Research Council at the Freie Universität Berlin.

to the internal policies of the new emperor, whose important measures—such as abolition of the terrifying secret police—relied on theatrical patterns of manipulating public emotion in favor of the ruler-as-actor.

On May 21, 1762, King Frederick of Prussia wrote to his Field Marshal, Prince Ferdinand of Braunschweig-Lüneburg: "Ce changement qui m'arrive, est ce que les Grecs appellent dans leur tragédies péripetie. Le Ciel nous seconde encore et mène tout à une bonne fin!" (This change which occurred with me, is what the Greeks call in their tragedies "peripeteia." Heaven still supports us and leads everything to a good end!)[1] The king was referring to a series of events that shaped the outcome of the Seven Years' War. On the verge of 1762, after the death of the Russian Empress Elizabeth, her successor Peter III, an outspoken admirer of Frederick, withdrew from the anti-Prussian coalition formed by France and Austria. In this way, he prevented the imminent ruin of the Prussian state, instead allowing Frederick to conclude an honorable peace.

By the time Elizabeth died, Frederick, who was increasingly overstrained by the prolonged war against overwhelming enemy forces, had already several times conjured a "miracle of the house of Brandenburg." Judging by Johannes Kunisch's well-known monograph, this concept has not lost its viability for discussing the events of 1762, even in the era of rationalist historiography. The notion of "miracle," a figment of self-referential "discoursivity" inimical to any elucidation, conveys the powerful presence of symbolic patterns, which inform the experience of history beyond explanations and—contrary to Hayden White's assertion that "stories are not lived,"—embed tropes of representation into the very core of fact, the "factum."[2] As Reinhold Koser has established, Frederick's own miracle belonged to an archaic political theology that was modeled after a long-standing tradition of the "miracles of the House of Austria," which proved the divine election of the Habsburgs.[3]

However, unlike some of his pious subjects, who literally accepted and propagated this theology, Frederick was schooled in skepticism and keenly appreciated the powers of manipulation and distortion accessible to authority

---

1 Frederick II, *Politische Correspondenz Friedrichs des Großen*, Band 21 (Berlin: Dunker, 1894), 462; Johannes Kunisch, *Das Mirakel des Hauses Brandenburg: Studien zum Verhältnis von Kabinettspolitik und Kriegführung im Zeitalter des Siebenjährigen Krieges* (Munich: Oldenbourg, 1978), 12.

2 Hayden White, "Literary Theory and Historical Writing," in *Figural Realism: Studies in the Mimesis Effect* (Baltimore, MD: John Hopkins University Press, 1999), 9.

3 Reinhold Koser, *Geschichte Friedrichs des Großen,* Band 3 (Stuttgart: Cotta'sche Buchhandlung Nachfolger, 1913), 38.

and authorship.[4] These powers were revealed and tested on the occasion of the war: as its instigator—its *auteur*—Frederick devised both its military operations and its glorifying narrative, culminating in his own *Histoire de la guerre de Sept Ans* (1763). In his letter to Braunschweig, the suggestion of divine intervention is both diluted by a vague reference to *le ciel,* a mere figure of speech as much as a confession of faith, and—in a self-conscious reminder of the authorial powers of representation—counterbalanced by the notion of "péripetie," a technical term from pagan poetics.

It is a reference to tragedy and its Aristotelian theory that allows Frederick to grasp the fateful events that saved his kingdom from the brink of ruin. Indeed tragedy, as it was practiced and theorized in early modern Europe, provided a paradigm for a historical sensibility, which as White argues, was dominated by the tension between a methodology of historical representation dependent on "classical rhetoric and poetics," on the one hand, and a mistrust of the irrational and "the fabulous" in history, on the other.[5] In his seminal study of the genre, Walter Benjamin has demonstrated that early modern tragedy (Trauerspiel) was conceived as a medium of reflection on history identified with "the insight into diplomacy and the manipulation of all the political schemes." Moreover, this vision of history was centered upon the figure of the sovereign, its "principal exponent" and "representative," and thus "the main character of the *Trauerspiel.*"[6] According to Benjamin, who builds in turn on Carl Schmitt's readings of baroque political theology and theory, the royal history of the *Trauerspiel* is permeated with a constant "tension between immanence and transcendence," which shapes the troubled status of the sovereign, who cannot cast off his own "immanence," or "the disproportion between the unlimited hierarchical dignity, with which he is divinely invested and the humble estate of his humanity."[7]

This tension was reenacted in Frederick's intellectual trajectory during the Seven Years War. As the records of Henri de Catt, the king's reader, confirm, his self-consciousness as a political actor and a "warrior king" was largely shaped by a constantly reconsidered relationship with the divine. Frederick's view oscillated

---

[4] Kunisch, *Mirakel,* 12. The distortions inherent in Frederick's double role as his own chronicler were recognized by Klopstock in an ode addressed to the king: "Mehr trübt der Nebel, wenn, was du tatest, du / Selbst redest." For the full text, see Friedrich Gottlieb Klopstock, "Die Verkennung (1779)," in *Friedrich II, König von Preußen, und die deutsche Literatur des 18. Jahrhunderts. Texte und Dokumente,* edited by Horst Steinmetz (Stuttgart: Reclam, 1985), 57.

[5] Hayden White, "The Irrational and the Problem of Historical Knowledge in the Enlightenment," in *Tropics of Discourse: Essays in Cultural Criticism* (Baltimore, MD: John Hopkins University Press, 1985), 142–143.

[6] Walter Benjamin, *The Origin of the German Tragic Drama,* translated by John Osborne (London: Verso, 1985), 62–65.

[7] Ibid, 67–70.

between his usual metaphysical skepticism (which informs many of his poems composed during the war) and occasional outbreaks of religious zeal reinforced by the political theology of divine election. On July 28, 1760, Frederick said, for example: "Pour me tirer d'affaire, il faut un miracle, et il ne s'un fait plus." (In order to get out of this business, I need a miracle, and there are no more.)[8] Frederick's construal of tragedies, mostly Racine's, which were known to have been his favorite reading in the war years, reflected this set of issues.[9] Among the tragedies he recited to de Catt, he especially favored Racine's *Athalie* (1691), which adapted a biblical plot and staged the restoration of the divine kingship of the house of David, which became emblematic of direct divine intervention into royal politics. In 1758 Frederick "fervently" quoted the prayer of the high priest Joad directed against the usurper Queen Athalie and her councilor Mathan, adapting the verses to include a reference to Empress Queen Maria Theresa, the leader of the anti-Prussian coalition, and her minister Kaunitz:

> *Daigne, daigne, mon Dieu, sur Kaunitz et sur elle*
> *Répandre cet esprit d'imprudence et d'erreur,*
> *De la chute des rois funeste avant-coureur!*
> *(Deign, Deign, My God, to shed on Kaunitz and on her*
> *This spirit of imprudence and error,*
> *A fateful precursor of the fall of kings!)*[10]

It is the idiom of tragedy that allows Frederick to interpret political events in a theological perspective. Joad's prayer provided a pattern for the king's assessment of his position a year later when he wrote that things were going so badly that a favorable outcome could only originate from "quelque miracle ou de la divin ânerie des mes ennemis" (some miracle or the heaven sent imbecility of my enemies).[11] Anticipating the "miracle" of 1762, the king's use of tragic discourse nourished a fascination with political mysticism quite remote from his usual skeptical intellectual stance. He enthusiastically recited to de Catt verses from

---

[8] Reinhold Koser, ed., *Unterhaltungen mit Friedrich dem Großen: Memoiren und Tagebücher von Heinrich de Catt* (Leipzig: Hirzel, 1884), 432. On the religious and metaphysical issues in the cultural experience of the Seven Years' War, see Karl Schwarze, *Der Siebenjährige Krieg in der zeitgenössischen deutschen Literatur. Kriegserleben und Kriegserlebnis in Schrifttum und Dichtung des 18. Jahrhunderts* (Berlin: Junker und Dunhaupt, 1936), 94–116.

[9] On Frederick's reading, see Jorg Ulbert, "Friedrichs Lektüren während des Siebenjährigen Krieges," in *Friedrich der Große als Leser,* edited by Brunhilde Wehinger and Günther Lottes (Berlin: Akademie Verlag, 2012), 71– 98.

[10] Koser, *Unterhaltungen,* 130; *Frederick the Great: The Memoirs of his Reader, Henri de Catt (1758–1760),* translated by F. S. Flint (Boston: Houghton Miflin, 1917), 1:238. See also Jean Racine, *Athalie,* I:2, in Racine, *Théâtre complet*, edited by Jean-Pierre Collinet (Paris: Gallimard, 1983), 2:420.

[11] *Politische Correspondenz Friedrich's des Großen* (Berlin, 1890), 18:516, #11403.

Athalie on the divine supervision of earthly rulers and immediately declared them to be false.[12] In 1763, in an intriguing train of thought, he told D'Alembert that he would rather have written *Athalie* than won the war, since the war was mostly a work of chance. Thus, he simultaneously negated the divine intervention he had so often conjured forth, while affirming the value of its tragic representation.[13] The parallel between drama and the war (meant to problematize the comparative strengths and weaknesses of authorial and royal agency) relied on the intrinsic affinity between the literary mode of tragedy and the experience of history: "The *Trauerspiel*, it was believed, could be directly grasped in the events of history itself; it was only a question of finding the right words."[14]

In the letter to Braunschweig, Frederick juxtaposes "miracle" with "péripetie," thereby linking it to a mode of representation that simultaneously functioned as a performative theory of political action.[15] In 1778, writing amidst a political crisis where Frederick II figured prominently, another German statesman and man of letters, Johann Wolfgang Goethe, noted: "ich scheine dem Ziele dramatischen Wesens immer näher zu kommen, da michs nun immer näher angeht, wie die Großen mit den Menschen, und die Götter mit den Großen spielen."(It seems that I am approaching closer and closer the aim of dramatic essence, as I am more and more affected by the ways in which the great play with men, and the gods play with the great.)[16] Goethe summarizes his experience of absolutist politics with a reference to dramatic "essence," which again discerns a divine will behind political shifts and then reduces it to a poetic trope.

Readings of tragedy seem to reflect the genealogy of "all significant concepts of the modern theory of state" as "secularized theological concepts . . . transferred from theology to the theory of state," so that "the omnipotent God became the omnipotent lawgiver," while the "exception in jurisprudence is analogous to the miracle in theology."[17] Together these mutually intertwined notions provided a conceptual framework for political crises, or "states of exception," which according to Benjamin had crystallized in the practice and theory of tragedy. Indeed, according to d'Aubignac, one of the most influential theorists of the French neoclassical canon, the specific goal of tragedy

---

12 Koser, *Unterhaltungen*, 132; *Frederick the Great*, 243.

13 *Correspondance complète de la Marquise du Deffand avec ses amis (*Paris, 1865), 1:276.

14 Benjamin, *The Origin of the German Tragic Drama*, 63.

15 Louis Marin, "Théâtralité et pouvoir: Magie, machination, machine: *Médée* de Corneille," in *Politiques de la représentation* (Paris: Editions Kimé, 2005), 263–285.

16 Goethe an Charlotte von Stein, letter of May 14, 1778, cited in Katharina Mommsen, *Goethe und der Alte Fritz* (Leipzig: Lehmstedt, 2012), 71. On the political context of Goethe's phrase, see Mommsen, 69–81.

17 Carl Schmitt, *Political Theology: Four Chapters on the Concept of Sovereignty,* translated by George Schwab (Cambridge, MA: Harvard, 1985), 36.

was to represent "the Life of Princes and great People full of disquiets, suspicions, troubles, rebellions, wars, murders, and all sorts of violent passions, and mighty adventures."[18]

By characterizing the "miracle of the house of Brandenburg" with a term of tragic poetics signifying a reversal of a dramatic situation, Frederick exposed it as a trope, a metaphor for political triumph. The triumph of sovereignty in a state of emergency, its ultimate action, was often conceived in early modern thinking as a "miraculous" restoration after a cosmic catastrophe.[19] Aligning this analogy with "peripeteia," a technique of dramatic representation, Frederick fashioned the genre of tragedy as an aestheticized paradigm for the interpretation of political crises. (Several decades later another warrior monarch and an interested spectator of tragedies, Napoleon, in his conversations with Goethe and others condemned appeals to fate in contemporary drama since "in our age . . . politics is fate" and "the principle of political necessity is . . . a fertile germ of the most dramatic situations, a modern fate no less imperious, no less ineluctable than that of the ancients."[20]) In a letter to Voltaire written after the bloody battle of Zorndorf, Frederick again resorts to this recurrent conceit when he compares his situation to a tragedy by Racine (where, as the letter's editors put it, "the mortality . . . equals that of *Hamlet*"), and himself to an actor:

> "Ce don Quichotte mène la vie des comédiens de campagne, jouant tantôt sur un théâtre, tantôt sur l'autre, quelquefois sifflé, quelquefois applaudi. La dernière pièce qu'il a jouée était la *Thébaïde*; à peine y resta-t-il le moucheur de chandelles."
>
> (This Don Quixote leads the life of a country comedian, playing in one theater as often as another, sometimes booed, sometimes applauded. The last play in which he performed was *Thebaïde*; hardly the extinguisher of candles was left.)[21]

---

18 [François-Hédelin d'Aubignac], *The Whole Art of the Stage* (London, 1684), 140.

19 Benjamin, *The Origin of the German Tragic Drama,* 65–66.

20 J. Christopher Herold, *The Age of Napoleon* (Boston: Houghton Mifflin Harcourt, 2002), 121; Frank George Healey, *The Literary Culture of Napoléon* (Geneva: Droz, 1959), 88–112, here 103–104.

21 Voltaire, *Complete Works*, vol. 103 (=*Correspondence,* vol. 19) (Oxford: The Voltaire Foundation, 1971), 192–193, #D7884. The importance of French tragedy for Frederick's political self-fashioning has been often noted by scholars, from Wilhelm Dilthey and Norbert Elias to Christiane Mervaud, see Wilhelm Dilthey, "Friedrich der Große und die deutsche Aufklärung," *Gesammelte Schriften*, Studien zur Geschichte des deutschen Geistes (Göttingen: Vandenhoeck & Ruprecht, 1992), 3:103–104; Norbert Elias, "The Fate of German Baroque Poetry: Between the Traditions of Court and Middle Class," in *The Collected Works* (Dublin:

The persistence of "the old form of tragedy—and the way of defining it" in the eighteenth century, as Matthew Wikander has suggested, arose from continued public fascination for "the mystique of royalty" and "the royal role."[22] Conversely, during the war and its resolution, both Frederick and his Russian counterpart, Emperor Peter III, largely relied on established patterns of action and domination elaborated in tragedy and the closely related genre, *opera seria.* This type of dramatic patterning, which Richard Wortman calls "scenarios of power," was calculated to reaffirm royal charisma by means of artfully manipulated public emotion.[23]

I

In October 1757, when Frederick's military situation after his defeat at Kolin in June of the same year was nearly catastrophic, he wrote and sent to Voltaire what is probably his best and best-known poem:

> *Croyez que si j'étais Voltaire,*
> *Particulier aujourd'hui,*
> *Me contentant du nécessaire,*
> *Je verrais envoler la fortune légère,*
> *Et m'en moquerais comme lui.*
> *Je connais l'abus des richesses,*
> *Je connais l'ennui des grandeurs*
> *Le fardeau des devoirs, le jargon des flatteurs . . .*
> *La vive et naïve allégresse,*
> *Ont toujours fui des grands la pompe et les faisceaux.*
> *Nés pour la liberté, leur troupe enchanteresse*
> *Préfère l'aimable paresse*
> *Aux austères devoirs, guides de nos travaux. . . .*

University College Dublin Press, 2010), 12:8–9; Christiane Mervaud, *Voltaire et Frédéric II: une dramaturgie des lumières, 1736–1778,* Studies on Voltaire and the Eighteenth Century, vol. 234 (Oxford: Oxford University Press, 1985), 274.

22 Matthew H. Wikander, *Princes to Act: Royal Audience and Royal Performance, 1578–1792* (Baltimore, MD: Johns Hopkins University Press, 1993), 12.

23 Richard Wortman, *Scenarios of Power: Myth and Ceremony in Russian Monarchy* (Princeton: Princeton University Press, 1995), vol. 1. On *opera seria* and the artistic (de)mystification of sovereignty, see, e.g., Ethel Matala de Mazza, "Die Regeln der Ausnahme. Zur Überschreitung der Souveränität in Fénelons *Télémaque* und Mozarts *Idomeneo,*" in *Transgressionen. Literatur als Ethnographie,* edited by Gerhard Neumann and Rainer Warning (Freiburg: Rombach, 2003), 257–286; Martha Feldman, *Opera and Sovereignty: Transforming Myths in Eighteenth-Century Italy* (Chicago: University of Chicago Press, 2007).

Mais notre état nous fait la loi;
Il nous oblige, il nous engage
A mesurer notre courage
Sur ce qu'exige notre emploi.
Voltaire, dans son ermitage,
Dans un pays dont l'héritage
Est son antique bonne foi,
Peut s'adonner en paix à la vertu du sage,
Dont Platon nous marqua la loi.
Pour moi, menacé du naufrage,
Je dois, en affrontant l'orage,
Penser, vivre et mourir en roi.[24]

Cf. a contemporary English translation:

Voltaire, believe me, were I now
In private life's calm station plac'd,
Let Heav'n for Nature's wants allow,
With cold indifference would I view
Departing Fortune's winged haste,
And at the Goddess laugh like you.
Th' insipid farce of tedious state,
Imperial duty's real weight,
The faithless courtier's supple bow,
The fickle multitude's caress,
And flatt'rer's wordy emptiness,
By long experience well I know …
Sweet ease, and unaffected joy,
Domestic peace and sportive pleasure.
The regal throne and palace fly,
And, born for liberty, prefer
Soft silent scenes of lovely leisure
To, what we Monarchs buy so dear,
The thorny pomp of scepter'd care. …
But from our stations we derive
Unerring precepts how to live,

[24] For the most recent scholarly edition of the poem, see Voltaire, *Complete Works*, vol. 102 (= *Correspondance*, vol. 18), (Oxford: The Voltaire Foundation, 1971), 198 (D7414). For its insightful and informed discussion, see Christiane Mervaud, *Voltaire et Frédéric II: une dramaturgie des lumières*, 276–278.

And certain deeds each rank calls forth,
By which is measur'd human worth.
Voltaire, within his private cell,
In realms where ancient honesty
Is patrimonial property,
And sacred Freedom loves to dwell,
May give up all his peaceful mind,
Guided by Plato's deathless page,
In silent solitude resign'd
To the mild virtues of a sage;
But I, 'gainst whom wild whirlwinds wage
Fierce war with wreck-denouncing wing,
Must be, to face the tempest's rage,
In thought, in life, and death a King.[25]

Written in the lighter diction of *poésie légère* and conceived as little more than a trifle reiterating the political stoicism of Frederick's grand epistles (*Épître à ma sœur de Baireuth*, 1757, *Épître sur le hasard. À ma sœur Amélie*, 1760), this poem claims a central place in the complex dynamic of literary authorship and political (self-)representation that permeated the king's oeuvre. As Brunhilde Wehinger suggests, the verses to Voltaire ostensibly amount to the king's renunciation of authorship, driven by social protocols that made it impossible to combine public literary ambition with royal status. However, on another level the royal persona fashions itself through a speech act, both drawing from and relying on techniques of poetic expression. This reading, which confirms the general approach to Frederick's writings suggested by Andreas Pečar, is enhanced by what seems to be the text's special status. While Frederick generally avoided wide dissemination of his poems and only published an authorized collection after a "pirated" edition had appeared in 1760, the verses in question were printed in January 1758 as "Réponse de S. M. le roi de Prusse au M. de Voltaire" in Berlin's semi-official newspaper *Vossische Zeitung*.[26]

[25] "Epistle from the King of Prussia to Monsieur Voltaire. Translated by J. G. Cooper, Esq.," *The Annual Register, or A View of the History, Politicks and Literature of the Year 1758* (London, 1759), 413–414.

[26] Brunhilde Wehinger, "Denkwürdigkeiten des Hauses Brandenburg—Friedrich der Große als Autor der Geschichte seiner Dynastie," in *Vom Kurfürstentum zum Königreich der Landstriche. Brandenburg-Preußen im Zeitalter von Absolutismus und Aufklärung*, edited by Günther Lottes (Berlin: Berliner Wiss.-Verlag, 2004), 147–148; Andreas Pečar, "Friedrich der Große als Autor. Plädoyer für eine adressatenorientierte Lektüre seiner Schriften," in *Friedrich300—Eine perspektivische Bestandsaufnahme. Beiträge des ersten Colloquiums in der Reihe "Friedrich300"*

In a dialogue qualified as a *dramaturgie des lumières* (drama of Enlightenment), Frederick taps into older but still meaningful "tragic" and "baroque" visions of sovereignty to style his public performance in a way that associates it with martyrdom. Benjamin discerns a paradoxical relationship among these concepts in that sovereignty as a worldly institution becomes aligned with martyrdom, but martyrdom itself, as understood in "baroque" and "tragic" discourse, was aligned to the "sphere of immanence" and conceived in stoic rather than truly religious terms. Frederick's reference to "l'ennui des grandeurs" (the tedium of grandeur) and "le fardeau des devoirs" (the burden of duty) inscribes into a baroque tradition which viewed the prince as the "paradigm of the melancholy man." Benjamin illustrates this point with a passage from Pascal's *Pensées* (1669), arguing that if a king should be left alone, "l'on verra, un Roi qui se voit, est un homme plein de misères" ("one will see that a king who sees himself, is a man full of misery"), and further draws four lines from a seventeenth-century emblem book that serve as a commentary for a picture of a crown:

> *Ce fardeau paroist autre à celuy qui le porte,*
> *Qu'à ceux qu'il esblouyt de son lustre trompeur,*
> *Ceuxcy n'en ont jamais conneu la pesanteur,*
> *Mais l'autre sçait expert quel tourment il apporte.*
> *(This burden appears differently to him who bears it,*
> *Than to those who are dazzled by its deceptive brilliance,*
> *These men have never known that weight,*
> *But the other knows expertly what torment he carries.)*[27]

This tradition was still quite alive in the eighteenth century. Frederick is known to have read Pascal during the war, and his instructor in poetic art, Voltaire (also an avid reader of the *Pensées*), wrote in his 1740 poem "Sur l'usage de la vie" some lines that could have provided a model for Frederick's own verses:

> *On voit souvent plus d'un roi*
> *Que la tristesse environne;*
> *Les brillants de la couronne*
> *Ne sauvent point de l'ennui:*
> *Ses valets de pied, ses pages,*

---

vom 28./29. September 2007, edited by Michael Kaiser und Jürgen Luh, accessed August 28, 2013, http://www.perspectivia.net/content/publikationen/friedrich300-colloquien/friedrich-bestandsaufnahme.

[27] Benjamin, *The Origin of the German Tragic Drama,* 72–73, 142–145.

Jeunes, indiscrets, volages,
Sont plus fortunés que lui.
(One often sees a king
Surrounded by sorrow;
The diamonds of a crown
Cannot save from tedium:
His footmen, his pages,
Young, indiscreet, flighty,
Are more fortunate than he.)[28]

However, it was ultimately the tragedy rather than *poésie légère* that provided the literary pattern for the double act of royal introspection and self-exposure suggested by Pascal. In conversations with de Catt, Frederick bitterly derided the common opinion of those "stupid people" who wish to "be happy as a king," complained about "this burden that weighs on me so," the moral corruption of the courts, the anxiety engendered even in peaceful years by premonitions of "the storm," and "since then, what troubles, what unprecedented fatigues, and what reverses!" He would conclude: "As a private individual—which I have often desired to be—I should live in quiet and as I pleased." The royal poet, who readily admitted to imitating Racine's tragic diction even in shorter lyric pieces, often adorned the laments for private happiness unattainable to kings, which he summarized in his "Réponse [. . .] au M. de Voltaire," with Agamemnon's lines from Racine's *Iphigénie* (1674; I:1, I:5):

Heureux! qui, satisfait de son humble fortune,
Libre du joug superbe où je suis attaché,
Vit dans l'état obscur où les dieux l'ont caché . . .
Triste destin des rois!
(Oh Happy Man! He who is satisfied with his humble fortune,
Free of the supreme yoke to which I am bound,
He lives in the obscure state in which the gods have hidden him . . .
Sad destiny of kings![29]*)*

References to the tragic figure of Agamemnon, a king and commander of the Greek army who is compelled by a divine decree to sacrifice his daughter to secure military success, permitted Frederick to inscribe his personal suffering

---

28 Voltaire, *Complete Works*, 16: 313.

29 *Frederick the Great: The Memoirs of His Reader,* 1:86; Koser, *Unterhaltungen*, 48, 350, 366, 374, 409; cf. Racine, *Théâtre complet*, 2:207, 219. On Frederick's imitation of Racine, see Koser, *Unterhaltungen*, 300, 423.

into a "scenario of power," a recognizable royal role. The inherent theatricality of this emotional pattern was revealed when Frederick quoted *Iphigénie* to convey his grief over the death of his deeply loved sister and then immediately came to speak of theater and the opera. This time the reference was taken from a scene where Ulysses urges Agamemnon to overcome his hesitation and accomplish the horrific sacrifice in exchange for royal glory and military triumph.[30] The "Réponse [. . .] au M. de Voltaire" reenacts a similar emotional dynamic in which the ruler's public "austères devoirs" (austere obligations) subordinate his own "private" emotions. In this way, the violence of war molds Frederick's intimate emotional experience into a culturally charged public spectacle of sovereignty, as announced by the last verse: "vivre et mourir en roi."

The tragic resonance of the poem's finale was evident to its contemporaries. Voltaire wrote later: "Rien n'est plus beau que ces derniers vers; rien n'est plus grand. Corneille dans son bon temps ne les eût pas mieux faits. Et quand, après de tels vers, on gagne une bataille, le sublime ne peut aller plus loin." (Nothing is as beautiful as these last lines; nothing is more grand. Corneille at his best could not have crafted them better. And when, after such verses, one wins a battle, the sublime could go no further.)[31] Elias, whose fundamental studies of court culture reflect a specific interest in Frederick II and his relationship to belles-lettres, discussed the same lines in one of his less-known articles: "Here, the tragic pathos of Corneille, which sometimes seems over-theatrical to later generations, served as a pattern to a real king in expressing his agitated feelings with great reserve in an extremely real and entirely untheatrical situation."[32]

In his poetic staging of kingship, Frederick relied on performative techniques of tragedy where sovereignty itself is constituted by acts of speech.[33] While older scholarship, which made "Réponse [. . .] au M. de Voltaire" a matter of some debate, failed to identify the poem's tragic models, Christiane Mervaud points to a scene in Corneille's *Sophonisbe* (1663), where a king and his queen share a common vow before a decisive battle: "je sais vivre et mourir en reine," (I know how to live and die as a queen) and "je saurai, pour vous, vaincre ou mourir en roi" (I know, for you, how to conquer or die as

---

[30] Koser, *Unterhaltungen*, 379.

[31] Voltaire, *Écrits autobiographiques,* présentation par Jean Goldzink (Paris: Flammarion, 2006), 157–158.

[32] Elias, "The Fate of German Baroque Poetry," 8.

[33] Rüdiger Campe, "Der Befehl und die Rede des Souveräns im Schauspiel des 17. Jahrhunderts. Nero bei Busenello, Racine und Lohenstein," in *Übertragung und Gesetz. Gründungsmythen, Kriegstheater und Unterwerfungstechniken von Institutionen*, edited by A. Adam and M. Stingelin (Berlin: Akademie Verlag, 1995), 55–71.

a king; I:4). An abbreviated version of this vow reappears in Racine's second tragedy, *Alexandre le Grand* (1665), which shows the Indian king Porus engaged in heroic but hopeless resistance to Alexander's overwhelming forces. Like Corneille's Sophonisbe, Porus's lover, Queen Axiane, assures him that the conquering enemy "me verra, toujours digne de toi, / Mourir en reine, ainsi que tu mourus en roi" (will see me, always worthy of you, / Dying as a queen, just as you die as a king; IV:1). In Racine's play, which was closer to Frederick's reading habits, although certainly not his favorite, this line resonated with a later scene where victorious Alexander questions the captive Porus:

> *Alexandre*
> *. . . Parlez donc, dites-moi :*
> *Comment prétendez-vous que je vous traite?*
> *Porus*
> *En roi.*
> *(Alexander*
> *So, speak, tell me:*
> *How do you claim that I should treat you?*
> *Porus*
> *As a king; V: 3)*[34]

Racine borrows Porus' famous answer from Plutarch, whose *Parallel Lives,* including the "Life of Alexander," were well known to the European courtly audiences. Frederick found inspiration in them during the war.[35] The last line of the "Réponse [. . .] au M. de Voltaire," both a poetic and a political gesture, reenacts the powerful rhetorical effect of Porus's laconic formula, an assertion of royal grandeur paradoxically reaffirmed by the momentarily suspended reality of defeat.

Frederick's insistence on his ability to "die as a king" referred to the plans of suicide that he contemplated during the war and often discussed in his conversations and correspondence, making them an important element of his self-dramatization.[36] Once again, visions of historical and political action were aligned with tragic patterns. Referring to the historical suicides of Cato the Younger and the Emperor Otho (recorded by Plutarch), Frederick applauded them and even used his own poetic voice to embody them in two *heroides,* in

---

[34] Racine, *Théâtre complet*, 1:166.

[35] *Œuvres de Frédéric le Grand* (Berlin, 1852), 19:311; Ulbert, "Friedrichs Lektüren während des Siebenjährigen Krieges," 96.

[36] Florian Kühnel, *Kranke Ehre?: Adlige Selbsttötung im Übergang zur Moderne* (Munich: Oldenbourg Verlag, 2013), 135–170.

essence isolated tragic monologues, written in their names.[37] The possibility of his own suicide, he often justified with a couplet from Voltaire's tragedy *Mérope* (1743; "Quand on a tout perdu, quand on n'a plus d'espoir, / La vie est un opprobre et la mort un devoir " [When one has lost everything, when one has no more hope, / Life is a disgrace and death an obligation]).

Frederick repeatedly claimed his suicide would "end the tragedy."[38] In a letter to Voltaire composed shortly before the "Réponse," the king suggested that his ruin would provide "un bon sujet de tragédie" (a good subject for a tragedy) characteristic of the times when "un petit particuillér seroit roué tout Vif pour avoir fait la Centième partie du Mal que ces Maîtres de la Terre Cometent Impunémant" (the common man would have been broken on the wheel for having committed a hundredth of the evil that these masters of the earth commit with impunity).[39] Frederick blamed the anti-Prussian coalition for the beginning of hostilities, and resorted in his accusations to the commonplace critique of war and conquest popular in early modern literature.

This critique was utilized in Racine's *Alexandre le Grand,* in which Porus exposes the destructive ambition of Alexander, the paragon of military valor and triumph: "nous l'aurons vu, par tant d'horribles guerres, / Troubler le calme heureux dont jouissaient nos terres." (We have seen him, through so many horrible wars, / disrupt the happy peace of our lands; I:2.) Just as Porus is prepared to perish for "la liberté de l'Inde" (the freedom of India) and despises the "esclavage" (slavery) imposed by Alexander (I:1–2), Frederick incites the Germans to resist the ambition of the Habsburgs and their allies, whom he calls "éternels ennemis / De votre liberté, de vos droits, de vos princes" (the eternal enemies / of your freedom, of your rights, of your princes).[40] The drama of Porus, a performative reenactment, or "emplotment," of this conceptual framework, includes the verbal gesture of royal self-sacrifice as a *coup de théâtre,* a ploy which, instead of annihilating royal charisma, only reenhances it through an intrinsically theatrical appeal to the emotions of an audience

---

[37] Frederick II, "Discours de l'empereur Othon à ses amis, après la perte de la bataille de Bédriac" and "Discours de Caton d'Utique à son fils et à ses amis, avant de se tuer," *Œuvres de Frédéric le Grand*, Bd 12 (Berlin, 1849), 12:237–245; Werner Langer, *Friedrich der Große und die geistige Welt Frankreichs* (Hamburg: Seminar für romanische Sprachen und Kultur, 1932), 142.

[38] Koser, *Unterhaltungen mit Friedrich dem Großen*, 374.

[39] Voltaire, *Complete Works*, vol. 102 (=*Correspondence,* vol. 18), 152 (D 7373).

[40] Racine, *Théâtre complet*, 1:122–124; "Ode aux Germains," *Œuvres de Frédéric le Grand* (Berlin, 1849), 12:20. On the contexts of Porus's denunciation of conquest, see Pia Claudia Doering, *Jean Racine zwischen Kunst und Politik: Lesarten der Alexandertragödie* (Heidelberg, 2010), 155–172. On the concept of liberty in Frederick's political rhetoric during the Seven Years' War, see, e.g., Ullrich Sachse, *Cäsar in Sanssouci: die Politik Friedrichs des Großen und die Antike* (Munich: Allitera Verlag, 2008), 213–216.

transformed into a political community. This mechanism was explored by the pan-European court theater, an institution equally important for the dramatist Racine and King Frederick, who inaugurated his rule by establishing an opera theater under his own close supervision and famously encouraged the "reformed" *opera seria* modeled on French neoclassical tragedy.

Among the operas performed in Berlin before the beginning of the Seven Years' War were two different musical settings of Pietro Metastasio's libretto *Alessandro nell'Indie* (1729), which treated the Porus plot and loosely followed Racine's tragedy. The opera opens with a scene on a "Field of Battle on the Banks of Hydaspes, with the Remains of Porus's Army, defeated by Alexander," to quote a contemporary English translation. Porus attempts to stop his fleeing soldiers, crying out to them,

> *Stay, ye pale Cowards! I command ye, stay!*
> *Life is Dishonour when bestow'd by Flight . . .*
> *His Term of Life is full that dies in Freedom!*
> *(Offers to kill himself.)*

He is interrupted by his general, Gandarte, who rushes to save his king and partake of the royal sacrifice, assuming "the Regal Diadem, that now, / Points all the Danger at your sacred Head." Gandarte's actions are immediately explicated in terms of monarchist political morality:

> *A Subject pays for Publick Good,*
> *A frugal Purchase with his Blood,*
> *If, by a private Death alone,*
> *His Prince preserves the Indian Throne.*[41]

The spectacular effects of stage drama provided the blueprint for the emotional economy of monarchy. In a scene that is itself a tragedy in miniature, the display of a king in danger evokes pity and fear, the two fundamental emotions that shaped the aesthetic effects of tragedy in Aristotelian theory. The Porus plays converted them into a political sentiment, pro-royalist enthusiasm enacted on stage by Gandarte and suggested to the play's audience. This fundamentally theatrical vision of the mobilizing effects of the threatened

---

[41] [Pietro Metastasio] *Poro, Re Dell'Indie. Drama* . . . Done Into English by Mr. Humphreys (London, 1731), 9–10. On Frederick's opera and its repertoire, see Michele Calella, "Metastasios Dramenkonzeption und die Ästhetik der friderizianischen Oper," *Metastasio im Deutschland der Aufklärung: Bericht über das Symposium Potsdam 1999*, edited by Laurenz Lütteken and Gerhad Splitt (Tübingen: Niemeyer, 2002), 103–123. The settings in question are Graun's *Allesandro e Poro* and Agricola's *Cleofide*.

royal charisma on a nation of subjects was developed in Thomas Abbt's vigorous manifesto of Prussian martial patriotism published during the Seven Years' War, *Vom Tode fürs Vaterland (On Dying for the Fatherland,* 1761). Abbt specifically refers to the Porus plot, writing:

> Porus und seine Untertanen teilen mit Alexanders Armee die Lorbeern, mit welcher sich die letztere umkränzt hat. Denn nach einem tapfern Widerstand überwunden werden, heißt nicht, seine Größe verlieren [. . .] Ich erinnere mich noch mit dem melancholischen Vergnügen, das unsre Seele bei der Vorstellung einer Tragischen Begebenheit überströmt, eine ganze Stadt über die falsche Nachricht von dem Unglück ihres Friederichs in Bestürzung, Greise in Tränen zerfließend, und Jünglinge in männlichen Ernst gesehen zu haben. [. . .] Hier sehe ich nicht nur mein Vaterland vor mir, ich sehe auch meinen König. Sein Anblick ist beredter, als Demosthene, und erregt die Leidenschaften heftiger. Mit der Blutfahne in der Hand geht er vor seinem Heer dem Feind entgegen. Die Gefahren umzingeln ihn; jedes tödtliche Blei, das neben ihm niederfallt, schlägt den Gedanken meiner eigenen Gefahr aus mir heraus. Ich sehe auf sein Leben, und vergesse darüber, daß das meinige vielleicht den nächsten Augenblick mir entrissen wird. [. . .] Aus dieser Denkungsart, aus dieser Leidenschaft, die allezeit unter einem guten, einem tapfern, Monarchen entstehen muß, rührt es her, daß die Soldaten Alexanders, wenn sie sein Leben in Gefahr sehen, mit einer Wut fechten, welche kaum bey Republikanern angetroffen wird [. . .]
>
> ("Porus and his subjects share with Alexander's army the laurels that it has crowned itself with. For to be defeated after a brave resistance does not mean to lose your greatness [. . .] I still remember with a melancholic delight that overwhelms our soul when a tragic event is presented to us, seeing a whole city thrown into confusion by a false news of their Frederick's misfortune, the elderly shedding tears, the young in manly earnestness. [. . .] Here I do not only see my fatherland before me, I also see my king. His look is more eloquent than Demosthenes, and he awakens stronger passions. With a banner in his hand, he rides towards the enemy ahead of his troops. Dangers surround him; each deadly bullet which falls near him drives the thoughts of my own danger away from me. I look after his life, and I forget that my own could be taken from me in the next moment. [. . .]

> This sentiment, this passion, which always inevitably arises under a good and valorous monarch, is the reason why Alexander's soldiers, when they saw his life at risk, fought with a rage that could scarcely be seen among republicans [. . .]")[42]

Abbt's influential treatise occupies an important place in the early history of German national sentiment. In it, he outlines what has been called an "aesthetic patriotism," grounding the monarchist solidarity of Prussia's subjects in the mechanics of collective sensibility. This mechanism is paradigmatically developed in tragedy, the genre where "tragic events" do indeed appear as fictional representations tailored to arouse a public reaction of "melancholic delight." As the influential critic Johann Christoph Gottsched argued, the Porus plot was well suited for public theater in absolutist polities, and audiences' admiration for Porus's resistance to Alexander provided an aesthetic paradigm for the exalted public devotion to Frederick II as it was fashioned in different genres and media.[43]

During the battle of Kolin in June 1757, Frederick experienced his first major defeat, one which eventually compelled him to resort to the rhetoric of desperation that he would come to use in his "Réponse [. . .] à M. de Voltaire." The king supposedly attempted to stop his fleeing soldiers with a risk of his

---

[42] Thomas Abbt, "Vom Tode für das Vaterland," in *Aufklärung und Kriegserfahrung. Klassische Zeitzeugen zum Siebenjährigen Krieg,* edited by Johannes Kunisch (Frankfurt am Main: Deutscher Klassischer Verlag, 1996), 612, 615, 633.

[43] Johann Christoph Gottsched, "Die Schauspiele und besonders die Tragödien sind aus einer wohlbestellten Republik nicht zu verbannen," [1729], in *Schriften zur Literatur* (Stuttgart: Reclam, 1972), 7. On Abbt's construction of patriotism, see Eva Piirimäe, "Dying for the Fatherland: Thomas Abbt's Theory of Aesthetic Patriotism," *History of European Ideas* 35 (2009): 194–208; Klaus Bohnen, *Von den Anfängen des Nationalsinns,* "Von den Anfängen des Nationalsinns. Zur literarischen Patriotismus-Debatte im Umfeld des Siebenjährigen Kriegs," *Dichter und ihre Nation,* edited by Helmut Scheuer (Frankfurt am Main: Suhrkamp, 1993), 121–137; Kunisch, [Kommentar], *Aufklärung und Kriegserfahrung,* 971–1008. On Abbt and the cult of Frederick, which emphasized royal grief and martyrdom, see, e.g., Eckhart Hellmuth, "Die 'Wiedergeburt' Friedrichs des Großen und der 'Tod fürs Vaterland.' Zum patriotischen Selbstverständnis in Preußen in der zweiten Hälfte des 18. Jahrhunderts," in *Nationalismus vor dem Nationalismus? = Aufklärung. Interdisziplinäre Halbjahresschrift zur Erforschung des 18. Jahrhunderts* 10/2 (1998), edited by E. Hellmuth and R. Stauber, 21–52. On the Seven Years' War as a crucial juncture for the emergence of printed mass media and the corresponding modes of public reaction, see *"Krieg ist mein Lied": der Siebenjährige Krieg in den zeitgenössischen Medien,* edited by Wolfgang Adam and Holger Dainat (Göttingen: Wallstein-Verlag, 2007); Manfred Schort, *Politik und Propaganda: der Siebenjährige Krieg in den zeitgenössischen Flugschriften* (Frankfurt am Main: Lang Verlag, 2006). For more on the public image and perception of Frederick, see *Friedrich der Große in Europa: Geschichte einer wechselvollen Beziehung,* edited by Bernd Sösemann and Gregor Vogt-Spira (Stuttgart: Steiner, 2012), volumes 1–2.

own life, shouting to them: "Rascals, would you live forever?"[44] This phrase entered into Fridérician lore after it appeared in print, only days after the battle. It appears to translate into colloquial German the operatic exclamations of Metastasio's Porus, balancing between Porus's praise of a death on the battlefield over a life of disgrace and the implication of immortal fame suggested in Frederick's own "Ode à mon frère Henri" written later that year. The king writes that calamities and defeats, identified once again with "images tragiques" (tragic images), inevitably occur in the history of any great nation and must be overcome with "noble désespoir" (noble despair) and heroic patriotism, which acknowledge that "La mort est un tribut qu'on doit à la nature . . . Aucun n'en fut exempt" (death is a tribute one owes to nature . . . No one is exempt from it), while a death suffered for the fatherland secures immortality.[45]

Reducing dramatic polyphony to a unity of poetic voice and political perspective appropriate for the occasion, the lyrical idiom of the war nevertheless built upon the emotional economy of tragic representation in order to mobilize and manipulate public sensibilities. Whereas Frederick exploited this aestheticized fascination for military adversity for a limited readership, Johann Wilhelm Ludwig Gleim explored it in his *Preußische Kriegslieder*, lyric utterances of Prussian martial sentiment published in the course of the war for the use of broader German audiences. Styling Frederick's battles as a "great tragedy" ("große[r] Trauerspie[l]"), Gleim once again represented the threat to the body of the king as a spectacle with mobilizing effects:

Da, Friedrich, gieng dein Grenadier
Auf Leichen hoch einher.
Dacht, in dem mörderischen Kampf,
Gott, Vaterland, und Dich;
Sah, tief in schwarzem Rauch und Dampf,
Dich seinen Friederich.
Und zitterte, ward feuerroth,
Im kriegrischen Gesicht,
(Er zitterte vor Deinem Tod,
Vor seinem aber nicht.)
Verachtete die Kugelsaat,
Der Stücke Donnerton,
Stritt wütender, that Heldenthat,

[44] On the origins and history of this anecdote reported, among others, by Goethe, see Gerhard Knoll, "'Hunde, wollt Ihr ewig leben?' oder Goethe und die 'Hunde' des Großen Königs," *Aus dem Aniquariat. Zeitschrift für Aniquare und Büchersammler* 2 (2005): 22–27.
[45] *Œuvres de Frédéric le Grand*, 12:1–8.

Bis deine Feinde flohn.
Then, Frederick, your grenadier
Climbed over the corpses.
He thought in the midst of a murderous battle
Of God, of the Fatherland, and of you;
Deep in black smoke and fumes he saw
You, his Frederick.
He trembled, his warlike face
Turned red as fire
(He trembled for your life,
Not for his own.)
He despised the crop of bullets
And the cannons' thunder,
He fought with even more rage, and performed heroic deeds
Until your enemies fled.[46]

It is the "tragic" fear for the chief actor that overwhelms the grenadier when he momentarily finds himself a spectator of the battle, which intensifies his patriotic fervor and incites him to action. He emulates the show of royalist self-sacrifice put on by Metastasio's Gandarte; however, he achieves victory where operatic heroes failed. While this emotional economy was unsuccessful on the battlefield (at Kolin the soldiers allegedly told Frederick they had done enough for their miserable salaries), it was crucial for the public resonance of Gleim's immensely popular songs.[47]

Aesthetic mobilization of pro-Prussian political sentiment during the Seven Years' War largely contributed to the emergence of public opinion in Germany. According to Goethe's famous formulation, it also shaped the development of German "national poetry" in which the "war-songs struck by Gleim maintain so high a rank" because Frederick's military exploits for the first time provided them with "true and really vital material of a higher order." Goethe

---

[46] Wilhelm Ludwig Gleim, *Preußische Kriegslieder von einem Grenadier* (Heilbronn, 1882; rpt. Nendeln/Liechtenstein, Kraus Reprint, 1968), 9, 15.

[47] On Gleim and the Prussian martial patriotism of the Seven Years' War, see Hans-Martin Blitz, *Aus Liebe zum Vaterland: die deutsche Nation im 18. Jahrhundert* (Hamburg: Hamburger Ed., 2000), 145–280; Jörg Schönert, "Schlachtgesänge vom Kanapee. Zu den 'Preußischen Kriegsliedern' des Kanonikus Gleim," *Gedichte und Interpretationen. Aufklärung und Sturm und Drang*, edited by Karl Richter (Stuttgart: Reclam, 1983), 126–139; Hans Peter Herrmann, "Individuum und Staatsmacht. Preußisch-deutscher Nationalismus in Texten zum Siebenjährigen Krieg" in *Machtphantasie Deutschland. Nationalismus, Männlichkeit und Fremdenhaß im Vaterlandsdiskurs deutscher Schriftsteller des 18. Jahrhunderts,* edited by Hans Peter Herrmann, Hans Martin Blitz, and Susanna Moßmann (Frankfurt am Main: Suhrkamp, 1996), 66–79.

explains further that poetry becomes "hollow" unless it is based upon subjects such as "the events of nations and their shepherds, when both stand for one man. Kings are to be represented in war and danger, where on that account they appear as the first, because they determine and share the fate of the very least, and therefore become much more interesting than the gods themselves."[48] In this way, literature (*Dichtung*) is entrusted with upholding the royalist mystique of political incorporation and forging a community of subjects. Royal charisma is produced as an equivalent of literary "interest" through the techniques of aesthetic engagement. Along these lines, Frederick's charismatic popularity during the war was propelled by the public fascination for adversity, crystallized in tragedy, and exploited in poetic dramatizations of his royal role.[49]

II

The earliest among the startling measures that shaped the short reign of Peter III (who succeeded to the Russian throne after the death of Empress Elizabeth in the first days of 1762) was his handling of the onerous and expensive war. He immediately ceased all hostilities against Prussia, restituted the territories occupied by Russian troops, and offered Frederick a military alliance. This unpopular decision contributed to Peter's fall six months later, when he was overthrown by his wife, the future Catherine II, and assassinated. However, contrary to a popular anecdotal view of events, this politically tactless peace was more than the personal whim of the famously Prussophile monarch. In fact, Chancellor Mikhail Vorontsov had elaborated plans for a peace with Frederick and the restitution of East Prussia even before Elizabeth's death.[50]

---

[48] Johann Wolfgang von Goethe, *Poetry and Truth from my Own Life,* translated b y R. O. Moon (Washington, DC: Public Affairs Press, 1949), 241.

[49] Goethe, *Dichtung und Wahrheit.* Gisbert Ter-Nedden in an important essay discusses the processing of the conceptual challenges posed by the war in drama; namely, in Lessing's *Philotas* and responses to it, and points to the public interest in calamity as a driving force behind the war's media impact: Gisbert Ter-Nedden, "*Philotas* und *Aias* oder Der Kriegsheld im Gefangenendilemma. Lessings Sophokles-Modernisierung und ihre Lektüre durch Gleim, Bodmer und die Germanistik," in *Krieg ist mein Lied: Der Siebenjahrige Krieg in den Zeitgenössischen Medien* (Göttingen: Wallstein, 2007), 317–378. On the affinities between royal charisma and dramatic interest, see Stephen Greenblatt, *Shakespearean Negotiations: The Circulation of Social Energy in Renaissance England* (Berkeley: University of California Press, 1988), 62–65.

[50] *Arkhiv kniazia Vorontsova* (Moscow, 1872), 4:173–178. Arguments for a favorable view of the peace (as well as all other measures undertaken by Peter) have been assembled by Carol Leonard, *Reform and Regicide: The Reign of Peter III of Russia* (Bloomington: Indiana University Press, 1993), 117–137. On the shifting logic behind Russian involvement in the war, see Michael Müller, "Rußland und der Siebenjährige Krieg. Beitrag zu einer Kontroverse," *Jahrbücher für Geschichte Osteuropas* 28 (1980): 198–219.

Vorontsov, the cautious and experienced master of foreign affairs who kept his post under Peter III, had ties to Prussia dating back to the 1740s. Generally, pro-Prussian sympathies were not uncommon at the Russian court, despite the personal animosity towards Frederick affected by Empress Elizabeth. These sympathies, strengthened after 1756 by the Empress's serious illness and the constant expectation of Peter's succession, stimulated interest in Frederick's literary works. Secret correspondence entertained in 1756–57 by Catherine, who was at that point still Peter's political ally, and the English ambassador, Hanbury Williams, in the course of an ambitious and dangerous pro-Prussian intrigue, includes references to Frederick's "writings" ("écrits") secretly procured by the ambassador for the heir apparent and his spouse. Catherine professed to share the ambassador's admiration for Frederick, who "écrit aussi bien qu'il se bat" (writes as well as he fights), and to read his works "avec le meme empressement que ceux de Voltaire" (with the same eagerness as those of Voltaire).[51] Even as a code, this confession certainly attested to the relevance of Frederick's double performance as a political actor and writer for Russia's courtly public.

According to Stanisław Poniatowski (Catherine's lover, who was also involved in Williams's intrigue), Peter's fascination with Prussia was so focused on the military that he refused to believe that Frederick enjoyed reading and wrote poetry. This suggests that Frederick's intellectual standing and poetic compositions were at least a matter of some debate in Petersburg.[52] This half-illicit interest must have provided the backdrop for the Russian reception of the "Réponse [. . .] au M. de Voltaire." By March 1758 it was forwarded by Gottsched from Leipzig to Aleksandr Sumarokov, one of Russia's two prominent poets. As a resident of a city occupied by Prussian troops, Gottsched was compelled by signs of favor shown to him by Frederick to employ his influential journal, *Das Neueste aus der anmuthigen Gelehrsamkeit* (*The News of Delightful Learning*), and his wide network of correspondents for the king's publicity. Gottsched contributed to the propagandistic success of Frederick's poem, which "soon splashed across the pages of European journals, in the original French and in translations" (including the English rendering quoted above). Gottsched reprinted the "Réponse [. . .] au M. de Voltaire" with a translation into German verse and sent it to Russia at a time when, as Lessing reported, his relationship

[51] *Correspondance de Catherine Alexéievna, Grande-Duchesse de Russie, et de Sir Charles H. Williams, Ambassadeur d'Angleterre, 1756 et 1757* (Moscow, 1909), 241, 281.

[52] Stanislas Auguste [Poniatowski], *Mémoires*, edited by Anna Grzeskowiak-Krwawicz (Paris: Institut d'Études Slaves, 2012), 129.

with Frederick grew "immer bekannter, immer vertrauter" (closer and more intimate by the minute).[53]

Sumarokov, the author of neoclassical tragedies, director of the Russian royal dramatic company, and recently elected member of Gottsched's German Society, sought the patronage of Peter's and Catherine's "young court," and in 1759 dedicated to Catherine his own journal, *Trudoliubivaia pchela* (*The Industrious Bee*). Reflecting the tensions of the political thinking at the Russian court, Sumarokov paradoxically combined exalted martial patriotism with an undercurrent of admiration for Frederick in his odes commemorating Russia's involvement in the "Prussian war." At one point, he apostrophized the enemy king: "Velik ty, ia skazhu to smelo" (Great you are, I will say it boldly), and elsewhere praised his courage in facing three hostile powers, thus reproducing a central motif of Frederick's own narrative of the war. At some point, Sumarokov drafted a translation of the "Réponse [. . .] au M. de Voltaire," which was not finished and was published posthumously, possibly because it would have broadcasted all too potently the heroic self-dramatization of a long-time adversary to the Russian general public.[54]

The response of the ruling elite, however, did not depend on Russian translations. Frederick's literary display of valor and endurance, enhanced by the appearance of the first publicly available editions of his poetry during the war in 1760, was not lost on the Russian court. If Frederick resorted to the rhetoric of hopeless resistance associated with Porus, the peace offered to him by Peter III, which included the restoration of territory officially known as the "Kingdom of Prussia," resembled the benevolent actions of Alexander, who accepted the defeated Porus as his friend and returned him his kingdom "through the Admiration he conceived of his extraordinary Courage in his Adversity:"

He that could preserve,
Amidst such Injuries of adverse Fate,

---

[53] Lessing an Ewald von Kleist, 14 März 1758, *Werke (Tempel Klassiker Sonderausgabe),* Wiesbaden s.d., 1:1079; *Das Neueste aus der anmuthigen Gelehrsamkeit* 3 (1758), 214–218.

[54] Amanda Ewington, *A Voltaire for Russia: A. P. Sumarokov's Journey from Poet-Critic to Russian Philosophe* (Evanston: Northwestern University Press, 2010), 154; Ulf Lehmann, *Der Gottschedkreis und Russland* (Berlin: Akad. Verlag, 1966), 102; Aleksandr Sumarokov, *Ody torzhestvennyia. Elegii lubovnyia. Reprintnoe vosproizvedenie sbornikov 1774 goda* (Moscow: OGI, 2009), Prilozhenie: Redaktsii i varianty, Dopolneniia. Kommentarii, 42, 46; Aleksandr Sumarokov, *Polnoe sobranie vsekh sochinenii* (Moscow, 1787), ch. 1, 309–310. On Gottsched and Frederick, see Werner Rieck, "Gottsched und Friedrich II," *Wissenschaftliche Zeitschrift der Pädagogischen Hochschule Potsdam, Gesell.-Sprachw. Reihe,* 2 (1966): 221–230.

A royal Soul, is worthy of a Crown.
I give thee Freedom with thy Queen and Kingdom . . .[55]

Alexander's treatment of Porus, as reported by Plutarch and Quintus Curtius, who were both well known to eighteenth-century Russian audiences (Curtius was twice translated into Russian by 1750), presented the most famous case in a "scenario of power" often enacted by Alexander. According to Curtius, Alexander tended to show "clemency towards the vanquished . . . returning so many kingdoms to those from whom he had taken them in war."[56] The Alexander-Porus plot often served for absolutist representation. Specifically, Racine's tragedy emerged from a vibrant cult of Louis XIV as Alexander, also reflected in a series of monumental paintings by Charles Le Brun, which included *Alexandre et Porus* (1673). In 1738 this plot was revived by Charles André van Loo, a painter with close ties the French court.[57]

The same patterns of domination and representation were explored all over absolutist Europe, including mid-eighteenth century Russia. In 1743, shortly after the new empress Elizabeth summoned her nephew, the future Peter III and proclaimed him her heir apparent, the festivities commemorating her ascension were amplified by the military triumph over Sweden, followed by the peace of Abo in which Elizabeth affected a magnanimous concession of the conquered territory to the defeated enemy in exchange for the designation of a pro-Russian successor to the Swedish crown.[58] This symbolic

---

55 *Poro, Re Dell'Indie,* 6, 66.

56 Quintus Curtius, *[History of Alexander],* translated by John C. Rolfe (Cambridge, MA: Harvard University Press, 1985), 2:523 (X, 5, 28).

57 On the absolutist uses of the Alexander legend, see Chantal Grell, Christian Michel, and Pierre Vidal-Naquet, *L'école des princes, ou Alexandre disgracié: essai sur la mythologie monarchique de la France absolutiste* (Paris: Les Belles Lettres, 1988); Doering, *Jean Racine zwischen Kunst und Politik.* Both works emphasize the fundamental ambiguity of Alexander's image, which simultaneously stood for successful rule and the destructive violence of conquest. Thanks to this ambiguity, comparisons to Alexander proved an important and meaningful political trope in the literature of the Seven Years' War. They were often applied to Frederick himself, a conscientious ruler and a foolhardy invader of Silesia and Saxony. Prince de Ligne, fascinated with the Prussian king, wrote that in the future "au lieu de la bataille de Porus, on saura celle de Lissa," a battle won by Frederick in 1757 (Charles-Joseph de Ligne, *Mes écarts ou ma tête en liberté: et autres pensées et réflexions*, edited by Jeroom Vercruysse and Daniel Acke [Paris: H. Champion, 2007], 146). In Russia, Sumarokov recognized Frederick as the "new Alexander" and simultaneously denied him any superiority over the Russian empress and her troops (Aleksandr Sumarokov, *Ody torzhestvennyia. Prilozhenie,* 46, 263).

58 S. M. Solov'ev, *Istoriia Rossii s drevneishikh vremen*, Kniga XI (Moscow: Prosveshchenie, 1993), 212. The relevance of the Swedish peace for Peter was enhanced by the fact that it immediately concerned his dynastic status as a possible heir to the Swedish throne.

scenario was celebrated in the opera *Il Seleuco* (1744), specifically written for the occasion by Elizabeth's librettist Giuseppe Bonecchi, in which a victorious king cedes occupied lands to the legitimate heir. In this case, foreign policy was reconciled with operatic poetics in a finale imitating Metastasio's *Alessandro nell'Indie.* In its turn, *Alessandro* was twice performed and printed in Petersburg in 1755 and 1759, the second time during the Seven Years' War on direct orders from the heir apparent and on his very own stage at the summer residence of Oranienbaum, as the title page of the respective printing announced.[59]

Operatic reenactments restored the theatricality inherent in Alexander's conduct: according to Curtius, Alexander himself professed to be acting "in the theater of the whole world."[60] Racine's tragedy, conceived as a dramatic reenactment of the emerging cult of the Sun King, fashioned his charisma in theatrical terms, grounding royal (majesté) on a display of "présence auguste" (august presence): "Ses yeux comme son bras font partout des sujets" (His eyes, as his arms make him subjects everywhere; III:3).[61] The final reconciliation with Porus, amalgamating military domination with a personalized sway over the emotions of subjects, represented both the peak of dramatic action and a foundational act of Alexander's power, the essential "gesture of executive power" (die Geste der Vollstreckung) which, in Carl Schmitt's political theory and Benjamin's reading of early modern tragedy, is constitutive of sovereignty.[62] The French version of the 1759 Petersburg edition of Metastasio's libretto praised Alexander's act as a model for rulers:

Que d'un Héros si magnanime
Les grands exploits soient célebrés [. . .]
D'un si beau nom que la douce harmonie
Inspire tous les Courtisans:

---

[59] Pierre Metastasio, *Alexandre aux Indes, opera . . . representé . . . par ordre de Son Altesse Imperiale monseigneur le grand duc de toutes les Russies* . . . St. Petersbourg 1759; V. N. Vsevolodskii-Gerngross, *Teatr v Rossii pri imperatritse Elizavete Petrovne* (Saint Petersburg: Giperion, 2003), 52–54, 107 ; *Teatral'naia zhizn' Rossii v epokhu Elizavety Petrovny. Dokumental'naia khronika. 1751–1761,* edited by by L. M. Starikova, vyp. 3, kn. 1 (Moscow: Nauka, 2011), 291–295, 318–321. A German company that occasionally played in Petersburg is known to have performed Racine's Alexander tragedy in Riga on Elizabeth's coronation day, see Vsevolodskii-Gerngross, *Teatr v Rossii,* 173. This tragedy was certainly known to the Russian public, along with other plays by Racine. Sumarokov translated an excerpt from it into Russian: Aleksandr Sumarokov, *Polnoe sobranie vsekh sochinenii,* ch. I, 316.

[60] Quintus Curtius, *[History of Alexander]*, 2:421 (IX:6, 21).

[61] Racine, *Théâtre complet*, 1:145.

[62] Benjamin, *The Origin of the German Tragic Drama,* 69–71.

Aux plus grands vertus si la gloire est unie,
Que tous les souverains en soient les partisans.[63]

(Of a hero so magnanimous
Let the exploits be renowned.
Of one such beautiful name the sweet harmony
Inspires all those at Court,
If glory is united with such great virtues
Let all sovereigns partake of it.)

In the opera, according to these verses, the aesthetic effects of musical drama ("douce harmonie") are merged with the effects of Alexander's charisma, which should be emulated by sovereigns whose power rests on the emotional engagement of their subjects. The Porus plays dramatized this mechanism of emotional submission. In Racine's rendering, overwhelmed by Alexander's display of "vertu" and "amitié" (virtue and friendship), Porus recognizes his dominion and joins his military effort in order to give the world "un maître aussi grand qu'Alexandre" (a master as great as Alexander). In his response to Peter's advances, Frederick, who once noted that Charles XII of Sweden was so fond of Alexander that he made Stanisław Leszczynski king of Poland "d'après Porus"(after Porus), resorted to a similar rhetoric, praising Peter who "donne un exemple de vertu à tous les souverains" (gives an example of virtue to all sovereigns) and declaring himself the emperor's "ami inseparable et qui coopérera … à tous ce Votre Majesté désirera," "j'irais moi-même contre Ses ennemis" (inseparable friend who cooperates with all Your Majesty would desire, I would go [to war] myself against Your enemies).[64]

The instant reconciliation with Frederick, usually considered as a sign of Peter's inadequacy, could be construed as a spectacular manifestation of his recently acquired sovereignty. The Alexander of the Porus plot, as Racine makes

[63] Pierre Metastasio, *Alexandre aux Indes,* 123. On the staging of sovereignty in Metastasio's *Allesandro,* see Reinhard Wiesend, "Metastasios Alexander: Herrscherfigur und Rollentypus. Aspekte der Rezeptionsgeschichte," in *Opernheld und Opernheldin im 18. Jahrhundert. Aspekte der Librettoforschung,* edited by K. Hortschansky (Hamburg: Eisenach, 1991), 139–152; Martha Feldman, *Opera and Sovereignty* (Chicago: University of Chicago Press, 2007), 255–258.

[64] *Politische Correspondenz Friedrichs des Großen,* 21:314, 391, 413 (#13552, 13637, 13656); "Réfutation du prince de Machiavel," *Œuvres de Frédéric le Grand* (Berlin 1848), 8:222. The final text corrected by Voltaire, as well as Voltaire's own earlier *Histoire de Charles XII, Roi de Suede* instead of Porus mentions Abdalonymus, a poor nobleman enthroned by Alexander. His story, too, was dramatized by Metastasio in *Il re pastore,* most famous in Mozart's setting. Frederick referred to Abdalonymus's story and its operatic treatments during the war: *Unter haltungen mit Friedrich dem Großen,* 345.

clear in the dedication of his play to the king, combined the two faces of royal power, the glorious yet violent conqueror and the wise peacemaker. Peter's actions displayed a similar combination: a German oration commemorating the Russo-Prussian peace contrasted the "Verwüstungen und Verheerungen ganzer Länder" (devastation and ruin of entire nations) by conquerors to the policy of the Russian monarch, who had demonstrated "daß Tapferkeit mit Menschenliebe verknüpffet, einen Helden in seiner Größe darstelle" (that valor combined with charity shows a hero in his greatness).[65]

Peter's peace initiative—which seemed to make Russia "la bienfaitrice de l'Europe" (the benefactress of Europe) and "l'arbitre du nord" (the arbiter of the north), as Voltaire put it—was only one of several measures devised for a spectacular inauguration of his reign and aligned with a common "scenario of power," which was largely inherited from Elizabeth and revolved around the notion of clemency. According to a contemporary account, the empress extracted from her successor "la promesse de pardonner à ses Ennemis, et de ne point affermir son trône par le sang de ses Sujets" (the promise of pardoning his enemies, and of not affirming his throne with the blood of his subjects).[66] Under Elizabeth this scenario was both reflected in policy, most famously in the suspension of death sentences, and reenacted on court stages. Indeed, *Alessandro nell'Indie* belonged to a rich tradition of dramatic representations of royal clemency that derived from Corneille's tragedy *Cinna* (1639) and its operatic imitation, Metastasio's *La clemenza di Tito* (1734), performed at Elizabeth's coronation.[67]

---

[65] Racine, *Théâtre complet,* 1:113–114; Samuel Tiefensee, [Carl Wilhelm Schulz], *Rede und Ode auf den zwischen den hohen Höfen Berlin und Petersburg Anno 1762. glücklich geschlossenen Frieden abgelesen in dem Gröningischen illustren Collegio zu Stargard an der Jhna* (Stargard, 1762), 19. The same author compares the Seven Years' War to a "traurige Schauspiel," 15.

[66] Voltaire, *Complete Works,* vol. 108 (=*Correspondence,* vol. 24), The Voltaire Foundation 1972, 330 (D10369), 326 (D10366); *Anecdotes russes, ou lettres d'un officier allemand à un gentilhomme livonien, écrites de Petersbourg en 1762; tems du règne et du détrônement de Pierre III. Empereur de Russie* (London, 1764), 10. Peter's double role as conqueror and peacemaker, as well as his claims to a hegemonic position in European politics, was broadcast in contemporary Russian panegyrics, first of all the odes by Sumarokov, Lomonosov, and Barkov. Barkov authored the Russian translation of the festive opera written for the peace celebrations: *Mir geroev. Drama na muzyke predstavlennaia vo vremia torzhestva blagopoluchno zaklyuchennago mira mezhdu . . . Petrom tret'im . . . i . . . Friderikom Tret'im korolem prusskim . . . Prelozhenie rossiiskimi stikhami . . . Ivana Barkova* (Saint Petersburg, 1762).

[67] On the politics of royal clemency and early modern drama, see Armin Schäfer, "Der Souverän, die *clementia* und die Aporien der Politik. Überlegungen zu Daniel Casper von Lohensteins Trauerspielen," in *Theatralität und die Krisen der Repräsentation,* edited by Erika Fischer-Lichte (Stuttgart: Weimar, 2001), 101–124; Armin Schäfer "Die Wohltat in der Politik. Über Souveränität und Moral im barocken Trauerspiel," *per imaginem. Bildlichkeit und*

Peter's reconciliation with Frederick stood for a scenario of clemency developed with an eye for internal use, just as Alexander's treatment of Porus could be construed as an allegory for the monarchy's relations to its subjects. (Racine's play, for example, glorified Louis XIV's handling of the Fronde of the Princes.) According to commonly held political conceptions, clement actions reinforced subjects' obedience to the monarchy with emotionally charged allegiance, or "love," for the ruler. This pattern could be recognized as the driving force behind Peter's policies. In the words of another contemporary, "Wer sollte nun nicht glauben, daß die guldenen Zeiten in Rußland angehen und die Anstalten, Großmuth und Milde des Kaisers ihm Liebe und Treue in allen Herzen erwerben würden?" (Who would not believe that the golden age is coming to Russia, and that the emperor's measures, his magnanimity and mildness would earn him love and loyalty in all hearts?)[68]

Traditional measures such as gifts, promotions, and the restitution of political exiles were reinforced by two legislative acts published one after another in February 1762. The first decree, the Manifesto on the Freedom of the Russian Nobility, allowed the nobles to retire from state service and to travel abroad, whereas the second abolished the secret police, together with the notorious system of political surveillance and persecution known as *slovo i delo.* Both decrees were recognized as displays of royal clemency (*shchedrost'* or *shchedrota,* in contemporary encomiastic idiom), strong gestures inscribed into the complex dynamic of collective emotion crucial for the functioning of Russian monarchy. The second decree claimed a semi-theatrical effect, attempting to reform any dissenters by a public "example" (*primerom*) of royal "mildness" (a scenario dramatized in *Cinna* and *La clemenza di Tito*).[69] In one of the many odes celebrating Peter's ascension, Aleksei Rzhevskii, a young nobleman and aspiring servitor, praised the royal decision to "forgive the guilty" and "accept the enemies as sons" ("Ty vinnykh poshchadil s okhotoi, / I prinial v synov'ia

---

Souveränität, edited by Anne von der Heiden (Zürich: Diaphanes, 2005), 79–99; Hélène Bilis, "Corneille's *Cinna*, Clemency, and the Implausible Decision," *The Modern Language Review* 108.1 (January 2013): 68–89. On the Russian performances of *La clemenza di Tito,* see Vsevolodskii-Gerngross, *Teatr v Rossii,* 19–25.

[68] Georg A. Will, *Merkwürdige Lebensgeschichte Peter des Dritten, Kaiser . . . aller Reußen* (Frankfurt, 1762), 19. On political contexts of Racine's play, see the much-mocked but still valuable René Jasinski, *Vers le vrai Racine* (Paris: A. Colin, 1958), 1:101–120.

[69] *Polnoe sobranie zakonov Rossiiskoi imperii*, 1-e izd., T. 15 (Saint Petersburg, 1830), 917–918. On the undercurrent of public perception of Peter's two decrees as foundational acts of a benevolent monarchy a generation later, see: Iu. M. Lotman, "Cherty real'noi politiki v pozitsii Karamzina 1790–kh gg. (K genezisu istoricheskoi kontseptsii Karamzina)," *Karamzin* (Saint Petersburg: Isskustvo-SPB, 1997), 479, 481; "A. S. Kaisarov i literaturno-obshchestvennaia bor'ba ego vremeni," Ibid., 658–660.

vragov"), reviving the pattern of power symbolized by Alexander's pardon for Porus. In another ode, Rzhevskii exalted the Manifesto on the Freedom of the Russian Nobility as a centerpiece of Peter's rule, rooted in the nation's "love" for him rather than armed force:

> Иной себя прославил,
> Кровь неповинных лив;
> Но славу Ты возставил
> Меча не обагрив;
> Щедротою одною,
> Над подданной страною,
> Героев превзошел,
> С мечем не кровавленным,
> В храм славы ты вошел,
> И мил своим плененным.
> Ты вольность даровавши,
> Всех вольность погубил,
> И всем свободу давши,
> Всех ныне нас пленил:
> Пленил ты нас любовью.
> Своей готовы кровью
> Мы то Тебе воздать,
> Трудом все безконечным,
> Мы будем исполнять
> С желанием сердечным.
> Ко смертоносну ль бою
> Охотно все идем,
> Охотно пред тобою
> Кровь нашу всю прольем.
> (Others have attained fame
> By shedding innocent blood
> But you have established your glory
> Without bloodying your sword.
> By sheer clemency
> To your dominion
> You have surpassed heroes and
> With a sword pure from blood
> You entered into the temple of fame
> Dear to your captives.
> Having granted us freedom
> You have taken it from us, and

Having taken us all captive,
You made us love's captives.
Ready with our own blood,
We will repay you
With endless toil
Accomplished with heartfelt zeal.
If we go into deadly battle,
We will gladly, before your very eyes
Pour out all of our own blood.)[70]

Rzhevskii's lyric idiom was artfully tuned to authentic political sensibilities of the Russian public. A Russian diplomat in Vienna admitted in a private letter that upon receiving news of the Manifesto he was "overwhelmed" (enthousiasmé) with Peter's "grandeur" and "une clemence aussi inatendue que surprenant" (a clemency as unexpected as [it was] surprising), and that the "chaines" (chains) abolished by the decree have to be replaced in the hearts of the nobility "avec de beaucoup plus fortes qui sont ceux de devoir de sujets fidel, zelé et reconaissant [sic]" (by those much stronger, namely those of the duty of loyal subjects, zealous and grateful).[71] In order to convey this new understanding of obedience, Rzhevskii adapts an erotic conceit (underscored by a meter unusual for political panegyric but common for "tender" songs and arias). In rejecting customary coercion, Peter's gift of freedom redefines his sway over his "captives," or subjects, in terms of love, conventionally described by the paradox of voluntary captivity. While Rzhevskii's verses do not necessarily refer to Racine's *Alexandre le Grand*, this play notably explored the affinities between the idioms of gallant love and political submission in the subplot of Queen Cléofile who, after her kingdom was conquered by Alexander, fell in love with him and gladly accepted "ses fers" (her bonds), "sa liberté perdant le souvenir" (losing the memory of her liberty; II: 1).[72] Showcasing the collective experience of subjection refashioned by the Manifesto, the lyric idiom once again unmasked the quasi-theatrical dynamic of royal gesture and public emotional engagement. This dynamic, which blurred

---

[70] Aleksei Rzhevskii, "Oda . . . imperatoru Petru Feodorovichu . . . na vseradostnoe vosshestvie na vserossiiskii prestol," *Poleznoe uveselenie*, 1762, March, 99; Aleksei Rzhevskii, "Oda . . . imperatoru Petru Feodorovichu . . . v znak blagodarnosti za . . . pozhalovan'e vol'nostiiu Rossiiskikh dvorian," *Ibidem*, 109–110. On erotic metaphors of power in absolutist literature, see Ziad Elmarsafy, *Freedom, Slavery, and Absolutism: Corneille, Pascal, Racine* (Lewisburg, PA: Bucknell University Press, 2003).

[71] I. G. Chernyshev and I. I. Shuvalovu, 7/18 fevrier 1762, *Russkii arkhiv*, 1869, 1822–1823.

[72] Racine, *Théâtre complet*, t. 1, 131–132.

the boundary between action and representation, was equally important for dramatic reenactments of monarchy and its actual functioning.

The political anthropology of monarchy, outlined in classical histories and explored by political theory from Machiavelli to Frederick's *Anti-Machiavel*, implied a constant oscillation between peace and conquest, clemency and violence, as foundations of sovereignty. It is deeply characteristic that Peter both mitigated political persecution and privately deplored his own "abuse of clemency," declaring that he should again "take to the gallows."[73] Just as in the Alexander plays, his reconciliation with the enemy was to be followed by its direct opposite: a war with Denmark for Holsteinian interests in which Peter could rely on his newly won ally. Peter's handling of the Prussian peace brought to light what Greenblatt calls "paradoxes, ambiguities, and tensions of authority"[74] and proved concomitantly to be both the central act of his reign and the ultimate manifestation of his failed sovereignty. His rapid fall in June 1762 was made possible by the public disapproval for the emperor's exaggerated Prussophilia.[75]

In order to defend Peter's decisions, his contemporary biographer had to remind readers that a "Souverain absolû" is not obliged to ask "ses Sujets la permission . . . de donner la paix à son païs" (his subjects for permission . . . to give peace to his [own] country) and that they do not possess "le pouvoir de le punir, parce qu'il ne veut pas s'accommoder à leur caprice" (the power to punish [the monarch], when he does not wish to give in to their caprice).[76] In displays of clemency, the idea of absolute royal sovereignty was reconciled with the monarchy's practical dependence on public approval. A semi-official account of Peter's Manifesto heralded "un Monarque qui a l'âme assez grande, pour renoncer à un droit aussi étendu dans la seule vue de rendre se sujets plus heureux" (a monarch who has a soul grand enough to renounce his privilege so vast in the only goal of making his subjects happier).[77] Unlike his Prussian counterpart, Peter, however, proved unable to fully acknowledge and master the patterns of performative engagement of the public. The peace

---

73 Ja. Shtelin [Jacob Stählin], "Zapiski o Petre III," *Ekaterina. Put' k vlasti* (Moscow: Fond Sergeia Dubova, 2003), 37.

74 Greenblatt, *Shakespearean Negotiations*, 65.

75 I build on the reading of Peter's fall suggested by Ronald Vroon, who demonstrates the importance of literary evidence for its comprehension: Ronald Vroon, "'Ekaterina plachet yavno…': k predystorii perevorota 1762 g.," *I vremia i mesto: Istoriko-filologicheskii sbornik k shestidesiatiletiiu A. L. Ospovata* (Moscow: Novoe Izdatel'stvo, 2008), 40–54.

76 *Anecdotes russes, ou lettres d'un officier allemand*, 205–206.

77 François Pierre Pictet to Voltaire, [2 March 1762], in Voltaire, *Complete Works*, vol. 108 (=*Correspondence*, vol. 24), 312 (D10355).

with Prussia, juxtaposed with his favor for his German entourage, was largely perceived as a violation of the body politic rather than a show of clemency.

In his poetic defense of Catherine's coup, the classically trained Mikhail Lomonosov complained that under Peter "torzhestvuiushchii narod / Predalsia v ruki pobezhdennykh . . . /O styd, o strannoi oborot!"(a people of victors had submitted to the defeated, what a shame, a strange twist), echoing the Macedonian troops' reproaches to Alexander as they rebelled against his acceptance of the customs of conquered lands, which "by a novel fashion made the victors pass under the yoke."[78] In a gesture equally eccentrically theatrical and drastically differing from public sensibility, Peter's failure to accommodate the attitudes of his audience fundamentally undermined his performance of sovereignty. While Frederick II successfully exploited dramatic patterns to refashion his defeat as a source of charisma, a misguided display of triumph precipitated Peter's ruin. If, as Benjamin suggests, tragic visions of kingship revolved around the "antithesis between the power of the ruler and his capacity to rule," Voltaire was right to remark: "Si Pierre III n'avait pas été un ivrogne, son aventure serait un beau sujet de tragédie." (If Peter III had not been a drunkard, his story would have made a great subject for a tragedy.)[79]

BIBLIOGRAPHY

Abbt, Thomas. "Vom Tode für das Vaterland." In *Aufklärung und Kriegserfahrung. Klassische Zeitzeugen zum Siebenjährigen Krieg*, edited by Johannes Kunisch, 598–650. Frankfurt am Main: Deutscher Klassischer Verlag, 1996.

Adam, Wolfgang, and Holger Dainat, eds. *"Krieg ist mein Lied": der Siebenjährige Krieg in den zeitgenössischen Medien*. Göttingen: Wallstein-Verlag, 2007.

Araja, Francesco, and Pierre Metastasio. *Alexandre aux Indes, opera . . . representé . . . par ordre de Son Altesse Imperiale monseigneur le grand duc de toutes les Russies*. Saint Petersburg: De l'imprimerie de l'Academie impe'riale des Sciences, 1759.

Bartenev, P. I., ed. *Arkhiv kniazia Vorontsova*. Moscow: Tip. A. I. Mamontova, 1872.

Benjamin, Walter. *The Origin of the German Tragic Drama*. Translated by John Osborne. London: Verso, 1985.

[78] Mikhail Lomonosov, *Izbrannye proizvedeniia*, sost. A. A. Morozov, Leningrad 1986, 170; Quintus Curtius, *[History of Alexander]*, vol. II, 295 (VIII, 7, 11).

[79] Walter Benjamin, *The Origin of the German Tragic Drama*, 70; Voltaire, *Complete Works*, vol. 109 (=*Correspondence*, vol. 25), The Voltaire Foundation 1973, 198 (D10685).

Bilis, Hélène. "Corneille's Cinna, Clemency, and the Implausible Decision" *The Modern Language Review* 108, no. 1 (January 2013): 68–89.

Blitz, Hans-Martin. *Aus Liebe zum Vaterland: die deutsche Nation im 18. Jahrhundert*. Hamburg: Hamburger Ed., 2000.

Bohnen, Klaus. "Von den Anfängen des Nationalsinns'. Zur literarischen Patriotismus-Debatte im Umfeld des Siebenjährigen Kriegs." In *Dichter und ihre Nation*, edited by Helmut Scheuer, 121–137. Frankfurt am Main: Suhrkamp, 1993.

Calella, Michele. "Metastasios Dramenkonzeption und die Ästhetik der friderizianischen Oper." In *Metastasio im Deutschland der Aufklärung: Bericht über das Symposium Potsdam 1999*, edited by Laurenz Lütteken and Gerhard Splitt, 103–123. Tübingen: Niemeyer, 2002.

Campe, Rüdiger. "Der Befehl und die Rede des Souveräns im Schauspiel des 17. Jahrhunderts. Nero bei Busenello, Racine und Lohenstein." In *Übertragung und Gesetz. Gründungsmythen, Kriegstheater und Unterwerfungstechniken von Institutionen*, edited by A. Adam and M. Stingelin, 55–71. Berlin: Akademie Verlag, 1995.

Catherine, Empress of Russia. *Correspondance de Catherine Alexéievna, Grande-Duchesse de Russie, et de Sir Charles H. Williams, Ambassadeur d'Angleterre, 1756 et 1757*. Moscow: Lissner & Sobko, 1909.

I. G. Chernyshev to I. I. Shuvalovu, 7/18 fevrier 1762, Russkii arkhiv, 1869, [column nos.] 1822–1823.

d'Aubignac, François-Hédelin. *The Whole Art of the Stage . . . Written in French by M.H. . . . and now made English*. London, 1684.

de Ligne, Charles-Joseph. *Mes écarts ou ma tête en liberté: et autres pensées et réflexions*, edited by Jeroom Vercruysse and Daniel Acke. Paris: H. Champion, 2007.

Dilthey, Wilhelm. "Friedrich der Große und die deutsche Aufklärung." In *Studien zur Geschichte des deutschen Geistes*, 81–205. Göttingen: Vandenhoeck & Ruprecht, 1992.

Doering, Pia Claudia. *Jean Racine zwischen Kunst und Politik: Lesarten der Alexandertragödie*. Heidelberg: Winter, 2010.

Du Deffand, Marie de Vichy Chamrond. *Correspondance complète de la Marquise du Deffand avec ses amis*, edited by Mathurin Francois Adolphe de Lescure. 2 vol. Paris: Plon, 1865.

Elias, Norbert. "The Fate of German Baroque Poetry: Between the Traditions of Court and Middle Class." In *The Collected Works*, 8–9. Dublin: University College Dublin Press, 2010.

Elmarsafy, Ziad. *Freedom, Slavery, and Absolutism: Corneille, Pascal, Racine*. Lewisburg, PA: Bucknell University Press, 2003.

Ewington, Amanda. *A Voltaire for Russia: A. P. Sumarokov's Journey from Poet-Critic to Russian Philosophe*. Evanston, IL: Northwestern University Press, 2010.

Feldman, Martha. *Opera and Sovereignty: Transforming Myths in Eighteenth-Century Italy.* Chicago: University of Chicago Press, 2007.

Frederick II. *Politische Correspondenz Friedrichs des Großen*. Berlin: Dunker, 1879.

Frederick II. "Epistle from the King of Prussia to Monsieur Voltaire." In *The Annual Register, or A View of the History, Politics and Literature of the Year 1758*. Translated by J. G. Cooper, 413–414. London: 1759.

———. *The Memoirs of his Reader, Henri de Catt (1758–1760)*. Translated by F. S. Flint. Boston: Houghton Mifflin, 1917.

———. *Œuvres de Frédéric le Grand*. 30 vol. Berlin: Imprimerie royale, 1852.

Gleim, Wilhelm Ludwig. *Preußische Kriegslieder von einem Grenadier.* Heilbronn: 1882. Reprint. Nendeln: Kraus, 1968.

Gottsched, Johann Christoph. "Die Schauspiele und besonders die Tragödien sind aus einer wohlbestellten Republik nicht zu verbannen" [1729]. In *Schriften zur Literatur*, 3–11. Stuttgart: Ph. Reclam, 1972.

Greenblatt, Stephen. *Shakespearean Negotiations: The Circulation of Social Energy in Renaissance England.* Berkeley: University of California Press, 1988.

Grell, Chantal, Christian Michel, and Pierre Vidal-Naquet. *L'école des princes, ou Alexandre disgracié: essai sur la mythologie monarchique de la France absolutist*. Paris: Les Belles Lettres, 1988.

Healey, F. G. *The Literary Culture of Napoléon*. Geneva: Droz, 1959.

Hellmuth, Eckhart. "Die 'Wiedergeburt' Friedrichs des Großen und der 'Tod fürs Vaterland.' Zum patriotischen Selbstverständnis in Preußen in der zweiten Hälfte des 18. Jahrhunderts." In *Nationalismus vor dem Nationalismus?*, edited by E. Hellmuth and R. Stauber, 21–52; Hamburg: Meiner, 1998 (= Aufklärung: interdisziplinäres Jahrbuch zur Erforschung des 18. Jahrhunderts und seiner Wirkungsgeschichte 10, no. 2).

Herrmann, Hans Peter. "Individuum und Staatsmacht. Preußisch-deutscher Nationalismus in Texten zum Siebenjährigen Krieg." In *Machtphantasie Deutschland. Nationalismus, Männlichkeit und Fremdenhaß im Vaterlandsdiskurs deutscher Schriftsteller des 18. Jahrhunderts*, edited by Hans Martin Blitz and Susanna Moßmann, 66–79. Frankfurt am Main: Suhrkamp, 1996.

Herold, J. Christopher. *The Age of Napoleon*. Boston: Houghton Mifflin Harcourt, 2002.

Jasinski, René. *Vers le vrai Racine*. Paris: A. Colin, 1958.

Klopstock, Friedrich Gottlieb. "Die Verkennung (1779)." In *Friedrich II, König von Preußen, und die deutsche Literatur des 18. Jahrhunderts. Texte und Dokumente*, edited by Horst Steinmetz, 56–57. Stuttgart: Reclam, 1985.

Knoll, Gerhard. "'Hunde, wollt Ihr ewig leben?' oder Goethe und die 'Hunde' des Großen Königs." *Aus dem Aniquariat. Zeitschrift für Aniquare und Büchersammler* 2 (2005): 22–27.

Koser, Reinhold. *Geschichte Friedrichs des Großen.* Vol. 3. Stuttgart: Cotta'sche Buchhandlung Nachfolger, 1913.

Koser, Reinhold, ed. *Unterhaltungen mit Friedrich dem Großen: Memoiren und Tagebücher von Heinrich de Catt*. Leipzig: Hirzel, 1884.

Kühnel, Florian. *Kranke Ehre?: Adlige Selbsttötung im Übergang zur Moderne.* Munich: Oldenbourg Verlag, 2013.

Kunisch, Johannes. *Das Mirakel des Hauses Brandenburg: Studien zum Verhältnis von Kabinettspolitik und Kriegführung im Zeitalter des Siebenjährigen Krieges*. Munich: Oldenbourg, 1978.

Langer, Werner *Friedrich der Große und die geistige Welt Frankreichs.* Hamburg: Seminar für romanische Sprachen und Kultur, 1932.

Lehmann, Ulf. *Der Gottschedkreis und Russland.* Berlin: Akademie Verlag, 1966.

Leonard, Carol. *Reform and Regicide: The Reign of Peter III of Russia*. Bloomington: Indiana University Press, 1993.

Lessing an Ewald von Kleist, 14 März 1758, Werke (Tempel Klassiker Sonderausgabe), Wiesbaden s.d., Bd 1, 1079.

Lomonosov, Mikhail. *Izbrannye proizvedeniia*, edited by A. A. Morozov. Leningrad: Sovetskii Pisatel', 1986.

Lotman, Iu. M. "Cherty real'noi politiki v pozitsii Karamzina 1790-kh gg. (K genezisu istoricheskoi kontseptsii Karamzina)." In *Karamzin*, 456–483. Saint Peterburg: Isskustvo-SPB, 1997.

Marin, Louis. "Théâtralité et pouvoir: Magie, machination, machine: Médée de Corneille." In Louis Marin, *Politiques de la representation.* 263–285. Paris: Editions Kimé, 2005.

Matala de Mazza, Ethel. "Die Regeln der Ausnahme. Zur Überschreitung der Souveränität in Fénelons Télémaque und Mozarts Idomeneo." In *Transgressionen. Literatur als Ethnographie,* edited by Gerhard Neumann and Rainer Warning, 257–286. Freiburg: Rombach, 2003.

Mervaud, Christiane. *Voltaire et Frédéric II: une dramaturgie des lumières, 1776–1778*. Oxford: The Voltaire Foundation; Paris: J. Touzot, 1985.

[Metastasio, Pietro]. *Poro, Re Dell'Indie. Drama . . . Done Into English by Mr. Humphreys*. London: n.p., 1731.

Mommsen, Katharina. *Goethe und der Alte Fritz*. Leipzig: Lehmstedt, 2012.

Michael Müller. "Rußland und der Siebenjährige Krieg. Beitrag zu einer Kontroverse." *Jahrbücher für Geschichte Osteuropas* 28 (1980): 198–219.

Mir geroev. Drama na muzyke predstavlennaia vo vremia torzhestva blagopoluchno zaklyuchennago mira mezhdu . . . Petrom tret'im . . . i . . . Friderikom Tret'im korolem prusskim . . . Prelozhenie rossiiskimi stikhami . . . Ivana Barkova. Saint Petersburg: Pri Imperatorskoi Akademii nauk, 1762.

Pečar, Andreas. "Friedrich der Große als Autor. Plädoyer für eine adressatenorientierte Lektüre seiner Schriften." In *Friedrich300*—*Eine perspektivische Bestandsaufnahme. Beiträge des ersten Colloquiums in der Reihe "Friedrich 300,"* edited by Michael Kaiser und Jürgen Luh, accessed August 28, 2013, http://www.perspectivia.net/content/publikationen/friedrich300-colloquien/friedrich-bestandsaufnahme.

Piirimäe, Eva. "Dying for the Fatherland: Thomas Abbt's Theory of Aesthetic Patriotism." *History of European Ideas* 35 (2009): 194–208.

Polnoe sobranie zakonov Rossiiskoi imperii, 1-e izd. Saint Petersburg: Otdeleniia Sobstvennoi Ego Imperatorskago Velichestva Kantseliarii, 1830.

[Poniatowski], Stanislas Auguste. *Mémoires*, edited by Anna Grzeskowiak-Krwawicz. Paris: Institut d'Études Slaves, 2012.

Quintus Curtius. *[History of Alexander]*. Translated by John C. Rolfe. Cambridge, MA: Harvard University Press, 1985.

Racine, Jean. *Racine, Théâtre complet*, edited by Jean-Pierre Collinet. Paris: Gallimard, 1983.

Reponse de S. M. le Roi de Prusse. *Das Neueste aus der anmuthigen Gelehrsamkeit* 3 (1758): 214–218.

Rieck, Werner. "Gottsched und Friedrich II." *Wissenschaftliche Zeitschrift der Pädagogischen Hochschule Potsdam, Gesell.-Sprachw. Reihe*, 2 (1966): 221–230.

Rzhevskii, Aleksei. "Oda . . . imperatoru Petru Feodorovichu . . . na vseradostnoe vosshestvie na vserossiiskii presto." In *Poleznoe uveselenie*, 99. Moscow: Pechatana pri Imperatorskom Moskovskom Universitete, 1762.

Sachse, Ullrich. *Cäsar in Sanssouci: die Politik Friedrichs des Großen und die Antike*. Munich: Allitera Verlag, 2008.

Schäfer, Armin. "Der Souverän, die clementia und die Aporien der Politik. Überlegungen zu Daniel Casper von Lohensteins Trauerspielen." In *Theatralität und die Krisen der Repräsentation*, edited by Erika Fischer-Lichte, 101–124. Stuttgart: Weimar, 2001.

———. "Die Wohltat in der Politik. Über Souveränität und Moral im barocken Trauerspiel." In *Imaginem. Bildlichkeit und Souveränität*, edited by Anne von der Heiden, 79–99. Zürich: Diaphanes, 2005.

Schmitt, Carl. *Political Theology: Four Chapters on the Concept of Sovereignty*. Translated by George Schwab. Cambridge, MA: Harvard University Press, 1985.

Schönert, Jörg. "Schlachtgesänge vom Kanapee. Zu den 'Preußischen Kriegsliedern' des Kanonikus Gleim." In *Gedichte und Interpretationen. Aufklärung und Sturm und Drang*, edited by Karl Richter, 126–139. Stuttgart: Reclam, 1983.

Schort, Manfred. *Politik und Propaganda: der Siebenjährige Krieg in den zeitgenössischen Flugschriften*. Frankfurt am Main: Lang Verlag, 2006.

Schwan, Christophe Friedrich. *Anecdotes russes, ou lettres d'un officier allemand à un gentilhomme livonien, écrites de Petersbourg en 1762; tems du règne & du détrônement de Pierre III. Empereur de Russie*. London: aux de'pens de la Compagnie, 1764.

Schwarze, Karl. *Der Siebenjährige Krieg in der zeitgenössischen deutschen Literatur. Kriegserleben und Kriegserlebnis in Schrifttum und Dichtung des 18. Jahrhunderts*. Berlin: Junker und Dunhaupt, 1936.

Shtelin, Ja. [Jacob Stählin]. "Zapiski o Petre III." In *Ekaterina. Put' k vlasti*, 9–50. Moscow: Fond Sergeia Dubova, 2003.

Solov'ev, S. M. *Istoriia Rossii s drevneishikh vremen*. Moscow: Prosveshchenie, 1993.

Starikova, L. M., ed. *Teatral'naia zhizn' Rossii v epokhu Elizavety Petrovny. Dokumental'naia khronika. 1751–1761*. Moscow: Nauka, 2011.

Sumarokov, Aleksandr. *Ody torzhestvennyia. Elegii lubovnyia. Reprintnoe vosproizvedenie sbornikov 1774 goda*. Moscow: OGI, 2009.

———. *Polnoe sobranie vsekh sochinenii*. 10 vol. Moskva: Univ. tip. N. Novikova, 1787.

Tiefensee, Samuel. [Carl Wilhelm Schulz], *Rede und Ode auf den zwischen den hohen Höfen Berlin und Petersburg Anno 1762. glücklich geschlossenen Frieden abgelesen in dem Gröningischen illustren Collegio zu Stargard an der Jhna*. Stargard: Johann Ludwig Kunst, 1762.

Ter-Nedden, Gisbert. "Philotas und Aias oder Der Kriegsheld im Gefangenendilemma. Lessings Sophokles-Modernisierung und ihre Lektüre durch Gleim, Bodmer und die Germanistik." In *Krieg ist mein Lied: Der Siebenjahrige Krieg in den Zeitgenössischen Medien*, 317–378. Göttingen: Wallstein, 2007.

Ulbert, Jorg. "Friedrichs Lektüren während des Siebenjährigen Krieges." In *Friedrich der Große als Leser*, edited by Brunhilde Wehinger and Günther Lottes, 71–98. Berlin: Akademie Verlag, 2012.

Voltaire. *Complete Works*. Oxford: The Voltaire Foundation, 1971.

Voltaire. *Écrits autobiographiques*. Edited by Jean Goldzink. Paris: Flammarion, 2006.

Vroon, Ronald. "'Ekaterina plachet yavno . . .': k predystorii perevorota 1762 g." *I vremia i mesto: Istoriko-filologicheskii sbornik k shestidesiatiletiiu A. L. Ospovata*, 40–54. Moscow: Novoe Izdatel'stvo, 2008.

Vsevolodskii-Gerngross, V.N. *Teatr v Rossii pri imperatritse Elizavete Petrovne.* Saint Petersburg: Giperion, 2003.

Wehinger, Brunhilde. "Denkwürdigkeiten des Hauses Brandenburg—Friedrich der Große als Autor der Geschichte seiner Dynastie." In *Vom Kurfürstentum zum Königreich der Landstriche. Brandenburg-Preußen im Zeitalter von Absolutismus und Aufklärung*, edited by Günther Lottes, 137–174. Berlin: Berliner Wiss.-Verlag, 2004.

White, Hayden. "Literary Theory and Historical Writing." In *Figural Realism: Studies in the Mimesis Effect*, 1–26. Baltimore, MD: Johns Hopkins University Press, 1999.

———. "The Irrational and the Problem of Historical Knowledge in the Enlightenment." In *Tropics of Discourse: Essays in Cultural Criticism*, 142–143. Baltimore, MD: Johns Hopkins University Press, 1985.

Wiesend, Rienhard. "Metastasios Alexander: Herrscherfigur und Rollentypus. Aspekte der Rezeptionsgeschichte." In *Opernheld und Opernheldin im 18. Jahrhundert. Aspekte der Librettoforschung*, edited by K. Hortschansky, 139–152. Hamburg: Eisenach, 1991.

Wikander, Matthew H. *Princes to Act: Royal Audience and Royal Performance, 1578–1792.* Baltimore, MD: Johns Hopkins University Press, 1993.

Will, Georg A. *Merkwürdige Lebensgeschichte Peter des Dritten, Kaiser . . . aller Reußen.* Frankfurt: n.p., 1762.

Wortman, Richard. *Scenarios of Power: Myth and Ceremony in Russian Monarchy.* Princeton: Princeton University Press, 1995.

GLEAMS OF THE WEST: DISTRIBUTION AND RECEPTION OF EUROPEAN FILMS IN SOVIET RUSSIA OF THE 1920S–1940S

Peter Bagrov*

Abstract

Political isolation of the USSR in Stalin's era led to an aesthetic isolation of Soviet art—including cinema. Nevertheless, throughout all of Soviet history, foreign cinema "percolated" through the Iron Curtain. At certain points, the amount of foreign films—European ones in the first place—was quite significant (several thousand in the 1920s). During other periods, their number was strictly limited (twelve features in the 1930s). Censorship led not only to a rigorous ideological selection of films, but to their extensive re-editing as well, which was quite possible in the silent era. The arrival of sound was followed by a rapid decrease in imported foreign films; thus, every single one of them was received enthusiastically as a window to the Western world. Soviet filmmakers and the Soviet audience studied and admired the "Soviet edition" of European cinema. The influence of European cinema on the Soviet one did exist, but it was highly peculiar. If carefully examined, the nature of this influence could enrich our understanding of the common European space of the 1920s–1940s.

The political isolation of the Soviet Union in the Stalinist era led to an aesthetic isolation of Soviet art—cinema included. But throughout the whole Soviet history, foreign cinema "percolated" through the Iron

* Peter Bagrov is a Senior Curator at Gosfilmofond of Russia (National Film Foundation of Russian Federation).

Curtain. The nature and the content of this "pernicious influence of the West" varied. My goal is rather modest—to trace an outline, for the topic of Western films on Soviet screens could provide enough material for an exciting nonfiction book.

But first a little flashback is necessary. In the era of primitives (1896–1913), the Russian film market mostly consisted of imported material. In addition, some of the major local production companies were no more than branches of European ones (Pathé Frères, Gaumont, Ambrosio, Eclair), and the production itself was Europe-oriented.

The major changes came in 1914—because of the war. The importing of films was neither halted nor even regulated by the government. But the trade connections were severely damaged and shipment became an issue of the greatest difficulty. For example, in Great Britain any export of film stock was forbidden. The Swedish government was consistently neutral and stopped all negotiations with combatant countries when "strategic materials" were concerned: among those was nitrocellulose—the base for films. Naturally, the leading position of the Germans at the Russian film market was shattered, even though paradoxically Russia continued receiving a certain amount of German film as late as 1915: war is war, business is business.

There were still Danish and American films, but they couldn't have provided enough entertainment for such a vast territory. And a country at war needed entertainment desperately. So the Russians had to enforce domestic film production. A quantitative leap eventually led to a qualitative one. Thus, the year 1914 marks the beginning of the Golden Age of early Russian cinema.

This Golden Age lasted no more than five years. The First World War was transformed into the Civil War and lasted for almost a decade. By the end of 1919, most of the leading Russian filmmakers had emigrated to Europe.

The 1920s

Yet the country still needed entertainment. At first sight, the picture looks quite impressive. With no financial resources, almost no film stock (Russia didn't produce its own blank film until the early 1930s), and very few experienced filmmakers, the Soviets managed to release almost 150 films in 1918–1923. Even the most committed Soviet historians were bound to admit their artistic insufficiency, but they claimed that the films fulfilled their purpose and were able to mobilize and educate the audience. Yet even a most sketchy analysis of the press reveals a rather bizarre situation. The films were indeed made, but hardly ever screened. There were absolutely no new foreign pictures either—for neither the Americans nor the Europeans were eager to establish connections with the Bolsheviks. So what did the public watch in the theaters? Mostly early, pre-revolutionary films—films that were not only aged but quite peculiar in terms of their content, ideology, and thus their suitability for Soviet audiences who were supposed to be building the new morals.

The New Economic Policy (NEP) changed everything. Proposed by Lenin in 1921 as an interim measure, it might be called the last outburst of capitalism in Soviet Russia. It allowed the opening of small businesses and shops—or even the reopening of confiscated ones. But the state still controlled large industries, factories, banks, etc. Gradually declining in the mid-1920s following Lenin's death, the NEP was completely abandoned in 1928 and replaced by Stalin's Five-Year Plan.

Lenin was a great supporter of the cinema. He had set great hopes on its propagandistic and ideological potential and arguably went as far as proclaiming it "the most important of all arts." By early 1920s, it became evident that the Soviets would have to purchase foreign films—and not just foreign films but the commercially successful ones—so that the profit from their distribution in Russia would provide enough funds for launching domestic filmmaking.

The turning point was 1923, the beginning of foreign film distribution in Soviet Russia. We still don't have complete statistics, but even the numbers available are quite impressive. Here is some data for Leningrad, the second-largest city in the country and an ex-capital. The information was recorded by Sergei Bratoluibov, one of the heads of Sevzapkino (Northwestern Photo-Cinema Management). In 1924 Sevzapkino purchased 500 films in Germany, 500 films in the United States, and 100 films in Denmark (Bratoliubov 1976, 50). The number of Soviet films produced that same year was only 78 (*Sovetskie khudozhestvenyye filmy-1* 1961).

As one of the critics recalled, "in those days one *Battleship 'Potemkin'* [a 1925 film by Sergei Eisentein and the symbol of the Soviet avant-garde—P.B.] accounted for a dozen 'old-fashioned' films and ten times more foreign ones . . . In the season of 1925 there were 183 films released on our screens: 103 American, 30 German, 25 Soviet, 7 Swedish, 7 French, 4 Italian, and one of each for the others" (Arnoldi, *Kinokriticheskoe "podrytie,"* 2).

In the early 1960s, a group of historians from Gosfilmofond, the Russian state film archive, tried to come up with a catalog of foreign silent films available for Soviet screens. The work was never completed, but three minor catalogs have been published, for French [Greiding], German [Yegorova], and American [Kartseva] films. According to those publications, the number of French silents in 1923–1931 was 195, German ones—561, and 945 American titles. Yet numerous research projects in the last half a century have proved that many titles were omitted in those pioneer works. What is more, we still have no catalogs for Scandinavian, Italian, British, and Asian films. The total number could be estimated as high as 3,000 or even 4,000 titles. The calculation of domestic production in 1923–1931 provides us with a number of 946 fiction films (*Sovetskie khudozhestvenyye filmy-1*).

Jay Leyda—not only the first Western historian of Russian cinema but also a contemporary of the events described, in his classic book *Kino* (1960) recalls:

> Fortunately for Russian film-makers, the end of NEP in the film industries did not mean the end of foreign film on Russian screens. The film-making country whose post-NEP connection stayed firmest was Germany, while French films dropped to a lesser place, as they did generally in the post-war film world. In Russia Gance was the most admired French director, Griffith and Cruze represented the serious American film, while the whole range of German work was familiar, to a remarkably full extent—Lang's *Dr Mabuse* and both parts of his *Nibelungen*, Pabst's *Freudlose Gasse*, Murnau's *Letze Mann* had all been seen in Russia by the end of 1925; Lubitsch was known both for his comedies and his historical spectacles, and Oswald for his social films and handsome costume tragedies.

One can add to that an impressive list of Mary Pickford's and Douglas Fairbanks's vehicles, dozens of American comedies (Charlie Chaplin, Buster Keaton, Harold Lloyd, Harry Langdon, Monty Banks, and many others), a whole set of Jackie Coogan melodramas (he made sixteen pictures as a child star; eight of them were shown in the Soviet Union). If we talk about European films there'll be—besides the titles mentioned—numerous comedies with Pat and Patachon, a popular Swedish duo known in the United States as Thick and Thin; German-made and American-styled action films with Harry Piel, and even two or three dozen films produced in France by Russian émigrés—proclaimed in their native country as traitors and enemies.

So how could those "politically incorrect" films be screened all over the country with strict censorship, a one-party system, and severe ideological control of all cultural events?

The solution was—"reediting." This meant changing the intertitles, omitting unsuitable content, and sometimes even replacing risky material with safe. Not much has been written on the exciting topic of reediting in Soviet Russia, but to those interested in the subject I would recommend a brilliant article by Yuri Tsivian called—quoting the famous Soviet critic Viktor Shklovsky—"The Wise and Wicked Game" (Tsivian 1996). I have nothing to add to Tsivian's article with reference to concept or analysis, so instead of theorizing I will quote a large excerpt from a piece of memoir that has been never before been published. It explains the practice clearly and adds new material to Tsivian's collection. The memoir belongs to Edgar Arnoldi, one of the leading film critics of the time:

> "Thus a critic was facing a difficult task of educating the viewer, raising his consciousness in the question of preferring the more useful films to the less useful ones. But the viewer had worked out a critical immunity and he would definitely try to see the criticized films and to avoid the praised ones. Yet this circumstance did not shatter at all the critics' assurance that they know best what the viewer needs. The critics were oriented towards the proletarian audience and were certain that the only reason they would fall for 'petty-bourgeois tinsel' was their lack of knowledge and competence—but that would soon pass. As for the non-proletarian layers—well, they won't last forever, so there is no need to worry about them . . .
>
> Deactivation of the bourgeois films was conducted extensively as a crucial remedy for releasing foreign production. It was impossible to simply turn down the import, for our films were few and they couldn't fulfill the economic needs of the existing network. That's why—by means of excluding certain scenes, changing the intertitles, re-accentuating the meanings—a certain opposition to the bourgeois poison was reached, and thus it became possible to release the films onto our screens. . . .
>
> I myself had a chance to become familiarized in practice with the truly incredible power of reediting. Several times on various occasions I was commissioned by the Leningrad film distribution office to do a reediting job. Once a catastrophe occurred: the first reel of a Harry Piel film was burned in a projection booth of a movie theatre. I was sent for early in the morning and offered to urgently create some kind of an exposition from the other reels and Piel's other films—so that the evening screening wouldn't be scuttled. The task was painstaking and the time extremely limited.
>
> I had to come up with a combination suitable for the first turn of the plot. By splicing pieces of film turned backwards (from polish to mate), I've shown how Piel meets himself in a hall. One of the Piels inevitably turned out to be left-handed, but that shouldn't have struck anyone's eye. Thus, a double appeared for the sake of the exposition. The inserted subtitles justified his emerging and later his well-timed disappearance.

> Often the editors distorted and rehashed foreign films unmercifully and unconvincingly. They transposed beginnings and endings, interrupted the action in the middle, achieved the opposite sense through the intertitles. In such cases the audience was furious, and even the critics noted the plot as being disfigured to nonsense—or they intellectualized on the crisis of content in bourgeois cinema. 'There is no plot in the film,'—stated one of the reviewers.—'The salad they are trying to pass as a plot is the last thing to be called a plot.' It wouldn't take much effort to guess who is the cook that made this salad . . ." (Arnoldi, *Kinokriticheskoe podrytie*, 3-5).

Occasionally such a reediting was done by talented people who used this opportunity to master the art of filmmaking (which was quite difficult to do in a traditional way due to the lack of film stock). Sergei Eisenstein is a name that requires no commentary. In 1923 he reedited Fritz Lang's *Dr. Mabuse, der Spieler* under the title *Gilded Rot*—in fact it was his first experience as a filmmaker. Among other eminent reeditors were Esphir Shub, later a classic figure of documentary film and one of the first influential female directors in world cinema, and two namesakes, Sergei Vasiliev and Georgii Vasiliev, who teamed up under the pseudonym Vasiliev Brothers and directed in 1934 perhaps the most popular of all Soviet films of the pre-World War II era, *Chapayev*. Alas, most of their work is lost, but thanks to Eisenstein one of the elegant solutions—this time by Veniamin Boitler, an architect—became a most popular apocrypha:

> "A picture with [Emil] Jannings, *Danton*, came from abroad. It became *Guillotine* here. (Today hardly anyone remembers the film.) There was a scene in the Soviet version: Camille Desmoulins is sent to the guillotine. Agitated, Danton rushes to Robespierre. Robespierre turns aside and slowly wipes away a tear. The intertitle said, approximately: "In the name of freedom I had to sacrifice a friend..."
>
> – All is well.
>
> But who could have guessed that in the German original Danton, a playboy and a womanizer, a marvelous chap and the only positive figure amidst a pack of villains, that this Danton ran up to the evil Robespierre and... spat in his face? That Robespierre wiped the spit off his face with a handkerchief? And that the intertitle indicated Robespierre's threat, a threat that became reality when at the end of the film Danton-Jannings is the one to go to the guillotine?!

> Two tiny cuts extracted a little piece of the film – from the moment a spit is made till the moment it reaches the aim. And the insult of a spit becomes a tear of remorse for the fallen friend..." (Eisenstein 1968, 70)

Did such work deform the author's intentions? It certainly did. But how else could a film, unsuitable for the Soviet audience from the censor's point of view—such, for example, as *Danton* with its portrayal of Robespierre as a villain—how else could such a film be screened at all? When decades later Arnoldi asked Sergei Vasiliev in a private conversation whether the ghosts of slaughtered foreign film masterpieces haunt him in nightmares, Vasiliev replied "absolutely calmly that if our audience was able to get acquainted with many wonderful examples of the work of American and Western European actors and directors, it was only thanks to reediting" (Arnoldi. *Kinokriticheskoe podrytie*, 6).

So, one way or another, a Soviet filmgoer of the 1920s, professionals included, was familiar with the contemporary Western productions—the avant-garde as well as the mainstream. And this definitely was one of the main catalysts for the legendary Soviet silent cinema. They knew the context, they felt the times, and their film production was aimed for the outer world—even if they wanted to polemicize with it.

The 1930s

The next turning point in the history of Soviet film distribution could be stretched from 1929 to 1931. On December 7, 1929, Sovnarkom (Council of People's Commissars) issued an act entitled "On the Acquisition, Production, and Screening of Politically Enlightening Films," according to which no less than 30 percent of the film budget (and the film production was, I'd like to remind the reader, totally controlled and financed by the state) had to be spent on the so-called agit-prop films (Margolit 2007, 255-256).

The classic agit-prop film was a hybrid of fiction, documentary, and educational film, meant to illustrate the latest political slogans, such as, "There are no fortresses that Bolsheviks cannot storm" or "Cadres are the key to everything." But there could be no story and no real characters: everyone represented a certain profession or social layer. Psychology was replaced with endless diagrams and schemata demonstrating the increase of coal output or the daily milk yield. What made the situation hopeless was the increasing share of agit-prop films on production calendars: by 1930 they made up 55 percent of the total output, and the powers-that-be were complaining that even that number was too low. Avant-garde experiments and commercial "genre" films were equally unwelcome. Many exceptional works made at the turn of the decade were either banned (Vsevolod Pudovkin's *Prostoi sluchai* and Ivan Pyriev's *Gosudarstvennyi chinovnik*) or severely reedited (Evgenii Cherviakov's *Goroda i gody*, Lev Kuleshov's *Dva-Buldi-Dva*) by Party-commissioned craftsmen—just like the foreign films in the 1920s.

As for the foreign films themselves, starting from 1931 their amount was cut down to an absurd minimum. Of course there was an illusion of democracy and diversity: the import of foreign pictures was never banned officially. But the complete list of foreign films on Soviet screens of the prewar talking era (1931–41) could easily be fit on one page. Nineteen motion pictures—including shorts and animation! It might be impressive to provide the numbers for each year:

1932 – 0
1933 – 0
1934 – 1
1935 – 9 (3 of them animated shorts and 1 experimental color short)
1936 – 4
1937 – 1
1938 – 0
1939 – 1
1940 – 2
1941 – 1 (Source: *Katalog zvukovykh filmov* 1954)

Naturally, most of them made quite a splash, though there were a few awkward situations when a film went practically unnoticed—like the American melodrama *The Cabin in the Cotton* (1932) or a Polish comedy, *Antek policmajster* (1935). Yet, both were significant for different reasons: *The Cabin in the Cotton* was the only chance for Soviet audiences to see young Bette Davis, and *Antek policmajster* was the only film from Eastern Europe.

In fact, in these circumstances practically every picture became significant as being "the only" something. Lloyd Corrigan's 1934 short, *La Cucaracha,* was the only foreign color film in the USSR—and the first color picture to be widely shown in the country. The 1936 musical *Give Us This Night,* released in the Soviet Union five years later as Pesn o Liubvi [*Song of Love*], was the only example of the popular European genre of "tenor-film" with which the Soviet audience became familiar. No wonder its star, Jan Kiepura, became much more famous in the USSR than most of his fellow tenors.

By the mid-1930s Hollywood production was certainly leading at the European box offices, but not in Russia—even among the foreign releases. In the silent days, the amount of American pictures was definitely higher than that of the European ones—though it's hard to judge from the trade papers, mostly interested in the "artistic achievements" of the western avant-garde. Only four out of twelve foreign features released in the 1930s were made in the United States—and two of them were Chaplin's *City Lights* and *Modern Times* (Stalin was a great fan of Chaplin), which could hardly be referred to as Hollywood mainstream.

The most paradoxical situation was that of the film stars. The Russian public of the 1930s never saw Greta Garbo, Marlene Dietrich, Miriam Hopkins, Mae West, Danielle Darrieux, Lilian Harvey, etc. Thus, the most popular foreign film star in the USSR was an Austro-Hungarian comedienne, Francisca Gaal. Her work was represented by an incredibly high number of films—three: *Peter* (1934), *Kleine Mutti* (1935), and *Katharina, die Letzte* (1936). A marvelous actress, she was, of course, overshadowed in Europe by other stars. Only in the last several years have Austrian and Hungarian film scholars started to explore her phenomenon—and one of the main causes for that interest was her enormous popularity in Soviet Union (Geréb 2011/2012).

There was almost no reediting in the 1930s (though the happy ending in *Katharina, die Letzte* was "edited out"—for, according to Soviet standards, a poor servant in bourgeois Europe was not supposed to find happiness with a young and handsome millionaire). Instead the films themselves were picked much more carefully. Comedies were a pretty safe choice: they either simply entertained or even criticized "capitalistic jungle." That's why fourteen out of the nineteen films belonged to this genre.

Two of the dramas (*The Cabin in the Cotton* and *La Cucaracha*) were released relatively early—before the ideological control became particularly harsh. The choice of the only two French dramas must look extremely bizarre to a film historian: it's no wonder that one of the greatest French directors, Jean Renoir, was represented by two films, but instead of screening his masterpieces, *La Chienne*, *La Grande Illusion*, *La Règle du jeu*, etc.—two of his weakest pictures were chosen. Yet, the explanation was simple: *La Marseillaise* (1938) was a film about the French Revolution made from socialist positions, and *La vie est à nous* (1936) was even produced and commissioned by the French Communist party.

But thanks to that, Renoir earned a right to have a monograph on his work published in Russian (Avenarius 1938). So did René Clair (Otten 1937), two of whose comedies, *Sous les toits de Paris* (1930) and *Le Dernier milliarder* (1934), have been shown in the Soviet Union; Charlie Chaplin [Sokolov]; and

Francisca Gaal (Arnoldi and Yefimov 1937). Of course the authors couldn't build a whole book on just two or three films, so they had to describe the rest. The lucky ones had a chance to see one or two unreleased pictures—there were "closed" screenings occasionally at the embassies, consulates, and even film studios. But usually they were simply compiling materials from secondary sources. Edgar Arnoldi, who has been quoted here several times, co-authored the Francisca Gaal book and witnessed the making of several others by his friends. He recalled ironically:

> "The heavy torrent of films that poured in during the years of NEP subsequently ran dry. . . . Foreign press seeped in rather scantily. We've studied painstakingly everything we could attain and tried to get an idea of the new films, their actors and directors, and even their set designs, from these shreds of information. At times the press data turned out to be quite contradictory, but we tried to use this diversity of opinions for our critical conclusions.
>
> We called such an occupation 'shooting at invisible targets.' We laughed that a film one has never seen is easier to describe than the seen one, for it's done without preconception." (Arnoldi 1968, 227)

Indeed there were a few remarkable achievements in this field. For example, in 1936 Nikolai Yefimov published a book on Georg Wilhelm Pabst—yet none of his sound films were ever shown in the USSR, and the last silent film, *Die Büchse der Pandora* (1929), was released seven years before.

Thus the information on foreign cinemas—and any information was valuable—was smuggled in all the possible ways.

Perhaps the issue of *The Great Waltz* is the most symptomatic and the most famous one. This musical biopic on the life of Johann Strauss was a truly international film made by a group of successful European immigrants in Hollywood. The screenplay by the Austrian Walter Reisch was directed by one of France's leading directors, Julien Duvivier, starring the French Fernand Gravey, the German Luise Rainer, and the Polish-Russian soprano Miliza Korjus. It was first acquired after the Soviet invasion of Poland (AKA "the liberation of Western Ukraine and Belorus") in 1939, greatly admired by Stalin, and bought officially from MGM a year later. For the American audience it was just one of the lavish MGM musicals. But for the Soviet public, *The Great Waltz* became a symbol of musical film, a symbol of good entertainment, a symbol of foreign film—and even more than that. This picture is mentioned in numerous memoires and works of fiction; several short stories and songs were specially dedicated to it. But here I'll quote just one diary entry—that of Fyodor Nikitin, perhaps the greatest actor of the Soviet silent screen:

> I've watched *The Great Waltz*—an American picture from '39. (That's all from the Polish resources.) Wonderful picture, and wonderful acting. This picture has charmed me and for two days I couldn't get it out of my head. So I asked myself, what did it charm me with. With the art? Yes, with the art with no social scopes, no depth and truthfulness to the theme from our position—but there is the private life, there is the scent of this personal, deep, light, happy, and sad private life. We have forgotten about that. We have no private life. We live a harsh, courageous, heroic life, whether we want it or not, [everyone] till the last philistine. And we are the creators and the prisoners of this grandiose life. We are the ascetics of an idea—the whole nation carrying a great feat of the world's renewal. There is a lot of grandeur, beauty, courage in our life. But very often we lack the warmth and heartiness and the depth of private, personal manifestations of the spirit; those manifestations that couldn't be appreciated by our ratio from the point of their usefulness to our common dead, but exist by themselves by virtue of the need of the heart. It is difficult to live like this, but we have already accustomed ourselves, and we come across this light music of private life—for a moment our hearts fill with the sadness of memories or longing for them. (Nikitin, 26-26rev)

This intimate self-confession about the lack of personality is quite frightening in itself. It becomes even more impressive if you take into account Nikitin's career. In the 1920s he was indeed one of the most "personal" and "intimate" actors in Soviet Russia, mostly playing social outcasts of various sorts, but by early 1940, when this entry was made, he couldn't find a place for himself in the movies—and indeed the screen had no need for striking individualities—so he quit this medium for the theater to make a successful comeback only after the war.

Yet, what makes these few lines a truly powerful document of the time, with its morals and aspirations, is the final sentence. Nikitin (26rev-27) concludes his entry rather unexpectedly: "That is why I liked the film and why it shouldn't be shown at all!"

And I guess Nikitin was absolutely correct inasmuch as that must have been exactly the reason why in general such foreign films never reached the

Soviet people. The Soviet Union was meant to be something like Plato's cave: it "functioned" properly as long as its inhabitants were unaware of the things happening outside. Movies, even the production of completely fictionalized genres, inevitably reflected true life—from worries and joys to fashions, kitchenware, automobiles, and farming equipment. All that had to be concealed.

What did it lead to in terms of art? Naturally, to complete isolation and the uniqueness of Soviet cinema. The silents of the 1920s could easily be fit into the general tendencies and styles of the epoch. There were many remarkable motion pictures in the 1930s, but one could hardly find analogies for Western cinema: this singularity effected dialogue, acting style, camerawork, and set design. For a typical European or American viewer, a Soviet film seemed to be made on another planet—one can judge by the many existing reviews.

The War changed everything.

The 1940s

Today it is almost common knowledge that the Great Patriotic War (as World War II is usually called in Russia), in spite of all the losses and difficulties, became the first outburst of freedom in Stalin's era. Some historians even speak of a "wartime thaw."

I am not going to discuss the general outcome of this "thaw," for there is too much to be discussed. The churches closed down in the 1930s were now reopened. Many of the purged artists were given the possibility to return to full-fledged work: Sergei Prokofiev received three Stalin prizes in one year (the ceremony took place in 1946, but the work itself was done during the war), Yevgenii Shvarts published his daring anti-totalitarian play *The Dragon,* and Nikolai Akimov directed it in his Theatre of Comedy.

There were many changes in the film world as well. Sergei Eisenstein, Abram Room, and Boris Barnet, accused of formalism in the 1930s, were now given the possibility to make some of their best films (*Ivan the Terrible* [1944-45], *The Invasion* [1944], and *Once Upon a Time In the Night* [1944] respectively). Many of the exiled filmmakers returned to the "big land" and were allowed to work. Among them were the scriptwriter and playwright Nikolai Erdman, cameraman Daniil Demutskii, and set designers Yevgenii Yenei and Isaak Makhlis.

And—returning to the subject of this paper—the number and the quality of foreign films increased rapidly. The first few were received through lend-lease from the United States and mostly Great Britain—pure entertainment for the fighting country: melodramas (*That Hamilton Woman*, 1941), musicals

(*Let George Do It!*, 1940), action films (*In Old Chicago*, 1937). All three were released in 1943 and enjoyed tremendous success. Paradoxically—or maybe not—the only foreign release of the year to be practically ignored by the public and the critics was the only true masterpiece in the set—Noël Coward's and David Lean's semi-documentary drama . . . *In Which We Serve* (1942).

There were six foreign films released in 1943, ten in 1944, and seven in 1945. Cartoons, pro-Soviet war propaganda, several British Technicolor spectacles (color was still considered rather a novelty in the USSR), and musicals, musicals, musicals. Francisca Gaal was now firmly replaced by Deanna Durbin. (There was, indeed, something similar in their films—particularly since most of them were directed by the same person, Herman Kosterlitz/ Henry Koster.) But nothing could beat the insane box-office success of a silly German color musical, *Die Frau Meiner Träume* (1944). The modest eroticism of this title was excluded from a much more romantic Russian translation "Девушка моей мечты," which means "The Girl of My Dream." Yet nothing could abolish the seductive manners of Marika Rökk—particularly in the scene where she takes a bath in a wooden barrel. One of the apocrypha that even I heard as a "revelation" was that of the famous uncensored print where the barrel is transparent. That is not true, of course, and it corresponds neither with the German morals of the 1940s, nor with Rökk's style, nor even with the structure of the barrel.

A new turning of the political screw started in 1947 with a fresh set of arrests and purges; namely, the anti-cosmopolitan (i.e., anti-Jewish) campaign, another one of the numerous anti-formalist campaigns. The film situation of 1948–52 is usually described by the word *malokartinye* (from the Russian "мало картин" [few films]). In order to raise the quality of Soviet films, Stalin decided to decrease their quantity. The result could have been easily predicted. Horrified by the enormous responsibility and a whole staff of "political supervisors" (the fewer pictures there were, the easier it was to "supervise" and control them), those lucky filmmakers who did get a chance to direct a feature became extremely tense, formal, and as clichéd as possible. As for the numbers, they were ridiculous. Only thirteen features were produced in 1948, with the record achieved in 1951: nine features in all the Soviet Republics (*Sovetskie khudozhestvennye filmy* 1961, vol. 2).

What about the public? What about the box-office?

The public was watching foreign films. One of the main cultural trophies of the war was the collection of Reichsfilmarchiv. Aside from German films—many of which contained no evident Nazi ideology and thus were suitable for the Soviet audience—this archive contained many films from other European countries and the United States.

These films were displayed in the Soviet Union as "war trophies." What made the situation piquant was the fact that the Soviets never conquered the Americans, the British, or the French. So they had absolutely no right to their films. And yet . . . the public needed entertainment. The solution was found easily.

An "illegal" trophy was screened without the credits, with a new title, and with an epigraph at the beginning: "This film was obtained by the Red Army as a war trophy in Germany." This way the Soviet audience was able to see some of the most important Western films—often without even knowing what they had seen. Only years later did some of them find out that the mysterious film "Путешествие будет опасным" (*The Trip Is Going to Be Dangerous*) was John Ford's great *Stagecoach* (1939), a political comedy/drama "Сенатор" (*The Senator*) was Frank Capra's *Mr. Smith goes to Washington* (1939), and "Капитан армии Свободы" (*Captain of the Army of Liberty*) turned out to be *Viva Villa!* (1934). Some of the titles were impossible to conceal, like *The Hunchback of Notre Dame* (1939). On the other hand, *David Copperfield* (1935) was renamed *Hard Years*, which made no sense since Dickens was extremely popular in the USSR and the characters would have been recognized in no time.

After such a radical but technically and aesthetically simple reediting operation, the film was usually left untouched. After all, formally these were films captured from the enemy. And what could one expect from the enemy in terms of ideology!

Yet, sometimes the changes seemed to be necessary. Here is just one example—a German melodrama of boxing life, *Die Letze Runde* (1940). By pure accident, in the personal files of a film administrator I ran into an archival document on the dubbing—and eventual reediting—of this film "in order to broaden the social meaning of the picture" (the main body of such documents is yet to be found):

> "In the German version the general idea of the picture was limited to the fact that a boxer shouldn't have frivolous relations with women.
>
> In our dubbing we tried to demonstrate how in capitalistic conditions sport turns into a commercial enterprise, a dirty speculation, to show the backstage side of the match, the adventurers and gangsters who decide the destinies of the sportsmen.
>
> For that purpose the following has been done:
>
> 1. Grisha Shuvalov is represented not as a Russian émigré but as an Italian Rozelli—the head of the gangster band . . .

> 2. Lili's destiny is described as that of an unemployed actress who is gradually going to the bottom . . .
>
> 3. The theme of bringing up a German Nazi boxer is excluded from the picture.
>
> 4. The dialogue has been cleared from dirty jokes." (Kamenskii, 62)

So in many ways foreign film distribution returned to the 1920s: the percentage of these films was again much higher than that of the domestic production; reediting skills and techniques were reanimated. We still don't have a list of foreign films released from 1947 to 1954 (the year when the "trophy" politic was replaced with legal distribution); the records were hardly kept. In the late 1950s, the Soviet state film archive Gosfilmofond tried to come up with a catalog, according to which there were 48 foreign films in 1948, 44 in 1949, 27 in 1950, 37 in 1951, 39 in 1952, 34 in 1953 (*Katalog* 1954). The actual numbers were even higher: the published archival documents for 1948 alone mention more than 60 titles.

Once again foreign films became excellent catalysts. A whole generation was raised on—or, rather, formed by—those films. A generation with a new mentality, the generation that would form the new post-Stalinist Soviet society. There is a wonderful confession made by Gennadii Poloka, one of the leading Soviet avant-garde directors of the 1960s and 1970s, just recently, a few months ago:

> "If there wasn't that period of the trophy films: French, German, American, all sorts—if this ability to conceive the world and the art as a boundless diversity did not stick in us, we wouldn't have been prepared for those extremes that emerged in our cinema at the end of the 1960s and beginning of the 1970s. We wouldn't have achieved that level of artistic courage that we got in those years." (Poloka 2014)

And Poloka was not the only one to admit that. Paradoxically enough, the "new wave" of Soviet film avant-garde was nourished by the western mainstream in the harshest post-war Stalinist years, just as the first Soviet film avant-garde of the 1920s was nourished by the silent Western mainstream—also quite paradoxically for a country that was constantly fighting with the vestiges of capitalism.

All this might sum up to a collection of anecdotes. And perhaps Russian history is no more than a collection of anecdotes. Still I'll try to make a conclusion.

One of the main questions of European studies has always been: "What is Russia in regards to Europe? To what extent is Russia Europe?" In the years mentioned, cinema was one of the most—if not the most—mass-oriented arts. Analyzing film distribution—rather than filmmaking—could tell quite a lot about Europe and European society. If we ask a simple question: "What did they watch in Europe?," we would end up with Hollywood productions and—at different periods—with local outbursts of European films. And the Soviet Union/Russia turns out to be no exception. According to memoires and diaries, Russians watched and were impressed by the same types of motion picture as the rest of Europe. Thus, film distribution in Russia was an edition, or projection, of the European one. To a certain—and a very peculiar—extent.

And perhaps to the same extent could Russia be called an edition/ projection of Europe.

BIBLIOGRAPHY

Arnoldi, Edgar. 1968. "Iz vospominanii o pervykh shagakh leningradskogo kinovedeniia." In *Iz istorii Lenfilma: Statii, vospominaniia, dokumenty: 1920-e gody.* 1: 220–237. Leningrad: Iskusstvo.

———. *Kinokriticheskoe "podrytie" dvadtsatykh godov. Eskizy vospominanii.* 15 pp. (Typewrite in the collection of the Russian Instute of Art History, Film Cabinet, Edgar Arnoldi's papers).

Arnoldi, Edgar, and Yefimov Nikolai. 1937. *Francheska Gaal.* Leningrad: Iskusstvo.

Avenarius, Georgii. 1938. *Zhan Renuar.* Moscow: Goskinoizdat.

Bratoliubov, Sergei. 1976. *Na zare sovetskoi kinematografii: Iz istorii kinoorganizatsii Petrograda-Leningrada 1918-1925 gg.*, edited by Nina Gornitkaia. Leningrad: Iskusstvo.

Eisenstein, Sergei. 1968. "Sredniaia iz triokh." In *Izbrannye proizvedeniia v shesti tomakh.* Vol. 5: 53-78. Moscow: Iskusstvo.

Geréb, Anna. 2011/2012. "Franchesca Gaal: fragmenty odnoi sudby." *Kinovedcheskie zapiski* 100/101: 654-683.

Geréb, Anna. 2014. *Kariera Francheski Gaal. K 111-letiiu so dnia rozhdeniia.* Moscow: GTsTM im. Bakhrushina.

Greiding, Yurii. 1964. "Frantuzskie nemye filmy v sovetskom prokate." In *Kino i vremia: Biulleten'.* 4: 348-379. Moscow: Gosfilmofond.

Kamenskii-Ekshtein, Fedor Ivanovich: personal file // TSGALI SPb (Central State Archive of Literature and Art of St. Petersburg). 257/19/416. 106 pp.

Kartseva, Yelena. 1960. "Amerikanskie nemye filmy v sovetskom prokate." *Kino i vremia: Biulleten'.* Moscow: Gosfilmofond. 1: 193–325.

Katalog zvukovykh filmov, vyuschennykh na sovetskii ekran 1927-1954, edited Aleksandr Macheret. Moscow: Gosfilmofond, 1954.

Leyda, Jay. 1960. *Kino: A History of the Russian and Soviet Film*. London: George Allen & Unwin.

Macheret, Aleksandr, ed. *Sovetskie khudozhestvenyye filmy: Annotirovannyi katalog*. Vols. 1 and 2. Moscow: Iskusstvo, 1961.

———. *Katalog zvukovykh filmov, vyuschennykh na sovetskii ekran 1927-1954*. Moscow: Gosfilmofond, 1954.

Margolit, Yevgenii. 2007. "Fenomen agitpropfilma i prikhod zvuka v sovetskoe kino." *Kinovedcheskie zapiski* 84: 255–266.

Nikitin, Fedor. Diaries. No 3: October 1939–May 1940 // State Central Film Museum. 141/1/3.

Otten, Nikolai. 1937. *Rene Kler*. Leningrad: Iskusstvo.

Poloka, Gennadii. 2014. TV interview, http://tvkultura.ru/article/show/article_id/99456.

Sokolov, Ippolit. 1938. *Charli Chaplin: Zhizn i tvorchestvo: Ocherk po istorii amerikanskogo kino*. Moscow: Goskinoizdat.

Sovetskie khudozhestvenyye filmy: Annotirovannyi katalog. Vol. 1. Nemye filmy (1918-1935), edited by Aleksandr Macheret. Moscow: Iskusstvo, 1961.

Sovetskie khudozhestvenyye filmy: Annotirovannyi katalog. Vol. 2. Zvukovye filmy (1930-1957), edited by Aleksandr Macheret. Moscow: Iskusstvo, 1961.

Tsivian, Yuri. 1996. "The Wise and Wicked Game: Re-editing and Soviet Film Culture of the 1920s." *Film History* 8 (3): 327-343.

Yefimov, Nikolai. 1936. *Pabst*. Moscow: Iskusstvo.

Yegorova, Natalia. 1964. "Nemetskie nemye filmy v sovetskom prokate." *Kino i vremia: Biulleten'*. Moscow: Gosfilmofond. 4: 380-476.

SHAMED BY COMPARISON—EASTERN EUROPE AND THE "REST"[1]

Judit Bodnar*

Abstract

This paper is about the uneasy place East European experience has occupied in social theory, which was confounded by the coming and going of socialism. It will first examine the reasons behind this uneasiness, then make an attempt to use this tension productively and exploit the comparative potentials it entails. Its aims will be achieved by placing both Eastern Europe and state socialism in the global context of modernity, capitalism, and development. The paper ultimately argues for the promise globalization holds out for a more inclusive and democratic social theory.

"INTO THE GREYNESS OF THE EAST FLASHES THE DARKNESS OF THE WEST" captured popular wisdom the dialectics of change and continuity in a graffiti that appeared on the oldest bridge in Budapest in the early 1990s. The critique of the West mixes with a self-ironical admission that the "East is East" and the historical frustration felt over failed attempts, including the regime change of 1989, to change it—partly seen as a result of a general nonacceptance by the West. This is a way of postsocialist theorizing that is older than postsocialism.

* Judit Bodnar is an Associate Professor in the Department of Sociology and Social Anthropology at Central European University in Budapest.

[1] The arguments in this paper have long been in the making; thus, several versions have been presented, the first one in the Globalization Workshop at the University of Chicago in 2002.

This paper is about the uneasy place East European experience has occupied in social theory, which was only confounded by the coming and going of socialism. I will examine the reasons behind this uneasiness and the comparative potentials it entails. I will do so by placing both Eastern Europe and state socialism in the broader context of global modernity and development, which are comparative categories par excellence that cast most incarnations of modernity as inferior. This paper is about the symbolic geography of modernity and development, and the place of Eastern Europe on this map. This is not a historical writing but a speculative and analytical piece, an essay based on doing and discussing research on Eastern Europe in the United States, Western Europe, and Eastern Europe. It goes, however, beyond Eastern Europe, and argues for the promise globalization holds out for a more inclusive and democratic social theory.

Eastern Europe is suspended in an unresolved paradox: a rupture of ending and beginning, and a constant remembrance of times past by being classified as "postsocialist" or "postcommunist." The former produces a high-modernist zeal of erasing the past, while the latter sets an asymptotic limit on such a daring endeavor. The past is used as a constant referent, either as a mirror negation or as a mixture of negation and continuity, but the enormity of state socialist experience always looms in the background. Both go back to the same intellectual laziness: changes are conveniently explained by the withdrawal of state socialism, which makes the recent experience of these societies unique. Few make use of the fact that coming out of socialism coincided with the celebrated farewell to modernity and the process we call globalization. The uncanny survival of the capitalist/socialist dichotomy in the denotation "postsocialist" blurs the view we need in order to perform a proper comparative historical analysis, to see state socialism as part of European modernity and its transformation within the global restructuring of late modernity or capitalism.

"Postsocialist theorizing," writes Michael Burawoy, "still relies on socialism as a negation or a comparison—as a celebration of capitalist supremacy or, more rarely, a source of capitalist critique" (1999, 309). The main genre of postsocialist theorizing includes theories of transition explicitly or implicitly understood as a move from state socialism to capitalism. Single-model capitalism as a yardstick effectively limits "our unstoppable predilection for alternatives,"—socialism included—claims Burawoy, and posits a critical turn in postsocialist theory following its initial disillusionment with freedom—very much in the vein of postcolonial theory.

Postsocialist theorizing is indeed strongly marked by a break with, or the negation of, state socialism, but at least as much by an emphasis on the continuity of state socialist experience. Again, it is very much akin to postcolonial theory in this respect. One of course cannot proceed hastily with such parallels: while "posting" something signals a general attitude to the past, together with Kwame Anthony Appiah one can note that the "post" in postmodern is not the same as the "post" in postcolonial. We can continue in that vein by observing that the "post" in postsocialist is not the "post" in postcolonial either (Appiah 1991). Postsocialist and postcolonial societies share the shame of having lacked freedom once—a rather highly valued trait of both national and global modernity. More importantly, both postsocialist and postcolonial societies are part of our global modernity—with qualifications: they are special cases. They are in a constant state of "becoming"; if they still have not become like the pattern-setting part of the world, it is due to the ramifications of their past experience rather than the mechanisms of the current system they are part of.

At least as bothersome as the denial of the political alternative of socialism in the denotation "postsocialist" is the lack of alternative theorizing, revealing the insecurity of western-centered social theory when it has to come to grips with an experience that is different from the one that informed "universal" social theory, be that Eastern European, state socialist, postcolonial, or "Oriental."

The comparative analysis of East European state socialism has faced a severe problem of collinearity: these societies were state socialist and East European at the same time (Bodnár 2001). Consequently, postsocialism obscures the overlap of different historical legacies: those of Eastern Europe and socialism (Todorova 2010). In fact, Eastern Europe as a political (rather than a geographical) space is the socialist legacy (Todorova 2010). The fact that socialism happened in Eastern Europe generated some uneasiness among socialist-minded intellectuals in the "West" in the evaluation of "existing socialism." East European but especially some Central-East European cities looked like secondhand Parisian cityscapes of sorts, with less glamour, less extravagance, poorer and worse kept (Bodnár 2003). Was that "second-handedness," the inherent feature of state socialism, a result of Eastern and Central European cultural difference, or simply the symptom of unqualified poverty? Although comparative historical memory suggests that these differences date back well before state socialism, the difference between capitalism and state socialism served as the primary explanatory variable; differences were swept under this overarching distinction. State socialism is gone along with the dichotomy of capitalism/state socialism, but the simplifying slip of the comparative mind is reinvigorated in "postsocialist" theorizing. The problem of disentangling the bundle of characteristics assumed under (post) state socialism is back with full force (Bodnár 2001).

In the term "Eastern Europe," both parts are equally important. In a simple chain of equivalence, Europe stands for the West and the center of social theory. Eastern Europe thus signals a slightly off-western experience. But the East is fundamentally West (Böröcz 2001). Yet linguistic denotations often place it closer to marked categories, such as periphery or colony. The uneasy place Eastern Europe has occupied in critical political economic discourse points precisely at this tension; it has subverted the notion of center-periphery by inserting itself in between the two as semi-periphery. Although Eastern Europe made its debut as the periphery of the European world system and made it to the semi-periphery automatically by the extra-European extension of the world system, the term was originally invented in world systems analysis to cover its in-between development and extended only later to accommodate other regions. This in-between development is defined as displaying a different degree of the modern characteristics that mark the core; such as, the dominance of less profitable production activities, a greater retaining force of agriculture, a stronger developmental state, and a less urbanized population (Wallerstein 1974; Kennedy and Smith 1989). Even though not so different from the core, this designated transitory position is signified by reference to the periphery.

Eastern Europe has undeniably been part of European modernity, but it has been measured and has measured itself as inferior to the pattern-setting development of the Western part, inferior in the sense of incarnating *less* of the same substance. The defining categories of modernity emerged out of the West European experience, and even though modernity has admittedly become global, the natural home of urbanization, social class, public space, freedom, and citizenship has been the "West" ever since (Chakrabarty 2000). It is duly recognized today that conceptual uneasiness lingers in theorizing any non-Western experience. The most common comparative categories describing non-Western experience rely on capturing a lack or a lesser extent of features that define modernity, variations of such themes as "belated" or "distorted" development, "inorganic growth," "dual society," "over-urbanization," or "under-urbanization" for that matter—a category reserved exclusively for East European socialist urbanism (Bodnar 2001), and suggest some transitionalism where tensions are ultimately to be resolved along the lines of well-known and well-documented Western patterns. The difference Eastern Europe makes is partly temporal; in the grand narrative of modernity, its development is delayed, out of touch with the fast pace of time. It is the clearest incarnation of the temporalization of difference, which generates a catching-up rhetoric on the side both of those who are to be caught up with and the "latecomers."

Categories are blurred, yet we seem to insist on using them. The pressure to do so is entailed in the universalist projects of the Enlightenment, capitalism or modernity, the concomitant political, economic, and social development, as well as the emerging disciplinary divisions, as a result of which historiography has become explicitly national and implicitly comparative for most. The background assumption of unified world history, coupled with teleological development that "reorganizes discordant geographies into a single narrative, into universal modernity" (Mitchell 2000), makes comparisons possible and necessary, out of which the overwhelming majority of the world emerges as inferior, lacking something that is highly valued. They figure as representatives of some sort of incomplete or lesser modernity. Modernity and development—the need to correct incomplete modernity—are organized into a tidy symbolic geography of North and South, East and West.

The borderlands of European modernity, however, are vast, and the East sometimes starts as westward as the outskirts of Vienna or Germany and runs all the way to Siberia.[2] It is certainly true that while the "special" features of German social development are at times seen as positive, similar special features become more apologetic and the signs of unqualified backwardness as one continues eastward (Konrad 1999). Still, the German *Sonderweg* debate is but a particular instance of the temporalization of difference in the framework of unified world history that is teleological and unilinear. It is very telling for our purposes that the *Sonderweg* reproduces the East/West division: Germany could become "normal" only with its split into the GFR and GDR—relegating the heavy burden of *Sonderweg* to the latter (Kocka 1999). Seeing socialism as the culmination of a longue-durée, idiosyncratic, non-Western development was a common trait of Cold War rhetoric that filtered into social science discourse as well. But while GDR socialism was the last incarnation of the *Sonderweg*, Soviet and Asian communist totalitarianism were depicted as the continuation of traditional Oriental despotism—only intensified by modern police technology (Pietz 1988; Nguyên 1984). There was a switch point, or in fact several switch points, on the continuum of West-East that were made to overlay the homogenizing logic of state socialism. This rhetoric by and large had the unfortunate effect of placing state socialism outside European modernity and once again stepping over the problem of the unevenness of modern development, and the integration of different modernities into social theory.

Can we make meaningful comparisons once we give up the notion of unified and teleological development, and treat the signs of "transitional" development in their own right, as symptoms of qualitative differences rather than passing disturbances, failures, or inadequacies in a universally valid

[2] There is a vast and intriguing literature on how flexible the boundaries of Europe have been in both scholarly and lay discourses throughout history, as well as on the elusiveness of seemingly geographical categories, such as east/west, north/south (Antohi 1991; Wolff 1994; Todorova 1997). More systematic treatments emphasize the comprehensive ordering of these categories into a west/east slope (Melegh 2006) or nested Orientalism (Bakić-Hayden 1995).

system? A related question is how to deal with the geopolitics of knowledge that designates some histories as constituting general theory while relegating others to "area studies"—Communist Studies included—in need of constant justification. How can non-Western histories be integrated into social theory, and what becomes general? The relevance of these questions varies by discipline; it is less of a problem for history than for sociology or social theory.

Any radical transformation of such knowledge implies, as Walter Mignolo puts it, that what was only an object of knowledge should become a new locus of enunciation (Mignolo 2000). He proposes new forms of knowledge in the form of border thinking from an epistemological position that is located on the exterior borders of modernity. Border thinking is to be distinguished from the critique of modernity that emanates from its interior borders producing universal statements from a local history, as opposed to border thinking that does so from two local histories that are connected by coloniality. The dominant theme of interior critiques of modernity is class, while that of exterior critiques is coloniality and the question of race. Colonial difference does not dissolve; it is irreducible, according to Mignolo (Mignolo 2000). This excludes the possibility of including an East European epistemological position in the framework of border thinking even if some of their history is described as semicolonial or quasi-colonial vis-à-vis the center of an empire, whether the Ottoman, the Habsburg, or the Romanov. The distinction "quasi" is quite significant in this regard, both in its legal meaning and social-psychological, political, and epistemological implications. Todorova, when considering this possibility seriously for the turbulent history of the Balkans, makes a special point about the difference in the self-perception of the Balkans and the Orient proper, "the sensibility of victimization [being] much less acute" in the former (Todorova 1997, 17).

I indeed do not wish to argue for the sameness of coloniality and semicoloniality or that of East European histories of "lesser modernity" and postcolonial modernities. Yet, there is something similar regarding their position in the geopolitics of knowledge production; both the rise of this bold assumption and its criticism, by pointing at the precise nature of similarities and differences, show only from a global perspective. It is precisely this change in perspective and the recognition of similarities in terms of the relationship to the West, to modernity, and to general social theory, that inspired some exciting work on Eastern Europe as a region (Wolff 1994; Bakić-Hayden 1995; Todorova 1997; Melegh 2006; Böröcz 2009, Chari and Verdery 2009).

Orientalism overlaps, but not completely, with colonial discourse; it has a somewhat separate life that does not need the Orient or colonial encounters proper to be invoked. Edward Said's *Orientalism* was a revelation for historians and sociologists of the region: the similarity of the rhetorical position of the

West vis-à-vis the Orient and Eastern Europe was striking, and East European area studies did not look all that different from Orientalism (Wolff 1994; Bakić-Hayden 1995; Todorova 1997; Melegh 2006). This is Orientalism not in a historical sense but as a contrapuntal discourse on the East by the West underlined by a power differential between the two poles. This recognition was crucial for the generation of scholars and lay thinkers who were socialized into thinking that state socialism constituted their "difference."

Although the question of colonial difference was still lurking in the background and seemed too obvious to be conceptualized properly, waking to the common experience of marginality had fundamental methodological and theoretical consequences. It made East European historical and sociological thought less parochial and cracked its methodological nationalism in a context that did not enforce the consideration of colonial difference, which played such an instrumental role in correcting the nationalist orientation of West European and North American scholarship.

Still, any intelligent author following the footsteps of Said in his Orientalism had to consider the question of difference between the Orient and Eastern Europe or the Balkans. The two seminal works (Todorova 1997 and Bakić-Hayden 1995) on the Balkans both start relating these differences by underlining the historical and geographical concreteness of the Oriental "other." The concrete historical experience of imperial power in the Balkans follows from the distinction between contiguous and detached empires, or in more common historical language, land and sea empires. Distance and the concomitant possibility of physical contact imply a different epistemological position in the construction of East and West, dominators and dominated. Frequent and routinized contact with the "others"—often racially not distinct—within contiguous empires does not allow for the construction of such aesthetization of difference as in most detached empires. Physical contact tames both exoticization and (racial) inferiorization. The distinction between colonial and semi-colonial status lies partly in sorting out contiguous and detached, land and sea empires.

The semi-colonial status of the oppressed of contiguous empires is best captured in their transitory position, ambiguity, and in-betweenness, rather than their clear opposition to the West (Todorova 1997). These regions of Eastern Europe are semi-periphery, semi-colony, or "ferry land" as poetic-journalistic language captured the constant move of Hungary between east and west at the turn of the twentieth century so aptly that the term has stuck ever since. There is not much difference to counterpose. But that little is not insignificant. It is precisely the lesser degree of almost the same substance that is often enunciated in the dichotomous rhetoric of Orientalism, which reaches its crescendo in the juxtaposition of the capitalist West and the socialist East.

In this sense Eastern Europe has been different from the Orient that, although also inferior, represented a different substance (Said 1978, 1993), at least in Orientalist discourse, where the point of departure is the positing of an ontological difference between East and West. Eastern Europe embodies a particular combination of qualitative and quantitative difference; it is familiar and unfamiliar at the same time, a bothersome, slimy category.

Going back to Mignolo's geopolitics of knowledge, what is the place of a place like Eastern Europe in social theory, and especially, critical theory, if it has any?

Mignolo makes a distinction between the "global design," the hegemonic discourse of overarching modernity, and "local histories" that are the silenced critical voices of peripheral colonies, and designates places of enunciation accordingly. From an extra-European perspective, Eastern Europe is a site of critique from within. This is, however, exactly where this particular place of enunciation disappears, unlike the duly recognized postmodern critique of Derrida, Foucault, or others whom Mignolo mentions. This comes as no surprise, since he claims that modernity and its critical discourses are alternate processes, implying that the production of critical theory displays the same geopolitical design as theory production in general. The enunciation of criticism is also located in the pattern-setting part of the world; "reflexive" modernity seems to be the privilege of the West. In order to avoid this hegemonic trap, Mignolo and most postcolonial thinkers reserve a specific place for postcolonial theory as coming from outside the part of the world that has the hegemony in knowledge production. But where is the place of Eastern Europe? It seems to be lost between the global design and border histories. A characteristically East European pessimistic analysis would stop here and immerse in the lament of self-victimization, even though there is no reason to do so.

Whether an East European standpoint in the discussion of modernity is recognized as border thinking may not be as important as the fact that it points to the shifting symbolic geography of East and West, the flexibility of the borders of European modernity, and the fragility and unevenness of its main categories, not only when applied outside Europe but even within. Indeed, the decentering of Europe in social theory—a project that Dipesh Chakrabarty (2000) captures so subtly as the provincializing of Europe—cannot proceed without the deconstruction of European social modernity and without full recognition of European social theory and its historicity.

One strategy of integrating non-Western histories into social theory is the opening up of categories that were hitherto used almost exclusively to conceptualize non-Western experience. Eugen Weber's treatment of the unification of France and the building of the French nation-state as a "civilizing mission" is a paradigmatic example in this regard (Weber 1976). He shows that the language of race is applied not only to non-European people but is also found in the description of French peasants, who "lacked civilization" and thus had to be simultaneously "civilized" and integrated into national society, economy, and culture (Weber 1976). He suggests a strong parallel between the linguistic unification of France and the white man's burden of francophony. Nation- and empire-building were intertwined, the state simultaneously colonized difference on contiguous territories and overseas while making the French national and colonial state. Weber's uniqueness lies in his comparison: even the ideal-typical nation-state—an important building block of the infrastructure of modernity—is best described as a colonial empire, at least prior to World War I (Weber 1976).

The object of racial discourse is elusive and cannot be found exclusively in the colonies. It is a more general rhetoric that can be applied in historical Orientalist discourses on Eastern Europe (Todorova 1997), current discourses of EU enlargement (Böröcz 2009), or the modernization of French peasants (Weber 1976). Racial difference blends into class distinctions even in the treatment of West European working classes; race cannot be relegated to the problem of coloniality. As Etienne Balibar writes, "'class' and 'race' constitute the two antinomic poles of a permanent dialectic, which is at the heart of modern representations of history" (1991, 207).

The evolution of these representations has been intertwined. The modern notion of race acquired a national and ethnic signification following an initial class signification, which in turn originated partly in the slave owners' representation of their slaves as inferior races (*ibid.*). It was the industrial revolution that refocused racism and made the proletariat its target with the simultaneous expansion of colonial empires that further linked exploitation, skin color, and racial inferiority. Michel Foucault makes a similar point with an emphasis on the entangled genealogies of race and class and revolutionary struggles. The race struggle that appears in the sixteenth and seventeenth centuries is a counterhistory to the history of sovereignty, a "twin and simultaneous declaration of war and rights" (Foucault 2003, 73). In the first half of the nineteenth century, this race struggle is converted into class struggle and breeds a counterhistory of revolutionary discourse, while another counterhistory emerges, that of biological racism. Revolutionary discourse takes the idea of servitude and struggle, while modern racism replaces racial struggle with racial purity. Foucault even makes a reference, which is only partly correct, to Marx admitting to have found the idea of class struggle in the work of French historians on race struggle (Foucault 2003, 79n6).

It would be senseless to blend class and race and stretch colonial difference so that it can accommodate Eastern Europe, thus making Eastern Europe a legitimate place of border thinking in the manner of Mignolo. Yet in spite of all differences, placing Eugen Weber's "internal colonialism," the distancing and belittling rhetoric of Balkanism, and detached sea empires on the same conceptual map is a liberating exercise both methodologically and politically. Only by doing so can the recognition be reached that colonial difference based on race may be indissoluble yet quite informative for class rhetoric and uneven development.

Mignolo claims that the main theme of criticism from within European modernity is class, while criticism from the borders is that of race. Eastern Europe seems to be an unusually good case for pointing at the intertwining of class and racial difference, of inner and outer criticism. This may make a place for it in the geography of critical theory.

Modernity is an incomplete project, and perhaps bound to be so. This should be taken seriously. One way to do so is to apply this recognition to all parts of the world and simultaneously destabilize the conceptual staples of modernity from "within" and "without," from the "center" and the "border," and in-between, from the perspective of all kinds of "lesser" modernities. It entails a methodological reversal in which the West itself becomes the exception rather than the yardstick. The rest is then relieved from the social psychological effect of belittling comparisons, and more will find themselves on the border than inside or outside. A reversed and more inclusive comparative strategy can, and perhaps should, be quite unsettling, but only in this way will currant theories of global modernity not be a mere projection of classical theory on the global scale. Only this way can theories be more interrogative and constructively decentered, thus producing a "theory that is self-conscious about its historicity, its place in dialogue and among cultures, its irreducibility to facts, and its engagement in the practical world," in a word, critical as Craig Calhoun redefines critical theory (Calhoun 1995:11). The momentum must come from both inside and outside Europe, or the perceived core of theory production, with a lot of uncertainty concerning what is inside and what is outside, and the recognition that the border is vast and diverse.

BIBLIOGRAPHY

Antohi, Sorin. 1991. "Le stigmate éclaté. Les Roumains et l'Occident en 1991." *Vie sociale et traitements* 21: 14–15.

Appiah, Kwame Anthony. 1991. "Is the Post- in Postmodernism the Post- in Postcolonial?" *Critical Inquiry* 17 (Winter): 336–57.

Bakić-Hayden, Milica. 1995. "Nesting Orientalisms: The Case of Former Yugoslavia." *Slavic Review* 54 (4): 917–31.

Balibar, Etienne. 1991. [1988] "Class Racism." Pp. 204–216 in *Race, Nation, Class: Ambiguous Identities*, edited by Etienne Balibar and Immanuel Wallerstein. New York: Verso.

Bodnar, Judit. 2001. *Fin de Millénaire Budapest: Metamorphoses of Urban Life*. Minneapolis: University of Minnesota Press.

———. 2003. "'Paris of the East'—Urban Theory of the West: Comparative Thinking after the End of the East-West Divide" *Hintergrund* 21 (November): 7-23. Wien: Architekturzentrum. (in German)

Böröcz, József. 2001. "Change Rules." *American Journal of Sociology* 106 (4): 1152–69.

———. 2009. *The European Union and Global Social Change: A Critical Geopolitical-Economic Analysis*. London: Routledge.

Burawoy, Michael. 1999. "Afterward." Pp. 301–11 in *Uncertain Transition: Ethnographies of Change in the Postsocialist World*, edited by Michael Burawoy and Katherine Verdery. Lamham, MD: Rowman & Littlefield.

Calhoun, Craig. 1995. *Critical Social Theory: Culture, History and the Challenge of Difference*. Cambridge: Blackwell.

Chakrabarty, Dipesh. 2000. *Provincializing Europe: Postcolonial Thought and Historical Difference*. Princeton, NJ: Princeton University Press.

Chari, Sharad, and Katherine Verdery. 2009. "Thinking between the Posts: Postcolonialism, Postsocialism, and Ethnography after the Cold War." *Comparative Studies in Society and History* 51 (1): 6–34.

Foucault, Michel. 2003 [1997]. *"Society Must Be Defended": Lectures at the Collège de France, 1975–1976*. Edited by Mauro Bertani and Alessandro Fontana. Translated by David Macey. New York: Picador.

Kennedy, Michael D., and David A. Smith. 1989. "East Central European Urbanization: A Political Economy of the World System Perspective." *International Journal for Urban and Regional Research* 13 (4): 63–90.

Kocka, Jürgen. 1999. "Asymmetrical Historical Comparison: The Case of the German *Sonderweg*." *History & Theory* 38 (1): 40–50.

Konrad, Sebastian. 1999. "What Time is Japan? Problems of Comparative (Intercultural) Historiography." *History & Theory* 38, 1: 67-83.

Melegh, Attila. 2006. *On the East/West Slope: Globalization, Nationalism, Racism and Discourses on Eastern Europe*. New York: CEU Press.

Mignolo, Walter D. 2000. *Local Histories, Global Designs: Coloniality, Subaltern Knowledges, and Border Thinking*. Princeton, NJ: Princeton University Press.

Nguyên, duc Nhuân. 1984. "Do the Urban and Regional Management Policies of Socialist Vietnam Reflect the Patterns of Ancient Mandarin Bureaucracy?" *International Journal of Urban and Regional Research* 8 (1): 73–89.

Pietz, William. 1988. "The 'Post-Colonialism' of Cold War Discourse." *Social Text* 19–20 (Fall): 55–83.

Said, Edward. 1978. *Orientalism*. Vintage.

Said, Edward. 1993. "Secular Interpretation, the Geographical Element, and the Methodology of Imperialism." Chap. 1 in *After Colonialism: Imperial Histories and Postcolonial Displacements*, edited by Gyan Prakash. Princeton, NJ: Princeton University Press. Originally published in Edward Said, *Culture and Imperialism*. New York: Alfred A. Knopf.

Todorova, Maria. 2010. "Balkanism and Postcolonialism, or on the Beauty of the Airplane View." Pp. 175–95 in *In Marx's Shadow: Knowledge, Power, and Intellectuals in Eastern Europe and Russia*, edited by Costica Bradatan and Serguei Oushakine. New York: Lexington Books.

———. 1997. *Imagining the Balkans*. Oxford: Oxford University Press.

Weber, Eugen. 1976. *Peasants Into Frenchmen: The Modernization of Rural France, 1870–1914*. Stanford, CA: Stanford University Press.

Wallerstein, Immanuel. 1974. *The Modern World-System: Capitalist Agriculture and the Origins of the European World-Economy in the Sixteenth Century*. New York: Academic Press.

Wolff, Larry. 1994. *Inventing Eastern Europe: The Map of Civilization on the Mind of the Enlightenment*. Stanford, CA: Stanford University Press.

THE COSMOPOLITAN POLITICS OF COMPARATIVE URBANISM: TOWARD A EUROPEAN CONTRIBUTION*

Monika De Frantz

Abstract

As transnational processes transform governments and societies, as well as societal knowledge, cities have shifted within the focus of the scholarly search for collective legitimacy in an increasingly diverse and global world. The importance of cultural diversity for political and economic development has revived the urban idea of a public space beyond nation-states and corporate capital. Shared by different academic disciplines, the cosmopolitan ideal is also reinterpreted within the social sciences—either affirmatively or critically—by different approaches, and reflected in the contexts of different research interests, case studies, and epistemic communities. The increasing exchange between scholarly debates in the USA and the UK, as well as other European countries and recently the "Global South," has given rise to a growing interest in comparative urban studies in addition to raising culturalist skepticism of "large theories" and general models. Conceiving urban culture as a contested field of knowledge, this paper questions diversity and transnationality as cosmopolitan characteristics of urban knowledge in different contexts of the academic debate. A European perspective

* A previous version of this paper was presented at the 8th International Interpretive Policy Analysis Conference (IPA), Vienna, July 3–5, 2013.

may contribute to taking cosmopolitan urbanism from a normative philosophy toward a comparative methodology, epistemological approach, and reflective agency of the researcher in constructing institutional change as open-ended and plural interaction.

Introduction

At the centers of globalization, cities emerge as important social spaces where cultural and political notions of legitimacy are reconstructed in response to socio-cultural diversity, political transnationalization, and economic development competition. As states and societies change and markets seem to dominate these transformations, urban cultures move into the focus of political and economic development strategies. The challenges of dealing with cultural diversity and economic competition pose new—transnational—constraints and opportunities for civic and political leaders to mobilize shared visions and common responses. Almost emblematic for the public sphere as an ideal civic space of plural collective action, the urban context has historically posed a wide playing field for all kinds of utopian experiments, normative critique, analytical models, and best practice plans. In the present context of globalization, the market-dominated character of the urbanization process does not only stress the economic rise of cities. It also risks affecting the very notion of the urban as a diverse social place that fosters civic engagement, social solidarity, open interaction, and acceptance of difference. In this search for a collective future in a complex world, the urban debate addresses a set of core questions: How can culture serve political agency to mobilize shared notions of legitimacy in a transnational context? Does public space decline in neoliberal capitalism, or how does political legitimacy change as a result of the present transformations? How can conflict about difference give rise to collective action and institutional learning about diversity? And what could be the role of researchers in mediating diverse institutional changes in the fields of knowledge and societal practice?

In responding to transnational change, the contemporary challenge for political leaders is to combine both varied economic needs and diverse cultural claims in new political spaces and projects. Thus, urban development strategies use cultural instruments in order to redefine a negative image of a location and adjust it to a new, more market-oriented collective vision. Urban culture can serve as a locally specific asset to attract external resources, such as economic investment, residents, and tourism expenditure, as well as political support through subsidies, state legislation, or electoral votes. But the cultural character of places is also changed in the process; e.g., by city-marketing or gentrification or the promotion of creative industries and other strategies of culture-led urban regeneration. As a local capital in development competition, urban culture will be turned into a commercial good and thus gradually homogenized according to market demand. Therefore, urbanity requires not only a locally based enterprise, but also cultural diversity, social solidarity, and civic engagement to keep the specific local character alive. As an implicit connotation of common heritage, social capital, institutions, symbolic representations, myth, memory, or place, urban culture is thus also an endogenous local resource. But given the various functions and meanings of urban culture, its political use for urban development is often not as harmonious as policy makers expect. The historical identifications with urbanity tend to be deeply rooted but contested, so that governing urban change arises as a controversial issue in theory and practice.

Sometimes critically summarized as neoliberalism, market-driven development competition adds up to—or even dominates—socio-cultural and political transformations, such as individualization, pluralization, and transnationalization of the urban context. However, as cities move into the focus of cultural, political, and scholarly struggles over contemporary state-transformation, urban globalization is not only an economically influenced but also a politically constructed phenomenon. Diverse societal transformations associated broadly with urban globalization are reflected in different local contexts of urban development. Although local face-to-face interactions may be increasingly supplanted by transnational media and metropolitan mobility, we share urban space as a global concept. In some instances, this translates into a specific local consciousness and material reality of joint living, or at least a minimum need of interaction in everyday life. Yet, our understandings of the urban condition are very different—between different people, communities, and areas within the city, between different cities, countries and continents, between local, national, and transnational contexts, between social, cultural, economic, and political realms, between theory and practice, and between different academic disciplines. In some instances, these differences gives rise to fragmentation and deadlock; in others, the shared interest in an issue initiates conflictive interpretations and contesting interactions. We try to communicate in order to understand our different perspectives, sometimes even being convinced, or at least acknowledging the others' differing points of view, thus overcoming boundaries and possibly even establishing a shared understanding of collective action. These interactions of exchange and contestation may constitute a creative potential of cities—in the social and economic realms, and the symbolic political sphere, where public politics interpret, mediate, and negotiate institutional change. Though often associated with complexity, ungovernability, fragmentation, or corporate dominance, the plural claims evolving from urban centrality may offer a political resource for governing state-transformation.

But the institutional outcomes of such political interactions are contextually differentiated and thus little predictable, ranging from political deadlock to policy change and institutional reform, or any combination.

Elaborating the politics of institutional change, this paper inquires into the potential contribution of a European perspective to comparative urban research. It theorizes diversity and transnationality as cosmopolitan characteristics of urban culture and knowledge institutions. Their contentious potential may be a source of reflective agency in social reality as well as in its empirical analysis and theoretical interpretation. Against neoliberal doom scenarios of urban decline, the first section proposes an open-ended conception of the public sphere emerging from the creative potential of cosmopolitan interactions in the spheres of politics, culture, and civic society (De Frantz 2013, 2011, 2005; Keating and De Frantz 2004). Taking up my previous critique of the European institutional model (De Frantz 2008a, 2007), the second part inquires into the various institutional elements embedding cities in different local contexts of statehood and diverse urban policies. Drawing on postcolonial, transnational, and cosmopolitan perspectives, the third part of the paper refines the new institutional approach by comparative urban politics as an open-ended, contextually differentiated, and plural process. Since neoliberalism may be a dominant legitimacy but not one without alternatives, the paper concludes by conceiving culture-led urban development as reflective institutional learning. In order to refine the reflective agency of comparative urban research, a European contribution may take the cosmopolitan approach from a normative philosophy and analytical ideal model toward an epistemological meta-reflection and concrete empirical–analytical methodology. The paper thus highlights the cosmopolitan political character of urban research as a contested cultural process of knowledge construction.

The Politics of Culture-led Urban Regeneration: Political–Economic Potential or Decline

The cultural turn in the social sciences has tended to oscillate between two extremes resulting from critical reflections on the universal knowledge claims and the idea of progress associated with modernity. On one side, normative argumentation for culture and community has led to subjectivist or place-specific perspectives stressing the ambiguity of power and identity. On the other side, the fluidity of identities has implied that culture can be manipulated at the will of powerful interests. This ambivalence is also reflected in urban studies, and particularly urban political economy's takes on culture and politics. From their various political and economic conceptions of cities, the neo-classic public choice, the neo-Marxist globalization critique, and the new institutional perspective have come to acknowledge the relevance of culture and power for urban development. This has fostered a debate on the normative and empirical merits of culture-led urban regeneration as a model for economic, social, civic, or political development (Keating and De Frantz 2004). Now the meaning of the concept itself turns into a critical focus concerning the structural opposition of a cultural ideal of urban public or local community to the economic functions of urban regeneration.

The cases of cultural flagships in Vienna, Berlin, and Bilbao have highlighted the political-institutional processes complementing the material changes to cultural heritage and cityscape associated with culture-led urban regeneration (De Frantz 2013, 2011, 2005; Keating and De Frantz 2004). Given the various different interests, strategies, and effects that may be involved in urban policies using culture as an instrument for urban development, political discourses define the shared public meanings of such political investments in culture. Rather than a public-choice response to market competition, cultural policy-making initiated political processes of public contention from which emerged collective symbols of partially shared visions. Discourse as the source of agency and legitimacy connected the local micro-level of community identities and socio-cultural diversification to the macro-context of globalization. These plural political processes of institutional changes may be initiated by city-marketing strategies but yet transcended the neoliberal concept of place-branding. Their contextual, plural, and open-ended character stressed the diversity of urban culture, which may also imply a creative potential for societal change (De Frantz 2013, 2011, 2005).

In addition to cognitive elements of discursive deliberation, affective and aesthetic experience may give rise to participation, reflexivity, and a sense of sociability. Complementing political-institutional change, Sassatelli's (2011) cosmopolitan conception of urban cultural festivals focuses on the social interactions constituting the urban public sphere. While consumerism is certainly a part of contemporary mass culture, artistic expression and everyday people's celebratory practices may also give rise to playful experimenting with alternative cultural expressions. Thus, the theoretical and normative distinction of aesthetic cosmopolitanism as exclusive elitist consumerism from its ethic of cosmopolitan responsibility for the global total does not necessarily make sense.

The recent recovery of some American inner-city neighborhoods from blight and decline has revived the debate about the economic functions of culture for urban development. As a locally bound capital, urban cultural amenities offer an important locational factor in cities' competition for otherwise mobile resources, such as financial investment, tourism income, and tax-paying residents, as well as political support through subsidies or legislation (Florida 2012; Silver et al. 2011). Moreover, urban centers are specifically characterized by cultural diversity, which offers a resource of creative innovation in the knowledge economy. Florida's (2012) creative class thesis adds an affirmative element of cosmopolitanism defined by openness to diversity and to the collective attitude of economic activism that had been conceived more critically by the entrepreneurial cities thesis during the 1990s. Both share a focus on the economic functions of culture—either as a capital of production or a good of consumption, an attitude shared by individual economic actors or a collective characteristic of socio-economic relations. In addition to the conceptual blurriness and methodological flaws involved in measuring the economic value of culture, it is problematic how such analysis is transferred as best-practice models across different contexts (Pratt and Hutton 2012; Pratt 2010; Peck 2005; Martin and Sunley 2003).

Apart from doubts about the effectiveness of such policy models, the main critique of culture-led urban development concerns its instrumentality for the neoliberal restructuring of local communities in the interest of global capitalism (Young et al. 2006; Degen and Garcia 2012; Ponzini and Rossi 2009). While the creative class thesis speaks largely to the US context, the debate addresses a long series of works about the role of culture in urban development, associated with such terms as revitalization, regeneration, gentrification, and city branding; e.g., in New York, Glasgow, Bilbao, Barcelona, or London (Gonzalez 2011; Pollock and Paddison 2010; Zukin 2009; Plaza 2008; Miles 2005; Keating and De Frantz 2004; Bianchini 1993; Keating 1988; etc.). Most of these critical observers have followed in some way or other Philo and Kearns' (1993) notion of the cultural "selling" and "making" of places. The need to choose certain marketable aspects of urban culture in order to describe a development vision necessarily results in the exclusion of alternatives. Culture is thus remade, and diversity and openness as cosmopolitan characteristics reduced. In some cases the commercial adjustment to the rather homogenous tastes of global markets goes so far that local authenticity is lost and the competitive economic advantage itself destroyed in the process. Therefore, the contradictory forces of capitalism at work in global markets become manifest in negative social consequences, such as exclusion, alienation, homogenization, and thus the loss of the locational advantages for the local economy. Thus distinguishing the functions of culture as an economic capital and product from those of a local public good, critical political economists aim to explain disparities and uncover conflicts of interest between or within urban societies.

Responding to various comments concerning what could be called a "cultural turn" in critical political economy, MacLeod and Jones (2011; Boyle 2011) draw out six theoretical directions toward "renewing" urban politics: (1) the ontological definition of the research unit, (2) postcolonial epistemology critique, (3) the empirical focus on political and cultural stakes as well as economic interest, (4) analysis of discourse and identity politics, (5) the historical institutions of national government and its restructuring through governance, and (6) the relational space of politics of scale. Then, proposing an interdisciplinary dialogue, Ward and Imbroscio (2011) claim an urban politics beyond political science, focusing on (1) politics beyond government, (2) political economic power beyond pluralist politics, (3) the structure–agency question by focusing on the structuration of agency in intermediate organizations, and (4) relational power beyond the state.

Still, the critical interest in urban culture as a material spatial manifestation of the structural contradictions of neoliberalism is embedded in the assumption of capitalism and its historic transformations as the ultimate foundation of societal power. From a political science perspective (Sapotichne et al. 2007), however, the neo-Marxian determinism in urban studies has resulted in a divergence from theoretical developments and conceptual interests in other main subfields of the discipline. The reason may be that "(a)t least since the early 1960s, urban scholars have identified so closely with the object of their analysis that scholarship, advocacy, and ideology often have become hopelessly entangled" (Judd 2005, 102).

Urban Difference in the European Context: The New Institutional Approach

The beginning reflection of urban interdisciplinarity is yet little complemented by an international dialogue that would also consider the various knowledge models within the different societal contexts of knowledge generation. Beyond the comparison of national urban policies or urban government institutions between different states (Wollmann 2004; Keating 1991), the problem concerns the lack of a comparative analytical framework that focuses on a shared definition of the urban as a research unit. Various comparative studies of urban regimes have attempted to apply this political economic concept beyond its US origins to international case studies (Kantor and Savitch 2005). But despite a long-standing exchange between US and European—or rather UK—scholars, a systematic mutual reflection of the different epistemological foundations and empirical—and professional—contexts of knowledge generation has only just begun.

Questioning the economic bias and universal claims of urban political economy as general theories derived from North-American or British contexts, European research has stressed urban diversity and the role of the "local state" for urban cohesion (Löw 2012; Zimmermann 2012a; 2012b; Frey and Koch 2011; Häussermann and Haila 2005; Le Gales 2002). Also in Europe, recent transformations of urban government, economic deregulation, state decentralization, and EU integration have increased economic competition pressures and a turn to "neoliberal" urban policies. Certainly, the cultural heritage of European cities has gained importance as a locational advantage, resulting in commercial pressures and suburbanization. But most European cities appear still rather lively and robust, with relatively intact urban centers, and less affected by urban decline than many American cases. In addition to a comparative empirical perspective on the various institutional contexts, the findings of diverse local responses to political and economic transformations have established various theoretical and normative claims for European difference.

The European context with its complex historical state-building and present transformations illustrates a broad and diverse institutional spectrum of the social and political processes embedding urban political economies. A diversity of relatively small towns with old—medieval, early modern, up to industrial—roots share the history and characteristics of a pre-national urban system, the importance of town planning embedded in varying local and national state frameworks (Le Gales 2002). European states show various national, institutional structures of local and metropolitan governments, centralized and decentralized local competences, executive and legislative power, and party and corporatist systems (Wollmann 2004). European urban policies tend to be driven more by political parties and less by business lobbies, more by social or environmentalist objectives and less by economic pressure groups. The governments tend to provide for social welfare and infrastructural services, and local constituencies are less dependent on autonomous financial resources than in the US (Harding 2009). In addition, various transnational, intergovernmental regimes and particularly the supranational EU constitute a multifaceted and multi-level framework that regulates market integration, promotes state reforms, and offers post-national frames of identification. Europeanization, along with various national policies of state-decentralization and privatization, has resulted in local convergence toward informal and horizontal forms of governance and public-private partnership and a strengthening of local executives (Wolman 2004; Bache and Flinders 2004). Cultural policy in particular is rooted in old national legacies of European state-building that now meet, merge, or conflict with urban strategies for the economic promotion of cultural industries and city marketing (Wodak et al. 2009; Pratt 2010; Bianchini 1993).

Given the complex institutional matrix of local governance (Lowndes 2008, Davies and Trounstine 2009), the focus shifts from the structural opposition of states and markets to the policy processes in the local context. Reviving the community power debate in the context of globalization, urban political economy can be understood as structural tension between elite power and plural coalitions "of" or "within" local societies (Harding 2009). The question of how urban growth coalitions accommodate the plural politics of scale (McKinnon 2012) in a changing political economic environment has shifted the attention to the role of civic culture and informal institutions. The Weberian urban model of urban collective action stressed the common historical values of European urban citizenship as a good institutional fit with contemporary state transformation (Le Gales 2002). As the historical origin of European modernity, the bourgeois city-states of late medieval Europe still stand for a civic ideal of the public sphere. Combining path-dependent historical institutions with collective values associated with this urban heritage to overcome structural conflicts of class and identity, Weber's analytical ideal-type was then also translated into a normative political model, a historical myth, and political ideology guiding actions in congruent ways. Reversing the Marxist-influenced conception of culture as a representation of political, economic power, the institutional hypothesis in the European context is not so much one of state versus market, but one of relative local autonomy through mobilization of state and market resources by local government and civil society (De Frantz 2008).

Instead of a coherent urban model, however, the different institutional elements and concepts may rather be understood as variable components of a mutually constitutive, open-ended, differentiated political process with more or less stable institutional outcomes. Stressing contextual difference in the politics of urban political economies, the European critique of the globalization model questions the concept of urban development as ensuing from a universal conception of economic modernization. But turning the historical emergence of capitalism in European cities into a contemporary political counter-model to economic globalization poses a modernization claim that may imply a hint of essentialist cultural superiority. Taking up my earlier critical comments and proposal for a plural conception of local politics (De Frantz 2008), the German debate recently introduced the concept of "Eigenlogik" in order to explain differences in the institutional dynamics of urban policy (Zimmermann 2012a; 2012b; Löw 2012). But while taking account of political pluralism, this focus on the city as a unit of analysis as well as explanatory variable tends to presuppose the existence of local institutions as a relatively separate polity. Though this may be valid in the case of some German municipalities with constitutional autonomy, the open functional and symbolic context of cities rarely converges with the boundaries of local government. Thus, without a more refined analytical conception of political agency, the focus on historical institutions also may be misinterpreted as a structural-functionalist notion of local community. Therefore, it has been noted (De Frantz 2008) that some—analytical, normative, or empirical—claims for contemporary European cities as a separate urban category, a coherent institutional model, or a bounded territorial unit have been overstated (Le Galés 2002; Zimmermann 2012a).

Toward Comparative Urbanism: Postcolonial, Transnational, and Cosmopolitan Perspectives

Similarly to the European debate, the post-colonial literature stresses the geographical difference of knowledge traditions that may give rise to a broad range of alternative development paths in this world. In order to overcome theorizing that either universalizes some characteristics of specific cities or constructs them as separate categories, the concept of "ordinary cities" claims comparative reflection of difference as basic to any social abstraction. Thus, comparison is not only an analytical methodology, but also an anti-foundational, epistemological critique of political economic paradigms that define urban hierarchies, make some types of cities incommensurable, and create an ideational gap between rich Western cities and poorer cities of the South. The comparison of very different urban contexts also poses the ontological question of a shared urban definition that may justify the choice of the research unit. Instead of comparing the city as a predefined whole, the comparative focus can be on specific urban phenomena and their variation within or between different—or similar—urban contexts (Robinson 2011).

Complementing historical difference by transnational politics, the post-colonial debate has turned from culturalist critique of knowledge as power construct to political claims for empowerment through participation and reciprocity for the decolonialization of dominant institutions. Transnationalism criticizes the conceptual reduction of urban globalization to economic macro-processes and focuses on the socio-cultural interactions in specific local contexts. Cities all over the world are linked through international migration, interlocal communities, and other forms of cultural exchange that construct urban changes as transnational as well as local phenomena (Smith 2005). This epistemological critique deconstructs neoliberalism as a global knowledge construct that is reproduced by scholars through the global transfer of theories and research practices, be they critical or affirmative. Thus the comparative engagement also includes the analysis of transnational and interurban connections of scholarly exchange that interactively construct urbanity as a transnational field of knowledge production (Robinson 2011).

Contrary to a mere interconnectedness, the blurring and transcendence of group boundaries results in the involuntary confrontation with the unknown or "Other" everywhere. In response to these transnational challenges to societal organization, the acknowledgement of difference gives rise to efforts for the rethinking of new—democratic—forms of politics and power beyond the national state. Here, European integration provides an important field for cosmopolitan theorizing about post-national diversity—of utopian political projects, reflexive historical processes, complex institutions, their analytical concepts, normative models and real world power. To counter the transnational inequality inherent to the European market and military power, the European project also implies a cosmopolitan claim for a non-violent alternative to global neoliberalism (Beck 2009).

In addition to a normative philosophy of post-national legitimacy, cosmopolitanism also implies epistemological, ontological, and methodological propositions. Awareness of methodological nationalism now poses questions about the very foundations of knowledge, power, and reality in the social sciences. While not fully discarding national statehood as the historically dominant organization and concept, cosmopolitan research focuses on the politics of difference in various instances of boundary-crossings (Beck and Sznaider 2006). As an epistemological approach, a relational conception of the politics of scale poses an alternative to disposition-based agency in rational choice and systemic accounts of marxism and functionalism. As an ontological concept, cosmopolitanism is defined as the relativization of identity, the positive recognition of the other, the mutual evaluation of cultures, and the creation of a normative world culture, as well as various parts, weightings, or combinations of these components. As an open-ended methodological framework, cosmopolitanism explains macro-level societal change by comparing various institutional processes constituting public space as a historical reflection of modernity (Delanty 2012).

Thus, deconstructing the unity of Western knowledge models, the postcolonial perspective on the multiplicity, diversity, and connectedness of urban cultures also translates into a "comparative gesture" (Robinson 2011) of far-reaching consequences for European research. The cosmopolitan conception of a diverse and transnational urban context poses the postcolonial critique of dominant and coherent concepts and models of urban development from within Western metropoles. European urbanity draws on a broad range of historical paths and civic traditions. Some of this cultural heritage—including that of the city-state—originates on the continent with its rich and diverse history, some in the colonial and postcolonial world. And all of it gets transformed and reinterpreted in the diverse present context of political, economic, and socio-cultural transnationalization, including the complex process of European integration (De Frantz 2008). Thus, the interest in comparison shifts our attention to the European context—not as a normative model, but as a rich source of conceptual debate and empirical case studies. The various institutional components of societal transformation in the European context may provide some more refined conceptual tools for comparative reflection of urban processes and their analytical interpretation in different contexts in and beyond Europe. Also, the focus on institutional difference may contribute to a more reflective understanding of contextual specificity in Europe as well as in the US. Thus, urban comparison in different contexts within Europe, within British and American contexts, and particularly between Europe and the US can contribute to deconstruct the unity of Western knowledge models. By intervening into the dominant power claims of knowledge institutions, a more refined social-constructivist approach to new institutionalism may help to decolonize urban culture and political agency.

Cosmopolitan Urban Politics: A European Contribution to Comparing Local Institutional Change

As notions of national legitimacy are being weakened, cities emerge as centers of cosmopolitan politics in our global world. Reflecting these empirical transformations, the urban debate has brought together a diverse international field of scholars concerning questions about the societal relationship of power and space. The contemporary legitimacy crisis had resulted in a postmodern retreat to either local culturalism and methodological subjectivism or a deterministic critique of neoliberal capitalist globalization. More recently, some initially critical globalization accounts have been combined and transferred into a celebratory trend in policy consulting that advertises universal cultural models for public choice in global urban competition (Florida 2012). Questioning the economic bias and universal claims of both affirmative and critical globalization scenarios from various postcolonial (Parnell and Robinson 2012; Robinson and McFarlane 2012; Robinson 2011a, 2011b;) and European (Zimmermann 2012a, 2012b; Löw 2012; Frey and Koch 2011; De Frantz 2008; Häussermann and Haila 2005; Le Gales 2002; Hassenpflug 2002) perspectives, the "cultural turn" has come to stress the contextual diversity of open institutional processes.

In reaffirming European modernity, the new institutional urban model implies a normative ideal, societal reality, and political claim, as well as a comparative approach and analytical conception (De Frantz 2008). Indeed, new institutionalism is well set to conceptualize urbanity because it approaches societal power as a historically contingent process embedding politics, society, and economy in different forms of structures and agency beyond the nation-state. As a response to "old" legal analyses of formal government, the "new" definition of institutions also includes informal norms, values, and practices. But rather than a coherent theoretical model that would predefine any specific urban structure, new institutional political science comprises diverse schools and a broad range of different hypotheses, roughly associated with rational choice, historical, and social-constructivist approaches. Different conceptions of power serve to analyze different aspects of institutional processes in different empirical fields and result in often contradictory explanations of their form, origin, effect, persistence, and change (Lowndes and Roberts 2013). Expanding the socio-cultural dimension of local collective agency in a diverse urban context, a cosmopolitan approach compares the open-ended interactions of cultural politics ensuing from the confrontation with difference in response to transnational institutional transformation (Delanty 2012; Beck and Sznaider 2006).

Yet these recent developments in the social sciences (e.g., the new institutional debate as it has evolved over the last decade into a mainstream approach that reflects a cosmopolitan approach to social and political change in Europe) find rather little attention in urban studies. European integration has resulted in new empirical phenomena beyond national state, society, and government, as well as an internationalization of academic research. In addition to a growing dominance of British and American knowledge institutions, this has also given rise to a flourishing dialogue between different national traditions and epistemological communities. There is a growing body of research in comparative politics, but also a theoretical debate about new institutional power that also reflects empirical transformations of states, societies, and markets. The debate focuses to a large extent on the EU and its impact upon government. But, for example, the concepts of multi-level governance (Marks and Hooghe 2009), territorial politics (Keating 2009), and interpretative politics analysis (Hajer 2009; Gottweis and Fischer 2012) also address other—new or old—societal phenomena that transcend conventional ideas of national government policy. In questioning how public institutions embed the relation between the political and the social sphere, various cases of public–private, national–international, civic–political, and sub- and transnational power illustrate the varying relation between policy, politics, and policy. This more open-ended political conception of statehood as a contested societal process has also given rise to the European debate about a new institutional approach to urban politics and the specific institutional conditions of European cities in responding to globalization. Contributing to a comparative perspective of cosmopolitan urban politics, this promises a theoretical perspective on culture and power that may help fill the gap between political economy, cultural studies, and political science.

While promising a potential refinement to social-constructivist approaches to institutional change, so far the cosmopolitan debate about cities as contested centers and symbolic sites of reflective modernization remains rather theoretical (Delanty 2012; Beck 2009). For the most part, the social embeddedness of the planning process has translated, on one side, as a methodological tool to disclose the power structures and interest conflicts underlying local policy making as governmentality (Parker 2012); on the other side, as a normative claim for community participation in political deliberation (Healey 2012). Building on Hajer's (1989; Hajer and Reijndorp 2001) earlier work on planning and the urban public sphere respectively, "ground zero" in NYC exemplified a pilot study of performative planning (Hajer 2005, 2009), though without specific reference to the urban context. Recently, Healey (2013) proposed applying interpretative policy analysis as a methodology to knowledge transfer in planning, though as yet without debate of the epistemological implications or empirical operationalisation. Although a large body of research about culture-led urban regeneration addresses the role of culture for political and economic change, urban debate has just begun to research the dynamic relation of discourse and institutions (De Frantz 2013, 2011). Complementing a structural bias on the macro-foundational power of states and markets dominant in urban studies, this focuses on the creative political potential of interactive self-reflection for reconstructing collective legitimacy as a source of normative power.

Traditionally a highly interdisciplinary field of studies sharing a cosmopolitan ideal of public space, urbanity may be considered emblematic of contemporary diversity and transnationalization. As the social functions of culture in the urban context are multiple, culture can be turned to various strategic uses and in this way mobilize collective support for urban development. But as cities gain importance in political economic transformation, urban centrality also intensifies the socio-economic contrasts between winners and losers of globalization as well as initiating cultural conflicts and political contention. Reflecting the complex contemporary societal changes, the evolving public debates address the relation of culture and political economic power for the construction of cosmopolitan legitimacy—in theory and practice. Thus the success of urban development depends on the normative criteria applied, either from a specific political or epistemological perspective defined by the actor's societal position or from the legitimacy that is dominant in a specific context. From a neoliberal perspective, urban development will normally be interpreted as market performance and measured in terms of economic growth and, possibly, population increase. Critical researchers, however, would rather aim at redistributive justice or the normative acknowledgement associated with criteria such as social cohesion, cultural inclusion, community empowerment, or democratic legitimacy. While the empirical focus and normative criteria depend on the context, cosmopolitan research as a methodological approach may be interested in culture-led urban development as any social change through reflective learning in response to confrontation with difference. Due to the openness of the urban context, we can thus hardly analyze urban culture as a general model or a representative image of a whole city as a predefined unit. Translated as diverse cultural claims and more or less institutionalized meanings, cosmopolitan politics become manifest in a broad range of cultural phenomena, often attached to specific local symbols, such as places, buildings, or cultural institutions. Cosmopolitan research would pick out various cultural phenomena that exemplify different situations of societal functions of culture where dislocation of institutional practices gives rise to confrontation with difference within and between local contexts.

Cosmopolitanism is interested in the politics of difference, constituting historical change by reflecting the idea of modernity as a universal idea and societal project of self-transformation (Delanty 2012). As a normative political claim, empirical analytical approach, and critical societal reflection, the cosmopolitan research approach embeds European urbanity in a comparative perspective of institutional change. In response to the earlier doom scenarios of urban globalization, not only Europeans but also post-colonial and American researchers claim an urban revival. The various theoretical perspectives of public choice, cultural constructivism, and new institutionalism imply a normative claim for a creative force of urban culture supporting the economic, social, or political capacity of cities in a transnational context. Due to the historical model of the city-state, European cities have been thought of as a normative political model for combining cultural plurality and tolerance, social solidarity, and economic success as a good fit with cosmopolitan transnationalization. Countering the economic bias of urban political economy with a model of political agency, the European urban debate has begun to "bring the state back in," not only as a structural mechanism of market regulation but as a complex, plural, and differentiated institutional process (De Frantz 2008). Thus, rather than a coherent normative model or a predefined analytical framework, European political science may offer some conceptual tools for reflecting urban institutional change in a comparative perspective of state-transformation.

Various small-n case studies of urban development strategies should help to illustrate further the diverse spectrum of cosmopolitan politics in different local contexts of contemporary institutional changes. This comparative focus on European urbanity also contributes to challenging the assumed unity of Western modernization and associated universal knowledge claims. Contrasting European findings with the theorems originating from research in the United States underlines the empirical differences in historical and contemporary statehood and urbanization (Fabbrini 2004; Nivola 1999, 2007). Beyond an ideal-typical opposition of economic versus political models, a comparative perspective can also show the various national urban policies as well as the local differences within both Europe and the United States. In addition, comparison within European metropolitan areas may challenge the local unity of cities and the theoretical coherence of the institutional model. This diversification and transnationalization of the urban context as a relational space transfers the postcolonial claim for cosmopolitan difference into the European metropoles. The European institutional approach may not only contribute to the normative globalization critique of postcolonial culturalism; comparative research can also highlight the internal diversity of European urbanity. In return, the postcolonial perspective may contribute to a critical epistemological reflection on the context specificity of theory and implicit normative assumptions constituting dominant power in European statehood.

One challenge here is to embed the expertise and concepts existing in the various local and national research contexts and disciplines—e.g., even within Western academic traditions, between European countries, the UK and US debates—in a context-sensitive international comparison. Instead of a predefined analytical framework that would necessarily be based on a specific theory, cosmopolitan research approaches comparison through reflective knowledge exchange in the urban field. Communication about difference, between different empirical and institutional contexts and knowledge institutions, helps to make urbanity understood as a diverse and transnational process. This also requires appropriate tools to facilitate and promote knowledge exchange across the boundaries of academic disciplines, epistemic communities, and geographic cultures as well as the various fields of professional expertise. A deliberative research approach includes a self-reflective practice of urban knowledge production by learning about tacit knowledge underlying different theoretical paradigms and local experiences. The implicit normative and empirical assumptions constitute knowledge as power claims in the transnational urban field and locate European research in cosmopolitan political practice. Following the societal responsibility of offering knowledge models for collective action in urban practice, cosmopolitan research should inquire into the appropriate design of deliberative forums to facilitate interdisciplinary and international communication.

To conclude, by reflecting on the cosmopolitan contribution of the European debate to comparative urban politics, this paper has contributed to the exchange of knowledge in a diverse urban field of research and practice. Cities, as symbols of collective self-imagination past and present, are central places of the contested reinvention of modernity as an epistemological concept, a social-political reality, and a spatial-material representation. This cosmopolitan conception of urbanity implies a normative–theoretical claim for collective agency emerging from cultural diversity within as well as between cities; an analytical claim for comparing the plural urban politics of cities; and a practical political claim for reflective research intervention in the material and symbolic base of an increasingly urbanized, global, and transnational world. Against economically determined or culturally essential typologies, it conceives cities as differentiated multifaceted local and transnational contexts with deeply enshrined institutions that are yet open to endogenous political change. By addressing the cultural–political aspects of urban globalization and the contextuality of institutional change, this paper intends to help fill the gap between social sciences' cosmopolitan turn to difference and transnational diversity and the debate about power and institutions in urban studies.

BIBLIOGRAPHY

Beck, Ulrich. 2009. "Das kosmopolitsche Europa—Realität und Utopie." Pp. 57–78 in *Das Ende der Gewissheiten: Reden über Europa*, edited by Michael Thoss and Christina Weiss. Muenchen: Diederichs.

Beck, Ulrich, and Natan Sznaider. 2006. "Unpacking Cosmopolitanism for the Social Sciences: A Research Agenda." *The British Journal of Sociology* 57 (1): 1–23.

Bianchini, Franco. 1993. "Remaking European Cities: The Role of Cultural Policies." Pp. 1-20 in *Cultural Policy and Urban Regeneration: The West European Experience*, edited by Franco Bianchini and Michael Parkinson. Manchester: Manchester University Press.

Boyle, Mark. 2011. "Commentary: The New Urban Politics Thesis; Ruminations on MacLeod and Jones' Six Analytical Pathways." *Urban Studies* 48 (12): 2673–2685.

Davies, Jonathan, and Jessica Trounstine. 2009. "Urban Politics and the New Institutionalism." In *Oxford Handbook of Urban Politics*, edited by Karen Mossberger, Susan E. Clarke, and Peter John. Oxford: Oxford University Press.

De Frantz, Monika. 2005. "From Cultural Regeneration to Discursive Governance: Constructing the Flagship of the 'Museumsquartier Vienna' as a Plural Symbol of Change." *International Journal for Urban and Regional Research* 29 (1): 50–66.

———. 2006. "KulturPolitik im Wandel: Hauptstadtsymbolik in Wien und Berlin." *Österreichische Zeitschrift für Politikwissenschaft* 3: 237–253.

———. 2007. "'The City without Qualities': Political Theories of European Urbanity and Globalization." EUI-Working Paper. Florence: European University Institute.

———. 2008. "Contemporary Political Theories of the European City: Questioning Institutions." *European Journal of Social Theory* 11 (4): 443–463.

———. 2011. *Capital City Cultures: Two Narratives of European Change in Vienna and Berlin*. Multiple Europes, vol. 45. Brussels: PIE–Peter Lang.

———. 2013. "Culture-led Urban Regeneration: The Discursive Politics of Institutional Change." In *Routledge Companion to Urban Regeneration: Global Constraints, Local Opportunities*, edited by Mike Leary and John McCarthy. London: Routledge.

Degen, Monica, and Marisol Garcia. 2012. "The Transformation of the 'Barcelona Model': An Analysis of Culture, Urban Regeneration and Governance." *International Journal of Urban and Regional Research* 36 (5): 1022–1038.

Delanty, Gerard. 2012. "A Cosmopolitan Approach to the Explanation of Social Change: Social Mechanisms, Processes, Modernity." *The Sociological Review* 60 (2): 333–354.

Fabbrini Sergio. 2004. "The European Union in American Perspective: The Transformation of Territorial Sovereignty in Europe and the United States." In *Restructuring Territoriality: Europe and the United States Compared*, edited by K. Ansell and Giuseppe Di Palma. Cambridge: Cambridge University Press.

Florida, Richard. 2012. *The Rise of the Creative Class—Revisited*. New York: Basic Books.

Frey, Oliver, and Florian Koch. 2011. *Die Zukunft der Europäischen Stadt: Stadtpolitik, Stadtplanung und die Stadtgesellschaft im Wandel*. Wiesbaden: VS Verlag für Sozialwissenschaften, Springer.

Gonzalez, Sara. 2011. "Bilbao and Barcelona 'in Motion': How Urban Regeneration 'Models' Travel and Mutate in the Global Flows of Policy Tourism." *Urban Studies* 48 (7): 1397–1418.

Hajer, Maarten. 1989. *City Politics: Hegemonic Projects and Discourse*. Avebury: Aldershot, Hants, UK.

———. 2005. "Rebuilding Ground Zero: The Politics of Performance." *Planning Theory and Practice* 6 (4): 445–464.

———. 2009. *Authoritative Governance: Policy Making in the Age of Mediatization*. Oxford: Oxford University Press.

Hajer, Maarten, and A. Reijndorp. 2001. *In Search of New Public Domain: Analysis and Strategy*. Rotterdam: Nai Uitgevers Publishing.

Harding, Alan. 2009. "The History of Community Power." In *Theories of Urban Politics*, edited by J. Davies and D. Imbroscio. Los Angeles: Sage.

Häussermann, Hartmut, and Anna Haila. 2005. "The European City: A Conceptual Framework and Normative Project." In *Cities of Europe: Changing Contexts, Local Arrangements, and the Challenge to Urban Cohesion*, edited by Yuri Kazepov. Oxford: Blackwell.

Healey, Patsy. 2012. "Performing Place Governance Collaboratively: Planning as a Communicative Process." In *The Argumentative Turn Revisited: Public Policy as Communicative Practice*, edited by F. Fischer and H. Gottweis. Durham, NC: Duke University Press.

Judd, Dennis. 2005. "Everything is Always Going to Hell: Urban Scholars as End-Times Prophets." *Urban Affairs Review* 41 (2): 119–131.

Kantor, Paul, and H. V. Savitch. 2005. "How to Study Comparative Urban Development Politics: A Research Note." *International Journal of Urban and Regional Research* 29 (1): 135–151.

Keating, Michael. 1988. *The City That Refused to Die: Glasgow: The Politics of Urban Regeneration*. Aberdeen: Aberdeen University Press.

———. 1991. *Comparative Urban Politics: Power and the City in the United States, Canada, Britain, and France*. Aldershot, Hants, UK: Edward Elgar.

———. 2009. "Rescaling Europe." *Perspectives on European Politics and Society* 10 (1): 34–50.

Keating, Michael, and Monika De Frantz. 2004. "Culture-led Strategies for Urban Regeneration: A Comparative Perspective on Bilbao." *International Journal of Iberian Studies* 16 (3): 187–194.

Le Gales, Patrick. 2002. *European Cities: Social Conflicts and Governance*. Oxford: Oxford University Press.

Löw, Martina. 2012. "The Intrinsic Logic of Cities: Towards a New Theory on Urbanism." *Urban Research and Practice* 5 (3): 303–315.

Lowndes, Vivien. 2008. "Something Old, Something New, Something Borrowed . . . How Institutions Change (and Stay the Same) in Local Governance." In *Innovations in Urban Politics*, edited by Jonathan Davies. London: Routlege.

Lowndes, Vivien, and Mark Roberts. 2013. *Why Institutions Matter: The New Institutionalism in Political Science*. Basingstoke, UK: Palgrave Macmillan.

MacKinnon, Danny. 2012. "Reconstructing Scale: Towards a New Scalar Politics." *Progress in Human Geography* 35 (1): 21–36.

MacLeod, Gordon, and Martin Jones. 2011. "Renewing Urban Politics." *Urban Studies* 48 (12): 2443–2472.

Martin, R., and P. Sunley. 2003. "Deconstructing Clusters: Chaotic Concept or Policy Panacea?" *Journal of Economic Geography* 3 (1): 5–35.

Miles, Malcom. 2005. "Interruptions: Testing the Rhetoric of Culturally Led Urban Development." *Urban Studies* 42 (5/6): 889–911.

Nivola, Pietro. 2007. "Are Europe's Cities Better?" in *The Urban Politics Reader*, edited by Elizabeth Strom and John Mollenkopf. New York: Routledge.

Parker, Simon. 2012. "Urbanism as Material Discourse: Questions of Interpretation in Contemporary Urban Theory." *Urban Geography* 33 (4): 530–544.

Parnell, Susan, and Jennifer Robinson. 2012. "(Re)theorizing Cities from the Global South: Looking Beyond Neoliberalism." *Urban Geography* 33 (4): 593–617.

Peck, Jamie. 2005. "Struggling with the Creative Class." *International Journal of Urban and Regional Research* 29 (4): 740–770.

Philo, Chris, and Gerry Kearns. 1993. "Culture, History, Capital: A Critical Introduction to the Selling of Places." In *Selling Places: The City as Cultural Capital, Past and Present*, edited by Chris Philo and Gerry Kearns. Oxford: Pergamon Press.

Plaza, Beatriz. 2008. "On Some Challenges and Conditions for the Guggenheim Museum Bilbao to be an Effective Economic Re-activator." *International Journal of Urban and Regional Research* 32 (2): 506–517.

Pollock, Venda, and Ron Paddison. 2010. "Embedding Public Art: Practice, Policy and Problems." *Journal of Urban Design* 15 (3): 335–356.

Ponzini, Davide, and Ugo Rossi. 2009. "Becoming a Creative City: The Entrepreneurial Mayor, Network Politics and the Promise of an Urban Renaissance." *Urban Studies* 47 (5): 1037–1057.

Pratt, Andy. 2010. "Creative Cities: Tensions Within and Between Social, Cultural and Economic Development: A Critical Reading of the UK Experience." *City, Culture and Society* 1 (1): 13–20.

———. 2011. "The Cultural Contradictions of the Creative City." *City, Culture and Society* 2 (3): 123–130.

Pratt, Andy, and Thomas Hutton. 2013. "Reconceptualising the Relationship Between the Creative Economy and the City: Learning From the Financial Crisis." *Cities* 33: 86–95.

Robinson, Jennifer. 2011. "Cities in a World of Cities: The Comparative Gesture." *International Journal of Urban and Regional Research* 35 (1): 1–23.

Robinson, Jennifer, and Colin McFarlane. 2012. "Introduction—Experiments in Comparative Urbanism." *Urban Geography* 33 (6): 765–773.

Sapotichne, Joshua, Bryan Jones, and Michelle Wolfe. 2007. "Is Urban Politics a Black Hole? Analyzing the Boundary Between Political Science and Urban Politics." *Urban Affairs Review* 43 (1): 76–106.

Sassatelli, Monica. 2011. "Urban Festivals and the Cultural Public Sphere: Cosmopolitanism Between Ethics and Aesthetics." In *Festivals and the Cultural Public Sphere*, edited by Monica Sassatelli, Gerard Delanty, and Liana Giorgi. London: Routledge.

Sharp, Elaine. 2007. "Revitalizing Urban Research: Can Cultural Explanation Bring Us Back from the Periphery?" *Urban Affairs Review* 43 (1): 55–75.

Silver, Daniel, Terry Clark, and Chris Graziul. 2011. "Scenes, Innovation, and Urban Development." In *Handbook of Creative Cities*, edited by David Emanuel Andersson, Åke E. Andersson, and Charlotta Mellande. Cheltenham, UK: Edward Elgar.

Smith, Michael. 2005. "Transnational Urbanism Revisited." *Journal of Ethnic and Migration Studies* 31 (2): 235–244.

Ward, Kevin, and David Imbroscio. 2011. "Urban Politics: An Interdisciplinary Dialogue." *International Journal of Urban and Regional Research* 35 (4): 853–71.

Wodak, R., R. De Cillia, M. Reisigl, and K. Liebhart. 2009. *The Discursive Construction of National Identity*. Edinburgh: Edinburgh University Press.

Wollmann, Hellmut. 2004. "Local Government Reforms in Great Britain, Sweden, Germany and France: Between Multi-function and Single-purpose Organisations." *Local Government Studies* 30 (4): 639–665.

Young, Craig, Martina Diep, and Stephanie Drabble. 2006. "Living with Difference? The 'Cosmopolitan City' and Urban Reimagining in Manchester, UK." *Urban Studies* 43 (10): 1687–1714.

Zimmermann, Karsten. 2012a. "Organisationsfelder, Arenafärbungen und städtische Eigenlogiken. Einige konzeptuelle Überlegungen zum Repertoire lokaler Politikforschung." In *Regieren: Festschrift für Hubert Heinelt*, edited by Björn Egner, Michael Haus, and Georgios Terizakis. Wiesbaden: VS Verlag für Sozialwissenschaften.

———. 2012b. "Eigenlogik of Cities —Introduction to the Themed Section." *Urban Research and Practice* 5 (3): 299–302.

Zukin, Sharon. 2009. *Naked City: The Death and Life of Authentic Urban Places*. New York: Oxford University Press.

THE LONG-TERM IMPACT OF AUTHORITARIANISM IN POST-DICTATORIAL EUROPE: A COMPARATIVE CASE STUDY BASED UPON THE MYTH SURROUNDING THE AUSTRIAN DICTATOR ENGELBERT DOLLFUSS

Lucile Dreidemy*

Abstract

Most European societies in which authoritarian and/or fascist regimes came to power in the 1920s, 1930s, and 1940s, have faced and are still facing difficulties in dealing with their dictatorial past. In all countries concerned, these difficulties are mainly due to the persistence of tenacious myths about the former regimes and their leading figures. From within the wide range of European case studies, the Austrian case, and more precisely the myth surrounding the Austrian dictator Engelbert Dollfuss since his death in 1934, appears particularly enlightening, for it illustrates how such myths come about and the long-term impact they can have on politics and the culture of memory. Based upon the analysis of the Dollfuss myth from a comparative perspective, this contribution will cast a critical light on the impact of consensual politics

* Lucile Dreidemy is a Maître de conférences in the Department of German Studies at the University of Toulouse-Jean Jaurès.

of memory in post-dictatorial societies and raise the topical question of the relation between authoritarian legacy and modern authoritarianism in today's Europe.

Most European societies in which authoritarian and/or fascist regimes came to power in the 1920s, 1930s, and 1940s, have faced and are mostly still facing difficulties in dealing with their dictatorial past. While the people of Germany were forced to come to terms with Nazism immediately after the end of World War II, most countries postponed this public confrontation, leading to numerous memory scandals and repeated (and mostly unpunished) acts of revisionism. In Italy, for instance, although a law implemented in 1952 makes it a criminal offence punishable by up to two years in prison for anyone "publicly to celebrate the exponents, principles, actions, or methods of fascism,"[1] the country has experienced a growing tendency to neglect the totalitarian elements of the regime and to play down its repressive character.[2]

The last decade offers many illustrations of this phenomenon of "de-fascisation of fascism":[3] Besides the repeated glorifying statements of Mussolini's granddaughter Alessandra,[4] one can mention the most recent revisionist statement by former Prime Minister Silvio Berlusconi at the ceremony marking International Holocaust Remembrance Day in January 2013, where he qualified Mussolini's anti-Semitic laws as a "mistake" and praised "other good things" done by the *Duce* "in so many areas."[5] In Spain, the unearthing of mass graves in 2011 has focused attention on the fact that Spaniards have only recently begun to revisit their past, while further recent events show the obstacles critical voices are facing in their attempt to confront Franco's legacy publicly. When the artist Eugenio Merino, for instance, recently chose to confront the public with this legacy by putting a replica of the late dictator in a drinks refrigerator under the title "Always Franco," he was immediately prosecuted by the Franco Foundation, which protects the

---

[1] "Law of June 20, 1952, n. 645," accessed February 15, 2014, http://www.normattiva.it/uri-res/N2Ls?urn:nir:stato:legge:1952;645.

[2] Didier Musiedlack, *Mussolini* (Paris: Presses de sciences po, 2005), 306.

[3] Emilio Gentile, *Qu'est-ce que le fascisme ? Histoire et interprétation* (Paris: Gallimard, 2004), 12.

[4] See Alessandra Mussolini, interview by Frank Bruni, "A Proud Mussolini Refuses To Let 'Il Duce' Be Vilified," *New York Times*, November 30, 2003, accessed February 15, 2014, http://www.nytimes.com/2003/11/30/world/a-proud-mussolini-refuses-to-let-il-duce-be-vilified.html.

[5] See Nick Squires, "Silvio Berlusconi could be prosecuted for Mussolini comments," *The Telegraph*, January 28, 2013, accessed February 15, 2014, http://www.telegraph.co.uk/news/worldnews/silvio-berlusconi/9832191/Silvio-Berlusconi-could-be-prosecuted-for-Mussolini-comments.html. Several observers interpreted this statement as part of Berlusconi's attempt to address the far-right voters, in view of the imminent general elections.

memory of the "Generalissimo" and is headed by Franco's daughter, Carmen Polo Franco.[6] Furthermore, Hungary has been experiencing a revival of the cult of dictator Miklós Horthy in the last decade. Horthy installed one of the earliest right-wing dictatorships of the European interwar period in 1919–1920 and collaborated with the National Socialists from 1933 until 1944, when they occupied the country.

In all countries concerned, these difficulties to cope with the dictatorial past go along with tenacious myths about the former regimes and their leading figures. From within the wide range of European case studies, the Austrian case, and more precisely the myth surrounding the Austrian dictator Engelbert Dollfuss, although internationally little known, appears particularly enlightening, for it illustrates how such myths come about and the long-term impact they can have on politics and on the culture of memory in post-dictatorial societies.

Dollfuss became Austrian Chancellor in May 1932. In March 1933, his government, a coalition of Dollfuss's Catholic Conservative Party, the fascist *Heimatblock* (the political arm of the paramilitary organization *Heimwehr*—Home Guard), and the small Pan-German party *Landbund* (Farmers' League) took the occasion of a parliamentary crisis to disable parliamentary democracy and to install a dictatorship. Right from the start, the regime was heavily opposed by different political currents, the most influential of them being the Social Democrats and, at the other end of the political scale, the National Socialists. The resulting political crisis led on the one hand to a civil war in February 1934 between the forces of the regime and the left-wing opposition, and on the other hand to a putsch attempt by the National Socialists on July 25 1934, during which Dollfuss was killed.

Between 1934 and 1938, the government of Dollfuss's successor, Kurt Schuschnigg, set up a state cult for the so-called "dead leader," which became the core of the regime's propaganda. After 1945, Dollfuss became one of the most controversial personalities of Austria's contemporary history, as illustrated by the recurrent phrase "*Arbeitermörder oder Heldenkanzler*" ("murderer of workers," a term coined by the communicative memory of the Communist and Social Democratic victims of the civil war, versus "hero chancellor," a term which was always associated with the Conservative Dollfuss cult). Today, even though a large part of the Austrian population is now

---

[6] Belén Palanco, "Franco can stay in the fridge," *The Art Newspaper*, August 26, 2013, accessed February 15, 2014, http://www.theartnewspaper.com/articles/Franco-can-stay-in-the-fridge/30239. The court found in favor of the artist on the grounds of freedom of art; the Foundation has appealed. Meanwhile, it is also suing him for his latest work, "Punching Franco," in which the artist transformed Franco's head into a punching ball.

ignorant of him,[7] the so-called Dollfuss-myth continues to divide Austrian academic, political, and public discourse on the interwar period. This is best illustrated by the controversies raised on the occasion of the 80th anniversary of the civil war in February 2014 by newly discovered archive sources that refer to an informal proposal made by Dollfuss to use poison gas against striking workers.[8]

This contribution will focus on two aspects that make the Dollfuss-myth interesting for a comparative analysis on the question of authoritarian legacies in post-dictatorial Europe. By comparing the politics of reconciliation conducted in Austria and Spain, this contribution will cast a critical light on the long-term impact of consensual memory politics in these countries. The analysis will raise the question of the relation between authoritarian legacy and modern authoritarianism in today's Europe, which will again be illustrated by a comparison between the situation in Austria and in neighboring Hungary.

The Dilemma of Consensual Memory Politics

Especially in countries that experienced a civil war, such as Austria and Spain, the immediate post-dictatorial (in Austria, simultaneously post-WWII) phase was dominated by the issue of reconciliation between the former adversaries, for reconciliation was considered the very key to a successful transition to democracy. In both cases, reconciliation was only considered possible by forgetting the conflictive past, which is why the former adversaries tacitly agreed upon a form of collective amnesia. At first glance, this pragmatic choice may have appeared successful, as both countries have been praised for their transition to democracy and their consensual achievements, especially in terms of political and social peace. The ongoing controversies about the dictatorship in both countries invite us nevertheless to question how far these politics of the "final stroke" were effective in the long term.

The year 1945 marks a turning point in Austrian domestic politics, not only as the end of World War II and the starting point of the Second Austrian Republic, but also as the beginning of the historic "Great Coalition"

---

[7] A survey held in 2008 among 1,000 people in Austria shows that fewer than half the people could associate the name Dollfuss with the creation of a dictatorship in Austria. Cf. Günther Guggenberger, "The Reflection of Authoritarianism, Anomia and Group-related Misanthropy in Remembrance of the Authoritarian Regime and World War II in Austria," in *Authoritarianism, History and Democratic Dispositions in Austria, Poland, Hungary and the Czech Republic*, edited by Oliver Rathkolb and Günther Ogris (Innsbruck: Studien Verlag, 2010), 47.

[8] Herbert Lackner, "1934: Wollte Kanzler Dollfuß E-Werks-Arbeiter 'überfallsartig vergasen'?" *Profil*, January 25, 2014, accessed February 15, 2014, http://www.profil.at/articles/1404/985/371968/1934-wollte-kanzler-dollfuss-e-werks-arbeiter-ueberfallsartig.

between the former adversaries of the civil war, namely the Catholic Conservatives (now ÖVP) and the Social Democrats (SPÖ). Concerned about restoring Austria's international image, the coalition partners tacitly agreed to avoid memorial and political conflicts by adopting a historical discourse that considered Social Democrats and Conservatives equally responsible for the breakdown of the First Republic in 1933. Forgetting the conflictive past also meant avoiding controversial topics, which is why the Dollfuss/Schuschnigg dictatorship of 1933–1938, and above all its main actor Dollfuss, became a consensual taboo.

Another main pattern of the coalition discourse that strongly contributed to the postponement of the confrontation with the Austrian dictatorship was the so-called *Opferthese* (victim theory), which declared Austria the first victim of Nazism and denied any Austrian responsibility both for what was called Austria's "annexation" in 1938, and for any other form of collaboration during the Nazi era. This theory, which is often considered the founding myth of the Second Austrian Republic, was mainly based upon a partial interpretation of the Moscow Declaration signed by the Allies in 1943, in which Austria was officially declared "the first free country to fall a victim to Hitlerite aggression," even though the last part of the same declaration also clearly stated: "Austria is reminded, however, that she has responsibility which she cannot evade for participation in the war on the side of Hitlerite Germany, and that in the final settlement account will inevitably be taken of her own contribution to her liberation."[9]

From this balanced assessment, the short-lived provisional government (April–October 1945) and the Great Coalition selected and emphasized the victim aspect in order to recover full sovereignty more quickly, but also in order to ward off any blame, and therefore also any claims for reparations.[10] The coalition discourse about the interwar period mainly benefited the new Conservative ÖVP, since it enabled many former prominent figures of the dictatorship to keep leading positions in the party, and above all in the government: Leopold Figl, for instance, a former member of the Federal Council of Economic Policy of the Austrofascist[11] regime and leader of its paramilitary

---

[9] "The Moscow Conference, Joint Four Nation Declaration, October 1943," *The Avalon Project: Documents in Law, History and Diplomacy, Yale Law School*, accessed February 15, 2014, http://avalon.law.yale.edu/wwii/moscow.asp.

[10] Cf. Wolfgang Neugebauer, *Der österreichische Widerstand 1938–1945* (Vienna: Edition Steinbauer, 2008), 239.

[11] Historiography on the Dollfuss-/Schuschnigg-regime is still divided on the question of its relation to fascism. Despite the ongoing debate, "austrofascism" appears to me as the most appropriate category regarding (1) the undeniable fascist leaning of the regime, and (2) at the same time its concern about establishing a specific system based upon a specific "Austria"-ideology.

organization, the *Ostmärkische Sturmscharen* (literally: storm troopers of the Ostmark, or Austria), in Lower Austria, became First Chancellor of the new Republic; his predecessor, Julius Raab, was the former Chief of the fascist paramilitary army *Heimwehr* in Lower Austria and later Minister of Commerce under Schuschnigg.

Despite these consensual measures, coalition policy and consensual historical discourse were not enough to override the ideological cleavage between "reds" (Social Democrats) and "blacks" (Conservatives). On the contrary, official compromises and taboos contributed, behind the coalition scene, to strengthen the latent antagonisms in both political camps. The gap between coalition discourse and party narratives became particularly obvious during the commemorations of the civil war in 1954 and on the occasion of the electoral campaigns in 1959.[12] However, this situation was already about to change, especially since the SPÖ was at that time gradually changing from a "class party" to a "mass party," isolating thereby the more left-wing branch of the party which was always the most likely to refuse any consensus with the Conservative "archenemy."[13] The first official commemoration of the civil war, organized by the coalition in February 1964,[14] is striking evidence of what could be called the "victory of consensus" in post–civil-war Austria.

This consensual memory discourse, reinforced by the theory of the first victim, had a tremendous impact on the political and memorial culture of the Second Republic even after the end of the Great Coalition in 1966. For instance, after the short-lived Conservative government of Josef Klaus (1966–1970) was replaced by the first solely Social Democratic government in 1970, the new Chancellor, Bruno Kreisky, did not use this occasion to reverse the coalition discourse that had prevailed until that moment, even though he was himself a former victim of the Dollfuss/Schuschnigg regime. On the contrary, the charismatic politician seemed to be very keen to overcome the latent civil-war spirit between both parties (the so-called *Lagermentalität*) and to be the first "midway" Chancellor. One of the most symbolic expressions of this midway orientation was his decision to tolerate the annual memorial

---

[12] Concerning the antagonistic memory discourse during the commemoration year 1954, cf. Paul Pennerstorfer, "Das Gedenken an die Februarkämpfe 1934. Geschichtsbilder und Geschichtspolitiken von ÖVP und SPÖ 1946–1964" (Vienna: Diplomarbeit, University of Vienna, 2012), 69–105, especially 103–105. On the electoral campaign of 1959, see for instance the election posters of the SPÖ, on which the politics of the ÖVP were described as "Dollfuss-path."

[13] Robert Kriechbaumer, *Parteiprogramme im Widerstreit der Interessen. Die Programmdiskussion und die Programme von ÖVP und SPÖ 1945–1986* (Vienna: Verlag für Geschichte und Politik, 1990), 330–334.

[14] Cf. Pennerstorfer, "Gedenken," 159–162.

mass for Dollfuss in the Chancellery, which had been implemented by the Conservatives during their sole control of the government from 1966–1970.

There is little doubt that Kreisky's decision was part of an electoral strategy aiming to appeal to Conservatives, who traditionally voted for the ÖVP. Nevertheless, these commemorative concessions had tremendous consequences in terms of memorial politics. For, since even a former prisoner of Dollfuss's regime like Kreisky had made such a concession, his Social Democratic successors Fred Sinowatz (1983–86), Franz Vranitzky (1986–97) and Viktor Klima (1997–2000), followed suit. After the coalition between the Conservatives and the radical right FPÖ, which led to a stronger revival of the Dollfuss cult (2000–2006), it was four more years before the mass was finally abolished in 2010 under Chancellor Werner Faymann (SPÖ).

These consensual politics of memory also dominated the academic historical discourse on the interwar period until the second half of the 1960s. Things started to change as contemporary history became an established academic discipline and as a new generation of historians started to cast a critical light on the Austrian interwar period and thus on the conservative paradigm of "shared responsibility" for the failure of the First Republic. Yet, even though the critical research on the dictatorship made undeniable progress, some taboos remained untouched, such as the one surrounding the politics, ideology, and historical responsibility of Dollfuss.

Consequently, most Austrian academics avoided the topic, so that until today, most biographical works on Dollfuss have been published either by non-Austrians or by exiled Austrians, and none of them ever chose a really critical approach to his politics and ideology. Indeed, even the most recent biographical works present apologetic patterns similar to those used in the early hagiographies of the 1930s: These modern apologies continue to blame the regime opponents, especially the Social Democrats, for Dollfuss's reprehensible decisions. They still also take Dollfuss's legitimation rhetoric for granted; for example, by asserting, just as he once did, that the authoritarian path was the only way to secure Austria's independence in the 1930s and that he actually did not wish to rule but only did it because he felt invested with a sense of duty and mission.[15]

The long-term impact of consensual memory politics, together with the survival of a neo-apologetic Dollfuss discourse and the lack of a critical academic counterpart, all contributed to create the image of an almost

---

[15] On the evolution of the apologetic Dollfuss-literature, cf. Lucile Dreidemy, "Dollfuß—biografisch: Eine Längsschnittanalyse des biografischen Diskurses über Engelbert Dollfuß," in *Österreich 1918–1938: Interdisziplinäre Bestandsaufnahmen und Perspektive*, edited by Ilse Reiter-Zatloukal et al. (Vienna: Böhlau, 2012), 230–244.

"acceptable" dictator. Dollfuss's remaining presence in Austria's memorial landscape is striking evidence of this phenomenon. Already in the first years following WWII, the official taboo surrounding Dollfuss created room to manoeuver for local Dollfuss supporters. Accordingly, from the 1950s on, several local Dollfuss memorials that had been built under Schuschnigg and destroyed or hidden after 1938 were rebuilt or renovated; elsewhere, new memorials were built.

What will happen to the remnants of the Dollfuss cult still present in the public or semi-public sphere (for example, in churches)? The current tendency is not to remove, but to re-contextualize them; for instance, by adding small information plaques next to them. This happened in the Upper Austrian capital, Linz, where the Catholic Church and the SPÖ decided—against the will of the local ÖVP—to re-contextualize the Dollfuss memorial plaque on one of the Cathedral's front doors by adding a small statement underneath, in which the Church distances itself from Dollfuss's politics and stresses its adherence to democracy and pluralism. Meanwhile, even the Conservatives have started to support this compromise: In February 2014, for instance, the ÖVP proposed a similar solution regarding the controversial Dollfuss portrait, which is still prominently displayed in their clubroom in parliament, and many politicians and commentators from all political sides welcomed this initiative. Nevertheless, many other commentators continue to consider such compromises to be in many ways problematic, especially because they exemplify the widespread opinion that Dollfuss somehow deserves recognition despite his dictatorial politics.

At first glance, these compromises may appear contradictory to the progress made—not only since the 1970s in academic discourse, but also over the past few years in political discourse—towards a critical stand concerning the Dollfuss/Schuschnigg regime. This progress on the level of memory politics is best illustrated by the recent agreement between Social Democrats and Conservatives to officially rehabilitate the victims of the dictatorship. At closer look, this apparent contradiction bears something similar to the process of "de-fascisation of fascism" in Italy, by dissociating the Austrian dictatorship from its main architect, namely Dollfuss. The phenomenon is best illustrated by the fact that more and more Conservatives agree to call the regime a "dictatorship," yet without speaking about Dollfuss as a dictator.[16]

Complementarily, although the theory of "shared responsibility" has already been largely overcome, even from the Conservative side, its long-term

---

[16] Cf. for instance the words chosen by former ÖVP-President of the Austrian Parliament Andreas Khol in an interview with the daily newspaper *Die Presse*, where he called the regime a dictatorship, but said about Dollfuss that he was "not a democrat." Michael Fleischhacker, "Wer ist schon makellos?" *Die Presse*, March 5, 2005, 2.

impact is still visible in popular history discourse. For instance, according to a recent survey conducted in Austria, Poland, the Czech Republic, and Hungary about the relation between authoritarian legacy and modern authoritarian potential, 34.8% of the one thousand Austrians interviewed agreed with the assertion that "Democracy failed because the political parties of the time were not prepared to seek compromises" (against 9% rejection). Even more interesting are the party preferences of the respondents (48.5% of FPÖ voters, 36.9% for the SPÖ, and 34.1% for the ÖVP agreed with the statement, with only 9.5% of SPÖ voters rejecting it), which clearly underpin the idea of the ongoing cross-party impact of the myth of "shared guilt."[17]

The initial role of consensual memory politics in Austria as an instrument of political reconciliation, and its long-term impact on the political culture of the country, show many similarities to the post-dictatorial evolution in Spain. Even though the dictatorships are barely comparable when it comes to their length and, above all, to their repressive character, the fact that both societies had to recover from a civil war led them to comparable political compromises and politics of memory.

According to political scientist Omar Encarnación, Spain is probably "the most famous case in recent history of a new democracy dealing with a difficult and painful past by choosing not to deal with it at all."[18] After almost 40 years of dictatorship under Francisco Franco, both right-wing and left-wing parties agreed upon a collective amnesia, the so-called Pact of Oblivion.[19] Two years after Franco's death, this informal agreement was given a legal basis in form of the so-called Amnesty Law of October 1977, which shielded any crime committed in the Franco era from being put under trial.[20] Yet, even more puzzling than this consensual agreement upon collective oblivion itself is, similarly to the Austrian case, its long-term persistence, and especially the fact that it was maintained even after the Social Democrats (PSOE—*Partido Socialista Obrero Español*), the historic opponents of the Franco regime, took power in 1982.[21]

---

[17] Cf. Guggenberger, "The Reflection of Authoritarianism," 46 and 49–50.

[18] Omar Encarnación, "Reconciliation after Democratization: Coping with the Past in Spain," *Political Science Quarterly* 123 (2008): 436.

[19] Omar Encarnación, *Spanish Politics: Democracy after Dictatorship* (Cambridge, UK: Polity Press, 2008), 2.

[20] "Ley 46/1977," *Boletin Oficial del Estado*, accessed February 15, 2014, http://www.boe.es/buscar/doc.php?id=BOE-A-1977-24937.

[21] Antonio C. Pinto, "The Authoritarian Past and South European Democracies: An Introduction," in *Dealing with the Legacy of Authoritarianism: The "Politics of the Past" in Southern European Democracies*, edited by António C. Pinto (London: Routledge, 2013), 12.

After the PSOE came into power again in 2004, the Congress of Deputies passed the so-called Historical Memory Law,[22] a law that was meant to provide definitive reparation and recognition for the rehabilitation and compensation of those who suffered prosecution or violence in the civil war and the dictatorship. This law was the government's response to the pressure exercised by grassroots organizations such as the Association for the Recovery of Historical Memory (*Asociación para la Recuperación de la Memoria Histórica*—ARHM), which was founded in 2000 and started to collect testimonies of witnesses from the Civil War and the Francoist dictatorship and to excavate and identify bodies of victims, often dumped into mass graves. Even though the law already went too far for the conservative *Partido Popular,* who therefore voted against it, it was in fact still marked by the idea of reconciliation, as illustrated by the first two paragraphs of the law, which Hispanist Luis Martin Cabrera has interpreted as "a plea in defense of the Spanish transition to democracy and its 'spirit of reconciliation.'"[23] Indeed, the law condemned the Franco regime only on moral terms but not on juridical grounds, it recognized the victims on both sides of the Civil War, and what is even more striking, it did not abolish the amnesty law of 1977, which has remained in force until today. As a consequence, when Judge Baltasar Garzón opened a national investigation on crimes committed in the Franco era in 2008, the inquiry was suspended on the basis of the amnesty law.

The main provisions of the Historical Memory Law of 2007 also include the removal of all Francoist symbols from public buildings and spaces, and of Franco's grave from the "Valley of the Fallen" (*Valle de Los Caidos*), a gigantic commemoration area close to Madrid that had been built on Franco's request and was initially dedicated to the "heroes and martyrs of the Crusade"—in other terms, the Francoist victims of the Civil War. According to the law, the memorial area should not be used anymore for political celebrations honoring the former dictator, but transformed into a center for collective and democratic memory, reparation, truth, and reconciliation.[24] Paradoxically, this concept established by the Expert Commission for the Future of the Valley appointed by Zapatero's government, reproduces the idea already developed

---

[22] "Ley 52/2007," *Boletin Oficial del Estado,* accessed February 15, 2014, http://www.boe.es/boe/dias/2007/12/27/pdfs/A53410-53416.pdf.

[23] Luis M. Cabrera, *Radical Justice: Spain and the Southern Cone beyond Market and State* (Lewisburg, PA: Bucknell University Press, 2011), 16.

[24] Cf. "Report of the Expert Commission for the Future of the Valley of the Fallen," accessed February 15, 2014, http://www.memoriahistorica.gob.es/ValleCaidos/enlaces/ComisionExpertosVCaidos.htm.

by Franco himself in the late 1950s, as he decided to transform the *Valle de Los Caidos* into a place of reconciliation after the Civil War.

While in the construction phase in the 1950s, this aim must have appeared cynical to the political prisoners who took part in the construction of the memorial, it is doubtful how far this concept makes sense today considering the dark history of the memorial and its infamous reputation as the biggest symbol of the dictatorship. The transformation project was, however, set aside again after the Conservative *Partido Popular* came back to power in 2011. Besides, in spite of the Historical Memory Law being formally maintained, the government reopened the *Valle de Los Caidos* to political celebrations honoring the late dictator and also rejected the recommendation made by the Commission to remove Franco's grave from the Valley.[25] These measures are a logical continuation of the refusal of the PP to confront the Francoist past, as seen for instance in the statement given by former president José María Aznar in May 2007 regarding the question of the excavation of mass graves: "Spain does not need to look back, to remove bones, nor to look at the past."[26]

But "how can there be reconciliation if there is still denial of the atrocities committed in the Civil War and the dictatorship?," Spanish Civil War expert Luis Martin-Cabrera asks.[27] Even though the Austrian Civil War and the Dollfuss/Schuschnigg dictatorship do not offer any point of comparison in terms of atrocities with the Spanish case, the situation in Austria raises a similar question, especially when one recalls the fact that despite the progress made towards a critical confrontation with Austrofascism, the implementation of the recent Rehabilitation Act was also marked by the refusal of the Conservative party to add a historic preamble, which would have enshrined a common recognition of the illegal and unjust nature of the regime.[28]

In both countries, the political will to overcome the trauma of both the civil war and the dictatorship led the Social Democrats to accept a partially consensual interpretation of the past based upon the historical narratives of

---

[25] Cf. "El PP pretende que el Valle de Los Caídos se quede tal y como está," *eldiario.es*, July 8, 2013, accessed February 15, 2014, http://www.eldiario.es/politica/PP-expertos-Valle-Caidos-enterrados_0_151535517.html.

[26] Aznar: "Cada voto que no vaya al PP será un voto para que ETA esté en las instituciones," *ElPais.com*, May 22, 2007, accessed February 15, 2014, http://elpais.com/elpais/2007/05/22/actualidad/1179821827_850215.html.

[27] Cabrera, *Radical Justice*, 166.

[28] Harald Walser, "Austrofaschismus—'sagen wir es nur ganz offen und ehrlich!,'" *Die Presse*, October 3, 2011, accessed February 15, 2014, http://diepresse.com/home/meinung/gastkommentar/697770/Austrofaschismus-sagen-wir-es-nur-ganz-offen-und-ehrlich.

their Conservative counterparts. If this strategy may have appeared beneficial to the democratic transition in the short term, the fact that both countries still cannot get rid of this past rather seems to illustrate the thesis supported by ethnologist Francisco Ferrandiz in relation to Spain that "societies eventually need to confront head-on the most disquieting elements of the past and that political strategies that privilege sweeping such history 'under the rug,' while potentially effective for limited periods of time, may be destabilizing in the long term."[29]

The outcome of the recent survey mentioned above about the relation between authoritarian legacy and modern authoritarian potential in Austria, Poland, the Czech Republic, and Hungary illustrates the validity of this theory in the case of Austria.[30] From all four countries analyzed in this survey, the correlation appeared particularly clear in Austria, which was the only country to show a direct relation between sympathy for the former dictator (in this case Dollfuss) and inclination towards submissive authoritarian attitudes. This was, for instance, illustrated by the fact that interviewees who supported minority rights appeared mostly critical toward Dollfuss, while, on the contrary, supporters of Dollfuss were mostly distrustful of minority rights.[31]

The Paradox of Collaboration and Victimhood and Their Impact on Modern Authoritarianism

One particularly astonishing outcome of the survey concerns the political orientations of the Dollfuss supporters. On the one hand, ÖVP voters turned out, as expected, to be more sympathetic towards Dollfuss than all other voters. Only among ÖVP sympathizers was the proportion of people who disagreed with the proposition "Federal Chancellor Dollfuss destroyed democracy in Austria" higher (21.9%) than the number of people who agreed (13.8%). On the other hand, however, 14.9% of SPÖ voters also disagreed with the idea that Dollfuss destroyed democracy and 26.2% of SPÖ voters even granted Dollfuss "great respect."[32] This unexpected outcome underpins the idea of a dissociative memory process: even though the historical discourse

---

[29] Francisco Ferrandiz, "Exhuming the Defeated: Civil War Mass Graves in 21st-Century Spain," *American Ethnologist* 40 (2013): 39.

[30] This research project was based upon 1,000 telephone interviews conducted in all four countries in December 2007 by a team of historians and social scientists from the Institute for Contemporary History at the University of Vienna and from the Austrian Institute for Social Research and Consulting (SORA).

[31] Oliver Rathkolb, "Epilogue," in Rathkolb and Ogris, *Authoritarianism,* 135.

[32] Guggenberger, "Reflection of Authoritarianism," 45.

on the Dollfuss/Schuschnigg regime has become increasingly critical in the past decades, the fact that Dollfuss was killed by the Nazis constitutes a sort of mitigating circumstance in the global assessment of the dictator's politics. Despite all his political "mistakes," his death lets him appear retrospectively as a resistance fighter and a victim—in some interpretations even as "Austria's first victim" of the Nazis.

This dual perspective of Dollfuss as dictator and victim, or as a "light-and-shadow" personality has become more and more accepted in the past decade. The image is often used by Conservative politicians in order to legitimize the prominent display of Dollfuss's portrait in the party's clubroom in the parliament,[33] but the pattern is also illustrated in schoolbooks, which often contain pictures of Dollfuss in the typical dictator outfit and pictures of his dead body after the Nazi putsch.[34] The most likely explanation for the increasing acceptability of this new paradigm is that it complements perfectly the transformation of the Austrian victim theory that occurred after the so-called Waldheim Affair. Following the scandal concerning the Nazi past of presidential candidate—and former UN general secretary—Kurt Waldheim in 1986, the victim theory based upon the Moscow declaration of 1943 was seriously shaken, yet not abolished but transformed into a so-called Victim-culprit-myth ("*Opfer-Täter-These*").[35]

The 2007 survey illustrates very well the recent evolution of the Austrian victim discourse toward a mix of co-responsibility and victimhood. On the one hand, 52.7% of the interviewees agreed that "Austrians have to accept co-responsibility for the crimes of World War Two" (against 19.7% rejecting this idea), and 56.6% believed that "Austrians were co-responsible for the fate of the Jews between 1938 and 1945" (against 13.7% rejecting this idea).[36] On the other hand, 36.5% (against 25% of rejections) agreed with the idea that "Austria was the first victim of National Socialism."[37] This trend even seems to

---

[33] Cf. the argumentation of ÖVP-politician Michael Spindelegger in 2008 (at that time Austria's foreign minister) in an interview with the daily newspaper *Die Presse*: Alexander Pruger, "ÖVP mit Habsburg und Schuschnigg. Interview von Michael Spindelegger," *Salzburger Nachrichten*, February 14, 2008, 2.

[34] Cf. for example: *Durch die Vergangenheit zur Gegenwart 7*, edited by Alexander Pokorny et al. (Vienna: Veritas, 2004), 75 and 85.

[35] Cf. Gerhard Botz, "Opfer/Täter-Diskurse. Zur Problematik des 'Opfer'-Diskurses," in *Zeitgeschichte im Wandel*, edited by Gertraud Diendorfer et al. (Innsbruck: Studien Verlag, 1998), 223.

[36] Guggenberger, "Reflection of Authoritarianism," 54. However, it is striking that 26.5% of ÖVP voters and 21.8% of SPÖ voters still think that the degree of collaboration of the Austrians was low.

[37] Guggenberger, "Reflection of Authoritarianism," 51.

be rising: in a similar survey conducted in 1995, only 28% of the interviewees agreed with the victim theory, whereas a recent survey conducted in March 2013 suggested that 46% would agree with the victim theory.[38] Similarly, the number of people who consider that Austrian resistance was important for the liberation was much higher (about 50%) in 2007 than in a similar survey in 1996 (21%).[39]

These ambiguous results illustrate the specific difficulties for a society like Austria to reckon with a multiple dictatorial past; namely, both a "home-grown" and an imported dictatorship. The Austrian case thereby shows interesting similarities with its Hungarian neighbor, even though Hungary had not two, but three different anti-democratic and repressive legacies to cope with after 1945: the authoritarian Horthy regime of 1919-1944, and the period from October 1944 to May 1945 marked simultaneously by Nazi occupation and by a collaborationist regime, the so-called government of national unity led by the fascist Arrow Cross movement under Ferenc Szálasi.

According to the 2007 survey, Austrian and Hungarian memory discourses reveal a similar tension between responsibility and victimhood—yet not in the same way. On the one hand, Hungarian answers reveal a similar trend of criticism of collaboration during World War II, with about one-third agreeing that "Hungarians share responsibility regarding WWII crimes" and that "Many Hungarians benefited materially from the extermination."[40] In contrast to Austria, however, about the same percentage of interviewees rejected these ideas, and about a quarter of the respondents supported the idea that "Jews are co-responsible for their fate" (against 38% rejecting this idea). Hungarians appear, therefore, much more divided than Austrians on the question of collaboration. They nevertheless share with Austria a large acceptance of the resistance myth, with 54.2% of the interviewees believing that resistance played an important role in the country's liberation.[41] As with Austria, this shows the long-term impact of a myth that was actively created by the Hungarian government immediately after 1945 in order to downplay the importance of collaboration and to regain the confidence of the Allies.[42]

---

[38] Guggenberger, "Reflection of Authoritarianism," 51.

[39] Hilde Weiss, *Nation und Toleranz?* (Vienna: Braumüller Verlag, 2004), 136.

[40] Árpád v. Klimó, "Hungary," in Rathkolb and Ogris, *Authoritarianism*, 83.

[41] Klimó, "Hungary," 88.

[42] On the construction of the myth of resistance in post-war Hungary, cf. Regina Fritz, *Nach Krieg und Judenmord: Ungarns Geschichtspolitik seit 1944* (Göttingen: Wallstein, 2012), 309–311.

However, the myth that dominates Hungarian memory discourse is the complex of victimhood. Unlike in Austria, this myth is not only based upon the externalization of guilt concerning World War II, but also marked by the ongoing emotional impact of the Treaty of Trianon of 1920, following which Hungary lost two-thirds of its territory and more than half of its population. About 80% of the respondents consider this treaty unfair.[43] One may wonder why this event remains such a decisive *lieu de mémoire* for Hungarians almost a century later. As the historian Árpád von Klimó observes, Hungarians are indeed not really seeking the return of Great Hungary. Instead, Trianon has rather become the symbol of the continuous suffering and injustice imposed by foreign powers.[44]

Nevertheless, the inflationary reference to Trianon bears at the same time a sort of "silent" revisionist potential, especially towards the Horthy era, since the treaty played a decisive role in the aggressive nationalism developed by the regime. It is no coincidence that the memory of the Horthy regime became a current reference in the context of the nationalist revival in Hungary after 1989. The first step towards a rehabilitation of the Horthy regime was the decision taken in 1993 by the new center-right government under Prime Minister József Antall (Hungarian Democratic forum - MDF) to bring back Horthy's remains from Portugal, where he had lived undisturbed from 1944 until his death in 1957. More than 10,000 people attended the reburial ceremony, which took place in his hometown of Nagybány and was simultaneously broadcast on state television.[45] The event was preceded by several interviews of Prime Minister Antall praising Horthy as a "Hungarian patriot" and calling for his international recognition.[46]

From then on, the rehabilitation of the Horthy regime was closely related to the increasing power of the Hungarian right-wing parties, and first of all to the rise of the national conservative *Fidesz* party of Viktor Orbán, who built his first government in 1998 together with the MDF. This revisionism was, for instance, reflected in the concept of the museum, "The House of Terror," which

---

[43] Klimó, "Hungary," 83.

[44] Klimó, "Hungary," 83.

[45] Jane Perlez, Reburial Is Both a Ceremony and a Test for Today's Hungary, September 5, 1993, accessed February 15, 2014, http://www.nytimes.com/1993/09/05/world/reburial-is-both-a-ceremony-and-a-test-for-today-s-hungary.html?pagewanted=all&src=pm.

[46] The politics of memory of the Antall government were highly ambiguous: it was, for example, the first government to pass a restitution law awarding compensation to Jewish victims. Christian Gerbel and Rossalina Latcheva, "Cultures of Remembrance of World War II and the Holocaust in Austria, Poland, Hungary and the Czech Republic," in Rathkolb and Ogris, *Authoritarianism*, 110–11.

was set up under Orbán's government and inaugurated in Budapest shortly before the elections in 2002. The exhibit insists upon the allegedly democratic aspects of the Horthy regime and presents its anti-Semitic policies as a consequence of German pressure.[47] This argument also fits into the second main pattern of the exhibit; namely, the presentation of Hungary as an eternal victim of foreign powers, as reflected in its first room, entitled "Double Occupation," where Hungary is presented as victim and survivor, and Nazism and Stalinism are equated as similarly totalitarian regimes.[48] The victim myth and the totalitarian paradigm are also at the core of the online presentation of the museum, which reads: "Having survived two terror regimes, it was felt that the time had come for Hungary to erect a fitting memorial to the victims, and at the same time to present a picture of what life was like for Hungarians in those times."[49]

The 2007 survey suggested that Horthy, contrary to Dollfuss in Austria, did not play any decisive role for Hungarians anymore; Klimó even concluded that the responses of the Hungarian interviewees showed "only weak correlation between authoritarianism and memory." However, the political evolution in Hungary since the survey invites us to reconsider these observations. In fact, politically motivated revisionism and especially the rehabilitation of the Horthy regime reached new heights after the nationalist landslide which followed the parliamentary elections of 2010. Backed by a two-third majority in parliament, Prime Minister Orbán began to centralize power and to increase the government's influence in the judicial domain and in the media. This authoritarian turn was given a legal basis in 2011 in the form of a new constitution, which reflected at the same time the revisionist tendency of the government. The constitution's preamble repeated the old myth of Hungary as an eternal victim of foreign powers. Moreover, by dating the loss of the country's "self-determination" to March 19, 1944 (the date of Nazi-occupation) and its restoration on May 2, 1990, the preamble not only assimilated Nazism and Stalinism once again, but it also ignored the non-communist period of 1945–1949, and by taking the period 1944–1990 as a negative reference, it established a continuity with the Horthy regime and legitimized it de facto.[50]

The second biggest winner of the 2010 elections was the far-right *Jobbik*, the "Movement for a Better Hungary," a rather young party created in 2003,

---

[47] Cf. Fritz, *Nach Krieg und Judenmord*, 303.

[48] Cf. Fritz, *Nach Krieg und Judenmord*, 289.

[49] "Description of the Exhibition of the House of Terror," accessed February 15, 2014, http://www.terrorhaza.hu/en/exhibition/exhibition.html.

[50] "The Fundamental Law of Hungary," April 25, 2011, Website of the Hungarian Government, accessed February 15, 2014, http://www.kormany.hu/download/4/c3/30000/THE%20FUNDAMENTAL%20LAW%20OF%20HUNGARY.pdf.

which jumped from less than 5% of the votes in 2006 to 16.67% in 2010, and hence became the second largest opposition group after the Socialists with 47 of 386 parliamentary seats. This party has since become *Fidesz*'s biggest challenger and flirts openly with revisionism: In 2007, its leaders founded the "Hungarian Guard," a paramilitary organization clearly inspired by the fascist Arrow Cross movement. At the same time, they started to revive the Horthy cult; for example, by putting up statues of Horthy in local municipalities under *Jobbik*'s control.

Fidesz reacted with a typical double-speak strategy: on the one hand, Orbán's government incriminated the anti-Semitic and xenophobic propaganda of *Jobbik* and even banned the Hungarian Guard. On the other hand, it tried to outpace the far right by increasing its own nationalist and revisionist attitude. Recent events illustrate *Fidesz*'s zigzag course: In April 2012, the city council of Gyömro in Pest County accepted *Jobbik*'s proposal to rename the town square after Horthy. Two months later, a Horthy statue was unveiled by the *Fidesz* mayor of Csókako, a small municipality near Budapest.[51] Asked by the Austrian newspaper *Die Presse* about the ongoing revival of the Horthy cult in his country, Orbán warded off any blame and claimed that these initiatives were the exclusive responsibility of the concerned municipalities. At the same time, he refused to call Horthy a dictator and labeled only Ferenc Szálasi as such.[52]

These few examples underpin the idea of an increasing correlation between authoritarianism and memory in Hungary. In addition, the bad economic situation of the country creates an even more fertile ground for anti-democratic and revisionist ideas. In this context, revisionist narratives and symbolic politics are often instrumentalized in order to distract the public's attention from topical issues, such as the government's mismanagement of the tremendous consequences of the economic crisis.

Conclusion

The analysis of memory politics in Austria, Spain, and Hungary brings to the fore the fact that societies which avoid an official confrontation with the dictatorial past are doomed to see it come back in the form of tenacious

---

[51] Cf. "Does Hungary Have a new Hero?" *The Economist*, June 18, 2012, accessed February 15, 2014, http://www.economist.com/blogs/easternapproaches/2012/06/hungarian-history.

[52] Michael Fleischhacker and Christian Ultsch, "Orban im Interview: 'Wir haben die Linke zertrümmert,'" *Die Presse*, June 16, 2012, accessed February 15, 2014, http://diepresse.com/home/politik/aussenpolitik/766412/Orban-im-Interview_Wir-haben-die-Linke-zertruemmert?from=suche.intern.portal.

myths, memory scandals, and revisionist attitudes. The situations in Austria and Hungary also show that such myths and revisionist attitudes create a fertile ground for modern forms of authoritarianism. Moreover, the analysis of the correlation between authoritarian legacy and modern authoritarianism underpins the idea that reductionist ideologies and authoritarian potential are strengthened by a lack of critical historical consciousness. In both countries, many interviewees, for instance, were of the opinion that the debate on WWII should be terminated (47% agreeing with this idea in Austria,[53] 75.8% in Hungary[54]). In another survey organized in March 2013, an astonishing 61% of 502 Austrian interviewees supported the idea that WWII has received enough attention, and 57% thought that the victims and their descendants have received enough compensation.[55]

These results are mainly due to a growing historical ignorance in all political camps. As historian Oliver Rathkolb observes in the case of Austria, "even those who are prepared in principle to take a critical look at National Socialism do not necessarily arrive at a sufficiently differentiated view of history and are therefore liable to make assessments that are not founded on facts."[56] The same interpretation could be made in relation to the Dollfuss/Schuschnigg regime in Austria and to the Horthy regime in Hungary: In contrast to the impressions of the interviewees, there is still a lot to be done in terms of critical confrontation with the dictatorial past in these countries. Furthermore, the case of countries that experienced both a dictatorship and a civil war, such as Spain and Austria, shows that the legitimate wish to overcome the trauma of the civil war and to reach a certain level of political peace (which appears less illusionary than "reconciliation") must not prevent a society, and above all its main political actors, from a critical confrontation with its dictatorial past, for this confrontation appears as a necessary condition for democratic development in the long term.

In conclusion, the long-term impact of authoritarianism in Spain, Austria, and Hungary not only reminds us that critical historical consciousness is a key component of democratic consciousness and, therefore, also one of the most efficient walls against modern authoritarianism. At the same time, it raises the question of how far the perpetuation of political and historical *impunity*, be it explicit or implicit, might gradually turn into a rampant

53 Cf. Guggenberger, "The Reflection of Authoritarianism," 45–46.

54 Cf. Klimó, "Hungary," 88.

55 Conrad Seidl, "Umfrage: 42 Prozent sagen 'Unter Hitler war nicht alles schlecht,'" *Der Standard*, March 8, 2013, accessed February 15, 2014, http://derstandard.at/1362107918471/Umfrage-42-Prozent-sagen-Unter-Hitler-war-nicht-alles-schlecht.

56 Rathkolb, "Epilogue," 136.

acceptability and even open the door to a renewed *legitimacy* of this latent authoritarian legacy.

BIBLIOGRAPHY

Botz, Gerhard. "Opfer/Täter-Diskurse. Zur Problematik des 'Opfer'-Diskurses." in *Zeitgeschichte im Wandel*, edited by Gertraud Diendorfer et al. Innsbruck: Studien Verlag, 1998.

Cabrera, Luis M. *Radical Justice: Spain and the Southern Cone beyond Market and State*. Lewisburg, PA: Bucknell University Press, 2011.

Dreidemy, Lucile. "Dollfuß—biografisch: Eine Längsschnittanalyse des biografischen Diskurses über Engelbert Dollfuß." in *Österreich 1933–1938: Interdisziplinäre Bestandsaufnahmen und Perspektive*, edited by Ilse Reiter-Zatloukal et al. Vienna: Böhlau, 2012.

Encarnación, Omar. "Reconciliation after Democratization: Coping with the Past in Spain." *Political Science Quarterly* 123 (2008).

———. *Spanish Politics: Democracy after Dictatorship*, Cambridge, UK: Polity Press, 2008.

Ferrandiz, Francisco. "Exhuming the Defeated: Civil War Mass Graves in 21st-Century Spain." *American Ethnologist*, vol. 40 (2013).

Fritz, Regina. *Nach Krieg und Judenmord: Ungarns Geschichtspolitik seit 1944*. Göttingen: Wallstein, 2012.

Gentile, Emilio. *Qu'est-ce que le fascisme? Histoire et interprétation*. Paris: Gallimard, 2004.

Gerbel, Christian, and Rossalina Latcheva. "Cultures of Remembrance of World War II and the Holocaust in Austria, Poland, Hungary and the Czech Republic." in *Authoritarianism, History and Democratic Dispositions in Austria, Poland, Hungary and the Czech Republic*, edited by Oliver Rathkolb and Günther Ogris. Innsbruck: Studien Verlag, 2010.

Guggenberger, Günther. "The Reflection of Authoritarianism, Anomia and Group-related Misanthropy in Remembrance of the Authoritarian Regime and World War II in Austria." in *Authoritarianism, History and Democratic Dispositions in Austria, Poland, Hungary and the Czech Republic*, edited by Oliver Rathkolb and Günther Ogris. Innsbruck: Studien Verlag, 2010.

Klimó, Árpád v. "Hungary." in *Authoritarianism, History and Democratic Dispositions in Austria, Poland, Hungary and the Czech Republic*, edited by Oliver Rathkolb and Günther Ogris. Innsbruck: Studien Verlag, 2010.

Kriechbaumer, Robert. *Parteiprogramme im Widerstreit der Interessen: Die Programmdiskussion und die Programme von ÖVP und SPÖ 1945–1986*. Vienna: Verlag für Geschichte und Politik, 1990.

Musiedlack, Didier. *Mussolini*. Paris: Presses de sciences po, 2005.

Neugebauer, Wolfgang. *Der österreichische Widerstand 1938–1945*. Vienna: Edition Steinbauer, 2008.

Pennerstorfer, Paul. "Das Gedenken an die Februarkämpfe 1934: Geschichtsbilder und Geschichtspolitiken von ÖVP und SPÖ 1946–1964." Vienna: Diplomarbeit, University of Vienna, 2012.

Pinto, Antonio C. "The Authoritarian Past and South European Democracies: An Introduction." in *Dealing with the Legacy of Authoritarianism: The "Politics of the Past" in Southern European Democracies*, edited by António C. Pinto. London: Routledge, 2013.

Pokorny, Alexander, et al., eds. *Durch die Vergangenheit zur Gegenwart 7*. Vienna: Veritas, 2004.

Rathkolb, Oliver. "Epilogue." in *Authoritarianism, History and Democratic Dispositions in Austria, Poland, Hungary and the Czech Republic*, edited by Oliver Rathkolb and Günther Ogris. Innsbruck: Studien Verlag, 2010.

Weiss, Hilde. *Nation und Toleranz?* Vienna: Braumüller Verlag, 2004.

Figure 1. Pian della Mussa, Italy.

Figure 2. First publication of the Montanara.

Figure 3. Monument of the Bersaglieri, Pian della Mussa, Italy.

Figure 4. Sarcophagus of Saint Charles Borromeo, Milan Cathedral, Milan (Italy).

Figure 5. *Magasin Pittoresque* 1843, p. 209. Gallica (Bibliothèque Nationale de France, NUMP-360).

Figure 6. Plague column in Vienna (Austria).

Figure 7. Plague column in Vienna (Austria). Johann August Corvinus (nach Salomon Kleiner): *Die Pestsäule in Wien*, Kupferstich, 1724.

Figure 8. Plague column in Vienna (Austria). Coat of arms of Austria.

Figure 9. Plague column in Vienna (Austria). Coat of arms of Austria.

Figure 10. Plague column in Vienna (Austria). Coat of arms of Hungary.

Figure 11. Plague column in Vienna (Austria). Coat of arms of Bohemia.

Figure 12. Plague column in Klagenfurt (Austria).

Figure 13. *Der liebe Augustin* (1940), film directed by E. W. Emo.

Berühmte

Unglücksfälle

von

M. D. Chavannes.

Wien.

Jacob Wallner's Verlags-Buchhandlung.

Stadt, Petersplatz Nr. 562 alt; 2 neu.

Figure 14. *Berühmte Unglücksfälle* by H. de Chavannes de la Giraudière.

Figure 15. Mirosław Bałka, *AuschwitzWieliczka*, Kraków June 2014, photograph by Tomasz Łysak.

Figure 16. Wojciech Wilczyk, *Lubań Śląski, synagogue, 11.04.2007,* from the series *Niewinne oko nie istnieje/There's No Such Thing As an Innocent Eye*, 2009.

Figure 17. Łukasz Baksik, *Surface of a square. Zator, a town in the Małopolska Province. 1939–45,* 2012.

Figure 18. Sławomir Sierakowski as a young Polish leader in Yael Bartana's *Mary Koszmary,* 2008, video still by Tomasz Łysak.

Figure 19. Rafał Betlejewski, *I miss you, Jew,* in Brzeska Street, Warsaw, February 2013, photograph by Tomasz Łysak.

Figure 20. Diorama of the Czech sea in the film *Jára Cimrman, ležící, spící* (screenshot).

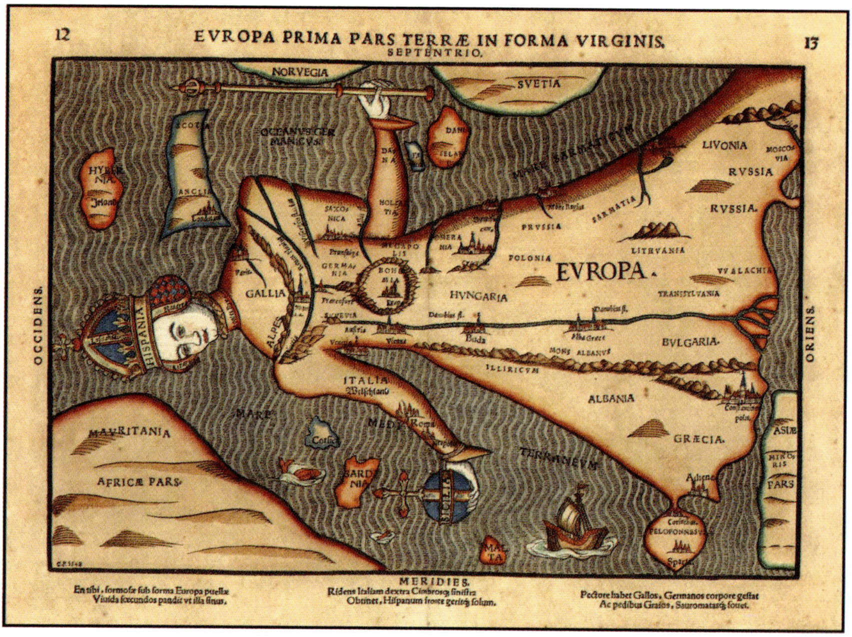

Figure 21. Heinrich Bunting, *Europa Prima Pars Terrae In Forma Virginis*, 1548.

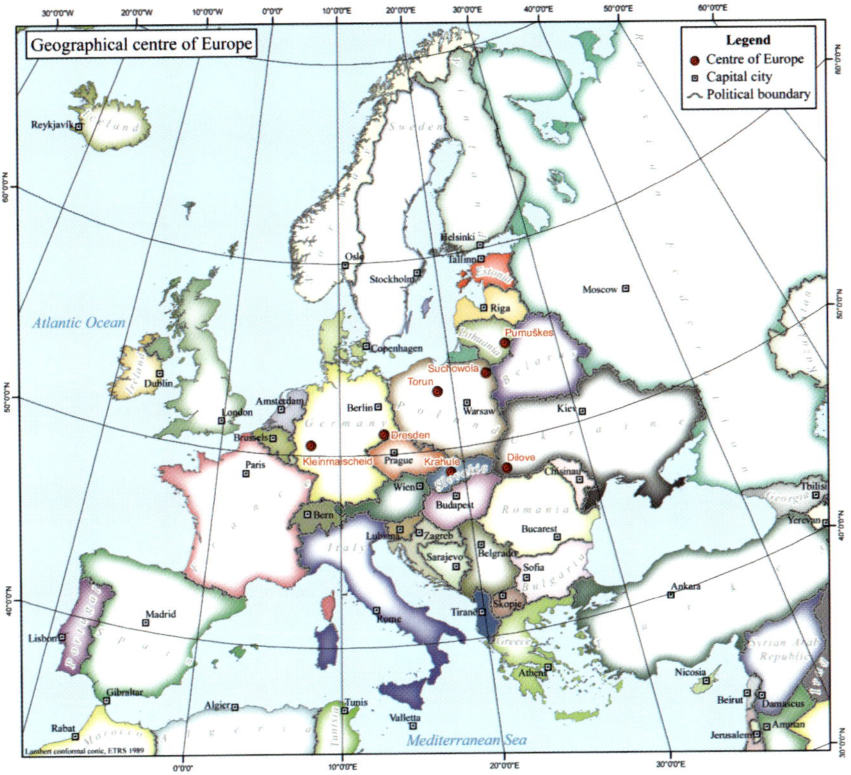

Figure 22. Seven "Centers of Europe" according to Wikipedia. http://en.wikipedia.org/wiki/Geographical_midpoint_of_Europe#mediaviewer/File:Centre_of_Europe.jpg.

Figure 23. "Continental drift" according to *The Economist*, April 29, 2010.

Figure 24. Cover of the novel *Les années Lamalif* by Zakya Daoud.

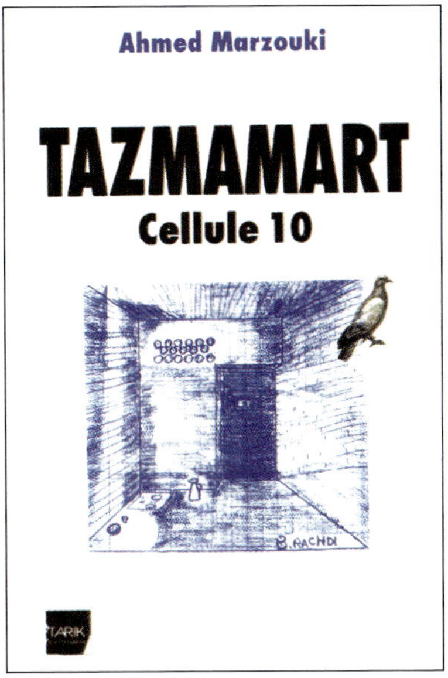

Figure 25. Cover of the novel *Tazmamart Cellule 10* by Ahmed Marzouki.

Figure 26. Cover of the novel *Le Couloir* by Abdelfettah Fakihani.

Figure 27. Cover of the novel *Présumé coupable* by Khalid Jamaï.

Figure 28. Cover of the novel *Une odeur de mantèque* by Mohamed Khair-Eddine.

Figure 29. Cover of the novel *Le plumier* by Henri Michel Boccara.

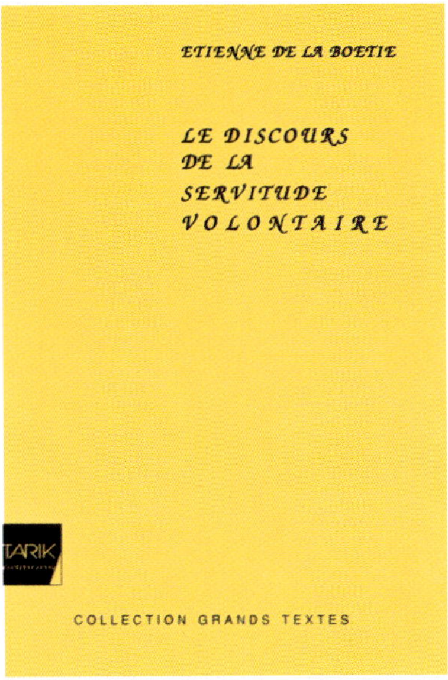

Figure 30. Cover of *Le Discours de la servitude volontaire* by Etienne de La Boétie.

The picture sequence on the pages that follow was prepared by Jason Francisco (Emory University) to accompany Roma Sendyka's paper "Prism: Understanding Non-Sites of Memory." On each page, Francisco juxtaposes archival photographs of the former Płaszów concentration camp in Kraków, and his own contemporary photographs of Płaszów. The wartime photographs (except one) were done by Raimund Titsch in 1943–1944 and are part of the Leopold Page Photographic Collection [now in the holdings of the US Holocaust Memorial Museum, the collections of Yad Vashem, Instytut Pamieci Narodowej (Poland), Bildarchiv Preussischer Kulturbesitz (Germany)]. The anonymous photograph comes from the archives of Interpress (Poland). For more on Jason Francisco's work on Płaszów, see his project, *Time in Płaszów* [http://jasonfrancisco.net/time-in-paszw].

Trailhead sign at an entrance to the Płaszów camp, 2011.

Jewish prisoners in Płaszów at forced labor, 1943-44 (USHMM #03400).

Jewish prisoners in Płaszów at forced labor, 1943-1944 (USHMM #05272).

Mother and child playing beside a Płaszów memorial, 2011.

Friends relaxing beside a mass grave at Płaszów, 2011.

View of a barracks at the Płaszów camp, 1943-1944 (USHMM #02318).

Jewish prisoners in Płaszów at forced labor, 1943-1944 (USHMM #50701).

Sunbathers in the former Płaszów camp, 2010.

Sunbather atop Jewish gravestones in the former Płaszów camp, 2010.

Jewish prisoners in Płaszów at forced labor, 1943-1944 (USHMM #03391).

Jewish prisoners carry cloth to the Madritch factor in Płaszów, 1943-1944 (USHMM #50666).

Teenagers relaxing in the former Płaszów camp, 2011.

A man at target practice in the former Płaszów camp, 2011.

Jewish prisoners in Płaszów at forced labor, 1943-1944 (USHMM #50704).

The Płaszów camp, 1943-1944 (USHMM #32058).

Boys playing war games in the former Płaszów camp, 2011.

FORGOTTEN HISTORIES: WORKERS AND THE NEW CAPITALISM IN EAST GERMANY AND HUNGARY*

Eszter Bartha**

Abstract

By drawing on Kideckel (2002) and Todorova and Gille (2010), this article seeks to (1) explore forms of workers' new subalternity in the new capitalist regimes in East Germany and Hungary, and (2) argue that nostalgia for the socialist regimes functions as a means and claim of the "little man" to express social criticism. Under state socialism, workers constituted the emblematic class of the regime. After the collapse of the socialist regimes in Eastern Europe, workers faced the double challenge of the decline of the political weight and significance of the working class and the devaluation of production work in a postindustrial society.

The essay analyzes the postsocialist experience of East German and Hungarian workers in three main dimensions: (1) the experience of post-Fordist development in the factory, (2) the subjective evaluation of the standard of living, and (3) interpersonal relations. Lastly, I examine the social and political attitudes of the workers in the mirror of their postsocialist experience.

I argue that Hungarians had a more direct experience of peripheral development than East Germans. While East Germany's more successful integration into the capitalist world economy was accompanied by a change of mentality and the

---

* This paper was written with the support of the Bolyai Fellowship of the Hungarian Academy of Sciences.

** Eszter Bartha is a Senior Research Fellow in the Center for Social Sciences of the Hungarian Academy of Sciences.

appearance of post-materialistic values, in Hungary nationalism seemed to be the only alternative to capitalism, which had disappointed and effectively impoverished many people. This explains the ambiguous evaluation of the socialist Kádár regime, as the vision of greater social and material equality came to be confused with a longing for a strong state, order, and an autocratic government.

New Capitalism and the Socialist Working Class

David Kideckel recalled his first trip to the Jiu Valley mining town in Romania with the observation that people to whom he told of his interest in labor, miner working conditions and the impact of unemployment, would ask him in return whether he was a Communist (Kideckel 2002). Later he went on to argue that

> the region's problematic is not too slow a movement to capitalism (as "transition" would have it) but too fast; not too little capitalism but too much. Rather than postsocialist, it is better understood as "neo-capitalist," a social system that reworks basic capitalist principles in new, even more inegalitarian ways than the Western model from which it derives. . . . There have been some exceptions. Some joint ventures with enterprises of the developed capitalist world have given workers reasonable wages and job security. The dominant trends, however, have been to sanctify individualized ownership at the expense of social equity, to pursue inappropriate loan policies, and to facilitate a corrupt bargain between owning and political classes at the expense of labor. Industrial workers have fallen to near the bottom of the economic and social scale, there is still no effective middle class, and class boundaries are further solidified. (Kideckel 2002, 115)[1]

These observations show a remarkable similarity to the arguments of left-wing intellectuals in Hungary. Erzsébet Szalai, for instance, also prefers to call postsocialist societies "neocapitalist regimes,"[2] while Nigel Swain, who conducted fieldwork in Hungary in the 1970s and wrote a book about the socialist system as it existed after the economic reforms (Swain 1992), speaks of postsocialist capitalism (Swain 2011). The reason why I cited Kideckel at length is twofold. First, he offers an explanation for the "blank spot" in the Hungarian (and,

---

[1] This criticism is shared by Gowan (1995); Watson (1993); Amsden et al. (1994); Slomczynski and Shabad (1997); Wedel (1998). From the Hungarian literature see also Huszár (2012; 2013).

[2] Szalai (2001; 2004a). On the unmaking of the Hungarian working class, see Szalai 2004b, although it should be noted that she does not consider the working class to be a class under socialism (Szalai 1986).

indeed, in general in the East-Central European) literature covering working-class life under postsocialism. Secondly, while Kideckel is critical of transition theory[3] (as is clear from the citation), he indeed argues that anthropology can offer a panacea for the shortcomings of the great paradigms and the dominant (legitimating) narratives as constructed by the new capitalist elites of the region.

As is well known, the "working class" throughout the Soviet bloc was closely linked with the Marxist-Leninist legitimating ideology of the state socialist regimes. This ideology proclaimed the working class to be the ruling class, in whose name the Communist Parties of the region governed the working people, the party serving as the vanguard of the working class.[4] The eventual and rapid collapse of Communist regimes across the region in 1989 discredited the legitimizing narratives of official working-class histories; the events of the year disproved notions of a simple equivalence between class position and class consciousness characterized by dominant trends in Marxist thought. In 1989 many Western left-wing intellectuals hoped that the socialist working classes, after getting rid of the tutelage of the Communist parties, would be mobilized against the restoration of capitalism and establish a democratic socialism based on workers' councils and self-governance.[5] Of course, this expectation proved to be wrong, and there was little effective working-class resistance to the introduction of a capitalist economy.[6] There was no country in Eastern Europe where workers supported any kind of democratic socialist alternative to the existing system. Nor was the East European political and intellectual climate favorable for revisiting working-class histories after the change of regimes: all forms of class theory were regarded as utterly discredited, and the working class was often uncritically associated with the state socialist past, as intellectual elites invested in a future based on "embourgeoisiement," which downplayed the social and political roles of industrial workers (Burawoy 1992).

Indeed, after the change of regimes anthropologists argued that the working class became the new subaltern class (Kideckel 2002; 2008; Buchowski 2001; Kalb 2009; Kalb and Halmai 2011). While subalternity was used by Rudolph Bahro (1977) to explain workers' location at the bottom

---

[3] For a discussion of the terminology, see Verdery (1996); Snyder and Vachudova (1997); Hann (2002); Humphrey (2002); Verdery (2002); Bartha (2010).

[4] For a review of the Western left-wing critical discourses of the Soviet Union, see Linden (2007).

[5] Burawoy, for instance, expressed this hope of the Western left-wingers in Burawoy (1985). Burawoy and Lukács (1992) rethink the potential of a socialist turn in the region.

[6] In Hungary the organization of workers' councils was a short-lived experiment. See Szalai (1994); Nagy (2012). After the political failure of this project, the Eszmélet-kör and the journal *Eszmélet* sought to preserve this intellectual tradition, which goes back to thinkers such as György Lukács and István Mészáros.

of a knowledge-based division of labor in socialism,[7] the transformation of socialist political economies has deepened the subalternalization of labor. Kideckel (2002) identifies eight key factors, which explain renewed and reinvigorated worker subalternity and its social decline, out of which this article mainly builds on two: (1) the devaluation of industrial work and loss of symbolic capital due to the expansion of the information society and globalized culture, and (2) the general dissolution of working-class social networks, encouraging their loss of energy and physical incapacity.

The loss of symbolic capital coincides with the economic processes of "transition." Even though the working class was nowhere a ruling class, the Communist parties held the large industrial working class to be their main social base and centered their social policy on this group. I argued elsewhere (Bartha 2013) that the standard-of-living policy implemented in Honecker's GDR and Kádár's Hungary did, in fact, orient working-class consciousness towards consumerism, which the socialist economies could not satisfy, and they had to finance their policies increasingly from loans (Steiner 2004; Földes 1995). Politically, however, the parties could not afford to reduce their outdated heavy industries because it would have destroyed the very basis of their social support.

After the change of regimes, the new elites constructed a legitimating narrative in which workers had no place other than as people who are "lazy," "unfit for a modern, capitalist society," "lacking the entrepreneurial spirit and initiative to set up their own business," and who "expect the state to support them." These stereotypes are by far not limited to Hungary. Dominic Boyer (2006) reports that in East Germany several journalists told him that speaking critically of unified German society was something they were loath to do because such criticism was immediately taken by their Western colleagues as a lack of commitment to democracy and a yearning for a return of the GDR. To illustrate the point of the essentially different *rights* of talking about the future as compared to the totality of a society, he cites a journalist who complained that while it was natural of the West Germans to ask their "Ossi" counterparts how they could have lived in such a totalitarian regime, they would not understand the reverse question: how can one live in a society where so many people are unemployed or threatened with unemployment (Boyer 2006, 374) or where—as in the case of Hungary—sociologists showed the existence of a large underclass? (Ladányi 2012; Ferge 2012). Or take the example of Poland, where Michal Buchowksi writes: "The voice of the powerless and the poor passes virtually unheard. They have to resort to radical methods if they want to articulate their interests. Then, however, they are described as uncouth and ignorant about the new deal. They are simply created as 'new others' of transitions" (Buchowski 2001; 15).

[7] See also Konrád and Szelényi (1979). For a discussion of the internal stratification of labor under socialism, see Kemény (1990); Héthy and Makó (1975).

While it counts as a truism that the workers' state—as it was understood from a left-wing, socialist perspective—was not realized anywhere in Eastern Europe, it is worth asking the reverse question: what actually *has been* realized? The clarification of this question would help us revisit the nostalgia for the Kádár regime in Hungary: we should not explain everything through comments such as "the workers are nostalgic for a regime where they did not have to work so hard" or where "they had a better position," nor with statements that nostalgia serves as a means through which the losers of the change of regimes seek to upgrade their self-esteem. Eastern European nostalgia (*Ostalgie*) has been a topic of recent discussions in order to explain the eventual disappointment of Eastern European citizens with the newly established, capitalist regimes.[8] It cannot be the intention here to give a review of this literature; I just want to clarify my own position in the debate. I argue that the validity of the memories of the socialist past should not be dismissed as a mere nostalgia for a lost youth or for a time when workers were ranked higher in society than today. I cite here Frances Pine: "When people evoked the 'good' socialist past, they were not denying the corruption, the shortages, the queues and the endless intrusions and infringements of the state; rather, they were choosing to emphasize other aspects: economic security, full employment, universal healthcare and education" (Pine 2002, 111). Working-class community life was recalled with a sense of loss in both the German and Hungarian interviews. While in East Germany we cannot, of course, observe the growth of an underclass, the Hartz legislation introduced between 2003 and 2005 rendered the situation of the unemployed more difficult, and one can, indeed, observe the "ghettoization" of the formerly privileged Neubau (blocks of flats), where only the unemployed, the poor, and immigrants live today. *Ostalgie* can thus be understood as a *conscious comparison* between a however malfunctioning socialism and the hard, everyday life reality of neoliberal capitalism (Boyer 2010). I therefore underline that *Ostalgie* is not a discourse constructed by the losers of the change of regime; it is, essentially a way and *claim* to express social criticism.

The Data

I examine workers' everyday life experience and collective memory of the change of regimes in East Germany and Hungary through life-history interviews that I collected in both countries between 2002 and 2004. I focus on the group that was supposed to be the main beneficiary of the party's policy towards labor in both countries: the large skilled and urban industrial working class.[9] I collected forty life-history interviews in both Carl Zeiss Jena and

---

[8] See, e.g., Todorova and Gille (2010). See also Todorova's introduction (Todorova 2010).

[9] Pittaway (2011; 2012) and Földes (1989) argue that the support of the large, skilled, urban industrial working class was crucial for Hungary's Communist Parties.

Rába in Győr, the two large factories whose state socialist pasts I examined in the light of archival sources. There were an equal number of men and women among my interview partners, and also of workers who could keep their jobs after the change of regimes (both factories survived the change with radically reduced personnel) and those who were dismissed/retired. The majority of the interview partners were 38–60 years old at the time of interviewing; namely, I looked for workers who had work experience under both regimes. The majority of them were skilled workers; however, I also interviewed foremen, white-collar workers, and the retrained employees of the new service sector (mainly in the East German case). In some stories we can observe an upward social mobility: among the pensioners there were skilled workers, who were educated under state socialism and promoted to be engineers, production managers, or economists; they, however, continued to have a working-class identity or they preserved their ties to the working class (therefore they wanted to be interviewed). In quoting the interviews, I sought to preserve the individual language use of the speakers, which I tried to give back in translation (although the majority of the German workers made a conscious effort to use "standard" German). In addition, I used forty other interviews conducted in 2010 with Hungarian workers of the catering sector and the building industry,[10] and ten interviews that I conducted in Halle with workers and foremen in 2014.

"This market economy knocked us out"

The immediate experience of the change of regimes was different in the two countries. In East Germany mass demonstrations indicated the collapse of the legitimation of the Honecker regime, while in Hungary the ruling Communist Party MSZMP (Magyar Szocialista Munkáspárt, Hungarian Socialist Workers' Party) agreed with the opposition about holding democratic elections.[11] To contrast these two essentially different experiences of the change of regimes (in the GDR people participated, whereas in Hungary they felt that the negotiations were a "business" of the new elite), it is worth citing from an interview I conducted in an unusual "terrain" in East Germany with a Zeiss worker (*Zeissianer*) who had been imprisoned in the Honecker era for his oppositionist political activity. In the summer of 1989, he left the GDR

[10] The interviews were used with the permission of András Tóth.

[11] The change of regime in Hungary has been referred to as "negotiated revolution" or "constitutional revolution." On the political history of the roundtable discussions (the negotiations among MSZMP and the new parties), see Bozóki (2000). For a study of the historical roots of the peaceful transition, see Tokés (1996). For the GDR, see Maier (1997).

and he found new employment in Münich as a transport worker. After suffering an injury, he lost his job and he failed to find a new one. At the time of interviewing, he lived in a hostel for homeless people. This is how he recalled the socialist past in the light of his experience in the new, capitalist society:

> We were fifty people in the [oppositionist] group. We did not do big things: we published some posters and a journal in which we wrote that there is political repression in the GDR. In 1982 they [the Party] took the case very seriously. I was arrested and I spent six months in prison. When I was released, the organization had already been dissolved. There was no point to continue. I did not have any problem in the factory, I earned good money. What I did not like was that I could not have my own opinion. You could not say openly what you thought because there was constant spying on you, even in the pub or within the factory.
>
> They [the Party] declared everything to be anti-state activity and subversion. "You [the Party] made a mistake"—this was impossible to say. "The Party decides everything, without the Party the grass does not grow and people can't breathe"—this was the general attitude. People wanted to think for themselves, make suggestions, better things—no one listened. The Party is always right, you should not think, you should just do your work. They wanted to deprive people of their ability to think. People should just do their work and leave the serious things to the leadership. I don't see a change in this. Those who are at the top don't want people to think. *Today I don't see a really big difference between the two systems, socialism and capitalism.*[12]

Jan's life history is not a typical East German working-class career. The citation, however, reflects a crucial difference between the subjective evaluations of the two welfare dictatorships. In East Germany, no one, including Jan, who lost his job and his home in the new regime, wanted Honecker's state back. In the Hungarian interviews we meet a more ambiguous picture: the desire for greater social and material equality triggers a longing for a strong state, order, and an autocratic government, which is expected to restore national pride, protect Hungarian industry, and increase the standard of living

[12] Citation from an interview conducted with Jan (52), an East German male production worker, in a hostel for homeless people in Jena in 2004. He was a skilled worker in Zeiss until 1989; at the time of the interview he was unemployed.

of the working people—the latter being the most attractive "catchword" of the Kádár regime.[13]

On the basis of the interviews, I distinguished between three dimensions of postsocialist experience: (1) the world of labor, (2) subjective evaluation of the standard of living and the level of integration into consumer society, and (3) interpersonal relations. The first dimension is divided into two different types of experience: half of the interviewees in both groups experienced transition in the factory, while the other half lost their jobs or were sent to early retirement. The transition to post-Fordism was an essentially different experience in the two countries.[14] The Rába workers unanimously constructed "narratives of decline" about the postsocialist history of their factory: the managers decreased production, the new proprietors refused to invest in innovation and the technical development of the factory, and they profited by selling the valuable estates of Rába and laying off workers who had worked there for many years, since the plants had been built by the legendary Communist manager Ede Horváth. Many workers argued that the proprietors intentionally destroyed production in order to make a profit from the sale of the estates. Workers' grievances were frequently translated into full-fledged conspiracy theories, as we see below:

> Because you can see that in the West, the state protects the national enterprises. But look at the Wagon Factory.[15] It was a profitable enterprise, and now I think that there is a will to destroy it so that it can't be a competitor. I can see through these practices. Győr had famous textile factories. All of them were sold to the competitor [Western] firms, and they were all closed or destroyed otherwise.[16]

The above citation nicely illustrates how the workers' grievances are translated into an ethnic–populist discourse, in which the "multinational" (Western) capital identified with the "traitor" domestic elite destroys Hungarian industry, thereby becoming responsible for the misery of the workers, who lose the secure existence guaranteed under the Kádár regime. To stress the decline, many workers explicitly contrasted the glorious era of Rába under Ede

---

13 See also Bartha (2011).

14 For a criticism of post-Fordism, see Boltanski and Chiapello (2005).

15 The local name of Rába.

16 Citation from an interview conducted with Péter (49), a Hungarian male production worker, in Rába in 2002. He was a skilled worker and a shop steward.

Horváth, when Rába exported its products to the COMECON–countries and the United States and enjoyed wide press and media coverage as a successful socialist company, with the "lean years" of the 1990s:

> In the old times it was an honor to work in the Wagon Factory. I was so proud when my father first took me here at the age of eighteen, and that I am going to work in the famous Wagon Factory . . . and now here I am [sigh]. And if they give me notice, I don't know what I will do. Distributing newspapers, cleaning offices or flats . . . sadly, there is nothing else. And this is so frightening! In addition, I married late: my daughter has just started secondary school and my son will go to university next year. If we were only the two of us, my husband and me, it would not be so bad. But I have to support them, and both of them are excellent students, which is my biggest problem because both will go to university because I cannot let them go to work after secondary school.[17]

The Hungarian workers unanimously argued that the history of their factory was that of a history of decline after 1989, which they blamed on management at the local level and on the multinational companies and the state's failure to protect successful enterprises at the national level. Post-Fordist innovation and development was represented by Audi, which they experienced as the humiliation of their company: Audi, in fact, bought the giant hall, which Ede Horváth built with the purpose of bringing the production of motor cars back to Győr. Rába workers recalled bitterly that under Ede Horváth, Rába was the main sponsor of the town: it built a stadium, and it could boast about a football team, a house of culture, a well-equipped library, an orchestra, a choir, and a dance group. After the change of regimes, Audi became the main sponsor of Győr, which Rába workers held to be the unjust consequence of tax exemption (which they blamed on the government).

The Zeiss experience differed from the "narratives of decline" characteristic of the Rába workers. The company implemented massive lay-offs: the chairman of the enterprise council (*Betriebsrat*) estimated that around 16,000 people lost their jobs in the first few years after the *Wende*. The company mainly lost the young work force because young skilled workers were expected

[17] Citation from an interview conducted with Judit (50), a Hungarian female production worker, in Rába in 2002. She was a skilled worker who finished secondary school.

to find new jobs in West Germany more easily than middle-aged family men. In 1995 a further 600 workers had to be given notice.[18] The Zeiss picture was, however, more ambiguous than the Hungarian experience. Workers in fact had positive experiences with the post-Fordist model of production because the new proprietor, the West German Zeiss, modernized the plants, bought new machines and technology and made significant investments in the town of Jena. Workers reported improving working conditions (competitive salaries, the installation of air conditioning, new bathrooms and canteens, flexible working hours). They noted, however, that they had to work under greater stress and tension than in the old production regime.

"Narratives of decline" are essentially missing from the East German interviews. Unlike the Hungarians, the East German workers, including a former party secretary who told me that he continued to hold himself to be a Communist, did not mention such cases of corruption and the deception of the people in relation to privatization. Instead, the East Germans explained the massive layoffs through the collapse of the COMECON-market and the rise in the price of production.

Unemployment was unmistakably the most negative experience that the East German interviewees had to face after the change of regimes. In contrast, this was a far less palpable fear and experience in Győr.[19] The Hungarian interviewees thought that whoever wanted to work could find "something" in Győr; indeed, anti-Roma attitudes were often justified with the reasoning that Roma people who lived from social security and child-care allowances could find employment if they really wanted to work. For the East German workers privatization was not associated with corruption, the decline of the company, and the rise of a rival Western firm such as Audi in Győr. Unemployment was, however, a constant source of tension and fear, which all interviewees had to face either personally or through the fate of their relatives/partners/children. Long-term unemployment meant not only exclusion from the respected world of labor but also social isolation, which often led to severe psychological problems. Some interviewees even spoke of the clinical treatment and eventual suicide of their male partners, who were long-term unemployed.

---

[18] Information from an interview conducted with Thorsten (52), the chairperson of the enterprise council in Zeiss in 2003. He was a production worker before 1989, and a member of the Church opposition. He received a religious education, for which he was discriminated against at school and was rejected admission to an art school he had wanted to attend. One of his sisters immigrated to West Germany, which rendered him even more suspicious in the eyes of the authorities. After the *Wende* he became actively involved in the reorganization of the trade union.

[19] Official unemployment was less than 5% in Gyor at the time of the interviews, while it was twice as high in Jena.

The worst aspect of unemployment was not the material decline (although this, too, was mentioned) but the loss of face in front of other people, which had very negative psychological consequences. The interviewees who were affected by long-term unemployment would often mention that their working relatives/friends/acquaintances refused to believe that they couldn't find work, and some even held them to be lazy people, who lived on social benefits. Many voluntarily chose to lock themselves up in order to avoid the regrettable comments. Those who agreed to give me an interview all said that they made a conscious effort *not* to fall into this trap: they used existing networks that were formed in the GDR or joined other communities (e.g., one female production worker did voluntary work for the trade union) and self-help groups. (The son of one of the interviewees, who found no regular employment for many years, joined a group of unemployed people who exchanged services).

In the second dimension—a subjective evaluation of the standard of living—we can also observe striking differences between the two groups. The overwhelming majority of the German interviewees reported improvement in their material conditions: those who had work spoke of material prosperity, which allowed them to build family houses, buy new cars, and spend their vacations in exotic foreign countries, while the unemployed positively mentioned the improvement of services and the supply of consumer goods. The Hungarian interviewees, on the contrary, held their material situation to be the continuation of their "narratives of decline": they all reported stagnation or the decline of their standard of living, which they considered to be the most painful experience of the change of regimes. The Kádár regime was calculable: even though the urban skilled workers admitted that the regime could not fulfill great material aspirations, they held realistic goals for themselves: an urban flat or a family house in the country, a car, a weekend plot, and regular holidays. The new regime offered them no such possibilities; even those who said they could maintain their former standard of living claimed they no longer had to support their children, but if they had to, they would have to content themselves with a poorer quality of life. Those who had school-age children bitterly spoke of the rise of the new material inequalities:

> My children are not demanding and they fully understand that we can't afford as much as others. But I really feel guilty because they are left out of so many things . . . When there is a school excursion and we pick up my son, I always tell my husband: "Leave the car at the back of the parking lot so that the other children won't see that we have such an old car."[20]

---

[20] Citation from an interview conducted with Judit (50), a Hungarian female production worker, in Rába in 2002.

In the research, the overwhelming majority of the workers reported that they lived worse now than they had in the past. In order to make ends meet, many interviewees had to renounce such "luxuries" as traveling, eating out in restaurants (let alone cheap ones), and maintaining a car. People who lived in single-income households were in a particularly bad financial situation. They reported having experienced the most radical decline. I interviewed a female skilled worker who was divorced, and she provided for her three children from one wage in the Kádár regime until she met her second husband. At the time of the interview, she lived on a disability pension. Her second husband was a technician in Rába, and they raised one common child. After her illness, the family sold their urban flat, and they moved to a nearby village in the hope that life would be cheaper there:

> In Győr we lived in a block of flats, heating was very expensive, and we thought that it would be cheaper to live in the country. We spent all our savings, and now we literally live from one wage to the next, believe it or not. We support only one child, we spend only on the basic necessities, and here we are, because the wage is so low. My husband earns 100,000 HUF, but after taxation he brings 70,000 home, including the child-care allowance. And he is a leading technician. In the 1980s we lived much better, and we had to support four children back then. We fed them, they went to school, and we could still maintain a car, buy a TV, video, other things. But now we can buy nothing. *I think that the Kádár regime was much better for us than this system.*[21] Because it also gave something to the poor. There were not so great differences between people. Today, one to one-and-a-half million people live in real misery in Hungary.[22]

While the Hungarian interviewees unanimously held the working class to be the main loser of the change of regimes, the East Germans preferred to criticize the crystallization of social hierarchies in the new regime. The unemployed mentioned that they were "second-class" consumers in the German society because they could afford considerably less than their acquaintances with a job. However, while in Hungary many workers continued to measure the success of the government against the standard of living, the East Germans expressed no wish for the return of the Honecker regime. Not even Jan, who

---

[21] Emphasis is mine.

[22] Citation from an interview conducted with Éva (54), a Hungarian skilled female production worker, in her house in 2004.

lost his job and his home in the new regime, considered "the workers' state" a viable alternative. In the East German case, we can observe a gradual shift towards post-materialistic values: the unemployed Dora could have found a job in Hamburg, but she decided to live in Jena because of the proximity of her friends; many workers called attention to the new, environmentally friendly technologies, which cleared the air of the town; many explicitly criticized consumption for consumption's sake; and some participated in self-help groups or did some other form of voluntary work. In Hungary, the workers explicitly complained of the loss of existing networks; no one mentioned voluntary work; and many Hungarian rural female workers expressed an explicit wish for the return of the Kádár regime, when their families had a safer and often better life.[23] In the Hungarian case, material values continued to dominate political thinking. Since they saw no alternative value system to consumerism, the feelings of deprivation and frustration were prevalent among the interviewees.

The perceived lack of social integration takes us to the third dimension: interpersonal relations. Here we can find a common criticism of capitalist society, which can be explained through the shared experience in a system that advocated more egalitarianism. Interviewees in both groups reported negative changes in interpersonal relations: working-class communities were destroyed as a result of layoffs and a fierce competition for jobs, people at the workplace are individualized and atomized, solidarity has declined and everybody is focused only on himself/herself. People consciously reduce private contacts because they are afraid to open up and display their weaknesses, which the others can use against them. German interviewees used military terms to express the intensification of competition: they spoke of lonely fighters (*Einzelkämpfer*), two-thirds society (*Zwei-Drittel Gesellschaft*),[24] and racing society (*Ellbogengesellschaft*). Interviewees in both groups recalled the collegiality and intensive community life under socialism with a sense of loss:

> There was a great collegiality, which we could all feel at the festive occasions. On such occasions we all had to listen to the official political talks, but then we drank together, danced—I

[23] Unemployment can, of course, redefine gender relations within a family (see, e.g., Pine 2002; Rudd 2006).

[24] The two-thirds society refers to a society wherein two-thirds of the population belongs to the middle or upper classes. In Germany it was argued that the two-thirds would mean the employed, while one-third is condemned to live from social and unemployment benefits and/or "black work." In Hungary the interviewees did not use this term; however, the citations suggest that they would have agreed with the concept of the reverse two-thirds society developed for postsocialist Eastern Europe: that two-thirds of society fell out of the middle class.

> actually played Western music and all the comrades were dancing and no one cared who is party member and who is not. This collegiality does not exist anymore. Today I would rather speak of the freedom of race in society. Everybody pursues only his or her goals, and there is no solidarity. This was the advantage of the socialist system, and that's why—you see, I am interested in politics—what the leftists say, finds resonance in the GDR. We are responsive because what they say corresponds to the values according to which we were socialized. Perhaps we are also corrupted. [He laughs.][25]

Alex was a retired entrepreneur, who worked as a production manager until the Wende; then he founded his own firm, which was successful for ten years. Then, however, his firm, which was engaged in gardening and planting trees, won an order for the parking of a huge area of land:

> . . . and then all of a sudden, the chief entrepreneur who contracted us went bankrupt. That was pure capitalism as we learnt it at school. Marx…I am a kind of social democrat . . . that was pure capitalism. So, we went bankrupt. My wife earned well. She was a physiotherapist—she was also retrained—and this is how we survived.

Alex was later employed as a trainer for gardeners, and then he went into early retirement. In spite of his bad experience with capitalism, he did not want back the Honecker regime, but he remained critical of unified Germany:

> We became *die neue Bundesländer*—the Sicily of Italy. The poorhouse of West Germany. Unemployment, no money, social problems that we did not have under the GDR . . . you don't know the expression: the stupid who stayed? This is how the West Germans ridicule the East Germans. We don't want the GDR back, but we want them [the West Germans] to recognize our histories, our lives, our professions, our families, and our values. But the West refuses to do that.

Dominic Boyer depicts a similar picture of West Germany denying that the time of the socialist other is synchronous with their own time.[26] Hence, Boyer

---

[25] Citation from an interview conducted with Alex (65) in his home in 2014.
[26] See also Hann (2013).

argues, the whole concept of *Ostalgie* is a symptom less of East German nostalgia than of West German utopianism. Alex's criticism of "the stupid other" was developed along the same lines as Boyer's argument that future-orientedness is "reserved" for West Germans; East Germans are put in their place with the charge of being "corrupted" by a totalitarian regime or even contemptuously labeled as "homo Sovieticus."

But far from wishing Honecker's regime back, Alex later recalled his encounters with the Stasi with the observation that had the regime survived, he would have lost his position as a production manager because he was reported even on the eve of collapse to be critical of the GDR. (He had asked at a production conference how to explain the mass escape of East German citizens that occurred with the opening of the Hungarian borders). He, however, argued—alongside nearly all my German interview partners— that Nazism could not be compared to "actually existing" socialism because the original ideas that lay behind them were not comparable.

As is clear from Alex's story, he tried to preserve East German community values and was also socially engaged in the Church and in a music group. He admitted that as a capitalist, he was a failure ("I don't have a family house because I cannot afford it"), but he declared himself to be satisfied with his life.

While the Hungarians typically argued that their deteriorating material situation forced them to reduce social contacts (they could no longer afford restaurants, parties, and common holidays),[27] the East Germans like Alex explained the disintegration of the old communities through the fierce competition characteristic of the new regime. They argued that technological development renders part of society redundant, which creates a sharper competition for jobs than what they experienced in the old regime. This has resulted in an extensive individualization in society, the loss of the old collegial, communitarian spirit and more intensive fighting against rivals at the workplace, the reduction of private contacts among colleagues, secrecy (to prevent others benefitting from individual knowledge), and atomization. Workers in both groups stressed that under the socialist regime people related differently to each other: communities were stronger, and interpersonal relations were less directed towards profit-making, social advancement, and material interest. More people were willing to work voluntarily and free for the community than under the new regime. The disintegration of workplace

---

[27] Utasi conducted a nationwide survey in Hungary, from which she concluded that the poorer classes can only count on their immediate families and that social trust is very low in Hungary. See Utasi (2008).

communities was thus an equally negative experience for both groups—it is not accidental that this was the dimension triggering the most similar criticism of the new regime.

As the above comparison shows, the structural differences between the two countries essentially shaped the everyday experience of postsocialist change. The peripheral experience of post-Fordism in Hungary was reflected in the workers' construction of the "narratives of decline," which blame the failure of catching-up development on external factors, and frequently follow the logic of conspiracy theories. The essentially similar critique of the new regime developed in the third dimension, however, suggests that the workers had a shared human experience under socialism, which they recalled with a sense of loss. This experience was voiced similarly by the workers of the two groups although their fears differed: Hungarians were mainly afraid of the material decline, while the East Germans' greatest fear was unemployment. This experience, however, did not discredit the new regime in the eyes of the East German workers as much as was the case in Hungary. Hungarian interviewees had no direct experience of the change of the political regime: none participated in demonstrations, and many maintained a distance from 1989: "It was not important for me to have a say in politics. I don't want to embellish the truth, but for me this [free elections] was not so important. If I want to be honest, I had my secure existence: I lived my life and we raised our children. I achieved everything possible *at my level.*[28] For me it was not the most important thing in what kind of issues I should have a say. I worked 12 hours a day. I also worked during the weekends. This is my honest answer to you."[29]

While the East Germans identified themselves with the *Wende* (either because they did not like Honecker's dictatorship, or because they supported German unification, or both) the Hungarians did not feel that it was *their* change of regimes. For the majority, it was the "business" of the elite; and, as disappointment grew with the worsening of their material situation, so did people lose trust in the democratic institutions, which were believed to breed corruption, the rule of the rich over the poor, and dishonest and deceitful practices, which everybody associated with privatization:

> I don't know what people profited from 1989. I had a more relaxed life under socialism, and I think that the majority of Hungarian people lived better under the Kádár regime [than they live today]. When this democracy came in, they sold

---

[28] Emphasis is mine.

[29] Citation from an interview conducted with Péter (49), a Hungarian male production worker, in Rába in 2002.

> everything that was movable in this country. I think that it is a horrible sin to privatize hospitals, the electronic and gas industries, the ambulance, because the new proprietors will rob the working people of all their savings and property. We learnt this in the Party school, and it is true. Today's Hungary is ruled by plundering capitalism. There are no regulations, no law, and no respect for morality. Everybody steals as much as he can.[30]

Those who harbored left-wing sympathies were strongly opposed to privatization. However, those who declared themselves to be "committed" anti-Communists had an equally negative opinion of privatization and the working of capitalism—the only exception being that they blamed the malfunctioning of Hungarian capitalism on the Communist functionaries, who in their opinion continued to govern the country:

> It was the dream of my youth to be self-employed, in today's term: an entrepreneur. But I hate this new term because it can be applied for practically anything today. No one respects individual skills or good craftsmanship. If I have money, I can open a restaurant, a beauty salon or a pharmacy. But it does not mean that I know something of the trade or the profession. If you have money, you don't need to know anything and you just employ people who know the business. But I would never equate this with the entrepreneurs of the past, who mastered their profession. I think that entrepreneurship underwent a huge dilution. Those who work hard are downgraded in this system. The only thing that matters is how you can sell things—no one is interested in the quality. It is a very superficial system, with very superficial values; this is my opinion.[31]

---

[30] Citation from an interview conducted with Tibor (67), a retired male manager, in his house in 2004. He started his career as a skilled worker in Rába, and he obtained his degree in adult education.

[31] Citation from an interview conducted with Miklós (51), a male self-employed plumber, in his house in 2004. He started his career as a skilled worker in Rába, and he also spent two years in the Soviet Union as a guest worker, which was a good "business" because the workers earned very well. As he proudly said, he could credit this only to his good work because he was never a member of the Party, and he disliked communists. (His father was a peasant whose land was nationalized, and he never forgave the communists.) Miklós became self-employed in 1981; in the 1990s he expanded his business, but he could not bear the stress, and after an operation he gave up his business, and he accepted a job as a maintenance man. He also worked "off the books" to secure a "normal" income.

Based on his ethnographic research conducted with artists and Orthodox Christians in contemporary Moscow, Zigon (2009) observed that hope can function as a temporal orientation of intentional ethical action in moments of what he calls a moral breakdown. I argue that in these moments people can choose to build their own dignity based on a moral superiority which they consciously contrast with the elite-propagated system of values they perceive to be superficial or outright lies. The calculable and socially secure socialist past was frequently contrasted with today's "plundering capitalism." Workers drew a sharp line between those who shared the old values of the significance and prestige of physical work and those, who rejected these values and benefited from the new regime, often through dishonest means:

> Plundering capitalism . . . the Communist gang, which was close to the fire, gained fortunes after the change of regimes. Everybody knows this, and it is a different question that the newspaper *Kisalföld* is silent on these issues. He [the manager] bought two dredgers, which the factory bought for 100,000 HUF, but he could buy them for 5,000 HUF when the unit was privatized. Nine out of ten enterprises were created this way in this country. I ask you: what is the difference between socialism and today's system? What was advocated after 1945—that everything belongs to the working people . . . now I ask you where is that property? Either it was sold to foreigners, or it went to the bank account of such Hungarian businessmen. I mean also the management of this factory, who are stealing the last pennies from the workers—here is the property![32]

We can observe in these interviews that Hungarian workers frequently constructed moral boundaries to separate the dishonest, exploitive "them" from "us." Privatization was perceived as the means of dispossession of the working people, who had spent their whole lives in the factory. The devaluation of their work and symbolic capital in the new, capitalist regime was connected with this feeling of dispossession and deprivation; their way of resistance was the assertion of a moral superiority, which functioned as a means of constructing an alternative discourse where the disturbed moral order would be restored.[33] This explains the apparent paradox that while there was a widespread nostalgia for the social security under the Kádár regime, the post-Communist elite was

[32] Interview with Miklós (51), a Hungarian male building entrepreneur, in his house in 2003.
[33] See also Bartha (2004).

held to be "inherently" corrupt and immoral. Political catchwords, such as the restoration of a moral order, would therefore find resonance among my interview partners.

Conclusion

Ost (2005) develops the argument that in Poland the liberal intellectuals betrayed the alliance with the working class, which had been formed in the Solidarity movement, and in response the disappointed workers chose to vote for the right or the extreme right, which promised them the restoration of national pride and the protection of the interests of the "little man." In the Hungarian case we can't speak of an alliance between the workers and the intellectuals after 1956. My research concludes that workers were not familiar with the concepts of self-governance and self-management developed by left-wing intellectuals, who were critical of state socialism; and many interviewees did not consider free parliamentary elections as something that was very important for their life or their identity. The corruption they directly experienced with privatization greatly undermined the credibility of democratic institutions and a market economy, which instead of the promised and expected prosperity only gave them a stagnating or outright declining standard of living and the experience of a sharpening material inequality between the workers and the new bourgeois classes (managers, bankers, lawyers, doctors, and businessmen; in other words, those who could be seen as the winners of the change of regimes). Like their Polish counterparts, many Hungarian workers were susceptible to nationalistic, populist "catchwords," which operated with a concrete enemy picture: "foreign," exploitive capital, multinational enterprises, which take the profit out of the country, etc. The feeling of ressentiment was intensified by the "conspicuous consumption" of the new elite, which rendered their own impoverishment all the more visible. The reasoning that this was possible because of the weakness of the state found many receptive ears: workers argued that a strong government was needed to take a firm stance against global capital.

It can't be said that the East Germans were not critical of the new democracy. They, however, made no distinction (as did the Hungarians) between Western capitalism, globalization, and "national" capitalism. Neither did they hold the uniformly rejected Honecker regime to be a special East German path towards modernity. They counted such institutions and social practices as the positive heritage of the GDR, which could be easily incorporated into the new left-wing ideologies: socially responsible thinking, the strengthening of communities, more social solidarity, and the increase of reciprocity in social life. This East German "identity"—if we understand it as open towards communitarian values and less consumption-oriented than the more materialistic West, and which is best described in Alex's story—can be easily reconciled with a post-materialistic value system, which stands in direct opposition to the materialistic Honecker regime. Therefore many interviewees declared themselves to "be in agreement" (*einverstanden*) with such political "catchwords" as environmental consciousness, sustainable development, and greater social responsibility. The East Germans did not criticize globalization; on the contrary, many workers thought that the multinational companies established new jobs, and they brought capital and innovation to Jena. They had a positive attitude towards the multiculturalism of university life, and they positively spoke of the appearance of foreign students in Jena;[34] some criticized only the *Deutschrussen* (ethnic Germans who lived in the former Soviet Union and were given German citizenship).[35] Anti-Fascist education played an important role in the political and social thinking of this age group: they all argued that war is the most horrible experience possible and that humankind should avoid it at any price (the overwhelming majority were born after the Second World War), and even the committed anti-Communists refused to compare the Nazi dictatorship with the Honecker regime because the former was held to be a lot more monstrous.

Opinions of West Germany varied across the interviewed group, but in general, the East Germans were more conscious of the nature of peripheral capitalism than the Hungarians. Many admitted that before the *Wende* they felt inferior to West Germans because they were strongly influenced by the stereotypical representation of capitalism; namely, Western workers are more educated, more creative, more diligent, and more motivated than the Eastern workers of the state-owned enterprises, who were held in the West to be less disciplined and "brainwashed."[36] The postsocialist years modified these stereotypes as East Germans grew more critical of capitalism: they said that albeit their technology was not as advanced as the West German, their skills were

---

[34] Jena has a famous university, Friedrich-Schiller-Universität, which accepted many ERASMUS-exchange students and other students from all over the world.

[35] The East German interview partners all knew prior to the interview that they would talk to a Hungarian citizen. Therefore, those who held strongly nationalistic views were unlikely to have participated in the research.

[36] Concerning this topic, some interview partners explicitly told me that they would not give an interview to a West German researcher because of the mutual stereotypes. In this respect, it was an advantage that I also came from a socialist country; further, Hungary was held to be a "friendly" and politically "liberal" country where East Germans could meet their West German relatives. The "liberalism" of the Hungarian Communist Party was observed by the SED functionaries as well.

comparable, and in fact they had to be more creative than the West Germans because of the technological deficiencies. (One example that they mentioned: if a machine went wrong, they had to be able to fix it, while the West Germans called a maintenance man). The majority were skeptical of the prospects of catching up with West Germany: they estimated that leveling would take at least 20–30 years. While they were familiar with the terms *Wessi/Ossi*,[37] they argued that this distinction would disappear in their children's generation.

While the East Germans could reconcile the socialist values "they learnt at school" with the values propagated by the left-wing parties, in the Hungarian case, workers could only construct moral boundaries between the corrupt, immoral, exploiting "them" and "us," which proved to be attractive catchwords for the emerging nationalistic, populist discourse. The results help us to explain the ambiguous evaluation of the Kádár regime. The vision of greater social and material equality is confused with a longing for a strong state, order, and an autocratic government, which we can observe in many interviews. While the German interviewees identified with the *Wende* (if not all of them with the German unification), and not even the unemployed wanted Honecker's state back, few Hungarians thought they had profited from the change of regimes and the newly established democracy. Thanks to their negative experiences, which triggered the above described "narratives of decline," the majority were opposed to "Western" capitalism, and they thought that a stronger state and a distinctive Hungarian path towards modernity would offer a panacea for the sores of peripheral development. While East Germany's greater success with integration into the capitalist world economy was accompanied by a change of mentality and the appearance of post-materialistic values, in Hungary nationalism seemed to be the only alternative to capitalism, which disappointed and effectively impoverished many people.

Since this is qualitative research, I have to be very careful with my conclusions since I don't have enough dependent variables. However, as I tried to show on the basis of this small sample, working-class subalternity and the effective devaluation of workers' symbolic capital can channel working-class anger and frustration into a nationalistic, populist discourse that operates with catchphrases such as "moral" and "Christian superiority," "freedom fight against the EU and IMF," "strong state" and "the punishment of the corrupt ex-Communist elite." In East Germany, there was a strong perception among the interviewees that the observed anomalies of capitalism could be explained through structural reasoning. "This is the system" was frequently concluded during the interviews. While Hungarian workers also expressed strong doubts

[37] Pejorative distinction between the West and East Germans.

about the change of regimes, these doubts failed to translate into a criticism of capitalism. Instead, workers spoke of a "plundering" capitalism (capitalism distorted by the expansion of global capital or by a corrupt and trustworthy [post-]Communist elite), and they typically expected the State to act as a mediator between the interests of multinational and domestic companies and between the interests of the workers and capitalists.

I have argued that nostalgia for the socialist regimes can be understood as a means and, indeed, claim of the working people to express their social criticism. In the absence of an alternative (class-based) ideology, this criticism, as we have seen, could easily be channeled into a nationalistic, populist discourse. It would, however, be utterly wrong to disregard working-class opinions and narratives as the manifestations of a "Soviet habitus." One can, indeed, rather ask a different question: instead of blaming the workers, should not we blame rather the very intellectual and cultural context which renders it impossible for them to *otherwise* express any criticism? In East Germany, the political left has a much more powerful public presence and media coverage than in Hungary, which can be one explanation for the different outcomes in the two countries. Workers have a claim for the revaluation of their symbolic capital; if working-class histories are to be altogether forgotten as relics of a failed regime, one may not wonder that the outcome will be the rise of (new) ethnic communities.

BIBLIOGRAPHY

Amsden, Alice H., Jacek Kochanowicz, and Lance Taylor. 1994. *The Market Meets Its Match: Restructuring the Economies of Eastern Europe*. Cambridge: Harvard University Press.

Bahro, Rudolf. 1977. *The Alternative in Eastern Europe*. London: NLB.

Bartha, Eszter. 2004. "Szegény gazdagok: A késő Kádár-rendszer képe az ifjúsági irodalomban." *Magyar Hírlap*, máj. 15–16.

———. 2010. "Transition, Transformation, Postsocialism: Theorizing Systemic Change in Eastern Europe." In *After Twenty Years . . . Reasons and Consequences of the Transformation in Central and Eastern Europe*, edited by Krisztián Csaplár-Degovics, Miklós Mitrovits, and Csaba Zahorán, 9–29. Budapest: Terra Recognita Foundation.

———. 2011. *Magányos harcosok: Munkások a rendszerváltás utáni Kelet-Németországban és Magyarországon.* Budapest: L'Harmattan Kiadó—ELTE BTK Kelet–Európa Története Tanszék.

———. 2013. *Alienating Labour: Workers on the Road from Socialism to Capitalism in East Germany and Hungary*. International Studies in Social History. New York: Berghahn Books.

Boltanski, Luc, and Eve Chiapello. 2005. *The New Spirit of Capitalism*. London: Verso Books.

Boyer, Dominic. 2006. "Ostalgie and the Politics of Future in East Germany." *Public Culture* 18 (2): 361–381.

———. 2010. "From Algos to Autonomous: Nostalgic Eastern Europe as Postimperial Mania." In *Post-communist Nostalgia*, edited by Maria Todorova and Zsuzsa Gille, 17–28. New York: Berghahn Books.

Bozóki, András, ed. 2000. *A rendszerváltás forgatókönyve: kerekasztal-tárgyalások 1989-ben: alkotmányos forradalom: tanulmányok*. Budapest: Új Mandátum Könyvkiadó.

Bryant, Christopher G. A., and Edmund Mokrzycki. 1994. *The New Great Transformation? Change and Continuity in East Central Europe*. London: Routledge.

Buchowski, Michal. 2001. *Rethinking Transformation: An Anthropological Perspective on Postsocialism*. Poznan: Wydawn; Fundacji Humaniora.

Burawoy, Michael. 1985. *The Politics of Production: Factory Regimes under Capitalism and Socialism*. London: Verso.

———. 1992. "A View from Production: The Hungarian Transition from Socialism to Capitalism." In *Labour in Transition: The Labour Process in Eastern Europe and China*, edited by Chris Smith and Paul Thompson, 180–197. London: Routledge.

Burawoy, Michael, and János Lukács. 1992. *The Radiant Past: Ideology and Reality in Hungary's Road to Capitalism*. Chicago: The University of Chicago Press.

Csizmadia, Ervin. 1995. *A magyar demokratikus ellenzék 1968–1988*. Budapest: T-Twins.

Eyal, Gil, Iván Szelényi, and Eleanor Townsley. 1998. *Making Capitalism without Capitalists: The New Ruling Elites in Eastern Europe*. New York: Verso Books.

Ferge, Zsuzsa. 2012. *Vágányok és vakvágányok a társadalompolitikában*. Budapest: L'Harmattan Kiadó.

Földes, György. 1989. *Hatalom és mozgalom 1956–1989*. Budapest: Reform Könyvkiadó–Kossuth Könyvkiadó.

———. 1995. *Az eladósodás politikai története 1957–1986*. Budapest: Gondolat.

Gorz, André. [1982] 2001. *Farewell to the Working Class: An Essay on Post-Industrial Socialism*. Boston: Pluto Press.

Gowan, Peter. 1995. "Neo-liberal Theory and Practice for Eastern Europe." *New Left Review* 213 (September/October).

Hann, Chris. 2002. "Farewell to the Socialist 'Other.'" In *Postsocialism: Ideals, Ideologies and Practices in Eurasia*, edited by C. M. Hann, 1–11. London: Routledge.

———. 2012. "Merre forog az idő kereke Tázláron (és a társadalomnéprajzban)?" *Eszmélet* volume 100 (4).

Haraszti, Miklós. 1978. *A Worker in a Worker's State*. New York: Universe Books. [1979. Darabbér. Egy munkás a munkásállamban. Párizs: Magyar Füzetek Könyvei.]

Héthy, Lajos, and Csaba Makó. 1975. *Az automatizáció és a munkástudat*. Budapest: MTA Szociológiai Kutató Intézet Kiadványa.

Humphrey, Caroline. 2002. "Does the Category 'Postsocialist' Still Make Sense?" In *Postsocialism: Ideals, Ideologies and Practices in Eurasia*, edited by C. M. Hann, 12–15. London: Routledge.

Huszár, Ákos. 2012. "Osztályegyenlőtlenségek. Az egyenlőtlenségek ábrázolása Magyarországon." *Szociológiai Szemle* 22. évf. 2. sz. 4–26.

———. 2013. "Class and the Social Embeddedness of the Economy: Outline of a Normative–Functionalist Model of Social Class." *Szociológiai Szemle* volume 23 (4).

Kalb, Don. 2009. "Beszélgetések egy lengyel populistával: globalizáció, osztály és átmenet—emberközelből." *Eszmélet* 82.

Kalb, Don, and Gábor Halmai, eds. 2011. *Headlines of Nation, Subtexts of Class: Working-Class Populism and the Return of the Repressed in Neoliberal Europe*. Oxford: Berghahn Books.

Kapitány, Ágnes, and Gábor Kapitány. 2007. *Túlélési stratégiák. Társadalmi adaptációs módok*. Budapest: Kossuth Kiadó.

Kemény, István. 1990. *Velünk nevelkedett a gép: Magyar munkások a hetvenes évek elején*. Budapest: Muvelődéskutató Intézet.

Kideckel, David. 2002. "The Unmaking of an East-Central-European Working Class." In *Postsocialism: Ideals, Ideologies and Practices in Eurasia*, edited by C. M. Hann, 114–132. London: Routledge.

———. 2008. *Getting By in Postsocialist Romania: Labor, the Body, and Working-Class Culture*. Bloomington, IN: Indiana University Press.

Konrád, György, and Iván Szelényi. 1979. *The Intellectuals on the Road to Class Power*. New York: Harcourt Brace Jovanovich.

Ladányi, János. 2012. *Leselejtezettek: A kirekesztett népesség társadalom—és térszerkezeti elhelyezkedésének átalakulása Magyarországon a piacgazdasági átmenet időszakában*. Budapest: L'Harmattan Kiadó.

Losonczi, Ágnes. 2005. *Sorsba fordult történelem*. Budapest: Holnap Kiadó.

Maier, Charles. 1997. *Dissolution: The Crisis of Communism and the End of East Germany*. Princeton: Princeton University Press.

Nagy, Éva Katalin. 2012. "Munkástanácsok 1989-ben: A dolgozói tulajdon kérdése a rendszerváltás folyamatában." In *Határokon túl: Tanulmánykötet Mark Pittaway (1971–2010) emlékére*, edited by Eszter Bartha and Zsuzsanna Varga. Budapest: L'Harmattan Kiadó.

Ost, David. 2005. *The Defeat of Solidarity: Anger and Politics in Postcommunist Europe*. Ithaca, NY: Cornell University Press.

Pine, Frances. 2002. "Retreat to the Household? Gendered Domains in Postsocialist Poland." In *Postsocialism: Ideals, Ideologies and Practices in Eurasia*, edited by C. M. Hann, 95–113. London: Routledge.

Pittaway, Mark. 2011. "A magyar munkásság és a rendszerváltás." *Múltunk* 56 (1): 4–18.

———. 2012. *The Workers' State: Industrial Labor and the Making of Socialist Hungary, 1944–1958*. Pittsburgh: Pittsburgh University Press.

Rudd, Elizabeth. 2006. "Gendering Unemployment in Postsocialist Germany: 'What I do is work, even if it's not paid.'" *Ethnos* 71: 191–212.

Slomczynski, Kazimierz, and Goldie Shabad. 1997. "Systemic Transformation and the Salience of Class Structure in East Central Europe." *East European Politics and Societies* 11: 155–189.

Snyder, Tim, and Milada Vachudova. 1997. "Are Transitions Transitory? Two Types of Political Change in Eastern Europe Since 1989." *East European Politics and Societies* 11: 1–35.

Steiner, André. 2004. *Von Plan zu Plan: eine Wirtschaftsgeschichte der DDR*. Munich: Dt. Vrl.-Anst.

Swain, Nigel. 1992. *Hungary: The Rise and Fall of Feasible Socialism*. London: Verso.

———. 2011. "A Postsocialist Capitalism." *Europe-Asia Studies* 63 (9): 1671–1695.

Szalai, Erzsébet. 1986. *Beszélgetések a gazdasági reformról*. Budapest: Pénzügykutatási Intézet Kiadványai.

———. 1994. *A civil társadalomtól a politikai társadalom felé. Munkástanácsok 1989–93*. Budapest: T-Twins Kiadó.

———. 2001. *Gazdasági elit és társadalom a magyarországi újkapitalizmusban*. Budapest: Aula Kiadó.

———. 2004a. *Az első válaszkísérlet. A létezett szocializmus—és ami utána jön . . .* Budapest: Nemzeti Tankönyvkiadó.

———. 2004b. "Tulajdonviszonyok, társadalomszerkezet és munkásság.æ *Kritika*, 33 (9): 2–6.

Todorova, Maria. 2010 "From utopia to propaganda and back." In *Post-communist Nostalgia*, edited by Maria Todorova and Zsuzsa Gille, 1–13. New York: Berghahn Books.

Todorova, Maria, and Zsuzsa Gille, eds. 2010. *Post-communist Nostalgia*. New York: Berghahn Books.

Tóth, András. 2013. *The Collapse of Post-Socialist Industrial Relations System in Hungary.* Kézirat.

Tőkés, R. L. 1996. *Hungary's Negotiated Revolution: Economic Reform, Social Change, and Political Succession, 1957–1990.* New York: Cambridge University Press.

Utasi, Ágnes. 2008. *Éltető kapcsolatok: A kapcsolatok hatása a szubjektív életminőségre.* Budapest: Új Mandátum.

Van der Linden, Marcel. 2007. *Western Marxism and the Soviet Union: A Survey of Critical Theory and Debates Since 1917.* Leiden: Brill.

Verdery, Katherine. 1996. *What Was Socialism and What Comes Next?* Princeton: Princeton University Press.

———. 2002. "Whither Postsocialism?" In *Postsocialism: Ideals, Ideologies and Practices in Eurasia*, edited by C. M. Hann, 15–28. London: Routledge.

Watson, Peggy. 1993. "The Rise of Masculinism in Eastern Europe." *New Left Review* 198: 71–82.

Wedel, Janine R. 1998. *Collision and Collusion: The Strange Case of Western Aid to Eastern Europe, 1989–1998.* New York: St. Martin's Press.

Zigon, Jarrett. 2009. "Hope Dies Last: Two Aspects of Hope in Contemporary Moscow." *Anthropological Theory* 9: 253–271.

THE SEAS AND SKIES OF BOHEMIA: PROJECTIONS AND INVENTIONS OF THE NATIONAL SPACE

Petra Hanáková

Abstract

The label "Central Europe" has been for centuries more than a regional designation: it has always also represented a shared historical, cultural, and political experience. Central Europe is, therefore, most fittingly described and pictured metaphorically—as a "state of mind" (J. Rupnik), "a fate" (M. Kundera), or "an act of faith, a project, let us say, even utopia" (C. Miłosz). The imprecise and shifting borders between the European East and the West and the mystique of the Center (Herder's Mitte, also the original place of his vision of Humanität) have undergone a long and productive semiosis over several centuries.

The idea of Central Europe will be analyzed in this text based on a plethora of sources—starting with famous misplacements and negations in classic literary works (Shakespeare's placement of the sea in the middle of Europe, Jarry's claim of "Poland, that is to say nowhere," etc.), through its utopian status and presence in political and poetic texts (Kundera, Miłosz, Havel, Bachmann), to its most typical embodiments in visual (and gradually also popular) culture. Visions of Central Europe are also a particularly telling presence in the contemporary globalizing and transnational positioning of the region.

Položím Praze k nohám moře./ I shall lay the sea at the feet of Prague.

—Jára Cimrman, 1897

Kuřátko, Nickův pomocník: Kde to je, Praha?
Nick Carter: Ve Vídni./
Kuřátko, Nick's assistant: Where is this place, Prague?
Nick Carter: In Vienna.

—*Adéla ještě nevečeřela* (Ondřich Lipský, 1977)

From the standpoint of history, Europe can be divided into three blocks: the historicity of the West, the absurd history of Central Europe, and the ahistoricity of the East.

—Jacques Rupnik quoting "a Josef K." in *The Other Europe*

The 30 Minutes of Sea

In an epigrammatic scene from the mock-biopic *Jára Cimrman, ležící, spící* (directed by Ladislav Smoljak, 1983), the main character, the eponymous Czech/European genius[1] decides in 1897 to lay the sea at the feet of Prague. As the patriotic speech at the opening of the event reminds the crowd that "this sea was not given to us by nature as with other nations, but by the genius of the Czech artist," an enormous panorama, on a canvas so huge that it had to be painted on a football field, is extended between two Renaissance houses in one corner of the Old Town Square. (See insert, figure 20.) A nationalist celebration commences, complete with Sokol club parade, participants dressed up in national costumes, and the patriotic choir Hlahol performing a folk song in an elaborate canon. But this merry idyll does not last for more than thirty minutes, as specified by the permit from the Viennese authorities then still governing the Bohemian Lands, after which police on horseback start to dispel the crowd. The panorama is taken down, revealing wooden scaffolding behind it, and only an echo of the opening speech promises a better, albeit still mockingly compromising future for patriotic and national culture: "Moreover

[1] This "universal Czech genius" was invented in 1966 by the writers Jan Šebánek, Zdeněk Svěrák, and Ladislav Smoljak. Originally intended as a caricature of a national hero, Cimrman gained enormous popularity, and the Jára Cimrman Theatre, which stages "his" plays and organizes mock historical conferences about his life, has become one of the most popular stages in Prague, maintaining its popularity until today. In 2005, when Czech public TV organized "The Greatest Czech" contest, Cimrman immediately rose to first place in the popular vote, beating all important real historical figures, and so the rules of the show had to be changed to officially exclude fictional characters.

I firmly believe that the day will come when this our Czech sea will adorn Prague not just for a graciously permitted moment, but its waves will forever wash the walls of Old Prague houses, at least every Saturday afternoon and all day Sundays."

This brief and truly hilarious scene—at least to anyone familiar with the history of the nineteenth-century Czech Revivalist movement (which virtually invented anew the Czech and Slovak national project after three centuries of enforced Germanization)—also offers a condensed metaphor for visual culture functioning as a compensation for lack, inadequacy, and trauma. This "Czech sea" has a lot in its imaginary surf: the distress of a small country at the mercy of the neighboring political and cultural superpowers throughout its history; compensation for this smallness and oppression through an investment in culture; the creation of mediocre art as a patriotic event and political act, thus acknowledging the artist as the "consciousness of the nation"; and even the invented, imaginary, and by its nature absurd character of such an investment. Cimrman's sea functions here literally as a screen[2]—as the phantasmatic presence of the greatness of Czech spirit and culture (overcoming both the political constraints and often meager quality of late nineteenth-century patriotic culture) is staged, the real, threatening void is suspended for those thirty minutes. Reality becomes marginal in a literal way, making place for a fundamentally preposterous image, a projection of the desire to bring the sea to the center of Europe, which is, taken *ad litteram*, under the current geological conditions, basically a desire for self-annihilation. This simultaneity of the panorama as the product of a wish fulfillment machine, the emotional investment in it as the sign of national grandeur, and at the same time the threat of disappearance beyond this very image in its ludicrous rendering (as the fight for national and cultural independence is basically revealed as foolish by this projection of a sea) opens up the nationalist imaging in its absurdity. The sea, crudely depicted so that it never achieves the status of a full *trompe-l'oeil*, remains in many ways a stain, an amorphous specter, an impenetrable barrier, but also a vacuity, an empty space into which both aspirations and anxieties are projected.

What I'm attempting to do in this text (and hopefully a following book project) can in many ways be described metaphorically as a dissection through

---

[2] If we play the game along with the "cimrmanologists," who revel in inventing situations in which Cimrman inspired the greatest minds of Europe (like, meeting with Chekhov when he was working on "Two Sisters" and posing the seminal question: "You think *two* are enough, Anton Pavlovich?"), we might claim it was Cimrman's Prague sea that inspired Lacan in his work on the screen and its relation to the real; see Jacques Lacan, *Four Fundamental Concepts of Psychoanalysis* (New York: W. W. Norton, 1985), 105–108. The two could easily have met when Lacan traveled all the way to the Czech town of Mariánské lázně (Marienbad) to make his (in)famously interrupted attempt to present his report on the "mirror phase" for the first time.

the refracted national images that function like this "Czech sea" and appear as a screen; i.e., as paradoxical images infested with dreams and traumas in an awry verisimilitude. The Czech sea has become an imaginary and imagined topos and a poetic (and at times political) trope that recurs in several forms and variants, with a peculiar *Nachleben,* the principle of which gives the trope a twisted chronology. Both real and imaginary, tangible as a screen and elusive as an ideal, limited and perpetual, jubilant and anxious, the visions/projections of the national are broadly dealt with here on two levels: first, on the level of semiosis, as the process of investing a neutral space ("a sea") with new structures of meanings and projections of the national ("the Czech sea"); and on the second level, sometimes parallel, sometimes opposing, movement of deriving, deducing, (but also inducing) claims about national mentality and the supposed "destiny" of the nation from these primarily semiotic projections. The metaphor of the Czech sea, I believe, can conveniently introduce us to the journey through this loaded semiotic landscape as a space of the afterlife of images that is also always the space of negotiation between the (f)actual and the mythologizing needs of the national.

In many ways, the images of Bohemia (in the polyvalent versions disguised throughout history as the Celtic Boiohaemum, the Kingdom of Bohemia, the Lands of the Bohemian Crown, Czech Lands, Böhmen und Mähren, Czechoslovakia, up to the present Czech Republic) cannot be understood without considering this imaginary space, which always appears from the contested dynamics and interdependence between "a" Bohemia and Europe, the center and the limit, East and West, its discursive and imaginary borders being always more an abstract product of semiosis than a concrete, actual historical and political existence—there is always a Bohemia that is imagined, narrated, layered over actuality. Thinking through this topographical imaginary (never just topographical, but cultural and political as well) of Bohemia/Czech Lands, we can start to disentangle its layered and complex implications for the image of the national.

Although we leave Cimrman here as he supposedly departs from Prague after his ultimate patriotic gesture, with the dual aim to split the (Austro-Hungarian) Monarchy and to split the atom, let's stay with the Czech sea, as a paradoxical—both full and vacant—topos that will hopefully help us to understand the imagining of the national space of one small country hidden in the middle of Europe.

Ich grenz noch an ein Wort und an in andres Land

But the most renowned and most often analyzed image of the Bohemian sea does not actually come from the fictitious Czech genius. It is Ingeborg

Bachmann who in one of her most beautiful poems, *Böhmen liegt am Meer*, takes as the starting point of her vision the notorious Shakespearean misplacement of the landlocked Bohemian Lands to the seashore (see *The Winter's Tale*, scene III, which takes place in "Bohemia, a desert country near the sea . . . place famous for the creatures of prey that keep upn't")[3] and twists her poetic lesson into the belief in this sea: "If Bohemia still lies by the sea, I'll believe in the sea again./And believing in the sea, thus I can hope for land" (*Liegt Böhmen am Meer, glaub ich den Meeren wieder./Und glaub ich noch ans Meer, so hoffe ich auf Land*). This act of trust gives the image of sea-shored Bohemia the status of utopian homeland, an imaginary harbor and a place of retreat that has the power to soothe the restlessness of the modern soul and free artistic imagination from constraints. Bachmann recasts this fictive, mislaid site as the wished for, encountered homeland, which embraces the lyrical subject as its eventual, paradoxically selected, adopting/adopted *Heimat* (although she never uses this charged word in this poem,[4] referring to the fictive Bohemia as "the land of my choice" [*Land meiner Wahl*]).

To understand this gesture and its possible cultural, historical, and political readings, some basic biographical data and references might be useful at this point. As we know, Bachmann, originally an Austrian[5] author living at the time in the split city of Berlin (the only place where the iron curtain literarily materialized in the Wall), got the inspiration for this poem from her

---

[3] The debates regarding Shakespeare's "error" are well known, starting with Ben Jonson's mocking remark from 1619 that "Shakespear wanted Art, and sometimes Sense, for in one of his plays, he brought in a number of men, saying they had suffered a ship-wrack in Bohemia, where there is no sea near by 100 miles"; see Ben Jonson, *Conversations with Drummond of Hawthornden* (London: Shakespearean Society, 1842), 46. Some authors, evidently concerned to save the aura of the genial Shakespeare and to purge him of mistakes, claim that the "places remote in Bohemia/There weep, an leave it crying" actually may refer to either of the two periods when a Bohemian King ruled an area vast enough to reach to the sea—as was the case with Ottokar II of Bohemia (in power from 1253–1278)—, and the Bohemian King and Holy Roman Emperor (1576–1612) Rudolf II, well known around Europe in Shakespearean times for his support of the arts, including the high arts of alchemy. (Prague, then, in many ways served as the utopian land of artists and scientists, rather in the manner evoked here by Bachmann.)

[4] She uses the word *Heimstätte* for Prague in another fragment, *Heimkehr über Prag*, another ambivalent poem in which the journey home through Prague basically leads the author to state that this is both the transitory space of detour and the first *Heimstätte*, where she (in a condensed image) pays the toll to the river Moldau, not to be let home, but to "let the river flow on"; see Ingeborg Bachmann, *Ich weiss keine bessere Welt: unveröffentlichte Gedichte* (Munich: Piper, 2000), 161.

[5] More precisely, Bachmann was born in Klagenfurt, in the province of Carinthia, bordering on Slovenia and Italy, a city with historically high numbers of Slavic population (and also a history of Slavic occupation and the self-proclaimed South-Slav Kingdom of 1919 and 1920).

actual two short visits to Prague during the political thaw in the early 1960s, the years of cultural ferment leading to the Prague Spring of 1968. Bachmann wrote several poems and fragments inspired by the visit apart from the most well known, *Böhmen liegt am Meer*: *Prag Jänner 64*, *Jüdischer Friedhof*, *Poliklinik Prague, Heimkehr über Prag,* and *Wenzelsplatz.*[6] Spending most of her life as a migrant, living in a number of places in Central Europe, including Vienna, Berlin, and Rome, the author took both literal and metaphorical inspiration from her journeys, transmuting the actuality of traveling and the experience of moving through both imaginary and real European landscapes into existential parables of human vagrancy in the modern world.

Bachmann's lyrical subject thus often masquerades as wanderer, a figure that stands in a condensed reference to both Nietzsche's *Menschliches, Allzumenschiches* and Goethe's (i.e., "Werther's") idea of human fate as that of the *Wandrer* ("*Ja wohl bin ich nur ein Wandrer, ein Waller auf der Erde! Seid ihr denn mehr?*"[7]), but also brings a nostalgic allusion to the periods in the history of Europe when one could not become a savant or an artist without the concrete experience of visiting certain already globalized spaces of knowledge and culture. (We can think about the networks of medieval universities, monasteries, renaissance cultural centers, or the extremely elaborate knowledge-gathering networks of the Jesuits connecting the baroque with the Enlightenment, all of which basically created the European cultural and scientific tradition.) Traveling as a way of accumulating knowledge and inspiration, as well as the self-reflexive exploration of human nature, formally mixed with trips for pleasure and aesthetic contemplation at least since Petrarch's fabled ascent of Mount Ventoux. But it is the romantic soul of the wanderer-explorer in the work of

[6] Not many details are known about these visits. We know that Bachmann was in Prague in January and March 1964, but the reasons for the trip and the nature of her contacts with the pre-Prague Spring cultural environment remain unknown. Some authors suggest that she may have come for some medical treatment (as the fragment "Poliklinik Prag," which ruminates on the possibility of leaving life altogether, might suggest). Bachmann's Prague poems and fragments can be found in the following editions: Ingeborg Bachmann, *Ich weiß keine bessere Welt: unveröffentlichte Gedichte*, edited by Isolde Moser, Heinz Bachmann, and Christian Moser (Munich: Piper, 2000), and Ingeborg Bachmann, *Werke* [Erster Band] (Munich: Piper, 1993); see also Erich Fried, *Ich grenz noch an ein Wort und an ein andres Land: Über Ingeborg Bachmann—Erinnerungen, einige Anmerkungen zu ihrem Gedicht "Böhmen liegt am Meer" und ein Nachruf* (Berlin: Friedenauer Presse, 1983), and G. M. Roberts, ed., *Germany and the Imagined East* (Newcastle, UK: Cambridge Scholars Press, 2005).

[7] Nietzsche's most famous fragment from "The Wanderer" section of *Menschliches* reads: "He who has come only in part to a freedom of reason cannot feel on Earth otherwise than as a wanderer—though not as a traveller *towards* a final goal, for this does not exist"; see Friedrich W. Nietzsche, *Human, All Too Human: A Book for Free Spirits* (Lincoln: University of Nebraska Press, 1984), 266, fragment 638.

J. W. Goethe and A. von Humboldt,[8] the romantic picture of Wanderer as the embodiment of human soul eternalized in C. D. Friedrich's paintings, most notably *Der Wanderer über dem Nebelmeer* (1818), or, to bring the figure closer to home, the ultimate Czech romantic "poutník" (the poet-wayfarer) K. H. Mácha,[9] that are forerunners of Bachmann's wandering minstrel. It is also not a coincidence in this context that Friedrich's wanderer is literally transfixed by a protean cloud substance that forms an illusion of a sea, a *Nebelmeer*, almost a protoplasm of the spirit, evaporating from the European landscape we can only sense underneath—and, as if in a sacred transmutation, the wanderer/observer becomes almost a demiurge of the very spirit.

Bachmann's wanderer starts from constant motion, a constant state of exile, s/he is restless because of a lack, driven by the urge to cover up this lack by the dreamy yet intensely physical experience of traveling. But in *Böhmen Liegt am Meer,* this supposedly lifelong peregrination is punctuated by a closure, by landing in the mythical land "of choice." As the peregrine soul embraces it as the desired home that interrupts the trajectory of wandering, s/he finds its haven in one place, both imagined and real, foreign and surprisingly homelike, both subdued and victorious.[10]

But especially intriguing about Bachmann's traveler, who "has nothing, who is held by nothing, gifted only at seeing, by a doubtful sea, the land of my choice" ("*den nichts hält, begabt nur noch, vom Meer, das strittig ist, Land meiner Wahl zu sehen*"), is how in the final identification ("my choice") the author leaves behind all standard definitions of modern European nationality,

---

[8] Both Goethe and Humboldt are known to have traveled to Bohemia on several occasions, and the latter is often quoted to have proclaimed on one of his visits (supposedly in 1819) that the view from Milešovka (Mileschauer) Mountain in Central Bohemia was the third most beautiful in the world. See Johannes Urzidil, *Goethe v Čechách* (Prague: Pistorius & Olšanská, 2009).

[9] I'm tracing the metaphor of the traveler here mainly to the late eighteenth century and the first half of the nineteenth century as the period of the birth of modern nationalism; otherwise we can go as far back as to the baroque allegories of Johann Amos Comenius (especially the character of "Všudybyl" /"Searchall Ubiquitous"/ in his *Labyrint swěta a Lusthaus srdce*/ *Labyrinth of the World and Paradise of the Heart,* 1624).

[10] Bachmann's view of Europe is the very opposite of the paranoid, haunting vision of Apollinaire's in *Zone*, where he heaps horrifying scenes of the twentieth-century European cities. Even escaping from the modern buzzing Paris to the Czech countryside cannot appease him, and the especially drastic effect produces the encounter with the Prague ghetto as the relic of time:

> *Épouvanté tu te vois dessiné dans les agates de Saint-Vit*
> *Tu étais triste à mourir le jour où tu t'y vis*
> *Tu ressembles au Lazare affolé par le jour*
> *Les aiguilles de l'horloge du quartier juif vont à rebours*
> *Et tu recules aussi dans ta vie lentement.*

especially those traditionally dependent on the identification by and with language. The experience is translated into a recurrent metaphor of bordering ("I still border on a word and on another land, I border, like little else, on everything more and more"—*Ich grenz noch an ein Wort und an ein andres Land, ich grenz, wie wenig auch, an alles immer mehr* [note the homophony of *mehr* and *Meer*]), which in many respects opposes the common understanding of borders as a point of separation and alienation. The wanderer sheds all the material signifiers of his/her identity (in another poem, s/he even arrives in the world "free of charge," the *umsonst*[11]) and enters the sphere of bordering conceived of as an osmosis—bordering as touching, permeability, passage, in which one is not bound by linguistic and cultural differences anymore: "Since that night/ I go on and speak again/it sounds Czech" ("*Seit jener Nacht/gehe und spreche ich wieder/böhmisch klingt es*").

Centering the wanderer's quest around the loss and gain of language (especially in *Böhmen liegt am Meer* and *Prag Jänner 64*), Bachmann repeatedly crosses the barrier between German as the language of the historical oppressor and Czech (labeled here by the older term *böhmisch*) as the language of the subaltern; but not in terms of a switch, not as a political gesture of identification with the oppressed. She envisions a more paradoxical state, a strange equivalence and sudden stroke of understanding, thus a merging and transversing of the traditional linguistic identities. The radical gesture of this poem is the return to language not as a source of identity and isolation, nor as the mainstay of the struggle for independence (as it functioned in the forming of national cultures), but as a resurgence of a (pre?)linguistic envelope that provides identity and identification of another sort, since it can surround and console the subject by engulfing it in an illusion of sudden plenitude and fullness.

The self-contradictory image of the wandering poet who is un/bound by languages and travels across them organically, along with the paradoxical conception that one can choose and appropriate an imaginary homeland beyond the sphere of national and linguistic identity, stages the kind of refusal that

---

Appalled you see yourself reproduced in the agates of Saint Vitus
You were sad near to death to see yourself there
You looked as bewildered as Lazarus
In the Jewish ghetto the clock runs backwards
And you go backwards also through a slow life.

Guillaume Apollinaire, *Alcools* (Paris: Éditions Galimard, 1920), 11.

[11] See the fragment *Poliklinik Prag,* which introduces us to the passage of leaving the material world behind: "Da ist alles umsonst. Kostet nichts mehr." ("Everything is free here. Nothing costs anything any more.")

always borders on the abandonment of the *Vaterland; i.e., the-land-of the father* and *the name/non-of the father.* Thus it also subverts the linguistic and narrative formation[12] of the nation and the national in addition to the representation thereof. This already signals to us that Bachmann's Bohemia is in many ways the Bohemia of the *imaginaire*, as a place of fusion within the mixed national body before the linguistic separation and the formation of the nationalist screen. We cannot get further away from Cimrman's sea than here, yet at the same time, we are strangely close to it.

But what kind of space does this imaginary register of the national presuppose here, and how does it connect to the real Bohemia? Contemporary scholarship has typically focused on reading Bachmann's Bohemia as a purely utopian space, even as an ungeographical, untopographical place—as for example, Reingard Nethersole in her thoughtful analysis of Bachmann's poetry, which mainly focuses on another of her famous travel poems, *Ausfahrt* (*Journey Out*).[13] Nethersole basically relocates the focus of Bachmann's poetic work/travels from the actual and real to the textual and linguistic space—and stresses how here the nomadic, wandering subject is governed by "logic postulating the contradictory interdependence of two forces, namely the drive to flight and the desire for arrival at an utopian destination, whereby transience marks the writerly process and arrival inscribed in the text as 'land' signifies the space of the poem."[14] This premise is further expanded in the section that deals directly with *Böhmen Liegt am Meer:* "the idea of reaching land after

---

[12] It might be useful to state at this point that I conceive of the nation as a process in the active sense, as *narration*, *imagining*, or *mythologization*, as the constant re-telling and re-inventing of a narrative structure based on canonical references, motifs, and shared experiences, with undeniable and evident, often material, effects on people, but still only a fictional, invented, and in many ways arbitrary formation—in brief, as an imagined community, using Anderson's classic term, but also expanded by Arjun Appadurai's understanding of imagination as social practice: "The world we live in today is characterized by a new role for the imagination in social life. To grasp this new role, we need to bring together: the old idea of images, especially mechanically produced images (in the Frankfurt School sense): the idea of the imagined community (in Anderson's sense); and the French idea of the imaginary (*imaginaire*), as a constructed landscape of collective aspirations, which is no more and no less real than the collective representations of Emile Durkheim, now mediated through the complex prism of modern media." See Arjun Appadurai, "Disjuncture and Difference in the Global Cultural Economy," *Public Culture* 2, no. 2 (1990): 4–5; and also Stefan Berger, Linas Eriksonas, and Andrew Mycock, eds., *Narrating the Nation: Representations in History, Media and the Arts* (Oxford: Berghahn, 2008).

[13] Inspired also by a real journey of Bachmann's to England and France in the winter of 1950–1951.

[14] Reingard Nethersole, "Ingeborg Bachmann's Poetry: A Sense of Passing," in Gudrun Brokoph-Mauch, ed., *Thunder Rumbling At My Heels: Tracing Ingeborg Bachmann* (Riverside, CA: Ariadne Press, 1998), 143.

having been aground in the sea not only echoes the position of the subject in *Journey Out . . .* but also the last verses refer to the life of a 'vagrant,' in search of the 'chosen land.' Without possession other than the seer's gift, the nomadic self envisages this to be the domain of art and poetry where paroxysmal sadness reverses into mystical jubilation."[15]

Yet, mapping the spatial onto the textual[16] is only one (albeit important) part of the story of Bachmann's imagining. There is a cultural, historical, and political resonance and relevance in *Böhmen liegt am Meer* that definitely goes beyond any simple kind of retreat from the real world into the sphere of "beautiful language." While this is a standard aesthetic and modernist interpretation of retreat into poetic space, in the case of Bachmann's travel "diaries," more is at stake, and it enters into dialogue with national identity formation, cultural and political mappings and re-mappings—especially the important historical concept of Central Europe—in the context of which the landlocked country of Bohemia becomes a stage for the European historical conflict and drama.

Central Europe and Its Second Raptus

Central Europe is a topos and trope dear to many European intellectuals, but it has to be noted that the discourse on Central Europe comes to the fore especially as a retrograde projection, as a nostalgic contemplation of a historical space the loss of which is mourned by some as they ruminate on its disappearance. Historically, Central Europe essentially equals the strip of small nations sandwiched between two imperialist powers, Germany (in some periods represented mainly by the militaristic Prussia) and Russia, a compound of small countries constantly threatened by their elimination from the world map. The most typical state formation of this region would be the "Austrian Haus," the Austrian and later Austro-Hungarian Monarchy, granting at some periods relative autonomy to individual nations and especially allowing for the intense traffic of ideas and knowledge. We can heretically add that it was this relative freedom that brought the empire down, but the intense cultural exchange continued after the creation of independent nations in 1918 until the outbreak of WWII.[17] Poland

[15] Ibid., 148.

[16] I'm aware that I'm leaving aside for now, or at least simplifying too much, the whole problem of text–space as a semiotic paradox, but anyone who wants to continue in that direction can go to Winfried Nöth, "Der Text als Raum," in Dieter W. Halwachs, et al., eds., *Sprache, Onomatopöie, Rhetorik, Namen, Idiomatik, Grammatik. Festschrift für Karl Sornig* (Graz Institut für Sprachwissenschaft der Universtität Graz, 1994), 163–174.

[17] WWII, in fact, activated another concept connected to the idea of central Europe, the German concept of *Mitteleuropa*, which became part of the German *Lebensraum* plans for the

also partakes in the Central European heritage, although it was partitioned at the end of the eighteenth century among Austria, Prussia, and Russia, to be reconstituted only in 1918.

Kundera goes back to the Revivalist historian František Palacký for his definition, emphasizing the utopian dimension of the formation:

> Central Europe, according to Palacký, ought to be a family of equal nations, each of which—treating the others with mutual respect and secure in the protection of a strong, unified state—would also cultivate its own individuality. And this dream, although never fully realized, would remain powerful and influential. Central Europe longed to be a condensed version of Europe itself in all its cultural variety, a small arch-European Europe, a reduced model of Europe made up of nations conceived according to one rule: the greatest variety within the smallest space.[18]

The idea can be more clearly visualized as the Europe and Bohemia of Freud, Kafka, Hašek, Meyrink, Rilke, Husserl, Mahler (all of them born in Bohemia or Moravia), who were definitely not all *Tschechen* but clearly might be entitled *Böhmen*; i.e., by the term that does not necessarily have linguistic relation to Czech nationality but attests to the ethnic and national diversity of Bohemia. Both Prague and Vienna appear in this context as osmotic cities with enormously mixed populations. Prague in some respects really was "in" Vienna, not only in the Nick Carter joke from the crazy comedy *Adéla ještě nevečeřela* quoted at the beginning of this text.[19] We also know that although we can clearly distinguish specific ethnic and national groups, there was a high

---

expansion of the Reich to the East. Hitler reactivated these plans in several schemes, one of them being the project of the *Abschiebung* of the Czechs into Siberia; see Peter Bugge, "The Use of the Middle: Mittelleuropa vs. Střední Evropa," *European Review of History—Revue européenne d'Histoire* 6, no. 1 (1999): 15–34. Note also that a popular belief in the nineteenth century stated that the Germans wanted to turn Bohemia into a *sea of blood*; this conviction is famously pictured in Bedřich Smetana's opera *Braniboři v Čechách* (*The Brandenburgers in Bohemia*, 1862–1863).

[18] Milan Kundera, "The Tragedy of Central Europe," *New York Review of Books* 31, no. 7 (April 26, 1984): 33.

[19] Due to mass migration in the second half of the nineteenth century, Vienna was actually by the beginning of twentieth century sometimes described as "the second largest Czech city"—the estimated number of the Czech population was between 250,000 and 400,000 (out of approximately two million). See Vlasta Valeš, ed., *Doma v cizině. Češi ve Vídni ve 20. století / Zu Hause in der Fremde. Tschechen in Wien im 20. Jahrhundert* (Prague: Skriptorium, 2002).

bilingual or trilingual presence in both places.[20] German remained not only the official, but also the cultural language in Bohemia up to the first decades of the nineteenth century, but even as Czech starts to take over afterwards, it only adds to the linguistic variety, which was then drastically ended by the ethnic cleansing and emigration caused by WWII and the following *Abschieb* of the German population. With the installment of the iron curtain towards the end of the 1940s, the borders closed almost hermetically, and the fruitful migrations and heterogeneity of the area remained only a nostalgic memory, a space to be remembered and mourned.

This approach is especially palpable in the texts of the emigré authors like (originally Czech) Milan Kundera, (Polish) Czesław Miłosz, or (Hungarian) György Konrád, who in the 1980s in a way re-inscribe on the European body the story of the abduction of Europa.[21] Kundera particularly returns to the original mythical origin of Europa as symbolized in the rape and abduction of a Phoenician princess to a faraway land (as we know it already from Ovid), when he claims that Central Europe, a place of no return for him at the time, is doomed by a second *raptus*, being "kidnapped" by the East after the, in many respects, arbitrary redivision of Europe into the Western world and the "Soviet sphere of influence" at the Yalta conference in 1945. (As Jacques Rupnik claims, Yalta basically established "the last colonial empire," an ahistorical relict of cultural colonization of the Central European space by the Soviets.[22])

For Kundera, the tragedy of the political disappearance of Central Europe "is a drama of the West—a West that, kidnapped, displaced, and brainwashed, nevertheless insist[s] on defending its identity" in a series of revolts and especially in the investment into the mutual cultural legacy and understanding.[23] For Rupnik, this cultural investment in the European heritage is the natural result of political oppression: "nowhere is the identification with

[20] Recent research proved, for example, that Kafka was not only a regular visitor to Czech theatre performances and interacted often with Czech authors, but also wrote stylistically advanced texts in Czech; see Marek Nekula, *"...v jednom poschodí vnitřní babylonské věže..."/ Jazyky Franze Kafky* (Prague: Nakladatelství Franze Kafky, 2003).

[21] Roman Szporluk, "Defining 'Central Europe': Power, Politics, and Culture," *Cross Currents: A Yearbook of Central European Culture* 1 (1982): 30–38; Jan Patočka, "European Culture," *Cross Currents* 3 (1983), 3–6.

[22] Jacques Rupnik, *The Other Europe* (New York: Pantheon Books, 1988), iv.

[23] Kundera, "The Tragedy of Central Europe," 33. This is also one of the reasons why the forced cultural contacts between the "brotherly" Socialist republics and the USSR never fully replaced these more natural bonds, and the ideological support of this new orientation towards the East created so much resistance.

Europe as a whole stronger than where it is most threatened, where the defense of a culture is part of a search for alternatives to partition of the continent."[24] Central Europe here again stands for the idea of Europe in which languages, nations, and cultures interact to the extent that any political borders appear inauthentic, as a Europe that is both essentially national and deeply transnational, a super-structure created through ages by the traffic of intellectuals and communications in shared languages, starting with Latin as the language of clergy and literature or German as the language of philosophy and the state. Kundera sticks to his vision of Central Europe and its shared history and culture well into the present, even going further in inferring in *The Curtain* that Bohemia was the origin of this concept:

> Looking out from the Czech window, I see there, in the mid-fourteenth century, the first Central European university at Prague; in the fifteenth century I see the Hussite revolution foreshadowing the Reformation; in the seventeenth century I see the Hapsburg Empire gradually constructing itself out of Bohemia, Hungary, Austria; I see the wars that, over two centuries, will defend the West against the Turkish invasion; I see the Counter-Reformation, with the flowering of baroque art that stamps an architectural unity on the whole of that vast territory, right up to the Baltic counties.[25]

This vision of Europe is thus neither purely geographical, nor only political—it is mainly a cultural projection ("Europe united in baroque") in which the Czech lands play an important part, as they are suitably located in the very center, as a point of crossing. For Kundera, "Central Europe is not a state: it is a culture or a fate. Its borders are imaginary and must be drawn and redrawn with each new historical situation";[26] for Miłosz it is "an act of faith, a project, let us say, even utopia, but . . . reasons for adopting it are quite realistic";[27] for Rupnik it is "more a state of mind than a scientific concept";[28] for the

[24] Rupnik, *The Other Europe*, 4.

[25] Milan Kundera, *The Curtain: An Essay in Seven Parts* (New York: Harper Collins, 2005), 46–47. Kundera here comes back to the idea of Central Europe as "maximum diversity in minimal space," as a median context between the global (the world) and the local (the national).

[26] Milan Kundera, "Interview with Milan Kundera," by A. Finkielkarut, *Cross Currents* 1 (1982): 29.

[27] Czeslaw Milosz, "Central European Attitudes," *Cross Currents* 5 (1986): 101–108.

[28] Rupnik, *The Other Europe*, 4.

later historian Peter Bugge, it is a "discursive landscape" that presupposes the sentimental approach to its loss.[29]

Kundera's description attests to the uneasiness that most Czechs still feel when referred to as Eastern European, a term they would never use themselves—opting typically for "středoevropan," Central European, and identifying with the history of the West: "I am always shocked by the perfidious vocabulary that has transformed Central Europe into the East. Central Europe represents the destiny of the West, in concentrated form."[30] Similarly, in mocking gesture, Joseph Brodsky refused to use the expression "Eastern Europe" for the region and suggested taking it *ad absurdum,* replacing it by the invented and paradoxical label "West Asia."[31]

The East, as embodied in Russia, presented for the Central Europeans for centuries the very opposite of Europe. Kundera sums up this position in the incompatibility of the historical spheres of influence of the Roman Empire (Catholicism) vs. Byzantinum (Orthodoxy);[32] in modern terms it can be seen as the difference between the enlightened "heimlich" monarchism of the Austrian empire (the Austrian Haus of nations with an emperor about whom the subaltern nations can tell jokes without any fear of being executed) vs. the "devilish otherness" of Russian absolutisms and despotism, whose tyranny is absolute and foreign to the historical experience of the Western Slavs. This otherness already horrified the rather pro-Slavic Revivalists (notably K. Havlíček Borovský), and the pragmatic and transitory panslavism and Russophilia of some Revivalists (Kolár's imagining of Russia as "velké dubisko," the "big oak" we can lean on) was often seen as a short-sighted deviation from a natural inclination towards the West.[33] Austria in many respects was seen as the guardian, not the oppressor, of Central Europe (Palacký's austroslavism is especially well known). As the idea of Central Europe was deeply despised by the Soviet authorities during the whole occupation, it is not surprising that it

---

[29] Peter Bugge, "The Use of the Middle," 16.

[30] Finkielkarut, "Interview with Milan Kundera," 29.

[31] Milosz, "Central European Attitudes," 101–108.

[32] Kundera specifies: "The word 'Europe' does not represent a phenomenon of geography but a spiritual notion synonymous with the word 'West.' 'Geographic Europe' (extending from the Atlantic to the Ural Mountains) was always divided into two halves which evolved separately: one tied to ancient Rome and the Catholic Church, the other anchored in Byzantium and the Orthodox Church. After 1945, the border between the two Europes shifted several hundred kilometers to the west, and several nations that had always considered themselves to be Western woke up to discover that they were now in the East." See "The Tragedy of Central Europe," 33. This condensed argument is further expanded in Rupnik, *The Other Europe*, 7–14.

[33] See especially Václav Černý, *Vývoj a zločiny panslavismu* (Prague: ISE, 1989), and T. G. Masaryk, *Rusko a Evropa. Sociologické skizzy*, vols. 1–3 (Prague: Ústav TGM, 2001).

was illegal even to identify with this concept in socialist Czechoslovakia—as Rupnik reminds us, the official interpretation of paragraph 98 of the Czechoslovak penal code no.140 of 1961, dealing with treason and other "crimes against the republic," stated: "Among the subversive activities threatening the independence of the state it is possible to include, for instance, the advocacy of a Central European federation."[34]

If the decisive Central European experience has been defined as "the experience of a nation that chooses between its existence and its nonexistence," Central Europe itself faced seemingly irreparable extinction even after the reunification of Europe in 1990 and the expansion of the European Union to the East. The spiritual land of extinct brotherhoods, as envisioned by Bachmann, Kundera, and others, in many ways still remains an abstract, utopian space, a retrospective investment and wish, and so it sometimes reappears in cautious cultural references. The last I know of, Hans Magnus Enzesberger in the new edition of his book *Ach Europa!* from 2006 envisions in the last chapter the united Europe of artists and poets as the antipode to the gradually more bureaucratic European Union of politicians.[35]

The Power of the Center

The image of Central Europe and Bohemia is closely connected to much older imaginings of the European continent. One of the first historical inscriptions of Bohemia on the world map (and in the *Weltbilt*) comes to us from the engraving made by Johannes Putsch (Bucius) in 1537, labeled *Europa in forma virginis* ("Europe pictured as a maiden"), and later called *Europa regina* ("Europe as a queen"). This type of anthropomorphized map of Europe, combining a rather precise picture of the region with a metaphorical layer of imperial imagining stretched over it, became widely known when it was included in the editions of Sebastian Münster's highly influential *Cosmographia* (versions of which were appearing from 1544 to 1628) and Heinrich Bünting's (Buntingus) *Itinerarium Sacrae Scripturae* (first edition from 1581; the Czech edition was published in Prague in 1592 by M. Daniel Adam of Veleslavín and is still in the possession of the Library at the Royal Premonstratensian Canon Seat at Strahov).[36] These

---

[34] Rupnik, *The Other Europe*, 5.

[35] Hans Magnus Enzensberger, *Ach Europa! Wahrnehmungen aus sieben Ländern. Mit einem Epilog aus dem Jahre 2006* (Frankfurt am Main: Suhrkamp, 2006).

[36] Elke Anna Werner, "Triumphierende Europa—Klagende Europa. Zur visuellen Konstruktion europäischer Selbstbilder in der Frühen Neuzeit," in *Europa-Stier und Sternenkranz. Von der Union mit Zeus zum Staatenverbund: Gründungsmythen Europas in Literatur, Musik und Kunst*, edited by Roland Alexander Ißler, and Almut-Barbara Renger (Bonn: Vandenhoeck & Ruprecht, 2009), 241–260.

maps were produced not long after the rediscovery and reintroduction of Ptolemy's geography, which revolutionized the general practice of schematic map making, adding to it a new objectivity but also allowing for easier ideological bias. (Ptolemy's *Cosmographia,* or *Geographia,* was translated into Latin already in 1409, but only by the late 1470s did the Italian editions include engraved maps, the influence of which virtually ended the predominance of simplified, symbolic medieval T-O maps or subjective renderings of the landscape.)[37]

Putsch's *Europa regina* uncannily superimposes the specter of Europe as queen[38] on the continent, crowning Hispania, the main seat of the ruling Hapsburg monarchy, as her head, with the two major powers Gallia and Germania figuring as her chest, and the long tail of her dress covering the "dark parts" of Europe all the way down to Moscovia on the North and Pelopponesus in the South. All the variants of these maps seem to have a peculiar round spot in their very center: prominently separated from the enveloping Germania, we find a perfect circle of Bohemia marked by a *bordura*, being in one case a line of schematically drawn coniferous trees, in another a mountain ring that almost resembles a laurel wreath. The circle is pierced by Albis, the Elbe river. In some versions another vein-shaped line leads from the bordered territory to Frankfurt, probably depicting Via Carolina, and inside the circle there is a schematic rendering of spires, most probably of the St. Vitus Cathedral. (See insert, figure 21.)

This centrally positioned Bohemia has traditionally been read as representing the very heart of Europe, the true center of the European civilization. (It is sometimes also seen as a medallion hanging from the queen's neck.) The idea of Bohemia/Czech Republic as the center and the "heart of Europe" that survives in popular culture up to now had a highly formative influence on the often melodramatic discourse surrounding its role in Europe, at least since the Revival.[39] The cultural journal *Květy* writes in this tradition already in 1837: "the Czech, round, mountain-bordered lands rests on the heart of Europe unpretentiously as a tender little rose" ("česká, kulatá, horami olemovaná země—jak zřejmě co něžná růžinka na srdci Europinu spočívá").[40]

---

[37] The gist of this long story of map making is that they were invaded with the ideology of perspective; for more on this, see David Harvey, *The Condition of Postmodernity: An Enquiry into the Origins of Cultural Change* (Oxford: Blackwell, 1990), especially Part III, "The Experience of Space and Time."

[38] Although some sources argue that it is an image of Charles V, meant to celebrate the unification of Europe by the Hapsburg monarchy.

[39] The discussions about where the real heart and center of Europe is, are ongoing and can be followed in popular encyclopedias. If we believe Wikipedia, there are currently seven places claiming the official status of the geographic center of Europe, distributed geographically from Germany to Lithuania and Ukraine. (See insert, figure 22.)

[40] Quoted in Vladimír Macura, *Znamení zrodu: České národní obrození jako kulturní typ* (Jinočany: H & H 1995), 173.

Most of the Revivalist discussions surrounding this trope derive their legitimacy from the brief so-called Slaven Kapitel in J. G. Herder's *Ideen zur Philosophie der Geschichte der Menschheit* (1784–1791), which was already seminal for the Revivalists because of the central argument supporting the linguistic definition of the national (as recreation of the language after centuries of heavy Germanization was for them the necessary first step to political emancipation of the nation). But Herder also provides an idealized image of the Slavs ("Slavians") in *Ideen*, especially juxtaposing them to the bellicosity of the Germans: "they were never enterprising warriors or adventures, like the Germans" (482), but "industrious people that cultivated the land abandoned or plundered by others, people of agriculture and domestic arts, harbor building and trade" (482–483). Herder's ideal Slavs were interested in crafts and a gay, musical life, loved quiet and domestic industry, "were liberal, hospitable to excess, lovers of pastoral freedom, but submissive and obedient, enemies to spoil and rapine," were also peace-loving and thus often oppressed, and suffered under the yoke of other nations for centuries (483). But the fate of the Slavs was to see a bright, victorious future. Herder predicts:

> the wheel of changing Time . . . resolves without ceasing, these now deeply sunk, but one industrious and happy people, will at length awake from their long and heavy slumber, shake off the chains of slavery, enjoy the possession of their delightful lands from the Adriatic sea to the Carpathian mountains, from the Don to the Muldaw, and celebrate on them their ancient festivals of peaceful trade and industry. (483–484)

As some Revival scholars have proven, most compellingly Vladimír Macura in his groundbreaking book, *Znamení zrodu* (1983), the importance of Herder's philosophy for the Revivalists goes far beyond a simple identification with this idea of victorious Slavic rule from the Mediterranean sea to the sea of Azov. As Macura shows,[41] the Revivalists took from Herder not just the term *Humanität* (in their search for the Slavic tradition of humanity) but also explored the specific resonances in his concept of the *Mitte/mittel*, the center, the middle. It is evident in many Revivalist texts how this concept becomes the means to define the re-created Czech culture, then often presented as a center between the Greek (Hellenistic, meditated via Roman culture) and Germanic heritage of European culture. Macura talks about the Revivalist "mystique of the center," as a projection not only into the concept of the geographical,

[41] Vladimír Macura, *Znamení zrodu*; see also Macura, *Český sen* (Prague: Paseka, 1998); and Dušan Třeštík, *Mysliti dějiny* (Prague and Litomyšl: Paseka, 1999).

but also into the culturally mediating space of European knowledge (173), especially in the sphere of literary exchange, understood as an important root of literary European erudition.

The idea of the middle is often translated into the trope of a bridge: the center is understood as the sphere oriented towards the future in which the nation finally fulfills its "destiny" of bridging between the West and the East. (And we might also recall Bachmann here: "If bridges here are sound, I'll walk on solid ground."/ "*Sind hier die Brücken heil, geh ich auf gutem Grund.*") The bridging has often been pictured as a point of translation between Eastern (Slavic) emotionality and Western (German) rationality, the two traditions of *poesis* and *ratio*, and this concept was especially dear to Palacký, but strongly opposed by others, mainly later Masaryk, who claimed that imperialist nations actually preclude the possibility of tolerating a mediator between them.

The positive value of the middle also reflects how the concept of "prostřednost" ("mediocrity") is cherished in Czech and more broadly Central European culture, where the golden middle way ("zlatá střední cesta") as a balanced, rational, cautious attitude that excludes extremes plays an important role, and the position of the mediator is also understood as that of compromise, realism, and pragmatism; i.e., the features traditionally ascribed to Czech identity. And last but not least, the center and heart of Europe is quite often, at least since the Revival, seen as a condensation and synthesis of the "best European qualities."

As Above So Below

Yet, Bohemia actually does not lie by the sea, but on/upon it. Paleontological remains indicate the presence of a real Silurian sea, full of trilobites, that lays petrified in the geological layers of the Prague Basin, discovered and broadly studied by the French paleontologist Joachim Barrande since the 1840s.[42] What became to be called the Barrandien Area later turned into an attraction to other explorers and researchers, but was also used as another metaphorical proof of the ancient and seminal importance of this geographical space for the whole Europe, as the contemporaneous "colonies hypothesis" actually claimed that it was from these little seas that life spread gradually on the Earth.

[42] Barrande was publishing his encyclopedia, *Système silurien du centre de la Bohême*, from 1852–1881. In a famous speech at the inauguration of the collections in the National Museum, the geologist and director of the National Museum, Antonín Frič, praised Barrande in this way: "He brought for us from France, the cradle of noble ideas, a ray of light of the geological science, a ray, which enabled us to browse through the leaves of history of ancient ages, through the Earth´s beds in which a fossil speaks as writing. Barrande carried out the research of the Silurian system in Bohemia splendidly and honestly. Honestly, because his motto was: 'C´est ce que j´ai vu.'" Quoted in Horný, Radvan, and Vojtěch Turek, "Joachim Barrande, His Life, Work and Heritage to World Palaeontology," accessed March 21, 2010, http://www.trilobit.biz/joachim.html.

The hidden Silurian layers also soon became an important popular tropus, read as the traces of extinct civilizations, interfaces that connect not only prehistory and history, but also the world of the living with that of the dead, the spheres of the visible and invisible. In the flourishing esoteric literature at the turn of the nineteenth and twentieth centuries situated metonymically in Old Prague, the Silurian becomes synonymous with the saturnine and is evoked as a place with enormous effects on its inhabitants. This trope is well present in the work of Meyrink, Arbes and Karásek, but reached probably the clearest formulation in Crafword's *Witch of Prague*, in which the old alchemist claims: "have no thought of removing myself or my goods from Prague. (…) It is saturnine. The foundation of its houses rests on the Silurian formation, which is more than can be said for any other capital, as far as I know." The saturnine/Silurian sometimes reaches the extreme of becoming the place of a burial, a space of coffin (Karásek's *Romány tří mágů*: "If I want to see the world like the dead look at it from their coffins, I go to Prague"), with the reversal between the universe of the dead and the living—the spectral layers coming alive, the world of the living becoming zombiefied.[43]

Recent geological research introduced another interesting trope to the picturing of the Bohemian lands, as some geologists and astronomers started to work with the hypothesis that the Czech or Prague Basin is in fact a prehistoric impact crater, a phenomenon known as *astrobleme* (from Greek *astron, blema,* "star wound"), as the moldavites, tektites abundant in some parts of the country, are presumed to be "concrete" traces of the impact. This hypothesis was originally promoted by Michael D. Papagiannis and Farouk el Baz, who presented it in *The New Scientist* in the late 1980s,[44] to the dismay of some Czech geologists and the delight of others, especially the geo-climatologist–philosopher Václav Cílek.[45] But the first record of this premise is actually much older: it comes to us already from Galileo, who in *Sidereus nuncius* compares the craters he observes on the surface of the moon with the shape of Bohemia:

> There is one other point, which I must on no account forget, which I have noticed and rather wondered at. It is this:—The

[43] See Jiří Karásek ze Lovic, *Romány tří mágů* (Prague: Volvox Globator, 2012), 27, and F. Marion Crawford, *The Witch of Prague: A Fantastic Tale* (New York: Macmillan, 1919), 33. Gustav Meyring would even go so far as to read the Silurian as the doorway to Hell (his "chřtán pekelný" is supposedly located somewhere in Lesser Town in Prague) in his book *Valpurgisnacht*, and it is of note here that in Dante, the seventh circle of hell, the sphere of Saturn, is pictured as an *ocean* of blood and fire.

[44] M. D. Papagiannis, and F. El-Baz, "A 300-km Oval Feature in Central Europe Could Be the Remnant of a Huge Old Impact Crater," *Bulletin of the American Astronomical Society* 20 (1988): 1043; and M. D. Papagiannis, and F. El-Baz, "The Praha Basin: A Circular Feature in Central Europe," (Abstract), *EOS Trans. Amer. Geophys. Union* 69, no. 44 (1988), 1293.

[45] Václav Cílek, *Krajiny vnitřní a vnější* (Prague: Nakladatelství Dokořán, 2002).

> middle of the Moon, as it seems, is occupied by a certain cavity larger than all the rest, and in shape perfectly round. I have looked at this depression near both the first and third quarters, and I have represented it as well as I can in the second illustration already given. It produces the same appearance as to effects of light and shade as a tract like Bohemia would produce on the earth if it were shut in on all sides by very lofty mountains arranged on the circumference of a perfect circle; for the tract in the Moon is walled in with peaks of such enormous height that the furthest side adjacent to the dark portion of the Moon is seen bathed in sunlight before the boundary between light and shade reaches half-way across the circular space.[46]

Neither Galileo nor the American astronomers fill this alleged meteoric crater with any semiosis of the national, but the image of Czechs as the "offspring of the Stars" became surprisingly ubiquitous both during the Revival and in more recent periods. Cílek himself expands the geological hypothesis into a metaphorical statement about the Czech character, claiming that this might be the "metaphysical" reason why the Czechs so often feel crushed to the ground but also tempted by the universe. "My bychom vzhůru k nebesům a jsme zde Zemí spjatí" ("We would go up to the skies but are tied down to the Earth") is also the most famous verse from Jan Neruda's *Písně kosmické* (*Cosmic Songs*, 1878), in which he celebrates the scientific exploration of the universe but also constantly contrasts it with images of "smallness," immediately understandable as a meditation on the state of the national culture. The poem "Jsou-li tam žáby taky" ("Do Frogs Exist There Too?") from this collection offers the most typical example of this: "Frogs sat around a puddle/And gazed at heavens high/Frog teacher pounding into skulls/The science of the sky" ("Seděly žáby v kaluži,/hleděly vzhůru k nebi,/starý jim žabák učený/odvíral tvrdé lebi"). The image of frogs in a puddle is very close in symbolism to "worms in the puddle," which became the decadents' emblem of the nation.[47] But here, smallness combined with erudition and perseverance allows for the

---

[46] Quoted from the English translation of *Siderius Nuncius,* in Galileo Galilei, *The Sidreal Messenger of Galileo Galilei, and a part of the Preface to Kepler's Dioptrics,* ed. Edward Stafford Carlos (London: Rivingtons, 1880); Wikisource.

[47] One of the prominent Czech Decadents, Arnošt Procházka, talked about the Czechs as "worms in a puddle, long forgotten by the whole of Europe, the whole world." Rejecting any vision of "sweet Bohemia" and Biedermeier concepts of Czech pettiness, the Decadents particularly attacked the myth of the nation's "dove-like nature," which they read as cowardice and latent hostility combined with servility. For them, the "greatness" of the nation was nothing

exploration of space—as if Neruda, himself an amateur astronomer, could anticipate that his poems would actually reach space one day, as happened in 2009 when Andrew Feustel took *Cosmic Songs* on board the NASA expedition to fix the Hubble telescope.

But the presumed Czech national tendency to "raise the heads to the skies" more often than other nations reached its apotheosis already three decades before the NASA flight, in a heavily publicized and mythologized/semiotized event in March 1978, when the Czech astronaut–explorer Vladimír Remek spent a week onboard the Soviet space station Salyut 6 and significantly came back proclaiming that he had seen "the blaze of Prague from space." Vladimír Macura in one of his later essays, called simply "Remek," traces (among other important aspects) the process by which this achievement was immediately linked to the Revivalists' historical quest for the self-determination of the nation:

> Almost two centuries have passed since the scientist and Revivalist of Czech language Josef Dobrovský wrote its grammar in a foreign language [i.e., German] and did not hope for its resurrection, and when the attempts to show that Czech is as rich as other languages and that the works of world-famous authors can be translated into it were ridiculed. Now it became the third cosmic and the second Slavic language that resounds from space, about which only poets wrote their poems so far.[48]

Macura shows in his analysis how Remek's ascent crowns the Czech national fate, stretching presumably from the myths of the Bohemians coming to the mountain Říp and settling around it, through Countess Libuše's (the pagan queen's) famous prophecy in Vyšehrad that the glory of this nation and its main city will reach the stars.[49] By becoming the third nation to send its citizen into space, and Czech "the third language of the cosmos," heavy semiosis was set in motion again, not only aimed at proving the superiority of the Socialist block over the West in space exploration and science generally, but also to proclaim the Revivalist project of national imagining as having been accomplished and consummated via the alliance with the Soviet Union. The sky thus became the new sea.

---

more than a delusion—a result of false optics and an unwillingness to face the world—and the decaying state of the nation clearly manifested itself in the aggressiveness of people towards each other; see Robert Pynsent, *Questions of Identity: Czech and Slovak Ideas on Nationality and Personality* (Budapest: CEU Press, 1994).

[48] Václav Macura, *Šťastný věk* (Prague: Academia, 2009), 210–228.

[49] Ibid., 211.

Postscript

On April 29, 2010, the Czechs finally got their sea. The British newspaper *The Economist* proclaimed the European map as "outdated and illogical" and proposed in an ironic article a "continental drift" that would correct some of the illogical placements and soothe tensions among neighboring European nations. (See insert, figure 23.) As *The Economist* claims that "rejigging the map of Europe would make life more logical and friendlier," it suggests among other moves swapping the Czech Republic with Belgium because:

> Belgium's incomprehensible Flemish-French language squabbles (which have just brought down a government) are redolent of central Europe at its worst, especially the nonsenses Slovakia thinks up for its Hungarian-speaking ethnic minority. So Belgium should swap places with the Czech Republic. The stolid, well-organised Czechs would get on splendidly with their new Dutch neighbours, and vice versa.[50]

The idea met with jubilant reception in the Czech media and public, not only because of the flattering image of a disciplined country but because the swap would be a fulfillment of many wishes—it would mean staying in Europe but being finally far away from the East, and close to France, which for so long stood as the cultural model in Europe. And we would finally have a sea, although a cold one—a sea that would free us from the need to semiotize its supposed place or invest in the lack of it. And, it will not—I hope—surprise the reader at this point that one commentator longingly exclaimed, "it would be so easy to drive to Amsterdam, buy some pot, and then smoke it on the beach and watch the stars." It would be as above, so below, finally.

BIBLIOGRAPHY

Apollinaire, Guillaume. *Alcools*. Paris: Éditions Galimard, 1920.

Appadurai, Arjun. "Disjuncture and Difference in the Global Cultural Economy." *Public Culture* 2, no. 2 (1990): 295–310.

Bachmann, Ingeborg. *Ich weiß keine bessere Welt: Unveröffentlichte Gedichte*. Edited by Isolde Moser, Heinz Bachmann, and Christian Moser. Munich: Piper, 2000.

———. *Werke* (Erster Band). Munich: Piper, 1993.

Berger, Stefan, Linas Eriksonas, and Andrew Mycock, eds. *Narrating the Nation: Representations in History, Media and the Arts*. Oxford: Berghahn, 2008.

[50] *The Economist*, April 29, 2010. Web. <http://www.economist.com/world/europe/displayStory.cfm?story_id=16003661>

Bugge, Peter. "The Use of the Middle: Mittelleuropa vs. Střední Evropa." *European Review of History [Revue européenne d'Histoire]*, 6 no. 1 (1999): 15–34.

Cílek, Václav. *Krajiny vnitřní a vnější.* Prague: Nakladatelství Dokořán, 2002.

———. *Vývoj a zločiny panslavismu*. Prague: ISE, 1989.

Crawford, F. Marion. *The Witch of Prague: A Fantastic Tale.* New York: Macmillan, 1919.

Economist, online. April 29, 2010. http://www.economist.com/world/europe/displayStory.cfm?story_id=16003661.

Enzensberger, Hans Magnus. *Ach Europa! Wahrnehmungen aus sieben Ländern: Mit einem Epilog aus dem Jahre 2006.* Frankfurt am Main: Suhrkamp, 2006.

Fried, Erich. *Ich grenz noch an ein Wort und an ein andres Land: Über Ingeborg Bachmann—Erinnerungen, einige Anmerkungen zu ihrem Gedicht "Böhmen liegt am Meer" und ein Nachruf.* Berlin: Friedenauer Presse, 1983.

Galilei, Galileo. *The Sidereal Messenger of Galileo Galilei, and a Part of the Preface to Kepler's Dioptrics,* edited by Edward Stafford Carlos. London: Rivingtons, 1880. Wikisource.

Harvey, David. *The Condition of Postmodernity: An Enquiry into the Origins of Cultural Change*. Oxford: Blackwell Publishers, 1990.

Herder, Johann Gottfried. *Outlines of the Philosophy of the History of Man, vol. II.* New York: Bergman Publishers, 1800. Archive.org.

Horný, Radvan, and Vojtěch Turek. "Joachim Barrande, His Life, Work and Heritage to World Palaeontology." Accessed March 21, 2010. http://www.trilobit.biz/joachim.html.

Jonson, Ben. *Conversations with Drummond of Hawthornden*. London: Shakespearean Society, 1842.

Karásek ze Lovic, Jiří. *Romány tří mágů*. Prague: Volvox Globator, 2012.

Kundera, Milan. *The Curtain: An Essay in Seven Parts.* New York: Harper Collins, 2005.

———. "The Tragedy of Central Europe," *The New York Review of Books* 31 no. 7 (April 26, 1984).

———. Milan Kundera Interview. By A. Finkielkraut. *Cross Currents: A Yearbook of Central European Culture* 1 (1982): 15–29.

Lacan, Jacques. *Four Fundamental Concepts of Psychoanalysis.* New York: W.W. Norton, 1985.

Macura, Vladimír. *Český sen*. Prague: Paseka, 1998.

———. *Znamení zrodu: České národní obrození jako kulturní typ*. Jinočany: H&H 1995.

Masaryk, T. G. *Rusko a Evropa. Sociologické skizzy*. Prague: Ústav TGM, 2001.

Milosz, Czeslaw. "Central European Attitudes." *Cross Currents: A Yearbook of Central European Culture* 5 (1986): 101–108.

Nekula, Marek. *"...v jednom poschodí vnitřní babylonské věže..."/Jazyky Franze Kafky*. Prague: Nakladatelství Franze Kafky, 2003.

Nethersole, Reingard. "Ingeborg Bachmann's Poetry: A Sense of Passing." Pages 139–160 in *Thunder Rumbling At My Heels: Tracing Ingeborg Bachmann*, edited by Gudrun Brokoph-Mauch. Riverside, CA: Ariadne Press, 1998.

Nietzsche, Friedrich W. *Human, All Too Human: A Book for Free Spirits.* Lincoln: University of Nebraska Press, 1984.

Nöth, Winfried. "Der Text als Raum." In *Sprache, Onomatopöie, Rhetorik, Namen, Idiomatik, Grammatik: Festschrift für Karl Sornig*, edited by Dieter W. Halwachs et al., 163–174. Graz, Austria: Universität Presse, 1994.

Papagiannis, M. D., and F. El-Baz. "A 300-km Oval Feature in Central Europe Could Be the Remnant of a Huge Old Impact Crater." *Bulletin of the American Astronomical Society* 20 (1988): 1043.

———. "The Praha Basin: A Circular Feature in Central Europe." Abstract. EOS, Transactions American Geophysical Union 69 no. 44 (1988): 1293.

Patočka, Jan. "European Culture." *Cross Currents: A Yearbook of Central European Culture* 3 (1983): 3–6.

Pynsent, Robert. *Questions of Identity: Czech and Slovak Ideas on Nationality and Personality.* Budapest: CEU Press 1994.

Roberts, G.M., ed. *Germany and the Imagined East.* Newcastle, UK: Cambridge Scholars Press, 2005.

Rupnik, Jacques. *The Other Europe.* New York: Pantheon Books, 1988.

Szporluk, Roman. "Defining 'Central Europe': Power, Politics, and Culture." *Cross Currents: A Yearbook of Central European Culture* 1 (1982): 30–38.

Třeštík, Dušan. *Mysliti dějiny*. Prague and Litomyšl: Paseka, 1999.

Urzidil, Johannes. *Goethe v Čechách*. Prague: Pistorius & Olšanská, 2009.

Valeš, Vlasta, ed. *Doma v cizině. Češi ve Vídni ve 20. století / Zu Hause in der Fremde. Tschechen in Wien im 20. Jahrhundert.* Prague: Skriptorium, 2002.

Werner, Elke Anna. "Triumphierende Europa—Klagende Europa. Zur visuellen Konstruktion europäischer Selbstbilder in der Frühen Neuzeit." In *Europa—Stier und Sternenkranz. Von der Union mit Zeus zum Staatenverbund. Gründungsmythen Europas in Literatur, Musik und Kunst*, edited by Roland Alexander Ißler, and Almut-Barbara Renger, 241–260. Bonn: Vandenhoeck & Ruprecht, 2009.

NATIONALISM IN THE USSR AND YUGOSLAVIA: HISTORICAL AND COMPARATIVE PERSPECTIVES

Andrey Shcherbak*

Abstract

The late 1980s and early 1990s were characterized by the sudden rise of nationalist movements in almost all Soviet and Yugoslav ethnic regions. It is argued that the rise of political nationalism since the late 1980s can be explained by the development of cultural nationalism in the previous decades, as an unintended outcome of Communist nationalities policy. Soviet and Yugoslav political and cultural nationalism are studied in a historical and comparative perspective. All ethnic regions are examined throughout the entire history of both Communist states—the Soviet Union (49 regions, 1917–91) and Yugoslavia (8 regions, 1941–95), using the structural equation modeling (SEM) approach. This paper aims to make at least three contributions in the field. First, it offers a methodological contribution for studying nationalism: a "quantification of history" approach. Quantitative values are assigned to historical trends and events. Having constructed variables from historical data, I use conventional statistical methods like SEM. Second, this paper contributes to the theoretical debate about the role of cultural autonomy in multiethnic states. The results rethink the notion of "cultural autonomy" as a solution for interethnic conflict. Cultural nationalism matters: it indirectly reinforces political nationalism. In both cases, concessions in the cultural domain did not stop the growth of political nationalism in the late 1980s. Finally, the paper statistically proves that the break between early Soviet and Stalinist nationalities policy explains the entire Soviet nationalities policy. In

* Andrey Shcherbak is a Senior Research Fellow at the Laboratory for Comparative Social Research, National Research University Higher School of Economics in St. Petersburg, Russia.

fact, the late Soviet nationalities policy was inherited from the Stalinist period. This finding, revealed in other studies, is now supported by statistical evidence.

INTRODUCTION

The focus of this paper is nationalism in the Soviet and Yugoslav ethnic republics. The late 1980s and early 1990s were characterized by the sudden rise of nationalist movements across the Soviet Union and Yugoslavia. As a result, these states—Communist ethnic federations—collapsed. This paper aims to answer two questions. First, how may one explain nationalism in the Soviet and Yugoslav ethnic republics? Second, and perhaps more importantly, should the rise of ethnic nationalism in the Soviet Union and Yugoslavia be treated as a kind of deviation related solely to the crisis of the Communist state, or should it be regarded as a more complex phenomenon? Is there any difference between the roots of nationalism in the two states?

Cultural nationalism is crucial for understanding the roots of political nationalism. The USSR and Yugoslavia rejected any kind of assimilation policy, claiming the right of cultural and political autonomy for every nationality. The model of ethnic federalism created opportunities for the development of "ethnic institutions." As a result, most union and autonomous ethnic republics showed significant progress in national and cultural development.

I endeavor to study Soviet and Yugoslav nationalism from a historical and comparative perspective. All ethnic regions within each Communist state will be examined throughout their entire history—the Soviet Union (49 regions, 1917–91) and Yugoslavia (8 regions, 1941–95), using a structural equation modeling approach.

This paper aims to make at least three contributions to the field. First, it is a methodological contribution for studying nationalism in post-Communist countries. Instead of a conventional, descriptive, historical case study or survey-based quantitative approach, I use a combined one, a "quantification of history." I go deep into the history, back to 1917, and assign quantitative values to historical events and trends for use in statistical analysis.

Second, this paper contributes to the theoretical debate about the role of cultural autonomy in multiethnic states. The results challenge the concept of "cultural autonomy" as a solution to interethnic conflict. The USSR and Yugoslavia varied in the pace of the cultural nationalism developed within their borders; however, in both cases concessions in the cultural domain failed to stop the growth of political nationalism in the late 1980s.

Finally, the paper statistically proves that the break between early Soviet and Stalinist policy concerning nationalities explains the entire Soviet nationalities policy. In fact, the late-Soviet period nationalities policy was inherited from the Stalinist period.

The paper consists of five sections. The first section provides a theoretical framework. The second one contains a brief historical outline of nationalities policy in the USSR and Yugoslavia. The third describes data and methodology. The forth section includes results and interpretation. The last section concludes.

NATIONALISM AND MODERNIZATION

My theoretical approach lies within the modernist nationalism framework. This paper understands nationalism not as an idea or sentiment, but as a polity-seeking (or polity-upgrading) national movement that aims to establish or upgrade an autonomous national polity (Brubaker 1996, 411–412). Modernism holds that nationalism is a rather recent invention. As Benedict Anderson and Ernst Gellner argue, education, science, and technology are key factors in the emergence of nationalism in the modern era (Gellner 2008). Anderson (2006) focuses on print languages as starting points for nation-building, a linguistic approach. Gellner (2008) places emphasis on cultural homogeneity through mass education in a national language. Miroslav Hroch (2000) argues that nations emerge as a result of the activities of ethnic movements. National intellectuals—the by-product of modernization—play a significant role in the emergence of ethnic movements.

Two concepts are of crucial importance for my theoretical framework: the concepts of David Laitin and Dmitry Gorenburg. Laitin, in his book *Nations, States, and Violence* (2007) argues that nationalism is a privilege of rich societies. Only rich societies can afford to invest or spend resources in inventing/maintaining/spreading traditions, customs, beliefs, etc., and creating the “imagined communities” that we call nations.

Gorenburg’s (2001, 2003) concept is based on the division of nationalism into political nationalism and cultural nationalism. Political nationalism (separatism) may be defined as the demand for a declaration of national sovereignty and recognition of the right to national self-determination—up to the point of secession. Cultural nationalism is defined as support for a titular official language and culture, the expansion of its teaching in schools, and the introduction of a greater or lesser degree of requirements/incentives to learn the titular language by members of a non-titular nation. Gorenburg argues that the strength of political nationalism depends on the support for ethnic institutions. The level of support for ethnic institutions, in turn, heavily depends on the willingness/capacity of regional leadership to invest a sufficient amount of resources in them. In other words, nations emerge as the outcome of nation-building (Gorenburg 2001, 2003).

Ethnic institutions lead to the emergence of a national educated class/intellectuals (*intelligentsia*), who become the driving force of political mobilization. How does it happen? There are at least two possible explanations. First,

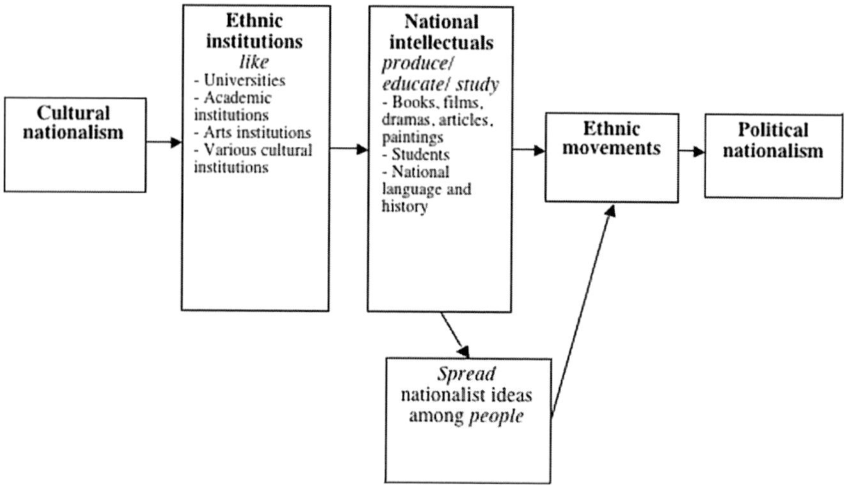

Figure 1. Theoretical model outline.

intellectuals are responsible for the creation of national identity (language, literature, culture, history, and so on). Second, through participating in the educational process, intellectuals create social networks among the students they teach in universities. Gorenburg (2001, 2003) claims that it was the national intelligentsia who established nationalist movements in the Russian ethnic republics in the late 1980s. The national intelligentsia is a key intermediary between ethnic institutions and the rise of political nationalism. Intellectuals are employed in education, science, the media, industry and culture. They are responsible for the creation and distribution of national culture—via books, journals, articles, paintings, films, and history textbooks, as well as lectures in universities and classes in schools.

To test this theoretical model, this paper focuses on two cases—the Soviet Union and Yugoslavia. The choice of these cases represents two extremes within the research design. The Soviet Union was a highly centralized state. Regional units could not spend resources on ethnic institution-building without Moscow's approval. Such investments depended on the region's formal status in the official administrative hierarchy: union republics had many more chances to invest in cultural nation-building than national administrative districts. Valerie Bunce (1998, 1989) argues that the difference in institutional structure between the USSR and Yugoslavia is the key factor in explaining the different outcomes of political mobilization in these states; namely, violence and non-violence.

Yugoslavia presents a contrasting case with at least three important distinctions. First, from the early 1960s Tito's response to Yugoslav nation-building

TABLE 1. Official administrative hierarchy in the USSR and Yugoslavia

USSR	Yugoslavia
Union Republic	Federal republic
Autonomous Republic (ASSR)	Autonomous province
Autonomous Oblast' (AO)	
National Autonomous District (NAD)	

was decentralization and confederation. Therefore, state-led intervention into cultural policy was less likely. Second, Yugoslavia existed for a shorter period than the Soviet Union. Collective memories about ethnic civil war (during World War II) were stronger in Yugoslavia than Soviet grievances lingering after the Russian Civil War of 1917–25. Third, nationalist movements among intellectuals emerged in the Yugoslav republics as early as the mid-nineteenth century. Some of these movements supported the idea of a united South Slavic state, but others stressed the salience of particular nationalities. These factors may have contributed to the relatively lower importance of cultural nationalism in the case of Yugoslavia, compared to the USSR.

According to Gorenburg (2001, 2003), the level of ethnic institutional development depended on the status of the region in the official Soviet national-administrative hierarchy (Table 1). The larger the investment in ethnic institutions, the larger the number of national intelligentsia. In its turn, the presence of numerous intellectuals also increases the probability of mass ethnic-movement emergence.

Within the enormous number of articles on post-Communist nationalism, quite a few focus on the relationship between cultural and political nationalism. Yet most of them focus only on some limited aspects of cultural nationalism.

In his recent book, Keith Darden (2014) links regional differences in the intensity of UPA (Ukrainian Insurgent Army) insurgents' activity in Western Ukraine from 1946–52 with the pre-Soviet education systems in two regions. David Laitin in his numerous papers (e.g., Laitin, Petersen, and Slogum 1992; Laitin 1998) has stressed the importance of titular language to nationalist movements. In the late Soviet context, language standardization and language rationalization were among the most important issues in the nationalist agenda on all administrative levels.

In this paper, both language and education are taken into consideration in addition to other factors. It is assumed that the extent of political nationalism in the USSR and Yugoslavia in the late 1980s and 1990s is explained by the history of cultural nationalism development over the previous decades.

Both the USSR and Yugoslavia were multiethnic Communist federations, and nationalities policy was an important part of their political agenda. The main goals of the central government were the maintenance of interethnic peace, the creation of supraethnic identity, and the prevention of secession. However, both the Soviet and Yugoslav governments failed at achieving any of these goals. The next section presents an overview of nationalities policy in Russia and Yugoslavia. In each case, the entire period of Communist rule is split into five periods.

HISTORY OF SOVIET AND YUGOSLAV NATIONALISM

The Soviet Union

1) The Revolution and Civil War (1917–25). The Russian Empire was a unitary state. The imperial political and administrative structure was not built for the rise of nationalism. Russian governors appointed by St. Petersburg managed all the provinces. The last two tsars—Alexander III and Nicholas II—were moderate nationalists who attempted to restrict the rights of some particular nationalities. Since the late nineteenth century, pan-Slavism was adopted as a kind of official ideology. The Imperial Russian government underestimated the power of nationalism and failed to implement policies to assimilate or at least pacify discontented ethnic groups. Ultimately, Russia's participation in World War I precipitated the collapse of the Tsarist Empire.

In an attempt to attract new allies, the Bolsheviks declared the right of self-determination as one of their political principles. Indeed, ethnic federalism was the Bolsheviks' political solution for the "national question." In the aftermath of the Civil War, in 1922, the USSR was established as a union of equal nations and republics. It was repeatedly stressed that the USSR was no longer a Russian empire. Moreover, all union republics were theoretically granted the right to secede.

2) The Early Soviet Period (1926–39). During the Civil War, the Bolsheviks were shocked by "the bloody lesson of 1919": Ukrainian peasants revolted against Bolshevik rule, having been mobilized along ethnic lines. Having repressed the revolt, the Bolsheviks had to admit that nationalism could not be ignored anymore.

The Bolsheviks adopted the "The Greater Danger" approach: Ignorance of the role of nationalism and national culture by the early Soviet regime could be understood as a continuation of Great-power Russian nationalism and colonialism. Therefore, the Bolsheviks chose to support minority nationalism against Great-power Russian nationalism. Russian chauvinism was treated as the Greater danger in comparison to local nationalism (Martin 2001). The political impact of this approach was the adoption of the original nationalities policy, aimed at promoting local nationalism and accelerating the social, economic, political, and cultural development of "backward" ethnic groups. Terry Martin (2001) defined this approach as "The Affirmative Action Empire." Rather than a melting pot, the Soviet Union became the incubator of new nations. The distinctive features of this so-called Affirmative Action Empire were as follows:

- *Korennizatsia (nativization).* Titular ethnic groups were given some politically biased advantages for development, like ethnic quotas in central universities, job quotas in government organizations, and resources to develop ethnic institutions. This policy indirectly endorsed anti-Russian sentiments; and the Bolsheviks had no choice but to tolerate their rise.
- *Latinization campaign.* The Soviet government assisted in spreading written language to all, even small ethnic groups. This policy coincided with numerous proposals by some linguists and intellectuals (from Turkic ethnic groups) to shift to the Latin script. By the early 1930s the Latinization campaign was completed.
- *Rapid state-led nation-building.* Soviet authorities invented new ethnic identities and ascribed them, drew national boundaries, established titular language schools, promoted local elites, printed books and newspapers in native languages, supported local intellectuals (writers, poets, artists, intellectuals, historians, etc.), and established national territorial units.

However, by the mid-1930s, the Affirmative Action Empire policy had reached its peak. The promotion of local nationalism resulted in a rise in local anti-Communist sentiments. Industrialization and collectivization had proven Russians to be the most loyal ethnic group in the USSR. By the late 1930s, Stalin had radically changed the Soviet nationalities policy. Local nationalisms were attacked as "bourgeois" and "pro-capitalist" political movements, and Great-power Russian nationalism was endorsed as the new official policy.

3) Great-Power Russian Nationalism (1940–55). Stalin's new nationalities policy stressed the pivotal role of Russians in the new Soviet state. This shift has several possible explanations. First, the Bolsheviks wanted to secure the political support they were receiving from Russians, the most loyal ethnic group. Due to the opposition of Russians to the anti-imperialist and anti-Russian campaign (which was endorsed by ethnic minorities), Stalin decided to meet their demands. Attacks on Russian culture were banned, and pro-Western cultural orientations were explicitly prohibited (Martin 2001). Second, the Bolsheviks perceived Russians as the ethnic glue for the USSR. In the 1920s, there was an effort to avoid discontent from local elites, so Russian settlement in other ethnic regions was not part of the nationalities policy. Following the policy change, the central government actively promoted Russian migration to other republics, regarding ethnic Russians as the main support group (Brandenberger 2000).

At the political level, Stalin implemented a policy of Russification: from the late 1930s, regional first party secretaries were predominantly Russian. The outbreak of the World War II again proved the loyalty of Russians to the Soviet regime. Realizing that Russians could be mobilized most effectively along ethnic lines, Stalin issued several decrees to endorse Russian ethnic sentiments. In 1944 several ethnic groups were accused of large-scale collaboration with the Nazis and were subsequently deported to Central Asia.

The promotion of Great-power Russian nationalism led to Russification in cultural and education policies as well. Prewar mass terror and emergency policies implemented during World War II had led to purges of the national intelligentsia in many ethnic republics. The Soviet government no longer promoted pro-nationalist cultural policies; for example, in autonomous republics the circulation of books printed in native languages dropped significantly. Moreover, almost all alphabets were shifted to Cyrillic script. The role of Russian language in the education system was also increased. Some autonomous republics in Russia—especially the Orthodox Finnish–Ugric peoples—started to show a significant drop in native language usage.

Postwar Great-power Russian nationalism adopted grotesque forms. The spread of Communism was equal to the spread of Russian influence, and the role of Russians in the new world order was incontestable. Therefore, the role of Russian culture, language, and literature was indisputable too. The Great Russian nationalism policy was revised only after Stalin's death.

4) The New Nativization, or "Trust the Local Elites" (1956–84). The Soviet nationalities policy from Stalin's death until Perestroika included three key elements: Anti-Stalinism, "Nativization," and a slow-pace Russification.

The new Soviet leader, Nikita Khrushchev, was quick to enact an anti-Stalinist policy. In 1956 he condemned the Great Purge and attacked Stalin for abusing his power. The Great-power Russian nationalism policy was revoked, and the new political leadership was strongly opposed to mass repression, including terror along ethnic lines. The main idea was peaceful coexistence, not only with the rest of the world but within the Soviet Union as well.

In 1964, Leonid Brezhnev replaced Khrushchev. At the nationalities policy level, Brezhnev pushed "Nativization." This time, "nativization" had a different meaning: it was not just a linguistic policy, but the "Trust the local elites" policy. The main feature of this policy was promotion of titular nationalities in local party leadership and government. At the same time, these leaders were obliged to maintain the political loyalty of local populations. Along with the official administrative hierarchy, Moscow also introduced an unofficial hierarchy of ethnic regions, at least on the RSFSR (Russian Soviet Federative Socialist Republic) level (Miller 1977). The most "trusted" regions had a titular first party secretary but a second secretary of Russian origin; the least trusted regions had a Russian first party secretary.

Khrushchev's and Brezhnev's tenures were the golden age of ethnic institutional development. National intellectuals were provided with copious opportunities for employment in education, science, and culture. The establishment of new universities and academic institutions also led to the creation of new jobs for the intelligentsia. Rising volumes of books printed in local languages also indicated an increasing number of national writers and scholars.

The third key element of late Soviet nationalities policy was slow-pace assimilation. In the late 1950s, the Soviet government announced new language and education reforms, which resulted in a reduction in the number of native-language schools in Russian autonomous republics. Official status in the Soviet administrative hierarchy mattered: nationalities with lower political status experienced a gradual curtailment of native language instruction (Silver 1974). Among all ethnic groups, Slavs, Orthodox Christians, and the more urbanized were exposed to Russification more than others (Silver 1974a). Non-Russians were opposed to Russification and tried to resist it. The roots of nationalism can be found in these late Soviet anti-Russification sentiments.

5) Perestroika and the New Political Mobilization (1986–2000). Mikhail Gorbachev came to power in 1985. A few years later he announced broad political reforms that radically changed the balance between Moscow and the regions. In almost all ethnic republics, nationalists came to power after the elections in 1990. Everywhere they adopted a similar political program: demands for political and economic autonomy, as well as ethnic cultural revival. By early 1991, six union republics had declared their *de facto* independence. After the hard-liners' coup attempt failed in August 1991, the collapse of the USSR was inevitable. In December 1991, the Soviet Union ceased to exist.

Due to the policy of "nativization," the union republics looked like quasi-sovereign states: they had state institutions, established native languages, and most importantly, identity. When the Russian second party secretaries (as well as the KGB, military, etc.) disappeared, local elites realized that they had had free hands to set up new political agendas and adopt and implement policies as they wished.

The rise of nationalism could also be found in autonomous republics within the RSFSR. In some ethnic regions, nationalist movements were powerful and strong, while in others they failed to recruit enough supporters and played no significant role in local politics. Sometimes the success of ethnic movements was explained by their ability to raise issues of job security for the native population (Giuliano 2011). The key troublesome regions for the new Russian state were Chechnya and Tatarstan. To keep Chechnya within Russia, the government fought two bloody wars. In the case of Tatarstan, President Yeltsin succeeded in finding a peaceful solution. In other regions, nationalist movements managed either to achieve policy changes or to secure the incorporation of their leaders into regional administrations. By the late 1990s, nationalist movements everywhere lost their influence and took on fairly marginal roles in local politics.

Yugoslavia

The South Slavic nationalist movement arose in the nineteenth century, spurred by the success of German and Italian unification. Proponents of Yugoslav nationalism claimed that the differences—linguistic or cultural—between any two South Slavs were in fact even less evident than between a Prussian and a Bavarian. The rise of popular Yugoslav nationalism peaked in the early twentieth century and coincided with the emergence of strong ethnic movements throughout the Habsburg Empire. When the Central Powers were defeated in 1918 and the Habsburg Empire collapsed, the Kingdom of Serbs, Croats, and Slovenes was established.

1) WWII and the Creation of Communist Yugoslavia (1941–45). The first iteration of Yugoslavia ceased to exist in April 1941, after the German invasion and rapid defeat of the royal military. As early as summer 1941, an armed rebellion against the Nazis spread throughout Serbia. Military struggle against the Nazis was followed by a bloody ethnic civil war, with Croatian nationalists, Serbian nationalists, and Yugoslav Communists all playing a major role. A former colonel of the royal army, Dragoljub Mihailovic, established a Serbian nationalist guerilla force, the Chetniks. Simultaneously, Yugoslav Communists created their own military force, the Partisans, under the command of Josip Broz Tito, the future leader of Yugoslavia. The Ustasha proclaimed an ethnically homogeneous Croatia as their primary political goal; ethnic cleansings and forced deportations of non-Croats, mostly Serbs, followed soon after. As a response, Serbian and Muslim populations took up arms, and the Chetniks sought revenge for the massacres of Serbs. Similar to the Ustasha, the Chetniks' political program included the ethnic cleansing of non-Serbs, mostly in Croatia and Bosnia. The Partisans, to the contrary, presented themselves as a multiethnic force committed only to the fight against the Nazis and their collaborators, but not with other ethnic groups.

By 1943, the Partisans had become the largest resistance force. In the same year, they declared a political program aimed at the creation of a new Yugoslav federal state, where all nations would have equal legal status and rights. Tito's goal was to transcend political, cultural, religious, and linguistic distinctions by creating a new supraethnic identity based on the "brotherhood and unity" of all South Slavic nations. Supplied with Allied arms, the Partisan Army annihilated the Chetniks and the Ustasha forces in 1945, and a second, Communist Yugoslavia was established in 1945.

2) Postwar "Brotherhood and Unity" (1946–62). In 1946, the new Yugoslav Constitution was adopted. It established a federal Yugoslavia with eight ethnic units: six federal republics and two autonomous provinces. New political vocabulary included terms such as "peoples of Yugoslavia" instead of "Yugoslav people" (Wachtel 1998), and ethnic homogeneity was not among the political goals anymore. Officially, all languages were equal, none being legally dominant or favored, regardless of the number of speakers (Bugarski 2001).

The new supraethnic Yugoslav identity was based upon the Partisan ideology of "brotherhood and unity"; the fraternal struggle against the Nazis became postwar Yugoslavia's creation myth. It appeared to be a powerful mechanism for reinventing the Yugoslav nation. The Communists never denied the existence of separate ethnic identities, but rather, wanted to transcend them.

The Yugoslav political leadership attempted to promote multiethnic cultural and professional organizations, supported republican education reforms, and stressed the uniqueness of the Yugoslav cultural and political experience. Despite political centralization and a relatively successful attempt to create and promote this supraethnic Yugoslav identity, regional authorities achieved significant progress in cultural nation-building. Such regions as Bosnia and Montenegro established their first universities. The number of students enrolled in higher education increased dramatically, especially in comparison with attendance rates in the first Yugoslavia.

However, Croatian and Slovene intellectuals tended to define the new Yugoslavism as an old Serb hegemonism (Pavkovic 1997, 62). By the early 1960s, localism, chauvinism, and national particularism had resurfaced (Ramet 1992).

3) Decentralization (1963–73). Tito's response to new challenges was the decentralization of the Yugoslav state. In 1963 he announced a broad economic reform that aimed to stem economic mismanagement and promote higher GDP growth rates. The reform had an unmistakably devolutionary character: its main feature was strengthening the role of the republics and industrial enterprises at the expense of the federal government (Ramet 1992, 85). Economic decentralization led to political decentralization. A series of amendments to the constitution was adopted, and Yugoslavia was transformed into a semi-confederative state. Further proposals from the republics included federalization of the party and veto power over the decisions of federal party organs (Seculic, Massey, and Hodson 1994).

Decentralization facilitated the development of ethnic institutions in the republics. The number of students enrolled in higher education increased dramatically. Kosovo was the last region to establish its own university. Across the republics, citizens gained broad access to books and magazines printed in their native language; circulations rose almost everywhere.

Political decentralization was followed by moderate political liberalization. The Croatian party organization supported the revival of Croatian nationalism in the late 1960s. Local nationalists articulated Croatian grievances; e.g., the repeated attempts to assimilate Croats, subordination of Croatian interests in favor those of Serbs, threats to Croatian culture and language, etc. The Croatian crisis peaked in late 1971 with anti-federal student riots and nationalist claims to parts of Bosnia. The federal center's decentralization had backfired. Tito decided to decapitate the Croatian party leadership: tens of thousands of members were expelled from the party. Pro-nationalist cultural organizations were banned and several newspapers were shut down.

At the cultural level, the main outcome of this crisis was the gradual collapse of a belief in any form of Yugoslav culture. Significant segments of the cultural elites gave up on the Yugoslav project. The void was filled by nation-based cultural formations, which tend to appear before the expression of political nationalism (Wachtel 1998, 184).

4) The Decay of Multinational Yugoslavia (1974–86). The Croatian crisis led to the further concentration of power in Tito's hands. At the same time, Tito moved to undercut the popular bases of Croatian nationalism by acceding to many nationalist demands (Ramet 1992, 131), in both the political and cultural spheres. In 1974 a new Constitution was adopted. Yugoslavia was transformed into a "semiconfederation of semisovereign states" (Pavkovic 1997, 70). For example, the Constitution attributed statehood and sovereignty to federal units, declared the right of self-determination for all republics, and introduced a collective state presidency (Lampe 1994). Until his death in 1980, Tito succeeded in resolving political disputes among the republics by using his undoubted political authority.

The 1980s saw a major economic slowdown of Yugoslavia, which contributed to a loss of perceived legitimacy: the "developed" republics (Slovenia and Croatia) were much less willing to contribute their revenues to the central funds that provided financial assistance to "backward" republics. The long-lasting economic decline caused a new rise in ethnic tensions throughout Yugoslavia, and the revival of Serbian nationalism was perhaps the most dangerous threat to the survival of Yugoslavia.

At the political level, Serbs were mostly concerned with the status and political situation in Kosovo—anti-Serbian Albanian riots in 1981 and a subsequent Serbian backlash—purges within the Kosovar party organization, arrests of nationalist activists and the deployment of additional police forces. At the cultural level, Serbian intellectuals initiated a gradual delegitimization of the supranational Yugoslav identity. The issue of discrimination against Serbs within Yugoslavia was raised; many Serbian writers articulated and decried disproportionate suffering among Serbs during the creation of Yugoslavia—and a lack of gratitude among other ethnic groups. Polarization was the last major cultural trend in the Yugoslav cultural life.

5) Political Crisis and Ethnic Wars (1987–95). Miloshevic, president of the Communist party of Serbia, derived his legitimacy from popular nationalism in Serbia. His first success was the imposition of Serbian rule in Vojvodina and Kosovo in the late 1980s. By this time the key element of his political program was not to preserve a unified Yugoslavia, but to create a new Great Serbian nation-state, including the Serb-populated parts of Croatia and Bosnia.

In 1990, the first free and democratic elections were held across the federal republics, but only in Serbia and Montenegro were Communists able to retain their power. In the aftermath of the elections, the new Slovenian and Croatian non-Communist governments declared their commitment to achieving independence in the near future. All attempts to negotiate an even more confederative state had failed by the summer of 1991. Yugoslav supraethnic identity had ceased to exist and was immediately replaced with particularistic ethnic identities that were dominated by grievances and collective war memories (Godina 1998). Nationalists radicalized their position and attacked their co-ethnic moderates even more fiercely than their opponents (Oberschall 2000). Serbs were strongly opposed to unilateral declarations of independence by Slovenia and Croatia and were preparing to strike back. The Serbs living in Croatia refused to accept an independent Croatian state and claimed their right to political autonomy, if not for secession and incorporation into Serbia.

The first republic to claim its independence was Slovenia in June 1991. The Serb-dominated Yugoslav National Army attempted to intervene, but after ten days of war it was forced to retreat. Indeed, Slovenia had become independent. Croatia was the second republic to claim independence, soon after which both Bosnia and Macedonia declared they would not remain within Yugoslavia. Only Serbia and Montenegro remained part of Yugoslavia, until 2006.

The Yugoslav succession wars—Serbs vs. Croats, Serbs vs. Muslims, and Croats vs. Muslims—lasted until 1995, stopped only by international intervention. They were followed by bloody ethnic cleansing and genocide. After the Dayton agreements were signed in 1995, Bosnia was established as a fragile federation of Bosnian Muslims, Croats, and Serbs. The history of South Slavic "brotherhood and unity" was over.

The two remaining multiethnic Communist states—Serbia and Montenegro—made a desperate effort to create ethnic federations with equal rights for all constituent nations. Nationalism and nationalities policies were a major source of legitimacy for these Communist states. However, Communist party rulers failed to create a legitimate supraethnic identity. Promoting broad cultural autonomy as a solution, Communists in fact contributed to the rise of single-culture nationalist movements.

DATA AND METHODS

This paper seeks to test the relationship between cultural and political nationalism with statistical methods. I split the history of the USSR and Yugoslavia into five periods, after which political and cultural nationalism are measured. Finally, the relationship between cultural and political nationalism is tested in both countries. To modify Gorenburg's model, I include the entire period of Soviet rule (1917–1985) and Yugoslav history (1941–1995) in my analysis; each one is split into five periods, with two being periods of political nationalism (the first and the last ones) and three in the middle, periods of cultural nationalism (Table 2). I take into account 49 Soviet and 8 Yugoslav ethnic units.

I have added several other factors to my model. I use the *formal status* of each region and trace its change since the emergence of the region. In general, almost all ethnic regions raised their formal status. *Religion* is another factor. One can assume that religion, as a primordial factor, can be an even more important predictor of nationalism than a region's rank in formal hierarchy.

Political Nationalism

I use D. Treisman's and E. Guiliano's approach to constructing indices for measuring political nationalism (Treisman 2003, Guiliano 2011). They use several dummy variables to compose the indices of political nationalism in Russia.

TABLE 2. Periodization of cultural and political nationalism in USSR and Yugoslavia

Period	USSR	Yugoslavia
Political nationalism	1917–25 The October Revolution and the Civil War (political mobilization)	1941–45 The Second World War and creation of Yugoslavia (Ethnic Civil War)
Cultural nationalism	1925–39 "The Affirmative Action Empire" (state-led nation-building)	1946–62 Postwar "brotherhood and unity" (creation of new supraethnic Yugoslav identity)
Cultural nationalism	1940–55 Great-power Russian nationalism (Russification campaign)	1963–73 Decentralization (Crisis of Yugoslav identity)
Cultural nationalism	1956–85 "Nativization," or "Trust the local elites" (creation of quasi-sovereign states on the basis of Union republics; regional cultural development)	1974–86 The decay of multinational Yugoslavia (transformation of Yugoslavia into a semi-confederative state)
Political nationalism	1986–2000 Perestroika and the crisis of the Soviet state (the collapse of the USSR and political mobilization)	1987–95 Political crisis and ethnic wars (the rise of particularistic nationalism and the disintegration of Yugoslavia)

I use 14/16 indicators for the USSR and 10 for Yugoslavia, respectively, to construct indices of political nationalism in the 1990s (Tables 3a and 3b). I then transfer this data into a "0–1" scale (mean value).

In a similar way, I compose an index of political nationalism in Russia for 1917–25 and for 1941–45 in Yugoslavia. I use 9 and 7 indicators respectively (Tables 4a and 4b). I then convert this data into a "0–1" scale (mean value).

Cultural Nationalism

The approach presented in this paper is based on the argument that cultural nationalism can be defined indirectly, via the development of ethnic institutions. These institutions—mostly in education and cultural spheres—create job opportunities for national intellectuals. I use some proxies that measure the growth of a national intelligentsia in ethnic regions in both countries. One of my indicators is *books printed in native language*: they reflect the number

TABLE 3a. The components of political nationalism in the USSR in the 1990s

USSR	
Union, autonomous republics, and NAD	
Declaration of sovereignty (0/1)	Referendum on sovereignty held (0/1)
Presidency established (0/1)	Priority of republican laws proclaimed (0/1)
Language law adopted (0/1)	Right to own currency declared (0/1)
Exclusiveness of titular language (0/1)	Priority right on national resources claimed (0/1)
Only union republics	
Territorial claims raised (0/1)	Boycott of the 1991 March referendum (0/1)[1]
Referendum on sovereignty held before August 1991 (0/1)	Ethnic paramilitary established before 1991 (0/1)
Ethnic pogroms/cleansings (0/1)	
Only autonomous republics and NAD	
Constitution adopted before 1993?[2] (0/1)	Formal administrative status raised (0/1)
Constitution adopted before 2000? (0/1)	Boycott of the 1993 April referendum[3] (0/1)
Including right for secession? (0/1)	Refusal to send soldiers to Russian army (0/1)
Boycott of the 1993 December referendum[4] (0/1)	

of writers and scholars. Another proxy is *number of students enrolled in higher education*: universities create jobs for national intellectuals. In the case of Yugoslavia, I also use such proxies as *magazines printed in native language*: they create jobs for local journalists. In the Soviet case, I use *titular language as primary language.*

For the USSR and Yugoslavia, I have constructed an index of cultural nationalism for 3 periods: in the case of the Soviet Union, 1925–39, 1940–55, and 1956–85, and in the Yugoslav case, 1946–62, 1963–73 and 1974–86. The index consists of three variables, and due to data limitations, I use one value for the entire period.

[1] The referendum on the preservation of the USSR.

[2] The Constitution of Russian Federation was adopted in December 1993.

[3] The referendum on the vote of confidence in President Yeltsin and the parliament.

[4] The referendum on the Constitution draft.

TABLE 3b. The components of political nationalism in Yugoslavia in the 1990s

Yugoslavia	
Presidency established (0/1)	Nationalist paramilitary established (0/1; either short-term existence, or occasional involvement in conflict—0,5)
Language law adopted (0/1; no separate law, but the Constitution contains language amendments—0,5)	Ethnic cleansings (0/1)
Exclusive status of titular language (0/1)	Ethnic non-violent protests against Belgrade (0/1)
Referendum on sovereignty held (0/1)	Right to own currency declared (0/1)
Priority of republican laws proclaimed (0/1)	Independence prior to 1995 (0/1)

TABLE 4a. The components of political nationalism in the USSR, 1917–25

USSR	
Declaration of sovereignty (0/1)	Uprising (0/1; single event, against the Reds or the Whites; small scale uprising—0,5)
Non-Soviet independent state declared (0/1)	Rebellion movement (0/1; long lasting guerilla war) (0/1)
A Constituent convention held (0/1; ethnic convention with broad powers and goals—0,5)	Occupation by the Whites (0/1)
A Soviet republic proclaimed (0/1; from below, not from above; as part of a broader state—0,5)	Own currency printed (0/1)
Constitution adopted (0/1; provisional political program—0,5)	

USSR

Books in native language—total circulation of books printed in native language. I take this data from official Soviet statistics: 1937/40, 1956, and 1980. I transform all values into a "0–1" scale in two steps: first, I compute all figures as shares of the 1925–40 period (1 = data for the period 1925–40); second, I recalculate these values: all values between 0 and 1 remain unchanged; values in the 1–2 range receive a value of "1"; values exceeding 2 receive a value of "1,1."

TABLE 4b. The components of political nationalism in Yugoslavia, 1941–45

Yugoslavia	
Constitution adopted (0/1; provisional political program—0,5)	Anti-Nazi guerilla war (0/1)
Independent nation-state proclaimed (0/1; annexing by other state—0,25)	Own currency printed (0/1)
Independent pro-Communist state proclaimed (0/1)	Ethnic cleansings (titulars vs. non-titulars; outside titular republic—0,5)
Nationalist paramilitary established (0/1)	

Titular language as primary language—share of titular population that claimed their native language as their primary language. I use census data—1959, 1970, and 1989. I recalculate all values in a "0–1" scale ("1" = 95–100%; "0,9" = 90–95%; "0,75" = 80–90%; "0,5" = 70–80%; "0,25" = 50–70%; "0" = 0–50%).

Students—number of students enrolled in higher education. Values are taken for the year of the republic's origin: 1940, 1956/60 and 1980. I recalculate all values in a "0–1" scale in two steps: first, I give values to the period 1917–25 ("0" = 0; "0,25" = 0–1000; "0,5" = 1000–2000; "0,75" = 2000–3000; "1" = 3000+). Second, I recalculate all other values as shares of the previous period ("0,25" = 1–1,5; "0,5" = 1,5–2; "0,75" = 2–3; "1" = 3–5; "1,1" = 5+).

Finally, I compose the *Index of cultural nationalism in the USSR* as the mean of these 3 aforementioned variables.

Formal status—the status of a given ethnic region in the official Soviet administrative hierarchy. This value was calculated in three steps. First, I assigned values for each status ("0" = no separate region; "0,25" = district in non-ethnic region; "0,5" = national district in autonomous republic, autonomous oblast; "0,75" = Autonomous republic; "1" = Union republic; "1,1" = independent state). Second, all republics were assigned values for each year. Third, I calculated the mean value for the entire period.

Non-Orthodox religion—variable for the predominant religion in an ethnic republic. I code "0" for Orthodoxy, "1"—for all others. In some cases, I assign the value "0,25" to those regions that were officially converted into Orthodoxy by Russians, but unofficially many titulars still practiced their traditional religion, like shamanism or paganism.

I take all data from the official Soviet statistical sources (Pod'yachikh 1961; Dinamika naseleniia 1985; Narodnoye khozyaystvo 1967, 1987; Naseleniie SSSR 1974, 1990).

Yugoslavia

Students—number of students enrolled in higher education. Values are taken for the years 1954/55, 1971/72, and 1986/87. I recalculate all values into a "0–1" scale in two steps: first, I assign values to the period 1946–62, as the proportion of students in the 1954/55 academic year to the population of the republic ("0" = 0; "0,25" = less than 0,1%; "0,5" = 0,1–0,3%; "0,75" = 0,3–0,5%; "1" = 0,5%+). Second, I recalculate all other values as shares of the previous period ("0,25" = less than 1; "0,5" = 1–2; "0,75" = 2–3; "1" = 3–5; "1,1" = 5+).

Books circulation—total circulation of books printed in a particular republic. Values are taken for the years 1962, 1973, and 1986. I transform all values in the "0–1" scale in two steps: first, I assign values to the period 1946–62, as the proportion of printed books per capita in a republic, so that in 1962 ("0,25"= less than 1 book per capita; "0,5"= 1–2 books per capita; "0,75" = 2–3 books per capita; "1" = 3+ books per capita). Second, I recalculate these values: all values between 0 and 1 remain unchanged; values in the 1–2 range are assigned a value "1"; values exceeding 2 are assigned a value of "1,1."

Serbs and Croats speak a single Serbian-Croatian language, and the main linguistic difference was in the use of a particular dialect, and use of the Latin or the Cyrillic script for writing. Montenegrins and Bosnians speak another dialect of the Serbo-Croatian language. Only the Slovenian, Macedonian, and Albanian languages can be defined as separate languages. Therefore, it is impossible to use the variable *Titular language as primary language* in the case of Yugoslavia.

Magazine circulation—total circulation of magazines printed in a republic. Values are taken for the years 1962, 1970, and 1986. I transform all values into a "0–1" scale in two steps: first, I assign values to the period 1946–62, as the number of printed magazines per capita in a republic, in 1962 ("0,25"= less than 10 copies per capita; "0,5"= 10–30 copies per capita; "0,75" = 30–50 copies per capita; "1" = 50+ copies per capita). Second, I recalculate these values as shares of the previous period ("0,25" = less than 1, "0,5" = 1–1,25; "0,75" = 1,25–1,5; "1"= 1,5–2; and "1,1" = 2+).

Finally, I composed the *Index of cultural nationalism in Yugoslavia* as the mean of these 3 variables.

All data was taken from the official Yugoslav statistical yearbooks for 1956, 1963, 1973, 1974, and 1986 (Statistički . . . 1956; 1963; 1973; 1974; 1986).

RESULTS

I use the *structural equation modeling* approach to test my hypotheses. This methodological approach allows testing the path-dependency relationship between variables. My dependent variables are political nationalism 1986–2000

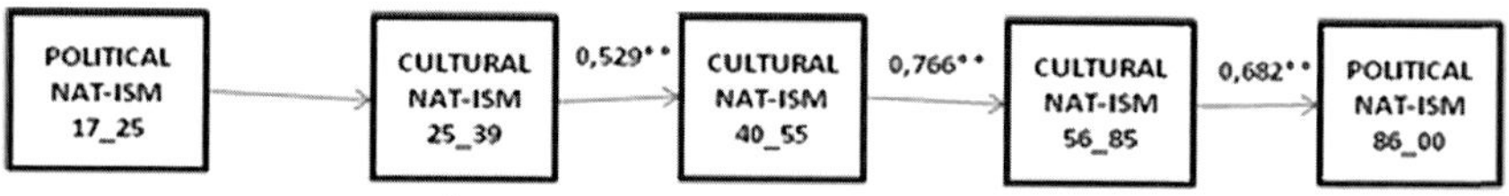

Figure 2. Model 1. $\chi^2 = 30.83$, df = 6, p = 0.000, CFI = 0.776, RMSEA = 0.291, SRMR = 0.165

(USSR[5]) and 1987–95 (Yugoslavia). Independent variables are earlier political nationalism and 3 periods of cultural nationalism. I expect all relationships between all periods to be significant.

The unit of analysis is the region. I use two sets of models. The first set includes only Soviet ethnic regions (N=49), and the second one includes both Soviet and Yugoslav regions (N=57). To balance the effects of a smaller number of Yugoslav regions, I give equal weight to both Soviet and Yugoslav samples (50/50).

I test my basic assumption on the path-dependency of nationalism among all periods (Models 1–2 and 4–5). Next, I add new variables—*Religion* and *Formal status*—in the basic model to test their influence on cultural nationalism (Model 3).

USSR

Model 1. This model tests only linear causal links between all periods of Soviet nationalism (Fig. 2). One can see that there is a causal link between cultural nationalism (1925–1939 and 1940–55; 1940–55 and 1956–85) and cultural nationalism and political nationalism (1956–85 and 1986–2000). However, fit indices for this model are quite poor.

Model 2. This model adds cross-temporal links into the overall model (Fig. 3). It finds links between all periods except "*Cultural nationalism 1926–39*" and "*Cultural nationalism 1940–55*"; all previous links remain significant. These results support my hypothesis: Cultural nationalism predicts political nationalism. "*Political nationalism 1917–25*" and "*Political nationalism 1986–2000*" have a significant relationship, but the coefficient (0.296) is lower than between "*Cultural nationalism 1956–85*" and "*Political nationalism 1986–2000*" (0.484).

The break between the two periods—1926–39 and 1940–55—might be considered as evidence of the inheritance of the Soviet nationalities policy. The 1926–39 period is defined as a period of "positive nationalism" and state-led nation-building. Stalin's nationalities policy, associated with the shift from the "Affirmative Action Empire" policy to "Great-power Russian Nationalism," is likely to be the turning point in the history of Soviet nationalism.

[5] Including nationalism in the Russian Federation (1991-2000).

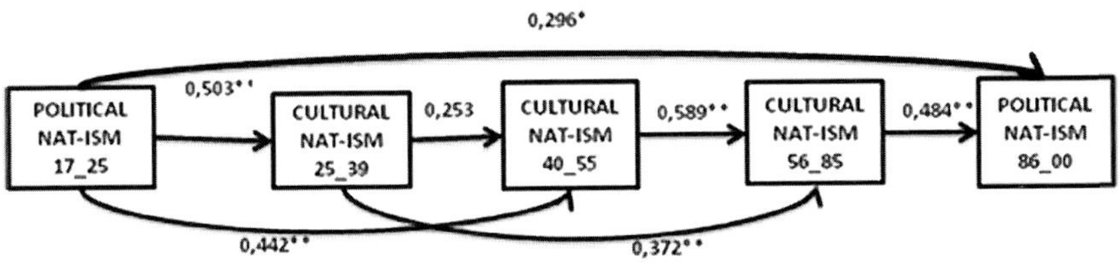

Figure 3. Model 2. $\chi^2 = 2.988$, df = 3, p = 0.394, CFI = 1.000, RMSEA = 0.000, SRMR = 0.026

The Soviet case shows that cultural nationalism was likely grown in ethnic republics throughout Soviet history. When political crisis broke out, the development of cultural nationalism was one of the predictors for political nationalism.

Model 3 (Fig. 4) also includes *Formal status* and *Religion* variables. Some links (between *Formal status* and political nationalism, *Religion* and all other nationalist periods) are omitted as insignificant, and their exclusion improved the model fit. The links between "*Political nationalism 1917–25*" and "*Cultural nationalism 1925–39*," "*Cultural nationalism 1925–39*" and "*Cultural nationalism 1940–55*" are fixed to 0. Model fit indices show that the model has good explanatory power.

The coefficient between "*Cultural nationalism 1926–39*" and "*Cultural nationalism 1940–55*" is insignificant. This insignificance may reflect a radical change in the Soviet nationalities policy: the rise of Great-power Russian nationalism, dissolution of some ethnic regions, and mass purges. The model shows that cultural nationalism grew since Stalin's late period and had a significant impact on political nationalism. *Formal status* is significant for the period 1917–55, and in fact was marginally significant for 1956–85 (r=0,237, p=0,067). This supports Gorenburg's findings on the role of higher formal status for the development of cultural institutions.

USSR and Yugoslavia. The Yugoslav sample is very small—8 cases. The solution chosen was to pool together all cases into one sample and to increase the weight of the Yugoslav cases by assigning equal weight to both parts of the sample. If the output of these models does not show similar results compared to the "pure" Soviet sample, it indicates that Yugoslav nationalism differs from that of the USSR. Different time periods are related respectively, assuming the logic of cultural nationalism development being quite similar among the periods.

Model 4. This model tests only linear causal links between the periods (Fig. 5). One can see that the results are identical to Model 1, with one insignificant coefficient between the periods "*Cultural nationalism 2*" and "*Cultural nationalism 3*." The model fit indices indicate that the model is quite poor.

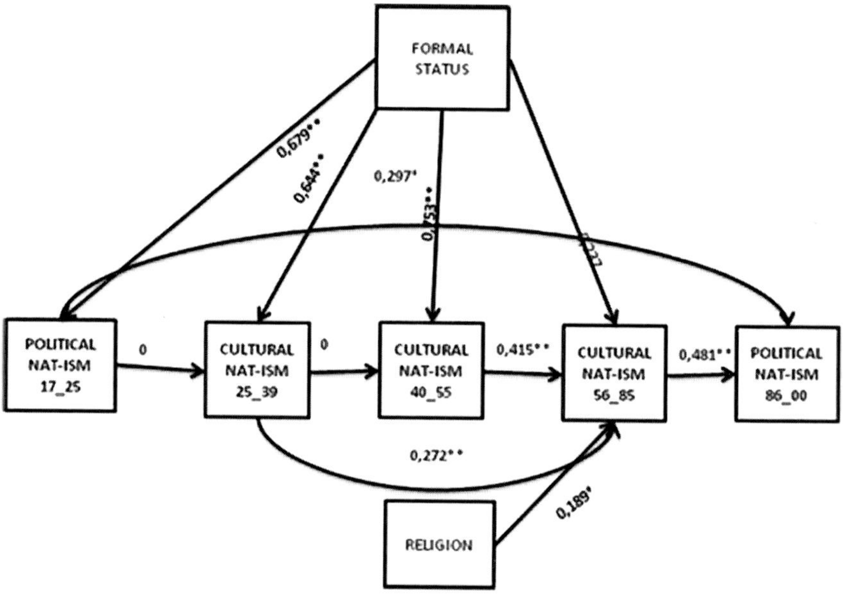

Figure 4. Model 3. χ^2 = 6.87, df = 11, p = 0.81, CFI = 1.000, RMSEA = 0.000, SRMR = 0.047

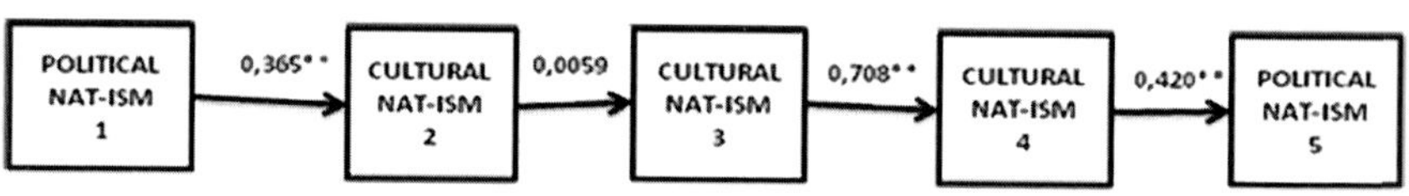

Figure 5. Model 4. χ^2 = 20.37, df = 6, p = 0.002, CFI = 0.613, RMSEA = 0.205, SRMR = 0.183

Model 5 (Fig. 6). This model includes some cross-temporal links between periods of nationalism in the USSR and Yugoslavia. Some insignificant links were omitted to improve the model fit. This model shows that there is no direct significant relationship between cultural nationalism and political nationalism (i.e., no link between "*Cultural nationalism 4*" and "*Political nationalism 5*"). Cultural nationalism influences indirectly: links from "*Cultural nationalism 2*" (0.287) and "*Cultural nationalism 3*" (0.353). The growth of cultural nationalism is also present to some degree: there is a significant link between "*Cultural nationalism 3*" and "*Cultural nationalism 4*" (0.708). The strongest predictor for political nationalism of the 1990s is early political nationalism (0.369), and this coefficient is higher than that of "*Cultural nationalism 2*" and "*Cultural nationalism 3*."

This finding contradicts the main theoretical argument of this paper, at least to some extent. However, the good news is that it reveals sharp contrasts between Russia and Yugoslavia in the nature of political nationalism. In the

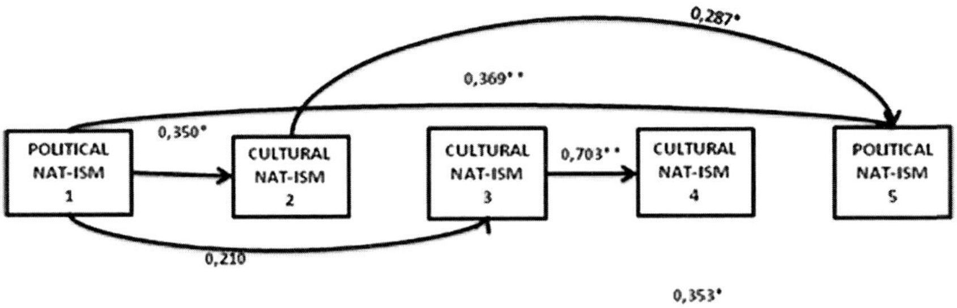

Figure 6. Model 5. χ^2 = 4.51, df = 4, p = 0.341, CFI = 0.986, RMSEA = 0.047, SRMR = 0.063

USSR, the outburst of political nationalism in the 1990s can be explained by the spread of cultural nationalism—as an unintended outcome of the Soviet nationalities policy. Conversely, the rise of political nationalism in Yugoslavia can be explained by previous nationalist experience. The legacy of the past likely had a much stronger impact on political nationalism in the 1990s than cultural policies. In the Soviet case, the temporal distance between the two periods of political nationalism was much longer.

An alternative explanation could be that the Yugoslav constituent nations had already completed their cultural nation-building by the mid-1940s and, therefore, were less affected by cultural and linguistic policies. The issues of cultural revival in terms of native language, local history, access to education, etc., were not as important in confederate Yugoslavia as in the heavily centralized USSR. Full-scale cultural autonomy was achieved with adoption of the 1974 Constitution. Therefore, political issues dominated the agenda following the late 1980s. This helps explain the relative importance of previous periods of cultural nationalism in Yugoslavia. Tito's solution was to expand the cultural and political autonomy of the constituent republics. In fact, it was not a good solution: extended cultural autonomy from Belgrade did not protect Yugoslavia from collapse.

CONCLUSION

Cultural nationalism was an important predictor of political nationalism, although it played different roles in Russia and Yugoslavia. In Russia it became one of the sources of political nationalism; in Yugoslavia it was subordinate to political nationalism.

The results show a certain level of path-dependency between all periods of Soviet history. The rise of political nationalism in the USSR was inherited from the earlier Soviet period. This paper attempted to show that latent cultural nationalism was one of the most significant factors. The permanent development of local culture led to the emergence of local national intellectuals who later became the driving force of ethnic movements during Perestroika.

In explaining political nationalism, the most important period was 1956–85. There was a radical policy change between two periods: 1925–39 and 1940–55. The rise of nationalism in the 1990s in ethnic republics in the USSR is likely to be explained by Stalin's nationalities policy. The statistical testing of this radical change is one of the major contributions of this paper. Stalin's rule in his later period was the peak of Great-power Russian nationalism, the last period of intensive Russification, and the last period of the empire-building. After Stalin, the Soviet rulers preferred to compromise with local elites to gain their support. The "trust to local elites" policy allowed ethnic regions to enjoy some degree of cultural autonomy. When Gorbachev launched Perestroika, he could not even imagine that the earlier nationalities policies had built ethnic institutions in almost all, both union and autonomous, republics. The emergence and rise in number of ethnic conflicts contrasted with the official Soviet nationalities doctrine.

Political nationalism was likely more important in Yugoslavia. Despite the salience of cultural and linguistic issues, the historical legacy of World War II was likely the most powerful predictor for political nationalism. Primordial cleavages among South Slavs—religion, institutional legacy, and a history of interethnic conflicts—could not be transcended by the "brotherhood and unity" policy. Nation-building was completed in constituent nations before the outbreak of the Second World War. Tito's policy of federation led to a radical extension of cultural and political autonomy in the republics. Having achieved cultural autonomy, the republics started to raise "purely" political issues. Cultural nationalism had only an indirect impact on political nationalism.

The rise of political nationalism in the late 1980s was not related solely to the crisis and the collapse of the Communist state. It could be predicted by the latent cultural nationalism that was an unintended byproduct of Communist cultural policy. In fact, these policies could be redefined as cultural nation-building. Paradoxically, Communist ideology argued that it had found a "true" solution to the national question—however, this solution ultimately contributed to the collapse of the Communist states.

BIBLIOGRAPHY

Anderson, Benedict. 2006. *Imagined Communities.* London: Verso.

Brandenberger, David. 2000. "Proletarian Internationalism, Soviet Patriotism, and the Rise of Russocentric Statism during the Stalinist 1930s." *Left History* 6 (2): 80–100.

Bugarski, Ranko. 2001. "Language, Nationalism and War in Yugoslavia." *International Journal of Sociology of Language* 51: 69–87.

Brubaker, Rogers. 1996. "Nationalizing States in the Old 'New Europe'—and the New." *Ethnic and Racial Studies* 19 (2): 411–437.

Bunce, Valerie. 1998. "Subversive Institutions: The End of the Soviet State in Comparative Perspective." *Post-Soviet Affairs* 14 (4): 323–354.

Bunce, Valerie. 1999. "Peaceful vs. Violent State Dismemberment: A Comparison of the Soviet Union, Yugoslavia and Czechoslovakia." *Politics and Society* 27 (2): 217–237.

Darden, Keith. 2014. *Resisting Occupation: Mass Schooling and the Creation of Durable National Loyalties.* Cambridge University Press. Forthcoming.

Gellner, Ernest. 2008. *Nations and Nationalism.* Ithaca, NY: Cornell University Press.

Godina, Vesna. 1998. "The Outbreak of Nationalism on Former Yugoslav Territory: A Historical Perspective on the Problem of Supranational Identity." *Nations and Nationalism* 4 (3): 409–422.

Gorenburg, Dmitry. 2001. "Nationalism for Masses: Popular Support for Nationalism in Russia's Ethnic Republics." *Europe–Asia Studies* 53 (1): 73–104.

———. 2003. *Minority Ethnic Mobilization in the Russian Federation.* Cambridge: Cambridge University Press.

Guiliano, Elise. 2011. *Constructing Grievances: Ethnic Nationalism in Russia's Republics.* Ithaca, NY: Cornell University Press.

Hroch, Miroslav. 2000. *Social Preconditions of National Revival in Europe: A Comparative Analysis of the Social Composition of Patriotic Groups Among the Smaller European Nations.* New York: Columbia University Press.

Laitin, David. 1998. *Identity in Formation: The Russian-speaking Populations in the Near Abroad.* New York: Cornell University Press.

Laitin, David, Roger Petersen, and John W. Slocum. 1992. "Language and the State: Russia and the Soviet Union in Comparative Perspective." Pp. 129–167 in *Thinking Theoretically About Soviet Nationalities: History and Comparison in the Study of the USSR,* edited by Alexander J. Motyl. New York: Columbia University Press.

Laitin, David. 2007. *Nations, State and Violence.* Oxford: Oxford University Press.

Lampe, John. 1994. "The Failure of the Yugoslav National Idea." *Studies in East European Thought* 46: 69–89.

Martin, Terry. 2001. *The Affirmative Action Empire: Nations and Nationalism in the Soviet Union, 1923–1939.* Ithica, NY: Cornell University Press.

Miller, John. 1977. "Cadres Policy in Nationalities Areas: Recruitment of CPSU First and Second Secretaries in Non-Russian Republics of the USSR." *Soviet Studies* 29 (1): 3–36.

Oberschall, Anthony. 2001. "The Manipulation of Ethnicity: From Ethnic Cooperation to Violence and War in Yugoslavia." *Ethnic and Racial Studies* 23 (6): 982–1001.

Pavkovic, Aleksandar. 1997. *The Fragmentation of Yugoslavia: Nationalism in A Multinational State.* New York: St. Martin's Press.

Ramet, Sabrina. 1992. *Nationalism and Federalism in Yugoslavia, 1962–1991.* Bloomington: Indiana University Press.

Seculic, Dusco, Garth Massey, and Randy Hodson. 1994. "Who Were the Yugoslavs? Failed Sources of a Common Identity in the Former Yugoslavia." *American Sociological Review* 59 (1): 83–97.

Silver, Brian. 1974. "The Status of National Minority Languages in Soviet Education: An Assessment of Recent Changes." *Soviet Studies* 26 (1): 28–40.

Silver, Brian. 1974a. "Social Mobilization and the Russification of Soviet Nationalities." *The American Political Science Review* 68 (1): 45–66.

Treisman, Daniel. 1997. "Russia's 'Ethnic Revival': The Separatist Activism of Regional Leaders in a Post-Communist Order." *World Politics* 49 (2): 212–249.

Wachtel, Andrew. 1998. *Making a Nation, Breaking a Nation: Literature and Cultural Politics in Yugoslavia.* Stanford, CA: Stanford University Press.

Dinamika naseleniia SSSR 1960–80 gg. 1985. Moscow: Finansy i statistika, 1985. (in Russian)

Narodnoye khozyaystvo RSFSR za 50 let. Statisticheskii sbornik. 1967 Moscow: Statistika. (in Russian)

Narodnoye khozyaystvo RSFSR za 70 let. Statisticheskii ezhegodnik. 1987. Moscow: Finansy i statistika. (in Russian)

Naseleniie SSSR. Spravochnik. 1974. Moscow: Politizdat. (in Russian)

Naseleniie SSSR. Po dannym vsesoyuznoy perepisi naseleniya 1989 g. 1990. Moscow: Finansy i statistika. (in Russian)

Pod'yachikh, P. 1961. *Naseleniie SSSR.* Moscow: Glavnoie izdatel'stvo politicheskoy literatury. (in Russian)

Statistički godišnjak Jugoslavije/Socijalistička Federativna Republika Jugoslavija, Savezni zavod za statistiku. 1956, 1963, 1973, 1974, 1986. Beograd. (in Croatian)

HETEROGLOSSIA AND HYBRIDITY IN GUSTAV MAHLER'S WUNDERHORN SYMPHONIES

Federico Celestini*

Abstract

Aesthetic experience and, more specifically in the context of my research, musical composition (and to some degree, musical listening), can be analyzed as the experience of a shift in the relationship between Self and Otherness. I propose calling this shift "de-identification" and suggest that this dynamic can be traced to the compositional level of music. This paper focuses on aspects of Otherness in the arts; namely, the plurality of idioms and styles, as well as the hybridization of expression. For this purpose, Michail M. Bakhtin's concepts of heteroglossia and hybridity in the literary novel are discussed in order to consider Gustav Mahler's music from this theoretical perspective.

Introduction

Aesthetic experience and, more specifically in the context of my research, musical composition (as well as to some degree, musical listening), can be analyzed as the experience of a shift in the relationship between Self and Otherness. I propose calling this shift "de-identification" and suggest that this dynamic can be traced to the compositional level of music.

Plato was one of the earliest thinkers to recognize de-identificatory forces in the arts. He condemned the destabilizing effect of arts on the individual (*Ion* 533e–534c), as well as on collective identities (*Republic* 397e–398b),

* Federico Celestini is a Professor in the Department of Music at the University of Innsbruck.

thus justifying his aversion to the arts.[1] It wasn't until 1872 that the first positive statement about the aesthetics of de-identification was made; namely, in Friedrich Nietzsche's *Birth of Tragedy*. Here, Nietzsche suggests that arts present us with a particularly intensive experience of Otherness. He substantiates this idea in two ways. His first example is the cultural history of Ancient Greece. Nietzsche describes the birth of Tragedy as the result of a cultural transfer from the "barbarian" Asian cults to the Apollonian culture of the Greeks. Hence, Nietzsche's celebrated first book presents a cultural theory based on the idea that hybridization is the fundamental principle governing cultural innovation and artistic creativity. Nietzsche's second example of an aesthetic experience as an experience of Otherness is the Dionysian principle, which is a core thread throughout his aesthetic thought. This principle represents not only an instance of cultural difference; i.e., a different Self. Rather, as the god of the pre-individualized world, Dionysus symbolizes the Otherness of the Self. In its aesthetic transformation, Dionysian intoxication leads to the fragmentation of the *principium individuationis*. By experiencing Dionysian arts, human beings overstep the limits of the Self. In Nietzsche's view, the Tragic consists in the frightening and at the same time fascinating violation of the borders between Self and the Otherness of the Self.

The simultaneity of horror and aesthetic pleasure in the experience of tragic arts reminds us of the aesthetics of the sublime, which were developed in the course of the eighteenth century, reaching a systematic formulation in Immanuel Kant's *Critique of the Power of Judgment* (1790).[2] However, Nietzsche differs from Kant's sublime in two substantial aspects. First, he opens the field of the arts to the experience of the sublime, which was limited only to natural phenomena by Kant. Secondly and more importantly in our context, according to Nietzsche the experience of the sublime doesn't end with the triumph of reason as predicted by Kant. On the contrary, it leads to the violation of the *principium individuationis*. Therefore, the intensive experience of Otherness presented by the arts emerges as a consequence of the post-Kantian, Nietzschean sublime as the "aesthetic sublimation of shock."[3]

In the past few decades, this approach to Otherness in the arts has received the most attention, not least due to Jean-François Lyotard's influential

[1] See Federico Celestini, "Gustav Mahler and the Aesthetic of De-Identification," in *Rethinking Mahler*, ed. Jeremy Barham (New York: Oxford University Press, forthcoming).

[2] Carsten Zelle, *Die doppelte Ästhetik der Moderne. Revisionen des Schönen von Boileau bis Nietzsche* (Stuttgart: Metzler, 1995); Paul Crowther, *The Kantian Sublime* (Oxford: Clarendon Press, 1989).

[3] Dieter Mersch, "Ästhetischer Augenblick und Gedächtnis der Kunst," in *Die Medien der Künste. Beiträge zur Theorie des Darstellens*, ed. Dieter Mersch (Munich: Fink, 2003), 167.

valuation of the sublime as the common denominator of modern arts.[4] In this paper, I would like to focus on a further aspect of Otherness in the arts; namely, the plurality of idioms and style as well as the hybridization of expression. For this purpose, I will discuss Michail Bakhtin's concept of heteroglossia in the literary novel in order to consider Gustav Mahler's first four symphonies from this theoretical perspective.

Mahler and the Novel

A connection between Mahler's symphonies and the novel was made relatively early in the musicological and critical reception of the composer. In 1930, in a short contribution for the journal of the publishing house Universal Edition, the former Schoenberg pupil Erwin Stein recognized a novel-like character in the symphonies of Mahler, due mainly to his unscholarly variation technique.[5] Stein underlined the flexibility of Mahler's themes and their characteristic of always appearing in new forms. According to Stein, it is impossible for the listener to determine their precise profile. Not even the first presentation of a theme has particular significance. The several occurrences of any theme are not hierarchically related like a classical series of theme and variations. Rather, they show a horizontal relationship typical for the variants in popular music. In this way, the thematic statements that follow as the symphony unfolds are similar to each other, but never identical, and assume a temporal significance that is characteristic of memory. The thematic modifications appear as consequences of the time elapsed and the experiences that have occurred. This way of handling themes, the character and the physiognomy of which are not immovable, but evolve over the course of time, seemed to Stein to be an important common trait between Mahler's symphonies and the literary genre of the novel.

Thirty years later, Theodor W. Adorno's seminal book on Gustav Mahler was published. The fourth chapter is titled "Novel" (Roman). Here, Adorno develops the ideas presented earlier by Stein. According to Adorno, a comparison with the great symphonic tradition of the nineteenth century demonstrates the innovative character of Mahler's compositional technique. Adorno considers the recapitulation to be the veritable crux of Sonata Form because it negates the dynamic of the development. In his eyes, the most problematic aspect in the recapitulation is that it is a confirmation of that which was

---

4 Jean-François Lyotard, *Lessons on the Analytic of the Sublime*, trans. Elizabeth Rottenberg (Stanford: Stanford University Press, 1994).

5 Erwin Stein, "Mahlers Sachlichkeit," *Musikblätter des Anbruch—Sonderheft Mahler* 12/3 (1930): 99–101.

presented at the beginning, as a result of the evolution during the development section. On the other hand, adds Adorno, music without a recapitulation gives the impression that a conclusion is missing. Mahler's compositional answer to this dilemma, claims Adorno, converges with that of the great novelists of his generation.[6] The memory of the past is conserved in the variant, without however pretending that it is returning, as it is not represented in its identical form. In their variant-like changeability, themes assume a vagueness suggesting musical memory.

Alluding to Henri Bergson, Adorno detects a new conception of musical time in Mahler's symphonic music, in which the measured, physical time has been transformed into the *durée* of experienced time.[7] As Stein already observed, Mahler's variant technique seems to be the main compositional trait responsible for the novel-like character in his music, but it is certainly not the only one. Adorno describes the popular tone often heard in Mahler's music as being trivial in content, but sublime in the execution, establishing a direct link with Gustave Flaubert's *Madame Bovary*.[8] Finally, Adorno sees a further novel-like feature in Mahler's symphonic unfolding, which seems to follow the carved narrative line of a novel, escalating toward high points and collapsing in the ruins of sudden breakdowns.[9] When narratological studies began to develop in musicology in recent decades, they found an already existent critical tradition in the field of Mahler scholarship with which to connect.[10]

The idea of a significant connection between Mahler's symphonies and the novel is supported by several elements of Mahler's biography. Admittedly, theories don't require biographical parallels. Nevertheless, if they are present, a sort of epistemological coherence between theoretical concepts and their object emerges that allows a mild adaptation of abstract thinking to the individuality of the empirical data. Mahler was an enthusiastic reader. Among his favorite literature were the humorous novels of Cervantes, Laurence Sterne, Jean Paul, and Charles Dickens. If the veneration of Goethe is not surprising for a German-educated composer like Mahler, his strong interest in Dostoevsky is unusual.[11] Furthermore, it is noticeable that each

---

[6] Theodor Adorno, "Mahler. Eine musikalische Physiognomik," in *Die musikalischen Monographien* (Gesammelte Schriften 13), ed. Rolf Tiedemann with Gretel Adorno, Susan Buck-Morss, and Klaus Schultz (Frankfurt am Main: Suhrkamp, 1971), 241–42.

[7] Ibid., 233–34.

[8] Ibid., 209.

[9] Ibid., 217–18.

[10] See on this Celestini, "Gustav Mahlers Fünfte Symphonie," in *Gustav Mahler. Interpretationen seiner Werke*, ed. Peter Revers and Oliver Korte (Laaber: Laaber-Verlag, 2011), 2: 4–10.

[11] On Mahler's interest in literature, see Jens Malte Fischer, *Gustav Mahler*, trans. Stewart Spencer (New Haven: Yale University Press, 2011), 125–39.

of these authors appears among the group most frequently mentioned in the literary criticism of Michail M. Bakhtin.[12] The latter's essays about heteroglossia and hybridity in the novel deliver a theory of Otherness in literature. According to Bakhtin, the polyphony of narrative voices, the plurality of consciousnesses, and the internal dialogicity of the word find expression in the novel that is denied to the monologic genres of poetry and drama. Drawing on Bakhtin, it seems possible to assume that in the novel-like character of Mahler's symphonies, a corresponding manifestation of plurality can be detected.

Heteroglossia and Plurality of Consciousnesses: Bakhtin on the Novel

In his studies on Dostoevsky conducted in the 1920s and re-elaborated in the 1960s, Bakhtin stressed the importance of plural voices and points of view in the novels of the Russian writer. This feature appeared to him to be an absolute novelty in the context of European literature of the nineteenth century, so he introduced a new literary genre able to encompass it; namely, the *polyphonic novel*.[13] Bakhtin defined this kind of polyphony as follows:

> In his work a hero appears whose voice is constructed exactly like the voice of the author himself in a novel of the usual type. A character's word about himself and his world is just as fully weighted as the author's word usually is; it is not subordinated to the character's objectified image as merely one of his characteristics, nor does it serve as a mouthpiece for the author's voice.[14]

The essential element in Bakhtin's definition of a *polyphonic novel* is not simply the presence of several voices, but the autonomy of these from the voice of the author, which in this way becomes just one amongst others. This distinguishes the *polyphonic* from the *monologic novel*; that is, according to Bakhtin, the usual kind of narrative in which the plurality of the characters' voices is subordinated to an authorial instance controlling and bringing it to a superior unity. In our context, it is also noteworthy that Bakhtin uses a musical model to describe Dostoevsky's new novelistic genre, and that the musical metaphor is properly used: the necessary feature of musical polyphony is the very same autonomy of single voices that Bakhtin attributes to the polyphonic novel.

---

[12] A significant exception is François Rabelais.

[13] Pam Morris, ed., *The Bakhtin Reader: Selected Writing of Bakhtin, Medvedev, Voloshinov* (London: Edward Arnold, 1994), 89.

[14] Ibid.

Thus, the parallels between music and literature extend in both directions: while on one hand the comparison with the novel is made by musicological scholars to explain some particular characteristics of Mahler's symphonies, on the other, Bakhtin's recourse to musical analogy qualifies a new genre of novel.

As Pam Morris observes, in describing the difference between monologic and polyphonic novels, Bakhtin shifts from the visual to the acoustic metaphoric field. The attitude of the monologic author is one of seeing from an outside perspective, which includes the views of the single characters. In a polyphonic novel however, the presence of simultaneous and autonomous voices annuls this manner of seeing.[15] As none of these voices are allowed to take an outside perspective, it follows that the characters no longer appear as objectified images observed by the totalizing consciousness of the monologic author, but that their voices assume a subjective prominence equal in quality to that of the author itself.

In the essay "Discourse in the Novel" (1935), Bakhtin further specifies the quality of novelistic polyphony. The single voices are not only autonomous from the authorial voice, they are also heterogeneous in style. And this stylistic heterogeneity mirrors the social diversity from which it originates:

> The novel can be defined as a diversity of social speech types (sometimes even diversity of languages) and a diversity of individual voices, artistically organized. The internal stratification of any single national language into social dialects, characteristic group behavior, professional jargons, generic languages, languages of generations and age groups, tendentious languages, languages of the authorities, of various circles and of passing fashions, languages that serve the specific sociopolitical purposes of the day, even of the hour… —this internal stratification present in every language at any given moment of its historical existence is the indispensable prerequisite for the novel as a genre.[16]

When Bakhtin tries to explain how such stylistic diversity can be artistically organized in the novel, he reverts to musical metaphors once again:

> The novel orchestrates all its themes, the totality of the world of objects and ideas depicted and expressed in it, by means of the

[15] Pam Morris, "Dostoevsky's Polyphonic Novel: a Plurality of Consciousnesses," in *The Bakhtin Reader*, 88.

[16] Mikhail Bakhtin, "Discourse in the Novel," in *The Dialogic Imagination: Four Essays by M. M. Bakhtin*, ed. Michael Holquist, trans. Caryl Emerson and Michael Holquist, 18th ed. (Austin: University of Texas Press, 2011), 262–63.

> social diversity of speech types and by the differing individual voices that flourish under such conditions.[17]

Finally, stylistic and social diversity imported into the novel are considered to be the prerequisite for *heteroglossia*:

> Authorial speech, the speeches of narrators, inserted genres, the speech of characters are merely those fundamental compositional unities with whose help heteroglossia can enter the novel; each of them permits a multiplicity of social voices and a wide variety of their links and interrelationships between utterances and languages, this movement of the theme through different languages and speech types, its dispersion into the rivulets and droplets of social heteroglossia, its dialogization—this is the basic distinguishing feature of the stylistics of the novel.[18]

As we will see, heteroglossia also enters Mahler's music. The question is, to what degree Bakhtin's categories can help to describe this phenomenon.

Fragmented Consciousness

In the recollections of Mahler's friend Natalie Bauer-Lechner, two holiday scenes from August 1900 are reported, once more giving biographical consistency to a compositional feature; namely, the plurality of stylistic voices in Mahler's symphonies. Both scenes depict experiences with incidental overlapping of music sources as different as several barrel organs, a military band, and a men's choir during a folk festival near Klagenfurt, and represent a genuine acoustic parallel to Bakhtin's metaphorical polyphony.[19] According to Bauer-Lechner, Mahler didn't only express his enthusiasm for this "musical pandemonium," but he also explicitly and firmly declared such phenomena to be the ideal and inspirational source for his own music.[20] After a comparison of these occurrences with non-human, natural rustling, including the singing of thousands of birds, the howling of storms, the lapping of waves and the crackling of fire, Mahler claimed that in order to achieve real polyphony in

---

[17] Ibid., 263.

[18] Ibid.

[19] Natalie Bauer-Lechner, *Recollections of Gustav Mahler*, ed. Peter Franklin, trans. Dika Newlin (Cambridge: Cambridge University Press, 1980), 155–56.

[20] To his later brother-in-law, Arnold Rosé, who expressed surprise at this, Mahler said: "If you like my symphonies, you must like that too!" Regarding the second, similar experience, Mahler exclaimed to Natalie: "You hear? That's polyphony, and that's where I get it from!" (Ibid., 155).

musical composition, themes must appear to originate from quite different spheres, as in the scenes reported.[21] Mahler's concluding sentence, however, seems to relativize the Bakhtinian sense of such a polyphony by invoking a superior order that serves to unify and harmonize the diversity: "The only difference is that the artist orders and unites them all into one concordant and harmonious whole."[22] We will discuss this aspect soon.

Looking for compositional manifestations of such stylistic heteroglossia in Mahler's symphonic work, we find one of the most impressive occurrences in the third movement of the First Symphony, where a minor-key version of the *Frère Jacques* canon in a funeral march adaptation, a Bohemian marching band with echoes of Klezmer music, and a self-quotation from the fourth of the *Lieder eines fahrenden Gesellen* form an astonishing polyphony in which disparate cultural worlds (by the way, also those of Mahler's own pluralistic cultural identity) are recognizable.[23] Mahler suggested a kind of plot to Natalie Bauer-Lechner for this enigmatic movement:

> A funeral procession passes our hero and the whole misery, the whole lament of the world with its incisive contrasts and the ghastly irony takes hold of him. Someone has thought for the funeral march "Bruder Martin" to be churned out by a really bad band, as is typical for such solemnities. In between, the whole crudeness, merriness and banality of the world resounds in the tones of a "Bohemian marching band" that butts in, as well as in the terribly painful elegy of the hero. The effect is shattering, with its acute irony and reckless polyphony, particularly where we see the cortege returning from the burial (after the middle section) and the funeral music intones the customary "cheerful tune."[24]

---

[21] Ibid., 155–56 (italics by Bauer-Lechner): "Just in this way—*from quite different directions* [von ganz verschiedenen Seiten her]—must the theme appear; and they must be just as different from each other in rhythm and melodic character (everything else is merely many-voiced writing, homophony in disguise) [alles andere ist bloß Vielstimmigkeit und verkappte Homophonie]."

[22] Ibid., 156.

[23] Celestini, "Gustav Mahler and the Aesthetic of De-Identification."

[24] Bauer-Lechner, *Gustav Mahler in den Erinnerungen von Natalie Bauer-Lechner*, ed. Herbert Killian, rev. and enl. ed. (Hamburg: Verlag der Musikalienhandlung Karl Dieter Wagner, 1984), 174: "An unserem Helden zieht ein Leichenbegängnis vorbei und das ganze Elend, der ganze Jammer der Welt mit ihren schneidenden Kontrasten und der gräßlichen Ironie faßt ihn an. Den Trauermarsch des 'Bruder Martin' hat man sich von einer ganz schlechten Musikkapelle, wie sie solchen Leichenbegängnis zu folgen pflegen, dumpf abgespielt zu denken. Dazwischen

In Mahler's explanation we again find the incidental overlapping of different music sources; namely, the funeral march and the Bohemian marching band. But there is no trace of the third musical voice; i.e., the quotation from the fourth of the *Lieder eines fahrenden Gesellen*. A more accurate examination of the score shows that the situation is actually quite complex. The movement consists of three sections. At the beginning of the first section (b. 1–38), the funeral march is introduced by the interval of a fourth in the timpani, repeated unchanged throughout the whole section and beyond. The heavy step of the funeral march is easily recognizable in this figure.[25] Played in a minor version of the popular *Frère Jacques* canon, the funeral march assumes an ironic tone, addressed by Mahler in his statement for Natalie Bauer-Lechner quoted above. The Bohemian marching band doesn't intrude into the funeral march. Rather, we hear a short dissolution of the canon, lasting six bars (b. 33–38), before the marching band begins. We sense the echo of a genuine succession of events as described by Mahler in his statement, yet transposed into the psychological state of memory.

If this impression is correct, we are not confronted with independent voices building polyphony in Bakhtin's sense, but with the perception of these voices by the hero. It is as if we can hear through his ears, feel and remember through his consciousness. Accordingly, the self-quotation from the *Lieder eines fahrenden Gesellen* in the second section of the movement (b. 83–112) doesn't represent a further musical incident, in this case an encounter with authentic folk music, but a psychological state in which the consciousness of the self is dissolved ecstatically. It is an idyllic state of painlessness and of forgetting, evoked through the allusion of a folk atmosphere, and suggesting the reaction of the hero's consciousness in the face of the triviality and hypocrisy represented by the preceding episodes in the first section of the movement.

In respect to Bakhtin's notion of the polyphonic novel and of plurality of consciousness, we observe that in Mahler's case, we are confronted with a single consciousness, which we can easily ascribe to the symphonic hero. Otherwise, unlike the monologic novel described by Bakhtin, it seems that

---

tönt die ganze Roheit [sic], Lustigkeit und Banalität der Welt in den Klängen irgend einer sich dreinmischenden 'böhmischen Musikantenkapelle' hinein, zugleich die furchtbar schmerzliche Klage des Helden. Es wirkt erschütternd in seiner scharfen Ironie und rücksichtlosen Polyphonie, besonders wo wir—nach dem Zwischensatz—den Zug vom Begräbnis zurückkommen sehen und die Leichenmusik die übliche (hier durch Mark und Bein gehende) 'lustige Weise' anstimmt." (Passage missing in the English edition). Translation by Celestini.

[25] For an extended analysis of this movement, see Celestini, "Literature as *Dèja vu*? The Third Movement of Gustav Mahler's First Symphony," in *Phrase and Subject: Studies in Literature and Music*, ed. Delia da Sousa Correa (London: Legenda, 2006), 153–66.

this consciousness is no longer able to unify the plurality of voices experienced and unite them to a superior whole. Rather, the hero's consciousness breaks down in face of the irreducible multiplicity of the real world. This seems to be the sense of the impressive passage in the third section (b. 113–168), when the three stylistic spheres of the movement (namely, the funeral march, the Bohemian marching band, and the self-quotation from the *Lieder eines fahrenden Gesellen*) sound concurrently in genuine polyphony (b. 138 ff.). If this strongly reminds us of the real experiences in the Klagenfurt woods recalled by Natalie Bauer-Lechner, it is clear that this astonishing polyphony doesn't portray specific dramatic events, but rather their traces in the consciousness of the hero. In this way, the plural voices of Bakhtin's polyphony resound within the hero's consciousness. The consequences of this are tragic.

Plurality of Voices and Symphonic Transcendence

The failure of the hero to bring the diversity experienced together into a unity in his consciousness leads to a symphonic breakdown at the beginning of the following movement, the Finale. Here, the sharply dissonant orchestral *tutti* that dramatically opens the movement, a diminished ninth chord, is reminiscent of the beginning of the Finale of Beethoven's Ninth Symphony. In a letter to the music critic Max Marschalk from 20 March 1896, Mahler describes this dramatic opening as the "desperate outcry of a deeply wounded heart, which is preceded by the eerie and ironically brooding sultriness of the Funeral March."[26]

In the first section of the Finale, the traditional dualism of Sonata Form escalates to the drastic opposition of the main thematic area in F minor (b. 1–174) and the secondary one in D flat major (b. 175–237). Mahler's score instructions demonstrate these irresolvable contrasts: "With stormy motion" (Stürmisch bewegt, b. 1), "Energetic" (Energisch, b. 55), and "With great wildness" (Mit großer Wildheit, b. 73) characterize the first thematic group, while the expressively beautiful second theme is marked "very singable" (Sehr gesangvoll, b. 175). In contrast to the symphonic tradition of the nineteenth century, no thematic integration occurs to mediate this opposition in the following section (Development, b. 238–427).[27] The diversity of these expressive worlds, as well as that of the voices and styles encountered in the course of

---

[26] Gustav Mahler, *Briefe*, ed. Herta Blaukopf, new ed. (Wien: Zsolnay, 1996), 170: "... einfach der Aufschrei eines im Tiefsten verwundeten Herzens, dem eben die unheimlich und ironisch brütende Schwühle des Trauermarsches vorhergeht." Translation by Celestini.

[27] Musicological criticism of the lack of mediation between the main themes is predominantly negative, see Bernd Sponheuer, *Logik des Zerfalls. Untersuchungen zum Finalproblem in den Symphonien Gustav Mahler* (Tutzing: Hans Schneider, 1978), 74; 79.

the whole symphony, is not unified or synthesized in the Finale. Rather, in the third section of the movement (reversed reprise and coda, b. 428–731) we are confronted with a grandiose symphonic manifestation of transcendence: the Finale, and with it the whole symphony, culminates in the exultant overcoming of the disruption and of the "desperate outcry" it induces through the solemn choral of the brass in D major (b. 623–656), followed by the apotheosis in the coda, marked with the explicit score instruction "Triumphant" (Triumphal, b. 657–731).

From a Bakhtinian perspective, this is an ambivalent solution, because the transcending of fragmentation and diversity cannot be equated with unification or synthesis. On the contrary, the *deus ex machina* intervention of transcendence, the most authoritarian instance we can imagine, reveals that neither unification nor synthesis is possible on the level of immanence. Mahler's staging of symphonic transcendence is aesthetically questionable.[28] But at the same time, it reveals that a monologic authority is no longer possible in the irreducible pluralistic world of phenomena.

In the Second Symphony, the narrative scheme of *per aspera ad astra* is further developed in regard to the dramaturgic design and the means employed. The polarity of breakdown and breakthrough that was concentrated in the last movement of the First Symphony is now broadened to embrace the whole symphony. Here, the "desperate outcry," a clash between a B-flat minor chord and the sustained C of the lower strings, already occurs in the third movement (b. 465–468). Before this, in the first movement, massive, violent orchestral outbreaks anticipate the explosion in the third movement (b. 291; 325–328), which is, in turn, recalled at the beginning of the Finale. Here, however, *arpeggio* figures in the trumpets and trombones (b. 5–6 and 9–10) introduce an element of breakthrough into the orchestral outcry. At b. 343, an escalation begins that leads once more to the outcry chord in triple *fortissimo* in b. 402, transposed a semitone higher. While the strings and woodwinds sustain the chord for nine bars, the brass arpeggiate the consonant core of the chord. In this way, the transformation of the breakdown into a breakthrough is developed further. In b. 418, the *fugato* theme is anticipated. Then follows the "Große Appell" episode (b. 448–471), in which military calls and birdsongs seem to signal the arrival of the *a cappella* choir in triple *pianissimo*, which itself heralds the final resurrection. A triumphal apotheosis, which surmounts that of the First Symphony through the employment of a

---

28 The conventional character of Mahler's Finale has been underlined by many commentators. Adorno is exemplary here: "Im Finale der ersten Symphonie steigert sich Zerrissenheit über alles vermittelnde Maß hinaus in ein Ganzes von Verzweiflung, hinter der dann freilich der bedenkenlose Schlußtriumph zu einer bloßen Regie verblaßt." See Adorno, "Mahler," 201.

choir and solo voices, concludes the movement, and the whole work, "with the greatest display of strength."[29]

The Second Symphony shows a remarkable compositional intensification of the idea of transcendence already presented in the First Symphony, as well as a switch from the "struggle-victory" scheme of the earlier work to the "death and transfiguration" paradigm of the later one.[30] This work doesn't, however, contribute any new elements to the Bakhtinian question of plurality and unification. The idioms of funeral march and lyric pathos prevalent in the first movement, the *laendler* dances of the second movement,[31] and the satiric irony of the third movement find no synthesis in the last movement. The "misterioso" tone of the final resurrection choir suggests a transcendent sphere in a manner even more explicit than in the Finale of the First Symphony, if that is possible. Nevertheless, the naïve, infantile irony of the fourth movement, *Urlicht*, anticipates a new path that Mahler will investigate in the Fourth Symphony and later; namely, the renunciation of the fictional presentation of transcendence in the immanent world of concert performances in favor of an ironic evocation thereof. In the Second Symphony, the emphatic Finale contradicts this promising alternative, but the seminal quality of this attempt is evident. We will come back to this.

The Symphony as a World

While still involved with the idea of symphonic transcendence, the Third Symphony is a key work for the discussion of heteroglossia in Mahler's music. The composer himself addressed this aspect explicitly in two significant statements:

> My calling it a "symphony" is really inaccurate, for it doesn't keep to the traditional form in any way. But to me "symphony" means constructing a world with all the technical means at one's disposal.[32]
>
> . . . the symphony must be like the world. It must embrace everything.[33]

---

[29] Score instruction at b. 752: "Mit höchster Kraftentfaltung."

[30] See on this Sponheuer, *Logik des Zerfalls*, 128–33.

[31] Here, the overlay of dance and song in b. 92–132 is also remarkable.

[32] Bauer-Lechner, *Recollections of Gustav Mahler*, 40.

[33] Remark to Jean Sibelius on the occasion of Mahler's concert journey to Helsinki in 1907 (Karl Ekman, *Jean Sibelius: His Life and Personality*, trans. Edward Birse (London: A. Wilmer, 1936), 176), here quoted after Donald Mitchell, *Gustav Mahler*, Vol. 1: *The Early Years*, rev. ed. (Berkeley: University of California Press, 1980), 115.

The French musicologist Marc Vignal reports (although without indicating references) that the last statement was made by Mahler in response to Jean Sibelius, who praised Mahler's motivic logic and sense of unity: "Non, la Symphonie doit être comme le monde. Elle doit tout embrasser."[34] Indeed, heteroglossia and centrifugal forces reach levels that are even exceptional for Mahler in this colossal work. The cosmological dimension of the symphony is already evident in the plan of the movements, as listed with Mahler's original descriptions in the autograph of the score:[35]

Symphony No. III in F major

First Part:	Introduction: Pan awakes/leading directly to Summer marches in ("Bacchic Procession")
Second Part:	What the flowers in the meadow tell me What the animals in the forest tell me What man tells me What the angels tell me What love tells me

If references to the whole human race were a typical feature of the symphonic genre from the last symphonies of Haydn and Mozart, and to an even greater extent from Beethoven onward, Mahler takes this attribute to an extreme degree. As Bernd Sponheuer observes, only an enlarged conception of symphonic totality saves Mahler from the collapse of the symphonic genre:

> The idiomatic diversity of the symphony is responsible for the impression of disparate, noncommittal, suite-like music. One could also say: un-symphonic [music], which initially imposes on the listener. But exactly this idiomatic diversity (this ostensibly un-symphonic character) is the precise consequence of a non-restrictive definition of the symphony.[36]

---

34 Marc Vignal, *Mahler* (Paris: Éditions du Seuil, 1966), 132, here quoted after Sponheuer, *Logik des Zerfalls*, 137–38n7.

35 Quoted after Peter Franklin, *Mahler: Symphony No. 3* (Cambridge: Cambridge University Press, 1991), 92–99. Mahler mentioned these titles in a letter to Max Marschalk on August 6, 1896 (Mahler, *Briefe*, 196). In a letter to Josef Krug-Waldsee in Summer 1902, Mahler withdrew them (Ibid., 297–98).

36 Sponheuer, *Logik des Zerfalls*, 141: "Die idiomatische Vielfalt der Symphonie ist verantwortlich für den Eindruck des Disparaten, Unverbindlich-Suitenhaften, man könnte auch sagen: Unsymphonischen, der sich zunächst dem Hörer aufdrängt. Aber eben diese idiomatische Vielfalt (dies vorgeblich *Un*symphonische) ist die präzise Konsequenz eines nicht restriktiven Symphoniebegriffs. . . ." Italics by Sponheuer, translation by Celestini.

Stylistic pluralism, the mixture of different idioms in Mahler's music, transforms the monologic universalism of the Classical symphony from the late Age of Enlightenment into an implicit denunciation of social inequality and a protest against the division between high and low music.

The German composer Dieter Schnebel underlines the stylistic pluralism of Mahler's Third Symphony and establishes a connection between the different idioms and social groups, a clear case of symphonic heteroglossia. According to him, the first movement "speaks" military band jargon, but with the inclusion of the higher sphere of a funeral march. Schnebel classifies the music of the second movement to be that of a middle-class concert hall, represented by a minuet in a slightly old-fashioned and nostalgic way, and the dance music in the contrasting sections, in which a polka is quoted. Music of the lower classes is to be heard in the third movement, according to Schnebel, followed by the grave church music idiom of the fourth. The fifth movement presents children's music, with pentatonic colors, whilst the music of the sixth and last movement appears to him to include both high and low spheres. Schnebel compares the Finale with a fan, in which everything is folded together.[37]

Crucial once more is the reading of the last movement of the symphony. If this is considered to be the synthesis of the preceding differences, then we are confronted with the final triumph of monologism over heteroglossia. This seems to be how Mahler's old friend Guido Adler understood this music, as he stressed the organic unity of Mahler's compositions.[38] A differentiated and stimulating answer is given by Julian Johnson in his recent book on *Mahler's voices*:

> Adler is surely correct in that Mahler's music opens up such acoustic chaos precisely in order to redeem it in a "higher" order; the earthy rawness of the earlier movements of the Third Symphony is, in the end, absorbed into the Adagio Finale, which ends with *a gesättigten Ton* (a saturated, noble tone). For Mahler himself, the plural and heterogeneous is a counterpart to the idea of a unitary voice that claims an authenticity in the face of the carnivalesque. But his oeuvre as a whole demonstrates that this tension is never wholly reconciliated.[39]

---

37 Dieter Schnebel, "Über Mahlers Dritte," *Neue Zeitschrift für Musik* 135 (1974): 284–85.

38 Guido Adler, *Gustav Mahler* [1914], repr. and trans. in Edward R. Reilly, *Gustav Mahler and Guido Adler: Records of a Friendship* (Cambridge: Cambridge University Press, 1982).

39 Julian Johnson, *Mahler's Voices: Expression and Irony in the Songs and Symphonies* (New York: Oxford University Press, 2009), 133. Italics by Johnson.

Referring to Bakhtin's analysis of the English comic novel, Johnson observes that in contrast to Laurence Sterne, who "makes use of 'the common language' of given social groups" without completely identifying with any of them, "keeping the boundaries shifting and ambiguous,"[40] a "Mahlerian symphony, taken individually in performance, proposes something different—that these multiple voices are, in the end, reconciled into the 'noble tone' of a summative finale."[41] But the state of things changes if we take the corpus of Mahler's music as a whole. In this case, according to Johnson, the reading "comes closer to Bakhtin's view of Sterne: that even the 'noble tone' is just another voice proposed by the symphony that moves between many, while 'completely identifying with none.'"[42]

The aesthetic dubiety of the symphonic presentation of transcendence mentioned above, which Mahler fabricates in his first three symphonies, also affects the question of disorder and its resolution. In the same degree to which a symphonic *deus ex machina* reveals its fictional character, it also fails as an overcoming instance. If the "higher order" loses its credibility, redemption of chaos is no longer possible. The consequence is paradoxical: instead of being redeemed by the "noble tone" of the "summative" Finale, the heterogeneity Mahler addresses finally absorbs this, which becomes just one among many fictional voices in the symphonic narrative.

Raymond Knapp also adopts Bakhtinian categories in his discussion of single movements of the Third Symphony and contrasts the "monologic sensibilities of Nietzsche's midnight poem," set to music in the fourth movement, with the "heteroglossia of 'Es sungen drei Engel'" in the following movement.[43] For this, Mahler chooses a poem from the folklike collection *Des Knaben Wunderhorn*, in which St. Peter confesses to have broken the ten commandments and is subsequently absolved by Jesus. As Knapp observes, the heteroglossia of the poem is constituted by three distinct voices; namely, the narrative voice, the angels, and St. Peter.[44] Despite the naïve and childish tone of both text and music,[45] real and metaphorical polyphony present quite a complex situation here. The narrative voice is sung by a three-part women's chorus, while a two-part boys' choir, located high up in

---

[40] Bakhtin, "The Dialogic Imagination," in *The Bakhtin Reader*, 116n3.
[41] Johnson, *Mahler's Voices*, 134.
[42] Ibid.
[43] Raymond Knapp, *Symphonic Metamorphoses: Subjectivity and Alienation in Mahler's Re-Cycled Songs* (Middletown: Weslayan University Press, 2003), 30.
[44] Ibid., 32.
[45] The score instruction is: "Lustig im Tempo und keck im Ausdruck" (Cheerful in tempo and perky in expression).

the concert hall, imitating the sound of bells, represents the singing angels evoked by the narrative voice. In this celestial environment, St. Peter sings with an alto voice. The contrast to the serious "monologic" inwardness of the Nietzschean setting in the preceding movement could hardly be stronger, illuminating Mahler's more general attitude toward monologism and heteroglossia in music.

Voices of Nature, Children, and Unconsciousness

Mahler's preference for the folklike poetry of *Des Knaben Wunderhorn* is nearly absolute until the early years of the twentieth century. As Adorno already observed, the archaistic texts Mahler chose are far removed from the psychologically individuated Self that characterizes lyric poetry.[46] "Es sungen drei Engel" is a clear example. Mahler was evidently interested in setting a kind of poetry to music that doesn't rise from the consciousness of the lyric Self, but mirrors the multiplication of voices and points of view of a world before individuation. Through the large spectrum of different instrumental voices and timbres, the orchestral accompaniment sustains the multitude of voices already present in the texts of these songs. Adorno considered the orchestral song, which Mahler so often integrated into his symphonies, to be the key to the novelistic character of Mahler's individual style. Regarded from a Bakhtinian perspective, this assertion gains a new light: the Wunderhorn songs are one of the most important gates through which heteroglossia enters Mahler's symphonies.

Mahler's choice of archaistic texts also seems to reflect an interest in a kind of expression which differs from that of a subjective, lyrical voice. This non-subjective sphere can be divided into three main areas; namely, the natural world with all its components, the world of childhood, and that of human unconsciousness. The first two fields are copiously represented in the poems of *Des Knaben Wunderhorn*. The 19-year-old Anton Webern already noted in his diary that Mahler's music makes a childish impression.[47] In the song *Ablösung im Sommer*, which Mahler published in 1892 with piano accompaniment and utilized for the Scherzo of his Third Symphony, stylized animal expression and a childlike world view are combined. Cynically, the

---

[46] Adorno, "Mahler," 223.

[47] Anton Webern, quoted after Adorno, "Zu einer imaginären Auswahl von Liedern Gustav Mahlers," in: Id., *Musikalische Schriften IV* (Gesammelte Schriften 17), ed. Rolf Tiedemann with Gretel Adorno, Susan Buck-Morss, and Klaus Schultz (Frankfurt am Main: Suhrkamp, 1982), 189.

death of the cuckoo causes concern only because the amusement it assured ceases. As soon as it is replaced by the nightingale, the cuckoo is forgotten. Mahler retains the tone of the text and composes childish music, even if somewhat uncanny.[48]

The second of Nietzsche's *Untimely Meditations*, "On the Use and Abuse of History for Life," opens with a definition of animal life. According to Nietzsche, this is completely centered in the present:

> Observe the herd which is grazing beside you. It does not know what yesterday or today is. It springs around, eats, rests, digests, jumps up again, and so from morning to night and from day to day, with its likes and dislikes closely tied to the peg of the moment, and thus is neither melancholy nor weary.[49]

The human being, unable to forget and always hanging onto things past, envies the animal, whose attitude Nietzsche calls unhistorical:

> For the man says, "I remember," and envies the beast, which immediately forgets and sees each moment really perish, sink back in cloud and night, and vanish forever. In this way the beast lives *unhistorically*. For it goes into the present like a number without any odd fraction left over; it does not know how to play a part, hides nothing, and appears in each moment exactly and entirely what it is.[50]

From this perspective, a child's manner of perception appears to Nietzsche to be very similar to that of animals. Both are a source of admiration for an adult, oppressed by the burden of the past and looking for release:

> And so it moves him, as if he imagined a lost paradise, to see the grazing herd, or something more closely familiar, the child, which does not yet have a past to deny and plays in blissful blindness between the fences of the past and future.[51]

---

[48] For more on this, see Celestini, *Die Unordnung der Dinge: Das musikalische Groteske in der Wiener Moderne (1885–1914)*, Beihefte zum Archiv für Musikwissenschaft, 56 (Stuttgart: Franz Steiner Verlag, 2006), 63–75.

[49] Friedrich Nietzsche, *On the Use and Abuse of History for Life* [1874], trans. Ian Johnston, August 19, 2013, http://records.viu.ca/~johnstoi/nietzsche/history.htm.

[50] Ibid. Italics by Nietzsche.

[51] Ibid.

Living in the sensations and perceptions of the present is what brings animals and children psychologically close to each other. It is noteworthy that Mahler observed and commented on animals using similar words:

> Lipiner claimed that Mahler practised animal psychology. And indeed, Mahler didn't pass a single dog or cat without making an observation about its character and to comment thus: he found it attractive "that an animal lives absolutely in the present, completely absorbed in every moment."[52]

The memory of past experiences is the substance of subjectivity. Thus, Mahler's interest leads to a kind of musical expression in which subjectivity is not yet, or no longer, active. This is the case with animals and children, as we have already seen, and in a special state of the human psyche. In this last aspect it is not difficult to recognize the main reason for Mahler's life-long attraction to Nietzsche's thoughts about Dionysian intoxication. Mahler called the third movement of the Third Symphony "Tierstück" (Animal Piece) and explained this as follows:

> That this nature contains everything that is horrible, great and also lovely (exactly this is what I wanted to express in the whole work, as a type of evolutionary development)—of course, nobody considers this. It strikes me as strange that most people, when they speak of "nature," only ever think about flowers, birdies, forest fragrances, etc. Nobody knows the god Dionysus, the great Pan.[53]

Like Nietzsche, Mahler was certain that there is a close relationship between animal psychology and that of people during a Dionysian intoxication. This conviction of Mahler is manifested in his enthusiastic commentary on the theatrical work *Adam,* written by his friend Siegfried Lipiner:

> That is a truly Dionysian work! . . . *What* is it then, that transports all living things into the force of Dionysus? Wine

[52] Killian, ed., *Gustav Mahler in den Erinnerungen von Natalie Bauer-Lechner*, 139: "Lipiner behauptete von Mahler, dass er Tierpsychologie betrieb. Und tatsächlich Mahler ging an keinem Hund und keiner Katze vorüber, ohne auf die Äußerung ihres Wesen zu achten und sich damit zu unterhalten: 'Dass so ein Tier immer absolut in der Gegenwart lebt, jeden Augenblick ohne Rest darin aufgeht,' zog ihn an." Translation by Celestini. This passage is missing in the English edition.

[53] Mahler, *Briefe*, 202–3 (to Batka on 18 November 1896): "Daß diese Natur alles in sich birgt, was an Schauerlichem, Großem und auch Lieblichem ist (eben das wollte ich in dem

> intoxicates and elevates the state of the drinker! But *what* is wine?—There has never been a representation as successful as that which arises by itself from every note in music. *This* music wafts in your poetry! It is really unique in the world.—It doesn't talk about wine and depict its effects. Rather, this [poetry] *is* the wine, it *is* Dionysus! By the way, it seems to me that the figure of Dionysus was the *drive* for the ancient Greeks in exactly the mystical, grandiose sense in which you understand it! There, too, the awestruck people are driven out to the animals, with whom they become *one*.[54]

Raymond Knapp considers one of the most fascinating aspects of the third movement to be the evocation of "a multitude of roughly equivalent voices, creating a conversational confusion as a metaphor for the animate forest."[55] With the inclusion of expressive spheres that lie beyond human subjectivity, Mahler presents a still more radical view of heteroglossia than Bakhtin himself. For he confronts us not only with the musical manifestation of several consciousnesses, but also with a kind of expression that lies beyond consciousness itself.[56]

Hybridity

Mahler seems to forge a new path with his Fourth Symphony. The differences to his preceding works, particularly the reduction of the orchestral forces and the temporal framework, are remarkable. The "chamber music tone" of the works that follow is already recognizable here. Nevertheless, there are many

---

ganzen Werk in einer Art evolutionistischer Entwicklung zum Aussprechen bringen), davon erfährt natürlich niemand etwas. Mich berührt es ja immer seltsam, daß die meisten, wenn sie von 'Natur' sprechen, nur immer an Blumen, Vöglein, Waldesduft etc. denken. Den Gott Dionysos, den großen Pan kennt niemand." Translated by Celestini.

[54] Ibid., 264 (to Lipiner Juli 1899): "Das ist ein wahrhaft dionysisches Werk! . . . *Was* ist es denn, was alle Lebende in die Gewalt des Dionysos gibt? Der Wein berauscht und erhöht den Zustand des Trinkenden! *Was* aber ist der Wein?—Der Darstellung ist es bis jetzt noch nie gelungen, was sich in der Musik in jeder Note von selbst ergibt. In deiner Dichtung weht *diese* Musik! Sie ist wirklich einzig auf der Welt.—Sie erzählt nicht vom Wein und schildert seine Wirkungen—sondern sie *ist* der Wein, sie *ist* Dionysos! Mir scheint es übrigens, daß die Gestalt des Dionysos bei den Alten eben der *Trieb* war, in diesem mystisch-grandiosen Sinn, wie Du ihn erfaßt! Auch dort treibt es die Ergriffenen hinaus zu den Tieren, mit denen sie *eins* warden." Italics by Mahler, translated by Celestini.

[55] Knapp, *Symphonic Metamorphoses*, 58–60.

[56] For an analytic examination of this kind of musical expression in Mahler and in Viennese Modernism, see Celestini, *Die Unordnung der Dinge*.

links to the first three symphonies, the most important being the explicit reference to the world of *Des Knaben Wunderhorn*. According to Bauer-Lechner, Mahler viewed his first four symphonies as a kind of "tetralogy," whereby a "particularly close relationship exists between the Third and the Fourth; in fact, the latter even has themes in common with the movement of the Third called 'Was mir die Engel erzählen.'"[57] The genesis of the Fourth Symphony demonstrates the strength of this relationship. Two undated sketches of the structure of the Third Symphony, published first by Paul Bekker and later in a slightly different version by Alma Mahler, attest that Mahler initially planned to conclude this symphony with *Das himmlische Leben*, an orchestral song composed in 1892 to a poem of *Des Knaben Wunderhorn*.[58] In both drafts, this movement appears with the title "Was mir das Kind erzählt" (What the child tells me). Evidently, Mahler wished the Third Symphony to end with a humoristic Finale in an ironic, childish tone. At the latest in June 1896, Mahler eliminated *Das himmlische Leben* from the plan of the work,[59] finally using this in the Fourth Symphony in an even more radical way. Here, *Das himmlische Leben* is not only the final movement of the symphony, but a sort of bud from which the whole work sprouts. According to Bekker,

> The Finale is thus the core of the work in a complete sense. It contains not only important thematic germs for the first movements. It encloses the whole intellectual layout of the work. It determines the style and character of the whole to a much higher degree than the final movements of the earlier works . . .[60]

As already observed by Adorno, the Fourth Symphony is completely permeated by childish imagery.[61] In the text of the poem, disparate and contradicting

---

[57] Bauer-Lechner, *Recollections of Gustav Mahler*, p. 154. On the thematic relationships, see Knapp, *Symphonic Metamorphoses*, 28–69.

[58] Paul Bekker, *Gustav Mahlers Sinfonien* (Berlin: Schuster & Loffler, 1921), 106; Alma Mahler-Werfel, *Erinnerungen an Gustav Mahler* [1940], ed. Donald Mitchell (Frankfurt a. M. and Berlin: Verlag Ullstein, 1971), 64–65. The original title of the poem is "Der Himmel hängt voll Geigen."

[59] Constantin Floros, *Gustav Mahler*, Vol. 3: *Die Symphonien* (Wiesbaden: Breitkopf & Härtel, 1985), 78.

[60] Bekker, *Gustav Mahlers Sinfonien*, 142: "Das Finale ist also hier in vollem Sinn der Kern des Werkes. Es enthält nicht nur wichtige thematische Keime für die Vordersätze. Es schließt in sich bereits den gesamten geistigen Grundplan des Werkes. Es bestimmt in noch weit höherem Maße als die Endsätze der früheren Werke Stil und Charakter des Ganzen . . ." Translated by Celestini.

[61] Adorno, "Mahler," 202.

elements, such as celestial peace, worldly pleasure, and bloody violence, are brought together in an infantile tone, which thus reveals its ambiguity: "The song about the heavenly delights is, like all utopias, in reality one about earthly suffering."[62] Mahler's music reflects this ambiguity, the infantile tone coexisting with structural complexity and compositional sophistication. He called the whole Fourth Symphony a "Humoresque." Many commentators have noted that Mahler's concept of humor refers to early romantic aesthetics, and particularly to the aesthetics of Jean Paul. Here, humor mediates between finiteness and infiniteness. According to Mirjam Schadendorf, humor in early romantic aesthetics is a way to represent ideal beauty in a reversed form; i.e., in its negative version, the model for which is reality.[63] As she observes, there are significant similarities between Mahler's music and the humor in Jean Paul's novels. The precise geographic and historic description of events during the course of his novels, the adoption of socially determined idioms and abrupt changes of style, are the most obvious examples here.[64]

The humorous depiction of reality in Jean Paul's novels evokes the "absolute" by presenting its negation; i.e., the ridiculous fragmentation of the empirical world. For this very reason, Mahler transforms the meaning of his musical heteroglossia by importing this concept of humor into the symphony. Instead of representing that which is to be transcended, heteroglossia becomes the humorously reversed image of transcendence itself. This spectacular transformation remains unrealized in the first three symphonies, where the theatrical seriousness of the final apotheoses contradicts the humor of the preceding movements, degrading it to a transitory stage on the way to the ultimate triumph. The Fourth Symphony is Mahler's first fully consequent realization of humoristic heteroglossia.

Humoristic heteroglossia is potentiated by hybridization, according to Bakhtin a "mixture of two social languages within the limits of a single utterance."[65] Defined as such, hybridization concentrates the spatial polyphony of heteroglossia into the internal dimension of a single voice. For this reason, Bakhtin speaks of the "internal, essentially dialogic quality of novelistic hybrids" and distinguishes "unintentional, unconscious hybridization" from intentional hybridization, which is "*an artistically organized system for bringing*

---

[62] Sponheuer, *Logik des Zerfalls*, 190–91: "Das Lied von den himmlischen Freuden ist, wie alle Utopie, in Wahrheit eines von den irdischen Leiden." For an extensive interpretation of the poem, see Ibid., 187–91.

[63] Mirjam Schadendorf, *Humor als Formkonzept in der Musik Gustav Mahlers* (Stuttgart und Weimar: Metzler, 1995), 4.

[64] Ibid., 74–78.

[65] Bakhtin, "Discourse in the Novel," 358.

different languages in contact with another."[66] As classic examples of intentional hybridization, Bakhtin mentions "Don Quixote, the English comic novel (Fielding, Smollett, Sterne) and the German Romantic comic novel (Hippel and Jean Paul)."[67] It is not surprising to find Mahler in this company. Mahler's humoristic hybridity results from the semantic ambivalence of his ironic utterances and in the co-existence of different stylistic spheres; e.g., childlike naivety and the compositional sophistication of the "high" music tradition, within the same music.

According to Bakhtin, in order to realize intentional hybridization, "it is obligatory for two linguistic consciousnesses to be present, the one being represented and the other doing the representation, with each belonging to a different system of language."[68] By referring to the Wunderhorn-World, Mahler is able to represent an expressive instance that is external from human consciousness.

Looking back and forwards

Erwin Stein, and more explicitly Theodor W. Adorno, regarded Mahler's variant technique as his compositional solution to the dilemma of the fictional character of literal repetition; i.e., of identity in music. Mahler himself considered identical repetition to be a "lie."[69] Bakhtin's categories of heteroglossia and hybridity represent instances of Otherness as against monologic writings. A consideration of the novelistic character in Mahler's symphonies is, to a great extent, a question about escaping identification in composition.

BIBLIOGRAPHY

Adler, Guido. *Gustav Mahler* [1916]. In *Gustav Mahler and Guido Adler: Records of a Friendship*. Edited by Edward R. Reilly. Cambridge: Cambridge University Press, 1982.

Adorno, Theodor W. "Mahler: Eine musikalische Physiognomik." In *Die musikalischen Monographien*. Edited by Rolf Tiedemann with Gretel Adorno, Susan Buck-Morss, and Klaus Schultz, 149–319. Gesammelte Schriften 13. Frankfurt am Main: Suhrkamp, 1971.

---

[66] Ibid., 360–61, italics by Bakhtin.

[67] Ibid., 361–62.

[68] Ibid., 359.

[69] Killian, *Gustav Mahler in den Erinnerungen von Natalie Bauer-Lechner*, 158: "Denn jede Wiederholung ist schon eine Lüge."

———. "Zu einer imaginären Auswahl von Liedern Gustav Mahlers." In *Musikalische Schriften IV*. Edited by Rolf Tiedemann with Gretel Adorno, Susan Buck-Morss, and Klaus Schultz, 189–197. Gesammelte Schriften 17. Frankfurt am Main: Suhrkamp, 1982.

Bakhtin, Mikhail. "Discourse in the Novel." In *The Dialogic Imagination: Four Essays by M. M. Bakhtin*. Edited by Michael Holquist. Translated by Caryl Emerson and Michael Holquist, 259–422. 18th ed. Austin: University of Texas Press, 2011.

Bauer-Lechner, Natalie. *Gustav Mahler in den Erinnerungen von Natalie Bauer-Lechner*. Edited by Herbert Killian. Revised and enlarged ed. Hamburg: Verlag der Musikalienhandlung Karl Dieter Wagner, 1984.

———. *Recollections of Gustav Mahler*. Edited by Peter Franklin. Translated by Dika Newlin. Cambridge: Cambridge University Press, 1980.

Bekker, Paul. *Gustav Mahlers Sinfonien*. Berlin: Schuster & Loffler, 1921.

Celestini, Federico. *Die Unordnung der Dinge: Das musikalische Groteske in der Wiener Moderne (1885–1914)*. Beihefte zum Archiv für Musikwissenschaft 56. Stuttgart: Franz Steiner Verlag, 2006.

———. "Gustav Mahler and the Aesthetic of De-Identification." In *Rethinking Mahler*. Edited by Jeremy Barham. New York: Oxford University Press. Forthcoming.

———. "Gustav Mahlers Fünfte Symphonie." In *Gustav Mahler: Interpretationen seiner Werke*. Edited by Peter Revers and Oliver Korte. 2: 3–51. Laaber: Laaber-Verlag, 2011.

———. "Literature as *Dèja vu*? The Third Movement of Gustav Mahler's First Symphony." In *Phrase and Subject: Studies in Literature and Music*. Edited by Delia da Sousa Correa, 153–66. London: Legenda, 2006.

Crowther, Paul. *The Kantian Sublime*. Oxford: Clarendon Press, 1989.

Ekman, Karl. *Jean Sibelius: His Life and Personality*. Translated by Edward Birse. London: A. Wilmer Ltd, 1936.

Fischer, Jens Malte. *Gustav Mahler*. Translated by Stewart Spencer. New Haven: Yale University Press, 2011.

Floros, Constantin. *Gustav Mahler*. Vol. 3: *Die Symphonien*. Wiesbaden: Breitkopf & Härtel, 1985.

Franklin, Peter. *Mahler: Symphony No. 3*. Cambridge: Cambridge University Press, 1991.

Johnson, Julian. *Mahler's Voices: Expression and Irony in the Songs and Symphonies*. New York: Oxford University Press, 2009.

Knapp, Raymond. *Symphonic Metamorphoses: Subjectivity and Alienation in Mahler's Re-Cycled Songs*. Middletown: Weslayan University Press, 2003.

Lyotard, Jean-François. *Lessons on the Analytic of the Sublime*. Translated by Elizabeth Rottenberg. Stanford: Stanford University Press, 1994.

Mahler, Gustav. *Briefe*. Edited by Herta Blaukopf. Wien: Zsolnay, 1996.

Mahler-Werfel, Alma. *Erinnerungen an Gustav Mahler* [1940]. Edited by Donald Mitchell. Frankfurt am Main: Verlag Ullstein, 1971.

Mersch, Dieter. "Ästhetischer Augenblick und Gedächtnis der Kunst." In *Die Medien der Künste. Beiträge zur Theorie des Darstellens*. Edited by Dieter Mersch, 151–176. Munich: Fink, 2003.

Mitchell, Donald. *Gustav Mahler*. Vol. 1: *The Early Years*. Revised ed. Berkeley: University of California Press, 1980.

Morris, Pam, ed., *The Bakhtin Reader: Selected Writing of Bakhtin, Medvedev, Voloshinov*. London: Edward Arnold, 1994.

Nietzsche, Friedrich. *On the Use and Abuse of History for Life*. 1874. Translated by Ian Johnston, August 19, 2013, http://records.viu.ca/~johnstoi/nietzsche/history.htm.

Schnebel, Dieter. "Über Mahlers Dritte." *Neue Zeitschrift für Musik* 135 (1974): 284–85.

Sponheuer, Bernd. *Logik des Zerfalls: Untersuchungen zum Finalproblem in den Symphonien Gustav Mahler*. Tutzing: Hans Schneider, 1978.

Schadendorf, Mirjam. *Humor als Formkonzept in der Musik Gustav Mahlers*. Stuttgart: Metzler, 1995.

Stein, Erwin. "Mahlers Sachlichkeit," *Musikblätter des Anbruch—Sonderheft Mahler* 12/3 (1930): 99–101.

Vignal, Marc. *Mahler.* Paris: Éditions du Seuil, 1966.

Zelle, Carsten. *Die doppelte Ästhetik der Moderne: Revisionen des Schönen von Boileau bis Nietzsche*. Stuttgart: Metzler, 1995.

FORMATTING THE TRUTH: THE TRANSFORMATION OF MOROCCAN PRISON WRITINGS INTO ARCHIVES[1]

Anouk Cohen*

Abstract

The Equality and Reconciliation Commission (ERC or in French: Instance Equité et Réconciliation*), created in Morocco in 2006, aims to "establish the truth about several historical facts," from the date of independence, 1956, to the end of the reign of Hassan II, 1999. The European Union (EU) made a significant contribution to setting up the ERC, both on a logistical and financial level. After Morocco became the first North African country to be granted "advanced status" by the EU, the Union stepped up its cooperation with the ERC. In 2009, Morocco and the EU signed a financing convention aimed "at reinforcing the wider process of democratic transition in Morocco" and "supporting the creation of a working group on history, memory and archives established by the CCDH [Conseil Consultatif des droits de l'Homme] . . . to consider the conservation of archives and the popularization and diffusion of knowledge in contemporary history." In the course of their investigations, and faced with the absence of "official archives for the years of lead," the ERC recommended adopting a new law regarding national archives that would impose an "obligation for public bodies . . . to preserve all documents attesting to their actions." Since then, the ERC has set out to collect "all*

---

* Anouk Cohen is chargée de recherche at the CNRS.

[1] This paper is a reworked version of a previous article published in French (Cohen 2012).

declarations and witness accounts liable to help in the quest for truth." It has, for instance, archived all prison literature published in Morocco. This raises a number of questions: How did prison stories shift from the status of literary compositions to that of archives? In what ways has the EU, and especially France, the former colonial power, participated in the archiving process, and how has it affected local historical production? How is the relationship between "witness accounts," "narratives," and "archives" understood and deployed by the different social actors who make use of it (ERC, authors, editors, readers)? And finally, what is the significance for authors of their works becoming archives? These questions lie at the heart of this article, which explores the transformation of prison writings into archives and the effects of the EU's interventions in this process.

THE PUBLISHING HOUSE TARIK (OR *TARÎQ*, "PATH" IN ARABIC) WAS FOUNDED in 1999. Since then, it has published some fifteen witness accounts or personal testimonies (prison literature) by former political prisoners during the so-called years of lead—the early part of Hassan II's reign (1961–1999), stretching from the early-1960s to the mid-1970s. This period had been very much a blank spot on the map of Moroccan historiography, until Mohammed VI created, five years into his reign, the Equity and Reconciliation Commission (ERC) in order to "find out the truth concerning several historical events (from Moroccan independence in 1956 to the end of Hassan II's reign in 1999) and several types of violation long kept silent or which are the object of rumor and taboo, foremost among which is the question of forced disappearances."[2]

The European Union made a significant contribution to setting up the ERC, both on a logistical and financial level.[3] After Morocco became the first North African country to be granted "Advanced status" by the EU,[4]

---

[2] See the official site of the ERC: www.ier.ma.

[3] As a part of the third Morocco–EU "Action Plan," the EU has given 8 million euros to support the ERC project; see the European Union of Morocco: ec.europa.eu.

[4] This agreement results from a long collaboration between Morocco and the EU, begun in 1963, when Morocco asked to open negotiations aimed at creating a commercial partnership by 1969. The respect of democratic and human rights principles also represents a central element of the association process. In 2003, the EU launched a program entitled European Neighborhood Policy, which sharpens and deepens the so-called Euro-Mediteranean partnership. This relationship is founded on a mutual engagement to promote shared values; i.e., the respect of rules of law, good governance, respect for human rights, the promotion of good neighborly relations, a market economy, and sustainable development: http://eeas.europa.eu/delegations/morocco/eu_morocco/political_relations/index_fr.htm.

the Union stepped up its cooperation with the ERC. In 2009, Morocco and the EU signed a financing convention aimed "at reinforcing the wider process of democratic transition in Morocco"[5] and "supporting the creation of a working group on history, memory and archives established by the CCDH [Conseil Consultatif des droits de l'Homme] . . . to consider the conservation of archives and the popularization and diffusion of knowledge in contemporary history."[6] In the course of their investigations, and faced with the absence of "official archives for the years of lead,"[7] the ERC recommended adopting a new law regarding national archives that would impose an "obligation for public bodies...to preserve all documents attesting to their actions."[8] Since then, the ERC has set out to collect "all declarations and witness accounts liable to help in the quest for truth."[9] It has, for instance, archived all prison literature published in Morocco.

This initiative raises a number of questions: How have prison writings shifted from being literary texts to becoming archives? How has the ERC transformed them into historical documents? In what ways has the EU, and especially France, the former colonial power, participated in the archiving process, and how has it affected local historical production? How is the relationship between "witness accounts," "narratives," and "archives" understood and deployed by the different social actors who make use of it (ERC, authors, editors, readers), and why do they use this terminology? And finally, what is the significance for authors of their works becoming archives? These questions lie at the heart of this article, which explores the transformation of prison writings into archives and the effects of the EU's interventions in this process.[10]

---

[5] www.ccdh.org.ma.

[6] Cf. the website of the Conseil national des droits de l'homme: www.ccdh.org.ma.

[7] Khalid Chegraoui, "Littérature carcérale et Histoire du présent au Maroc," *Moroccan History: Defining New Fields and Approaches* (Ifrane, Morocco: Al-Akhawayn University, 2004), 129–137.

[8] Driss El Yazami, "L'instance équité et réconciliation: transition politique, histoire et mémoire," *Confluences méditerranéennes* n° 62, summer, 2007, accessible at www.confluences-méditerranée.com.

[9] www.ier.ma.

[10] These questions were first raised during a stay in Casablanca and Rabat in 2006–2007 as part of my doctoral project on the Moroccan publishing industry, during which I worked as an intern at Tarik and was able to interview several of its authors. Alongside these interviews, I was able to meet a number of editors and readers, as well as to participate in the *Salon international de l'édition et du livre* (International Bookfair) in Casablanca, where I had the opportunity to explore the impact and social, cultural, and political repercussions of prison literature.

I. TRANSFORMING PRISON WRITINGS INTO TEXTS

Traces and Evidence

These texts devoted to the prison experience and to prison life emerged in a context characterized by increasing popular interest in the recent past. We can call to witness the publication of a large number of prisoners' testimonies, accounts, and interviews in the national press. They appeared in dedicated columns in the cultural pages of left-leaning newspapers, such as *Libération*, *al-Ahdath al-Maghribia*, *La Gazette du Maroc*, etc., or as single- or double-page spreads in weekly titles, such as *La Nouvelle Tribune*.

Only later did they begin to appear in book form. For instance, Christine Daure-Serfaty's[11] *Tazmamart, une prison de la mort* (Tazmamart, a death camp), which discussed conditions in the camp (where political militants were imprisoned and tortured), was banned in Morocco when it first appeared in France in 1992. Tazmamart no longer exists, having been destroyed in 1991 by the Makhzen,[12] who had long denied its very existence. In the words of Hassan II, "Tazmamart only ever existed in the imaginations of the enemies of Morocco." Thus, just as the Makhzen was setting out to erase all trace of "Tazmamart," as is generally known, Christine Daure-Serfaty's book was denouncing the atrocities committed there. It was not until eight years after its publication in France that the work appeared in Morocco, as a weekly supplement to a magazine.

Publication in Serial Form: Authority, Medium, and Materiality

The technique of using weekly supplements was designed not only to reel readers in and increase sales, but also to publish censored texts, which were allowed to appear in fragmentary form at a time when they still could not be imported or sold in Morocco as full books. Many prisoner accounts first appeared in the press and only later were published in book form. Such serial publications are subject to Article 1 of the Press Code, which is the only legal text affecting the press and which stipulates that "the printing and distribution of the press shall not be restricted." This shows how a text may be received in different ways according to the form it takes. A book can be banned, but

---

[11] Her husband, Abraham Serfaty, was a renowned opponent of Hassan II's regime. Exiled to France, he only returned to Morocco after Mohammed VI explicitly invited him to do so upon assuming the throne.

[12] The term *makhzen* (literally "warehouse," whence our word "magazine") is used to describe the Moroccan state apparatus, its ruling elite, and, by extension, the forces of law and order. While not necessarily negatively connoted, it typically refers to the state's authoritarian or repressive qualities.

tolerated if it appears as a weekly supplement. The composite structure of the serial is deemed less threatening than the unity of a book. Thus, prison writings were permitted to circulate in fragmentary form, but censored if gathered together as a book. This raises interesting questions about the relationship between the format a text takes (fragment vs. book) and its legitimacy, and shows how the perceived authority of a text is affected by its format.

Prison writings, be they direct accounts, narratives, novels, plays, or poetry, only began to take pride of place in editorial projects after Mohammed VI's accession to the throne. The recent past became a key concern of publishers and editors, especially Bichr Bennani of Tarik, whose stated goal was to "inform the Moroccan people" about a little studied period of their history.[13]

Indeed, Morocco's recent history remains only partially explored. Torn between the desire to shed light on certain periods of the recent past and efforts to buttress the foundations of the nation-state, historians have written a partial history that is today being contested and rewritten by the protagonists themselves.[14] Discourses about the recent past are the work of the press and of the witness/participant. It is worth noting that both arabophone and francophone readers (male and female, young and old, of all social classes) declare that they read prison literature in order "to know what really happened."[15] This is something that Bichr Bennani and Marie-Louise Belarbi, founders of Tarik, are well aware of and, indeed, it is the very goal of many of their publications. *Les années Lamalif* (The Lamalif years), named after a militant Moroccan journal that was repeatedly censured, recounts, in the words of the author Zakya Daoud, "the history of the country from 1958 to 1988." Here again, personal testimony becomes authoritative history. The way Tarik's

---

[13] There are a number of reasons for this lack of academic interest. Cf. Raji (2006), Baïda (2005), Benjamin Stora (2002), Brahim Boutaleb (1996), and Driss El Yazami (2007).

[14] These questions surrounding the writing of recent Moroccan history were addresed in a conference in 2005, which gave rise to a volume entitled *From the Protectorate to Independence: Present-Day Problematics*, which notes that "*Faced both with a lack of any dedicated methodology seminars, as well as the extreme difficulty of accessing archival material, scholars tended to focus on the pre-colonial era, particularly the 19th century.*" The author attributes this to "[the historian's] tendency to turn first and foremost to state archives, which are his habitual point of departure. The lack of such material, as well as its inaccessibility, encourages him to leave the present (of which he is both witness and contemporary) to journalists and political scientists (2005, 8)." See the papers by Jamaâ Baïda, Abdelahad Sebti, and Mohamed Kenbib, which sketch the current state of play with regard to contemporary history.

[15] This at least was the principal reason put forward in the interviews I carried out at two Casablancan bookshops, Carrefour des Livres and Dar Attakafa. In other words, readers see them as historical documents.

editorial board reacted allowed me to witness this transformation firsthand and to study its implications.

The Book as Historical Source

On December 12, 2006, Tarik's editorial board convened its monthly meeting to discuss the manuscripts currently under review. The meetings seemed more like a reading group than a gathering of specialists focused on discovering authors and developing their work. The problem, according to Marie-Louise, was that the board was insufficiently representative of their readership: "too few men and too few Moroccans." (Half of the board was French.) For Bichr, meanwhile, it did a good job of predicting what the public would like, as it did, for instance, with Zakya Daoud's book, which provoked widespread debate upon its presentation at the Casablanca bookfair. Two months earlier, it had been at the center of a heated discussion at an editorial meeting that had dragged on until the early hours—"a first!" in the words of Bichr. *Les années Lamalif* was on the agenda (See insert, figure 24).

At that time, Marie-Paule and I had been presenting and advocating for Daoud's publication. For Marie-Paule, a 46- year-old librarian at the French lycée in Casablanca and a member of Tarik's editorial board, there could be no doubt:

"It is an authoritative work on a little explored aspect of Moroccan history under Hassan II that Tarik absolutely must publish." Denise, a retired Frenchwoman married to a Moroccan for the last 40 years, and Tbeur, a thirty-something professor of French Literature at the faculty of Aïn Chock, both shared her opinion. Denise, seconded by Marie-Paule, professed herself to be horrified at her own ignorance. Marie-Paule: "How can I have lived here all those years, all those discussed by Zakya Daoud, and not known about that?" Denise: "I didn't know either; from 1970 to 1980 I lived here, but I didn't know what was going on in this country." Bichr did not share their enthusiasm. For him, there was a major problem linked to the veracity of the account and the legitimacy of the author's claim to "write history":

> As a journalist, it's not her role to write the history of Morocco, especially as she only devotes a small part of the text, barely ten pages, to Moroccan history from 1955–1960, which is when all [recent] Moroccan history was made. You'd need thousands of pages to cover it. And her perspective is very personal and likely controversial. There are even outright errors. I was there: I know what happened and it wasn't like that.

Bichr and his family were key actors in recent Moroccan history. His father and his uncle, Ahmed Balafrej, were founding members of the Independence

Party, Istiqlal, which had helped construct the newly independent country. Meanwhile, his cousin, Anis Balafrej, was at the center of the trial in 1972 that followed from the attempt on Hassan II's life. Indeed, both he and Amale, a pensioner on the board whose father had also fought against the French protectorate and helped create the Moroccan nation-state, were intimately familiar with the period and they shared the same position. For Amale, Zakya's text was only surprising for French people ignorant of Moroccan history. But Tbeur responded: "I had the same impression of discovering something new as Marie-Paule did, and I'm Moroccan," which led Amale to remark: "You're young, and so that's normal. But then yeah, it might indeed be of interest to young Moroccans unfamiliar with this period of their history."

In the end, they decided to publish, and the book appeared a few months later. Marie-Louise, however, remained shaken by the debate. For several days, her interactions with Bichr were cordial, but distant. For her, Bichr's reaction was proof of Moroccans' refusal to "accept that a foreigner (Zakya Daoud is a French citizen who has been resident in Morocco for the last sixty years; Daoud is her husband's surname, and Zakya a pseudonym) could write history from the inside." But beyond this, it testified to the blurring of lines between professional historians and participants/witnesses and highlighted the tensions surrounding the publication of a text treating this difficult period.

The debate provoked by *Les années Lamalif* raised questions of legitimacy and legitimation regarding the conditions of production and publication of accounts that assume the status of "documents." At the heart of the debate lay the following questions: Who has the right to produce a source and to what end? Can witnesses/participants assume the role of historian by "speaking like a book"?[16] The conflict also showed the part played by editors and editorial committees in producing texts that are also sources. *Les années Lamalif* is not an isolated example of this. Many of Tarik's publications, as well as articles in the press, have (as we shall see) assumed the status of "documents," not only for the ERC, but also for ordinary readers, who are extremely interested in their own secret history (as regards both particular events and the modalities of political action). I have frequently witnessed people exchanging articles and dossiers about the prison camps or exclusive interviews with former political prisoners, as well as discussing these issues in front of the books and newspapers artfully arranged on the pavement or in kiosks, or sitting on the terrace of a café. This impression is confirmed by booksellers working at Livre Service or

[16] François Hartog, "Le témoin et l'historien," paper presented at the 19th International Congress of Historical Sciences, Oslo, 6-13 August 2000. Accessed 25 October 2014. http://www.oslo2000.uio.no/program/papers/m3a/m3a-hartog.pdf, 1.

at the Carrefour des Livres in Casablanca, who claim that prison writings are still their best sellers, even if interest seems to have peaked a few years back. Editors like Bichr Bennani (Tarik), Abdelkader Retnani (Eddif) and Rachid Chraïbi (Marsam), who specialize in French language texts, listened to their readers, and these accounts took pride of place in their catalog.

The Popular Aesthetics of Published Prison Literature: Graphic Representations of Subjectivity

The publishing house Tarik was born in 1999, a child of the sudden wave of testimonies by former political prisoners. In 2000, its founders, namely Marie-Louise and Bichr, published Ahmed Marzouki's prison camp account, *Tazmamart, cellule 10*. The book sold several thousand copies, becoming a rare example of a local best seller. The book's success (and the profits it generated) encouraged Bichr and Marie-Louise to continue in the same vein, publishing another ten such books. Some of these, such as *Tazmamart, cellule 10* and *Héros sans gloire* (Hero without glory), were translated into Arabic. For the first few years, these texts lay at the heart of Tarik's editorial project. Their goal, in the words of Bichr, was to help "preserve Morocco's collective memory," for "society cannot progress without a memory." Tarik's editorial line was the preservation of memory. This could be seen in the book display at their premises (a converted apartment on the first floor of a building just outside central Casablanca). A large bookcase along one wall of the main room housed all the books published by Tarik since it was founded. On the upper shelves were arranged the ten or so prison texts they had published over the years. By grouping them together, Tarik enabled visitors to "read them relationally".[17] The potential reader was able to compose and construct a slice of history that had yet to be written and, by deploying certain cognitive strategies (comparison, explanation, criticism, deepening of analysis, and filling in the blanks), elaborate her own historical analysis.

Tarik, then, provided ordinary readers with effective instruments of knowledge. And this allows us to reconsider the question raised earlier regarding the circulation of serials. Their fragmentary form (both temporally and in the space of a disconnected and distributed text) complicates the task of reconstructing the facts of history by placing different events alongside one another. And this is precisely how ordinary readers can freely and progressively reconstruct unexplored periods of their history. (An image of the cover of *Tazmamart cellule 10* can be found in the insert, figure 25.)

---

[17] Christian Jacob, "Rassembler la mémoire. Réflexions sur l'histoire des bibliothèques," Diogène 196 (4): 53–76, here 56.

The book is 14 by 21 centimeters, with a white cover. The author's name appears in blue, top-center, and beneath it is the title of the book in bolder black lettering. The blue of Ahmed Marzouki's name reflects the blue of the image in the center of the cover, which sketches out a prison cell whose ornaments and spatial organization are characteristic of penitentiary existence: emptiness, enclosure, the absence of light, a rudimentary meal tray, and eyes peering in through the viewing hatch.

Together, these elements tell the reader something about the book's content and narrative drift. This aesthetic frame appears to have influenced the design of Tarik's later publications. Many of these are also prison writings, but some are not. Witness, for instance, the covers of Abdelfettah Fakihani's *Couloir* (Corridor) and Khalid Jamaï's *1973. Présumés Coupables* (Presumed guilty). (See insert, figures 26 and 27.)

These kinds of illustrations are also used with other literary genres, what Bichr and Marie-Louise call "mémoires," "narratives," and "novels." Novels by Henri-Michel Boccara (*Le Plumier* [The pencil case]—document 17), Gilbert Torres (*Une odeur de mantèque* [The scent of lard]—document 16), and the famous Moroccan writer Mohamed Khaïr-Eddine all have similar cover designs with muted colors and somber images. (See insert, figures 28 and 29.)

The same is true of most books published by Tarik, with the exception of a few more scholarly works whose aesthetic is somewhat flatter, with just a photo or a blank cover (e.g., Ignace Dalle's *Le Maroc*, Etienne de la Boétie's *Le Discours de la servitude volontaire* [Discourse on voluntary servitude]—document 18, and the Arabic translation of Vermeren's *Le Maroc en transition* [Changing Morocco]). These sober front covers reflect the authors' and editors' attempt to stress the works' objective and analytical qualities. As such, they form a sharp contrast with the pictures that adorn the accounts, narratives, and novels, whose subjectivity is clearly displayed. (See insert, figure 30.)

In short, the functional aesthetic originally designed for the covers of prison writings has come to serve as a template for a whole aesthetic tradition of expressive covers that stretches beyond Tarik to define that part of the Moroccan publishing industry that pays attention to its front covers.

INTERWOVEN HISTORIES

From Manuscript to Book: The Parallel Lives of Prison Writings

Marie-Louise and Bichr were not the only editors to construct their catalog around prison literature. The wave of such texts and the undeniable interest they provoked, encouraged everybody but textbook publishers to try their hand at the genre. The appearance of this cluster of prison texts in the years 1999 to 2004 was not anodyne. On the one hand, as we have seen, it reflected the wider spirit of political liberalization and, on the other, increasing numbers of former prisoners chose to express themselves through narrative, publishing first in the press and later in book form, rather than via photography, documentary films, or music. This choice was due, in part, to the very nature of the writing process, which requires only pen and paper—objects that could be procured in the prison camps. Like other prisoners, Raymond Benhaïm, who was held for some ten years, kept his manuscript "in a drawer" for a long while before showing it to others: friends, militants, journalists, and editors, who gradually coalesced into a network of readers and critics as the manuscript passed from hand to hand.

Manuscripts change in form when they are sent to readers: they are typed up rather than handwritten, and bound rather than stapled or loose. What is more, when they are published in the press or, *a fortiori*, in book form, the original version is structured and laid out to maximize readability. The text is, in some sense, (re)defined and (re)created in slightly modified form. First, it is reshaped into article or book format. It is handed over as a manuscript to the person responsible for layout and data input, who types it up and digitizes it in preparation for later alterations. The editor and layout specialist shape the text, deciding on a font, setting paragraphs, inserting titles and subtitles, restructuring certain sections, cutting and elaborating, etc. The original version may also be rewritten to increase its public appeal. In short, this process consists (especially with books) in a restructuring of the narrative by setting paragraphs and chapters, reformulating sentences, and sometimes by inserting literary conceits such as dialogue, stylistic devices, etc.

I participated in this process of recomposition and rewriting for the text of *Les années Lamalif* after Bichr decided that at 450 pages it was too long for a Moroccan readership in search of "short, straightforward books." I was tasked with cutting it to 300 pages (also to reduce printing costs) and decided to cut whole passages, thus rewriting a future "historical source." Marie-Louise objected strongly to the new streamlined version, adding that the author, "Zakya" (an old friend of hers), categorically refused to rework the text. Bichr, she said, should come to a decision soon or she would send the manuscript to other publishers, notably PUF, which had shown an interest.[18] The committee members deemed it better to publish it as it was, rather than "miss out on such an opportunity." For them, this "groundbreaking" text dealt with seminal events that deserved to be

[18] Zakya Daoud preferred her book to be published in Morocco, rather than in France (even by a well-known publisher). This allowed it to be priced affordably (7 euros rather than 20) and so to reach a wider audience.

recounted in full. Bichr, meanwhile, stressed the importance of reducing printing costs, and so the book's cover price. Here we can clearly see the gulf between what an editor considers "publishable" and what readers expect. In the end (some few weeks later), a decision was made to publish the original version in partnership with Sense Unico, a Moroccan publisher that accepted to co-finance the production costs. Some modifications were nonetheless made to give it more the form of a book.

The layout and presentation of a text, in other words, necessarily alters the information it seeks to transmit, as well as its efficacy. Initially, Zakya Daoud's testimony (much like that of others) was fairly raw, but once caught up in the editorial process, it acquired new structure along with the potential readership offered by a book or magazine format with a print run of thousands. Publication of these personal narratives means not only wider distribution, but also coexistence alongside other such texts. They become one of a series of texts endowed with similar history-making force and which, in the words of Daniel Fabre "are meaningful by virtue of their juxtaposition with other similar texts".[19] Together, these texts produce a history that would have been unlikely without them. They interweave to create a narrative texture whose density enables it to bear the tangible trace of a historical event around which a shared community of language can be established. Whereas the publication of a single text is insufficient to establish the existence of the prison camps, multiplicity establishes and authorizes.

The mnemonic vocation of such texts is evident in the terms used by the editors at Tarik, Eddif, Marsam, and Le Fennec to present them to the general public: "Témoignage" (Testimony) or "Collection Témoignage" (Testimonial Series). Editors of Arab-language books publish more history texts (*tarîkh*), especially essays (*dirasât*) on pre-colonial Morocco, than do French-language publishers. Works looking at contemporary history are more the domain of political scientists than historians and often take the form of textbooks written by secondary school teachers. Noufisa, a 42-year-old history teacher in the suburbs of Casablanca, told me that these texts tended to focus on Independence and the nation-building roles of Mohammed V and Hassan II. They endeavor to iron out inconsistencies or contradictions and serve to legitimize the political system and reinforce social cohesion. Noufisa, who is also a volunteer and militant engaged in the struggle for human rights, rails against this: "A considerable part [of our history] is swept under the carpet, but I tell my students what I think. I tell them the other side of the story."

---

19 Daniel Fabre, "Vivre, écrire, archiver." Sociétés & Représentations 13/1 (2002): 17–42, here 23.

There are, nevertheless, a number of Arab-language testimonies from former political prisoners. Many of these take the form of poetry collections, and less frequently they appear as autobiographies or novels (*riwâyât*). Most of the latter are translated from the French and originally published overseas (in Lebanon, Syria, or Egypt) or by the authors themselves because local Arab-language publishers generally refuse such texts. Accordingly, when it comes to recent history, the market fractures along linguistic lines: Arabic is used to write official and often self-censored history that never oversteps the unwritten line by venturing to criticize the monarchy or the King, whereas French is used to denounce the atrocities of Hassan II's regime.

This linguistic and genre-based distinction is, as the *Nichane*[20] case shows (see Excursus 1), linked to questions of politics and religion. It is tied up with the construction of the nation-state, built around the power of the monarchy and the attempt to root its legitimacy in the *longue durée*. The Makhzen, symbol of Morocco's resistance to the French Protectorate (after the coronation of Mohamed V in 1956) traces its roots back to the prophet Mohammed. In so doing, it claims to guarantee the nation's Islamic status, enshrined in the preeminent position of the Arabic language. Arabic, the language of the Qur'an, replaced French, the language of the colonizer, as the country's official tongue. These references to history and to the Arabic language are integral elements of Moroccan nation-building, such that *tarîkh* (Arabic for history) exists in an uneasy relationship with the state, which continues to exercise authority over its conditions of production (both in terms of language and genre) and publication.

And as for the editors, who Bourdieu declared to possess "the extraordinary power of publication—i.e., the power to promote an author and a text to public existence" (1977: 3), they play a vital role in the production of contemporary historical sources, acting almost as guardians of collective, national memory. By refusing to publish prisoner accounts in Arabic, they help maintain the relationship of legitimization that exists between *tarîkh* and *makhzen*, as well as to transmit a particular vision of history that often differs from its French-language counterpart, largely published by Bichr, who also refuses to publish manuscripts that run counter to his vision of history (e.g., Abdallah Laroui's *Hassan II et le Maroc*).

---

[20] *Nichane* was the Arabic-language sister magazine of the critical Moroccan French-language weekly, *Tel Quel*. Their editorial lines were very similar, but whereas *Tel Quel* continues to be published, Nichane was banned for two years (2007–2009) after publishing some provocative jokes concerning Islam. It began to reappear from 2009, but finally closed the following year after a persistent advertising boycott.

Excursus 1: Different writing practices in Arabic and in French

In Morocco, French and Arabic are associated with different writing practices and styles of representation. The history of Arabic is marked by the phenomenon of diglossia; i.e., the coexistence of several variations of a same language. Two main categories are generally distinguished: the vernacular—called *darija* in Morocco—and the written or erudite language—classical Arabic or *fusha*. The latter is the country's official language. As the language of the Quran, *fusha* assumes particular status (Haeri 2003). Moroccans regard it as divine. Accordingly, for many authors and Moroccan journalists, the French language represents the language of "freedom," a concept that they themselves employ (Caubet 2004). The shift from one language to another, in this case from Arabic to French, opens a space of previously veiled expression. The French language is used to express what cannot or is not ordinarily said or written in one's mother tongue (Basfao 1987). An eloquent example is the *Nichane* scandal (Cohen 2011). Four months after its first publication in August 2006, the Arabic weekly *Nichane* was censured by decision of the Prime Minister after publishing an article entitled "Joking: How Moroccans Laugh at Religion, Sex and Politics." A similar article had previously been published in Nichane's French-language sister magazine without sanction. The heart of the scandal lay in the fact that these jokes had now been reported in Arabic. This raises the question of the status of Arabic and French with regard to religious and political considerations in urban Morocco. Thus, in a country marked by a history of bilingualism, the written word reveals the presence of a certain linguistic duality: the French and Arabic languages do not express the same ideas and are not confronted with the same censorship practices. French is used to question and publish certain taboo subjects referring to politics and religion. It appears that the different written uses of Arabic and French have little to do with an opposition between tradition and modernity. The tension rather seems to lie in the relation between freedom and constraint. We cannot ignore the influence of "Islamist" groups who claim monopoly over the moralization of public life.[21] They are able to get the state to

[21] Tozy Mohamed, "L'évolution du champ religieux marocain au défi de la mondialisation," Revue internationale de politique comparée 16/1 (2009): 63–81.

exercise censorship according to their conceptions of Arabic, the sacred language that cannot be contaminated by a certain type of discourse. This reinforces the taboo character of *fusha* as part of the sociocultural hierarchy inherent to the Arabic language, through which political and religious elites have access to the written language, while the common folk know only spoken Arabic. Another eloquent example of these different writing practices in Arabic and in French is the prison story genre.

However, it is interesting to observe that this constraint associated with the Arabic language has been increasingly bypassed these last few years due to the emergence of authors (both men and women) who take part in the literary movement of the truth. Even if it remains, in Arabic and in Morocco, a literary kind of gestation, its emergence indicates that besides a classical Arabic writing (mainly in the form of poetry), a writing of the self appears, local and Moroccan. As we've seen, the writing of contemporary history varies according to the language used. The choice of Arabic or French is linked to questions of legitimacy and legitimation, which are themselves linked to political and economic considerations. French and European institutions play a central role in that process, pursuing political agendas through the distribution of financial subsidies to the publishing sector.

Ideological explanations alone cannot account for the attitudes of both French and Arabic-language editors. The latter—generally specialized in textbooks—are also obliged to cultivate cordial relations with the monarchy if they wish to benefit from the large market for textbooks. Many French-language editors, meanwhile, only publish if a book is subsidized by the French embassy and the CCDH's cultural outreach program (supported by the EU), which aim to promote secular and democratic values and defend human rights. In other words, economic interests are also at play in editorial decision-making processes (See Excursus 2).

Excursus 2: "Race Grants"

Low demand leads publishers to decrease books' cover price. Accordingly, they depend on publishing subsidies, which allow them to compensate for production costs. Indeed, for most of them, especially small business publishers specializing in cultural books (any kind of books except textbooks), mainly in French, the publication of a text often depends on obtaining financing. Such a situation has concrete effects on both books and catalogs, and so on publishers' editorial policies. According to M.A. (the director of the "Bureau du Livre"), by providing these subsidies, the French Embassy's Cooperation and Cultural Action Service (SCAC) and the Council for the Moroccan Community Overseas (CCME) aspires to "support the development of Moroccan publishing." M.A. goes on to say: "My aim is to develop the Moroccan publishing sector, but obviously France has other, more strategic ambitions." adding that "with its publishing subsidies, France seeks to communicate certain values and convey modern ideas in Morocco, such as secularism or equality. France wants Morocco to open itself up, to develop its economy, and to become more modern." Thus, SCAC's objectives are not only close to the wider goals of "la francophonie" (the development of democracy, conflict prevention and resolution, and supporting the rule of law and human rights). but also to those of the EU, which has recently granted Morocco "advanced status."

Furthermore, M.A. adds, "It benefits France and the EU that Morocco be more developed, on the one hand because there is a huge immigration problem to resolve and this is essential and, on the other hand, because Morocco is an important economic partner of France and the EU." Thus, in addition to its economic interest, there is another goal associated with promoting the French language: to decrease illegal Moroccan immigration into France. To this end, the institution seeks to "modernize" the country "through the diffusion of certain values," such as human rights, secularism, democracy, peace, etc. In so doing, the SCAC hopes to discourage thousands of Moroccan people from coming to live in France in search of a better life. The other (supposed) objective of the Bureau du Livre is thus to keep the population of Morocco in Morocco through the promotion of a particular world vision.

Accordingly, Morocco is a good field site for observing the politics of publishing as developed by France and the EU, which endeavor to construct new spaces of knowledge founded on specific values, such as secularism and modernity. Their numerous interventions help weaken the center of power, whose reaction aims to prevent providers from using Morocco as their own stable space of knowledge, one that can be manipulated at will. A "knowledge-thing," to paraphrase Michel Callon's expression: "economy-thing."

As such, prison writings constitute a valuable editorial niche for those French-language editors whose goal is to publish supposedly raw, hard-hitting texts on national history narrated by the protagonists themselves. The idea of the "witness account" helps underscore the sincerity of the narrative by stressing the author's unique subject position, particular point of view, and the truth of his or her testimony. Moreover, this choice of terms reflects the authors' self-declared desire to "*take stock*" (*faire le point*) and to publish "to let Morocco know what happened."

The Creation of the ERC and the Archiving of Prison Writings

Abdelaziz Mouride, a former political prisoner an author of a comic book relating to prison life, eloquently expresses this idea when he states: "I bear no grudge and harbor no hatred for those who locked me away and tortured me. I simply want to recount what I endured so nobody ever has to endure it again. Let us turn the page, . . . but not before we have written it and it has been widely read" (quotation collected by Benjamin Stora). It is this same urge that drove many militants, including Bichr Bennani, Marie-Louise Belarbi, and Leila Chaouini (Le Fennec) to become authors or editors. It also underlay many Moroccan readers' decisions to study these texts, the better to know "their true history" as they put it. The sheer number of these prison texts (over 100 articles, witness accounts, and narratives were published between 2000 and 2004), along with their broad-reaching social impact, constitutes the wider context for Mohammed VI's creation of the Equity and Reconciliation Commission (ERC) in 2004 to "establish the truth" concerning the painful past and to work towards social "reconciliation."[22]

Confronted by a lack of archives, the commission, headed by Driss Benzekri, former president of the charitable Justice and Truth Forum, relied heavily on recently published prison writings (some of which were read aloud on television) as part of the process of historical reconstruction.[23] A bibliography of such texts is available on the ERC's website. According to one member of the commission, Salah El Ouadie, "These prison writings are historical documents." This idea is seconded by Abdesslam Ouzzani, rector of Mohammed V University in Rabat, who noted in 2005 that the "ERC is archiving prison writings." These statements make clear that the Equity and Reconciliation Commission has transformed the prison writings from literary documents into archives. Their historical importance is recognized by their being conserved in the ERC's headquarters.

---

[22] See www.ier.ma (consulted April 27 2010).

[23] See also Ali Kabbouss, Jaafar Ali, and Abdelali El Yazami, *D'ombre et de lumière, bibliographie sur les droits de l'Homme au Maroc* (Rabat: CFIDH, 2004).

In sum, the absence of historical material and the commission's need for veracity led to a complex transformation in which texts that were initially conceived of as cathartic, and once published as mnemonic, were finally transformed into "archives" (after their readers had already made them into historical documents). The editors set this process in motion by referring to them as "witness accounts" (*témoignages*). And the narrators themselves were also transformed—from militants into authors and then finally into witnesses: those who can testify to the actual unfolding of particular historical events.

The creation of the ERC and the collective movement from which it emerged led many former political prisoners who had not dared (or perhaps felt the need) to recount their (hi)story, either while in prison or after their release, to publish texts of their own. In these cases, it is the authors themselves, rather than the ERC, who conceive of the texts as "archives." By projecting them into a shared space, they partake of the collective attempt to author a slice of national history. As such, the process of autobiography becomes both a collective exercise and a singular practice, driven as much by the desire to tell one's own story as the desire to be published. It is noteworthy that none of the authors hides behind a pseudonym, despite the somewhat arbitrary nature of the lines in the sand drawn by the King, who is under increasing pressure from Islamist parties. Instead, authors actively endeavor to make themselves visible by using their real surnames, which in Morocco as elsewhere allows other people to discover their family history and their class background. The ostensibly very personal desire to publish so as to display one's name, to write so as to exist, has nonetheless to be understood in the wider context of a collective movement aimed at writing national history.

Investigating the Truthfulness of Archives

Not all former prisoners, however, are accomplished writers, and many of their books are ghostwritten. Sometimes editors recommend them to do so, especially when they commission a book. In such cases, they may call on the services of a Francophone journalist or French language teachers from local high schools or universities whose writing they admire. Ghostwriters receive a lump-sum payment determined by the number of pages and other relevant criteria, such as the "author's" personality, his grasp of French, travel time to the author's house (where interviews generally take place), etc. The ghostwriter records the protagonist's narrative and rewrites it accordingly. This writing process involves several distinct stages, each of which implies a shift of form (from aural to written) and medium (from soundtrack to digital format and then to printed page). These shifts necessarily affect the text's status as an archive. This is clear at a number of levels, the most significant of which is the way the text is composed. Though the ghostwriter is supposed to do little more than write up the "spoken word," in fact he takes an active part in the construction of the narrative. He polishes the style, corrects minor grammatical and vocabulary errors, and shuffles the various events around to make the oral testimony more accessible as a written text. In short, the ghostwriter adapts the narrative to a written medium and, in so doing, reconstructs it. For example, Ahmad Marzouki did not write his "witness account," *Tazmamart cellule 10*; it was in fact a friend of Bichr's who, in his own words, "recorded, formatted, and rewrote it."

It is in the nature of oral testimony to be fairly plastic: its form allows for the real-time alteration of an idea, sentence, or word. And part of the ghostwriter's task is to compensate for this by asking questions to clarify ambiguous passages and so better reconstruct the actual chain of events, rather than just passively listening. In so doing, he may lead the author to explore questions he might otherwise have left untouched. Thus, the oral archive that the prison narrative is destined to become contains, by virtue of its interactive nature, the possibility for it to be reshaped.[24] It is the product of subjective *and* objective construction that represents the two facets of a dual history—an official facet (insofar as the narrative is destined to be archived by the ERC, set up by the state and the EU) and a personal one.

This same duality is evident in the reception afforded prison writings by the ERC, on the one hand, and the wider public on the other. While the ERC uses the texts to write a slice of national and collective history, readers approach them in different and more open-ended ways. These are related to the form of the text-*cum*-archive, which is a narrative rather than a textbook or historical document. In this way, readers can access a part of their history independent of foreign scholars or state-employed academics. Instead, they do so in the company of social actors who directly or indirectly, with or without a ghost, have chosen to transform their life experiences and their testimony into archives.

---

[24] The opposition between oral and written forms of expression is not, however, so sharp as it might first appear to be. Patrick Williams makes this clear in his work on the interplay among French Gypsies. He notably cites Anne Marie-Chartier, who asserts that "*we need to escape from the tendency to confuse oral culture with illiteracy and written culture with writing, reading and making use of written material. Certain forms of oral expression may possess a written structure and oral cultural forms are quite compatible with ceratin uses of writing.*" Cf. Patrick Williams, "L'écriture entre l'oral et l'écrit. Six scénes de la vie tsigane en France." in *Par écrit. Ethnologie des écritures quotidiennes*. Edited by D. Fabre (Paris: Éditions de la Maison des Sciences de l'Homme, 1997), 77. In other words, oral and written forms of expression are always caught up with one another and the shift from one to the other never amounts to a total transformation, as the different modes of narration are often intertwined.

As a result, recent history does not follow a strictly determined official line, but is made up of multiple, fragmentary experiences. It draws on diverse personal life stories, which when woven together make up the History with a capital H that is gradually replacing traditional historical discourse. Authors and readers seize hold of this raw material and make it their own. Rather than leaving history to the state and to public institutions like schools and universities, they choose to read these diverse narratives that do not emerge from some vast, anonymous construct and that sidestep the narrative forms which were previously imposed on them. They pay particular attention to subjective, individual truth as it emerges in a saturated space and acquires weighty and authoritative status. The testimony is accepted as "true" and is not subjected to any analytical probing by professional historians. The actors themselves claim to be "telling these stories so that children know how their parents died." Speaking truth and breaking the silence that shrouds that truth—these are the goals of prison writing.

BIBLIOGRAPHY

Basfao, Kacem. 1987. "La littératuremaghrébine: une question de langue." *Annuaire de l'Afrique du Nord* 24, éditions du CNRS: 379–384.

Bourdieu, Pierre. 1992. *Les règles de l'art*. Paris: Le Seuil.

Bras, Jean-Philippe. 2008. "Introduction: la mémoire, idiome du politique au Maghreb." *L'Année du Maghreb* [En ligne] 4. Consulté le 28 avril 2010. http://anneemaghreb.revues.org/424.

Callon, Michel. 2006. "L'Egypte et les experts. Compte-rendu du livre de Tim Mitchell, Rule of Experts." *Gérer et comprendre* 86: 12–26.

Caubet, Dominique. 2004 *Les Mots du bled*. Paris: L'Harmattan.

Cohen, Anouk. 2011. "La langue du silence dans le Maroc urbain contemporain." *Revue d'Histoire des Religions* 3: 245–263.

———. 2012. "L'écriture de soi, et ses modalités de constitution en archives, Ateliers d'anthropologie." *Pratiques d'archives. Fabriques, modelages, manipulations* 36 [En ligne]. http://ateliers.revues.org/9062.

Chegraoui, Khalid. 2004. "Littérature carcérale et Histoire du présent au Maroc." Pages 129-137 in *Moroccan History: Defining New Fields and Approaches*. Ifrane, Morocco: Université Al-Akhawayn.

Daure Serfaty, Christine. 1992. *Tazmamart, une prison de la mort*. Paris: Stock.

El Ouazzani, Abdeslam. 2005. "Le récit carcéral, un nouveau genre littéraire au Maroc." Entretien avec le journaliste Abdelatif Kinini publié initialement dans le journal marocain *Libération*. http://www.casafree.com/modules/news/article.php?storyid=1171.

El Yazami, Driss. 2007. "L'instance équité et réconciliation: transition politique, histoire et mémoire." *Confluences méditerranéennes* 62 (3): 25–34. www.confluences-méditerranée.com.

Fabre, Daniel. 2002. "Vivre, écrire, archiver." *Sociétés & Représentations* 13 (1): 17–42.

Jacob, Christian. 2001. "Rassembler la mémoire. Réflexions sur l'histoire des bibliothèques." *Diogène*, 196 (4): 53–76.

Hartog, François. 2000. "Le témoin et l'historien." http://www.oslo2000.uio.no/program/papers/m3a/m3a-hartog.pdf.

Kabbouss, Ali, Jaafar Ali, and Abdelali El Yazami. 2004. *D'ombre et de lumière, bibliographie sur les droits de l'Homme au Maroc*. Rabat: CFIDH.

Laroui, Abdallah. 2005. *Le Maroc et Hassan II*. Cap rouge, Québec: Presses Inter Universitaire.

Sebti, Abdelahad. 2006. "Histoire et présent: interrogations sur la distance et la proximité." Pp. 47–54 in *Du protectorat à l'indépendance : problématiques du temps présent*. Rabat: Publications de la Faculté des Lettres et des Sciences Humaines.

Stora, Benjamin. 2002. *Algérie, Maroc. Histoires parallèles. Destins croisés*. Paris: Maisonneuve & Larose.

Tozy, Mohamed. 2009. "L'évolution du champ religieux marocain au défi de la mondialisation." *Revue internationale de politique comparée* 16 (1): 63–81.

Williams, Patrick. 1997. "L'écriture entre l'oral et l'écrit. Six scènes de la vie tsigane en France." Pp. 59–78 in *Par écrit. Ethnologie des écritures quotidiennes*. Edited by D. Fabre. Paris: Éditions de la Maison des Sciences de l'Homme.

ELLIPSIS PHENOMENA IN AMERICAN ENGLISH AND SELECTED EUROPEAN LANGUAGES

Joanna Nykiel

Abstract

In this chapter, I offer an overview of two of the better known elliptical constructions across three languages: American English, Norwegian, and Polish. The term ellipsis *refers to utterances that are incomplete because parts of them have been left unspoken. Such utterances are comprehensible only if accompanied by appropriate context, which is called the antecedent. I discuss two instances of ellipsis, the constructions sluicing* (Katie is staying in Paris with someone, but I don't know **who**) *and Bare Argument Ellipsis* (A: What meds are you on? B: **None**). *I discuss similarities and differences between these constructions in the three languages, focusing on what I dub ellipsis alternation. The alternation is between overt material that includes prepositions and overt material that does not include prepositions. For instance, the example* Katie is staying in Paris with someone, but I don't know **who**, *where the overt material does not include the preposition* with, *has an alternative,* Katie is staying in Paris with someone, but I don't know **with who**, *where the preposition is present in the overt material. I offer evidence that all three languages allow the alternation, but differ in terms of how frequent or acceptable the two alternatives are.*

1. Introduction: Ellipsis and Ellipsis Alternation

In this chapter, I offer an overview of two of the better known elliptical constructions across three languages: American English, Norwegian, and Polish.

The term *ellipsis* refers to utterances that are incomplete because parts of them have been left unspoken. Such utterances are anaphoric in the sense that they are comprehensible only if accompanied by appropriate context, which is called the antecedent and which supplies the meaning for these utterances. I discuss two instances of ellipsis, constructions sluicing, shown in example (1); and Bare Argument Ellipsis (BAE), shown in example (2). The two phrases marked in bold are referred to as remnants.

(1) Katie is staying in Paris with someone, but I don't know **who**.
(2) A: What meds are you on? B: **None**.

With respect to sluicing, what is left unspoken is an interrogative clause that could follow the wh-phrase, as in (3):

(3) I don't know who [Katie is staying in Paris with].

In the case of BAE, a declarative clause is left unspoken that could act as an answer to the question asked by speaker A, as in (4):

(4) A: What meds are you on? B: [I am on] none.

Although both constructions have overlapping properties across English, Norwegian, and Polish, there are two differences that have attracted considerable attention in the linguistic literature.

In a language with overt case marking, such as Polish (but not English or Norwegian), a remnant must be marked for the same case as its correlate, that is, the corresponding phrase in the antecedent. Example (5) from Polish illustrates.

(5) A: Anna czeka na kogoś z rodziny.
A: Anna waits for someone. ACC from family
B: **Kogo/ *komu**?
B: who.ACC/*who.DAT/
A: "Anna is waiting for a family member. B: Who?"[1]

The remnant's correlate is the prepositional phrase (PP) that contains the indefinite pronoun *kogoś* "someone," and this indefinite pronoun and the remnant must match in terms of the accusative case. Because the accusative case is assigned by the verb (or preposition) found in the antecedent, the case-matching requirement has led linguists to assume that a remnant is really just a fragment of a larger utterance that goes unpronounced (Ross 1969).

[1] Here and throughout, I use the following abbreviations to indicate case: X.ACC means that X is marked for accusative, X.GEN means that X is marked for genitive, X.DAT means that X is marked for dative, and X.INSTR means that X is marked for instrumental.

The second difference among the three languages concerns the possibility of using two kinds of remnants in certain contexts. Since the correlate is a PP, the remnant may be either a corresponding PP or a noun phrase (NP) without the preposition present in the correlate. This alternation, which I dub ellipsis alternation, is shown in (6) for English. Note that in both antecedents, the correlate is the PP *with someone*.

(6) a. Katie is staying in Paris with someone, but I don't know **with who**.
b. Katie is staying in Paris with someone, but I don't know **who**.

Ellipsis alternation was originally assumed to be available in a select few languages, including English and Norwegian (Merchant 2001). Its availability was believed to correlate with the availability of preposition stranding in a given language. Preposition stranding is a word order option that allows prepositions to occur separately from their objects in interrogative clauses. This is illustrated in (7)–(9) for English and Norwegian. The a-sentences illustrate the order where the prepositions precede their objects, and the b-sentences illustrate preposition stranding.

(7) a. On which level is our car?
b. Which level is our car on?

(8) a. På hva venter Jon?
on what waits Jon
"For what is Jon waiting?"
b. Hva venter Jon på?
what waits Jon on
"What is Jon waiting for?"

Polish is unlike English and Norwegian because it does not tolerate preposition stranding in interrogative clauses. Example (9) shows the two word orders, one of which is ill-formed.

(9) a. Na kim testowano nowe kosmetyki?
on who.INSTR they.tested new cosmetics
"On who did they test the new cosmetics?"
b. *Kim testowano nowe kosmetyki na?
who.INSTR they.tested new cosmetics on
"Who did they test the new cosmetics on?"

Based on Merchant's (2001) classification, the set of languages that behave like Polish includes: German, Yiddish, Greek, Czech, Russian, Slovene, Bulgarian, Serbo-Croatian, Persian, Hebrew, Moroccan Arabic, and Basque. The set of languages that behave like English and Norwegian includes: Danish, Swedish, Icelandic, and Frisian.

Connecting the availability of ellipsis alternation to the availability of preposition stranding offers a straightforward way to explain how different remnants derive from full clauses. Without going into the details of the analysis, the idea is that remnants are indeed incomplete utterances with full clausal sources that are unpronounced on the surface. The syntactic machinery that derives remnants first moves them to the clause-initial position and then deletes the rest of the clause. This derivation is shown in (10), with strikethrough indicating the deleted material. The a-sentence shows how to derive a remnant with a preposition, and the b-sentence shows how to derive a remnant without a preposition.

(10) a. Katie is staying in Paris with someone, but I don't know **with who** ~~Katie is staying in Paris~~.
b. Katie is staying in Paris with someone, but I don't know **who** ~~Katie is staying in Paris **with**~~.

Notice that the possibility of preposition stranding in English allows the preposition to remain at the end of the clause in (10b) so that only the remnant moves to the front. In languages that disallow preposition stranding, however, the remnant cannot move without the preposition, which predicts that remnants without prepositions cannot be generated, and hence, ellipsis alternation is unavailable. Example (11) shows this for Polish: the a-sentence is well-formed, but the b-sentence should not be.

(11) a. Nowe kosmetyki testowano na kimś, ale nie wiem
new cosmetics they.tested on someone.INSTR but not I.know
na kim ~~testowano nowe kosmetyki~~.
on who.INSTR they.tested new cosmetics
b. *Nowe kosmetyki testowano na kimś, ale nie wiem
new cosmetics they.tested on someone.INSTR but not I.know
kim ~~testowano nowe kosmetyki na~~.
who.INSTR they.tested new cosmetics on

More recent research on the link between preposition stranding and ellipsis shows that ellipsis alternation can be available independently of preposition stranding. Brazilian Portuguese, Spanish, French, Serbo-Croatian, Bahasa Indonesian, Czech, Polish, and Amis have all been found to allow the alternation despite disallowing preposition stranding in interrogative clauses (Almeida and Yoshida 2007, Rodrigues et al. 2009, Stjepanovic 2008, Fortin 2007, Sag and Nykiel 2011, Caha 2011, Wei 2011, Nykiel 2013a). A pattern recurring in this literature is that the alternation tends to be available in a specific environment. Because sluicing has been the focus of inquiry, I also illustrate this environment with examples from sluicing.

The correlate for a remnant usually hosts an indefinite pronoun or an NP, and the remnant correspondingly hosts a bare wh-phrase (*who, what*) or a which/what-NP phrase (*which documents, what party*). These possibilities are shown in (12).

(12) a. Katie is walking on egg shells around someone, but I don't know who.
b. Katie is walking on egg shells around a cousin, but I don't know which/what (cousin).

There is evidence that bare wh-phrases are consistently preferred when co-occurring with indefinite pronouns, and which/what-NP phrases are preferred when co-occurring with NPs (Nykiel 2013b). This distribution means that the two types of wh-phrases occur with correlates that differ in specificity. To see this, consider that the indefinite pronoun *someone* in example (12a) offers little information in terms of who its referent is: all we know is that the referent is human. In contrast, the NP *a cousin* in example (12b) specifies that the referent is not only human, but also a member of Katie's family. Hence, example (12b) provides the more specific correlate. It is the environment shown in (12b) that promotes the use of remnants without prepositions. Rodrigues et al. (2009) point out that this is the case in Spanish, and Nykiel (2013a) offers experimental evidence revealing the same pattern in Polish.

Even languages that tolerate preposition stranding in interrogative clauses show that ellipsis alternation is sensitive to how specific the correlate is. This sensitivity is observed in corpus data from American English: remnants without prepositions tend to be preferred over remnants with prepositions as the specificity of the correlates increases (Nykiel 2014). In my recent research on Norwegian sluicing, I found that while acceptability ratings for remnants with prepositions are generally lower than ratings for remnants without prepositions, using less specific correlates improves ratings for the former. Given that Polish, English, and Norwegian behave similarly in this respect, it is interesting to note that remnants without prepositions are preferred over remnants with prepositions in English and Norwegian, but not in Polish. I address this curious property of ellipsis alternation in the three sections that follow. I first discuss the reason why the specificity of a correlate influences the kind of remnant used and then proceed to suggest two ways in which English and Norwegian differ from Polish.

2. Specificity of a Correlate

A general property of an anaphoric expression is that it refers to another expression located in the previous discourse, whether spoken or written. For instance, in the passage shown in (13), the personal pronoun *them* is anaphoric to the NP *my parents.* Also anaphoric to the same pronoun and NP is the second occurrence of *my parents* in this passage.

(13) Many of **my parents'** Chinese friends would tell **them** it was a waste to spend money to educate a daughter because you wanted her to get married and have children. They'd say that if girls got too educated, it would be harder for them to find husbands. **My parents** didn't buy into that . . . (Ariel 2004, 103)

The passage raises the question of why the first NP is referred back to by means of a pronoun and then three lines later by means of the same NP. Ariel's (1990) work on NP anaphora provides an answer to this question: the type of anaphor selected reflects the accessibility of its antecedent. While the antecedent *my parents* remains accessible until the time that the pronoun *them* is uttered, this changes as more discourse referents are introduced (*Chinese friends*, *children*, *girls*, and *husbands*) into the passage. Notice also that the pronoun becomes the most recent mention of the antecedent, and in and by itself it is already less specific than the antecedent. The second appearance of the full NP *my parents* signals the decreased accessibility of the antecedent due to the reduced specificity of the pronoun appearing between the first and second NP, as well as potential interference from the other discourse referents.

NP anaphors range from full names to NPs to pronouns to zero, differing in terms of the amount of explicit information they provide about the antecedent. They provide more information in case the antecedent's accessibility is low. With respect to ellipsis alternation, it offers a way of selecting a more informative remnant to match a low-accessibility correlate. To see this, consider that a remnant with a preposition provides more information about its correlate: it specifies the correct phrasal category of the correlate (PP as opposed to NP), and hence, also its grammatical function in the antecedent clause (e.g., complement, adjunct, etc.). In contrast, a remnant without a preposition fails to unambiguously identify the function of its correlate. The choice of remnant is adjusted to the current accessibility of the correlate, which is mediated by its specificity, as described in section 1. This behavior is entirely expected, given that remnants are anaphors. I now turn to two differences between English/Norwegian and Polish in sections 3 and 4.

3. Lexical Dependencies

It is well known that some PPs have a more intimate relationship with verbs than other PPs. Hawkins (2000) argues that this relationship is motivated by how we process lexical items. In the example shown in (14) from Hawkins (2000, 243), the order of the two postverbal PPs is determined by whether each of the PPs can be processed in isolation from the verb *die*.

(14) Fatty died [PP1 of heat] [PP2 at Lake Rudolph].

While the PP *at Lake Rudolph* is understood as the location of the event specified by the verb, the PP *of heat* depends on the verb for its interpretation. Note that we can replace the verb with an appropriate proform, as in (15), and still be able to process the second PP, but the same is not true of the first PP, as shown in (16).

(15) Something happened to Fatty at Lake Rudolph.
(16) *Something happened to Fatty of heat.

Hawkins (2000) argues that the human parser cannot interpret the meaning of the preposition *of*, and hence the entire PP *of heat*, unless it has simultaneous access to the verb, and that this dependency is processed more efficiently if the verb and preposition are placed adjacent, since they are perceived as a lexical unit.

The effect of lexical dependencies is not only seen in the ordering of constituents, but also in the choice of ellipsis remnants. In English corpus data, a remnant without a preposition appears more often than a remnant with a preposition in those cases where the remnant shows some degree of dependency on the verb present in the antecedent, or the verb shows some degree of dependency on the remnant, or both (Nykiel 2014). This pattern can be explained in the following way: if a verb and a preposition are perceived as a unit by speakers, then they will not normally be separated from each other. As an illustration, let us consider the first PP in example (14). If we turn (14) into an instance of sluicing, then it will look like (17).

(17) Fatty died of something at Lake Rudolph, but I'm not sure what/of what.

The preposition *of* is more likely to be missing than not, because of its dependency relation with the verb, which is also missing from the remnant. This preference ensures that the two constituents forming a lexical unit are not separated. If, however, there is no dependency relation between a verb and preposition, then the verb's absence from the remnant does not lead to separating any constituents that form a lexical unit. Thus, the preposition is more likely to be used in (18) than in (17).

(18) Fatty can't live without someone, but I'm not sure who/without who.

I observed the same patterns in an acceptability study of Norwegian sluicing and an online comprehension study of the same construction, as well as in an acceptability study of Polish sluicing (Nykiel 2013c).

With regard to cross-linguistic differences, it is important to point out that more than one level of lexical dependency should be distinguished. Some languages exhibit one-level and two-level dependencies. For instance, the verb *die* in (17) does not depend on the preposition for interpretation, although the reverse holds. Notice that the parser can assign the correct interpretation to the sentence *Fatty died* (Fatty is no longer alive), whether or not it has access to the PP *of something*. Example (17) thus instantiates a one-level dependency. To take a different example, consider (19).

(19) Katie fell for something again, but she didn't say what/*for what.

The verb used in this example is the prepositional verb *fall for*, which is a combination of a verb and preposition whose meaning cannot be derived from the meanings of the two constituents. The lexical dependency is a two-level one, because neither the verb alone nor the preposition can receive an interpretation that corresponds in any way to the meaning that they have together in (19). The result of this dependency is that the remnant is not likely at all to include the preposition, as indicated by the asterisk in (19).

Two-level dependencies, in addition to one-level dependencies, are found in both English and Norwegian. In general, a language will have two-level dependencies if it has prepositional verbs. Like English, Norwegian has prepositional verbs (e.g., *gå inn for* "support," *se opp til* "look up to," or *ta etter* "take after"). Polish, however, only has one-level dependencies, because it lacks prepositional verbs. In Nykiel (2013c, 2014), I propose that an explanation for differences between Polish on the one hand and English and Norwegian on the other should be sought in the strength of lexical dependencies found in these languages, where the strength is a reflection of the different levels of dependency that are available.

4. Structural Persistence

The second difference between Polish and English/Norwegian concerns the effect of speakers' exposure to certain syntactic structures. Such exposure increases the likelihood with which similar utterances are subsequently generated in discourse. This well-studied phenomenon, called priming or structural persistence, occurs at different levels of linguistic description: semantics, syntax, morphology, lexis, and phonetic form. For example, seeing a passive construction (e.g., *Katie was missed at the meeting*) in previous discourse makes another passive construction likelier to be produced than an active one (e.g., *We missed Katie at the meeting*) (Bock 1986).

The relevance of structural persistence to ellipsis alternation is that the antecedent can host a correlate whose constituents are adjacent, discontinuous, or partly missing. These possibilities are shown in (20)–(23).

(20) A: Katie is staying in Paris with who?
B: With a co-worker.

(21) A: **Who** is Katie staying in Paris **with**?
B: A co-worker.

(23) A: Katie is staying in Paris with someone.
B: **Who**?
A: A co-worker, I think.

The correlate in A's question in (20) consists of a PP whose constituents are adjacent to each other. B's response is the more typical remnant used in such an environment, as shown by English corpus data (Nykiel 2014). In (21), the constituents of the correlate are discontinuous, that is, separated through preposition stranding. This promotes the use of remnants without prepositions, as in B's response. Finally, the correlate in (23) is itself elliptical (B's utterance) and contains no preposition. A's second utterance echoes the same structure (a remnant that is also an NP), a pattern that is robust in English corpus data. Of the three kinds of correlates, the one shown in (21) is present in English and Norwegian, but absent from Polish, reducing the range of environments that can support generation of remnants without prepositions. Modern quantitative methods, which I used in my study of American English, permit precise statements about the extent to which the presence of antecedents like (21) affects the frequency of the two types of remnants.

5. The Ellipsis Alternation Cross-Linguistically

A more detailed look at ellipsis alternation in American English, Norwegian, and Polish shows that these languages do not differ in terms of whether they allow this alternation. Nor do they differ in terms of how remnants with or without prepositions are selected, based on the current accessibility of their correlates. Rather, differences lie in the actual frequency of both types of remnants. I have identified two factors that underlie these differences.

These factors are rooted in language processing in the sense that they reflect choices that speakers make, based on which structures are easier to process or generate in a specific context. There is growing recognition in the linguistic literature that such preferences might underlie what later becomes conventionalized as grammatical rules (Hawkins 2004, 2009). This is because the ease with which some structures are generated can lead to their conventionalization, such that other competing structures become infrequent, or might even drop out of use with time, as the result. It is important that we distinguish such infrequent structures from unacceptable ones, because they have sometimes been considered unacceptable in the linguistic literature (Manning 2003). Data collected through controlled studies of grammatical variation, of which ellipsis alternation is an example, can help identify and account for frequent, infrequent, and unacceptable structures found in various languages.

6. Conclusion

In this chapter, I have overviewed selected features of two elliptical constructions, sluicing and BAE. My focus has been on ellipsis alternation, which these constructions make available, and three constraints on this alternation in three languages. Ellipsis alternation concerns the possibility of using either a remnant with a preposition or one without, given an appropriate antecedent. I have suggested that one of the three constraints is found to affect ellipsis alternation in a similar way across all three languages. However, the remaining two constraints lead to appreciable differences in the frequency of the two types of remnants in American English and Norwegian on the one hand, and Polish on the other.

Acknowledgements

I gratefully acknowledge the University of Chicago's offer of a six-month visiting position in 2013, which allowed me to discuss this research with colleagues in the Department of Linguistics. All errors are, of course, mine.

BIBLIOGRAPHY

Almeida, D. A. de, and M. Yoshida. 2007. "A Problem for the Preposition Stranding Generalization." *Linguistic Inquiry* 38 (2): 349–362.

Ariel, M. 1990. *Accessing Noun Phrase Antecedents*. London: Routledge.

———. 2004. "Accessibility Marking: Discourse Functions, Discourse Profiles, and Processing Cues." *Discourse Processes* 37 (2): 91–116.

Bock, J. K. 1986. "Syntactic Persistence in Language Production." *Cognitive Psychology* 18: 355–387.

Caha, P. 2011. "Case in Adpositional Phrases." Unpublished manuscript. Center for Advanced Study in Theoretical Linguistics, University of Tromsø.

Fortin, C. 2007. *Indonesian Sluicing and Verb Phrase Ellipsis: Description and Explanation in a Minimalist Framework*. Doctoral dissertation. Ann Arbor, MI: University Microfilms.

Hawkins, J. A. 2000. "The Relative Order of Prepositional Phrases in English: Going Beyond Manner–Place–Time." *Language Variation and Change* 11: 231–266.

———. 2004. *Efficiency and Complexity in Grammars*. Oxford: Oxford University Press.

———. 2009. "Language Universals and the Performance-Grammar Correspondence Hypothesis." In *Language Universals*, edited by M. H. Christiansen, C. Collins, and S. Edelman, 54–78. Oxford: Oxford University Press.

Manning, C. 2003. "Probabilistic Syntax." In *Probabilistic Linguistics*, edited by R. Bod, J. Hey, and S. Jannedy, 289–342. Cambridge, MA: The MIT Press.

Merchant, J. 2001. *The Syntax of Silence: Sluicing, Islands, and the Theory of Ellipsis*. Oxford: Oxford University Press.

Nykiel, J. 2013a. "Clefts and Preposition Omission in Sluicing." *Lingua* 123: 74–117.

———. 2013b. "Wh-phrases in Sluicing: An Interaction of the Remnant and the Antecedent." In *The Core and the Periphery. Data-Driven Perspectives on Syntax Inspired by I. A. Sag*, edited by P. Hofmeister, and E. Norcliffe, 251–271. Stanford, CA: Center for the Study of Language and Information Publications.

———. 2013c. "Syntactic Alternatives under Sluicing." Manuscript submitted for publication.

———. 2014. "The Ellipsis Alternation: Remnants With and Without Prepositions." Manuscript submitted for publication.

Rodrigues, C., A. Nevins, and L. Vicente. 2009. "Cleaving the Interactions between Sluicing and Preposition Stranding. In *Romance Languages and Linguistic Theory 2006*, edited by L. Wetzels and J. van der Weijer, 175–198. Amsterdam: John Benjamins Publishing Company.

Ross, J. R. 1969. "Guess Who?" In *Papers from the 5th Regional Meeting of the Chicago Linguistic Society*, edited by R. Binnick et al., 252–286. Chicago, IL: Chicago Linguistic Society.

Sag, I. A., and J. Nykiel. 2011. "Remarks on Sluicing." In *Proceedings of the HPSG 11 Conference*, edited by S. Mueller. Center for the Study of Language and Information Publications. http://csli-publications.stanford.edu/HPSG.

Stjepanovic, S. 2008. "P-stranding under Sluicing in a Non-P-Stranding Language?" *Linguistic Inquiry* 37 (1): 179–190.

Wei, T. 2011. "Parallelism in Amis Sluicing." *Concentric: Studies in Linguistics* 37 (1): 1–44.

THE POLITICS OF FORMALISM: PURITY, OBJECTIVITY, AND THE QUESTION OF SELF

Agnieszka Rejniak-Majewska*

Abstract

Formalism, especially in art history and art criticism, is notorious for its association with reductionist and limiting approaches, and especially with a mode of "preventive aesthetics" that cuts out all the emotional and contextual dimensions of a work of art. In my paper, I argue that this general opinion needs qualification, for it ignores both the historical complexity of modern formalist views and much of their philosophical and political motivations. In my analysis, I focus on some of the early twentieth- century European formalist conceptions of art, juxtaposing them against the foundation of formal aesthetics, namely Kant's Critique of Judgment, *and questioning the meanings they gave to such terms as purity, objectivity, aesthetic disinterestedness, and formal unity. My argument is that concepts such as purity and objectivity served, rather, as ideal terms that imposed a demand for one's attentive regard to an object; and, as the condition for the autonomy of aesthetic judgment, they related most of all to our subjective attitudes, unlike the uses of these terms in science. According to the formalist views I investigate, aesthetic perception and aesthetic emotion—pleasure in grasping a formal unity in the object—worked, in fact, to confirm subjective faculties of feeling and to give an aesthetic basis for the autonomy of self. It is worth pointing out that the notion of individual autonomy may lack its own grounds, but this notion nevertheless finds confirmation in the*

* Agnieszka Rejniak-Majewska is an Assistant Professor in the Institute of Philosophy at the University of Lodz.

faculty of subjective aesthetic apprehension and reflexive judgment, which involve the suspension of common beliefs in one's attentive concern with the object. In that point, I see a connection between the ethical and the aesthetic premises of European Enlightenment thought, a connection which I regard to be still valid in view of some supposed global universal humanism, even if modern formalist theories often failed in their universalist ambitions. At the same time, in my historical reconstruction, I try to emphasize how differently the meaning of individual autonomy in relation to aesthetic experience was interpreted, ranging from authors who, like Roger Fry, could have assumed their "universal" outlook as the cultural heirs of great empires, to others who, like Witkiewicz, culturally and politically, were speaking from the margins.

In modern (and postmodern) artistic vocabulary there are not many terms as often contested, as variously understood, rejected, and reappropriated, as formalism.[1] The usual approach in contemporary art criticism has been to criticize formalism wholesale, while thinking about particular schools or methods from the past, or to set "good" kinds of formalism against "bad" discredited counterparts that might be finally banished to the dustbin of history.[2] While this kind of approach seems to be rhetorically effective, and productive on the pragmatic level, what it often loses sight of is the wider motivation and complexity of the opposing views. In my analysis, I would like to propose a more sympathetic view, more focused on the conceptual backgrounds and objectives of formalist approaches than on their limitations

[1] The more recent turn towards "new formalism," observable over the last decade in the field of cultural studies and literature, claims the need to go back again to a closer analysis of "form," understood as a contingent particularity or way of structuring. The revalidation of formal interest—the new attention to how things are made, said, or shown—is encouraged as an antidote to the common fault of "moving too quickly through text to the context." For major statements, see: Marjorie Levinson, "What is New Formalism?," *PMLA* 122, no. 2 (2007): 558–569; W. J. T. Mitchell, "The Commitment to Form, or Still Crazy after All These Years," *PMLA* 118, no. 2 (2003): 321–325.

[2] A model example may be found in Rosalind Krauss, "Formalism and Structuralism," in *Art since 1900: Modernism, Antimodernism, Postmodernism*, edited by Hal Foster, et al. (London: Thames & Hudson, 2004), 32–39. See also: Whitney Davis, "Subjectivity and Objectivity in High and Historical Formalism," *Representations* 104, no. 1 (2008): 8–22. Krauss poses what she calls the "morphological" formalism of Wölfflin, Greenberg, and Fry against Russian formalism, which she praises for its more structural approach. Whitney Davis' text is a resolute rejection of aesthetic formalism, which he criticizes as ahistorical and irredeemably subjectivist; this critique extends partly to the formal method of historical analysis of style. The scope and critical variations of formalism are variously defined by different authors, even in general typologies; for example, Bohdan Dziemidok, "Artistic Formalism: Its Achievements and Weaknesses," *Journal of Aesthetics and Art Criticism* 51, no. 2 (1993): 185–193; and Paul Crowther,

and dead ends. My focus will be the relations between the formalist concept of the aesthetic autonomy of art and the idea of individual autonomy—the connection that points, in fact, beyond purely aesthetic issues, to questions of politics and ethics.

It would be precipitate to speak about any unified politics behind formalist views. To an art historian, a literary researcher interested in methodology, or to an art critic, formalism may mean quite different things. Thus, in questioning the politics of formalism, one should begin by asking: "Whose formalism?"[3] Moreover, what I would like to call the "politics of formalism" operates in variable contexts and on different levels, ranging from artistic views to institutionalized methodologies and interpretive standards.

Nevertheless, the term "formalism" used to be associated broadly with a flight from politics—a mode of lofty (elitist) disengagement, of limiting oneself blindly or opportunistically to the cultivation of artistic values. Significantly, when we look back at the twentieth century, the name "formalism" was more often imposed than voluntarily adopted. The proponents of artistic avant-gardes used to throw this term against their not-sufficiently-radical fellow artists, whom they accused of isolationism or aesthetic superficiality. It was a heavy charge to be called "formalist" in Communist Russia, or in the Communist-ruled countries of the Soviet Bloc. According to that rhetoric, "formalist art" or a "formalist standpoint" designated something inert and devoid of spirit, a stumbling block on the way to the future (either an artistic, or socialist, revolution).

In the 1960s and 1970s in America—another important moment when formalism earned its bad name—the roles were somehow reversed. If being called "formalist" in a Communist regime would line up with being a dissident, now, in this time of political and cultural turmoil, the contested formalist party was perceived as the dominant power, one that set standards of academic reading, imposed artistic hierarchies, and ruled the art market and institutions. The frames of artistic autonomy it established were regarded as too narrow and limiting; formalist criticism earned accusations equally for its elitist leanings as for its imperialist ambitions in imposing uniform and allegedly universal categories of artistic description.[4] It was simultaneously

---

"Formalism, Art History, and Effective Historical Difference," in *Transhistorical Image: Philosophizing Art and Its History* (Cambridge: Cambridge University Press, 2002), 7–21. A general difficulty in this context is how to locate critically and historically the main enemy; namely, "pure formalism," since even Fry's or Greenberg's formalist views could be proved to go beyond what the adversaries of formalism recognize as its "essence."

[3] See Yve-Alain Bois' contribution in a discussion on *Art History and Its Theories*, titled "Whose formalism?," *Art Bulletin* 78, no. 1 (1996): 9–12.

[4] David Summers, *Real Spaces: World Art History and the Rise of Western Modernism* (New York: Phaidon Press, 2003), 28ff.

criticized as a subjective judgmental approach and as a kind of "preventive aesthetics," raising associations with dull, systematic, and bureaucratic attitudes.[5]

The general effect of these attacks was to strengthen the negative connotations that formalism has with intellectual sterility and systematic abstraction. Thus, formalism came to be viewed as an almost paradigmatic embodiment of the repressive, disciplinary aspects of modernity. My attempt here is to point out the other side of the story. By turning to formalism's beginnings in the philosophy of Kant, and by examining some of its early twentieth-century modern variants, I would like to investigate the assumptions they made concerning the meaning of aesthetic experience and the subjective position it entailed.

From the Kantian tradition in aesthetics, there stemmed the connection between the idea of individual freedom and the autonomy of the aesthetic judgment, which was later developed and transformed in modern conceptions of art. While this concept of freedom was, from the very beginning, dialectically combined with a notion of inner subjective control, I would argue that modern formalist theories were intent on broadening rather than disciplining human sensibilities according to some established rules. As I would like to show, these theories wanted to preserve a firm notion of the individual, but they also came to acknowledge the modern crisis of a unified, self-conscious notion of self. In this respect, the conception of art by a Polish artist and theorist, Stanislaw Ignacy Witkiewicz (1885–1939), is an especially interesting case. I will discuss his conception separately later in the text, since this lesser known version of aesthetic formalism, created after World War I, in the shadow of the vanished empires, and in the midst of rapid modernization, shows another side of formalist claims to universalism, one that was later occluded in formalism's more triumphant discursive counterparts in the West.

Kantian Tropes

Although some formalist critics, notably Clement Greenberg, used to resort to the philosophical authority of Kant in defense of their views, the German philosopher appears rather as a distant patron of modern formalist conceptions of art. The easiest explanation for this is that Kant's interest in aesthetics

---

[5] Leo Steinberg, "Other Criteria," in *Other Criteria: Confrontations with Twentieth-Century Art* (Oxford: Oxford University Press, 1972), 64–66. See also a more recent, much broader and more nuanced interpretation of Greenberg's work: Caroline Jones, *Eyesight Alone: Clement Greenberg's Modernism and the Bureaucratization of the Senses* (Chicago: University of Chicago Press, 2008). According to Jones, Greenberg's formalism may be read precisely as aestheticism and bohemianism institutionalized and remade into authoritative discourse.

was not primarily related to art, which he considered, according to the dominant views of his epoch, as a socially useful practice dedicated to pleasurable representation or moral edification. Kant himself did not propose an autonomist conception of art, since artistic work was, for him, still a matter of skill and determinate purpose. Therefore, in the *Critique of Judgment*, the model of aesthetic experience was not the experience of art, but the experience of nature. In his discussion of the exercise of pure aesthetic judgment, Kant's main objective was to demonstrate the connection between the transcendental dimension of freedom (which is characteristic of our noumenal self) and the empirical realm of sensibility. The operation of judgment was not limited to any specific kind of objects. As he pointed out, the principle of judgment "has no field of objects appropriate to it as its realm."[6]

Hence, it was a subtle yet meaningful shift when Kant's arguments came to be used by his followers to validate the formal autonomy of art. The subsequent tradition of philosophic aesthetics offered various psychologized versions of Kant's views, starting with Friedrich Schiller's idea of "the aesthetic man," through Johann Herbart's and Konrad Fiedler's theories of perception, to Arthur Schopenhauer's philosophy of art, all of which placed more emphasis on human creative faculties and their artistic expression. Although in many respects divergent from the original Kantian concepts and from his critical method, these later conceptions bore responsibility for popular interpretations of his aesthetics and thus exerted a direct influence on modern conceptions of art.[7]

One of the main Kantian ideas that the subsequent tradition brought to the fore was the idea of contemplative detachment, regarded as the grounding condition of aesthetic experience. This followed Kant's argument that the judgment of beauty demands a purely disinterested attitude, one that excludes any preoccupation with the conceptual meaning of the object, any interest in sensual pleasure it may give, or even any question about the reality of its existence. In the idealistic frame of interpretation, most of all dictated by Schopenhauer's work, this notion was consequently developed to stress art's independence from and elevation over practical life. The separateness of a purely formal interest was identified with a subjective position of disen-

[6] Immanuel Kant, *Critique of Judgment*, translated by James Creed Meredith (Oxford: Oxford University Press, 2007), 13 [cited hereafter as CJ].

[7] For a classic and thorough critique of this interpretation of Kant, see Martin Heidegger, *Nietzsche*, vol. 1: *The Will to Power as Art*, translated by David Farrell Krell (San Francisco: HarperCollins, 1991), especially the chapter on "Kant's Doctrine of the Beautiful: Its Misinterpretation by Schopenhauer and Nietzsche" (107–114), where he refutes Nietzsche's identification of Kant's idea of disinterestedness with Schopenhauer's notion of will-less detachment.

gagement, a peaceful contemplative state in which one would surrender to a disinterested and passive observation of a given piece of art. This psychological interpretation dwelled on the specifically voiding effect of Kant's definition of beauty, which came in line with nineteenth-century aestheticism and its focus on inner subjective life.

However, even if such an interpretation had its grounds in the emphasis Kant put on the subjectivity of feeling and not on the inherent qualities of the object, this later reading of the third *Critique* was strikingly selective and did not do justice to the main core of its argument. Indeed, the meaning of subjectivity for Kant, and his demands concerning aesthetic reflection, were much higher than the subsequent versions of aestheticism might suggest. The demand for the "purity" of aesthetic judgment was also in a way a moral demand, one that presupposed one's detachment from subjective personal conditions of pleasure and dislike. In making a claim for the autonomy of taste,[8] Kant made it a part of his more general vision of the autonomous self, which he expressed in the "common maxims of human understanding"; that is: "(1) to think for oneself; (2) to think from the standpoint of everyone else; (3) always to think consistently."[9] As an extension of his earlier formulations concerning "the discipline of pure reason," Kant's incentive to profess these "mental habits" through their aesthetic exercise reveals a hidden connection he assumed between morality and aesthetics. Far from subjective exaltation, aesthetic experience implies a combination of subjective freedom and constraint. In Kant's view, this combination was the general condition of individual autonomy, which could be realized only by keeping in view the ideal horizon of a universal community.

Accordingly, Kant's stress upon the merely formal interest in aesthetic response served several aims at once. The infamous instruction to confine one's attention to the purely formal peculiarities of the object, while abstracting from its "charm and emotion,"[10] was intended to fend off all the personal and bodily affections that would make judgments of taste merely private, contingent affairs. This bracketing of the sensual and emotional dimension, as has often been remarked, reveals Kant's allegiance to the "traditional distinction between satisfactions of sensation and appetite, which are personally variable, and rational satisfactions which are universal to all men."[11]

---

[8] CJ, 112, 123.

[9] CJ, 124. If the first and the second maxim might seem to us somehow divergent, Kant assumes they must be combined. The last one, he says, should arise precisely from combining the two previous ones.

[10] CJ, 54, 123–24.

[11] Michael Podro, *The Manifold of Perception: Theories of Art from Kant to Hildebrandt* (London: Oxford University Press, 1972), 21.

One should not, however, lose sight of all the efforts Kant made to emphasize the particular, empirical grounding of an aesthetic judgment and to set it apart from the abstract generality of understanding. For this reason, the purely formal apprehension of the object, which allows for "a free play of imagination and understanding," is opposed to the conceptual grasp of reality, which would tie the object to the already established meanings. That this "free play" needs to have some grounding in a sensible manifold remains obvious for Kant when he considers the example of geometrically regular figures, like a circle, a square, or a cube, which were traditionally regarded as ideal instances of beauty. For Kant, they cannot be objects of reflective aesthetic judgment, precisely because they are directly comprehensible and identifiable for us as "the presentations of determinate concepts."[12]

Kant's dual move in his discussion of aesthetic judgment may be interpreted, therefore, as a revalidation of the sensible, subjective mode of apprehension and simultaneously as an attempt to ascribe to it a quasi-objective status. Judging individually, but "from the standpoint of everyone else," inscribes a singular judgment with an inherent claim for universal validity—without, however, making it objective in the correct sense of the word. As Kant put it himself: "We want to get a look at the object with our own eyes, just as if our delight depended on sensation. And yet, if upon so doing, we call the object beautiful, we believe ourselves to be speaking with a universal voice."[13] Kant makes it clear that the prescription to restrain one's personal likes and dislikes is not automatically a guarantee of such universality: "the universal voice is only an idea," he says, and purity of judgment remains an ideal to be approximated, in search of which one often may fail.[14]

In Kant's view, the aesthetic contemplation of form opens up a space of subjective freedom, a possibility of taking pleasure in the presentation of shapes and figurations, the purpose of which is beyond consideration and may remain unknown. This pleasure has no particular purpose in itself, apart from giving our cognitive faculties a sense of vitality and harmonious accord. Aesthetic freedom seems, therefore, to be a negative one, occasioned by the lack of determination of concepts, yet it is also an expression of our spontaneity, involving the enlivening of human faculties in their play.

Interestingly, Kant notes that while attending to some phenomena, such as a flowing stream or blazing fire, the play of imagination may bring us close to a pleasurable state of *rêverie*, where "the mind entertains itself as it is being

[12] CJ, 72. This point is emphasized by Rodolphe Gasché, *The Idea of Form: Rethinking Kant's Aesthetics* (Stanford, CA: Stanford University Press, 2003), 65.

[13] CJ, 47.

[14] CJ, 48.

continually stirred by the variety that strikes the eye." He immediately adds, however, that this may not be the case if an aesthetic judgment is delivered, since if one wants to tell one's judgment, it should be based in his grasp of the object.[15] If that condition might not speak strictly of the "objective" quality of aesthetic judgment (a contradiction in Kant's terms), it nevertheless clarifies that a certain attentive involvement with the object is deserved, or what in the language of phenomenology was later to be called "the intentionality of consciousness." Even if the aesthetic experience of beauty implies inner subjective satisfaction at the harmonious operation of our own faculties,[16] it needs an external object as an intermediary to which one should openly and actively turn.

Formal Regard, or Aestheticism Restrained

With the rise of *artistic* modernism at the beginning of the twentieth-century, formalist views constituted a diverse but powerful force in support of the autonomy of art. The position of defending artistic autonomy was to a large part coincident with the neo-romantic and symbolist movements, which claimed art's high status as an expression of transcendent, spiritual reality. Yet despite their closeness to late-romantic aestheticism and its belief in the inner force of artistic creation, formalist views, starting with Eduard Hanslick's famous

[15] CJ, 74.

[16] According to Kant, the purposiveness of our faculties, which we experience in a feeling of beauty, presents itself as a harmonious interplay without imposition of power. Here, as in the whole of his critical philosophy, one may be struck by the abundance of legal and political metaphors: human faculties of imagination and intellect, sensuality and reason, and sense particulars and concepts, all figure as opposite parties that should eventually come into some non-coercive unity without suppressing each other. On this topic, see Jonathan Hess, *Reconstituting the Body Politic: Enlightenment, Public Culture and the Invention of Aesthetic Autonomy* (Detroit: Wayne State University Press, 1999), 185. One may find a similar figurative vision of freedom in the objects Kant presents as examples of beauty. Without exception, he privileges the picturesque, the lively variety that contains the unpredictable and the new: "all stiff regularity is inherently repugnant to taste . . . On the other hand, anything that gives the imagination scope for unstudied and purposive play is always fresh to us" (CJ 73). Thus, a natural English garden is better than the absolute geometrical order of Versailles. Kant's preferences clearly reveal his political stand. This level of hidden political meaning in the valuation of form may be traced also in art-historical descriptions. Naming formal qualities such as "unity" or "subordination" on the one hand, and "equilibrium," "multiplicity," or compositional "independence" of parts that seem to exist "on their own rights," on the other, may bring up close associations with specific kinds of social organization and political systems of power (feudal, authoritarian, or liberal). Evonne Levy has argued that this connection might have been intended in the case of Adolph Wölfflin's contrasted definitions of Renaissance and Baroque, see "The Political Project of Wölfflin's Early Formalism," *October* 139 (2012): 39–52.

1854 discussion on musical form, *On the Musically Beautiful*, tended to give more focus to the object-like qualities of artistic work and to pay more attention to the particularities of artistic craftsmanship. This, and the resulting formalist disregard for art's emotional content and power to affect, led to serious antagonisms between formalist critics and those who championed romantic ideals.[17]

On the other hand, in their preoccupation with abstract qualities of form, and in defining the aesthetic object as a self-contained, self-sufficient entity, formalist theories of art showed much affinity with nineteenth-century strains of aestheticism. They manifested a similar disdain for bourgeois values, which found its expression in the ideal of "art for art's sake," as well as expressing the same demand for artistic freedom, voiced in the renouncing of more traditional mimetic and didactic conceptions of art. With its focus on artistic means, formalism came to support the typically modernist artistic demand to grant artists authority in the specific sphere of their craft, to "entrench [them] more firmly in their area of competence."[18]

Regarding the formalists' concern with issues of artistic medium and technique, it is worthwhile to point out the multiple connections that existed among modern artistic endeavors, critical approaches, and formalist definitions of art. Adolf Hildebrandt, the author of a seminal text, *The Concept of Form in the Visual Arts* (1893), which bore significant impact on Alois Riegl's and Adolph Wölfflin's writings in art history, was a sculptor himself. Roger Fry's career as an art critic and curator was also complemented by his artistic efforts, and his formalist conception of art was clearly influenced by the writings of another French painter, Maurice Denis. The champions of the first generation of Russian formalists were the friends of futurists, or even futurist poets themselves. Artists of the constructivist avant-garde showed their familiarity with the writings of Heinrich Wölfflin, while developing their own systematic explorations concerning visual forms.

This list could be further extended, but it is long enough to show that the connections were mutual and not limited to the role formalist criticism played

---

[17] The polemical war between Hanslick and his former friend Richard Wagner was an emblematic case of this antagonism. Against the emotional intoxication with music that he claimed to be "pathological," Hanslick argued that attentive perception is "the beginning and requirement of aesthetic pleasure and creates first the basis for emotion." Quoted after Robert M. Anderson, "Polemics or Philosophy: Musical Pathology in Eduard Hanslick's *Vom Musicalisch-Schönen*," *Musical Times*, 154, no. 1924 (2013): 74. Anderson notes the substantial influence of Kantian aesthetics on Hanslick's argument.

[18] This well-known formulation comes from Clement Greenberg, "Modernist Painting," *The Collected Essays and Criticism*, vol. 4: *Modernism with a Vengeance, 1957–1969*, edited by John O'Brien (Chicago: University of Chicago Press, 1993), 85.

in validating modern tendencies in art and in opening a path for modernism's institutional acceptance. Artists' voices and critical approaches worked in parallel lines towards securing and consolidating the inner autonomy of the artistic field, and soon the simple observation that "poetry is made out of words" (Viktor Shklovsky), or that "a picture, before being a battle horse, a nude, an anecdote or whatnot, is essentially a flat surface covered with colors assembled in a certain order" (Maurice Denis), became commonplaces of modern artistic discourse.

The formalist method of interpretation, developed in art history by Heinrich Wölfflin and Alois Riegl, served a similar aim, for it was expected to provide a firm and specific foundation for the discipline that still remained, somehow, a province of the historical sciences. The study of art history in terms of formal developments of style offered an "exact" method of a supposedly universal application, giving the discipline alleged sovereignty in its own distinct domain.

In art history writing, the method of formal analysis presupposed drawing systematic conclusions on the basis of empirical observation in a way that was supposed to resemble the standards of positive science. Ultimately, the judgment of formal relations needed to rely to some extent on subjective apprehension and feeling, but the unspoken objective of this method was to ward off the menace of personal, subjective projection. The ideal of objectivity in formalist analysis had much in common with the desire "to go back to the things themselves," which became at the time the watchword of Husserl's phenomenology.[19] The ideal of direct perception unhampered by practical considerations and habits was similarly advanced by formalist critics in connection with artistic work.[20] Almost the same observations on this topic may be found in the work of authors as different as Viktor Shklovsky and Roger Fry. While pointing towards art's recovering impact on our sensibilities, they both complained about the way we conceive of reality in our habitual perception:

> With an admirable economy we learn to see only so much as is needful for our purposes; but this is in fact very little, just enough to recognize and identify each object or person; that

---

[19] A broad discussion on the affinities of formalism with phenomenological approaches is given by Lambert Wiesing, *Die Sichtbarkeit des Bildes. Geschichte und Perspektiven der formalen Ästhetik* (Hamburg: Rowohlt Verlag, 1997).

[20] The roots of this idea may be also traced to Romantic conceptions of art. Shklovsky himself makes a quotation from Thomas Carlyle: "Thirst of concreteness constitutes the soul of art." Viktor Shklovsky, "The Resurrection of the Word," in *Russian Formalism: A Collection of Articles and Texts*, edited by Stephen Bann, and John E. Bowlt (Edinburgh: Scottish Academic Press, 1973), 43.

> done, they go into to an entry in our mental catalogue and are no more really seen. In actual life the normal person really only reads the labels as it were on the objects around him and troubles no further. Almost all the things which are useful in any way put on more or less this cap of invisibility. It is only when an object exists in our lives for no other purpose than to be seen that we really look at it, as for instance at a China ornament or a precious stone, and towards such even the most normal person adopts to some extent the artistic attitude of pure vision abstracted from necessity.[21]

That is what Roger Fry stated in his article from 1909; and a few years later, Shklovsky named the same illness:

> We do not sense the familiar, we do not see it, but recognize it. We do not see the walls of our rooms, it is so hard for us to spot a misprint in a proof—particularly if it is written in a language that is well known to us, because we cannot make ourselves see and read through, and not 'recognize' the familiar word.[22]
>
> By this algebraic method of thought we apprehend objects only as shapes with imprecise extensions, we do not see them in their entirety but rather recognize them by their main characteristics. We see the object as if it was enveloped in a sack. The object . . . fades and does not leave even a first impression; ultimately even the essence of what it was is forgotten.[23]

The famous distinction Shklovsky makes in his texts between automated, habitual vision and artistic perception may remind one of the romantic complaints concerning the deadening impact of mechanization and the opposite ideal of "pure" vision, characterized by its directness and clarity. Yet, according to Shklovsky, the renewed vision is not static or uniform—it is dialectically connected with our real-life perceptions and invited by the estranging effects of "semantic modifications" encountered in an artistic text. According to Shklovsky, the specific organization of the artistic material should bring the reader's or viewer's eyes to a new perception of the world. Shklovsky's notion

---

[21] Roger Fry, "An Essay in Aesthetics," in *Vision and Design* (London: Penguin, 1937), 29-30.

[22] Shklovsky, "The Resurrection of the Word," 41–42.

[23] Viktor Shklovsky, "Art as Technique," in *Russian Formalist Criticism: Four Essays,* edited by Lee T. Lemon and Marion J. Reiss (Lincoln: University of Nebraska Press, 1965), 17. The apparent similarity between Shklovsky and Fry may be due to the common impact of Henri Bergson, whose philosophy must have been known to them both. Their common distinction

of the artistic device of estrangement does not refer to some specific kind of sensibility highly removed from practical live, but to artistic techniques and their subjective effects, which allow us to find a new grasp of reality and rediscover it again.

If Fry's theory seems somehow divergent in spirit from the Russian theorist's—and his championship of modern art was certainly not in tune with the violent disturbances of futurist avant-gardes—what he expected from art was also a certain enlivening of our sensibilities and emotional understanding. "Aesthetic feeling," as he defined it, had something of a redemptive value, as it offered a fuller sense of life, more "free" and "universal" than ordinary emotions.[24] This redemptive quality meant breaking free from the "mechanisms of civil life" (i.e., social conventions, which he conceived mainly as hypocritical snobbery), and from the excessive emotions they propel. As in scientific research, the contemplation of form was for Fry a kind of "spiritual exercise," a training in disinterestedness crucial for cultivating one's internal consistency and composure.[25] According to Fry, art, which he called "the chief organ of our imaginative life," simultaneously offered a space for the free exercise of imagination and also gave imagination clear limits: "In dreams and under the influence of drugs the imaginative life passes out of our control, and in such cases its experiences may be highly undesirable," whereas in attending a work of art, our imagination is both stimulated and controlled.[26] (This remark seems strikingly close to Kant's own reservations, mentioned above.) As a coherent formal unity, a work of art imposes on the attending subject its own logic and discipline; therefore, Fry understood it as a sensible embodiment of the same qualities of self-restraint, control, and moderation he valued as characteristics of the individual self.

"Insatiability for Form"

The same connection Fry made between individual integrity and the formal unity of a work of art was also at the center of another formalist theory of art, which was proposed in the 1920s by a Polish artist, Stanisław Ignacy

---

between pure perception and recognition was probably taken form Bergson's *Matter and Memory* and related to his idea of an "immediate intuition" in which we can sense the true reality of the object. On Bergson's possible influence, see James Curtis, "Bergson and Russian Formalism," *Comparative Literature* 28, no. 2 (1976): 109–121; and Mary Ann Gilles, *Henri Bergson and British Modernism* (Montreal: McGill-Queens University Press, 1996).

[24] Fry, "An Essay in Aesthetics," 28. For similar statements in his private correspondence, see also: Virginia Woolf, *Roger Fry: A Biography* (London: Vintage Press, 2003), 183.

[25] Ibid., 230–233.

[26] Fry, "An Essay in Aesthetics," 29.

Witkiewicz (Witkacy). Despite the general similarities between the two theories, however, Witkiewicz's interpretation may be viewed as a complete reversal of Fry's dispassionate, self-contained vision of artistic work and subjective self. Witkiewicz's definition of "pure form" in art and his simultaneous defense of the individual, which he combined with a fight for artistic autonomy, were manifestly imbued with a pressing sense of crisis, which made them very distant from the Apollonian detachment of Fry's theory.

Witkiewicz's conception of art was formulated after his return from Russia following World War I, as a general statement of his views on art and as an attempt to provide a conceptual explanation of his own artistic efforts in the various disciplines he practiced, especially painting and theater. Although his artistic personality was already relatively well-formed in the intellectual milieu of the Austro-Hungarian Galician cities of Cracow and Zakopane (and in his many tours of Paris and Vienna), the years spent in Russia marked a visible rift in his life and left a decisive stamp on his subsequent views on art and politics.

As a Russian citizen, Witkiewicz decided to serve in the Russian army at the outbreak of World War I. After preliminary training, he became an infantry officer in an elite Tsar's regiment and was sent to the front.[27] The injuries he sustained in 1916 brought him back to St. Petersburg, where he became involved in the February Revolution of 1917 (being elected political commissar by the soldiers of his regiment) and witnessed the Bolshevik Revolution. During this time, he may have been exposed to the experimental activities of the Russian futurist and suprematist avant-gardes. One may presume from his later writings that he might also have gained some acquaintance with Russian formalist theories at this time, but for the most part we can only rely on conjectures, since scant documentation has survived from his stay in Russia.[28]

Visions of the communist revolution or authoritarian rule do often recur later in Witkiewicz's literary and dramatic work, presented as an inevitable catastrophe that brings about the destruction of the former, decadent, absurdly chaotic world. Witkiewicz's theory of pure form in art was formulated simultaneously with his catastrophic visions of the future, and it was equally marked with his anxiety about modern social changes and the anticipated

---

[27] Daniel Gerould, "Introduction," in S. I. Witkiewicz, *The Mother & Other Savory Plays*, edited by Daniel Gerould, with a foreword by Jan Kott (New York: Applause Books, 1993), 31–34.

[28] All the surviving official military documents and the few personal records by Witkiewicz himself are analyzed and reprinted in Janusz Degler, *Witkacego portret wielokrotny. Szkice i materiały do biografii* (Warsaw: Panstwowy Instytut Wydawniczy, 2009), 470–515.

destruction of the individual. Witkacy might have called himself, like Roger Fry, "an individualistic anarchist,"[29] and his distinct behaviors—often including extravagant dress, theatrical attitudes, and parodic speech—were a constant provocation to established social mores. But his reasons to seek refuge in artistic work were more complex than the British aesthetician's desire "to fortify the individual against the herd."[30] Too well did he realize the force of social tensions and historical pressures, which were impossible to fend off. In contrast with Witkiewicz's Russian experiences, one may find it quite ironic that, also in 1917, Roger Fry in his *Art and Life* essay proclaimed a modern artistic "revolution," which in his view seemed "out of proportion to any corresponding change in life as a whole."[31]

Witkiewicz's concept of "pure form" was meant to point out the essential quality of artistic work, which would distinguish art in general from other objects and phenomena.[32] Although his theoretical approach may seem at this point strikingly essentialist, any attempt to find stable and objective criteria for the "purity" of form, he stated, must be condemned to failure because of the "essentially subjective" basis of art's reception and judgment.[33] In his general approach, Witkiewicz followed the dominant modernist claim that artistic work should be independent from illustrative concerns or naturalistic representations and not bound by the rules of verisimilitude and common-sense approaches. In various artistic media, he stated, the name of "pure form" may be applied only to "form that is felt, that acts directly upon us to evoke aesthetic satisfaction."[34] This definition, in his view, applied equally to the new and to earlier artistic phenomena.

Accordingly, a work of art that gives us a sense of "pure form" need not be deprived of content. It may be representational, but the question is whether it strikes us as a unique formal creation or whether we come to read it mostly as a representation of some external reality. In some arts, he claimed, especially in poetry or theater, form and content cannot be divorced from each other, but they should come together to constitute "poetic quality." As a general rule, Witkiewicz remarked, form completely deprived of content is impossible,

---

[29] Woolf, *Roger Fry*, 232.

[30] Ibid., 234.

[31] Fry, "Art and Life," 22.

[32] Stanislaw Ignacy Witkiewicz, "On Pure Form," translated by Catherine Leach, in *Aesthetics in Twentieth-Century Poland: Selected Essays,* edited by Alina Wierzbianska (Lewisburg, PA: Bucknell University Press, 1973) 44.

[33] Ibid., 57.

[34] Ibid., 51.

since "no living creature can create such a thing."[35] If, according to his view, real-world elements would adulterate even the most abstract artistic work, then we come up with a paradox; namely, that the immanent feature of "pure form" must be its impurity.

Witkiewicz's position at this point converges with the former theoretical suggestions that formal "purity" with regard to our real subjective attitudes is only an ideal term, which points toward a certain position of "disinterestedness," and as such may be only approximated. Here Witkiewicz goes a step further, however, by stressing the divergence between the mode of objective observation that strives for some generalizable criteria, and our "entirely subjective" approach to art. The affective dimension of artistic experience therefore gains more importance, although according to him this dimension should not arise from thematic content, but from the unique formal quality of artistic work.

The crucial formulation in Witkiewicz's theory of "pure" form was his claim that artistic work should strike us directly as a "unity in multiplicity," as if transporting the viewer to some other, inexplicable universe. According to Witkiewicz, this sense of unity in artistic work may be defined as an immediate presentation of the "basic law of existence," which is "unity in multiplicity." Clearly, a work of art could not be anything else, based on his argument that it is "an expression of the unity of personality" of the artist himself, and "a conception of the work of art must arise in one individual (even if it may be collectively made or performed)."[36] Witkiewicz's reasoning seems to come full circle here, without taking us much farther beyond a banal celebration of individual genius as a source of artistic expression.

What gives more depth and complexity to this view, however, is the realization, so strikingly present in all of his work, that this sense of totality is not easily granted. The unity in question is not some complacent harmony, but a vision of endless tension and contradiction, always on the verge of destruction. It is not a kind of unity that could be rationally conceived or imposed through some cognitive process. By "unity," Witkiewicz meant an intuition that comes to us only when we move beyond a common-sense, practical view of reality that provides us with a fairly clear understanding of its complex conditions and relations, when we come to experience the metaphysical dread of existence, the unexplained mystery of being.[37] The increasingly practical

[35] Ibid.

[36] Ibid., 53–54.

[37] This sense of anxiety of existence, in which one realizes his/her individual being as opposed to the infinite totality of the world (also sensed as a mysterious "unity in multiplicity"),

and effective organization of life in the twentieth century had brought about the social "tranquilization" of such feelings; artistic expression was the crucial means to bring such feelings to life and communicate them. For that communication to take place, however, artists had to propose ever new, unexhausted forms that would be able to move us, to be felt as a strange, unexplained "unity." This metaphysical urge for the new was what Witkiewicz called "insatiability for form," which he posited as the reason for the growing difficulty and "strangeness" of modern art:

> In our time, the highest art, in which the condition of modern man is expressed indirectly, without hypocrisy, must of necessity be complicated, or as the case may be, artificially simplified, artistically perverse, disturbing; and the old calm, with very few exceptions, can only be in the form of reproducing earlier now dead styles, but not in the creating of new formal values.[38]

The principle of "unity in multiplicity" did not relate only to the aesthetic experience of artistic form, but it served also in defining the structure of the individual. According to Witkiewicz's conception, the emotion that is implicit in the apprehension of a work of art parallels our immediate sense of existence as distinct beings, thus pointing to our existential status as individuals. For Witkiewicz this was the crucial although inherently "inexplicable" argument that made him resist the contemporary philosophical and psychological conceptions that undermined the notion of a singular, unified, and consistent self.

Sigmund Freud's theory of psychoanalysis and Ernst Mach's philosophy of empirio-criticism argued that the notion of the individual was only a fictional label without substance, concealing only competing drives, or changing sensations. Witkiewicz himself was significantly influenced by these views, especially by Ernst Mach and his *Analysis of Sensations* (1897), and he accepted many of their points. His philosophical texts, and especially his literary and

---

Witkiewicz termed "metaphysical feelings" and regarded as the common source of religion, philosophy, and art, each trying to express this sense in its own specific way. According to Witkiewicz, "the price mankind must pay for its full socialization" would be the suppression of metaphysical feelings and, consequently, "the death of religion as the primary metaphysical approach," "the suicide of philosophy," and "the decline of art." With reference to religion and philosophy, Witkiewicz was of the opinion that this had already happened. See Stanislaw Ignacy Witkiewicz, "Unwashed Souls," in *The Witkiewicz Reader*, edited by Daniel Gerould (Evanston, IL: Northwestern University Press, 1992), 319. See also Witkiewicz's text in the same volume: "Metaphysical Feelings," 285–286.

[38] Witkiewicz, "On Pure Form," 55–56.

dramatic works, show his skepticism concerning humans as rational, self-conscious, and responsible beings.[39] Like many intellectuals of his time, he experimented with drug-induced mental states to investigate the unexplored potentialities of human consciousness.[40] He stressed the inner multiplicity, or even the schizophrenic quality of his own troubled personality, through his continuous "theater of life," the infinite parade of social masks he assumed.[41] At the same time, however, Witkiewicz did not want to succumb to views that in his opinion could suppress or annihilate the meaning of the individual subjective self. An aesthetic experience of a work of art acted, in his view, as a direct sensible confirmation of our being as autonomous individuals. It reminded a person of one's irreducible situation as a "singular being."

Witkiewicz's theory was, in many respects, atypical in the context of formalist conceptions of art. It testifies to the wide circulation of modern formalist views throughout Europe in the early twentieth century, demonstrating some affinities with British formalism on the one hand, and with the poetic conceptions of Russian formalists on the other. By its very specificity, however, it also points towards the cultural variability of formalist theories, thus partly undermining their own claims to universality. While Roger Fry's and Clive Bell's art theories, or Alois Riegl's art-historical method of formal research, with their "tone of certainty" and universalist ambitions may be viewed as imperial constructions born in the peaceful atmosphere of the great and long-lived world-powers, Witkiewicz's conception of "pure form" visibly lacked this positive basis. His statements were not an assertion of some critical

---

[39] Unlike Roger Fry, Witkiewicz agreed with many of Freud's observations concerning the libidinal sources of human activity, the meaning of sexuality, and sublimation. He even tried to apply a Freudian analytical approach to the unconscious in his own exploration of the typical historically and socially ingrained attitudes of the Polish people. The full title of this ironic and self-critical text from 1936 was: "Unwashed Souls: A Psychological Study into the Inferiority Complex Carried Out According to Freud's System with Special Attention to Polish Problems," *The Witkiewicz Reader*, 310–326.

[40] Witkiewicz conducted a systematic observation of himself under the influence of drugs, see Stanislaw Ignacy Witkiewicz, "Narcotics: Nicotine, Alcohol, Cocaine, Peyote, Morphine, and Ether," in *The Witkiewicz Reader*, 243–269.

[41] An interesting example of such theatrical behavior connected with the issue of "pure" art was the story related by a Polish poet, Julian Przybos. During the visit they paid to Witkiewicz in Zakopane in the 1930s, Przybos and Wladyslaw Strzeminski, the leader of the modern constructivist avant-garde, found him attempting to "make the situation strange" and to demonstrate what he thought on the question of artistic purity. "Every few minutes, Witkiewicz interrupted the conversation, went out, came back and washed his hands!" Julian Przybos, *Linia i gwar*, vol. 1 (Kraków, 1959), 147–149. This practical joke clearly indicated Witkiewicz's opinion on the "pure" abstract art Strzeminski wanted to champion—a mixture of mocking respect and doubt in the possibilities of art so radically abstracted from life.

superiority and universality of view, but a desperate defense of the individual, based on the no less fragile claim for the autonomy of artistic form—made more desperate the more aware he was of his own position of marginality, and of the immanent difficulties and complication of his theory.

In Witkiewicz's work, the ideals of "objectivity" and formal "purity" seem to be undermined from within. What remains, however, is a faith in the value of art and aesthetic experience as the means to assert and to communicate our being as distinct, reflexive self. This, as I have herein set out to demonstrate, was the crucial point behind various strands of formalist criticism: they were not just attempts to confine our senses to superficial formal distinctions, or to impose a similarly limited view of art. Rather, in their focus on aesthetic particularity, they proposed a certain ethics of attention,[42] which was dialectically related to a validation of our inner subjective freedom as individuals. This, I would argue, has been a crucial legacy of European aesthetics since Kant, and one in which modern formalist views played an important part. Last but not least, the validity of this claim of subjective freedom that allows us to go beyond common opinions and views, finds its practical confirmation today in contemporary artistic work that, admittedly, has moved beyond any traditional limits and formal conventions but still demands our individual concern and subjective response.

BIBLIOGRAPHY

Anderson, Robert M. "Polemics or Philosophy. Musical Pathology in Eduard Hanslick's *Vom Musicalisch-Schönen*" *Musical Times* 154, no. 1924 (2013): 65–76.

Bois, Yve-Alain. "Whose formalism?" *Art Bulletin* 78, no. 1 (1996): 9–12.

Crowther, Paul. "Formalism, Art History, and Effective Historical Difference." In *Transhistorical Image: Philosophizing Art and Its History*, 7–21. Cambridge: Cambridge University Press, 2002.

Davis, Whitney. "Subjectivity and Objectivity in High and Historical Formalism." *Representations* 104, no. 1 (2008): 8–22.

Degler, Janusz. *Witkacego portret wielokrotny. Szkice i materiały do biografii*, Warsaw: Panstwowy Instytut Wydawniczy, 2009.

Dziemidok, Bohdan. "Artistic Formalism: Its Achievements and Weaknesses." *Journal of Aesthetics and Art Criticism* 51, no. 2 (1993): 185–193.

Fry, Roger. *Vision and Design.* London: Penguin, 1937.

---

[42] This formulation was proposed and developed by Margaret Olin with reference to Alois Riegl, in her *Forms of Representation in Alois Riegl's Theory of Art* (University Park, PA: Pennsylvania State University Press, 1992), 155–170.

Gasché, Rodolphe. *The Idea of Form: Rethinking Kant's Aesthetics.* Stanford, CA: Stanford University Press, 2003.

Gerould, Daniel, ed. *The Witkiewicz Reader*. Evanston, IL: Northwestern University Press, 1992.

Greenberg, Clement. "Modernist Painting." In *The Collected Essays and Criticism*, vol. 4, edited by John O'Brien, 85–93. Chicago: University of Chicago Press, 1993.

Hess, Jonathan. *Reconstituting the Body Politic: Enlightenment, Public Culture and the Invention of Aesthetic Autonomy*. Detroit: Wayne State University Press, 1999.

Jones, Caroline. *Eyesight Alone: Clement Greenberg's Modernism and the Bureaucratization of the Senses.* Chicago: University of Chicago Press, 2008.

Kant, Immanuel. *Critique of Judgment*, translated by James Creed Meredith. Oxford: Oxford University Press, 2007.

Krauss, Rosalind. "Formalism and Structuralism." In *Art since 1900: Modernism, Antimodernism, Postmodernism*, edited by Hal Foster et al., 32–39. London: Thames & Hudson, 2004.

Levinson, Marjorie. "What is New Formalism?" *PMLA* 122, no. 2 (2007): 558–569.

Levy, Evonne. "The Political Project of Wölfflin's Early Formalism." *October* 139 (2012): 39–52.

Mitchell, W. J. T. "The Commitment to Form, or Still Crazy after All These Years." *PMLA* 118, no. 2 (2003): 321–325.

Olin, Margaret. *Forms of Representation in Alois Riegl's Theory of Art.* University Park, PA: Pennsylvania State University Press, 1992.

Podro, Michael. *The Manifold of Perception: Theories of Art from Kant to Hildebrandt.* London: Oxford University Press, 1972.

Przybos, Julian. *Linia i gwar.* Kraków: Wydawnictwo Literackie, 1959.

Shklovsky, Viktor. "Art as Technique." In *Russian Formalist Criticism: Four Essays,* edited by Lee T. Lemon and Marion J. Reiss, 17–23. Lincoln: University of Nebraska Press, 1965.

Shklovsky, Viktor. "The Resurrection of the Word." In *Russian Formalism: A Collection of Articles and Texts,* edited by Stephen Bann and John E. Bowlt, 41–47. Edinburgh: Scottish Academic Press, 1973.

Steinberg, Leo. *Other Criteria: Confrontations with Twentieth-Century Art.* Oxford: Oxford University Press, 1972.

Summers, David. *Real Spaces: World Art History and the Rise of Western Modernism.* New York: Phaidon Press, 2003.

Wiesing, Lambert. *Die Sichtbarkeit des Bildes. Geschichte und Perspektiven der formalen Ästhetik.* Hamburg: Rowohlt Verlag, 1997.

Witkiewicz, Stanislaw Ignacy. "On Pure Form." In *Aesthetics in Twentieth-Century Poland: Selected Essays,* edited by Jean G. Harrell and Alina Wierzbianska, 41–65. Lewisburg, PA: Bucknell University Press, 1973.

Witkiewicz, Stanislaw Ignacy. *The Mother and Other Savory Plays*, edited by Daniel Gerould, with a foreword by Jan Kott. New York: Applause Books, 1993.

Woolf, Virginia. *Roger Fry: A Biography*. London: Vintage Press, 2003.

APPENDIX

TEACHING IN CHICAGO, TEACHING AT HOME

THE EUROPES CAPSTONE CONFERENCE INCLUDED A WIDE-RANGING roundtable conversation about teaching. As part of their consideration of their contact with students inside and outside the classroom, as well as the University of Chicago's deepening global engagement, the conference participants discussed the relationships between research and teaching, effective methods of communication within the classroom, and ways in which the University of Chicago has and can continue to contribute to and learn from the development of pedagogies around the world.

Central to the discussion were the ongoing changes in American and European educational environments and the global conversations about education that they provoke. From the European Union to the campuses of American universities, educators and officials are asking broad questions: What are the appropriate goals and content of undergraduate education? What impact does private or public funding have on classroom teaching? How can educators respond to changing student demographics and needs? The Mellon and Endeavor Fellows, who represented seven countries and who taught at the University of Chicago, contributed their perspectives.

The Fellows discussed their continued interest in the University's Core curriculum. Chicago's orientation toward liberal arts education emphasizes the development in students of a spirit of inquiry, one that will shape their approaches to the humanities, the sciences, and the social sciences. In the Core, students and faculty engage rigorously with primary texts and unearth assumptions beneath arguments. Fellows noted that they found this environment "intellectually refreshing," that it created "new space within which to think" and "an opportunity for cross-fertilization" between teaching and research. Reading outside their research fields and teaching students from different backgrounds with different knowledge bases challenged the Fellows to rethink their teaching and research for more general audiences. This positive experience seems to have helped to bridge the sometimes yawning divide between research and teaching. Rather than one being privileged at the expense of the other—a situation found all too often in many countries—Fellows found at the University of Chicago a dialectical engagement mutually beneficial to both.

Repeatedly, however, some positive experiences (such as the satisfaction inherent in teaching highly motivated students) met with the question of how well the sort of dialogue favored in American liberal arts institutions travels. The group seemed to feel a tension between the kind of education practiced at the University of Chicago and its applicability elsewhere.

Fellows pondered how much of their University of Chicago experience could transfer to their present teaching in Europe. One Fellow felt that "the American university cannot serve as a global paradigm." While liberal arts curricula are gaining traction outside of the United States, early specialization is still a predominant feature of post-secondary education elsewhere. Differences in legal structures, traditions, histories, and socioeconomic contexts make for different educational expectations and needs. One scholar felt that the ambitious syllabus characteristic of the University of Chicago may be less well suited to an educational context where students are trained in a philological tradition of reading, which requires close, time-consuming engagement with a single text. Perhaps implicit in this critique was a question about how closely one can engage with numerous primary texts, the practice in the Core. Some Fellows felt that the success of Chicago-style education, which emphasizes student discussion, favors a particular kind of instructor and depends greatly on the chemistry, smarts and motivated participation among the students. They raised questions about the portability and reproducibility of an educational structure that seems to depend so strongly on the characteristics of individual agents.

Other pedagogical strategies first encountered in Chicago have proven more readily portable. Innovations brought back from Chicago have included more interactive classes, less codified assignments, and weekly comment papers. One Fellow noted that, following the Core model, she has instituted weekly meetings between instructors and course assistants. Another noted that after her return from Chicago she switched from using a bibliography to using a syllabus. As a kind of contract between the instructor and students, the syllabus restructured the power relationship in the classroom, and she reported that her students greatly appreciated the change. Other Fellows, impressed by the centrality of student discussion at the University of Chicago, noted that it seems to cultivate "a spirit of adventure in the academic world."

These observations suggest that teaching in Chicago has stimulated these scholars to reflect upon the instructor–student relationship and how pedagogic methods shape learning and research experience. The scholars themselves reflect a rich blend of "Europe," for not only have they taught in a range of countries, some of them are of one national origin who work in another country. The session concluded with a shared sense that the teaching experience at Chicago provided rich possibilities for transforming the traditional authority of teacher-to-student relationships into an intellectual exchange, in which faculty and students benefit by learning from each other.